DATE DUE

			Printed in USA

Documents of
American Diplomacy

DOCUMENTS OF AMERICAN DIPLOMACY

*From the American Revolution
to the Present*

MICHAEL D. GAMBONE

Documentary Reference Collections

GREENWOOD PRESS
Westport, Connecticut • London

Library of Congress Cataloging-in-Publication Data

Documents of American diplomacy from the American Revolution to the present /
[compiled] by Michael D. Gambone.
      p. cm.—(Documentary reference collections)
      Includes bibliographical references (p.) and index.
      ISBN 0–313–31064–5 (alk. paper)
      1. United States—Foreign relations—Sources. I. Gambone, Michael D., 1963– II.
Series.
    E183.7.D63   2002
    327.73—dc21   2001018021

British Library Cataloguing in Publication Data is available.

Library of Congress Catalog Card Number: 2001018021
ISBN: 0–313–31064–5

First published in 2002

Greenwood Press, 88 Post Road West, Westport, CT 06881
An imprint of Greenwood Publishing Group, Inc.
www.greenwood.com

Printed in the United States of America

The paper used in this book complies with the
Permanent Paper Standard issued by the National
Information Standards Organization (Z39.48–1984).

10 9 8 7 6 5 4 3 2 1

Copyright Acknowledgments

The author and publisher gratefully acknowledge permission for use of the following material:

DOCUMENT 134: Excerpts from Henry Kissinger, *White House Years* (New York: Little, Brown
and Company, 1979), pp. 135–36. Used by permission of International Creative Management and
Henry Kissinger.

DOCUMENT 163: Excerpts from Madeleine K. Albright, "Enlarging NATO: Why Bigger is
Better," *The Economist* 342 (February 15, 1997): 21–23. © 1997 The Economist Newspaper
Group, Inc. Reprinted with permission. Further reproduction prohibited. www.economist.com

Every reasonable effort has been made to trace the owners of copyright materials in this book,
but in some instances this has proven impossible. The author and publisher will be glad to
receive information leading to more complete acknowledgments in subsequent printings of the
book and in the meantime extend their apologies for any omissions.

For Rachel

Contents

Part Six: The First World War   151

Part Seven: The Interwar Period   189

Contents   xiii

Preface

Throughout its history the United States had a pivotal influence on world affairs. As a young republic, with its promise of a government based on public consent, the United States excited the minds of revolutionaries as far apart as Paris, France and Buenos Aires, Argentina. During the nineteenth century, the United States struggled to reconcile this ideal with its hunger for territory and markets overseas. During the twentieth century, the role of the United States in the world underwent an evolution. Situated atop a global community of nations deeply wounded by two world wars, it assumed a position of world leadership and, on an unprecedented scale, began to contemplate the complex issues of world development and stability. With the advent of the Cold War, U.S. policymakers added to its formidable list of tasks the challenge of Communism and the possibility of thermonuclear war. Today, American diplomacy continues to try to resolve the old East-West dispute, while it tackles a host of new problems. As the last remaining superpower, the United States must address the breakdown of stability (and all its potential consequences and opportunities) that the Cold War maintained.

Through documents drawn from every period of American history, this book offers a complete examination of the evolution of U.S. diplomacy from its revolutionary beginnings to the twenty-first century. It tracks the first uncertain steps of a young nation to the weighty responsibilities that capture the attention of policy makers today.

More important, this book offers the reader an opportunity to compare the evolutionary stages of American diplomacy across the entirety of the country's historical experience. It provides students of the topic the ability to see both the deeply rooted concepts of American foreign affairs and the important interpretations of America's changing role. It also provides a significant framework for the interested observer to understand the future directions that America might someday pursue.

Acknowledgments

I am indebted to the many helpful professionals who populate the archives and historical collections used in this work. I am especially grateful for the assistance provided by the staffs of the National Archives and the Library of Congress. Special thanks goes to Barbara Kegerreis in Kutztown University's Rohrbach Library who provided me with a great deal of assistance in the pursuit of primary source collections. I must also recognize Dr. John Delaney, a friend and colleague, who provided the early stages of this manuscript with an important and necessary degree of focus.

Last, I offer my sincere gratitude to my wife Rachel. Throughout the hectic years that I worked on this project, she was a constant source of encouragement. There is no question that her insight and skepticism served this manuscript extremely well in the early draft stages. Her quick reflexes were also instrumental in keeping my laptop computer out of the clutches of our young toddler Michael.

Part One

The Colonial Era

From the very beginning, the United States struggled to define its role in the world. In the earliest years of colonization, those who arrived first fashioned the country to suit their own preferences. Some sought sanctuary from the Old World so they could recreate society and polity in a new, utopian form. John Winthrop's observation that civilization in the new colonies could serve as a beacon, "a city upon a hill," for what had been left behind introduced a degree of moral certainty that has been present in American public policy ever since.[1]

Others came to the New World looking for an opportunity for expansion. Settlement was the product of it. After first landfall, expansion would reflect the larger pursuit of dominion over a continent whose boundaries were undefined but broad in the seventeenth century.[2] The lure of wealth and opportunities that lay to the west would define Americans for the next three centuries.[3]

The juxtaposition of the two was apparent in the clumsy unity provoked by the contingencies of war during the Colonial Era. The individual settlements had proven adequate for the initial construction of enclaves scattered along the eastern seaboard, but were poorly prepared to cooperate in times of crisis. During the course of King Philip's War in 1675, troubles between New York and the New England colonies regarding mutual defense and the treatment of Native American tribes resulted in considerable suffering on the part of the latter.[4] Nearly three-quarters of a century later, similar problems bedeviled colonial efforts to defend the Americas against the French and Spanish incursions. In 1747, after raids by privateers from both nations, Benjamin Franklin would urge Pennsylvanians to consider that: "At present we are like the separate Filaments of Flax before the Thread is form'd, without Strength, because without Connection; but UNION would make us strong, and even formidable."[5] Franklin would promote the same idea seven years later, when the much greater threat of the French and Indian War embroiled the colonies. His 1754 Plan of Union was an attempt to extend cooperation beyond war into the normal civil relations that existed between individual settlements. Franklin called for one "general government" to be formed from the American colonies. His plan was limited to the extent that it proposed that a united colonial structure act as an agent for the crown. Its purview was limited to relations with the various Native American tribes to the west, land purchases from them, and war. Its failure—not a single delegate to the Albany convention endorsed the idea—was a signal that American colonists remained unprepared for collective action.[6]

The revolution against England did little to clarify the basic approach Americans took to foreign affairs. The actual conduct of foreign policy initially became the purview of a tiny circle of individuals within the Continental Congress. Formed in November 1775 to maintain contact with foreign nations, the Committee of Secret Correspondence became the first agency to govern the affairs of the young nation.[7] Abroad, the United States was represented by a loosely organized corps of former colonial agents. Benjamin Franklin—a former representative of Georgia, New Jersey, Massachusetts, and Pennsylvania—became the dean of the overseas American diplomatic effort. The first complete American mission to France was formed in 1776 by Arthur Lee and Silas Deane, respectively a former colonial agent to England and a former congressional representative.

Forming a consensus on foreign affairs proved elusive. From the start, the very idea of separation from England provoked considerable debate for more than a year. The Continental Congress did not begin a discussion on correspondence with foreign allies until November 1775. It was not until April 1776 that the legislature consented to open American ports to non-English ships.[8]

When Americans finally did agree on a permanent separation from England, the means to maintain independence remained unclear. They recognized that a strong military and the protection of foreign military alliances was critical to secure freedom. However, many rejected the idea that the United States would have to reciprocate with its own allegiances to other nations. The military disasters that followed in the summer and fall of 1776 soon altered this position to one that solicited open alliances with France and Spain.

Control of the war at home proved equally problematic. As the conflict wore on, the leaders of the national government found themselves duly checked by representatives of the thirteen states. The war effort was too often stymied by suspicion and parochialism. As American commissioners sought out military assistance from France and Spain—contracting massive orders of weapons, uniforms, and ships—the financial condition of the United States unraveled into bankruptcy. In the short term, this situation led to interminable problems for General George Washington as he attempted to sustain his armies in the field and coordinate strategic plans with the French. Over the longer term, the issue of state sovereignty would interfere with efforts to regulate trade, stabilize currency, and provide adequate compensation for loyalist property seized during the war.

In contrast, the tiny American contingent stationed abroad produced some considerable achievements. The capstone of this effort was treaties of commerce and alliance signed by Franklin and Comte de Vergennes in February 1778. The latter would pledge the two nations to make common cause until U.S. independence from England was a fact. (It would become America's only treaty of alliance until 1949.) The commercial treaty allowed the United States to secure more than $8 million in loans and subsidies from the government of Louis XVI. Holland was also convinced to provide a loan of $1.8 million. Military assistance, in the form of weapons and the timely arrival of a French naval squadron and 5,500 regular soldiers to the United States in 1780, proved decisive in the final campaign against the British.[9]

After the British surrender at Yorktown, the focus of American diplomacy turned toward peace. As was the case in the past, the country was of a divided mind regarding proper objectives. Regional priorities asserted themselves at the conclusion of the war. Americans bickered incessantly over the preconditions necessary for a peace treaty. New Englanders wanted the issue of fishing rights off the coast of Newfoundland resolved. States adjacent to the frontier desired clarification of the western U.S. border and a resolution to navigation rights along the Mississippi River. As negotiations for a final treaty progressed, the outline of the American position began to grow clearer. Complete independence from England remained the foremost prerequisite for peace. Agreement was also reached on secondary objectives that included access to the western frontier and navigation of the Mississippi. In exchange, American negotiators made concessions on the northern border with Canada and fishing rights to the north of New England, but ambiguities in the final treaty language would plague relations between the United States and England for the next two decades.

In the end, the young nation was able to reach a modus vivendi with Great Britain. However, the exact future diplomatic role the United States would hold was uncertain. America emerged from its revolution as a potentially useful ally or a dangerous opponent. The concessions made on the territory to the east of the Mississippi reflected a British desire to cultivate the American market and a possible strategic ally. France, too, hoped to retain its wartime relationship. The dilemma for policy makers was to determine the extent of these contacts and the degree to which a vulnerable new country would enter into the arena of international diplomacy.

Post-Revolutionary diplomacy was a reflection of this important decision. The American Revolution had been predicated on the separation of the colonies from the existing system of global affairs under the ancien régime. In terms of its basic philosophical principles, it was a rejection of the separation of the interests of the state and those of civil society. For American leaders, the true value of republican government was its ability to reform the basic nature of governance. The justification of sovereignty was based on the principle of public consent and not law dictated from above. This granted the United States, so it was believed, the freedom to exercise choice in foreign interactions as defined by law and morality and not on expediency.

For a statesman like Thomas Jefferson, this offered America a unique opportunity to transform modern eighteenth-century diplomacy. Jefferson proposed a system that could avoid open conflict and the labyrinth of intrigues that defined European relations at that moment in time. He believed that commerce might serve as a vehicle that would cultivate peaceful relations between sovereign states, asserting the mutual benefits of prosperity, while highlighting the potential costs of warfare to the common welfare.[10]

Despite the potential of Jefferson's proposal, Americans realized that they could not wholly abandon the existing European system of international relations. Ironically, American commerce with the Old World did grow, but it also served as a point of political division in the postwar period. The eastern seaboard, particularly New England, developed a lucrative trade with Europe that fueled American economic prosperity for two decades after the Revolution. Between 1790 and 1807, American exports grew from $20.2 million to $108.3 million, primarily as a result of trade with England.[11] This evolving linkage significantly shaped American attitudes regarding the outside world. When the French Revolution finally erupted in 1789, American commerce established the country's closest links with Europe and heavily influenced American attitudes toward the warfare that followed in its wake. The mercantile interests of cities such as Boston became the primary proponents of London, while others sided with the new French nation.

The often bitter partisan debates that emerged between Federalist and Republican added yet another politicized layer to American diplomacy. Foreign allegiance defined domestic politics in the astoundingly bitter contests of the late 1790s. In Philadelphia, pitched street battles between Federalists wearing a black cockade (denoting support for England) and Republicans brandishing a red, white, and blue cockade (denoting support for France) were a disturbing measure of the high passions of the era.[12] In time, these passions would find their way into the law. The Sedition Act of 1798 was a milestone to the extent that it addressed a legitimate shortfall in American law pertaining to conspiracy against the government of the United States. The darker side of the Sedition Act was its impact on free speech. The portions of it prohibiting libels on high officials had a chilling effect on opponents of Samuel Adams's administration.

It was Alexander Hamilton, Washington's secretary of the treasury, who delivered the most articulate attack on Republican principles of diplomacy. He desired to construct American foreign policy on the basis of what he considered fundamental practicalities. From the start he contested Jefferson's assertion that commerce would become the universal balm of international relations. Hamilton argued instead that the young country could be damaged far more severely than England if commerce was to be used as a sanction to assert American prerogatives. He sought first to construct commercial institutions of a modern nation, specifically a national bank and a solvent treasury.[13] Interestingly, neither Jefferson nor Hamilton endeavored to pursue an aggressive foreign policy. Despite their ideological differences, both promoted an essentially passive American position in world affairs, one designed to shield the United States from foreign intrigue while it refined the mechanisms of governance.

In no case was a need for diplomacy more necessary than in regard to foreign relations. The Constitution, the very blueprint of the new republic, was mostly mute regarding diplomacy. Lacking practical experience in foreign affairs, the delegates who were composing the document in Philadelphia relied on the writings of Sir William Blackstone in which he described royal prerogatives concerning diplomacy. The final product, according to Forrest McDonald, addressed the "form rather than substance" of the proper conduct of foreign relations.[14] Beyond the fundamental consideration of war and treaty making, it was vague on the exact duties of the executive branch. Similarly, the Constitution empowered Congress to check executive authority through a variety of measures but, again, failed to prescribe a specific framework for action.

Despite these early problems, the first Federalist administration of George Washington was able to achieve some notable successes after the Revolution. Through the Jay Treaty (1794) and the Pinckney Treaty (1795), the United States was able to reduce the British presence in the northwest and open the lower Mississippi to American commerce. More important, America was able to prevent Spain and England from presenting a united front against American expansion, a propitious outcome given the Spanish-English alliance against France that would develop. Although John Jay was burned in effigy for his treatment of commerce on the high seas, his efforts were a major boon to an American government interested in limiting European influence on the western frontier.[15]

Diplomacy, however, could not wholly prevent war. In the area of the Ohio Valley, General "Mad Anthony" Wayne resolved the problem of the British alliance with Native Americans at the Battle of Fallen Timbers in 1794. Four years later, the United States unleashed commerce raiders against the French as part of the Quasi-War of 1798. More than a thousand armed merchantmen supplemented the fifty-four ships of the U.S. Navy in one of America's first undeclared wars.[16]

As the new century began, American diplomacy focused on two primary goals. Expanding the western frontier continued to capture the imagination of Americans and their new president, Thomas Jefferson. As the settlement of the west proceeded, the United States would also seek out the concurrent expansion of its global commerce. Both objectives would define the opportunities open to the young nation. Both would also eventually lead America toward war.

NOTES

1. Bradford Perkins, ed., *The Cambridge History of American Foreign Relations: The Creation of a Republican Empire*, vol. 1 (New York: Cambridge University Press, 1993), 6–9.

2. Ibid. See also William Appleman Williams, *The Tragedy of American Diplomacy* (New York: Dell Publishing, 1962).

3. David M. Wrobel, *The End of American Exceptionalism: Frontier Anxiety from the Old West to the New Deal* (Lawrence: University Press of Kansas, 1993), 3–12.

4. Douglas Edward Leach, *Flintlock and Tomahawk: New England in King Philip's War* (East Orleans, MA: Parnassus Imprints, 1958), 155–77; Walter Millis, *Arms and Men: A Study in American Military History* (New Brunswick, NJ: Rutgers University Press, 1984), 13–71.

5. Gerald Stourzh, *Benjamin Franklin and American Foreign Policy* (Chicago: University of Chicago Press, 1969), 43.

6. Ibid., 48–53.

7. Jonathan R. Dull, *A Diplomatic History of the American Revolution* (New Haven, CT: Yale University Press, 1985), 50–57, 75–106.

8. Thomas J. Schaeper, *France and America in the Revolutionary Era: The Life of Jacques-Donatien Leray de Chaumont, 1725–1803* (Providence, R.I.: Berghahn Books, 1995), 38–62.

9. Dull, *A Diplomatic History of the American Revolution*, 50–57, 75–106.; Perkins, *Cambridge History of American Foreign Relations*, 29.

10. Robert W. Tucker and David C. Hendrickson, *Empire of Liberty: The Statecraft of Thomas Jefferson* (New York: Oxford University Press, 1990), 11–20.

11. Paul A. Groves, "The Northeast and Regional Integration," in *North America: The Historical Geography of a Changing Continent*, ed. Robert D. Mitchell and Paul A. Groves (New York: Rowan & Littlefield, 1987), 200. See also Charles Sellers, *The Market Revolution: Jacksonian America, 1815–1846* (New York: Oxford University Press, 1991), 34–69.

12. For an excellent recent example of this conflict, see Richard N. Rosenfeld, *American Aurora: A Democratic-Republic Returns* (New York: St. Martin's Press, 1997).

13. Tucker and Hendrickson, *Empire of Liberty*, 14, 33–47.

14. Forrest McDonald, *Novus Ordo Seclorum: The Intellectual Origins of the Constitution* (Lawrence University Press of Kansas, 1985), 247–49.

15. Tucker and Hendrickson, *Empire of Liberty*, 65.

16. Allan R. Millett and Peter Maslowski, *For the Common Defense: A Military History of the United States of America* (New York: Free Press, 1994), 97–98, 102–3.

1. THE DECLARATION OF INDEPENDENCE
4 July 1776

The signing of the Declaration of Independence *marked the final, formal break with England. It came after more than a year of debate and discussion within the Continental Congress and the editorial pages of individual state newspapers. Its presentation of "laws of nature" established a new standard for the legitimacy of governance in the eighteenth century and inspired generations of revolutionaries thereafter.*

WHEN IN THE COURSE OF HUMAN EVENTS, it becomes necessary for one people to dissolve the political bands which have connected them with another, and to assume the Powers of the earth, the separate and equal station to which the Laws of Nature and of Nature's God entitle them, a decent respect to the opinions of mankind requires that they should declare the causes which impel them to the separation.

We hold these truths to be self-evident, that all men are created equal, that they are endowed by their Creator with certain unalienable rights, that among these are Life, Liberty, and the pursuit of Happiness. That to secure these rights, Governments are instituted among Men, deriving their just powers from the consent of the governed. That whenever any Form of Government becomes destructive of these ends, it is the Right of the People to alter or to abolish it, and to institute new Government, laying its foundation on such principles and organizing its powers in such form, as to them shall seem most likely to effect their Safety and Happiness. Prudence, indeed, will dictate that Governments long established should not be changed for light and transient causes; and accordingly all experience hath shown, that mankind are more disposed to suffer, while evils are sufferable, than to light themselves by abolishing the forms to which they are accustomed. But when a long train of abuses and usurpations, pursuing invariably the same Object evinces a design to reduce them under absolute Despotism, it is their right, it is their duty, to throw off such Government, and to provide new Guards for their future security.—Such has been the patient sufferance of these Colonies; and such is now the necessity which constrains them to alter their former Systems of Government. The history of the present King of Great Britain is a history of repeated injuries and usurpations, all having in direct object the establishment of an absolute Tyranny over these States. To prove this, let Facts be submitted to a candid world.

He has refused his Assent to Laws, the most wholesome and necessary for the public good.

He has forbidden his Governors to pass Laws of immediate and pressing importance, unless suspended in their operation till his Assent should be obtained; and when so suspended, he has utterly neglected to attend to them.

He has refused to pass other Laws for the accommodation of large districts of people, unless those people would relinquish the right of Representation in the Legislature, a right inestimable to them and formidable to tyrants only.

He has called together legislative bodies at places unusual, uncomfortable, and distant from the depository of their public Records, for the sole purpose of fatiguing them into compliance with his measures.

He has dissolved Representative Houses repeatedly, for opposing, with manly firmness his invasions on the rights of the people.

He has refused for a long time, after such dissolutions, to cause others to be elected; whereby the Legislative powers, incapable of Annihilation, have returned to the People at large for their exercise; the State remaining in the mean time exposed to all dangers of invasion from without, and convulsions within.

He has endeavoured to prevent the population of these States; for that purpose obstructing the Laws of Naturalization of Foreigners; refusing to pass others to encourage their migrations hither, and raising the conditions of new Appropriations of Lands.

He has obstructed the Administration of Justice, by refusing his Assent to Laws for establishing judiciary powers.

He has made Judges dependent on his Will alone, for the tenure of their offices, and the amount and payment of their salaries.

He has erected a multitude of New Offices, and sent hither swarms of Officers to harass our People, and eat out their substance.

He has kept among us, in times of peace, Standing Armies without the Consent of our legislature.

He has affected to render the Military independent of and superior to the Civil Power.

He has combined with others to subject us to a jurisdiction foreign to our constitution, and unacknowledged by our laws; giving his Assent to their Acts of pretended Legislation:

For quartering large bodies of armed troops among us:

For protecting them, by a mock Trial, from Punishment for any Murders which they should commit on the Inhabitants of these States:

For cutting off our Trade with all parts of the world:

For imposing taxes on us without our Consent:

For depriving us of many cases, of the benefits of Trial by jury:

For transporting us beyond Seas to be tried for pretended offences:

For abolishing the free System of English Laws in a neighbouring Province, establishing therein an Arbitrary government, and enlarging its Boundaries so as to render it at once an example and fit instrument for introducing the same absolute rule into these Colonies:

For taking away our Charters, abolishing our most valuable Laws, and altering fundamentally the Forms of our Governments:

For suspending our own Legislatures, and declaring themselves invested with Power to legislate for us in all cases whatsoever.

He has abdicated Government here, by declaring us out of his Protection and waging War against us.

He has plundered our seas, ravaged our Coasts, burnt our towns, and destroyed the lives of our people.

He is at this time transporting large armies of foreign mercenaries to compleat the works of death, desolation, and tyranny, already begun with circumstances of Cruelty & perfidy scarcely paralleled in the most barbarous ages, and totally unworthy the Head of a civilized nation.

He has constrained our fellow Citizens taken Captive on the high Seas to bear Arms against their Country, to become the executioners of their friends and Brethren, or to fall themselves by their Hands.

He has excited domestic insurrections amongst us, and has endeavoured to bring on the inhabitants of our frontiers, the merciless Indian Savages, whose known rule of warfare, is an undistinguished destruction of all ages, sexes, and conditions.

In every stage of these Oppressions We have Petitioned for Redress in the most humble terms: Our repeated Petitions have been answered only by repeated injury. A Prince, whose character is thus marked by every act which may define a Tyrant, is unfit to be the ruler of a free people.

Nor have We been wanting in attention to our British brethren. We have warned them from time to time of attempts by their legislature to extend an unwarrantable jurisdiction over us. We have reminded them of the circumstances of our emigration and settlement here. We have appealed to their native justice and magnanimity, and we have conjured them by the ties of our common kindred to disavow these usurpations, which, would inevitably interrupt our connections and correspondence. They too must have been deaf to the voice of justice and of consanguinity. We must, therefore, acquiesce in the necessity, which denounces our Separation, and hold them, as we hold the rest of mankind, Enemies in War, in Peace Friends.

WE, THEREFORE, the Representatives of the UNITED STATES OF AMERICA, in General Congress, Assembled, appealing to the Supreme Judge of the world for the rectitude of our intentions, do, in the Name, and by Authority of the good People of these Colonies, solemnly publish and declare, That these United Colonies are, and of Right ought to be FREE AND INDEPENDENT STATES; that they are Absolved from all Allegiance to the British Crown, and that all political connection between them and the State of Great Britain, is and ought to be totally dissolved; and that as Free and Independent States, they have full Power to levy War, conclude Peace, contract Alliances, establish Commerce, and to do all other Acts and Things which Independent States may of right do. And for the support of this Declaration, with a firm reliance on the

Protection of Divine Providence, we mutually pledge to each other our Lives, our Fortunes, and our sacred Honor.

The foregoing Declaration was, by order of Congress, engrossed, and signed by the following members:

John Hancock

New Hampshire
Josiah Bartlett
William Whipple
Matthew Thornton

Massachusetts Bay
Samuel Adams
John Adams
Robert Treat Paine
Elbridge Gerry

Rhode Island
Stephen Hopkins
William Ellery

Connecticut
Roger Sherman
Samuel Huntington
William Williams
Oliver Wolcott

New York
William Floyd
Philip Livingston
Francis Lewis
Lewis Morris

New Jersey
Richard Stockton
John Witherspoon
Francis Hopkinson
John Hart
Abraham Clark

Pennsylvania
Robert Morris
Benjamin Rush
Benjamin Franklin
John Morton
George Clymer
James Smith
James Wilson
George Taylor
George Ross

Delaware
Caesar Rodney
George Read
Thomas M'Kean

Maryland
Samuel Chase
William Paca
Thomas Stone

Charles Carroll, of Carrollton

Virginia
George Wythe
Richard Henry Lee
Thomas Jefferson
Benjamin Harrison
Thomas Nelson Jr.
Francis Lightfoot Lee
Carter Braxton

North Carolina
William Hooper
Joseph Hewes
John Penn

South Carolina
Edward Rutledge
Thomas Heyward, Jr.
Thomas Lynch, Jr.
Arthur Middleton

Georgia
Button Gwinnett
Lyman Hall
George Walton

Source: James D. Richardson, ed., *A Compilation of the Messages and Papers of the Presidents*, vol. 1 (New York: Bureau of National Literature, 1897), 1–4.

2. TREATY OF ALLIANCE WITH FRANCE
6 February 1778

The Treaty of Alliance with France *linked the American Revolution with its most powerful European patron and proved decisive toward its final victory. It was the first treaty of alliance made by the United States. Accompanied by the Treaty of Amity and Commerce (1778) it provided the young nation with the financing, military assistance, and the prestige of Louis XVI's government.*

ART I. If war should break out between France and Great Britain during the continuance of the present war between the United States and England, His Majesty and the said United States shall make it a common cause and aid each other mutually with their good offices, their counsels and their forces, according to the exigence of conjunctures, as becomes good and faithful allies.

ART. II. The essential and direct end of the present defensive alliance is to maintain effectually the liberty, sovereignty and independence absolute and unlimited, of the said United States, as well in matters of government as of commerce.

ART. III. The two contracting parties shall each on its own part, and in the manner it may judge most proper, make all the efforts in its power against their common enemy, in order to attain the end proposed.

ART. IV. The contracting parties agree that in case either of them should form any particular enterprise in which the concurrence of the other may be desired, the party whose concurrence is desired, shall readily, and with good faith, join to act in concert for that purpose, as far as circumstances and its own particular situation will permit; and in that case, they shall regulate, by a particular convention, the quantity and kind of succour to be furnished, and the time and manner of its being brought into action, as well as the advantages which are to be its compensation.

ART. V. If the United States should think fit to attempt the reduction of the British power, remaining in the northern parts of America, or the islands of Bermudas, those countries or islands, in case of success, shall be confederated with or dependent upon the said United States.

ART. VI. The Most Christian King renounces forever the possession of the islands of Bermudas, as well as of any part of the continent of North America, which before the treaty of Paris in 1763, or in virtue of that treaty, were acknowledged to belong to the Crown of Great Britain, or to the United States, heretofore called British Colonies, or which are at this time, or have lately been under the power of the King and Crown of Great Britain.

ART. VII. If His Most Christian Majesty shall think proper to attack any of the islands situated in the Gulph of Mexico, or near that Gulph, which are at present under the power of Great Britain, all the said isles in case of success, shall appertain to the Crown of France.

ART. VIII. Neither of the two parties shall conclude either truce or peace with Great Britain without the formal consent of the other first obtained; and they mutually engage not to lay down their arms until the independence of the United States shall have been formally or tacitly assured by the treaty or treaties that shall terminate the war.

ART. IX. The contracting parties declare that being resolved to fulfill each on its own part the clauses and conditions of the present treaty of alliance, according to its own power and circumstances, there shall be no afterclaim of compensation on one side or the other, whatever may be the event of the war.

ART. X. The Most Christian King and the United States agree to invite or admit other powers who may have received injuries from England, to make common cause with them, and to accede to the present alliance, under such conditions as shall be freely agreed to and settled between all the parties.

ART. XI. The two parties guarantee mutually from the present time and forever against all other powers, to wit: The United States to His Most Christian Majesty, the present possessions of the Crown of France in America, as well as those which it may acquire by the future treaty of peace: And His Most Christian Majesty guarantees on his part to the United States their liberty, sovereignty and independence, absolute and unlimited, as well in matters of government as commerce, and also their possessions, and the additions or conquests that their confederation may obtain during the war, from any of the dominions now, or heretofore possessed by Great Britain in North America, conformable to the 5th and 6th articles above written, the whole as their possessions shall be fixed and assured to the said States, at the moment of the cessation of their present war with England.

ART. XII. In order to fix more precisely the sense and application of the preceding article, the contracting parties declare, that in case of a rupture between France and England the reciprocal guarantee declared in the said article shall have its full force and effect the moment such war shall break out; and if such rupture shall not take place, the mutual obligations of the safe guarantee shall not commence until the moment of the cessation of the present war between the United States and England shall have ascertained their possessions. . . .

Done at Paris, this sixth day of February, one thousand seven hundred and seventy eight.

Source: W. M. Malloy, ed., *Treaties, Conventions, International Acts, Protocols, and Agreements between the United States of America and Other Powers, 1776–1909*, vol. 1 (Washington, DC: Government Printing Office, 1910), 479–82.

---

3. TREATY OF PEACE WITH GREAT BRITAIN
3 September 1783

The Treaty of Peace with Great Britain *finalized the defeat at Yorktown and represented a formal recognition of the United States as an independent nation. Although Congress appointed such notables as John Adams, John Jay, Henry Laurens, and Benjamin Franklin as the negotiators of the treaty, it was Franklin who carried the burden of the American effort. The final document addressed a host of issues from the national boundaries of the United States, to the treatment of property and debt, and fishing rights.*

ART. I. His Britannic Majesty acknowledges the said United States, viz. New Hampshire, Massachusetts Bay, Rhode Island, and Providence Plantations, Connecticut, New York, New Jersey, Pennsylvania, Delaware, Maryland, Virginia, North Carolina, South Carolina, and Georgia, to be free, sovereign and independent States; that he treats with them as such, and for himself, his heirs and successors, relinquishes all claims to the Government, proprietary and territorial rights of the same, and every part thereof.

ART. II. And that all disputes which might arise in future, on the subject of the boundaries of the said United States may be prevented, it is hereby agreed and declared, that the following are, and shall be their boundaries, viz.: From the northwest angle of Nova Scotia, viz: that angle which is formed by a line drawn due north from the source of Saint Croix River to the Highlands which divide those rivers that empty themselves into the river St. Lawrence, from those which fall into the Atlantic Ocean, to the northwesternmost head of Connecticut River; thence down along the middle of that river, to the forty-fifth degree of north latitude; from thence, by a line due west on said latitude, until it strikes the river Iroquois or Cataraquy; thence along the middle of said river into Lake Ontario, through the middle of said lake until it strikes the communication by water between that lake and Lake Erie; thence along the middle of said communication into Lake Erie, through the middle of said lake until it arrives at the water communication between that lake and Lake Huron; thence along middle of said water communication into Lake Huron; thence through the middle of said lake to the water communication between that lake and Lake Superior; thence through Lake Superior northward of the Isles Royal and Phelipeaux, to the Long Lake; thence through the middle of said Long Lake, and the water communication between it and the Lake of the Woods, to the said Lake of the Woods; thence through the said lake to the most northwestern point thereof, and from thence on a due west course to the river Mississippi; thence by a line to be drawn along the middle of the said river Mississippi until it shall intersect the northernmost part of the thirty-first degree of north latitude. South, by a line to be drawn due east from the determination of the line last mentioned, in the latitude thirty-one degrees north the middle of the Equator, to the middle of the river Appalachicola or Catahouche; thence along the middle thereof to its junction with the Flint River; thence straight to the head of the St. Mary's River; and thence down the middle of St. Mary's River to the Atlantic Ocean. East, by a line to be drawn along the middle of the river St. Croix, from its mouth in the Bay of Fundy to its source, and from its source directly north to the aforesaid Highlands, which divide the rivers that fall into the Atlantic Ocean from those which fall into the river St. Lawrence; comprehending all islands within twenty leagues of any part of the shores of the United States, and lying between lines to be drawn due east from the points where the aforesaid boundaries between Nova Scotia on the one part, and East Florida on the other, shall respectively touch the Bay of Fundy and the Atlantic Ocean; excepting such islands as now are, or heretofore have been, within the limits of the said province of Nova Scotia.

ART. III. It is agreed that the people of the United States shall continue to enjoy unmolested the right to take fish of every kind on the Grand Bank, and on all the other banks of Newfoundland; also in the Gulph of Saint Lawrence, and at all other places in the sea where the inhabitants of both countries used at any time heretofore to fish. And also that the inhabitants of the United States shall have liberty to take fish of every kind on such part of the coast of Newfoundland as British fishermen shall use (but not to dry or cure the same on that island) and also on the coasts, bays and creeks of all other of His Britannic Majesty's dominions in America; and that the American fishermen shall have liberty to dry and cure fish in any of the unsettled bays, harbours and creeks of Nova Scotia, Magdalen Islands, and Labrador, so long as the same shall remain unsettled; but so soon as the same or either of them shall be settled, it shall not be lawful for the said fishermen to dry or cure fish at such settlements, without a previous agreement for that purpose with the inhabitants, proprietors or possessors of the ground.

ART. IV. It is agreed that creditors on either side shall meet with no lawful impediment to the recovery of the full value in sterling money, of all *bona fide* debts heretofore contracted.

ART. V. It is agreed that the Congress shall earnestly recommend it to the legislatures of the respective States, to provide for the restitution of all estates, rights and properties which have been confiscated, belonging to real British subjects, and also of the estates, rights and properties of persons resident in districts in the possession of His Majesty's arms, and who have not borne arms against the said United States. And that persons of any other description shall have free liberty to go to any part or parts of any of the thirteen United States, and therein to remain twelve months, unmolested in their endeavours to obtain the restitution of such of their estates, rights and properties as may have been confiscated; and that Congress shall also earnestly recommend to the several States a reconsideration and revision of all acts or laws regarding the premises, so as to render the said laws or acts perfectly consistent, not only with justice and equity, but with that spirit of conciliation which, on the return of the blessings of peace, should universally prevail. And that Congress shall also earnestly recommend to the several States, that the estates, rights and properties of such last mentioned persons, shall be restored to them, they refunding to any persons who may be now in possession, the *bona fide* price (where any has been given) which such persons may have paid on purchasing any of the said lands, rights or properties, since the confiscation. And it is agreed, that all persons who have any interest in confiscated lands, either by debts, marriage settlements or otherwise, shall meet with no lawful impediment in the prosecution of their just rights.

ART. VI. That there shall be no future confiscations made, nor any prosecutions commenced against any person or persons for, or by reason of the part which he or they may have taken in the present war; and that no person shall, on that account, suffer any future loss or damage, either in his person, liberty or property; and that those who may be in confinement on such charges, at the time of the ratification of the treaty in America, shall be immediately set at liberty, and the prosecutions so commenced be discontinued.

ART. VII. There shall be a firm and perpetual peace between His Britannic Majesty and the said States, and between the subjects of the one and the citizens of the other, wherefore all hostilities, both by sea and land, shall from henceforth cease; All prisoners on both sides shall be set at liberty, and His Britannic Majesty shall, with all convenient speed, and without causing any destruction, or carrying away any negroes or other property of the American inhabitants, withdraw all his armies, garrisons and fleets from the said United States, and from every post, place and harbour within the same; leaving in all fortifications the American artillery that may be therein; And shall also order and cause all archives, records, deeds and papers, belonging to any of the said States, or their citizens, which, in the course of the war, may have fallen into the hands of his officers, to be forthwith restored and deliver'd to the proper States and persons to whom they belong.

ART. VIII. The navigation of the river Mississippi, from its source to the ocean, shall forever remain free and open to the subjects of Great Britain, and the citizens of the United States.

ART. IX. In case it should so happen that any place or territory belonging to Great Britain or to the United States, should have been conquer'd by the arms of either from the other, before the arrival of the said provisional articles in America, it is agreed, that the same shall be restored without difficulty, and without requiring any compensation. . . .

Source: Hunter Miller, ed., *Treaties and Other International Acts of the United States of America*, vol. 1 (Washington, DC: Government Printing Office, 1931), 151–57.

4. TREATY WITH THE CHEROKEE
28 November 1785

As the United States began to expand beyond its wartime boundaries, it began to construct treaties with Native American tribes to its west. The Treaty with the Cherokee *was one of the first of hundreds convened between the United States and these independent cultures. Its contents would be emblematic of many of the documents that opened the frontier to settlement.*

Articles concluded at Hopewell, on the Keowee, between Benjamin Hawkins, Andrew Pickens, Joseph Martin, and Lachlan M'Intosh, Commissioners Plenipotentiary of the United States of America of the one Part, and the Head-Men and Warriors of all Cherokees of the other.

The Commissioners Plenipotentiary of the United States, in Congress assembled, give peace to all the Cherokees, and receive them into the favor and protection of the United States of America, on the following conditions:

ARTICLE I.

The Head-Men and Warriors of all the Cherokees shall restore all the prisoners, citizens of the United States, or Subjects of their allies, to their entire liberty: They shall also restore all the Negroes, and all other property taken during the late war from the citizens, to such person, and at such time and place, as the Commissioners shall appoint.

ARTICLE II.

The Commissioners of the United States in Congress assembled, shall restore all the prisoners taken from the Indians, during the late war, to the Head-Men and Warriors of the Cherokees, as early as is practicable.

ARTICLE III.

The said Indians for themselves and their respective tribes and towns do acknowledge all the Cherokees to be under the protection of the United States of America, and of no other sovereign whosoever.

ARTICLE IV.

The boundary allotted to the Cherokees for their hunting grounds, between the said Indians and the citizens of the United States, within the limits of the United States of America, is, and shall be the following viz. Beginning at the mouth of Duck river, on the Tennessee; thence running north-east to the ridge dividing the waters running into Cumberland from those running into the Tennessee; thence eastwardly along the said ridge to a north-east line to be run, which shall strike the river Cumberland forty miles above Nashville; thence along the said line to the river; thence up the said river to the ford where the Kentucky road crosses the river; thence to Campbell's line, near Cumberland gap; thence to the mouth of Claud's creek on Holstein; thence to the Chimney-top mountain; thence to Camp-creek, near the mouth of Big Limestone, on Nolichuckey; thence a southerly course six miles to a mountain; thence south to the North-Carolina line; thence to the South-Carolina Indian boundary, and along the same south-west over the top of the Oconee mountain till it shall strike Tugaloo river; thence a direct line to the top of the Currohee mountain; thence to the head of the south fork of Oconee river.

ARTICLE V.

If any citizen of the United States, or other person not being an Indian, shall attempt to settle on any of the lands westward or southward of the said boundary which are hereby allotted to the Indians for their hunting grounds, or having already settled and will not remove from the same within six months after the ratification of this treaty, such person shall forfeit the protection of the United States, and the Indians may punish him or not as they please: Provided nevertheless, That this article shall not extend to the people settled between the fork of French Broad and Holstein rivers, whose particular situation shall be transmitted to the United States in Congress assembled for their decision thereon, which the Indians agree to abide by.

ARTICLE VI.

If any Indian or Indians, or person residing among them, or who shall take refuge in their nation, shall commit a robbery, or murder, or other capital crime, on any citizen of the United States, or person under their protection, the nation, or the tribe to which such offender or offenders may belong, shall be bound to deliver him or them to be punished according to the ordinances of the United States; Provided, that the punishment shall not be greater than if the robbery or murder, or other capital crime had been committed by a citizen on a citizen.

ARTICLE VII.

If any citizen of the United States, or person under their protection, shall commit a robbery or murder, or other capital crime, on any Indian, such offender or offenders shall be punished in the same manner as if the murder or robber or other capital crime, had been committed on a citizen of the United States; and the punishment shall be in presence of some of the Cherokees, if any shall attend at the time and place, and that they may have any opportunity to do, due notice of the time of such intended punishment shall be sent to some one of the tribes.

ARTICLE VIII.

It is understood that the punishment of the innocent under the idea of retaliation, is unjust, and shall not be practiced on either side, except where there is a manifest violation of this treaty; and then it shall be preceded first by a demand of justice, and if refused, then by a declaration of hostilities.

ARTICLE IX.

For the benefit and comfort of the Indians, and for the prevention of injuries or oppressions on the part of the citizens or Indians, the United States in Congress assembled shall have the sole and exclusive right of regulating the trade with the Indians, and managing all their affairs in such manner as they think proper.

ARTICLE X.

Until the pleasure of Congress be known, respecting the ninth article, all traders, citizens of the United States, shall have liberty to go to any of the tribes or towns of the Cherokees to trade with them, and they shall be protected in their persons and property, and kindly treated.

ARTICLE XI.

The said Indians shall give notice to the citizens of the United States, of any designs which they may know or suspect to be formed in any neighboring tribe, or any person whosoever, against the peace, trade or interest of the United States.

ARTICLE XII.

That the Indians may have full confidence in the justice of the United States, respecting their interests, they shall have the right to send a deputy of their choice, whenever they think fit, to Congress.

ARTICLE XIII.

The hatchet shall be forever buried, and the peace given by the United States, and friendship re-established between the said states on the one part, and all the Cherokees on the other, shall be universal; and the contracting parties shall use their utmost endeavors to maintain the peace given as aforesaid, and friendship re-established.

In witness of all and every thing herein determined, between the United States of America and all the Cherokees, we, their underwritten Commissioners, by virtue of our full powers, have signed this definitive treaty, and have caused our seals to be hereunto affixed.

Done at Hopewell, on the Keowee, this twenty-eighth of November, in the year of our Lord one thousand seven hundred and eighty-five.

Benjamin Hawkins,	[L.S.]	Chesecotetona, or Yellow Bird of the Pine Log, his x mark,	[L.S.]
And'w Pickens,	[L.S.]		
Jos. Martin,	[L.S.]	Sketaloska, Second Man of Tillico, his x mark,	[L.S.]
Lach'n McIntosh,	[L.S.]	Chokasatahe, Chickasaw Killer Tasonta, his x mark,	[L.S.]
Koatohe, or Corn Tassel of Toquo, his x mark,	[L.S.]	Onanoota, of Koosoate, his x mark,	[L.S.]
Scholauetta, or Hanging Man of Chota, his x mark,	[L.S.]	Ookoseta, or Sower Mush of Kooloque, his x mark,	[L.S.]
Tuskegatahu, or Long Fellow of Chistohoe, his x mark	[L.S.]	Umatooetha, the Water Hunter Choikamawga, his x mark	[L.S.]
Ooskwha or Abraham of Chilkowa, his x mark	[L.S.]	Wyuka, of Lookout Mountain, his x mark	[L.S.]
Kolakusta, or Prince of Noth, x mark	[L.S.]	Tulco, or Tom of Chatuga, his x mark	[L.S.]
Newota, or the Gritzs of Chicamaga, his x mark	[L.S.]	Will, of Akoha, his x mark	[L.S.]
Konatota, or the Rising Fawn of Highwassay, his x mark	[L.S.]	Necatee, of Sawta, his x mark	[L.S.]
Tuckasee, or Young Terrapin of Allajoy, his x mark	[L.S.]	Amokontakona, Kutcloa, his x mark	[L.S.]
Toostaka, or the Waker of Oostanawa, his x mark	[L.S.]	Kowetatahee, in Frog Town, his x mark	[L.S.]
Untoola, or Gun Rod of Seteco, his x mark	[L.S.]	Keukuck, Talcoa, his x mark	[L.S.]
Unsuokanail, Buffalo White Calf New Cussee, his x mark	[L.S.]	Tulatiska, of Chaway, his x mark	[L.S.]
Kostayeak, or Sharp Fellow Wataga, his x mark	[L.S.]	Wooaluka, the Waylayer, Chota his x mark	[L.S.]
Chonosta, of Cowe, his x mark	[L.S.]	Tatliuska, or Porpoise of Tilassi, his x mark	[L.S.]
Chescoonwho, Bird in Close of Tomotlug, his x mark	[L.S.]	John, or Little Tallico, his x mark	[L.S.]
Tuckasee, or Terrapin of Hightowa, his x mark	[L.S.]	Skelelak, his x mark	[L.S.]
Chesetoa, or Rabbit of Tlacoa, his x mark	[L.S.]	Akonoluchta, the Cabin, his x mark	[L.S.]
		Cheanoka, of Kawetakac, his x mark	[L.S.]
		Yellow Bird, his x mark	[L.S.]

Witness:

Wm. Blount,	Thos. Gregg,
Sam'l Taylor, Major,	W. Hazzard,
John Owen,	James Madison,

Jess. Walton,   Arthur Cooley,
Jno. Cowan, capt. comm'd't,   Sworn interpreters.

Source: Charles J. Kappler, ed., *Indian Treaties, 1778–1883* (New York: Interland Publishing, 1972), 8–11.

5. NORTHWEST ORDINANCE
13 July 1787

The Northwest Ordinance *created a basic model for the governance of western expansion. Originally the product of pressure from land speculators, it created the fundamental steps necessary for a territory to become a permanent part of the union. The ordinance established the principle that newly established territories did not exist for the sole benefit of the country but were distinct, sovereign extensions of the United States.*

An Ordinance for the government of the Territory of the United States northwest of the River Ohio

Be it ordained by the United States in Congress assembled, That the said territory, for the purposes of temporary government, be one district, however, to be divided into two districts, as future circumstances may, in the opinion of Congress, make it expedient.

Be it ordained by the authority aforesaid, That the estates, both of resident and non-resident proprietors in the said territory, dying intestate shall descend to, and be distributed among their children, and the descendants of a deceased child, in equal parts; the descendants of a deceased child or grandchild to take the share of their deceased parent in equal parts among them; And where there shall be no children or descendants, then in equal parts to the next of kin in equal degree; and among collaterals, the children of a deceased brother or sister of the intestate shall have, in equal parts among them, their deceased parents' share; and there shall in no case be a distinction between kindred of the whole and half-blood; saving, in all cases, to the widow of the intestate her third part of the real estate for life, and one-third of the personal estate; and this law relative to descents and dower, shall remain in full force until altered by the legislature of the district. And until the governor and judges shall adopt laws as hereinafter mentioned, estates in the said territory may be devised or bequeathed by wills in writing, signed and sealed by him or her in whom the estate may be (being of full age), and attested by three witnesses; and real estates may be conveyed by lease and release or bargain and sale, signed sealed and delivered by the person, being of full age, in whom the estate may be, and attested by two witnesses, provided such wills be duly proved, and such conveyances be acknowledged, or the execution thereof duly proved, and be recorded within one year after proper magistrates, courts, and registers shall be appointed for that purpose; and personal property may be transferred by delivery; saving, however to the French and Canadian inhabitants, and other settlers of the Kaskaskies, St. Vincents and the neighboring villages who have heretofore professed themselves citizens of Virginia, their laws and customs now in force among them, relative to the descent and conveyance, of property.

Be it ordained by the authority aforesaid, That there shall be appointed from time to time by Congress, a governor, whose commission shall continue in force for the term of three years, unless sooner revoked by Congress; he shall reside in the district, and have a freehold estate therein in 1,000 acres of land, while in the exercise of his office.

There shall be appointed from time to time by Congress, a secretary, whose commission shall continue in force for four years unless sooner revoked; he shall reside in the district, and have a freehold estate therein in 500 acres of land, while in the exercise of his office. It shall be his duty to keep and preserve the acts and laws passed by the legislature, and the public records of the district, and the proceedings of the governor in his executive department, and transmit authentic copies of such acts and proceedings, every six months, to the Secretary of Congress: There shall also be appointed a court to consist of three judges, any two of whom to form a court, who shall have a common law jurisdiction, and reside in the district, and have each therein a freehold estate in 500 acres of land while in the exercise of their offices; and their commissions shall continue in force during good behavior.

The governor and judges, or a majority of them, shall adopt and publish in the district such laws of the original States, criminal and civil, as may be necessary and best suited to the circumstances of the district, and report them to Congress from time to time: which laws shall be in force in the district until the organization of the General Assembly therein, unless disapproved of by Congress; but afterwards the Legislature shall have authority to alter them as they shall think fit.

The governor, for the time being, shall be commander-in-chief of the militia, appoint and commission all officers in the same below the rank of general officers; all general officers shall be appointed and commissioned by Congress.

Previous to the organization of the general assembly, the governor shall appoint such magistrates and other civil officers in each county or township, as he shall find necessary for the preservation of the peace and good order in the same: After the general assembly shall be organized, the powers and duties of the magistrates and other civil officers shall be regulated and defined by the said assembly; but all magistrates and other civil officers not herein otherwise directed, shall, during the continuance of this temporary government, be appointed by the governor.

For the prevention of crimes and injuries, the laws to be adopted or made shall have force in all parts of the district, and for the execution of process, criminal and civil, the governor shall make proper divisions thereof; and he shall proceed from time to time as circumstances may require, to lay out the parts of the district in which the Indian titles shall have been extinguished, into counties and townships, subject however to such alterations as may thereafter be made by the legislature.

So soon as there shall be five thousand free male inhabitants of full age in the district, upon giving proof thereof to the governor, they shall receive authority, with time and place, to elect representatives from their counties or townships to represent them in the general assembly: *Provided*, That, for every five hundred free male inhabitants, there shall be one representative, and so on progressively with the number of free male inhabitants shall the right of representation increase, until the number of representatives shall amount to twenty-five; after which, the number and proportion of representatives shall be regulated by the legislature: *Provided*, That no person be eligible or qualified to act as a representative unless he shall have been a citizen of one of the United States three years, and be a resident in the district, or unless he shall have resided in the district three years; and, in either case, shall likewise hold in his own right, in fee simple, two hundred acres of land within the same: *Provided*, also, That a freehold in fifty acres of land in the district, having been a citizen of one of the states, and being resident in the district, or the like freehold and two years residence in the district, shall be necessary to qualify a man as an elector of a representative.

The representatives thus elected, shall serve for the term of two years; and, in case of the death of a representative, or removal from office, the governor shall issue a writ to the county or township for which he was a member, to elect another in his stead, to serve for the residue of the term.

The general assembly or legislature shall consist of the governor, legislative council, and a house of representatives. The Legislative Council shall consist of five members, to continue in office five years, unless sooner removed by Congress; any three of whom to be a quorum: and the members of the Council shall be nominated and appointed in the following manner, to wit: As soon as representatives shall be elected, the Governor shall appoint a time and place for them to meet together; and, when met, they shall nominate ten persons, residents in the district, and each possessed of a freehold in five hundred acres of land, and return their names to Congress; five of whom Congress shall appoint and commission to serve as aforesaid: and, whenever a vacancy shall happen in the council, by death or removal from office, the house of representatives shall nominate two persons, qualified as aforesaid, for each vacancy, and return their names to Congress; one of whom Congress shall appoint and commission for the residue of the term. And every five years, four months at least before the expiration of the time of service of the members of council, the said house shall nominate ten persons, qualified as aforesaid, and return their names to Congress; five of whom Congress shall appoint and commission to serve as members of the council five years, unless sooner removed. And the governor, legislative council, and house of representatives, shall have authority to make laws in all cases, for the good government of the district, not repugnant to the principles and articles in this ordinance established and declared. And all bills, having passed by a majority in the house, and by a majority in the council, shall be referred to the governor for his assent; but no bill, or legislative act whatever, shall be of any force without his assent. The governor shall have power to convene, prorogue, and dissolve the general assembly, when, in his opinion, it shall be expedient.

The governor, judges, legislative council, secretary, and such other officers as Congress shall appoint in the district, shall take an oath or affirmation of fidelity and of office; the governor before the president of congress, and all other officers before the Governor. As soon as a legislature shall be formed in the district, the council and house assembled in one room, shall have authority by joint ballot, to elect a delegate to Congress, who shall have a seat in Congress with a right of debating but not of voting during this temporary government.

And, for extending the fundamental principles of civil and religious liberty, which form the basis whereon these republics, their laws and constitutions are erected; to fix and establish those principles as the basis of all laws, constitutions, and governments, which forever hereafter shall be formed in the said territory: to provide also for the establishment of States, and permanent government therein, and for their admission to a share in the federal councils on an equal footing with the original States, at as early periods as may be consistent with the general interest:

It is hereby ordained and declared by the authority aforesaid, That the following articles shall be considered as articles of compact between the original States and the people and States in the said territory and forever remain unalterable, unless by common consent, to wit:

ART. 1. No person, demeaning himself in a peaceable and orderly manner, shall ever be molested on account of his mode of worship or religious sentiments, in the said territory.

ART. 2. The inhabitants of the said territory shall always be entitled to the benefits of the writ of *habeas corpus*, and of the trial by jury; of a proportionate representation of the people in the legislature; and of judicial proceedings according to the course of the common law. All persons shall be bailable, unless for capital offences, where the proof shall be evident or the presumption great. All fines shall be moderate; and no cruel or unusual punishments shall be inflicted. No man shall be deprived of his liberty or property, but by the judgment of his peers or the law of the land; and, should the public exigencies make it necessary, for the common preservation, to take any person's property, or to demand his particular services, full compensation shall be made for the same. And, in the just preservation of rights and property, it is understood and declared, that no law ought ever to be made, or have force in the said territory, that shall, in any manner whatever, interfere with or affect private contracts or engagements, *bona fide*, and without fraud, previously formed.

ART. 3. Religion, morality, and knowledge, being necessary to good government and the happiness of mankind, schools and the means of education shall forever be encouraged. The utmost good faith shall always be observed towards the Indians; their lands and property shall never be taken from them without their consent; and, in their property, rights, and liberty, they shall never be invaded or disturbed, unless in just and lawful wars authorized by Congress; but laws founded in justice and humanity, shall from time to time be made for preventing wrongs being done to them, and for preserving peace and friendship with them.

ART. 4. The said territory, and the States which may be formed therein, shall forever remain a part of this Confederacy of the United States of America, subject to the Articles of Confederation, and to such alterations therein as shall be constitutionally made; and to all the acts and ordinances of the United States in Congress assembled, conformable thereto. The inhabitants and settlers in the said territory shall be subject to pay a part of the federal debts contracted or to be contracted, and a proportional part of the expenses of government, to be apportioned on them by Congress according to the same common rule and measure by which apportionments thereof shall be made on the other States; and the taxes for paying their proportion shall be laid and levied by the authority and direction of the legislatures of the district or districts, or new States, as in the original States, within the time agreed upon by the United States in Congress assembled. The legislatures of those districts or new States, shall never interfere with the primary disposal of the soil by the United States in Congress assembled, nor with any regulations Congress may find necessary for securing the title in such soil to the *bona fide* purchasers. No tax shall be imposed on lands the property of the United States; and, in no case, shall non-resident proprietors be taxed higher than residents. The navigable waters leading into the Mississippi and St. Lawrence, and the carrying places between the same, shall be common highways and forever free, as well to the inhabitants of the said territory as to the citizens of the United States, and those of any other States that may be admitted into the confederacy, without any tax, impost, or duty therefor.

ART. 5. There shall be formed in the said territory, not less than three nor more than five States; and the boundaries of the States, as soon as Virginia shall alter her act of cession, and consent to the same, shall become fixed and established as follows, to wit: The western State in the said territory, shall be bounded by the Mississippi, the Ohio, and Wabash Rivers; a direct line drawn from the Wabash and Post Vincents, due North, to the territorial line between the United States and Canada; and, by the said territorial line, to the Lake of the Woods and Mississippi. The middle State shall be bounded by the said direct line, the Wabash from Post Vincents to the Ohio, by the Ohio, by a direct line, drawn due north from the mouth of the Great Miami, to the said territorial line, and by the said territorial line. The eastern State shall be bounded by the last mentioned direct line, the Ohio, Pennsylvania, and the said territorial line: *Provided, however*, and it is further understood and declared, that the boundaries of these three States shall be subject so far to be altered, that, if Congress shall hereafter find it expedient, they shall have authority to form one or two States in that part of the said territory which lies north of an east and west line drawn through the southerly bend or extreme of lake Michigan. And, whenever any of the said States shall have sixty thousand free inhabitants therein, such State shall be admitted, by its delegates, into the Congress of the United States, on an equal footing with the original States in all respects whatever, and shall be at liberty to form a permanent constitution and State government: *Provided*, the constitution and government so to be formed, shall be republican, and in conformity to the principles contained in these articles; and, so far as it can be consistent with the general interest of the confederacy, such admission shall be allowed at an earlier period, and when there may be a less number of free inhabitants in the State than sixty thousand.

ART. 6. There shall be neither slavery nor involuntary servitude in the said territory, otherwise than in the punishment of crimes whereof the party shall have been duly convicted: *Provided, always*, That any person escaping into the same, from whom labor or service is lawfully claimed in any one of the original States, such fugitive may be lawfully reclaimed and conveyed to the person claiming his or her labor or service as aforesaid.

Be it ordained by the authority aforesaid, That the resolutions of the 23rd of April 1784, relative to the subject of this ordinance, be, and the same are hereby repealed and declared null and void.

Source: Henry Steele Commager, *Documents of American History*, vol. 1 (Englewood Cliffs, NJ: Prentice Hall, 1973), 128–32.

---

6. PROCLAMATION OF NEUTRALITY
22 April 1793

In 1793, George Washington wished to avoid the war that had begun to engulf Europe. Recognizing the inherent weaknesses of a young country, he attempted to distance the United States from any one combatant and offered a warning to individual citizens contemplating involvement in the conflict.

By the President of the United States of America
A Proclamation

Whereas it appears that a state of war exists between Austria, Prussia, Sardinia, Great Britain, and the United Netherlands, on the one part and France on the other, and the duty and interest of the United States require that they should with sincerity and good faith adopt and pursue a conduct friendly and impartial toward the belligerent powers:

I have therefore thought fit by these presents to declare the disposition of the United States to observe the conduct aforesaid toward those powers respectively, and to exhort and warn the citizens of the United States carefully to avoid all acts and proceeding whatsoever which may in any manner tend to contravene such disposition.

And I do hereby also make known that whosoever of the citizens of the United States shall render himself liable to punishment or forfeiture under the law of nations by committing, aiding, or abetting hostilities against any of the said powers, or by carrying to any of them those articles which are deemed contraband by the modern usage of nations, will not receive the protection of the United States against such punishment or forfeiture; and further, that I have given instructions to those officers to whom it belongs to cause prosecutions to be instituted against all persons who shall, within the cognizance of the courts of the United States, violate the law of nations with respect to the powers at war, or any of them. . . .

Philadelphia, the 22d of April 1793

Source: James D. Richardson, ed., *A Compilation of the Messages and Papers of the Presidents*, vol. 1 (New York: Bureau of National Literature, 1897), 148–49.

---

7.   THE JAY TREATY
19 November 1794

A decade after the conclusion of the Revolution, Anglo-American relations began to suffer. Americans on the Atlantic seaboard complained of English interference in neutral shipping. Along the border of the northwest, British posts remained, obstructing American access to the Ohio Valley. Envoy extraordinary John Jay was able to satisfactorily include both issues in the final treaty. His major accomplishment was averting war with England in 1794.

ART. I. There shall be a firm, inviolable and universal peace, and a true and sincere friendship between his Britannic Majesty, his heirs and successors, and the United States of America; and between their respective countries, territories, cities, towns and people of every degree, without exception of persons or places.

ART. II. His Majesty will withdraw all his troops and garrisons from all posts and places within the boundary lines assigned by the treaty of peace to the United States. This evacuation shall take place on or before [June 1, 1796,] . . . : The United States in the mean time at their discretion, extending their settlements to any part within the said boundary line, except within the precincts or jurisdiction of any of the said posts. All settlers and traders, within the precincts or jurisdiction of the said posts, shall continue to enjoy, unmolested, all their property of every kind, and shall be protected therein. They shall be at full liberty to remain there, or to remove with all or any part of their effects; and it shall also be free to them to sell their lands, houses, or effects, or to retain the property thereof, at their discretion; such of them as shall continue to reside within the said boundary lines, shall not be compelled to become citizens of the United States, or to take any oath of allegiance to the government thereof; but they shall be at full liberty so to do if they think proper, and they shall make and declare their election within one year after the evacuation aforesaid. And all persons who shall continue there after the expiration of the said year, without having declared their intention of remaining subjects of his Britannic Majesty, shall be considered as having elected to become citizens of the United States.

ART. III. It is agreed that it shall at all times be free to his Majesty's subjects, and to the citizens of the United States, and also to the Indians dwelling on either side of the said boundary line, freely to pass and repass by land or inland navigation, into the respective territories and countries of the two parties, on the continent of America (the country within the limits of the Hudson's bay Company only excepted) and to navigate all the lakes, rivers and waters thereof, and freely to carry on trade and commerce with each other. . . . The river Mississippi shall, however, according to the treaty of peace, be entirely open to both parties; and it is further agreed, that all the ports and places on its eastern side, to whichsoever of the parties belonging, may freely be resorted to and used by both parties, in as ample a manner as any of the Atlantic ports or places of the United States, or any of the ports or places of his Majesty in Great-Britain. . . .

ART. IV. Whereas it is uncertain whether the river Mississippi extends so far to the northward, as to be intersected by a line to be drawn due west from the Lake of the Woods, in the manner mentioned in the treaty of peace . . . it is agreed, that measures shall be taken . . . for making a joint survey of the said river from one degree of latitude below the falls of St. Anthony, to the principal source or sources of the said river, and also of the parts adjacent thereto, and that if on the result of such survey, it should appear that the said river, would not be intersected by such a line as is above mentioned, the two parties will thereupon proceed by amicable negotiation, to regulate the boundary line in that quarter. . . .

ART. V. Whereas doubts have arisen what river was truly intended under the name of the river St. Croix, mentioned in the said treaty of peace, and forming a part of the boundary therein described; that question shall be referred to the final decision of commissioners to be appointed. . . . The said commissioners shall, by a declaration, under their hands and seals, decide what river is the river St. Croix, intended by the treaty. . . . And both parties agree to consider such decision as final and conclusive, so as that the same shall never thereafter be called into question, or made the subject of dispute or difference between them.

ART. VI. Whereas it is alleged by divers British merchants and others his Majesty's subjects, that debts, to a considerable amount, which were bona fide contracted before the peace, still remain owing to them by citizens or inhabitants of the United States, and that by the operation of various lawful impediments since the peace, not only the full recovery of the said debts has been delayed, but also the value and security thereof have been, in several instances, impaired and lessened, so that by the ordinary course of judicial proceedings, the British creditors cannot now obtain, and actually have and receive full and adequate compensation for the losses and damages which they have thereby sustained. It is agreed, that in all such cases, where full compensation for such losses and damages cannot, for whatever reason, be actually obtained, and had been received by the said creditors in the ordinary course of justice, the United States will make full and complete compensation for the same to the said creditors: But it is distinctly understood, that this provision is to extend to such losses only as have been occasioned by the lawful impediments aforesaid. . . .

ART. VII. Whereas complaints have been made by divers merchants and others, citizens of the United States, that during the war in which his Majesty is now engaged, they have sustained considerable losses and damage, by reason of irregular or illegal captures or condemnations of their vessels and other property, under colour of authority or commissions from his Majesty, and that from various circumstances belonging to the said cases, adequate compensation for the losses and damages so sustained cannot now be actually obtained, had and received by the ordinary course of judicial proceedings; it is agreed, that in all such cases, where adequate compensation cannot, for whatever reason, be now actually obtained, had and received by the said merchants and others, in the ordinary course of justice, full and complete compensation for the same will be made by the British government to the said complainants. But it is distinctly understood, that this provision is not to extend to such losses or damages as have been occasioned by the manifest delay or negligence, or willful omission of the claimant. . . .

ART. X. Neither the debts due from individuals of the one nation to individuals of the other, nor shares, nor monies which they may have in the public funds, or in the public or private banks, shall ever in any event of war or national differences be sequestered or confiscated. . . .

ART. XI. It is agreed between his Majesty and the United States of America, that there shall be a reciprocal and entirely perfect liberty of navigation and commerce between their respective people, in the manner, under the limitations and on the conditions specified in the following articles:

[Art. XII., relating to trade with the West Indies, was suspended.]

ART. XIII. His Majesty consents that the vessels belonging to the citizens of the United States of America, shall be, admitted and hospitably received, in all the sea-ports and harbours of the British territories in the East-Indies. And that the citizens of the said United States, may freely carry on a trade between the said territories and the said United States, in all articles of which the importation or exportation respectively, to or from the said territories, shall not be entirely prohibited. . . . The citizens of the United States shall pay for their vessels when admitted into the said ports no other or higher tonnage-duty than shall be payable on British vessels when admitted into the ports of the United States. And they shall pay no other or higher duties or charges, on the importation or exportation of the cargoes of the said vessels than shall be payable on the same articles when imported or exported in British vessels. But it is expressly agreed, that the vessels of the United States shall not carry any of the articles exported by them from the said British territories, to any port or place, except to some port or place in America, where the same shall be unladen, and such regulations shall be adopted by both parties, as shall from time to time be found necessary to enforce the due and faithful observance of this stipulation. It is also understood that the permission granted by this article, is not to extend to allow the vessels of the United States to carry on any part of the coasting-trade of the said British territories; but vessels going with their original cargoes, or part thereof, from one port of discharge to another, are not to be considered as carrying on the coasting-trade. Neither is this article to be construed to allow the citizens of the said states to settle or reside within the said territories, or to go into the interior parts thereof, without the permission of the British government established there. . . .

ART. XIV. There shall be between all the dominions of his Majesty in Europe and the territories of the United States, a reciprocal and perfect liberty of commerce and navigation. The people and inhabitants of the two countries respectively, shall have liberty freely and securely, and without hindrance and molestation, to come with their ships and cargoes to the lands, countries, cities, ports, places and rivers, within the dominions and territories aforesaid, to enter into the same, to resort there, and to remain and reside there, without any limitation of time. Also to hire and possess houses and warehouses for the purposes of their commerce, and generally the merchants and traders on each side, shall enjoy the most complete protection and security for their commerce; but subject always as to what respects this article to the laws and statutes of the two countries respectively.

ART. XV. It is agreed that no other or higher duties shall be paid by the ships or merchandise of the one party in the ports of the other, than such as are paid by the like vessels or merchandise of all other nations. Nor shall any other or higher duty be imposed in one country on the importation of any articles the growth, produce or manufacture of the other, than are or shall be payable on the importation of the like articles being of the growth, produce, or manufacture of any other foreign country. Nor shall any prohibition be imposed on the exportation or importation of any articles to or from the territories of the two parties respectively, which shall not equally extend to all other nations. . . .

The two parties agree to treat for the more exact equalization of the duties on the respective navigation of their subjects and people, in such manner as may be most beneficial to the two countries. . . . In the interval it is agreed, that the United States will not impose any new or additional tonnage duties on British vessels, nor increase the now-subsisting difference between the duties payable on the importation of any articles in British or in American vessels. . . .

ART. XVII. It is agreed, that in all cases where vessels shall be captured or detained on just suspicion of having on board enemy's property, or of carrying to the enemy any of the articles which are contraband of war; the said vessel shall be brought to the nearest or most convenient port; and if any property of an enemy should be found on board such vessel, that part only which belongs to the enemy shall be made prize, and the vessel shall be at liberty to proceed with the remainder without any impediment. . . .

ART. IX. And that more abundant care may be taken for the security of the respective subjects and citizens of the contracting parties, and to prevent their suffering injuries by the men of war, or privateers of either party, all commanders of ships of war and privateers, and all others the said subjects and citizens, shall forbear doing any damage to those of the other party, or committing any outrage against them, and if they act to the contrary, they shall be punished, and shall also be bound in their persons and estates to make satisfaction and reparation for all damages, and the interest thereof, of whatever nature the said damages may be. . . .

ART. XXII. It is expressly stipulated, that neither of the said contracting parties will order or authorize any acts of reprisal against the other, on complaints of injuries or damages, until the said party shall first have presented to the other a statement thereof, verified by competent proof and evidence, and demanded justice and satisfaction, and the same shall either have been refused or unreasonably delayed. . . .

ART. XXVI. If at any time a rupture should take place, (which God forbid) between his Majesty and the United States, the merchants and others of each of the two nations, residing in the dominions of the other, shall have the privilege of remaining and continuing their trade, so long as they behave peaceably, and commit no offence against the laws; and in case their conduct should render them suspected, and the respective governments should think proper to order them to remove, the term of twelve months from the publication of the order shall be allowed them for that purpose, to remove with their families, effects and property; but this favour shall not be extended to those who shall act contrary to the established laws; . . .

ART. XXVIII. It is agreed, that the first ten articles of this treaty shall be permanent, and that the subsequent articles, except the twelfth, shall be limited in their duration to twelve years, . . .

Source: Hunter Miller, ed., *Treaties and Other International Acts of the United States of America*, vol. 1 (Washington, DC: Government Printing Office, 1931), 245–74.

8. THE PINCKNEY TREATY
TREATY OF FRIENDSHIP, BOUNDARIES, COMMERCE AND NAVIGATION BETWEEN THE UNITED STATES OF AMERICA, AND THE KING OF SPAIN
27 October 1795

After the American Revolution, Spain refused to recognize the Treaty of
Peace with Great Britain *(1783) that granted the United States access
to the Mississippi River. There was also disagreement between the two
nations over the exact boundary of western Florida and how to handle the
ongoing conflict between settlers and local Native Americans. After long
negotiations the United States and Spain signed The Pickney Treaty,
which avoided war and provided a resolution of the border issue and the
question of navigation along the Mississippi. The pertinent articles of this
treaty are listed herein.*

ART. I. THERE shall be a firm and inviolable peace and sincere friendship
between His Catholic Majesty, his successors and subjects, and the United
States, and their citizens, without exception of persons or places.

ART. II. To prevent all disputes on the subject of the boundaries which separate the territories of the two high contracting parties, it is hereby declared and
agreed as follows, to wit: The southern boundary of the United States, which
divides their territory from the Spanish colonies of East and West Florida, shall
be designated by a line beginning in the River Mississippi, at the northernmost
part of the thirty-first degree of latitude north of the equator, which from thence
shall be drawn due east to the middle of the River Apalachicola, or Catahouche,
thence along the middle thereof to its junction with the Flint: thence straight to
the head of St. Mary's river, and thence down the middle thereof to the Atlantic
ocean. . . .

ART. IV. It is likewise agreed that the western boundary of the United States
which separates them from the Spanish colony of Louisiana, is in the middle of
the channel or bed of the River Mississippi, from the northern boundary of the
said states to the completion of the thirty-first degree of latitude north of the
equator. And His Catholic Majesty has likewise agreed that the navigation of
the said river, in its whole breadth from its source to the ocean, shall be free
only to his subjects and the citizens of the United States, unless he should extend
this privilege to the subject of other Powers by special convention.

ART. V. The two high contracting parties shall, by all the means in their
power, maintain peace and harmony among the several Indian nations who in-

habit the country adjacent to the lines and rivers, which, by the preceding articles, form the boundaries of the two Floridas. . . .

And whereas several treaties of friendship exist between the two contracting parties and the said nations of Indians, it is hereby agreed that in future no treaty of alliance, or other whatever (except treaties of peace,) shall be made by either party with the Indians living within the boundary of the other, but both parties will endeavour to make the advantages of the Indian trade common and mutually beneficial to their respective subjects and citizens, observing in all things the most complete reciprocity. . . .

ART. XXII. . . . And in consequence of the stipulations contained in the IV. article, His Catholic Majesty will permit the citizens of the United States, for the space of three years from this time, to deposit their merchandises and effects in the port of New Orleans, and to export them from thence without paying any other duty than a fair price for the hire of the stores, and His Majesty promises either to continue this permission, if he finds during that time that it is not prejudicial to the interests of Spain, or if he should not agree to continue it there, he will assign to them, on another part of the banks of the Mississippi, an equivalent establishment. . . .

THOMAS PINCKNEY,
EL PRINCIPE DE LA PAZ,

Source: Hunter Miller, ed., *Treaties and Other International Acts of the United States of America*, vol. 1 (Washington, DC: Government Printing Office, 1931), 318–45.

---

9. WASHINGTON'S FAREWELL ADDRESS
17 September 1796

Ever since George Washington delivered his farewell address, it has been cited as a crucial document concerning America's role in the world. Ironically, its primary focus is the domestic state of the union at the time of his departure from government. However, his invocation of the need to not "entangle our peace and prosperity in the toils of European ambition, rivalship, interest, humor, or caprice" became a keystone of American isolationism in the nineteenth and twentieth centuries.

Friends and Fellow-Citizens:

The period for a new election of a citizen to administer the Executive Government of the United States being not far distant and the time actually arrived when your thoughts must be employed in designating the person who is to be clothed with that important trust, it appears to me proper, especially as it may conduce to a more distinct expression of the public voice, that I should now apprise you of the resolution I have formed to decline being considered among the number of those out of whom a choice is to be made. . . .

The impressions with which I first undertook the arduous trust were explained on the proper occasion. In the discharge of this trust I will only say that I have, with good intentions, contributed toward the organization and administration of the Government the best exertions of which a very fallible judgment was capable. Not unconscious in the outset of the inferiority of my qualifications, experience in my own eyes, perhaps still more in the eyes of others, has strengthened the motives to diffidence of myself; and every day the increasing weight of years admonishes me more and more that the shade of retirement is as necessary to me as it will be welcome. Satisfied that if any circumstances have given peculiar value to my services they were temporary, I have the consolation to believe that, while choice and prudence invite me to quit the political scene, patriotism does not forbid it. . . .

Here, perhaps, I ought to stop. But a solicitude for your welfare which can not end with my life, and the apprehension of danger natural to that solicitude, urge me on an occasion like the present to offer to your solemn contemplation and to recommend to your frequent review some sentiments which are the result of much reflection, of no inconsiderable observation, and which appear to me all important to the permanency of your felicity as a people. . . .

Interwoven as is the love of liberty with every ligament of your hearts, no recommendation of mine is necessary to fortify or confirm the attachment.

The unity of government which constitutes you one people is also now dear to you. It is justly so, for it is a main pillar in the edifice of your real independence, the support of your tranquility at home, your peace abroad, of your safety, of your prosperity, of that very liberty which you so highly prize. But as it is easy to foresee that from different causes and from different quarters much pains will be taken, many artifices employed, to weaken in your minds the conviction of this truth, as this is the point in your political fortress against which the batteries of internal and external enemies will be most constantly and actively (though often covertly and insidiously) directed, it is of infinite moment that you should properly estimate the immense value of your national union to your collective and individual happiness; that you should cherish a cordial, habitual, and immovable attachment to it; accustoming yourselves to think and speak of it as of the palladium of your political safety and prosperity; watching for its preservation with jealous anxiety; discountenancing whatever may suggest even a suspicion that it can in any event be abandoned, and indignantly frowning upon the first dawning of every attempt to alienate any portion of our country from the rest or to enfeeble the sacred ties which now link together the various parts.

For this you have every inducement of sympathy and interest. Citizens by birth or choice of a common country, that country has a right to concentrate your affections. The name of American, which belongs to you in your national capacity, must always exalt the just pride of patriotism more than any appellation derived from local discriminations. With slight shades of difference, you have the same religion, manners, habits, and political principles. You have in a common cause fought and triumphed together. The independence and liberty you possess are the work of joint councils and joint efforts, of common dangers, sufferings and successes.

But these considerations, however powerfully they address themselves to your sensibility, are greatly outweighed by those which apply more immediately to your interest. Here every portion of our country finds the most commanding motives for carefully guarding and preserving the union of the whole.

The *North*, in an unrestrained intercourse with the *South*, protected by the equal laws of a common government, finds in the productions of the latter great additional resources of maritime and commercial enterprise and precious materials of manufacturing industry. The *South*, in the same intercourse, benefiting by the same agency of the *North*, sees its agriculture grow and its commerce expand. Turning partly into its own channels the seamen of the *North*, it finds its particular navigation invigorated; and while it contributes in different ways to nourish and increase the general mass of the national navigation, it looks forward to the protection of a maritime strength to which itself is unequally adapted. The *East*, in a like intercourse with the *West*, already finds, and in the progressive improvement of interior communications by land and water will more and more find, a valuable vent for the commodities which it brings from abroad or manufactures at home. The *West* derives from the *East* supplies requisite to its growth and comfort, and what is perhaps of still greater consequence, it must of necessity owe the *secure* enjoyment of indispensable *outlets* for its own productions to the weight, influence, and the future maritime strength of the Atlantic side of the Union, directed by an indissoluble community of interest as *one nation*. Any other tenure by which the *West* can hold this essential advantage, whether derived from its own separate strength or from an apostate and unnatural connection with any foreign power, must be intrinsically precarious.

While, then, every part of our country thus feels an immediate and particular interest in union, all the parts combined can not fail to find in the united mass of means and efforts greater strength, greater resource, proportionably greater security from external danger, a less frequent interruption of their peace by foreign nations, and what is of inestimable value, they must derive from union an exemption from those broils and wars between themselves which so frequently afflict neighboring countries not tied together by the same governments, which their own rivalships alone would be sufficient to produce, but which opposite foreign alliances, attachments, and intrigues would stimulate and imbitter. Hence, likewise, they will avoid the necessity of those overgrown military establishments which, under any form of government, are inauspicious to liberty, and which are to be regarded as particularly hostile to republican liberty. In this sense it is that your union ought to be considered as a main prop of your liberty, and that the love of the one ought to endear to you the preservation of the other. . . .

Is there a doubt whether a common government can embrace so large a sphere? Let experience solve it. To listen to mere speculation in such a case were criminal. It is well worth a fair and full experiment. With such powerful and obvious motives to union affecting all parts of our country, while experience shall not have demonstrated its impracticability, there will always be reason to distrust the patriotism of those who in any quarter may endeavor to weaken its bands.

In contemplating the causes which may disturb our union it occurs as matter of serious concern that any ground should have been furnished for characterizing parties by *geographical* discriminations—*Northern* and *Southern, Atlantic* and *Western*—whence designing men may endeavor to excite a belief that there is a real difference of local interests and views. One of the expedients of party to acquire influence within particular districts is to misrepresent the opinions and aims of other districts. You can not shield yourselves too much against the jealousies and heartburnings which spring from these misrepresentations; they tend to render alien to each other those who ought to be bound together by fraternal affection. . . .

To the efficacy and permanency of your union a government for the whole is indispensable. No alliances, however strict, between the parts can be an adequate substitute. They must inevitably experience the infractions and interruptions which all alliances in all times have experienced. Sensible of this momentous truth, you have improved upon your first essay by the adoption of a Constitution of Government better calculated than your former for an intimate union and for the efficacious management of your common concerns. This Government, the offspring of our own choice, uninfluenced and unawed, adopted upon full investigation and mature deliberation, completely free in its principles, in the distribution of its powers, uniting security with energy, and containing within itself a provision for its own amendment, has a just claim to your confidence and your support. Respect for its authority, compliance with its laws, acquiescence in its measures, are duties enjoined by the fundamental maxims of true liberty. The basis of our political systems is the right of the people to make and to alter their constitutions of government. But the constitution which any time exists till changed by an explicit and authentic act of the whole people is sacredly obligatory upon all. The very idea of the power and the right of the people to establish government presupposes the duty of every individual to obey the established government. . . .

Toward the preservation of your Government and the permanency of your present happy state, it is requisite not only that you steadily discountenance irregular oppositions to its acknowledged authority, but also that you resist with care the spirit of innovation upon its principles, however specious the pretexts. One method of assault may be to effect in the forms of the Constitution alterations which will impair the energy of the system, and thus to undermine what can not be directly overthrown. In all the changes to which you may be invited remember that time and habit are at least as necessary to fix the true character of governments as of other human institutions; that experience is the surest standard by which to test the real tendency of the existing constitution of a country; that facility in changes upon the credit of mere hypothesis and opinion exposes to perpetual change from the endless variety of hypothesis and opinion; and remember especially that for the efficient management of your common interests in a country so extensive as ours a government of as much vigor as is consistent with the perfect security of liberty is indispensable. Liberty itself will find in such a government, with powers properly distributed and adjusted, its surest guardian. It is, indeed, little else than a name where the government is too feeble to withstand the enterprises of faction, to confine each member of the society within the limits prescribed by the laws, and to maintain all in the secure and tranquil enjoyment of the rights of person and property.

I have already intimated to you the danger of parties in the State, with particular reference to the founding of them on geographical discriminations. Let me now take a more comprehensive view, and warn you in the most solemn manner against the baneful effects of the spirit of party generally.

This spirit, unfortunately, is inseparable from our nature, having its root in the strongest passions of the human mind. It exists under different shapes in all governments, more or less stifled, controlled, or repressed; but in those of the popular form it is seen in its greatest rankness and is truly their worst enemy. . . .

It serves always to distract the public councils and enfeeble the public administration. It agitates the community with ill-founded jealousies and false alarms; kindles the animosity of one part against another; foments occasionally riot and insurrection. It opens the door to foreign influence and corruption, which find a facilitated access to the government itself through the channels of party passion. Thus the policy and the will of one country are subjected to the policy and will of another.

There is an opinion that parties in free countries are useful checks upon the administration of the government, and serve to keep alive the spirit of liberty. This within certain limits is probably true; and in governments of a monarchical cast patriotism may look with indulgence, if not with favor, upon the spirit of party. But in those of the popular character, in governments purely elective, it is a spirit not to be encouraged. From their natural tendency it is certain there will always be enough of that spirit for every salutary purpose; and there being constant danger of excess, the effort ought to be by force of public opinion to mitigate and assuage it. A fire not to be quenched, it demands a uniform vigilance to prevent its bursting into a flame, lest, instead of warming, it should consume.

It is important, likewise, that the habits of thinking in a free country should inspire caution in those intrusted with its administration to confine themselves within their respective constitutional spheres, avoiding in the exercise of the powers of one department to encroach upon another. The spirit of encroachment tends to consolidate the powers of all the departments in one, and thus to create, whatever the form of government, a real despotism. . . . If in the opinion of the people the distribution or modification of the constitutional powers be in any particular wrong, let it be corrected by an amendment in the way which the Constitution designates. But let there be no change by usurpation; for though this in one instance may be the instrument of good, it is the customary weapon by which free governments are destroyed. The precedent must always greatly overbalance in permanent evil any partial or transient benefit which the use can at any time yield.

Of all the dispositions and habits which lead to political prosperity, religion and morality are indispensable supports. In vain would that man claim the tribute of patriotism who should labor to subvert these great pillars of human happiness—these firmest props of the duties of men and citizens. The mere politician, equally with the pious man, ought to respect and to cherish them. A volume could not trace all their connections with private and public felicity. Let it simply be asked, Where is the security for property, for reputation, for life, if the sense of religious obligation *desert* the oaths which are the instruments of investigation in courts of justice? And let us with caution indulge the supposition that morality can be maintained without religion. Whatever may be conceded to the influence of refined education on minds of peculiar structure, reason and experience both forbid us to expect that national morality can prevail in exclusion of religious principle.

It is substantially true that virtue or morality is a necessary spring of popular government. The rule indeed extends with more or less force to every species of free government. Who that is a sincere friend to it can look with indifference upon attempts to shake the foundation of the fabric? Promote, then, as an object of primary importance, institutions for the general diffusion of knowledge. In proportion as the structure of a government gives force to public opinion, it is essential that public opinion should be enlightened.

As a very important source of strength and security, cherish public credit. One method of preserving it is to use it as sparingly as possible, avoiding occasions of expense by cultivating peace, but remembering also that timely disbursements to prepare for danger frequently prevent much greater disbursements to repel it; avoiding likewise the accumulation of debt, not only by shunning occasions of expense, but by vigorous exertions in time of peace to discharge the debts which unavoidable wars have occasioned, not ungenerously throwing upon posterity the burthen which we ourselves ought to bear. . . .

Observe good faith and justice toward all nations. Cultivate peace and harmony with all. Religion and morality enjoin this conduct. And can it be that good policy does not equally enjoin it? It will be worthy of a free, enlightened, and at no distant period a great nation to give to mankind the magnanimous and too novel example of a people always guided by an exalted justice and benevolence. Who can doubt that in the course of time and things the fruits of such a plan would richly repay any temporary advantages which might be lost by a steady adherence to it? Can it be that Providence has not connected the permanent felicity of a nation with its virtue? The experiment, at least, is recommended by every sentiment which ennobles human nature. Alas! is it rendered impossible by its vices?

In the execution of such a plan nothing is more essential than that permanent, inveterate antipathies against particular nations and passionate attachments for others should be excluded, and that in place of them just and amicable feelings toward all should be cultivated. The nation which indulges toward another an habitual hatred or an habitual fondness is in some degree a slave. It is a slave to its animosity or to its affection, either of which is sufficient to lead it astray from its duty and its interest. Antipathy in one nation against another disposes each more readily to offer insult and injury, to lay hold of slight causes of umbrage, and to be haughty and intractable when accidental or trifling occasions of dispute occur.

So, likewise, a passionate attachment of one nation for another produces a variety of evils. Sympathy for the favorite nation, facilitating the illusion of an imaginary common interest in cases where no real common interest exists, and infusing into one the enmities of the other, betrays the former into a participation in the quarrels and wars of the latter without adequate inducement or justification. It leads also to concessions to the favorite nation of Privileges denied to others, which is apt doubly to injure the nation making the concessions by unnecessarily parting with what ought to have been retained, and by exciting jealousy, ill will, and a disposition to retaliate in the parties from whom equal privileges are withheld; and it gives to ambitious, corrupted, or deluded citizens (who devote themselves to the favorite nation) facility to betray or sacrifice the interests of their own country without odium, sometimes even with popularity, gilding with the appearances of a virtuous sense of obligation, a commendable deference for public opinion, or a laudable zeal for public good the base or foolish compliances of ambition, corruption, or infatuation. . . .

Against the insidious wiles of foreign influence (I conjure you to believe me fellow citizens) the jealousy of a free people ought to be *constantly* awake, since history and experience prove that foreign influence is one of the most baneful foes of republican government. But that jealousy, to be useful, must be impartial, else it becomes the instrument of the very influence to be avoided, instead of a defense against it. Excessive partiality for one foreign nation and excessive dislike of another cause those whom they actuate to see danger only on one side, and serve to veil and even second the arts of influence on the other. Real patriots who may resist the intrigues of the favorite are liable to become suspected and odious, while its tools and dupes usurp the applause and confidence of the people to surrender their interests.

The great rule of conduct for us in regard to foreign nations is, in extending our commercial relations to have with them as little political connection as possible. So far as we have already formed engagements let them be fulfilled with perfect good faith. Here let us stop.

Europe has a set of primary interests which to us have none or a very remote relation. Hence she must be engaged in frequent controversies, the causes of which are essentially foreign to our concerns. Hence, therefore, it must be un-wise in us to implicate ourselves by artificial ties in the ordinary vicissitudes of her politics or the ordinary combinations and collisions of her friendships or enmities.

Our detached and distant situation invites and enables us to pursue a different course. If we remain one people, under an efficient government, the period is not far off when we may defy material injury from external annoyance; when we may take such an attitude as will cause the neutrality we may at any time resolve upon to be scrupulously respected; when belligerent nations, under the impossibility of making acquisitions upon us, will not lightly hazard the giving us provocation; when we may choose peace or war, as our interest, guided by justice, shall counsel.

Why forego the advantages of so peculiar a situation? Why quit our own to stand upon foreign ground? Why, by interweaving our destiny with that of any part of Europe, entangle our peace and prosperity in the toils of European am-bition, rivalship, interest, humor, or caprice?

It is our true policy to steer clear of permanent alliances with any portion of the foreign world, so far. I mean, as we are now at liberty to do it; for let me not be understood as capable of patronizing infidelity to existing engagements. I hold the maxim no less applicable to public than to private affairs that honesty is always the best policy. I repeat, therefore, let those engagements be observed in their genuine sense. But in my opinion it is unnecessary and would be unwise to extend them.

Taking care always to keep ourselves by suitable establishments on a respect-able defensive posture, we may safely trust to temporary alliances for extraor-dinary emergencies.

Harmony, liberal intercourse with all nations are recommended by policy, humanity, and interest. But even our commercial policy should hold an equal and impartial hand, neither seeking nor granting exclusive favors or preferences; consulting the natural course of things; diffusing and diversifying by gentle means the streams of commerce, but forcing nothing; establishing with powers so disposed, in order to give trade a stable course, define the rights of our merchants, and to enable the Government to support them, conventional rules of intercourse, the best that present circumstances and mutual opinion will per-mit, but temporary and liable to be from time to time abandoned or varied as experience and circumstances shall dictate; constantly keeping in view that it is folly in one nation to look for disinterested favors from another; that it must pay with a portion of its independence for whatever it may accept under that character; that by such acceptance it may place itself in the condition of having given equivalents for nominal favors, and yet of being reproached with ingrat-itude for not giving more. There can be no greater error than to expect or calculate upon real favors from nation to nation. It is an illusion which expe-rience must cure, which a just pride ought to discard. . . .

Though in reviewing the incidents of my Administration I am unconscious of intentional error, I am nevertheless too sensible of my defects not to think it probable that I may have committed many errors. Whatever they may be, I fervently beseech the Almighty to avert or mitigate the evils to which they may tend. I shall also carry with me the hope that my country will never cease to view them with indulgence, and that, after forty-five years of my life dedicated to its service with an upright zeal, the faults of incompetent abilities will be consigned to oblivion, as myself must soon be to the mansions of rest.

Relying on its kindness in this as in other things, and actuated by that fervent love toward it which is so natural to a man who views in it the native soil of himself and his progenitors for several generations, I anticipate with pleasing expectation that retreat in which I promise myself to realize without alloy the sweet enjoyment of partaking in the midst of my fellow-citizens the benign influence of good laws under a free government—the ever-favorite object of my heart, and the happy reward, as I trust, of our mutual cares, labors, and dangers.

Geo. WASHINGTON.

Source: James D. Richardson, ed., *A Compilation of the Messages and Papers of the Presidents*, vol. 1 (New York: Bureau of National Literature, 1897), 205–16.

Part Two

The Early Republic

Americans began the nineteenth century hotly contesting the core principles of U.S. diplomacy. Thomas Jefferson, newly arrived in the White House in 1801, resumed his attempts to revive the practice of international relations. He continued his advocacy of free commerce as a universal pursuit that could draw together the common interests of the world community. His approach embodied the old standard that dictated a departure from existing European practice in favor of American innovation. Conversely, Jefferson also embraced the concurrent standard that measured the young nation's vitality and security in terms of its ability to expand. At the root of his thinking, Jefferson believed America could only preserve its liberty with the resources gained from the frontier.

Jefferson's election, the so-called Republican "revolution of 1800," was produced by the Federalists' missteps of the late 1790s. The war scare of 1798, the Alien and Seditions Acts, arguments over military readiness, and the need to increase taxation to rearm for war prepared the way for the first Republican administration. Jefferson's vision, as expressed in his inaugural address, was to use government to "restrain men from injuring one another."[1] This sentiment was essentially reflected in his foreign policy. Shortly after becoming president, Jefferson said that "We are firmly convinced, and we act on that conviction, that with nations, as with individuals, our interests soundly calculated, will ever be found inseparable from our moral duties."[2] Jefferson saw in this principle a guiding light for American diplomacy and a first step toward a new universal standard for international relations.

In the meantime, he looked to the west. There, he envisioned a landed frontier that would offer America its best chance of preserving the prosperity and liberty of its people. To confirm his belief, Jefferson dispatched Meriwether Lewis and William Clark to explore this unknown territory. He requested extensive reports on the nature of flora and fauna, information on Native Americans, and maps of navigable river systems. The mission was a success. Lewis and Clark planted the American flag in the west, blazing a trail for the country to follow before rival nations could shut off this important outlet.[3]

Diplomacy was a very important part of Lewis and Clark's journey, because it ultimately allowed Jefferson to purchase the Louisiana Territory from France without the traditional act of conquest that often accompanied national expansion. This was a time when foreign events favored the United States. The ongoing challenges faced by France created an important opportunity for Jefferson. The enormous cost of the Napoleonic wars, most notably Napoleon's plans for dominion in the Western Hemisphere that had been stymied by his failure to effectively suppress a rebellion in Santo Domingo, left France's coffers empty. Because of this, France agreed to sell the Louisiana Territory to the United States for approximately $15 million in cash and claims.

The legality of the Louisiana Purchase was something Jefferson agonized over throughout his first term. He had negotiated the purchase with France without significant congressional consultation, which was a far cry from the promises he had made only three years before as a presidential candidate when he declared a departure from the arbitrary policies of the Federalists. Members of the Virginia delegation to Congress, such as John Randolph, lost few opportunities denouncing what they considered abject hypocrisy. Jefferson further eroded his standing during U.S. negotiations with Spain over the status of Florida. Attempts to bully the Spanish and manipulate previous treaties, and the lack of success this produced, did little to endear Jefferson to members of his own party. In the end, Jefferson essentially preferred to risk the constitutionality of his policies rather than accept the risk of losing territory. In doing so, he succeeded in establishing a U.S. claim on the frontier to the west of the original colonies for the remainder of the nineteenth century.

Unfortunately, the war in Europe intruded on this scene. British seizures of neutral American shipping began again after the Peace of Amiens (1802) proved untenable and war with France was renewed. The United States retaliated, attempting to use commerce as a weapon against England. To the world, Jefferson claimed, "Let us see whether having taught so many other useful lessons to Europe, we may not add that of showing them that there are peaceable means of repressing injustice, by making it to the interest of the aggressor to do what is just."[4] The Non-Importation Act (1806) became an early sop to anti-British sentiments in America. In reality, it was a toothless law that did little but cause a mild disruption of trade. The British practice of impressment and the Orders in Council of 1807, endorsing the seizure of U.S. shipping, inflamed Congressional passions to a degree not seen since the crisis of 1798. The British attack on the USS *Chesapeake* in June 1807 antagonized the country almost to the point of war. It was followed by the passage and implementation of the much more stringent Embargo Act in December 1807. The act struck a massive blow against trade at a time when American exports had grown from $300,000 per annum in 1790 to more than $59 million by the time the embargo was implemented.[5] The Embargo Act backfired on the country, causing many regions to plummet into recession. The situation was further exacerbated by the heavy-handed efforts of the Jefferson administration to see the embargo implemented, recalling the past abuses of the Federalists ten years earlier.

Many viewed the arrival of James Madison with a sense of relief when he was sworn in in 1809. The Embargo Act was repealed. Military expenditures for the Army and Navy declined. Yet, American diplomacy drifted without substantive guidance, allowing a war to begin for which the United States was fundamentally unprepared. Deteriorating events in Europe created this situation. American shipping on the high seas was battered by British and French seizures. Impressment continued to be a public scandal. By 1812, passions again drew the country into war.[6] On 18 June 1812, only two days after Viscount Castlereagh announced that the orders in council would be revoked, Congress declared war. The war itself was a tragicomic affair, punctuated by the abortive invasion of Canada and the successful British occupation and destruction of the capital. It concluded on a note of diplomatic irony. The Treaty of Ghent, concluded on Christmas Eve 1814, failed to prevent the costly British defeat at New Orleans on 8 January 1815, an event that stoked American patriotic fervor and made Andrew Jackson a national figure.[7]

The search for western territories continued virtually uninterrupted after the war. Population growth west of the Appalachians was explosive. In 1790, 100,000 settlers occupied Kentucky and Tennessee. Twenty years later, the number had increased more than sixfold.[8] While the total number was modest by contemporary European standards, it created a sense in the United States that the frontier was the only place Americans could go to alleviate the pressure of an ever-increasing population. Accompanying this conventional wisdom was a prevailing sense that Americans were destined to spread out over the continent. At the start of the century, one Kentucky settler commented, "On the east we are bounded by the rising sun, on the north by the aurora borealis, on the west by the procession of the equinoxes, and on the south by the Day of Judgment."[9] Accordingly, Americans began their migration into the Mississippi valley and the Mexican province of Texas, and as far afield as the Pacific northwest and the California coast. Over time, as innovations in steam technology were applied to water travel and railroads, the settlement of the 1790s would seem small in comparison.

New settlement inevitably brought Americans into contact with the previously undisturbed Native American tribes of the new frontier, a development that necessitated a new evolution in American diplomacy. As early as 1790, George Washington had attempted to rationalize the conduct of Indian relations through the adoption of the Indian Trade and Intercourse Act (1790). In the context of this law, U.S. diplomatic contact with Native Americans was the province of Secretary of War Henry Knox. Both Knox and Washington determined that the federal government had an obligation to preserve and protect the Native American. Through the provisions of the Indian Trade and Intercourse Act, the purchase of land was to be governed by tribal councils and federal commissioners, and the impact of the settlement would be mitigated by mutually observed treaties. In principle, tribes were to be treated as quasi-states within the territorial boundaries of the United States.[10]

Rarely was Native American sovereignty observed in practice. During treaty negotiations with the major European powers after the Revolution, the interior tribes were treated as proxies of London or Madrid. The sore spot created by Native American alliances was addressed, but not resolved, by The Jay Treaty (1794) and The Pinckney Treaty (1795). British meddling along the Ohio frontier produced almost constant conflict between Native Americans and the United States. The same situation prevailed in Spanish Florida. As a consequence, war became a familiar means to resolve territorial disputes. Anthony Wayne's decisive victory at the Battle of Fallen Timbers (1794) set a long-standing precedent that would be repeated often on the American frontier.

The insidious cycle of white encroachment on Native American territory accompanied this development. Population pressure on sparsely populated tribal land continued unabated along the vast western frontier. Despite official prohibitions against land seizures, enforcement of treaty agreements by the minuscule American military proved impossible.[11] Instead, the displacement of Native Americans became the official goal of U.S. policy. By 1830, through the auspices of the Indian Removal Act, the United States attempted to divine a means to take indigenous peoples out of the path of expansion.[12]

Enormous changes to America's south also prompted an evolution of U.S. diplomacy. In the years after 1810, Latin America freed itself from Spanish dominion. Although many Americans doubted the Latin Americans' ability to sustain their independence or create viable democratic republics, they resented that the reimposition of Spanish authority by Ferdinand VII might provide a precedent for further European intrusions into the hemisphere.[13] Formulating a policy to counter Spain offered many possibilities. Close ties with sister republics to the south brought the possibility of new trading partnerships. Perhaps more important, by halting Spain, the United States could make an explicit statement against similar intrusions by England and Russia in the Western Hemisphere.[14]

British support of this idea was critical to its success. At the moment in history that Latin Americans declared their independence, the British Royal Navy dominated the sea, and London openly worried about French designs on a declining Spain and the concurrent need to redraw British alliances. James Monroe's doctrine was an opportunity for London, one that would keep British rivals out of the Western Hemisphere and, in the meantime, reinforce a link with the burgeoning United States that would give pause to British enemies in the future.

The final outcome of the Monroe Doctrine (1823) was to establish the principle of American dominion in the Western Hemisphere. As a statement of policy, it was remarkable, albeit unilaterally unenforceable. It could not prevent the arrival of British investors and banking interests in Latin America. Nor could it halt the French occupation of Mexico in 1862.[15] However, the Monroe Doctrine was an important measure of an American nation that had begun to look beyond its own borders.

A yardstick to measure this new perspective could be found in the southwestern frontier. In the northern Mexican province of Texas, years of unregulated settlement and growing friction led American settlers to war in 1836. Their victory did not end American pressure on Mexican territory. As early as 1841, Texans began to penetrate into the Santa Fe region, seeking additional territory for their fledgling republic.[16] The incorporation of Texas into the United States in 1845 merely passed the problem to Washington, D.C.

By the mid-1840s, expansion had become an important part of the national lexicon, embellished by John L. O'Sullivan's explanation of America's "Manifest Destiny" to prevail over the frontier and translated into actionable policy by James K. Polk. Polk entered office in 1845 determined to annex Texas and to expand the United States at the expense of Mexico. His pretense was the disputed southern boundary of Texas along the Rio Grande River. Under the able leadership of Zachary Taylor and Winfield Scott, his administration was able to prevail over Mexico, adding, through the Treaty of Guadalupe Hidalgo, over 500,000 square miles of territory to the United States.[17]

Historically, the success produced by the Mexican War proved to be a pyrrhic victory for American domestic stability. By providing an enormous territorial windfall, the war reopened and sharpened the bitter contemporary debate as to whether the new land should be slave or free. For years, policy makers had attempted to maintain a balance between the two. Prohibited by the Northwest Ordinance, the decision had been left to the petitioning territories afterward. The institution of slavery, forcing redress from advocates of free states, was adopted by Louisiana (1812), Mississippi (1817), Alabama (1819), Missouri (1821), Arkansas (1836), Florida (1845), and Texas (1845). When David Wilmot, a Democratic congressman from Pennsylvania, offered his proviso to an 1846 wartime spending bill that "neither slavery nor involuntary servitude shall exist" in territories gained from the conflict, he added another chapter to a divisive discourse that led America inexorably toward war.[18] Ultimately, the failure of compromise at home would leave the United States dangerously vulnerable in the arena of world affairs.

NOTES

1. James D. Richardson, ed., *A Compilation of the Messages and Papers of the Presidents*, vol. 1 (New York: Bureau of National Literature, 1897), 309–12.

2. Robert W. Tucker and David C. Hendrickson, *Empire of Liberty: The Statecraft of Thomas Jefferson* (New York: Oxford University Press, 1990), 11; Peter Onuf and Nicholas Onuf, *Federal Union, Modern World: The Law of Nations in an Age of Revolutions, 1776–1814* (Madison, WI: Madison House Publishers, 1993), 156–78.

3. Stephen E. Ambrose, *Undaunted Courage: Meriwether Lewis, Thomas Jefferson, and the Opening of the American West* (New York; Simon & Schuster, 1996), 68–79.

4. Samuel Eliot Morison, Henry Steele Commager, and William E. Leuchtenberg, *The Growth of the American Republic*, vol. 1 (New York: Oxford University Press, 1969), 352.

5. Ibid., 252.

6. Peter Onuf and Nicholas Onuf, *Federal Union, Modern World* (Madison, WI: Madison House Publishers, 1993), 211–18.

7. Robert V. Remini, *The Jacksonian Era* (Wheeling, IL: Harlan Davidson, 1997), 1–24.

8. Sam B. Hilliard, "A Robust New Nation," in *North America: The Historical Geography of a Changing Continent*, ed. Robert D. Mitchell and Paul A Groves (New York: Rowman & Littlefield, 1987), 165–67.

9. William Earl Weeks, *Building the Continental Empire: American Expansion from the Revolution to the Civil War* (Chicago: Ivan R. Dee, 1996), 60.

10. Theda Pudue and Michael D. Green, *The Cherokee Removal: A Brief History with Documents* (New York: St. Martin's Press, 1995), 9–12.

11. Robert M. Utley, *Frontier Regulars: The United States Army and the Indian, 1866–1891* (Lincoln: University of Nebraska Press, 1973), 1–10.

12. Pudue and Green, *The Cherokee Removal*, 58–173.

13. Charles Sellers, *The Market Revolution: Jacksonian America, 1815–1846* (New York: Oxford University Press, 1991), 70–102; Bradford Perkins, ed., *The Cambridge History of American Foreign Relations: The Creation of a Republican Empire, 1776–1865*, vol. 1 (New York: Cambridge University Press, 1995), 150.

14. James E. Lewis, *The American Union and the Problem of Neighborhood: The United States and the Collapse of the Spanish Empire, 1783–1829* (Chapel Hill: University of North Carolina Press, 1998), 165.

15. John A. Crow, *The Epic of Latin America*, 4th ed. (Berkeley: University of California Press, 1992), 649–66.

16. Dean B. Mahin, *Olive Branch and Sword: The United States and Mexico, 1845–1848* (Jefferson, NC: McFarland Publishers, 1997), 24; Frederick Merk, *The Monroe Doctrine and American Expansionism, 1843–1849* (New York: Knopf, 1966), 9–39.

17. Merk, *Monroe Doctrine and American Expansionism*, 9–39, 133–60.

18. Morison, Commager, and Leuchtenberg, *The Growth of the American Republic*, vol. 1, 1557.

10. THE CESSION OF LOUISIANA
30 April 1803

The Jefferson administration's $15 million purchase of the Louisiana Territory effectively doubled the size of the United States. The treaty that accompanied the acquisition was a landmark because it ended France's role as a major power on the continent. More important, it opened up a vast amount of land to Americans for future settlement.

ART. I. Whereas, by the article of the treaty concluded at St. Idelfonso, the 1st October, 1800 between the First Consul of the French Republic and his

Catholic Majesty, it was agreed as follows: "His Catholic Majesty Promises and engages on his part, to cede to the French Republic, six months after the full and entire execution of the conditions and stipulations herein relative to his royal highness the duke of Parma, the colony or province of Louisiana, with the same extent that it now has in the hands of Spain, and that it had when France possessed it; and such as it should be after the treaties subsequently entered into between Spain and other states." And *whereas*, in pursuance of the Treaty, and particularly of the third article, the French Republic has an incontestable title to the domain and to the possession of the said territory:—The First Consul of the French Republic desiring to give to the United States a strong proof of his friendship, doth hereby cede to the said United States, in the name of the French Republic, forever and in full sovereignty, the said territory with all its rights and appurtenances, as fully and in the same manner as they have been acquired by the French Republic, in virtue of the above-mentioned Treaty, concluded with his Catholic Majesty.

ART. II. In the cession made by the preceding article are included the adjacent islands belonging to Louisiana, all public lots and squares, vacant lands, and all public buildings, fortifications, barracks, and other edifices which are not private property.—The Archives, papers, and documents, relative to the domain and sovereignty of Louisiana, and its dependencies, will be left in the possession of the Commissaries of the United States, and copies will be afterwards given in due form to the Magistrates and Municipal officers, of such of the said papers and documents as may be necessary to them.

ART. III. The inhabitants of the ceded territory shall be incorporated in the Union of the United States, and admitted as soon as possible, according to the principles of the Federal Constitution, to the enjoyment of all the rights, advantages and immunities of citizens of the United States; and in the mean time they shall be maintained and protected in the free enjoyment of their liberty, property, and the Religion which they profess. . . .

ART VII. It has been agreed between the contracting parties, that the French ships coming directly from France or any of her colonies, loaded only with the produce and manufactures of France or her said Colonies; and the ships of Spain coming directly from Spain or any of her colonies, loaded only with the produce or manufactures of Spain or her Colonies, shall be admitted during the space of twelve years in the ports of New Orleans, and in all other legal ports of entry within the ceded territory, in the same manner as the ships of the United States coming directly from France or Spain, or any of their colonies, without being, subject to any other or greater duty on merchandize, or other or greater tonnage than that paid by the citizens of the United States. . . .

Source: Hunter Miller, ed., *Treaties and Other International Acts of the United States of America*, vol. 1 (Washington, DC: Government Printing Office, 1931), 498–511.

11.　THE EMBARGO ACT
22 December 1807

By 1807, British seizures of neutral American shipping and Britain's on-going practice of impressment had pushed the United States to the brink of war. However, it was Thomas Jefferson's belief that he could use the power of a trade embargo to bring England to heel and resolve the conflict without bloodshed. On 22 December 1807, Congress passed The Embargo Act, *which forbade all exports from the United States whether by sea or by land and prohibited the import of certain British manufactures.*

An Act laying an Embargo on all ships and vessels in the ports and harbors of the United States.

Be it enacted, That an embargo be and hereby is laid on all ships and vessels in the ports and places within the limits or jurisdiction of the United States, cleared or not cleared, bound to any foreign port or place and that no clearance be furnished to any ship or vessel bound to such foreign port or place, except vessels under the immediate direction of the President of the United States: and that the President be authorized to give such instructions to the officers of the revenue, and of the navy and revenue cutters of the United States, as shall appear best adapted for carrying the same into full effect: *Provided*, that nothing herein contained shall be construed to prevent the departure of any foreign ship or vessel, either in ballast, or with the goods, wares and merchandise on board of such foreign ship or vessel, when notified of this act.

SEC. 2. That during the continuance of this act, no registered, or sea letter vessel, having on board goods, wares and merchandise, shall be allowed to depart from one port of the United States to any other within the same, unless the master, owner, consignee or factor of such vessel shall first give bond, with one or more sureties to the collector of the district from which she is bound to depart, in a sum of double the value of the vessel and cargo, that the said goods, wares, or merchandise shall be relanded in some port of the United States, dangers of the seas excepted, which bond, and also a certificate from the collector where the same may be relanded, shall by the collector respectively be transmitted to the Secretary of the Treasury. All armed vessels possessing public commissions from any foreign power, are not to be considered as liable to the embargo laid by this act.

Source: Henry Steele Commager, *Documents of American History*, vol. 1 (Englewood Cliffs, NJ: Prentice Hall, 1973), 202–3.

12.   THE NON-INTERCOURSE ACT
1 March 1809

In the spirit of greeting the newly arrived James Madison as a peacemaker, Congress repealed The Embargo Act *and substituted it with* The Non-Intercourse Act. *Aimed at both England and France, it held out the offer of repeal if either nation interfered with American shipping. George Canning, the British Minister of Foreign Affairs, denounced the act, setting the stage for a further decline in Anglo-American relations.*

An Act to interdict the commercial intercourse between the United States and Great Britain and France, and their dependencies; and for other purposes.

Be it enacted, That from and after the passing of this act, the entrance of the harbors and waters of the United States and of the territories thereof, be, and the same is hereby interdicted to all public ships and vessels belonging to Great Britain or France. . . . And if any public ship or vessel as aforesaid, not being included in the exception above mentioned, shall enter any harbor or waters within the jurisdiction of the United States, or of the territories thereof, it shall be lawful for the President of the United States, or such other person as he shall have empowered for that purpose, to employ such part of the land and naval forces, or of the militia of the United States, or the territories thereof, as he shall deem necessary, to compel such ship or vessel to depart.

SEC. 2. That it shall not be lawful for any citizen or citizens of the United States or the territories thereof, nor for any person or persons residing or being in the same, to have any intercourse with, or to afford any aid or supplies to any public ship or vessel as aforesaid, which shall, contrary to the provisions of this act, have entered any harbor or waters within the jurisdiction of the United States or the territories thereof; and if any person shall, contrary to the provisions of this act, have any intercourse with such ship or vessel, or shall afford any aid to such ship or vessel, either in repairing the said vessel or in furnishing her, her officers and crew with supplies of any kind or in any manner whatever, . . . every person so offending, shall forfeit and pay a sum not less than one hundred dollars, nor exceeding ten thousand dollars; and shall also be imprisoned for a term not less than one month, nor more than one year.

SEC. 3. That from and after the twentieth day of May next, the entrance of the harbors and waters of the United States and the territories thereof be, and the same is hereby interdicted to all ships or vessels sailing under the flag of Great Britain or France, or owned in whole or in part by any citizen or subject of either. . . . And if any ship or vessel sailing under the flag of Great Britain or France . . . shall after the said twentieth day of May next, arrive either with or without a cargo, within the limits of the United States or of the territories thereof, such ship or vessel, together with the cargo, if any, which may be found on board, shall be forfeited, and may be seized and condemned in any court of the United States or the territories thereof, having competent jurisdiction. . . .

SEC. 4. That from and after the twentieth day of May next, it shall not be lawful to import into the United States or the territories thereof, any goods, wares or merchandise whatever, from any port or place situated in Great Britain or Ireland, or in any of the colonies or dependencies of Great Britain, nor from any port or place situated in France, or in any of her colonies or dependencies, nor from any port or place in the actual possession of either Great Britain or France. Nor shall it be lawful to import into the United States, or the territories thereof, from any foreign port or place whatever, any goods, wares or merchandise whatever, being of the growth, produce or manufacture of France, or of any of her colonies or dependencies, or being of the growth, produce or manufacture of Great Britain or Ireland, or of any of the colonies or dependencies of Great Britain, or being of the growth, produce or manufacture of any place or country in the actual possession of either France or Great Britain. . . .

SEC. 11. That the President of the United States be, and he hereby is authorized, in case either France or Great Britain shall so revoke or modify her edicts, as that they shall cease to violate the neutral commerce of the United States, to declare the same by proclamation: after which the trade of the United States, suspended by this act, and by the [Embargo Act] and the several acts supplementary thereto, may be renewed with the nation so doing. . . .

SEC. 12. That so much of the . . . [Embargo Act] and of the several acts supplementary thereto, as forbids the departure of vessels owned by citizens of the United States, and the exportation of domestic and foreign merchandise to any foreign port or place, be and the same is hereby repealed, after March 15, 1809, except so far as they relate to Great Britain or France, or their colonies or dependencies, or places in the actual possession of either. . . .

SEC. 19. That this act shall continue and be in force until the end of the next session of Congress, and no longer; and that the act laying an embargo on all ships and vessels in the ports and harbors of the United States, and the several acts supplementary thereto, shall be, and the same are hereby repealed from and after the end of the next session of Congress.

Source: Henry Steele Commager, *Documents of American History*, vol. 1 (Englewood Cliffs, NJ: Prentice Hall, 1973), 203–4.

13. MADISON'S WAR MESSAGE
1 June 1812

For the majority of James Madison's first term in office, attempts to avert war were successful. However, after numerous clashes with the Royal

Navy and London's continued refusal to repeal the Orders in Council, he asked the Congress for war. The consummate irony of this act was that the British finally decided to repeal the Orders on 16 June 1812. Two days later Congress declared war.

To the Senate and House of Representatives of the United States:
I communicate to Congress certain documents, being a continuation of those heretofore laid before them on the subject of our affairs with Great Britain.

Without going back beyond the renewal in 1803 of the war in which Great Britain is engaged, and omitting unrepaired wrongs of inferior magnitude, the conduct of her Government presents a series of acts hostile to the United States as an independent and neutral nation.

British cruisers have been in the continued practice of violating the American flag on the great highway of nations, and of seizing and carrying off persons sailing under it, not in the exercise of a belligerent right founded on the law of nations against an enemy, but of a municipal prerogative over British subjects. British jurisdiction is thus extended to neutral vessels in a situation where no laws can operate but the law of nations and the laws of the country to which the vessels belong, and a self-redress is assumed which, if British subjects were wrongfully detained and alone concerned, is that substitution of force for a resort to the responsible sovereign which falls within the definition of war. . . .

The practice, hence, is so far from affecting British subjects alone that, under the pretext of searching for these, thousands of American citizens, under the safeguard of public law and of their national flag, have been torn from their country and from everything dear to them; have been dragged on board ships of war of a foreign nation and exposed, under the severities of their discipline, to be exiled to the most distant and deadly climes, to risk their lives in the battles of their oppressors, and to be the melancholy instruments of taking away those of their own brethren.

Against this crying enormity, which Great Britain would be so prompt to avenge if committed against herself, the United States have in vain exhausted remonstrances and expostulations, and that no proof might be wanting of their conciliatory dispositions, and no pretext left for a continuance of the practice, the British Government was formally assured of the readiness of the United States to enter into arrangements such as could not be rejected if the recovery of British subjects were the real and the sole object. The communication passed without effect.

British cruisers have been in the practice also of violating the rights and the peace of our coasts. They hover over and harass our entering and departing commerce. To the most insulting pretensions they have added the most lawless proceedings in our very harbors, and have wantonly spilt American blood within the sanctuary of our territorial jurisdiction. . . .

Under pretended blockades, without the presence of an adequate force and sometimes without the practicability of applying one, our commerce has been plundered in every sea, the great staples of our country have been cut off from their legitimate markets, and a destructive blow aimed at our agricultural and maritime interests. In aggravation of these predatory measures they have been considered as in force from the dates of their notification, a retrospective effect being thus added, as has been done in other important cases, to the unlawfulness of the course pursued. And to render the outrage the more signal these mock blockades have been reiterated and enforced in the face of official communications from the British Government declaring as the true definition of a legal blockade "that particular ports must be actually invested and previous warning given to vessels bound to them not to enter."

Not content with these occasional expedients for laying waste our neutral trade, the cabinet of Britain resorted at length to the sweeping system of blockades, under the name of orders in council, which has been molded and managed as might best suit its political views, its commercial jealousies, or the avidity of British cruisers. . . .

Abandoning still more all respect for the neutral rights of the United States and for its own consistency, the British Government now demands as prerequisites to a repeal of its orders as they relate to the United States that a formality should be observed in the repeal of the French decrees no wise necessary to their termination nor exemplified by British usage, and that the French repeal, besides including that portion of the decrees which operates within a territorial jurisdiction, as well as that which operates on the high seas, against the commerce of the United States should not be a single and special repeal in relation to the United States, but should be extended to whatever other neutral nations unconnected with them may be affected by those decrees. . . .

It has become, indeed, sufficiently certain that the commerce of the United States is to be sacrificed, not as interfering with the belligerent rights of Great Britain; not as supplying the wants of her enemies, which she herself supplies; but as interfering with the monopoly which she covets for her own commerce and navigation. She carries on a war against the lawful commerce of a friend that she may the better carry on a commerce with an enemy—commerce polluted by the forgeries and perjuries which are for the most part the only passports by which it can succeed. . . .

In reviewing the conduct of Great Britain toward the United States our attention is necessarily drawn to the warfare just renewed by the savages on one of our extensive frontiers—a warfare which is known to spare neither age nor sex and to be distinguished by features peculiarly shocking to humanity. It is difficult to account for the activity and combinations which have for some time been developing themselves among tribes in constant intercourse with British traders and garrisons without connecting their hostility with that influence and without recollecting the authenticated examples of such interpositions heretofore furnished by the officers and agents of that Government.

Such is the spectacle of injuries and indignities which have been heaped on our country, and such the crisis which its unexampled forbearance and conciliatory efforts have not been able to avert. . . .

Our moderation and conciliation have had no other effect than to encourage perseverance and to enlarge pretensions. We behold our seafaring citizens still the daily victims of lawless violence, committed on the great common and highway of nations, even within sight of the country which owes them protection. We behold our vessels, freighted with the products of our soil and industry, or returning with the honest proceeds of them, wrested from their lawful destinations, confiscated by prize courts no longer the organs of public law but the instruments of arbitrary edicts, and their unfortunate crews dispersed and lost, or forced or inveigled in British ports into British fleets, whilst arguments are employed in support of these aggressions which have no foundation but in a principle equally supporting a claim to regulate our external commerce in all cases whatsoever.

We behold, in fine, on the side of Great Britain a state of war against the United States, and on the side of the United States a state of peace toward Great Britain.

Whether the United States shall continue passive under these progressive usurpations and these accumulating wrongs, or, opposing force to force in defense of their national rights, shall commit a just cause into the hands of the Almighty Disposer of Events, avoiding all connections which might entangle it in the contest or views of other powers, and preserving a constant readiness to concur in an honorable reestablishment of peace and friendship, is a solemn question which the Constitution wisely confides to the legislative department of the Government. In recommending it to their early deliberations I am happy in the assurance that the decision will be worthy the enlightened and patriotic councils of a virtuous, a free, and a powerful nation. . . .

Source: James D. Richardson, ed., *A Compilation of the Messages and Papers of the Presidents*, vol. 2 (New York: Bureau of National Literature, 1897), 484–90.

14. RUSH-BAGOT AGREEMENT
28 April 1818

In 1818, England and the United States agreed to neutralize the Great Lakes region and create an unfortified border along the Canadian frontier. The action served as a building block for Anglo-American rapprochement after the War of 1812 and allowed the United States to focus attention on other areas of the western frontier.

ARRANGEMENT

BETWEEN, the United States and Great Britain, between Richard Rush, Esq., acting as Secretary of the Department of State, and Charles Bagot, His Britannic Majesty's Envoy Extraordinary, &c.

The naval force to be maintained upon the American lakes, by his majesty and the government of the United States, shall henceforth be confined to the following vessels on each side; that is—

On lake Ontario, to one vessel not exceeding one hundred tons burden, and armed with one eighteen pound cannon.

On the upper lakes, to two vessels, not exceeding like burden each, and armed with like force.

On the waters of lake Champlain, to one vessel not exceeding like burden, and armed with like force.

All other armed vessels on these lakes shall be forthwith dismantled, and no other vessels of war shall be there built or armed.

If either party should hereafter be desirous of annulling this stipulation, and should give notice to that effect to the other party, it shall cease to be binding after the expiration of six months from the date of such notice.

The naval force so to be limited shall be restricted to such services as will, in no respect, interfere with the proper duties of the armed vessels of the other party.

Source: Henry Steele Commager, *Documents of American History*, vol. 1 (Englewood Cliffs, NJ: Prentice Hall, 1973), 213.

---

15. FLORIDA TREATY
22 February 1819

Prompted by Andrew Jackson's invasion of Florida in 1818, Spain decided to finally cede the territory to the United States. As a result of the treaty, America was able to take possession of Florida and define its boundary with Mexico. Spain also relinquished its claim on the Oregon Territory. While the agreement was being finalized, James Monroe withheld recognition of the newly independent Latin American republic for fear of provoking the Spanish.

ART. I. There shall be a firm and inviolable peace and sincere friendship between the United States and their Citizens, and His Catholic Majesty, his Successors and Subjects, without exception of persons or places.

ART. II. His Catholic Majesty cedes to the United States, in full property and sovereignty, all the territories which belonged to him, situated to the eastward of the Mississippi, known by the name of East and West Florida. The adjacent islands dependent on said provinces, all public lots and squares, vacant lands, public edifices, fortifications, barracks, and other buildings, which are not private property, archives and documents, which relate directly to the property and sovereignty of said provinces, are included in this article. . . .

ART. III. The boundary line between the two countries, west of the Mississippi shall begin on the Gulph of Mexico, at the mouth of the river Sabine, in the sea, continuing north, along the western bank of that river, to the 32d degree of latitude; thence, by a line due north, to the degree of latitude where it strikes the Rio Roxo of Natchitoches, or Red River; thence following the course of the Rio Roxo westward, to the degree of longitude 100 west from London and 23 from Washington; then, crossing the said Red River, and running thence, by a line due north, to the river Arkansas, thence, following the course of the southern bank of the Arkansas, to its source, in latitude 42 north; and thence, by that parallel of latitude, to the South Sea. The whole being as laid down in Melish's map of the United States, published at Philadelphia, improved to the first of January, 1818. But if the source of the Arkansas River shall be found to fall north or south of latitude 42, then the line shall run from the said source due north or south, as the case may be, till it meets the said parallel of latitude 42, and thence, along the said parallel, to the South Sea: All the islands in the Sabine, and the said Red and Arkansas Rivers, throughout the course thus described, to belong to the United States; but the use of the waters, and the navigation of the Sabine to the sea, and of the said rivers Roxo and Arkansas, throughout the extent of the said boundary, on their respective banks, shall be common to the respective inhabitants of both nations. . . .

ART. V. The inhabitants of the ceded territories shall be secured in the free exercise of their religion, without any restriction. . . .

ART. VI. The inhabitants of the territories which His Catholic Majesty cedes to the United States, by this treaty, shall be incorporated in the Union of the United States, as soon as may be consistent with the principles of the Federal Constitution, and admitted to the enjoyment of all the privileges, rights, and immunities of the citizens of the United States. . . .

ART. XI. The United States, exonerating Spain from all demands in future, on account of the claims of their citizens to which the renunciations herein contained extend, and considering them entirely canceled, undertake to make satisfaction for the same, to an amount not exceeding five millions of dollars. To ascertain the full amount and validity of those claims, a commission, to consist of three Commissioners, citizens of the United States, shall be appointed by the President, by and with the advice and consent of the Senate. . . .

ART. XV. Spanish vessels, laden only with productions of Spanish growth or manufacture, coming directly from Spain, or her colonies shall be admitted, for the term of twelve years, to the ports of Pensacola and St. Augustine, without paying other or higher duties on their cargoes, or of tonnage, than will be paid by the vessels of the United States. During the said term no other nation shall enjoy the same privileges within the ceded territories. . . .

Source: Hunter Miller, ed., *Treaties and Other International Acts of the United States of America*, vol. 3 (Washington, DC: Government Printing Office, 1933), 3–64.

---

16.   MONROE DOCTRINE
2 December 1823

At the end of 1823, James Monroe made a statement of principle denying the right of European powers to emplace colonies in the Western Hemisphere. Undertaken with explicit British support, the doctrine represented a solidification of U.S. relations with England and an important step forward for American hegemony.

. . . At the proposal of the Russian Imperial Government, made through the minister of the Emperor residing here, a full power and instructions have been transmitted to the minister of the United States at St. Petersburg to arrange by amicable negotiation the respective rights and interests of the two nations on the northwest coast of this continent. A similar proposal had been made by His Imperial Majesty to the Government of Great Britain, which has likewise been acceded to. The Government of the United States has been desirous by this friendly proceeding of manifesting the great value which they have invariably attached to the friendship of the Emperor and their solicitude to cultivate the best understanding with his Government. In the discussions to which this interest has given rise and in the arrangements by which they may terminate the occasion has been judged proper for asserting, as a principle in which the rights and interests of the United States are involved, that the American continents, by the free and independent condition which they have assumed and maintain, are henceforth not to be considered as subjects for future colonization by any European powers. . . .

It was stated at the commencement of the last session that a great effort was then making in Spain and Portugal to improve the condition of the people of those countries, and that it appeared to be conducted with extraordinary moderation. It need scarcely be remarked that the result has been so far very different from what was then anticipated. Of events in that quarter of the globe, with which we have so much intercourse and from which we derive our origin, we have always been anxious and interested spectators. The citizens of the United States cherish sentiments the most friendly in favor of the liberty and happiness of their fellow-men on that side of the Atlantic. In the wars of the European powers in matters relating to themselves we have never taken any part, nor does it comport with our policy so to do. It is only when our rights are invaded or seriously menaced that we resent injuries or make preparation for our defense. With the movements in this hemisphere we are of necessity more immediately connected, and by causes which must be obvious to all enlightened and impartial observers. The political system of the allied powers is essentially different in this respect from that of America. This difference proceeds from that which exists in their respective Governments; and to the defense of our own, which has been achieved by the loss of so much blood and treasure, and matured by the wisdom of their most enlightened citizens, and under which we have enjoyed unexampled felicity, this whole nation is devoted. We owe it, therefore, to candor and to the amicable relations existing between the United States and those powers to declare that we should consider any attempt on their part to extend their system to any portion of this hemisphere as dangerous to our peace and safety. With the existing colonies or dependencies of any European power we have not interfered and shall not interfere. But with the Governments who have declared their independence and maintained it, and whose independence we have, on great consideration and on just principles, acknowledged, we could not view any interposition for the purpose of oppressing them, or controlling in any other manner their destiny, by any European power in any other light than as the manifestation of an unfriendly disposition toward the United States. In the war between those new Governments and Spain we declared our neutrality at the time of their recognition, and to this we have adhered, and shall continue to adhere, provided no change shall occur which, in the judgment of the competent authorities of this Government, shall make a corresponding change on the part of the United States indispensable to their security.

The late events in Spain and Portugal shew that Europe is still unsettled. Of this important fact no stronger proof can be adduced than that the allied powers should have thought it proper, on any principle satisfactory to themselves, to have interposed by force in the internal concerns of Spain. To what extent such interposition may be carried, on the same principle, is a question in which all independent powers whose governments differ from theirs are interested, even those most remote, and surely none more so than the United States. Our policy in regard to Europe, which was adopted at an early stage of the wars which have so long agitated that quarter of the globe, nevertheless remains the same, which is, not to interfere in the internal concerns of any of its powers; to consider the government *de facto* as the legitimate government for us; to cultivate friendly relations with it, and to preserve those relations by a frank, firm, and manly policy, meeting in all instances the just claims of every power, submitting to injuries from none. But in regard to those continents circumstances are eminently and conspicuously different. It is impossible that the allied powers should extend their political system to any portion of either continent without endangering our peace and happiness; nor can anyone believe that our southern brethren, if left to themselves, would adopt it of their own accord. It is equally impossible, therefore, that we should behold such interposition in any form with indifference. If we look to the comparative strength and resources of Spain and those new Governments, and their distance from each other, it must be obvious that she can never subdue them. It is still the true policy of the United States to leave the parties to themselves, in the hope that other powers will pursue the same course. . . .

Source: James D. Richardson, ed., *A Compilation of the Messages and Papers of the Presidents*, vol. 2 (New York: Bureau of National Literature, 1897), 778–89.

---

17. THE PANAMA CONGRESS
MESSAGE OF PRESIDENT ADAMS ON THE
PARTICIPATION OF THE UNITED STATES IN THE
PANAMA CONGRESS
26 December 1825

In an effort to unify Latin America, Simón Bolívar called for a Congress of American nations to meet in Panama in 1826. The United States was invited to attend after some prompting by Mexico and Colombia. Although Congress was not in favor of sending American delegates, it endorsed the idea with the condition that representatives not approve any resolution limiting the freedom of the participating countries.

To the Senate of the United States:

In the message to both Houses of Congress at the commencement of the session it was mentioned that the Governments of the Republics of Colombia, of Mexico, and of Central America had severally invited the Government of the United States to be represented at the Congress of American nations to be assembled at Panama to deliberate upon objects of peculiar concernment to this hemisphere, and that this invitation had been accepted.

Although this measure was deemed to be within the constitutional competency of the Executive, I have not thought proper to take any step in it before ascertaining that my opinion of its expediency will concur with that of both branches of the Legislature, first, by the decision of the Senate upon the nominations to be laid before them, and, secondly, by the sanction of both Houses to the appropriations, without which it can not be carried into effect. . . .

It will be seen that the United States neither intend nor are expected to take part in any deliberations of a belligerent character; that the motive of their attendance is neither to contract alliances nor to engage in any undertaking or project importing hostility to any other nation.

But the Southern American nations, in the infancy of their independence, often find themselves in positions with reference to other countries with the principles applicable to which, derivable from the state of independence itself, they have not been familiarized by experience. The result of this has been that sometimes in their intercourse with the United States they have manifested dispositions to reserve a right of granting special favors and privileges to the Spanish nation as the price of their recognition. At others they have actually established duties and impositions operating unfavorably to the United States to the advantage of other European powers, and sometimes they have appeared to consider that they might interchange among themselves mutual concessions of exclusive favor, to which neither European powers nor the United States should be admitted. In most of these cases their regulations unfavorable to us have yielded to friendly expostulation and remonstrance. But it is believed to be of infinite moment that the principles of a liberal commercial intercourse should be exhibited to them, and urged with disinterested and friendly persuasion upon them when all assembled for the avowed purpose of consulting together upon the establishment of such principles as may have an important bearing upon their future welfare.

The consentaneous adoption of principles of maritime neutrality, and favorable to the navigation of peace, and commerce in time of war, will also form a subject of consideration to this Congress. The doctrine that free ships make free goods and the restrictions of reason upon the extent of blockades may be established by general agreement with far more ease, and perhaps with less danger, by the general engagement to adhere to them concerted at such a meeting, than by partial treaties or conventions with each of the nations separately. An agreement between all the parties represented at the meeting that each will guard by its own means against the establishment of any future European colony within its borders may be found advisable. This was more than two years since announced by my predecessor to the world as a principle resulting from the emancipation of both the American continents. It may be so developed to the new southern nations that they will all feel it as an essential appendage to their independence.

There is yet another subject upon which, without entering into any treaty, the moral influence of the United States may perhaps be exerted with beneficial consequences at such a meeting—the advancement of religious liberty. Some of the southern nations are even yet so far under the dominion of prejudice that they have incorporated with their political constitutions an exclusive church, without toleration of any other than the dominant sect. The abandonment of this last badge of religious bigotry and oppression may be pressed more effectually by the united exertions of those who concur in the principles of freedom of conscience upon those who are yet to be convinced of their justice and wisdom than by the solitary efforts of a minister to any one of the separate Governments. . . .

In fine, a decisive inducement with me for acceding to the measure is to show by this token of respect to the southern Republics the interest that we take in their welfare and our disposition to comply with their wishes. Having been the first to recognize their independence, and sympathized with them so far as was compatible with our neutral duties in all their struggles and sufferings to acquire it, we have laid the foundation of our future intercourse with them in the broadest principles of reciprocity and the most cordial feelings of fraternal friendship. To extend those principles to all our commercial relations with them and to hand down that friendship to future ages is congenial to the highest policy of the Union, as it will be to that of all those nations and their posterity. In the confidence that these sentiments will meet the approbation of the Senate, I nominate Richard C. Anderson, of Kentucky, and John Sergeant, of Pennsylvania, to be envoys extraordinary and ministers plenipotentiary to the assembly of American nations at Panama, and William B. Rochester, of New York, to be secretary to the mission.

Source: James D. Richardson, ed., *A Compilation of the Messages and Papers of the Presidents*, vol. 2 (New York: Bureau of National Literature, 1897), 884–86.

18. JACKSON'S MESSAGE ON THE REMOVAL OF SOUTHERN INDIANS TO THE INDIAN TERRITORY
7 December 1835

The removal of the Creeks, Cherokee, and other tribes located in the southeastern part of the United States reached its final stages in 1835. Andrew Jackson's refusal to acknowledge (or accept) the Supreme Court's recognition of Native American rights was followed by plans to displace the collected tribes to a reservation west of the Mississippi.

WASHINGTON, *December 7, 1835*

... The plan of removing the aboriginal people who yet remain within the settled portions of the United States to the country west of the Mississippi River approaches its consummation. It was adopted on the most mature consideration of the condition of this race, and ought to be persisted in till the object is accomplished, and prosecuted with as much vigor as a just regard to their circumstances will permit, and as fast as their consent can be obtained. All preceding experiments for the improvement of the Indians have failed. It seems now to be an established fact that they can not live in contact with a civilized community and prosper. Ages of fruitless endeavors have at length brought us to a knowledge of this principle of intercommunication with them. The past we can not recall, but the future we can provide for. Independently of the treaty stipulations into which we have entered with the various tribes for the usufructuary rights they have ceded to us, no one can doubt the moral duty of the Government of the United States to protect and if possible to preserve and perpetuate the scattered remnants of this race which are left within our borders. In the discharge of this duty an extensive region in the West has been assigned for their permanent residence. It has been divided into districts and allotted among them. Many have already removed and others are preparing to go, and with the exception of two small bands living in Ohio and Indiana, not exceeding 1,500 persons, and of the Cherokees, all the tribes on the east side of the Mississippi, and extending from Lake Michigan to Florida, have entered into engagements which will lead to their transplantation.

The plan for their removal and reestablishment is founded upon the knowledge we have gained of their character and habits, and has been dictated by a spirit of enlarged liberality. A territory exceeding in extent that relinquished has been granted to each tribe. Of its climate, fertility, and capacity to support an Indian population the representations are highly favorable. To these districts the Indians are removed at the expense of the United States, and with certain supplies of clothing, arms, ammunition, and other indispensable articles; they are also furnished gratuitously with provisions for the period of a year after their arrival at their new homes. In that time, from the nature of the country and of the products raised by them, they can subsist themselves by agricultural labor, if they choose to resort to that mode of life; if they do not they are upon the skirts of the great prairies, where countless herds of buffalo roam, and a short time suffices to adapt their own habits to the changes which a change of the animals destined for their food may require. Ample arrangements have also been made for the support of schools; in some instances council houses and churches are to be erected, dwellings constructed for the chiefs, and mills for common use. Funds have been set apart for the maintenance of the poor; the most necessary mechanical arts have been introduced, and blacksmiths, gunsmiths, wheelwrights, millwrights. etc., are supported among them. Steel and iron, and sometimes salt, are purchased for them, and plows and other farming utensils, domestic animals, looms, spinning wheels, cards, etc., are presented to them. And besides these beneficial arrangements, annuities are in all cases paid, amounting in some instances to more than $30 for each individual of the tribe, and in all cases sufficiently great, if justly divided and prudently expended, to enable them, in addition to their own exertions, to live comfortably. And as a stimulus for exertion, it is now provided by law that "in all cases of the appointment of interpreters or other persons employed for the benefit of the Indians a preference shall be given to persons of Indian descent, if such can be found who are properly qualified for the discharge of the duties." Such are the arrangements for the physical comfort and for the moral improvement of the Indians. The necessary measures for their political advancement and for their separation from our citizens have not been neglected. The pledge of the United States has been given by Congress that the country destined for the residence of this people shall be forever "secured and guaranteed to them." A country west of Missouri and Arkansas has been assigned to them, into which the white settlements are not to be pushed. No political communities can be formed in that extensive region, except those which are established by the Indians themselves or by the United States for them and with their concurrence. A barrier has thus been raised for their protection against the encroachment of our citizens, and guarding the Indians as far as possible from those evils which have brought them to their present condition. Summary authority has been given by law to destroy all ardent spirits found in their country, without waiting the doubtful result and slow process of a legal seizure. I consider the absolute and unconditional interdiction of this article among these people as the first and great step in their melioration. Halfway measures will answer no purpose. These can not successfully contend against the cupidity of the seller and the overpowering appetite of the buyer. And the destructive effects of the traffic are marked in every page of the history of our Indian intercourse. . . .

Source: James D. Richardson, ed., *A Compilation of the Messages and Papers of the Presidents*, vol. 3 (New York: Bureau of National Literature, 1897), 1390–96.

---

19. TEXAS DECLARATION OF INDEPENDENCE
2 March 1836

For many years the American settlers in Texas were at odds with the government of Mexico. They had been invited to colonize Mexico's wilderness with the promise that they would continue to enjoy the "constitutional liberty and republican government to which they had been habituated in the land of their birth, the United States of America." But this promise was not kept. After many attempts to resolve their differences with Mexico failed, the American settlers declared their independence. That same week, with the intention of restoring order, General Antonio López de Santa Anna, leading a Mexican army, marched into the territory. After a series of short, sharp battles that culminated in Santa Anna's defeat at San Jacinto, Texas's separation from Mexico became a reality.

When a government has ceased to protect the lives liberty and property of its people, from whom its legitimate powers are derived, and for the advancement of whose happiness it was instituted, and so far from being a guarantee for the enjoyment of those inestimable and inalienable rights, becomes an instrument in the hands of evil rulers for their oppression: When the Federal Republican Constitution of their country, which they have sworn to support, no longer has a substantial existence, and the whole nature of their government has been forcibly changed without their consent, from a restricted federative republic, composed of sovereign states to a consolidated central military despotism in which every interest is disregarded but that of the army and the priesthood—both the eternal enemies of civil liberty, the ever-ready minions of power, and the usual instruments of tyrants:

When, long after the spirit of the constitution has departed, moderation is at length so far lost by those in power that even the semblance of freedom is removed, and the forms, themselves, of the constitution discontinued; and so far from their petitions and remonstrances being regarded, the agents who bear them are thrown into dungeons; and mercenary armies sent forth to force a new government upon them at the point of the bayonet: When, in consequence of such acts of malfeasance and abdication, on the part of the government, anarchy prevails, and Civil Society is dissolved into its original elements. In such a crisis, the first law of nature, the right of self-preservation the inherent and unalienable right of the people to appeal to first principles and take their political affairs into their own hands in extreme cases enjoins it as a right towards themselves and a sacred obligation to their posterity to abolish such government and create another in its stead, calculated to rescue them from impending dangers, and to secure their future welfare and happiness.

Nations, as well as individuals, are amenable for their acts to the public opinion of mankind. Statement of a part of our grievance is, therefore, submitted to an impartial world, in justification of the hazardous but unavoidable step now taken of severing our political connection with the Mexican people, and assuming an independent attitude among the nations of the earth.

The Mexican government, by its colonization laws, invited and induced the Anglo-American population of Texas to colonize its wilderness under the pledged faith of a written constitution that they should continue to enjoy that constitutional liberty and republican government to which they had been habituated in the land of their birth, the United States of America. In this expectation they have been cruelly disappointed, in as much as the Mexican nation has acquiesced in the late changes made in the government by General Antonio Lopez de Santa Anna, who, having overturned the constitution of his country, now offers as the cruel alternative either to abandon our homes, acquired by so many privations, or submit to the most intolerable of all tyranny, the combined despotism of the sword and the priesthood.

It has sacrificed our welfare to the State of Coahuila, by which our interests have been continually depressed through a jealous and partial course of legislation carried on at a far distant seat of government by a hostile majority, in an unknown tongue; and this to, notwithstanding we have petitioned in the humblest terms, for the establishment of a separate state government, and have, in accordance with the provisions of the national constitution presented to the General Congress a republican constitution which was, without just cause, contemptuously rejected.

It incarcerated in a dungeon, for a long time, one of our citizens, for no other cause but a zealous endeavor to procure the acceptance of our constitution and the establishment of a state government.

It has failed and refused to secure on a firm basis, the right of trial by jury, that palladium of civil liberty, and only safe guarantee for the life, liberty, and property of the citizen.

It has failed to establish any public system of education, although possessed of almost boundless resources (the public domain) and although it is an axiom in political science, that unless a people are educated and enlightened it is idle to expect the continuance of civil liberty, or the capacity for self-government.

It has suffered the military commandants stationed among us to exercise arbitrary acts of oppression and tyranny; thus trampling upon the most sacred rights of the citizen and rendering the military superior to the civil power.

It has dissolved by force of arms, the State Congress of Coahuila and Texas, and obliged our representatives to fly for their lives from the seat of government; thus depriving us of the fundamental political right of representation.

It has demanded the surrender of a number of our citizens and ordered military detachments to seize and carry them into the interior for trial; in contempt of the civil authorities, and in defiance of the laws and the constitution.

It has made piratical attacks upon our commerce, by commissioning foreign desperadoes, and authorizing them to seize our vessels, and convey the property of our citizens to far distant ports for confiscation.

It denies us the right of worshipping the Almighty according to the dictates of our own conscience, by the support of a national religion calculated to promote the temporal interest of its human functionaries rather than the glory of the true and living God.

It has demanded us to deliver up our arms, which are essential to our defence, the rightful property of freemen, and formidable only to tyrannical governments.

It has invaded our country by sea and by land, with intent to lay waste our territory and drive us from our homes, and has now a large mercenary army advancing to carry on against us a war of extermination.

It has, through its emissaries, incited the merciless savage, with the tomahawk and scalping knife, to massacre the inhabitants of our defenceless frontiers.

It hath been, during the whole time of our connection with it, the contemptible sport and victim of successive military revolutions, and hath continually exhibited every characteristic of a weak, corrupt, and tyrannical government.

These, and other grievances were patiently borne by the people of Texas until they reached that point at which forbearance ceases to be a virtue. We then took up arms in defence of the national constitution. We appealed to our Mexican brethren for assistance. Our appeal has been made in vain. Though months have elapsed, no sympathetic response has yet been heard from the interior. We are, therefore, forced to the melancholy conclusion that the Mexican people have acquiesced in the destruction of their liberty and the substitution therefore of a Military Government—that they are unfit to be free and incapable of self-government.

The necessity of self-preservation, therefore, now decrees our eternal political separation.

We therefore, the delegates with plenary powers, of the people of Texas, in solemn convention assembled, appealing to a candid world for the necessities of our condition, do hereby resolve and declare that our political connection with the Mexican Nation has forever ended; that the people of Texas do now constitute a free sovereign and independent republic, and are fully invested with all the rights and attributes which properly belong to independent nations; and conscious of the rectitude of our intentions, we fearlessly and confidently commit the issue to the decision of the Supreme Arbiter of the destinies of Nations.

Source: Henry Steele Commager, *Documents of American History*, vol. 1 (Englewood Cliffs, NJ: Prentice Hall, 1973), 281–83.

20.   THE WEBSTER-ASHBURTON TREATY
9 August 1842

Conflicts along the U.S.–Canadian border punctuated Anglo-America relations for much of the early nineteenth century. The most important point of contention was the exact boundary between the Canadian province of New Brunswick and Maine. In 1842, both countries were able to successfully resolve the issues, establishing a precedent for diplomatic cooperation that would continue to grow throughout the remainder of the century.

Treaty to Settle and Define Boundaries; for the Final Suppression of the African Slave Trade; and for the Giving up of Criminals Fugitive from Justice.

ART. I. It is hereby agreed and declared that the line of boundary shall be as follows: Beginning at the monument at the source of the river St. Croix as designated and agreed to by the Commissioners under the fifth article of the treaty of 1794, between the Governments of the United States and Great Britain; thence, north, following the exploring line run and marked by the surveyors of the two Governments in the years 1817 and 1818, under the fifth article of the treaty of Ghent, to its intersection with the river St. John, and to the middle of the channel thereof; thence, up the middle of the main channel of the said river St. John, to the mouth of the river St. Francis; thence, up the middle of the channel of the said river St. Francis, and of the lakes through which it flows, to the outlet of the Lake Pohenagamook: thence, southwesterly, in a straight line, to a point on the northwest branch of the river St. John, which point shall be ten miles distant from the main branch of the St. John, in a straight line, and in the nearest direction; but if the said point shall be found to be less than seven miles from the nearest point of the summit or crest of the highlands that divide those rivers which empty themselves into the river St. Lawrence from those which fall into the river St. John, then, the said point shall be made to recede down the said northwest branch of the river St. John, to a point seven miles in a straight line from the said summit or crest; thence, in a straight line, in a course about south, eight degrees west, to the point where the parallel of latitude of 46' 25' north intersects the southwest branch of the St. John's; thence, southerly, by the said branch, to the source thereof in the highlands at the Metjarmette portage; thence, down along the said highlands which divide the waters which empty themselves into the river St. Lawrence from those which fall into the Atlantic Ocean, to the head of Hall's Stream; thence, down the middle of said stream, till the line thus run intersects the old line of boundary surveyed and marked by Valentine and Collins, previously to the year 1774, as the 45th degree of north latitude, and which has been known and understood to be the line of actual division between the States of New York and Vermont one side, and the British province of Canada on the other; and from said point of intersection, west, along the said dividing line, as heretofore known and understood, to the Iroquois or St. Lawrence River. . . .

ART. II. It is moreover agreed, that, from the place where the joint commissioners terminated their labors under the sixth article of the treaty of Ghent, to wit: at a point in the Neebish channel, near Muddy Lake, the line shall run into and along the ship channel between St. Joseph and St. Tammany islands, to the division of the channel at or near the head of St. Joseph's island; thence, turning eastwardly and northwardly around the lower end of St. George's or Sugar island, and following the middle of the channel which divides St. George's from St. Joseph's island; thence up the east Neebish channel, nearest to St. George's island, through the middle of Lake George; thence, west of Jonas' island, into St. Mary's river, to a point in the middle of that river, about one mile above St. George's or Sugar island, so as to appropriate and assign the said island to the United States; thence, adopting the line traced on the maps by the commissioners, through the river St. Mary and Lake Superior, to a point north of Ile Royale in said lake, one hundred yards to the north and east of Ile Chapeau, which last-mentioned island lies near the northeastern point of Ile Royale, where the line marked by the commissioners terminates; and from the last-mentioned point, southwesterly, through the middle of the sound between Ile Royale and the northwestern main land, to the mouth of Pigeon river, and up the said river, to and through the north and south Fowl Lakes, to the lakes of the height of land between Lake Superior and the Lake of the Woods; thence, along the water communication to Lake Saisaginaga, and through that lake; thence, to and through Cypress Lake, Lac du Bois Blanc, Lac la Croix, Little Vermilion Lake, and Lake Namecan, and through the several smaller lakes, straits, or streams, connecting the lakes here mentioned, to that point in Lac la Pluie, or Rainy Lake, at the Chaudiere Falls, from which the commissioners traced the line to the most northwestern point of the Lake of the Woods; thence, along the said line, to the said most northwestern point, being in latitude 49° 23' 55" north, and in longitude 95° 43' 38" west from the observatory at Greenwich; thence, according to existing treaties, due south to its intersection with the 49th parallel of north latitude, and along that parallel to the Rocky mountains. It being understood that all the water communications and all the usual portages along the line from Lake Superior to the Lake of the Woods, and also Grand portage, from the shore of Lake Superior to the Pigeon river, as now actually used, shall be free and open to the use of the citizens and subjects of both countries. . . .

ART. VIII. The parties mutually stipulate that each shall prepare, equip, and maintain in service, on the coast of Africa, a sufficient and adequate squadron, or naval force of vessels, of suitable numbers and descriptions, to carry in all not less than eighty guns, to enforce, separately and respectively, the laws, rights, and obligations, of each of the two countries, for the suppression of the slave trade; the said squadrons to be independent of each other; but the two Governments stipulating, nevertheless, to give such orders to the officers commanding their respective forces as shall enable them most effectually to act in concert and co-operation, upon mutual consultation, as exigencies may arise, for the attainment of the true object of this article; copies of all such orders to be communicated by each Government to the other, respectively.

Source: Hunter Miller, ed., *Treaties and Other International Acts of the United States of America*, vol. 4 (Washington, DC: Government Printing Office, 1934), 363–478.

21. THE ANNEXATION OF TEXAS
1 March 1845

American leaders began to speculate on the annexation of Texas almost as soon as it became independent. The Senate's rejection of just such a treaty became a major issue in the election of 1844. When James K. Polk prevailed, on a platform that heartily endorsed the addition of Texas to the United States, a joint resolution was submitted to Congress for the purpose of annexation.

Resolved . . . , That Congress doth consent that the territory properly included within, and rightfully belonging to the Republic of Texas, may be erected into a new State, to be called the State of Texas, with a republican form of government, to be adopted by the people of said republic, by deputies in convention assembled, with the consent of the existing government, in order that the same may be admitted as one of the States of this Union.

2. That the foregoing consent of Congress is given upon the following conditions, and with the following guarantees, to wit: *First*, Said State to be formed, subject to the adjustment by this government of all questions of boundary that may arise with other governments; and the constitution thereof, with the proper evidence of its adoption by the people of said Republic of Texas, shall be transmitted to the President of the United States, to be laid before Congress for its final action, on or before the first day of January, one thousand eight hundred and forty-six. *Second*, Said State, when admitted into the Union, after ceding to the United States; all public edifices, fortifications, barracks, ports and harbors, navy and navy yards, docks, magazines, arms, armaments, and all other property and means pertaining to the public defence belonging to said Republic of Texas,

shall retain all the public funds, debts, taxes, and dues of every kind, which may belong to or be due and owing said republic; and shall also retain all the vacant and unappropriated lands lying within its limits, to be applied to the payment of the debts and liabilities of said Republic of Texas, and the residue of said lands, after discharging said debts and liabilities, to be disposed of as said State may direct; but in no event are said debts and liabilities to become a charge upon the Government of the United States. *Third*, New States, of convenient size, not exceeding four in number, in addition to said State of Texas, and having sufficient population, may hereafter, by the consent of said State, be formed out of the territory thereof, which shall be entitled to admission under the provisions of the federal constitution. And such States as may be formed out of that portion of said territory lying south of thirty-six degrees thirty minutes north latitude, commonly known as the Missouri compromise line, shall be admitted into the Union with or without slavery, as the people of each State asking admission may desire. And in such State or States as shall be formed out of said territory north of said Missouri compromise line, slavery, or involuntary servitude, (except for crime) shall be prohibited.

3. That if the President of the United States shall in his judgment and discretion deem it most advisable, instead of proceeding to submit the foregoing resolution to the Republic of Texas, as an overture on the part of the United States for admission, to negotiate with that Republic; then

Be it resolved, That a State, to be formed out of the present Republic of Texas, with suitable extent and boundaries and with two representatives in Congress, until the next apportionment of representation, shall be admitted into the Union, by virtue of this act, on an equal footing with the existing States, as soon as the terms and conditions of such admission, and the cession of the remaining Texian territory to the United States shall be agreed upon by the Governments of Texas and the United States: And that the sum of one hundred thousand dollars be, and the same is hereby, appropriated to defray the expenses of missions and negotiations, to agree upon the terms of said admission and cession, either by treaty to be submitted to the Senate, or by articles to be submitted to the two houses of Congress, as the President may direct.

Source: Henry Steele Commager, *Documents of American History*, vol. 1 (Englewood Cliffs, NJ: Prentice Hall, 1973), 306–7.

22. POLK'S REASSERTION OF THE MONROE DOCTRINE
2 December 1845

In his first annual message to Congress, James K. Polk restated his adherence to the idea that no European power establish colonies in the West-

ern Hemisphere. In this version of the Monroe Doctrine, *Polk made a clear link between foreign competition and America's "rising greatness as a nation" and staked out a distinct claim on "territories heretofore unoccupied" such as Oregon and Texas.*

. . . The rapid extension of our settlements over our territories heretofore unoccupied, the addition of new States to our Confederacy, the expansion of free principles, and our rising greatness as a nation are attracting the attention of the powers of Europe, and lately the doctrine has been broached in some of them of a "balance of power" on this continent to check our advancement. The United States, sincerely desirous of preserving relations of good understanding with all nations, can not in silence permit any European interference on the North American continent, and should any such interference be attempted will be ready to resist it at any and all hazards.

It is well known to the American people and to all nations that this Government has never interfered with the relations subsisting between other governments. We have never made ourselves parties to their wars or their alliances; we have not sought their territories by conquest; we have not mingled with parties in their domestic struggles; and believing our own form of government to be the best, we have never attempted to propagate it by intrigues, by diplomacy, or by force. We may claim on this continent a like exemption from European interference. The nations of America are equally sovereign and independent with those of Europe. They possess the same rights, independent of all foreign interposition, to make war, to conclude peace, and to regulate their internal affairs. The people of the United States can not, therefore, view with indifference attempts of European powers to interfere with the independent action of the nations on this continent. The American system of government is entirely different from that of Europe. Jealousy among the different sovereigns of Europe, lest any one of them might become too powerful for the rest, has caused them anxiously to desire the establishment of what they term the "balance of power." It can not be permitted to have any application on the North American continent, and especially to the United States. We must ever maintain the principle that the people of this continent alone have the right to decide their own destiny. Should any portion of them, constituting an independent state, propose to unite themselves with our Confederacy, this will be a question for them and us to determine without any foreign interposition. We can never consent that European powers shall interfere to prevent such a union because it might disturb the "balance of power" which they may desire to maintain upon this continent. Near a quarter of a century ago the principle was distinctly announced to the world, in the annual message of one of my predecessors, that—

The American continents, by the free and independent condition which they have assumed and maintain, are henceforth not to be considered as subjects for future colonization by any European powers.

This principle will apply with greatly increased force should any European power attempt to establish any new colony in North America. In the existing circumstances of the world the present is deemed a proper occasion to reiterate and reaffirm the principle avowed by Mr. Monroe and to state my cordial concurrence in its wisdom and sound policy. The reassertion of this principle, especially in reference to North America, is at this day but the promulgation of a policy which no European power should cherish the disposition to resist. Existing rights of every European nation should be respected, but it is due alike to our safety and our interests that the efficient protection of our laws should be extended over our whole territorial limits, and that it should be distinctly announced to the world as our settled policy that no future European colony or dominion shall with our consent be planted or established on any part of the North American continent. . . .

Source: James D. Richardson, ed., *A Compilation of the Messages and Papers of the Presidents*, vol. 5 (New York: Bureau of National Literature, 1897), 2248–49.

23. O'SULLIVAN ON MANIFEST DESTINY
1845

John L. O'Sullivan spoke for many Americans when he expressed his desire for the country to fill the entire continent from coast to coast. His description of "manifest destiny" became a clarion call for expansionists intent on occupying not only the remaining frontier between the Mississippi and California, but the attainable portions of Mexico and Canada as well.

ANNEXATION

It is time now for opposition to the Annexation of Texas to cease, all further agitation of the waters of bitterness and strife, at least in connexion with this question,—even though it may perhaps be required of us as a necessary condition of the freedom of our institutions, that we must live on for ever in a state of unpausing struggle and excitement upon some subject of party division or other. But, in regard to Texas, enough has now been given to Party. It is time for the common duty of Patriotism to the Country to succeed;—or if this claim will not be recognized, it is at least time for common sense to acquiesce with decent grace in the inevitable and the irrevocable.

Texas is now ours. Already, before these words are written, her Convention has undoubtedly ratified the acceptance, by her Congress, of our proffered invitation into the Union; and made the requisite changes in her already republican form of constitution to adopt it to its future federal relations. Her star and her stripe may already be said to have taken their place in the glorious blazon of our common nationality; and the sweep of our eagle's wing already includes within its circuit the wide extent of her fair and fertile land. She is no longer to us a mere geographical space—a certain combination of coast, plain, mountain, valley, forest and stream. She is no longer to us a mere country on the map. She comes within the dear and sacred designation of Our Country; no longer a *"pays,"* she is a part of *"la patrie;"* and that which is at once a sentiment and a virtue, Patriotism, already begins to thrill for her too within the national heart. It is time then that all should cease to treat her as alien, and even adverse—cease to denounce and vilify all and everything connected with her accession—cease to thwart and oppose the remaining steps for its consummation; or where such efforts are felt to be unavailing, at least to embitter the hour of reception by all the most ungracious frowns of aversion and words of unwelcome. There has been enough of all this. It has had its fitting day during the period when, in common with every other possible question of practical policy that can arise, it unfortunately became one of the leading topics of party division, of presidential electioneering. But that period has passed, and with it let its prejudices and its passions, its discords and its denunciations, pass away too. The next session of Congress will see the representatives of the new young State in their places in both our halls of national legislation, side by side with those of the old Thirteen. Let their reception into "the family" be frank, kindly, and cheerful, as befits such an occasion, as comports not less with our own self-respect than patriotic duty towards them. Ill betide those foul birds that delight to 'file their own nest, and disgust the ear with perpetual discord of ill-omened croak.

Why, were other reasoning wanting, in favor of now elevating this question of the reception of Texas into the Union, out of the lower region of our past party dissensions, up to its proper level of a high and broad nationality, it surely is to be found, found abundantly, in the manner in which other nations have undertaken to intrude themselves into it, between us and the proper parties to the case, in a spirit of hostile interference against us, for the avowed object of thwarting our policy and hampering our power, limiting our greatness and checking the fulfillment of our manifest destiny to overspread the continent allotted by Providence for the free development of our yearly multiplying millions. This we have seen done by England, our old rival and enemy; and by France, strangely coupled with her against us, under the influence of the Anglicism strongly tinging the policy of her present Prime Minister, Guizot. The zealous activity with which this effort to defeat us was pushed by the representatives of those governments, together with the character of intrigue accompanying it, fully constituted that case of foreign interference, which Mr. Clay himself declared should, and would unite us all in maintaining the common cause of our country against the foreigner and the foe. We are only astonished that this effect has not been more fully and strongly produced, and that the burst of indignation against the unauthorized, insolent and hostile interference against us, has not been more general even among the party before opposed to Annexation, and has not rallied the national spirit and national pride unanimously upon that policy. We are very sure that if Mr. Clay himself were now to add another letter to his former Texas correspondence, he would express this sentiment, and carry out the idea already strongly stated in one of them, in a manner which would tax all the powers of blushing belonging to some of his party adherents.

It is wholly untrue, and unjust to ourselves, the pretence that the Annexation has been a measure of spoliation, unrightful and unrighteous—of military conquest under forms of peace and law—of territorial aggrandizement at the expense of justice, and justice due by a double sanctity to the weak. This view of the question is wholly unfounded, and has been before so amply refuted in these pages, as well as in a thousand other modes, that we shall not again dwell upon it. The independence of Texas was complete and absolute. It was an independence, not only in fact but of right. No obligation of duty towards Mexico tended in the least degree to restrain our right to effect the desired recovery of the fair province once our own—whatever motives of policy might have prompted a more deferential consideration of her feelings and her pride, as involved in the question. If Texas became peopled with an American population, it was by no contrivance of our government but on the express invitation of that of Mexico herself, accompanied with such guarantees of State independence, and the maintenance of a federal system analogous to our own, as constituted a compact fully justifying the strongest measures of redress on the part of those afterwards deceived in this guaranty, and sought to be enslaved under the yoke imposed by its violation. She was released, rightfully and absolutely released, from all Mexican allegiance, or duty of cohesion to the Mexican political body, by the acts and fault of Mexico herself, and Mexico alone. There never was a clearer case. It was not revolution; it was resistance to revolution; and resistance under such circumstances as left independence the necessary resulting state, caused by the abandonment of those with whom her former federal association had existed. What then can be more preposterous than all this clamor by Mexico and the Mexican interest, against Annexation, as a violation of any rights of hers, any duties of ours?

Source: Stephen J. Valone, *Two Centuries of U.S. Foreign Policy: The Documentary Record* (Westport, CT: Praeger, 1995), 21–22.

24. POLK'S MESSAGE TO CONGRESS ON WAR WITH MEXICO
11 May 1846

In January 1846, James K. Polk ordered an Army detachment, commanded by General Zachary Taylor, across the Nueces River to take up positions along the left bank of the Rio Grande del Norte, a territory claimed as part of Mexico. On 25 April, Mexican cavalry engaged in a brief skirmish

with American forces, killing and capturing a number of soldiers. Polk,
declaring that "[t]he cup of forbearance has been exhausted," asked Con-
gress for war.

To the Senate and House of Representatives:

The existing state of the relations between the United States and Mexico
renders it proper that I should bring the subject to the consideration of Congress. . . .

In my message at the commencement of the present session I informed you
that upon the earnest appeal both of the Congress and convention of Texas I
had ordered an efficient military force to take a position "between the Nueces
and the Del Norte." This had become necessary to meet a threatened invasion
of Texas by the Mexican forces, for which extensive military preparations had
been made. The invasion was threatened solely because Texas had determined,
in accordance with a solemn resolution of the Congress of the United States, to
annex herself to our Union, and under these circumstances it was plainly our
duty to extend our protection over her citizens and soil.

This force was concentrated at Corpus Christi, and remained there until after
I had received such information from Mexico as rendered it probable, if not
certain, that the Mexican Government would refuse to receive our envoy.

Meantime Texas, by the final action of our Congress, had become an integral
part of our Union. The Congress of Texas, by its act of December 19, 1836,
had declared the Rio del Norte to be the boundary of that Republic. Its jurisdiction had been extended and exercised beyond the Nueces. The country between that river and the Del Norte had been represented in the Congress and in
the convention of Texas, had thus taken part in the act of annexation itself, and
is now included within one of our Congressional districts. Our own Congress
had, moreover, with great unanimity, by the act approved December 31, 1845,
recognized the country beyond the Nueces as a part of our territory by including
it within our own revenue system, and a revenue officer to reside within that
district has been appointed by and with the advice and consent of the Senate.
It became, therefore, of urgent necessity to provide for the defense of that portion of our country. Accordingly, on the 13th of January last instructions were
issued to the general in command of these troops to occupy the left bank of the
Del Norte. This river, which is the southwestern boundary of the State of Texas,
is an exposed frontier.

The movement of the troops to the Del Norte was made by the commanding
general under positive instructions to abstain from all aggressive acts toward
Mexico or Mexican citizens and to regard the relations between that Republic
and the United States as peaceful unless she should declare war or commit acts
of hostility indicative of a state of war. . . .

The Mexican forces at Matamoras assumed a belligerent attitude, and on the
12th of April General Ampudia, then in command, notified General Taylor to
break up his camp within twenty-four hours and to retire beyond the Nueces

River, and in the event of his failure to comply with these demands announced that arms, and arms alone, must decide the question. But no open act of hostility was committed until the 24th of April. On that day General Arista, who had succeeded to the command of the Mexican forces, communicated to General Taylor that "he considered hostilities commenced and should prosecute them." A party of dragoons of 63 men and officers were on the same day dispatched from the American camp up the Rio del Norte, on its left bank, to ascertain whether the Mexican troops had crossed or were preparing to cross the river, "became engaged with a large body of these troops, and after a short affair, in which some 16 were killed and wounded, appear to have been surrounded and compelled to surrender." . . .

The cup of forbearance had been exhausted even before the recent information from the frontier of the Del Norte. But now, after reiterated menaces, Mexico has passed the boundary of the United States, has invaded our territory and shed American blood upon the American soil. She has proclaimed that hostilities have commenced, and that the two nations are now at war.

As war exists, and, notwithstanding all our efforts to avoid it, exists by the act of Mexico herself, we are called upon by every consideration of duty and patriotism to vindicate with decision the honor, the rights, and the interests of our country. . . .

In further vindication of our rights and defense of our territory, I invoke the prompt action of Congress to recognize the existence of the war, and to place at the disposition of the Executive the means of prosecuting the war with vigor, and thus hastening the restoration of peace. . . .

Source: James D. Richardson, ed., *A Compilation of the Messages and Papers of the Presidents*, vol. 5 (New York: Bureau of National Literature, 1897), 2287–93.

25. TREATY OF GUADALUPE HIDALGO
2 February 1848

After numerous false starts by the head of the American delegation, Nicholas P. Trist, the United States and Mexico were able to formally end their war in February 1848. The treaty gained for America the Rio Grande boundary for Texas and the 500,000 miles of territory contained in California and New Mexico.

ART. I. THERE shall be firm and universal peace between the United States of America and the Mexican Republic, and between their respective countries, territories, cities, towns, and people, without exception of place or persons. . . .

ART. V. The boundary line between the two Republics shall commence in the Gulf of Mexico, three leagues from land, opposite the mouth of the Rio

Grande, otherwise called Rio Bravo del Norte, or opposite the mouth of its deepest branch, if it should have more than one branch emptying directly into the sea; from thence up the middle of that river, following the deepest channel, where it has more than one, to the point where it strikes the southern boundary of New Mexico (which runs north of the town called Paso) to its western termination; thence, northward, along the western line of New Mexico, until it intersects the first branch of the River Gila; (or if it should not intersect any branch of that river, then to the point on the said line nearest to such branch, and thence in a direct line to the same;) thence down the middle of the said branch and of the said river, until it empties into the Rio Colorado; thence across the Rio Colorado, following the division line between Upper and Lower California, to the Pacific Ocean. . . .

ART. VII. The River Gila, and the part of the Rio Bravo del Norte lying below the southern boundary of New Mexico, being, agreeably to the fifth article, divided in the middle between the two republics, the navigation of the Gila and of the Bravo below said boundary shall be free and common to the vessels and citizens of both countries; and neither shall, without the consent of the other, construct any work that may impede or interrupt, in whole or in part, the exercise of this right; not even for the purpose of favoring new methods of navigation. . . .

ART. VIII. Mexicans now established in territories previously belonging to Mexico, and which remain for the future within the limits of the United States, as defined by the present treaty, shall be free to continue where they now reside, or to remove at any time to the Mexican republic, retaining the property which they possess in the said territories, or disposing thereof, and removing the proceeds wherever they please, without their being subjected, on this account, to any contribution, tax, or charge whatever. . . .

ART. XII. In consideration of the extension acquired by the boundaries of the United States, as defined in the fifth article of the present treaty, the Government of the United States engages to pay to that of the Mexican Republic the sum of fifteen millions of dollars. . . .

ART. XIII. The United States engage, moreover, to assume and pay to the claimants all the amounts now due them, and those hereafter to become due, by reason of the claims already liquidated and decided against the Mexican Republic, under the conventions between the two republics severally concluded on the eleventh day of April, eighteen hundred and thirty-nine, and on the thirtieth day of January, eighteen hundred and forty-three; so that the Mexican Republic shall be absolutely exempt, for the future, from all expense whatever on account of the said claims.

ART. XIV. The United States do furthermore discharge the Mexican Republic from all claims of citizens of the United States, not heretofore decided against the Mexican Government, which may have arisen previously to the date of the signature of this treaty; which discharge shall be final and perpetual, whether the said claims be rejected or be allowed by the board of commissioners provided for in the following article, and whatever shall be the total amount of those allowed. . . .

ART. XV. The United States, exonerating Mexico from all demands on account of the claims of their citizens mentioned in the preceding article, and considering them entirely and forever canceled, whatever their amount may be, undertake to make satisfaction for the same, to an amount not exceeding three and one quarter millions of dollars. . . .

ART. XXI. If unhappily any disagreement should hereafter arise between the governments of the two republics, whether with respect to the interpretation of any stipulation in this treaty, or with respect to any other particular concerning the political or commercial relations of the two nations, the said governments, in the name of those nations, do promise to each other that they will endeavor, in the most sincere and earnest manner, to settle the differences so arising, and to preserve the state of peace and friendship in which the two countries are now placing themselves; using, for this end, mutual representations and pacific negotiations. And if, by these means, they should not be enabled to come to an agreement, a resort shall not, on this account, be had to reprisals, aggression, or hostility of any kind, by the one republic against the other, until the Government of that which deems itself aggrieved shall have maturely considered, in the spirit of peace and good neighborship, whether it would not be better that such difference should be settled by the arbitration of commissioners appointed on each side, or by that of a friendly nation. And should such course be proposed by either party, it shall be acceded to by the other, unless deemed by it altogether incompatible with the nature of the difference, or circumstances of the case.

Source: Hunter Miller, ed., *Treaties and Other International Acts of the United States of America*, vol. 5 (Washington, DC: Government Printing Office, 1937), 207–428.

---

26. CLAYTON-BULWER TREATY
19 April 1850

By the mid-nineteenth century, numerous countries had begun exploring a possible trans-isthmian route through Central America. The United States, with its new claim to California, clearly had an important interest in hastening access to the Pacific. Previous treaties had granted the United States the right of transit through possible routes in Mexico and Panama. The Clayton-Bulwer Treaty *effectively neutralized a growing British presence in Central America by declaring that neither the United States nor England would fortify or obtain exclusive control over an isthmian canal.*

ART. I. The Governments of the United States and Great Britain hereby declare that neither the one nor the other will ever obtain or maintain for itself any exclusive control over the said ship canal; agreeing that neither will ever erect or maintain any fortifications commanding the same, or in the vicinity thereof, or occupy, or fortify, or colonize or assume, or exercise any dominion over Nicaragua, Costa Rica, the Mosquito coast, or any part of Central America; nor will either make use of any protection which either affords or may afford, or any alliance which either has or may have to or with any state or people, for the purpose of erecting or maintaining any such fortifications, or of occupying, fortifying, or colonizing Nicaragua, Costa Rica, the Mosquito coast, or any part of Central America, or of assuming or exercising dominion over the same; nor will the United States or Great Britain take advantage of any intimacy, or use any, alliance, connection or influence that either may possess with any State or Government through whose territory the said canal may pass, for the purpose of acquiring or holding, directly or indirectly, for the citizens or subjects of the one, any rights or advantages in regard to commerce or navigation through the said canal which shall not be offered on the same terms to the citizens or subjects of the other.

ART. II. Vessels of the United States or Great Britain traversing the said canal shall, in case of war between the contracting parties, be exempted from blockade, detention, or capture by either of the belligerents; and this provision shall extend to such a distance from the two ends of the said canal as may hereafter be found expedient to establish.

ART. III. In order to secure the construction of the said canal, the contracting parties engage that if any such canal shall be undertaken upon fair and equitable terms by any parties having the authority of the local Government or Governments through whose territory the same may pass, then the persons employed in making the said canal, and their property used, or to be used, for that object, shall be protected, from the commencement of the said canal to its completion, by the Governments of the United States and Great Britain, from unjust detention, confiscation, seizure or any violence whatsoever. . . .

ART. V. The contracting parties further engage, that when the said canal shall have been completed, they will protect it from interruption, seizure or unjust confiscation, and that they will guarantee the neutrality thereof, so that the said canal may forever be open and free, and the capital invested therein secure. Nevertheless, the Governments of the United States and Great Britain, in according their protection to the construction of the said canal, and guaranteeing its neutrality and security when completed, always understand that this protection and guarantee are granted conditionally, and may be withdrawn by both Governments, or either Government, if both Governments, or either Government, should deem that the persons or company undertaking or managing the same adopt or establish such regulations concerning the traffic thereupon as are contrary to the spirit and intention of this convention, either by making unfair discriminations in favor of the commerce of one of the contracting parties over the commerce of the other, or by imposing oppressive exactions or unreasonable tolls upon the passengers, vessels, goods, wares, merchandise or other articles. Neither party, however, shall withdraw the aforesaid protection and guarantee without first giving six months' notice to the other.

ART. VI. The contracting parties in this convention engage to invite every State with which both or either have friendly intercourse to enter into stipulations with them similar to those which they have entered into with each other, to the end that all other States may share in the honor and advantage of having contributed to a work of such general interest and importance as the canal herein contemplated. And the contracting parties likewise agree that each shall enter into treaty stipulations with such of the Central American States as they may deem advisable, for the purpose of more effectually carrying out the great design of this convention, namely, that of constructing and maintaining the said canal as a ship communication between the two oceans for the benefit of mankind, on equal terms to all, and of protecting the same; and they also agree that the good offices of either shall be employed, when requested by the other, in aiding and assisting the negotiation of such treaty stipulations; and should any differences arise as to right or property over the territory through which the said canal shall pass between the States or Governments of Central America, and such differences should in any way impede or obstruct the execution of the said canal, the Governments of the United States and Great Britain will use their good offices to settle such differences in the manner best suited to promote the interests of the said canal, and to strengthen the bonds of friendship and alliance which exist between the contracting parties.

ART. VII. It being desirable that no time should be unnecessarily lost in commencing and constructing the said canal, the Governments of the United States and Great Britain determine to give their support and encouragement to such persons or company as may first offer to commence the same, with the necessary capital, the consent of the local authorities, and on such principles as accord with the spirit and intention of this convention. . . .

ART. VIII. The Governments of the United States and Great Britain having not only desired, in entering into this convention, to accomplish a particular object, but also to establish a general principle, they hereby agree to extend their protection, by treaty stipulations, to any other practicable communications, whether by canal or railway, across the isthmus which connects North and South America, and especially to the interoceanic communications, should the same prove to be practicable, whether by canal or railway, which are now proposed to be established by the way of Tehuantepec or Panama. In granting, however, their joint protection to any such canals or railways as are by this article specified, it is always understood by the United States and Great Britain that the parties constructing or owning the same shall impose no other charges or conditions of traffic thereupon than the aforesaid Governments shall approve of as just and equitable; and that the same canals or railways, being open to the citizens and subjects of the United States and Great Britain on equal terms, shall also be open on like terms to the citizens and subjects of every other State which is willing to grant thereto such protection as the United States and Great Britain engage to afford.

Source: Hunter Miller, ed., *Treaties and Other International Acts of the United States of America*, vol. 5 (Washington, DC: Government Printing Office, 1937), 671–802.

27. OSTEND MANIFESTO
18 October 1854

In the aftermath of the war with Mexico, America began to look for more territories to acquire. Many seriously considered the addition of Spanish Cuba. Consequently, the American ministers to Spain, France, and Great Britain met in Ostend, Belgium, to discuss the possibility of purchasing the island. They allowed their recommendation to be leaked to the New York Herald; and, thus, the so-called "Ostend Manifesto" became the source of great political embarrassment for the administration of Franklin Pierce.

Aix la Chapelle. October 18, 1854.

Sir:—The undersigned, in compliance with the wish expressed by the President in the several confidential despatches you have addressed to us, respectively, to that effect, have met in conference, first at Ostend, in Belgium, on the 9th, 10th, and 11th instant, and then at Aix la Chapelle, in Prussia, on the days next following, up to the date hereof. . . .

We have arrived at the conclusion, and are thoroughly convinced, that an immediate and earnest effort ought to be made by the government of the United States to purchase Cuba from Spain at any price for which it can be obtained, not exceeding the sum of $—.

The proposal should, in our opinion, be made in such a manner as to be presented through the necessary diplomatic forms to the Supreme Constituent Cortes about to assemble. On this momentous question, in which the people both of Spain and the United States are so deeply interested, all our proceedings ought to be open, frank, and public. They should be of such a character as to challenge the approbation of the world. We firmly believe that, in the progress of human events, the time has arrived when the vital interests of Spain are as seriously involved in the sale, as those of the United States in the purchase, of the island and that the transaction will prove equally honorable to both nations.

Under these circumstances we cannot anticipate a failure, unless possibly through the malign influence of foreign powers who possess no right whatever to interfere in the matter.

We proceed to state some of the reasons which have brought us to this conclusion, and, for the sake of clearness, we shall specify them under two distinct heads:

1. The United States ought, if practicable, to purchase Cuba with as little delay as possible.

2. The probability is great that the government and Cortes of Spain will prove willing to sell it, because this would essentially promote the highest and best interests of the Spanish people.

Then, 1. It must be clear to every reflecting mind that, from the peculiarity of its geographical position, and the considerations attendant on it, Cuba is as necessary to the North American republic as any of its present members, and that it belongs naturally to that great family of States of which the Union is the providential nursery. . . .

The natural and main outlet to the products of this entire population, the highway of their direct intercourse with the Atlantic and the Pacific States, can never be secure, but must ever be endangered whilst Cuba is a dependency of a distant power in whose possession it has proved to be a source of constant annoyance and embarrassment to their interests. Indeed, the Union can never enjoy repose, nor possess reliable security, as long as Cuba is not embraced within its boundaries.

Its immediate acquisition by our government is of paramount importance, and we cannot doubt but that it is a consummation devoutly wished for by its inhabitants.

The intercourse which its proximity to our coasts begets and encourages between them and the citizens of the United States, has, in the progress of time, so united their interests and blended their fortunes that they now look upon each other as if they were one people and had but one destiny.

Considerations exist which render delay in the acquisition of this island exceedingly dangerous to the United States. . . .

Cuba has thus become to us an unceasing danger, and a permanent cause of anxiety and alarm.

But we need not enlarge on these topics. It can scarcely be apprehended that foreign powers, in violation of international law, would interpose their influence with Spain to prevent our acquisition of the island. . . .

Besides, the commercial nations of the world cannot fail to perceive and appreciate the great advantages which would result to their people from a dissolution of the forced and unnatural connexion between Spain and Cuba, and the annexation of the latter to the United States. The trade of England and France with Cuba would, in that event, assume at once an important and profitable character, and rapidly extend with the increasing population and prosperity of the island.

2. But if the United States and every commercial nation would be benefited by this transfer, the interests of Spain would also be greatly and essentially promoted.

She cannot but see what such a sum of money as we are willing to pay for the island would effect in the development of her vast natural resources. . . .

Should Spain reject the present golden opportunity for developing her resources, and removing her financial embarrassments, it may never again return. . . .

Under no probable circumstances can Cuba ever yield to Spain one per cent on the large amount which the United States are willing to pay for its acquisition. But Spain is in imminent danger of losing Cuba, without remuneration. . . .

It is not improbable, therefore, that Cuba may be wrested from Spain by a successful revolution; and in that event she will lose both the island and the price which we are now willing to pay for it—a price far beyond what was ever paid by one people to another for any province.

It may also be remarked that the settlement of this vexed question, by the cession of Cuba to the United States, would forever prevent the dangerous complications between nations to which it may otherwise give birth.

It is certain that, should the Cubans themselves organize an insurrection against the Spanish government, and should other independent nations come to the aid of Spain in the contest, no human power could, in our opinion, prevent the people and government of the United States from taking part in such a civil war in support of their neighbors and friends.

But if Spain, dead to the voice of her own interest, and actuated by stubborn pride and a false sense of honor, should refuse to sell Cuba to the United States, then the question will arise, What ought to be the course of the American government under such circumstances? Self-preservation is the first law of nature, with States as well as with individuals. All nations have, at different periods, acted upon this maxim. Although it has been made the pretext for committing flagrant injustice, as in the partition of Poland and other similar cases which history records, yet the principle itself, though often abused, has always been recognized. . . .

Our past history forbids that we should acquire the island of Cuba without the consent of Spain, unless justified by the great law of self-preservation. We must, in any event, preserve our own conscious rectitude and our own self-respect.

Whilst pursuing this course we can afford to disregard the censures of the world, to which we have been so often and so unjustly exposed.

After we shall have offered Spain a price for Cuba far beyond its present value, and this shall have been refused, it will then be time to consider the question, does Cuba, in the possession of Spain, seriously endanger our internal peace and existence of our cherished Union?

Should this question be answered in the affirmative, then, by every law, human and divine, we shall be justified in wresting it from Spain if we possess the power; and this upon the very same principle that would justify an individual in tearing down the burning house of his neighbor if there were no other means of preventing the flames from destroying his own home.

Under such circumstances we ought neither to count the cost nor regard the odds which Spain might enlist against us. We forbear to enter into the question, whether the present condition of the island would justify such a measure? We should, however, be recreant to our duty, be unworthy of our gallant forefathers, and commit base treason against our posterity, should we permit Cuba to be Africanized and become a second St. Domingo, with all its attendant horrors to the white race, and suffer the flames to extend to our own neighboring shores seriously to endanger or actually to consume the fair fabric of our Union.

We fear that the course and current of events are rapidly tending towards such a catastrophe. We, however, hope for the best, though we ought certainly to be prepared for the worst. . . .

> Yours, very respectfully,
> James Buchanan.
> J. Y. Mason.
> Pierre Soulé

Hon. Wm. L. Marcy, Secretary of State.

Source: Henry Steele Commager, *Documents of American History*, vol. 1 (Englewood Cliffs, NJ: Prentice Hall, 1973), 333–35.

Part Three

The Civil War

The costliest war—the Civil War—in U.S. history also presented the country with significant consequences in the international forum. While the leaders in Washington, D.C., and Richmond, Virginia, contemplated campaigns on a scale unprecedented in modern warfare, American rivals prepared to exploit the distractions created by civil war. As armies numbering hundreds of thousands endured battles that dwarfed Waterloo, the United States found its survival challenged by formidable powers outside its borders.

The internecine war between Liberals and Conservatives in Mexico left the door open for foreign intervention. Citing uncompensated losses for property destroyed during the civil strife and Mexico's refusal to pay its foreign debt, England, France, and Spain demanded satisfaction. All three powers agreed to a joint intervention in October 1861 and occupied the port of Veracruz three months later. While Mexican leaders were able to reach an agreement with England and Spain, the French remained to carve out a new part of their empire. For years, Napoleon III had eyed the Western Hemisphere, entertaining designs that would expand French imperial power and his prestige. To achieve this, he dispatched the Archduke Maximilian of Hapsburg (brother of the Austrian Emperor Franz Josef) to Mexico.[1]

In the early stages of the war, few Europeans expected that the American union would survive. Although the industrial resources and the population base of the North appeared more than adequate to protect the remainder of the United States from a Confederate victory, significant doubts existed as to whether the Union could muster the means necessary to reunite the country. It was an open question whether it was possible for northern armies to prevail in a continent where the distance from Washington, D.C. to New Orleans was greater than that from Berlin to Moscow.[2]

President Lincoln's most pressing diplomatic priority was to bide time adequate enough to stave off either foreign support of the Confederacy or open intervention to resolve the war. In 1861, he contended with British fears that his government would transform the conflict into a "servile war," a war against slavery.[3] At the same time, Richmond sought a means to bolster its financing of the war effort through the cotton trade and somehow promote British intervention either as an ally or a diplomatic arbitrator. Jefferson Davis hoped that European intervention on the diplomatic front might result in a negotiated settlement of the war, something that would provide de facto recognition of the Confederacy as a sovereign nation.

The United States' conduct of the blockade nearly provoked war with England. The capture of Confederate diplomats James M. Mason and John Slidell in November 1861 became the focal point of an international controversy. American Unionists applauded the capture. England denounced it as kidnapping and, with apparently a small sense of historical irony, a violation of previous agreements against impressment. In response, London threatened to dispatch regular troops to Canada.

The clash over the Mason-Slidell mission was but one sore point between the United States and England. As the war progressed, the issue of Confederate commerce raiders became a major point of contention. Throughout the conflict, British shipyards had outfitted and repaired Confederate ships. A British company had constructed the so-called "Laird Rams" for use against Union merchants. The fundamental conflict over American freedom of the seas threatened to destabilize Anglo-American relations to the same degree it had after the Revolution and in the years prior to the War of 1812.[4]

However, the Union was able to avoid a clash with England with a nimble combination of diplomacy and force. A patient approach to diplomacy allowed time to cool British interest in intervention. Secretary of State William Seward acceded to British demands that the United States observe the principle of neutrality on the high seas. Lincoln's celebrated letter to the workingmen of Manchester was a deft play on British public sentiments, which generally supported the Union cause:

Through the action of our disloyal citizens, the workingmen of Europe have been subjected to severe trials, for the purpose of forcing their sanction to that attempt. Under the circumstances, I cannot but regard your decisive utterances upon the question as an instance of sublime Christian heroism which has not been surpassed in any age or in any country. It is indeed an energetic and reinspiring assurance of the inherent power of truth and of the ultimate and universal triumph of justice, humanity, and freedom.[5]

Conversely, the Lincoln administration, through American minister Charles Francis Adams, threatened war when Prime Minister William E. Gladstone openly contemplated diplomatic intervention. The Union was also fully well aware of England's dependence on American wheat and was prepared to brandish it as a weapon.

Union victories in the field cemented American diplomacy abroad. The success of Union armies in the west forestalled any decisive diplomatic move on the part of Richmond for much of 1862. General George B. McClellan's tactical draw at Antietam in September of that year proved critical to holding off a final referendum on British intervention.[6] After General Robert E. Lee's critical defeat at Gettysburg, the shifting fortunes of military strategy all but precluded further European interest in the war.

Confederate blunders augmented its diplomatic isolation. Jefferson Davis was never able to muster an argument convincing enough to entice actual European involvement. His cause was severely handicapped by the institution of slavery, something virtually all major European powers had abolished by 1861. Moreover, Davis's attempt to use cotton as a means to coerce European intervention backfired. His decision to withhold raw cotton from export eventually forced more than 330,000 textile workers out of British mills by November 1862, a fact London attributed more to Southern intransigence than the Union blockade.[7]

NOTES

1. John A. Crow, *The Epic of Latin America*, 4th ed. (Berkeley: University of California Press, 1992), 660–66; Howard Jones, *Abraham Lincoln and a New Birth of Freedom: The Union and Slavery in the Diplomacy of the Civil War* (Lincoln: University of Nebraska Press, 1999), 132; Alfred J. Hanna and Kathryn Abbey Hanna, *Napoleon III and Mexico: American Triumph over Monarchy* (Chapel Hill: University of North Carolina Press, 1971), 3–10.

2. James M. McPherson, *Battle Cry of Freedom: The Civil War Era* (New York: Oxford University Press, 1988), 546–67.

3. Howard Jones, "History and Mythology: The Crisis over British Intervention in the Civil War," in *The Union, the Confederacy, and the Atlantic Rim*, ed. Robert E. May (West Lafayette, IN: Purdue University Press, 1995), 29–33.

4. McPherson, *Battle Cry of Freedom*, 546–67.

5. Henry Steele Commager, *Documents of American History*, vol. 1 (Englewood Cliffs, NJ: Prentice Hall, 1973), 418–19.

6. McPherson, *Battle Cry of Freedom*, 546–67.

7. Bruce Catton, *The Civil War* (Boston: Houghton Mifflin, 1988), 38, 72; D. P. Crook, *Diplomacy during the American Civil War* (New York: Wiley, 1975), 74.

---

28. LINCOLN'S BLOCKADE PROCLAMATION
19 April 1861

Faced with the prospect of a war the United States was unprepared to prosecute, Lincoln decided to begin sanctions against the Confederacy while his commanders readied his armies in the field. As part of Winfield Scott's "Anaconda Plan," the Union blockade was designed to isolate the southern states from foreign trade and potential allies. Ultimately, it would prove a critical component in the northern strategy of attrition against Richmond.

Whereas an insurrection against the Government of the United States has broken out in the States of South Carolina, Georgia, Alabama, Florida, Mississippi, Louisiana, and Texas, and the laws of the United States for the collection of the revenue cannot be effectually executed therein conformably to that provision of the Constitution which requires duties to be uniform throughout the United States; and

Whereas a combination of persons engaged in such insurrection have threatened to grant pretended letters of marque to authorize the bearers thereof to commit assaults on the lives, vessels, and property of good citizens of the country lawfully engaged in commerce on the high seas and in waters of the United States; and

Whereas an Executive proclamation has been already issued requiring persons engaged in these disorderly proceedings to desist therefrom, calling out a militia force for the purpose of repressing the same, and convening Congress in extraordinary session to deliberate and determine thereon:

Now, therefor, I, Abraham Lincoln, President of the United States, with a view to the same purposes before mentioned, and to the protection of the public peace, and the lives and property of quiet and orderly citizens pursuing their lawful occupations, until Congress shall have assembled and deliberated on the said unlawful proceedings, or until the same shall have ceased, have further deemed it advisable to set on foot a blockade of the ports within the States aforesaid, in pursuance of the laws of the United States, and of the law of Nations in such case provided. For this purpose a component force will be posted so as to prevent entrance and exit of vessels from the ports aforesaid. If, therefore, with a view to violate such blockade, a vessel shall approach or shall attempt to leave either of the said ports, she will be duly warned by the commander of one of the blockading vessels, who will indorse on her register the fact and date of such warning, and if the same vessel shall again attempt to enter or leave the blockaded port, she will be captured and sent to the nearest convenient port, for such proceedings against her and her cargo, as prize, as may be deemed advisable.

And I hereby proclaim and declare that if any person, under the pretended authority of the said States, or under any other pretense, shall molest a vessel of the United States, or the persons or cargo on board her, such person will be held amenable to the laws of the United States for the prevention and punishment of piracy.

Source: James D. Richardson, ed., *A Compilation of the Messages and Papers of the Presidents*, vol.7 (New York: Bureau of National Literature, 1897), 3215–16.

29.   THE HOMESTEAD ACT
20 May 1862

Faced with the necessity of feeding Union armies and motivated by the desire to improve exports of grain to Europe, the United States fundamentally altered land policy in 1862. The Homestead Act *gave farmers the option of gaining title to 160 acres of public land by farming it for five years or purchasing the land for $1.25 an acre after six months residency.*

AN ACT to secure homesteads to actual settlers on the public domain.

Be it enacted, That any person who is the head of a family, or who has arrived at the age of twenty-one years, and is a citizen of the United States, or who shall have filed his declaration of intention to become such, as required by the naturalization laws of the United States, and who has never borne arms against the United States Government or given aid and comfort to its enemies, shall, from and after the first of January, eighteen hundred and sixty-three, be entitled to enter one quarter-section or a less quantity of unappropriated public lands, upon which said person may have filed a preemption claim, or which may, at the time the application is made, be subject to preemption at one dollar and twenty-five cents, or less, per acre; or eighty acres or less of such unappropriated lands, at two dollars and fifty cents per acre, to be located in a body, in conformity to the legal subdivisions of the public lands, and after the same shall have been surveyed: *Provided,* That any person owning or residing on land may, under the provisions of this act, enter other land lying contiguous to his or her said land, which shall not, with the land so already owned and occupied, exceed in the aggregate one hundred and sixty acres.

SEC. 2. That the person applying for the benefit of this act shall, upon application to the register of the land office in which he or she is about to make such entry, make affidavit before the said register or receiver that he or she is the head of a family, or is twenty-one or more years of age, or shall have performed service in the Army or Navy of the United States, and that he has never borne arms against the Government of the United States or given aid and comfort to its enemies, and that such application is made for his or her exclusive use and benefit, and that said entry is made for the purpose of actual settlement and cultivation, and not, either directly or indirectly, for the use or benefit of any other person or persons whomsoever; and upon filing the said affidavit with the register or receiver, and on payment of ten dollars, he or she shall thereupon be permitted to enter the quantity of land specified: *Provided, however,* That no certificate shall be given or patent issued therefore until the expiration of five years from the date of such entry; and if, at the expiration of such time, or at any time within two years thereafter, the person making such entry—or if he be dead, his widow; or in case of her death, his heirs or devisee; or in case of a widow making such entry, her heirs or devisee, in case of her death—shall prove by two credible witnesses that he, she, or they have resided upon or cultivated the same for the term of five years immediately succeeding the time of filing the affidavit aforesaid, and shall make affidavit that no part of said land has been alienated, and that he has borne true allegiance to the Government of the United States; then, in such case, he, she, or they, if at that time a citizen of the United States, shall be entitled to a patent, as in other cases provided for by law: *And provided, further*, That in case of the death of both father and mother, leaving an infant child or children under twenty-one years of age, the right and fee shall inure to the benefit of said infant child or children; and the executor, administrator, or guardian may, at any time within two years after the death of the surviving parent, and in accordance with the laws of the State in which such children for the time being have their domicile, sell said land for the benefit of said infants, but for no other purpose; and the purchaser shall acquire the absolute title by the purchase, and be entitled to a patent from the United States, on payment of the office fees and sum of money herein specified. . . .

Source: Henry Steele Commager, *Documents of American History*, vol. 1 (Englewood Cliffs, NJ: Prentice Hall, 1973), 410–11.

---

30. ADDRESS TO PRESIDENT LINCOLN BY THE WORKING-MEN OF MANCHESTER
31 December 1862

England clearly was of a divided mind regarding the American Civil War. This letter, written before Lincoln's formal announcement of the Emancipation Proclamation, *expressed support of 6,000 workers for the new policy. Broadly held sentiments such as these were an important obstacle against a British alliance with the Confederacy.*

To Abraham Lincoln, President of the United States:

As citizens of Manchester, assembled at the Free-Trade Hall, we beg to express our fraternal sentiments toward you and your country. We rejoice in your greatness as an outgrowth of England, whose blood and language you share, whose orderly and legal freedom you have applied to new circumstances, over a region immeasurably greater than our own. We honor your Free States, as a singularly happy abode for the working millions where industry is honored. One thing alone has, in the past, lessened our sympathy with your country and our confidence in it—we mean the ascendancy of politicians who not merely maintained negro slavery, but desired to extend and root it more firmly. Since we have discerned, however, that the victory of the free North, in the war which has so sorely distressed us as well as afflicted you will strike off the fetters of the slave, you have attracted our warm and earnest sympathy. We joyfully honor you, as the President, and the Congress with you, for many decisive steps toward practically exemplifying your belief in the words of our great founders: "All men are created free and equal." You have procured the liberation of the slaves in the district around Washington, and thereby, made the centre of your Federation visibly free. You have enforced the laws against the slave-trade, and kept up your fleet against it, even while every ship was wanted for service in your terrible war. You have nobly decided to receive ambassadors from the negro republics of Hayti and Liberia, thus forever renouncing that unworthy prejudice which refuses the rights of humanity to men and women on account of their color. In order more effectually to stop the slave-trade, you have made with our Queen a treaty, which your Senate has ratified, for the right of mutual search. Your Congress has decreed freedom as the law forever in the vast unoccupied or half unsettled Territories which are directly subject to its legislative power. It has offered pecuniary aid to all States which will enact emancipation locally, and has forbidden your Generals to restore fugitive slaves who seek their protection. You have entreated the slave-masters to accept these moderate offers; and after long and patient waiting, you, as Commander-in-Chief of the Army, have appointed tomorrow, the first of January, 1863, as the day of unconditional freedom for the slaves of the rebel States. Heartily do we congratulate you and your country on this humane and righteous course. We assume that you cannot now stop short of a complete uprooting of slavery. It would not become us to dictate any details, but there are broad principles of humanity which must guide you. If complete emancipation in some States be deferred, though only to a predetermined day, still in the interval, human beings should not be counted chattels. Women must have the rights of chastity and maternity, men the rights of husbands, masters the liberty of manumission. Justice demands for the black, no less than for the white, the protection of law—that his voice be heard in your courts. Nor must any such abomination be tolerated as slave-breeding States, and a slave market—if you are to earn the high reward of all your sacrifices, in the approval of the universal brotherhood and of the Divine Father. It is for your free country to decide whether any thing but immediate and total emancipation can secure the most indispensable rights of humanity against the inveterate wickedness of local laws and local executives. We implore you, for your own honor and welfare, not to faint in your providential mission. While your enthusiasm is aflame, and the tide of events runs high, let the work be finished effectually. Leave no root of bitterness to spring up and work fresh misery to your children. It is a mighty task, indeed, to reorganize the industry not only of four millions of the colored race, but of five millions of whites. Nevertheless, the vast progress you have made in the short space of twenty months fills us with hope that every stain on your freedom will shortly be removed, and that the erasure of that foul blot upon civilization and Christianity—chattel slavery—during your Presidency will cause the name of Abraham Lincoln to be honored and revered by posterity. We are certain that such a glorious consummation will cement Great Britain to the United States in close and enduring regards. Our interests, moreover, are identified with yours. We are truly one people, though locally separate. And if you have any ill-wishers here, be assured they are chiefly those who oppose liberty at home, and that they will be powerless to stir up quarrels between us, from the very day in which your country becomes, undeniably and without exception, the home of the free. Accept our high admiration of your firmness in upholding the proclamation of freedom.

Source: Henry Steele Commager, *Documents of American History*, vol. 1 (Englewood Cliffs, NJ: Prentice Hall, 1973), 418–19.

---

31. LINCOLN'S REPLY TO THE WORKING-MEN OF MANCHESTER
19 January 1863

After he issued the formal Emancipation Proclamation, *Lincoln offered his gratitude to the workers of Manchester. His letter was a rare example of an American president communicating directly to a foreign constituency. It also included several clear encouragements that the British government refrain from intervention.*

To the working-men of Manchester:
   I have the honor to acknowledge the receipt of the address and resolutions which you sent me on the eve of the new year. When I came, on the 4th of March, 1861, through a free and constitutional election to preside in the Government of the United States, the country was found on the verge of civil war. Whatsoever might have been the cause, or whosoever the fault, one duty, paramount to all others, was before me, namely, to maintain and preserve at once the Constitution and integrity of the Federal Republic. A conscientious purpose to perform this duty is the key to all the measures of administration which have been and to all which will hereafter be pursued. Under our frame of government and my official oath, I could not depart from this purpose if I would. It is not always in the power of governments to enlarge or restrict the scope of moral results which follow the policies that they may deem it necessary for the public safety from time to time to adopt.
   I have understood well that the duty of self-preservation rests solely with the American people; but I have at the same time been aware that favor or disfavor

of foreign nations might have a material influence in enlarging or prolonging the struggle with disloyal men in which the country is engaged. A fair examination of history has served to authorize a belief that the past actions and influences of the United States were generally regarded as having been beneficial toward mankind. I have, therefore, reckoned upon the forbearance of nations. Circumstances—to some of which you kindly allude—induce me especially to expect that if justice and good faith should be practised by the United States, they would encounter no hostile influence on the part of Great Britain. It is now a pleasant duty to acknowledge the demonstration you have given of your desire that a spirit of amity and peace toward this country may prevail in the councils of your Queen, who is respected and esteemed in your own country only more than she is by the kindred nation which has its home on this side of the Atlantic.

I know and deeply deplore the sufferings which the working-men at Manchester, and in all Europe, are called to endure in this crisis. It has been often and studiously represented that the attempt to overthrow this government, which was built upon the foundation of human rights, and to substitute for it one which should rest exclusively on the basis of human slavery, was likely to obtain the favor of Europe. Through the action of our disloyal citizens, the working-men of Europe have been subjected to severe trials, for the purpose of forcing their sanction to that attempt. Under the circumstances, I cannot but regard your decisive utterances upon the question as an instance of sublime Christian heroism which has not been surpassed in any age or in any country. It is indeed an energetic and reinspiring assurance of the inherent power of truth and of the ultimate and universal triumph of justice, humanity, and freedom. I do not doubt that the sentiments you have expressed will be sustained by your great nation; and on the other hand, I have no hesitation in assuring you that they will excite admiration, esteem, and the most reciprocal feelings of friendship among the American people. I hail this interchange of sentiment, therefore, as an augury that whatever may happen, whatever misfortune may befall your country or my own, the peace and friendship which now exist between the two nations will be, as it shall be my desire to make them, perpetual.

ABRAHAM LINCOLN

Source: Henry Steele Commager, *Documents of American History*, vol. 1 (Englewood Cliffs, NJ: Prentice Hall, 1973), 418–19.

32. SUSPENSION OF THE MONROE DOCTRINE
3 March 1862

In July 1861, Mexico suspended all payments on foreign debts, prompting France, Spain, and England to jointly seize the country's customhouses.

Spain and England were able to reach an agreement with Mexico City and withdrew. France, however, expanded its occupying force and invaded Mexico, posing a direct challenge to the Monroe Doctrine *as the United States struggled through the early stages of the Civil War.*

Department of State,
Washington, March 3, 1862

Sir: We observe indications of a growing opinion in Europe that the demonstrations which are being made by the Spanish, French, and British forces against Mexico are likely to be attended with a revolution in that country which will bring in a monarchical government there, in which the crown will be assumed by some foreign prince.

This country is deeply concerned in the peace of nations, and aims to be loyal at the same time in all its relations, as well to the allies of Mexico. The President has therefore instructed me to submit his views on the aspect of affairs to the parties concerned. He has relied upon the assurances given to this government by the allies that they were seeking no political objects and only a redress of grievances. He does not doubt the sincerity of the allies, and his confidence in their good faith, if it could be shaken, would be reinspired by explanations apparently made in their behalf that the governments of Spain, France, and Great Britain are not intending to intervene and will not intervene to effect a change of the constitutional form of government now existing in Mexico, or to produce any political change there in opposition to the will of the Mexican people. Indeed, he understands the allies to be unanimous in declaring that the proposed revolution in Mexico is moved only by Mexican citizens now in Europe.

The President, however, deems it his duty to express to the allies, in all candor and frankness, the opinion that no monarchical government which could be founded in Mexico, in the presence of foreign navies and armies in the waters and upon the soil of Mexico, would have any prospect of security or permanency. Secondly, that the instability of such a monarchy there would be enhanced if the throne should be assigned to any person not of Mexican nativity. That under such circumstances the new government must speedily fall unless it could draw into its support European alliances, which, relating back to the present invasion, would, in fact, make it the beginning of a permanent policy of armed European monarchical intervention injurious and practically hostile to the most general system of government on the continent of America, and this would be the beginning rather than the ending of revolution in Mexico.

These views are grounded upon some knowledge of the political sentiments and habits of society in America.

In such a case it is not to be doubted that the permanent interests and sympathies of this country would be with the other American republics. It is not intended on this occasion to predict the course of events which might happen as a consequence of the proceeding contemplated, either on this continent or in

Europe. It is sufficient to say that, in the President's opinion, the emancipation of this continent from European control has been the principal feature in its history during the last century. It is not probable that a revolution in the contrary direction would be successful in an immediately succeeding century, while population in America is so rapidly increasing, resources so rapidly developing, and society so steadily forming itself upon principles of democratic American government. Nor is it necessary to suggest to the allies the improbability that European nations could steadily agree upon a policy favorable to such a counter-revolution as one conducive to their own interests, or to suggest that, however studiously the allies may act to avoid lending the aid of their land and naval forces to domestic revolutions in Mexico, the result would nevertheless be traceable to the presence of those forces there, although for a different purpose, since it may be deemed certain that but for their presence there no such revolution could probably have been attempted or even conceived.

The Senate of the United States has not, indeed, given its official sanction to the precise measures which the President has proposed for lending our aid to the existing government in Mexico, with the approval of the allies, to relieve it from its present embarrassments. This, however, is only a question of domestic administration. It would be very erroneous to regard such a disagreement as indicating any serious difference of opinion in this government or among the American people in their cordial good wishes for the safety, welfare, and stability of the republican system of government in that country.

I am, sir, your obedient servant,

William H. Seward.

Source: Henry Steele Commager, *Documents of American History*, vol. 1 (Englewood Cliffs, NJ: Prentice Hall, 1973), 424–25.

33. REASSERTION OF THE MONROE DOCTRINE 1866

With the Civil War finally resolved, America was able to turn its attention to the French emperor ensconced in Mexico. Secretary of State Seward's letter reflected not only Maximilian's rapidly declining fortunes in Mexico, but also a new American resolve to reassert the principle of noninterference in hemispheric affairs.

Department of State,
Washington, April 16, 1866

SIR: I have had the honor to receive your despatch of the 27th of March, No. 155, which brings the important announcement that a treaty, called a "military supplementary convention," was ratified on the 15th of that month between the Emperor of Austria and the Prince Maximilian, who claims to be an emperor in Mexico.

You inform me that it is expected that about one thousand volunteers will be shipped (under this treaty) from Trieste to Vera Cruz very soon, and that at least as many more will be shipped in autumn.

I have heretofore given you the President's instructions to ask for explanations, and, conditionally, to inform the government of Austria that the despatch of military expeditions by Austria under such an arrangement as the one which seems now to have been consummated would be regarded with serious concern by the United States.

The subject has now been further considered in connexion with the official information thus recently, received. The time seems to have arrived when the attitude of this government in relation to Mexican affairs should be once again frankly and distinctly made known to the Emperor of Austria, and all other powers whom it may directly concern. The United States, for reasons which seem to them to be just, and to have their foundation in the laws of nations, maintain that the domestic republican government with which they are in relations of friendly communication is the only legitimate government existing in Mexico; that a war has for a period of several years been waged against that republic by the government of France; which war began with a disclaim of all political or dynastic designs that that war has subsequently taken upon itself, and now distinctly wears the character of an European intervention to overthrow that domestic republican government, and to erect in its stead a European, imperial, military despotism by military force. The United States, in view of the character of their own political institutions, their proximity and intimate relations towards Mexico, and their just influence in the political affairs of the American continent, cannot consent to the accomplishment of that purpose by the means described. The United States have therefore addressed themselves, as they think, seasonably to the government of France and have asked that its military forces, engaged in that objectionable political invasion, may desist from further intervention and be withdrawn from Mexico.

A copy of the last communication upon this subject, which was addressed by us to the government of France, is herewith transmitted for your special information. This paper will give the true situation of the question. It will also enable you to satisfy the government of Vienna that the United States must be no less opposed to military intervention for political objects hereafter in Mexico by the government of Austria, than they are opposed to any further intervention of the same character in that country by France.

You will, therefore, at as early a day as may be convenient, bring the whole case, in a becoming manner, to the attention of the imperial royal government. You are authorized to state that the United States sincerely desire that Austria may find it just and expedient to come upon the same ground of non-intervention in Mexico which is maintained by the United States, and to which they have invited France.

You will communicate to us the answer of the Austrian government to this proposition.

This government could not but regard as a matter of serious concern the despatch of any troops from Austria for Mexico while the subject which you are thus directed to present to the Austrian government remains under consideration.

I am, sir, your obedient servant,
WILLIAM H. SEWARD

Source: U.S. Department of State, *Papers Relating to the Foreign Relations of the United States, 1866*, vol. 3 (Washington, DC: Government Printing Office, 1866), 833.

Part Four

The Gilded Age

Peace after the Civil War brought with it rapid military demobilization and a lengthy involvement in southern Reconstruction. The ranks of the Union Army, which numbered over a million men in May 1865, diminished drastically once the guns had been silenced. By November 1866, only 11,043 volunteers remained in uniform. And within five years, the U.S. Navy was left with only 52 ships; a dramatic loss considering that at the peak of the war there were 700 vessels of all sizes.[1] During this period, the nation focused on the monumental task of rebuilding the physical damage wrought by the war and reforming its basic social institutions. The partisan bitterness over southern Reconstruction unleashed within the halls of government eventually consumed the administration of Andrew Johnson.[2]

Because of the cutbacks in the armed services and the reconstruction going on in the south, America's forays into foreign affairs during the decade after the Civil War were limited. Postwar U.S. diplomacy reflected a loose, reactive style, lacking an overall centralized direction or strategy. Individual representatives stationed abroad—a group that included officially recognized diplomats as well as merchants, missionaries, and entrepreneurs—were granted considerable leeway in the way they conducted American affairs.[3]

Despite these handicaps, the United States was able to register some early successes. In 1867, Alaska became an American territory. Although derided by many contemporaries as an expensive ($7.2 million) boondoggle, Secretary of State William H. Seward believed that possession of the Alaska territory could serve as a means to expedite American occupation of Canada.[4] Over the longer term, American ownership of Alaska halted Russian efforts to extend its domain across the Bering Strait; and the territory proved to be a veritable treasure trove of natural resources. During the same year, the United States also occupied Midway Island, considerably extending the range of American naval power into the Pacific.

However, American diplomats also registered some remarkable failures after the Civil War. Seward entertained designs on an array of new territories that included Haiti, Martinique, the Virgin Islands, Iceland, and Hawaii, among many others. Unfortunately, U.S. attempts at new expansion often ran afoul of the incompetence and inexperience that too often characterized post-1865 administrations. Ulysses S. Grant's impressive travails over Santo Domingo marked a definite low point in the history of American diplomacy. Grant's appeal for support in the acquisition of the Caribbean island, literally with hat in hand, to the powerful Senator Charles Sumner in January 1870 was rebuffed and parlayed into an embarrassing spectacle for the White House as the Senate Committee on Foreign Relations opened up the malfeasance of American agents to the public record.[5] Similarly, American demands that England pay reparations for losses suffered from Confederate commerce raiders in the case of the *Alabama* Affair (1871) proved unsupportable when matched against British power.[6] Perhaps the nadir of American power abroad appeared in the insignificant effort to intervene in Cuba. The crisis was provoked by the Spanish capture of the USS *Virginius* in 1873. After executing fifty crewmen, a brief war scare rippled across America and provoked a mobilization of haphazard proportions. A fleet, assembled for maneuvers a year later, was a decrepit collection of ships. According to one newspaper it was "almost useless for military purposes."[7]

While America explored the limits of its international role, the western frontier captured the nation's attention. The final settlement of the land to the west of the Mississippi absorbed the energies of civilians and federal officials alike for a quarter of a century. According to Warren W. Hassler, the American Army would fight 13 different campaigns and 1,067 separate engagements against Native Americans in the years between 1865 and 1891.[8] In this arena, American diplomacy was reduced to a series of treaty negotiations that neither adequately regulated the expansion of white settlement nor protected the land or rights of Native Americans. Instead, it produced a pattern, in the words of president Chester A. Arthur, that led "to frequent and disastrous conflicts between the races."[9] By 1890, most remaining Native American enclaves had been subsumed by war, disease, and the 8 million new settlers who had streamed west in the preceding twenty years.[10]

The waning influence of the frontier encouraged renewed interest in America's role outside the continent. The 1890s saw a rebirth of internationalism. The period was perhaps best characterized by the writings of Alfred Thayer Mahan. His book, *The Influence of Sea Power on History* (1890), was the primer for contemporary expansionists. The two principles featured in the work, the necessity of the "due use and control" of sea lanes and the need to accumulate overseas bases to sustain a fleet, became the clarion call of a generation of American navalists.[11] Mahan's book found a ready audience in a young Theodore Roosevelt, himself a formidable authority on naval affairs.[12]

Armed forces modernization accompanied new strategic theory. The U.S. Navy began its belated transition to all-steel vessels during the administration

of Chester A. Arthur, who approved the first protected cruisers in 1883 as part
of the so-called "Squadron of Evolution" or "White Squadron."[13] The same year
that Mahan published his book was a momentous year for American sea power.
In 1890, Secretary of the Navy Benjamin Franklin Tracey recommended a 100-
ship fleet that would include 20 new battleships. Congress responded by ap-
proving the construction of three first-class battleships, the *Oregon*, the *Indiana*,
and the *Massachusetts*.[14] A new age of American naval power had begun.

To a large extent American foreign affairs were subsequently shaped by the
search for strategic bases for this modern Navy. The United States craved coaling facilities and deep-water ports that would sustain fleets comprised of ships
built in excess of 10,000 tons. The vast expanses of the Pacific represented a
particular challenge and drew the United States to territories that could support
naval base construction and protect American trade with Asia. In 1878, America
gained naval base rights in Samoa. Eight years later, the U.S. Navy received
access to the excellent facility at Pearl Harbor. Annexation of Hawaii followed
in 1898.[15]

Closer to home, the United States appeared more willing to flex its muscles
in international affairs. Latin America evolved as an area of specific U.S. interest. In the years after the Civil War, American capital flowed into agriculture,
textiles, and oil. By 1900, the U.S. stake in Mexico alone had reached $500
million.[16] Latin American economies also drew closer to their northern neighbor.
The United States signed reciprocal trade agreements with six Latin American
nations in the 1880s. At the conclusion of the century, diplomacy increasingly
focused on protecting this stake and preventing foreign competition.[17]

Direct U.S. intervention in Latin America also became commonplace by the
close of the century. The American Navy intervened in the Haitian civil war of
1888 on the side of the rebels and secured base rights and a commercial treaty.
In 1891, the United States became entangled in a Chilean insurgency, this time
on the side of the President José Balmaceda against his own Congress. Three
years later, U.S. assistance helped break a rebellion in Brazil.

The Venezuelan crisis of 1895–1896 was a point of demarcation for the
United States. For years, European powers had intervened in Latin America.
England had intruded upon Chile, Brazil, and Nicaragua affairs. France was
involved in a border conflict between its Guiana colony and Brazil. These conflicts peaked during a dispute between England and Venezuela over the mouth
of the Orinoco River in 1895. The territory contained goldfields and controlled
access to the entire Andean region and was vital to American commerce with
South America. Venezuela granted an American mining company a lucrative
concession in the disputed region, hoping to draw the United States into the
conflict. The tactic worked. Citing the Monroe Doctrine as its precedent, Washington declared its intention to intervene when European power in the Western
Hemisphere posed a "serious and direct menace to its own integrity and welfare." Although the British scoffed at this threat, the Cleveland administration
made it clear that the United States was prepared to go to war to enforce its

decision.[18] According to historian Robert L. Beisner, "Cleveland's bombshell ignited an explosion of patriotism and Anglophobia."[19] London, with one eye on the emergence of an increasingly belligerent Germany and in need of future allies, wisely agreed to an international tribunal to settle the dispute and essentially relinquished future territorial designs in Latin America. American public passions calmed, but only served to presage the war with Spain that would arrive in only two years.

NOTES

1. Allan R. Millett and Peter Maslowski, *For the Common Defense: A Military History of the United States of America* (New York: Free Press, 1994), 248–49.

2. Eric Foner, *A Short History of Reconstruction, 1863–1877* (New York: Harper & Row, 1990), 82–103.

3. Robert L. Beisner, *From the Old Diplomacy to the New, 1865–1900* (Arlington Heights, IL: Harlan Davidson, 1986), 60–71, 88.

4. John M. Taylor, *William Henry Seward: Lincoln's Right Hand* (New York: HarperCollins, 1991), 275.

5. William S. McFeeley, *Grant: A Biography* (New York: W.W. Norton, 1982), 340–45.

6. Ibid., 332–36.

7. Millett and Maslowski, *For the Common Defense*, 249.

8. Warren W. Hassler, *With Shield and Sword: American Military Affairs, Colonial Times to the Present* (Ames: Iowa State University Press, 1982), 193–208.

9. Henry Steele Commager, *Documents of American History*, vol. 1 (Englewood Cliffs, NJ: Prentice Hall, 1973), 557.

10. Samuel Eliot Morison, Henry Steele Commager, and William E. Leuchtenburg, *The Growth of the American Republic*, vol. 2 (New York: Oxford University Press, 1969), 22.

11. Beisner, *From the Old Diplomacy to the New*, 84–95; Walter Millis, *Arms and Men: A Study in American Military History* (New Brunswick, NJ: Rutgers University Press, 1984), 155–67.

12. Edmund Morris, *The Rise of Theodore Roosevelt* (New York: Ballantine Books, 1979), 154–56.

13. Bernard Ireland, *Jane's Battleships of the 20th Century* (New York: HarperCollins, 1996), 146.

14. Ibid., 144–45.

15. William H. Goetzman, *When the Eagle Screamed: The Romantic Horizon in American Diplomacy, 1800–1865* (New York: Wiley, 1966), 92–102.

16. Benjamin Keen and Mark Wasserman, *A History of Latin America* (Boston: Houghton Mifflin, 1988), 513.

17. Friedrich Katz, *The Secret War in Mexico: Europe, the United States, and the Mexican Revolution* (Chicago: University of Chicago Press, 1981), 21–29.

18. Beisner, *From the Old Diplomacy to the New*, 109–16.

19. Ibid., 111.

---

34. PURCHASE OF ALASKA
1867

Derided as "Seward's icebox," the American purchase of Alaska proved controversial to contemporaries who heartily criticized its $7.2 million cost. The commercial and strategic benefits of this far-off land were unclear when the initial proposal was made. However, bolstered by a friendly Senate and a Russian monarchy interested in relinquishing what it considered an expensive possession, Seward was able to realize his dream in 1867.

CONVENTION FOR THE CESSION OF THE RUSSIAN
POSSESSIONS IN NORTH AMERICA TO THE UNITED
STATES
Concluded March 30, 1867. Ratifications exchanged at
Washington, June 20 1867.
Proclaimed June 20, 1867.

. . . ART. I. . . . His Majesty the Emperor of all the Russias agrees to cede to the United States, by this Convention, immediately upon the exchange of the ratifications thereof, all the territory and dominion now possessed by his said Majesty on the continent of America and in the adjacent islands, the same being contained within the geographical limits herein set forth, to wit: The eastern limit is the line of demarcation between the Russian and the British possessions in North America, as established by the convention between Russia and Great Britain, of February 28–16, 1825, and described in Articles III. and IV. of said convention, in the following terms: . . .

IV. With reference to the line of demarcation laid down in the preceding article, it is understood

1st. That the island called Prince Of Wales Island shall belong wholly to Russia, . . .

2d. That whenever the summit of the mountains which extend in a direction parallel to the coast from the 56th degree of north latitude to the point of intersection of the 141st degree of west longitude shall prove to be at the distance of more than ten marine leagues from the ocean, the limit between the British possessions and the line of coast which is to belong to Russia as above mentioned, (that is to say, the limit to the possessions ceded by this convention,) shall be formed by a line parallel to the winding of the coast, and which shall never exceed the distance of ten marine leagues therefrom. . . .

ART. II. . . . In the cession of territory and dominion made by the preceding article are included the right of property in all public lots and squares, vacant lands, and all public buildings, fortifications, barracks, and other edifices which are not private individual property. It is, however, understood and agreed, that the churches which have been built in the ceded territory by the Russian Government, shall remain the property of such members of the Greek Oriental Church resident in the territory as may choose to worship therein. . . .

ART. III. . . . The inhabitants of the ceded territory, according to their choice, reserving their natural allegiance, may return to Russia within three years; but, if they should prefer to remain in the ceded territory, they, with the exception of uncivilized native tribes, shall be admitted to the enjoyment of all the rights, advantages, and immunities of citizens of the United States, and shall be maintained and protected in the free enjoyment of their liberty, property, and religion. The uncivilized tribes will be subject to such laws and regulations as the United States may from time to time adopt in regard to aboriginal tribes of that country. . . .

ART. VI. In consideration of the cession aforesaid, the United States agree to pay at the Treasury in Washington . . . seven million two hundred thousand dollars in gold. . . .

Source: William M. Malloy, ed., *Treaties, Conventions, International Acts, Protocols, and Agreements between the United States and Other Powers, 1776–1909*, vol. 2 (Washington, DC: Government Printing Office, 1910), 1521–23.

---

35. GRANT'S APPEAL FOR ANNEXATION OF SANTO DOMINGO
31 May 1870

In the interest of expanding American domain in the Caribbean, President Grant appealed to the Senate for the acquisition of Santo Domingo. Unfortunately, despite a personal appeal to Senate Foreign Relations Committee Chairman Charles Sumner, the treaty ran into trouble almost immediately, and it became a point of significant embarrassment for the administration in subsequent public hearings.

EXECUTIVE MANSION,
May 31, 1870.

To the Senate of the United States:

I transmit to the Senate, for consideration with a view to its ratification, an additional article to the treaty of the 29th of November last, for the annexation of the Dominican Republic to the United States, stipulating for an extension of the time for exchanging the ratifications thereof, signed in this city on the 14th instant by the plenipotentiaries of the parties.

It was my intention to have also negotiated with the plenipotentiary of San Domingo amendments to the treaty of annexation to obviate objections which may be urged against the treaty as it is now worded; but on reflection I deem it better to submit to the Senate the propriety of their amending the treaty as follows: First, to specify that the obligations of this Government shall not exceed the $1,500,000 stipulated in the treaty; secondly, to determine the manner of appointing the agents to receive and disburse the same; thirdly, to determine the class of creditors who shall take precedence in the settlement of their claims; and, finally, to insert such amendments as may suggest themselves to the minds of Senators to carry out in good faith the conditions of the treaty submitted to the Senate of the United States in January last, according to the spirit and intent of that treaty. From the most reliable information I can obtain, the sum specified in the treaty will pay every just claim against the Republic of San Domingo and leave a balance sufficient to carry on a Territorial government until such time as new laws for providing a Territorial revenue can be enacted and put in force.

I feel an unusual anxiety for the ratification of this treaty, because I believe it will redound greatly to the glory of the two countries interested, to civilization, and to the extirpation of the institution of slavery.

The doctrine promulgated by President Monroe has been adhered to by all political parties, and I now deem it proper to assert the equally important principle that hereafter no territory on this continent shall be regarded as subject of transfer to a European power.

The Government of San Domingo has voluntarily sought this annexation. It is a weak power, numbering probably less than 120,000 souls, and yet possessing one of the richest territories under the sun, capable of supporting a population of 10,000,000 people in luxury. The people of San Domingo are not capable of maintaining themselves in their present condition, and must look for outside support.

They yearn for the protection of our free institutions and laws, our progress and civilization. Shall we refuse them?

I have information which I believe reliable that a European power stands ready now to offer $2,000,000 for the possession of Samana Bay alone. If refused by us, with what grace can we prevent a foreign power from attempting to secure the prize?

The acquisition of San Domingo is desirable because of its geographical position. It commands the entrance to the Caribbean Sea and the Isthmus transit of commerce. It possesses the richest soil, best and most capacious harbors, most salubrious climate, and the most valuable products of the forest, mine, and soil of any of the West India Islands. Its possession by us will in a few years build up a coastwise commerce of immense magnitude, which will go far toward restoring to us our lost merchant marine. It will give to us those articles which we consume so largely and do not produce, thus equalizing our exports and imports.

In case of foreign war it will give us command of all the islands referred to, and thus prevent an enemy from ever again possessing himself of rendezvous upon our very coast.

At present our coast trade between the States bordering on the Atlantic and those bordering on the Gulf of Mexico is cut into by the Bahamas and the Antilles. Twice we must, as it were, pass through foreign countries to get by sea from Georgia to the west coast of Florida.

San Domingo, with a stable government, under which her immense resources can be developed, will give remunerative wages to tens of thousands of laborers not now on the island.

This labor will take advantage of every available means of transportation to abandon the adjacent islands and seek the blessings of freedom and its se-quence—each inhabitant receiving the reward of his own labor. Porto Rico and Cuba will have to abolish slavery as a measure of self-preservation to retain their laborers.

San Domingo will become a large consumer of the products of Northern farms and manufactories. The cheap rate at which her citizens can be furnished with food, tools, and machinery will make it necessary that the contiguous islands should have the same advantages in order to compete in the production of sugar, coffee, tobacco, tropical fruits, etc. This will open to us a still wider market for our products.

The production of our own supply of these articles will cut off more than one hundred millions of our annual imports, besides largely increasing our exports. With such a picture it is easy to see how our large debt abroad is ultimately to be extinguished. With a balance of trade against us (including interest on bonds held by foreigners and money spent by our citizens traveling in foreign lands) equal to the entire yield of the precious metals in this country, it is not so easy to see how this result is to be otherwise accomplished.

The acquisition of San Domingo is an adherence to the "Monroe doctrine;" it is a Measure of national protection: it is asserting our just claim to a con-trolling influence over the great commercial traffic soon to flow from east to west by the way of the Isthmus of Darien; it is to build up our merchant marine; it is to furnish new markets for the products of our farms, shops, and manufac-tories; it is to make slavery insupportable in Cuba and Porto Rico at once and ultimately so in Brazil; it is to settle the unhappy condition of Cuba, and end in exterminating conflict; it is to provide honest means of paying our honest debts, without overtaxing the people; it is to furnish our citizens with the nec-essaries of everyday life at cheaper rates than ever before; and it is, in fine, a rapid stride toward that greatness which the intelligence, industry, and enterprise of the citizens of the United States entitle this country to assume among nations.

                                                                    U.S. GRANT.

Source: James D. Richardson, ed., *A Compilation of the Messages and Papers of the Presidents*, vol. 8 (New York: Bureau of National Literature, 1897), 4015–17.

36. RESOLUTION OF THE *ALABAMA* AFFAIR
8 May 1871

England's support of Confederate commerce raiders proved to be a linger-
ing point of Anglo-American contention long after the end of the Civil
War. The Washington Treaty *allowed Britain to express official "regret"*
regarding the subject of commerce raiding and referred the question of
reparations to an international tribunal. The United States eventually re-
ceived $15 million for shipping losses suffered during the war.

TREATY RELATIVE TO CLAIMS, FISHERIES, NAVIGATION
OF THE ST. LAWRENCE, ETC., AMERICAN LUMBER ON
THE RIVER JOHN; BOUNDARY.

ART. I. Whereas differences have arisen between the Government of the
United States and the Government of Her Britannic Majesty, and still exist,
growing out of the acts committed by the several vessels which have given rise
to the claims generically known as the "Alabama Claims:"

And whereas Her Britannic Majesty has authorized her High Commissioners
Plenipotentiaries to express, in a friendly spirit, the regret felt by Her Majesty's
Government for the escape, under whatever circumstances, of the Alabama and
other vessels from British ports, and for the depredations committed by those
vessels:

Now, in order to remove and adjust all complaints and claims on the part of
the United States, and to provide for the speedy settlement of such claims which
are not admitted by Her Britannic Majesty's Government, the high contracting
parties agree that all the said claims, growing out of acts committed by the
aforesaid vessels and generically known as the "Alabama Claims," shall be
referred to a tribunal of arbitration to be composed of five Arbitrators, to be
appointed in the following manner, that is to say: One shall be named by the
President of the United States; one shall be named by Her Britannic Majesty;
His Majesty the King of Italy shall be requested to name one; the President of
the Swiss Confederation shall be requested to name one; and His Majesty the
Emperor of Brazil shall be requested to name one. . . .

ART. II. The Arbitrators shall meet at Geneva, in Switzerland, at the earliest
convenient day . . . and shall proceed impartially and carefully to examine and
decide all questions that shall be laid before them on the part of the Governments
of the United States and Her Britannic Majesty respectively. All questions considered by the tribunal, including the final award, shall be decided by a majority
of all the Arbitrators. . . .

ART. VI. In deciding the matters submitted to the Arbitrators, they shall be governed by the following three rules . . . and by such principles of international law not inconsistent therewith as the Arbitrators shall determine to have been applicable to the case.

RULES.

A neutral Government is bound—

First, to use due diligence to prevent the fitting out, arming, or equipping, within its jurisdiction, of any vessel which it has reasonable ground to believe is intended to cruise or to carry on war against any Power with which it is at peace; and also to use like diligence to prevent the departure from its jurisdiction of any vessel intended to cruise or carry on war as above, such vessel having been specially adapted, in whole or in part, within such jurisdiction, to warlike use.

Secondly, not to permit or suffer either belligerent to make use of its ports or waters as the base of naval operations against the other, or for the purpose of renewal or augmentation of military supplies or arms, or the recruitment of men.

Thirdly, to exercise due diligence in its own ports and waters, and, as to all persons within its jurisdiction, to prevent any violation of the foregoing obligations and duties.

Her Britannic Majesty has commanded her High Commissioners and Plenipotentiaries to declare that Her Majesty's Government cannot assent to the foregoing rules as a statement of principles of international law which were in force at the time when the claims mentioned in Article I. arose, but that Her Majesty's Government, in order to evince its desire of strengthening the friendly relations between the two countries, and of making satisfactory provision for the future, agrees that in deciding the questions between the two countries arising out of those claims, the Arbitrators should assume that Her Majesty's Government had undertaken to act upon the principles set forth in these rules.

And the high contracting parties agree to observe these rules as between themselves in future, and to bring them to the knowledge of other maritime Powers, and to invite them to accede to them.

ART. VII. . . . The said tribunal shall first determine as to each vessel separately, whether Great Britain has, by any act or omission, failed to fulfill any of the duties set forth in the foregoing three rules, or recognized by the principles of international law not inconsistent with such rules. . . . In case the tribunal find that Great Britain has failed to fulfill any duty or duties as aforesaid, it may, if it think proper, proceed to award a sum in gross to be paid by Great Britain to the United States for all the claims referred to it. . . .

Source: Henry Steele Commager, *Documents of American History*, vol. 1 (Englewood Cliffs, NJ: Prentice Hall, 1973), 517–18.

37. TREATY REGULATING CHINESE IMMIGRATION
17 November 1880

By 1880, Chinese immigration to the United States was the subject of significant controversy. Strident opposition by such organizations as the Workingman's Party of California had produced an 1879 bill abrogating reciprocal immigration privileges. Although Rutherford B. Hayes vetoed the bill, he appointed a committee to renegotiate the existing immigration treaty with China.

. . . Whereas the Government of the United States, because of the constantly increasing immigration of Chinese laborers to the territory of the United States, and the embarrassments consequent upon such immigration, now desires to negotiate a modification of the existing Treaties which shall not be in direct contravention of their spirit: . . .

ART. I. Whenever in the opinion of the Government of the United States, the coming of Chinese laborers to the United States, or their residence therein, affects or threatens to affect the interests of that country, or to endanger the good order of the said country or of any locality within the territory thereof, the Government of China agrees that the Government of the United States may regulate, limit, or suspend such coming or residence, but may not absolutely prohibit it. The limitation or suspension shall be reasonable and shall apply only to Chinese who may go to the United States as laborers, other classes not being included in the limitations. Legislation taken in regard to Chinese laborers will be of such a character only as is necessary to enforce the regulation, limitation or suspension of immigration, and immigrants shall not be subject to personal maltreatment or abuse.

ART. II. Chinese subjects, whether proceeding to the United States as teachers, students, merchants, or from curiosity, together with their body and household servants, and Chinese laborers who are now in the United States, shall be allowed to go and come of their own free will and accord, and shall be accorded all the rights, privileges, immunities and exemptions which are accorded to the citizens and subjects of the most favored nation.

ART. III. If Chinese laborers, or Chinese of any other class, now either permanently or temporarily residing in the territory of the United States, meet with ill treatment at the hands of any other persons, the Government of the United States will exert all its power to devise measures for their protection and to secure to them the same rights, privileges, immunities and exemptions as may be enjoyed by the citizens or subjects of the most favored nation, and to which they are entitled by treaty. . . .

Source: William M. Malloy, ed., *Treaties, Conventions, International Acts, Protocols, and Agreements between the United States and Other Powers, 1776–1909*, vol. 1 (Washington, DC: Government Printing Office, 1910), 241–44.

38. PRESIDENT ARTHUR ON THE INDIAN PROBLEM
6 December 1881

By the 1880s, the treatment of Native Americans had become the subject of scandal in many quarters of the United States. Chester A. Arthur's response was to propose a series of comprehensive reforms that would address the legal rights, access to land, and education of Native Americans. His recommendations later led to the Dawes Act of 1887.

. . . Prominent among the matters which challenge the attention of Congress at its present session is the management of our Indian affairs. While this question has been a cause of trouble and embarrassment from the infancy of the Government, it is but recently that any effort has been made for its solution at once serious, determined, consistent, and promising success.

It has been easier to resort to convenient makeshifts for tiding over temporary difficulties than to grapple with the great permanent problem, and accordingly the easier course has almost invariably been pursued.

It was natural, at a time when the national territory seemed almost illimitable and contained many millions of acres far outside the bounds of civilized settlements, that a policy should have been initiated which more than aught else has been the fruitful source of our Indian complications.

I refer, of course, to the policy of dealing with the various Indian tribes as separate nationalities, of relegating them by treaty stipulations to the occupancy of immense reservations in the West, and of encouraging them to live a savage life, undisturbed by any earnest and well-directed efforts to bring them under the influences of civilization.

The unsatisfactory results which have sprung from this policy are becoming apparent to all.

As the white settlements have crowded the borders of the reservations, the Indians, sometimes contentedly and sometimes against their will, have been transferred to other hunting grounds, from which they have again been dislodged whenever their new-found homes have been desired by the adventurous settlers.

These removals and the frontier collisions by which they have often been preceded have led to frequent and disastrous conflicts between the races.

It is profitless to discuss here which of them has been chiefly responsible for the disturbances whose recital occupies so large a space upon the pages of our history.

We have to deal with the appalling fact that though thousands of lives have been sacrificed and hundreds of millions of dollars expended in the attempt to solve the Indian problem, it has until within the past few years seemed scarcely nearer a solution than it was half a century ago. But the Government has of late been cautiously but steadily feeling its way to the adoption of a policy which has already produced gratifying results, and which, in my judgment, is likely, if Congress and the Executive accord in its support, to relieve us ere long from the difficulties which have hitherto beset us.

For the success of the efforts now making to introduce among the Indians the customs and pursuits of civilized life and gradually to absorb them into the mass of our citizens, sharing their rights and holden to their responsibilities, there is imperative need for legislative action.

My suggestions in that regard will be chiefly such as have been already called to the attention of Congress and have received to some extent its consideration.

First. I recommend the passage of an act making the laws of the various States and Territories applicable to the Indian reservations within their borders and extending the laws of the State of Arkansas to the portion of the Indian Territory not occupied by the Five Civilized Tribes.

The Indian should receive the protection of the law. He should be allowed to maintain in court his rights of person and property. He has repeatedly begged for this privilege. Its exercise would be very valuable to him in his progress toward civilization.

Second. Of even greater importance is a measure which has been frequently recommended by my predecessors in office, and in furtherance of which several bills have been from time to time introduced in both Houses of Congress. The enactment of a general law permitting the allotment in severalty, to such Indians, at least, as desire it, of a reasonable quantity of land secured to them by patent, and for their own protection made inalienable for twenty or twenty-five years, is demanded for their present welfare and their permanent advancement.

In return for such considerate action on the part of the Government, there is reason to believe that the Indians in large numbers would be persuaded to sever their tribal relations and to engage at once in agricultural pursuits. Many of them realize the fact that their hunting days are over and that it is now for their best interests to conform their manner of life to the new order of things. By no greater inducement than the assurance of permanent title to the soil can they be led to engage in the occupation of tilling it.

The well-attested reports of their increasing interest in husbandry justify the hope and belief that the enactment of such a statute as I recommend would be at once attended with gratifying results. A resort to the allotment system would have a direct and powerful influence in dissolving the tribal bond, which is so prominent a feature of savage life, and which tends so strongly to perpetuate it.

Third. I advise a liberal appropriation for the support of Indian schools, because of my confident belief that such a course is consistent with the wisest economy. . . .

Source: James D. Richardson, ed., *A Compilation of the Messages and Papers of the Presidents*, vol. 10 (New York: Bureau of National Literature, 1897), 4641–43.

---

39. PRESIDENT HARRISON'S MESSAGE ON THE ANNEXATION OF HAWAII
13 February 1893

In the last decade of the nineteenth century, America appeared poised to permanently extend its domain into the Pacific Ocean. Benjamin Harrison's call for the annexation of Hawaii in 1893 reflected growing American commercial interests on the island and the Navy's desire for an excellent harbor. A final treaty of annexation was not completed until 1898.

EXECUTIVE MANSION,
Washington, February 15, 1893.

To the Senate:

I transmit herewith, with a view to its ratification, a treaty of annexation concluded on the 14th day of February, 1893, between John W. Foster, Secretary of State . . . and Lorin A. Thurston, W. R. Castle, W. C. Wilder, C. L. Carter, and Joseph Marsden, the commissioners on the part of the Government of the Hawaiian Islands. . . .

I do not deem it necessary to discuss at any length the conditions which have resulted in this decisive action. It has been the policy of the Administration not only to respect but to encourage the continuance of an independent government in the Hawaiian Islands so long as it afforded suitable guaranties for the protection of life and property and maintained a stability and strength that gave adequate security against the domination of any other power. The moral support of this Government has continually manifested itself in the most friendly diplomatic relations and in many acts of courtesy to the Hawaiian rulers.

The overthrow of the monarchy was not in any way promoted by this Government, but had its origin in what seems to have been a reactionary and revolutionary policy on the part of Queen Liliuokalani, which put in serious peril not only the large and preponderating interests of the United States in the islands, but all foreign interests, and, indeed, the decent administration of civil affairs and the peace of the islands. It is quite evident that the monarchy had become effete and the Queen's Government so weak and inadequate as to be the prey of designing and unscrupulous persons. The restoration of Queen Liliuokalani to her throne is undesirable, if not impossible, and unless actively supported by the United States would be accompanied by serious disaster and the disorganization of all business interests. The influence and interest of the United States in the islands must be increased and not diminished.

Only two courses are now open—one the establishment of a protectorate by the United States, and the other annexation full and complete. I think the latter course, which has been adopted in the treaty, will be highly promotive of the best interests of the Hawaiian people, and is the only one that will adequately secure the interests of the United States. These interests are not wholly selfish. It is essential that none of the other great powers shall secure these islands. Such a possession would not consist with our safety and with the peace of the world. This view of the situation is so apparent and conclusive that no protest has been heard from any government against proceedings looking to annexation. Every foreign representative at Honolulu promptly acknowledged the Provisional Government, and I think there is a general concurrence in the opinion that the deposed Queen ought not to be restored.

Prompt action upon this treaty is very desirable. . . .

Source: James D. Richardson, ed., *A Compilation of the Messages and Papers of the Presidents*, vol. 12 (New York: Bureau of National Literature, 1897), 5783–84.

Part Five

The Early Empire

By the time the nineteenth century drew to a close, the United States was on a final trajectory toward becoming an empire. America had begun, according to diplomatic historian Robert L. Beisner, the transition toward a "new paradigm" of foreign policy. After 1890, a series of economic shocks created havoc throughout the United States, causing civil unrest and widespread uncertainty. Many saw, in foreign markets, a chance for American exports to drive the nation's future prosperity. By 1900, the enormous gains in the productive capacity and technological sophistication of American industry made this idea a plausible objective for both entrepreneurs and policy makers. Of equal importance to this equation was the passing of the generation shaped by the Civil War, one that generally eschewed aggressive policies that might lead to open conflict with American rivals. The younger leadership that replaced them, exemplified by men such as Theodore Roosevelt, Henry Cabot Lodge, and Alfred Thayer Mahan, advocated a modern military and a professional diplomatic corps on par with Europe to achieve the grand designs of a global power.[1] The 1890s consequently saw both the flourishing of professional military training and deliberate efforts to bring official representatives of the United States and private citizens to the service of the United States.

The war against Spain in 1898 served as a major milestone in America's accelerated movement toward becoming a global empire. Sick and on the decline at this point in history, Spain's remaining toehold in the Western Hemisphere represented a challenge to American hegemony. Its occupation of Cuba was an obstacle to the United States that considered the Caribbean a direct sphere of influence. Millions of dollars in American sugar investments was a tangible element in the much larger drive toward cementing U.S. dominance over Latin America.[2]

The conflict with Spain also revealed a new, unforeseen feature of modern diplomacy. Significant public excitement surrounded the gradual decline of

U.S.–Spanish relations into war. By 1898, a literate public followed unfolding international events. Encouraged at turns by the Hearst press, outspoken public leaders, and an emerging sense of American nationalism, the average citizen carved out a niche in the conduct of foreign affairs that has remained ever since.

The Spanish American War was almost anticlimactic in this heated context. As an exercise of military might, it was a study in contrasts. For the United States Army, the ground war was a litany of the travails of a military force woefully unprepared for mobilization or a sustained campaign against the Spanish enemy. The near collapse of William Shafter's disease-ridden and depleted 5th Corps outside Santiago, Cuba, in July 1898 later prompted investigations by the War Department. For the Navy, the Spanish-American War was a triumph capped by Admiral George Dewey's destruction of the Spanish fleet in Manila Harbor and victory over the failed attempt by Spanish naval units to escape Santiago Harbor. Victory on this front proved that the United States possessed a fleet more than adequate to extend its influence on a global level and maintain the far-flung elements of America's new territorial possessions.

The war also revealed the potency of the Executive branch in conducting American foreign affairs. Past scholarship has often depicted William McKinley as a rudderless leader buffeted by public opinion and jingoists within his own administration. However, there is general agreement among contemporary historians that as a wartime commander, he presented a formidable example of clarity and decisiveness. Linked to his military deployed throughout the world by telephone and telegraph, McKinley was able to successfully pursue Cuban independence and attacks upon Spanish colonies. He avoided direct war with Spain itself.[3] Once Spanish surrender was secured by the Treaty of Paris in December 1898, many Americans looked upon the victory as a remarkable achievement.

Counterbalancing this new sense of national pride was a debate over America's new imperial role. The 1899 platform of the Anti-Imperialist League expressed the thoughts of many who questioned the country's new direction:

The United States has always protested against the doctrine of international law which permits the subjugation of the weak by the strong. A self-governing state cannot accept sovereignty over an unwilling people. The United States cannot act upon the ancient heresy that might makes right.[4]

Many who saw America's rise to international power interpreted this as an opportunity for the United States to preside over a new form of international relations. Victory against Spain offered, according to anti-imperialist Jane Addams, an opportunity to usher in a form of communal internationalism, something that could exchange aggressive nationalism for greater attention to the practical needs of a global public. Others, such as Karl Schurz, were openly concerned that if the United States annexed new territories, their collective differences would erode the American social order.[5]

The actual responsibilities of global power provided a sober counterpoint to the victory against Spain. In Manila, victory over one Spanish fleet was but the first cursory chapter in a complicated story of the Filipino rebellion against Spain and, eventually, the United States. The struggle to overcome Emiliano Aguinaldo's independence movement dragged on for years. It encompassed American-sponsored campaigns to improve education, transportation, and public health. The war in the countryside inflicted atrocities on both sides. While American forces under the command of Arthur MacArthur eventually prevailed, capturing Aguinaldo in March 1901, the entirety of the insurrection left most Americans with a bitter aftertaste.[6] The burden of conquest in the Philippines established an important precedent for the cost America was willing to bear for the sake of empire.

The limits of American influence were even more apparent in Asia. By 1900, the United States observed what appeared to be the final stages of the European partition of China. While this process caused some consternation because of the threat it posed to American economic prospects, the nature of the territorial grab, undertaken without the United States, made the country's newly won status as an imperial power appear moot in this important corner of the world.[7] The tepid international response to John Hay's "Open Door" notes was an important measure of the lack of real diplomatic traction produced by American power.

The United States thus entered the new century with fewer illusions regarding its global status. For all his training and inclinations as an internationalist, Theodore Roosevelt oversaw an era distinct in its sense of limits. The importance of the Philippines receded in the discourse of American diplomatic energies, replaced by the intent of finally gaining a sea passage through Central America. Roosevelt's intervention for the sake of a canal in Panama defined both an important achievement of American foreign policy and its operational limits.[8] In the years preceding the First World War, American involvement in Latin America would deepen as the country contemplated the unfolding revolution in Mexico and fashioned appropriate policy to meet this new challenge.[9]

NOTES

1. Robert L. Beisner, *From the Old Diplomacy to the New, 1865–1900* (Arlington Heights, IL: Harlan Davidson, 1986), 72–91; Walter Licht, *Industrializing America: The Nineteenth Century* (Baltimore: Johns Hopkins University Press, 1995), 114–32, 138–43, 156–65.

2. Jorge I. Dominguez, *Cuba: Order and Revolution* (Cambridge, MA: Belknap Press, 1978), 11–54.

3. For a contemporary viewpoint of McKinley as a wartime leader, see Allan R. Millett and Peter Maslowski, *For the Common Defense: A Military History of the United States of America* (New York: Free Press, 1994), 286–92. See also Ernest R. May, *Imperial Democracy: The Emergence of America as a Great Power* (New York: Harcourt, Brace & World, 1961), 133–47, 152–59.

4. Henry Steele Commager, *Documents of American History*, vol. 2 (Englewood Cliffs, NJ: Prentice Hall, 1973), 11–12.

5. Robert L. Beisner, *Twelve against Empire: The Anti-Imperialists, 1898–1900* (New York: McGraw-Hill, 1968), 5–17; Sondra Herman, *Eleven against War: Studies in American Internationalist Thought, 1898–1921* (Stanford, CA: Hoover Institution Press, 1969), 10–20, 108–23.

6. See Peter W. Stanley, *A Nation in the Making: The Philippines and the United States, 1899–1921* (Cambridge: Harvard University Press, 1974).

7. Beisner, *From the Old Diplomacy to the New*, 144–53.

8. See Walter LaFeber, *The Panama Canal: The Crisis in Historical Perspective* (New York: Oxford University Press, 1978).

9. Friedrich Katz, *The Secret War in Mexico: Europe, the United States, and the Mexican Revolution* (Chicago: University of Chicago Press, 1981), 7–18, 21–29, 92–118.

40. McKINLEY'S WAR MESSAGE
11 April 1898

Citing a long history of abuses to both American property and Cuban lives, President McKinley asked Congress for war in April 1898. His request followed the destruction of the USS Maine *in Havana harbor on 15 February 1898 and a subsequent public uproar. A joint resolution was issued by Congress on 19 April authorizing McKinley to employ armed force to gain Cuban independence. Six days later, the United States formally declared war against Spain.*

EXECUTIVE MANSION, April 11, 1898.

To the Congress of the United States:

Obedient to that precept of the Constitution which commands the President to give from time to time to the Congress information of the state of the Union and to recommend to their consideration such measures as he shall judge necessary and expedient, it becomes my duty to now address your body with regard to the grave crisis that has arisen in the relations of the United States to Spain by reason of the warfare that for more than three years has raged in the neighboring island of Cuba. . . .

The present revolution is but the successor of other similar insurrections which have occurred in Cuba against the dominion of Spain, extending over a period of nearly half a century, each of which during its progress has subjected the United States to great effort and expense in enforcing its neutrality laws, caused enormous losses to American trade and commerce, caused irritation, annoyance, and disturbance among our citizens, and, by the exercise of cruel, barbarous, and uncivilized practices of warfare, shocked the sensibilities and offended the human sympathies of our people. . . .

Our trade has suffered, the capital invested by our citizens in Cuba has been largely lost, and the temper and forbearance of our people have been so sorely tried as to beget a perilous unrest among our own citizens, which has inevitably found its expression from time to time in the National Legislature, so that issues wholly external to our own body politic engross attention and stand in the way of that close devotion to domestic advancement that becomes a self-contained commonwealth whose primal maxim has been the avoidance of all foreign entanglements. All this must needs awaken, and has, indeed, aroused, the utmost concern on the part of this Government, as well during my predecessor's term as in my own.

In April, 1896, the evils from which our country suffered through the Cuban war became so onerous that my predecessor made an effort to bring about a peace through the mediation of this Government in any way that might tend to an honorable adjustment of the contest between Spain and her revolted colony, on the basis of some effective scheme of self-government for Cuba under the flag and sovereignty of Spain. It failed through the refusal of the Spanish government then in power to consider any form of mediation or, indeed, any plan of settlement which did not begin with the actual submission of the insurgents to the mother country, and then only on such terms as Spain herself might see fit to grant. The war continued unabated. The resistance of the insurgents was in no wise diminished. . . .

The overtures of this Government made through its new envoy, General Woodford, and looking to an immediate and effective amelioration of the condition of the island, although not accepted to the extent of admitted mediation in any shape, were met by assurances that home rule in an advanced phase would be forthwith offered to Cuba, without waiting for the war to end, and that more humane methods should thenceforth prevail in the conduct of hostilities. Coincidentally with these declarations the new government of Spain continued and completed the policy, already begun by its predecessor, of testifying friendly regard for this nation by releasing American citizens held under one charge or another connected with the insurrection, so that by the end of November not a single person entitled in any way to our national protection remained in a Spanish prison. . . .

The necessity for a change in the condition of the reconcentrados is recognized by the Spanish Government. Within a few days past the orders of General Weyler have been revoked. The reconcentrados, it is said, are to be permitted to return to their homes and aided to resume the self-supporting pursuits of peace. Public works have been ordered to give them employment and a sum of $600,000 has been appropriated for their relief.

The war in Cuba is of such a nature that, short of subjugation or extermination, a final military victory for either side seems impracticable. The alternative lies in the physical exhaustion of the one or the other party, or perhaps of both—a condition which in effect ended the ten years' war by the truce of Zanjon. The prospect of such a protraction and conclusion of the present strife is a contingency hardly to be contemplated with equanimity by the civilized world, and least of all by the United States, affected and injured as we are, deeply and intimately, by its very existence.

Realizing this, it appeared to be my duty, in a spirit of true friendliness, no less to Spain than to the Cubans, who have so much to lose by the prolongation of the struggle, to seek to bring about an immediate termination of the war. To this end I submitted on the 27th ultimo, as a result of much representation and correspondence, through the United States minister at Madrid, propositions to the Spanish Government looking to an armistice until October 1 for the negotiation of peace with the good offices of the President.

In addition I asked the immediate revocation of the order of reconcentration, so as to permit the people to return to their farms and the needy to be relieved with provisions and supplies from the United States, cooperating with the Spanish authorities, so as to afford full relief.

The reply of the Spanish cabinet was received on the night of the 31st ultimo. It offered, as the means to bring about peace in Cuba, to confide the preparation thereof to the insular parliament, inasmuch as the concurrence of that body would be necessary to reach a final result, it being, however, understood that the powers reserved by the constitution to the central Government are not lessened or diminished. As the Cuban parliament does not meet until the 4th of May next, the Spanish Government would not object for its part to accept at once a suspension of hostilities if asked for by the insurgents from the general in chief, to whom it would pertain in such case to determine the duration and conditions of the armistice. . . .

With this last overture in the direction of immediate peace, and its disappointing reception by Spain, the Executive is brought to the end of his effort.

In my annual message of December last I said.

Of the untried measures there remain only: recognition of the insurgents as belligerents; recognition of the independence of Cuba; neutral intervention to end the war by imposing a rational compromise between the contestants, and intervention in favor of one or the other party. I speak not of forcible annexation, for that can not be thought of. That, by our code of morality, would be criminal aggression.

Thereupon I reviewed these alternatives in the light of President Grant's measured words, uttered in 1875, when, after seven years of sanguinary, destructive, and cruel hostilities in Cuba, he reached the conclusion that the recognition of the independence of Cuba was impracticable and indefensible and that the recognition of belligerence was not warranted by the facts according to the tests of public law. I commented especially upon the latter aspect of the question, pointing out the inconveniences and positive dangers of a recognition of belligerence, which, while adding to the already onerous burdens of neutrality within our own jurisdiction, could not in any way extend our influence or effective offices in the territory of hostilities.

Nothing has since occurred to change my view in this regard, and I recognize as fully now as then that the issuance of a proclamation of neutrality, by which process the so-called recognition of belligerents is published, could of itself and unattended by other action accomplish nothing toward the one end for which we labor—the instant pacification of Cuba and the cessation of the misery that afflicts the island. . . .

There remain the alternative forms of intervention to end the war, either as an impartial neutral, by imposing a rational compromise between the contestants, or as the active ally of the one party or the other.

As to the first, it is not to be forgotten that during the last few months the relation of the United States has virtually been one of friendly intervention in many ways, each not of itself conclusive, but all tending to the exertion of a potential influence toward an ultimate pacific result, just and honorable to all interests concerned. The spirit of all our acts hitherto has been an earnest, unselfish desire for peace and prosperity in Cuba, untarnished by differences between us and Spain and unstained by the blood of American citizens.

The forcible intervention of the United States as a neutral to stop the war, according to the large dictates of humanity and following many historical precedents where neighboring states have interfered to check the hopeless sacrifices of life by internecine conflicts beyond their borders, is justifiable on rational grounds. It involves, however, hostile constraint upon both the parties to the contest, as well to enforce a truce as to guide the eventual settlement.

The grounds for such intervention may be briefly summarized as follows:

First. In the cause of humanity and to put an end to the barbarities, bloodshed, starvation, and horrible miseries now existing there, and which the parties to the conflict are either unable or unwilling to stop or mitigate. It is no answer to say this is all in another country, belonging to another nation, and is therefore none of our business. It is specially our duty, for it is right at our door.

Second. We owe it to our citizens in Cuba to afford them that protection and indemnity for life and property which no government there can or will afford, and to that end to terminate the conditions that deprive them of legal protection.

Third. The right to intervene may be justified by the very serious injury to the commerce, trade, and business of our people and by the wanton destruction of property and devastation of the island.

Fourth, and which is of the utmost importance. The present condition of affairs in Cuba is a constant menace to our peace and entails upon this Government an enormous expense. With such a conflict waged for years in an island so near us and with which our people have such trade and business relations; when the lives and liberty of our citizens are in constant danger and their property destroyed and themselves ruined; where our trading vessels are liable to seizure and are seized at our very door by war ships of a foreign nation; the expeditions of filibustering that we are powerless to prevent altogether, and the irritating questions and entanglements thus arising—all these and others that I need not mention, with the resulting strained relations, are a constant menace to our peace and compel us to keep on a semi-war footing with a nation with which we are at peace.

These elements of danger and disorder already pointed out have been strikingly illustrated by a tragic event which has deeply and justly moved the American people. I have already transmitted to Congress the report of the naval court of inquiry on the destruction of the battleship *Maine* in the harbor of Havana during the night of the 15th of February. The destruction of that noble vessel has filled the national heart with inexpressible horror. Two hundred and fifty eight brave sailors and marines and two officers of our Navy, reposing in the fancied security of a friendly harbor, have been hurled to death, grief and want brought to their homes and sorrow to the nation.

The naval court of inquiry, which, it is needless to say, commands the unqualified confidence of the Government, was unanimous in its conclusion that the destruction of the *Maine* was caused by an exterior explosion—that of a submarine mine. It did not assume to place the responsibility. That remains to be fixed.

In any event, the destruction of the *Maine*, by whatever exterior cause, is a patent and impressive proof of a state of things in Cuba that is intolerable. That condition is thus shown to be such that the Spanish Government can not assure safety and security to a vessel of the American Navy in the harbor of Havana on a mission of peace, and rightfully there. . . .

The long trial has proved that the object for which Spain has waged the war can not be attained. The fire of insurrection may flame or may smolder with varying seasons, but it has not been and it is plain that it can not be extinguished by present methods. The only hope of relief and repose from a condition which can no longer be endured is the enforced pacification of Cuba. In the name of humanity, in the name of civilization, in behalf of endangered American interests which give us the right and the duty to speak and to act, the war in Cuba must stop.

In view of these facts and of these considerations I ask the Congress to authorize and empower the President to take measures to secure a full and final termination of hostilities between the Government of Spain and the people of Cuba, and to secure in the island the establishment of a stable government, capable of maintaining order and observing its international obligations, insuring peace and tranquility and the security of its citizens as well as our own, and to use the military and naval forces of the United State as may be necessary for these purposes.

And in the interest of humanity and to aid in preserving the lives of the starving people of the island I recommend that the distribution of food and supplies be continued and that an appropriation be made out of the public Treasury to supplement the charity of our citizens.

The issue is now with the Congress. It is a solemn responsibility. I have exhausted every effort to relieve the intolerable condition of affairs which is at our doors. Prepared to execute every obligation imposed upon me by the Constitution and the law, I await your action.

Yesterday, and since the preparation of the foregoing message, official information was received by me that the latest decree of the Queen Regent of Spain directs General Blanco, in order to prepare and facilitate peace, to proclaim a suspension of hostilities the duration and details of which have not yet been communicated to me.

This fact, with every other pertinent consideration, will, I am sure, have your just and careful attention in the solemn deliberations upon which you are about to enter. If this measure attains a successful result, then our aspirations as a Christian, peace-loving people will be realized. If it fails, it will be only another justification for our contemplated action.

WILLIAM McKINLEY.

Source: James D. Richardson, ed., *A Compilation of the Messages and Papers of the Presidents*, vol. 13 (New York: Bureau of National Literature, 1917), 6281–92.

---

41. RESOLUTION FOR RECOGNITION OF THE INDEPENDENCE OF CUBA
20 April 1898

A joint resolution of Congress authorized the McKinley administration to use military force to free Cuba from Spanish control. *Explicitly included in this resolution was the so-called* Teller Amendment *which specifically removed the possibility that a free Cuba would be annexed by the United States.*

Joint resolution for the recognition of the independence of the people of Cuba, demanding that the Government of Spain relinquish its authority and government in the Island of Cuba, and to withdraw its land and naval forces from Cuba and Cuban waters, and directing the President of the United States to use the land and naval forces of the United States to carry these resolutions into effect.

Whereas the abhorrent conditions which have existed for more than three years in the Island of Cuba, so near our own borders, have shocked the moral sense of the people of the United States, have been a disgrace to Christian civilization, culminating, as they have, in the destruction of a United States battle ship, with two hundred and sixty-six of its officers and crew, while on a friendly visit in the harbor of Havana, and can not longer be endured, as has been set forth by the President of the United States in his message to Congress of April eleventh, eighteen hundred and ninety-eight, upon which the action of Congress was invited: Therefore,

Resolved, First. That the people of the Island of Cuba are, and of right ought to be, free and independent.

Second. That it is the duty of the United States to demand, and the Government of the United States does hereby demand, that the Government of Spain at once relinquish its authority and government in the Island of Cuba and withdraw its land and naval forces from Cuba and Cuban waters.

Third. That the President of the United States be, and he hereby is, directed and empowered to use the entire land and naval forces of the United States, and to call into the actual service of the United States the militia of the several States, to such extent as may be necessary to carry these resolutions into effect.

Fourth. That the United States hereby disclaims any disposition or intention to exercise sovereignty, jurisdiction, or control over said Island except for the pacification thereof, and asserts its determination, when that is accomplished, to leave the government and control of the Island to its people.

Source: Henry Steele Commager, *Documents of American History*, vol. 2 (Englewood Cliffs, NJ: Prentice Hall, 1973), 5.

42. THE ANNEXATION OF HAWAII
7 July 1898

American efforts to annex Hawaii predated the Spanish-American War. As early as 1893, Benjamin Harrison had attempted to husband a treaty through the Senate; however, his successor, Grover Cleveland, withdrew it amidst the controversy surrounding American support for a rebellion against the standing Hawaiian government. Five years later, flush with the victory over Spain, McKinley presented his proposal for a joint Congressional resolution to annex the islands.

Joint Resolution To Provide for annexing the Hawaiian Islands to the United States.

Whereas the Government of the Republic of Hawaii having, in due form, signified its consent, in the manner provided by its constitution, to cede absolutely and without reserve to the United States of America all rights of sovereignty of whatsoever kind in and over the Hawaiian Islands and their dependencies, and also to cede and transfer to the United States the absolute fee and ownership of all public, Government, or Crown lands, public buildings or edifices, ports, harbors, military equipment, and all other public property of every kind and description belonging to the Government of the Hawaiian Islands, together with every right and appurtenance thereunto appertaining: Therefore,

Resolved, That said cession is accepted, ratified, and confirmed, and that the said Hawaiian Islands and their dependencies be, and they are hereby, annexed as a part of the territory of the United States, and are subject to the sovereign dominion thereof, and that all and singular the property and rights hereinbefore mentioned are vested in the United States of America.

The existing laws of the United States relative to public lands shall not apply to such lands in the Hawaiian Islands; but the Congress of the United States shall enact special laws for their management and disposition: *Provided*, That all revenue from or proceeds of the same, except as regards such part thereof as may be used or occupied for the civil, military, or naval purposes of the United States, or may be assigned for the use of the local government, shall be used solely for the benefit of the inhabitants of the Hawaiian Islands for educational and other public purposes.

Until Congress shall provide for the government of such islands all the civil, judicial, and military powers exercised by the officers of the existing government in said islands shall be vested in such person or persons and shall be exercised in such manner as the President of the United States shall direct; and the President shall have power to remove said officers and fill the vacancies so occasioned.

The existing treaties of the Hawaiian Islands with foreign nations shall forthwith cease and determine, being replaced by such treaties as may exist, or as may be hereafter concluded, between the United States and such foreign nations. The municipal legislation of the Hawaiian Islands, not enacted for the fulfillment of the treaties so extinguished, and not inconsistent with this, joint resolution nor contrary to the Constitution of the United States nor to any existing treaty of the United States, shall remain in force until the Congress of the United States shall otherwise determine.

Until legislation shall be enacted extending the United States customs laws and regulations to the Hawaiian Islands the existing customs relations of the Hawaiian Islands with the United States and other countries shall remain unchanged.

The public debt of the Republic of Hawaii, lawfully existing at the date of the passage, of this joint resolution, including the amounts due to depositors in the Hawaiian Postal Savings Bank, is hereby assumed by the Government of the United States; but the liability of the United States in this regard shall in no case exceed four million dollars. So long, however, as the existing Government and the present commercial relations of the Hawaiian Islands are continued as hereinbefore provided said Government shall continue to pay the interest on said debt.

There shall be no further immigration of Chinese into the Hawaiian Islands, except upon such conditions as are now or may hereafter be allowed by the laws of the United States; and no Chinese, by reason of any thing herein contained, shall be allowed to enter the United States from the Hawaiian Islands.

The President shall appoint five commissioners, at least two of whom shall be residents of the Hawaiian Islands, who shall, as soon as reasonably practicable, recommend to Congress such legislation concerning the Hawaiian Islands as they shall deem necessary or proper. . . .

Source: Henry Steele Commager, *Documents of American History*, vol. 2 (Englewood Cliffs, NJ: Prentice Hall, 1973), 5–6.

---

43. TREATY OF PEACE WITH SPAIN
10 December 1898

After suffering devastating defeats at Manila Bay and Santiago Bay, Spain sued for peace in August 1898. Subsequent negotiations established the territories to be transferred to the victorious United States. The Spanish cession of the Philippines was the most controversial part of the treaty.

ART. I. Spain relinquishes all claim of sovereignty over and title to Cuba.

And as the island is, upon its evacuation by Spain, to be occupied by the United States, the United States will, so long as such occupation shall last, assume and discharge the obligations that may under international law result from the fact of its occupation, for the protection of life and property.

ART. II. Spain cedes to the United States the island of Porto Rico and other islands now under Spanish sovereignty in the West Indies, and the island of Guam in the Marianas or Ladrones.

ART. III. Spain cedes to the United States the archipelago known as the Philippine Islands, and comprehending the islands lying within the following line:

A line running from west to east along or near the twentieth parallel of north latitude, and through the middle of the navigable channel of Bachi, from the one hundred and eighteenth (118th) to the one hundred and twenty seventh (127th) degree meridian of longitude east of Greenwich, thence along the one hundred and twenty seventh (127th) degree meridian of longitude cast of Greenwich to the parallel of four degrees and forty five minutes (4° 45') north latitude, thence along the parallel of four degrees and forty five minutes (4° 45') north latitude to its intersection with the meridian of longitude one hundred and nineteen degrees and thirty five minutes (119° 35') east of Greenwich, thence along the meridian of longitude one hundred and nineteen degrees and thirty five minutes (119° 35') east of Greenwich to the parallel of latitude seven degrees and forty minutes (7° 40') north, thence along the parallel of latitude seven degrees and forty minutes (7° 40') north to its intersection with the one hundred and sixteenth (116th) degree meridian of longitude east of Greenwich, thence by a direct line to the intersection of the tenth (10th) degree parallel of north latitude with the one hundred and eighteenth (118th) degree meridian of longitude east of Greenwich, and thence along the one hundred and eighteenth

(118th) degree meridian of longitude east of Greenwich to the point of beginning.

The United States will pay to Spain the sum of twenty million dollars ($20,000,000) within three months after the exchange of the ratifications of the present treaty.

ART. IV. The United States will, for the term of ten years from the date of the exchange of the ratifications of the present treaty, admit Spanish ships and merchandise to the ports of the Philippine Islands on the same terms as ships and merchandise of the United States. . . .

ART. VII. The United States and Spain mutually relinquish all claims for indemnity, national and individual, of every kind, of either Government, or of its citizens or subjects, against the other Government, that may have arisen since the beginning of the late insurrection in Cuba and prior to the exchange of ratifications of the present treaty, including all claims for indemnity for the cost of the war.

The United States will adjudicate and settle the claims of its citizens against Spain relinquished in this article.

ART. VIII. In conformity with the provisions of Articles I, II, and III of this treaty, Spain relinquishes in Cuba, and cedes in Porto Rico and other islands in the West Indies, in the island of Guam, and in the Philippine Archipelago, all the buildings, wharves, barracks, forts, structures, public highways and other immovable property which, in conformity with law, belong to the public domain, and as such belong to the Crown of Spain.

And it is hereby declared that the relinquishment or cession, as the case may be, to which the preceding paragraph refers, cannot in any respect impair the property or rights which by law belong to the peaceful possession of property of all kinds, of provinces, municipalities, public or private establishments, ecclesiastical or civic bodies, or any other associations having legal capacity to acquire and possess property in the aforesaid territories renounced or ceded, or of private individuals, of whatsoever nationality such individuals may be.

The aforesaid relinquishment or cession, as the case may be, includes all documents exclusively referring to the sovereignty relinquished or ceded that may exist in the archives of the Peninsula. Where any document in such archives only in part relates to said sovereignty, a copy of such part will be furnished whenever it shall be requested. Like rules shall be reciprocally observed in favor of Spain in respect of documents in the archives of the islands above referred to.

In the aforesaid relinquishment or cession, as the case may be, are also included such rights as the Crown of Spain and its authorities possess in respect of the official archives and records, executive as well as judicial, in the islands above referred to, which relate to said islands or the rights and property of their inhabitants. Such archives and records shall be carefully preserved, and private persons shall without distinction have the right to require, in accordance with law, authenticated copies of the contracts, wills and other instruments forming part of notarial protocols or files, or which may be contained in the executive or judicial archives, be the latter in Spain or in the islands aforesaid. . . .

ART. X. The inhabitants of the territories over which Spain relinquishes or cedes her sovereignty shall be secured in the free exercise of their religion.

ART. XI. The Spaniards residing in the territories over which Spain by this treaty cedes or relinquishes her sovereignty shall be subject in matters civil as well as criminal to the jurisdiction of the courts of the country wherein they reside, pursuant to the ordinary laws governing the same; and they shall have the right to appear before such courts, and to pursue the same course as citizens of the country to which the courts belong. . . .

ART. XIII. The rights of property secured by copyrights and patents acquired by Spaniards in the Island of Cuba, and in Porto Rico, the Philippines and other ceded territories, at the time of the exchange of the ratifications of this treaty, shall continue to be respected. Spanish scientific, literary and artistic works, not subversive of public order in the territories in question, shall continue to be admitted free of duty into such territories, for the period of ten years, to be reckoned from the date of the exchange of the ratifications of this treaty. . . .

ART. XV. The Government of each country will, for the term of ten years, accord to the merchant vessels of the other country the same treatment in respect of all port charges, including entrance and clearance dues, light dues, and tonnage duties, as it accords to its own merchant vessels, not engaged in the coastwise trade.

This article may at any time be terminated on six months' notice given by either Government to the other.

ART. XVI. It is understood that any obligations assumed in this treaty by the United States with respect to Cuba are limited to the time of its occupancy thereof; but it will upon the termination of such occupancy, advise any Government established in the island to assume the same obligations.

Source: William M. Malloy, ed., *Treaties, Conventions, International Acts, Protocols, and Agreements between the United States and Other Powers, 1776–1909*, vol. 2 (Washington, DC: Government Printing Office, 1910), 1690–94.

44. HAY'S CIRCULAR LETTER
6 September 1899

Even before its victory over Spain was complete, American eyes turned toward Asia. Of particular concern were the intrusions made upon China by Europe and Japan and the ultimate impact they would have on American and British rights. Secretary of State John Hay's circular letter was an appeal for equal access to China by all the major powers.

Mr. Hay to Mr. White
Department of State
Washington, September 6, 1899.

SIR: At the time when the Government of the United States was informed by that of Germany that it had leased from His Majesty the Emperor of China the port of Kiao-chao and the adjacent territory in the province of Shantung, assurances were given to the ambassador of the United States at Berlin by the Imperial German minister for foreign affairs that the rights and privileges insured by treaties with China to citizens of the United States would not thereby suffer or be in anywise impaired within the area over which Germany had thus obtained control.

More recently, however, the British Government recognized by a formal agreement with Germany the exclusive right of the latter country to enjoy in said leased area and the contiguous "sphere of influence or interest" certain privileges, more especially those relating to railroads and mining enterprises; but, as the exact nature and extent of the rights thus recognized have not been clearly defined, it is possible that serious conflicts of interest may at any time arise, not only between British and German subjects within said area, but that the interests of our citizens may also be jeopardized thereby.

Earnestly desirous to remove any cause of irritation and to insure at the same time to the commerce of all nations in China the undoubted benefits which should accrue from a formal recognition by the various powers claiming "spheres of interest" that they shall enjoy perfect equality of treatment for their commerce and navigation within such "spheres," the Government of the United States would be pleased to see His German Majesty's Government give formal assurances and lend its cooperation in securing like assurances from the other interested powers that each within its respective sphere of whatever influence—

First. Will in no way interfere with any treaty port or any vested interest within any so-called "sphere of interest" or leased territory it may have in China.

Second. That the Chinese treaty tariff of the time being shall apply to all merchandise landed or shipped to all such ports as are within said "sphere of interest" (unless they be "free ports"), no matter to what nationality it may belong, and that duties so leviable shall be collected by the Chinese Government.

Third. That it will levy no higher harbor dues on vessels of another nationality frequenting any port in such "sphere" than shall be levied on vessels of its own nationality, and no higher railroad charges over lines built, controlled, or operated within its "sphere" on merchandise belonging to citizens or subjects of other nationalities transported through such "sphere" than shall be levied on similar merchandise belonging to its own nationals transported over equal distances.

The liberal policy pursued by His Imperial German Majesty in declaring Kiao-chao a free port and in aiding the Chinese Government in the establishment there of a customhouse are so clearly in line with the proposition which this

Government is anxious to see recognized that it entertains the strongest hope that Germany will give its acceptance and hearty support.

The recent ukase of His Majesty the Emperor of Russia declaring the port of Ta-lien-wan open during the whole of the lease under which it is held from China, to the merchant ships of all nations, coupled with the categorical assurances made to this Government by His Imperial Majesty's representative at this capital at the time, and since repeated to me by the present Russian ambassador, seem to insure the support of the Emperor to the proposed measure. Our ambassador at the Court of St. Petersburg has, in consequence, been instructed to submit it to the Russian Government and to request their early consideration of it. A copy of my instruction on the subject to Mr. Tower is herewith inclosed for your confidential information.

The commercial interests of Great Britain and Japan will be so clearly served by the desired declaration of intentions, and the views of the Governments of these countries as to the desirability of the adoption of measures insuring the benefits of equality of treatment of all foreign trade throughout China are so similar to those entertained by the United States, that their acceptance of the propositions herein outlined and their cooperation in advocating their adoption by the other powers can be confidently expected. I inclose herewith copy of the instruction which I have sent to Mr. Choate on the subject.

In view of the present favorable conditions, you are instructed to submit the above considerations to His Imperial German Majesty's minister for foreign affairs, and to request his early consideration of the subject.

Copy of this instruction is sent to our ambassadors at London and at St. Petersburg for their information.

I have, etc.   JOHN HAY.

Source: William M. Malloy, ed., *Treaties, Conventions, International Acts, Protocols, and Agreements between the United States and Other Powers, 1776–1909*, vol. 1 (Washington, DC: Government Printing Office, 1910), 244–59.

45. HAY'S LETTER OF INSTRUCTION
20 March 1900

John Hay's original circular letter garnered, at best, qualified support from Europe and Japan. Despite this, in instructions issued to American diplomats, he announced the acceptance of his circular letter as "final and definitive."

Instructions sent mutatus mutandis to the United States ambassadors at London, Paris, Berlin, St. Petersburg, and Rome, and to the United States Minister at Tokyo.

Department of State,
Washington, March 20, 1900.

SIR: The ——— Government having accepted the declaration suggested by the United States concerning foreign trade in China, the terms of which I transmitted to you in my instruction No. ——— of ———, and like action having been taken by all the various powers having leased territory or so-called "spheres of interest" in the Chinese Empire, as shown by the notes which I herewith transmit to you, you will please inform the government to which you are accredited, that the condition originally attached to its acceptance—that all other powers concerned should likewise accept the proposals of the United States—having been complied with, this Government will therefore consider the assent given to it by ——— as final and definitive.

You will also transmit to the minister of foreign affairs copies of the present inclosures, and by the same occasion convey to him the expression of the sincere gratification which the President feels at the successful termination of these negotiations, in which he sees proof of the friendly spirit which animates the various powers interested in the untrammeled development of commerce and industry in the Chinese Empire and a source of vast benefit to the whole commercial world.

I am, etc.,   JOHN HAY.

Source: William M. Malloy, ed., *Treaties, Conventions, International Acts, Protocols, and Agreements between the United States and Other Powers, 1776–1909*, vol. 1 (Washington, DC: Government Printing Office, 1910), 244–59.

---

46. HAY'S CIRCULAR LETTER
3 July 1900

The outbreak of the Boxer Rebellion in June 1900 led to the massacre of some 300 foreigners and the joint intervention of an international expedition that included almost 5,000 U.S. soldiers. Hay's letter of 3 July was an attempt to reassert the original objectives of the Open Door Policy.

Circular telegram sent to the United States embassies in Berlin, Paris, London, Rome, and St. Petersburg, and to the United States missions in Vienna, Brussels, Madrid, Tokyo, The Hague, and Lisbon.

Department of State,
Washington, July 3, 1900.

In this critical posture of affairs in China it is deemed appropriate to define the attitude of the United States as far as present circumstances permit this to be done. We adhere to the policy initiated by us in 1857, of peace with the

Chinese nation, of furtherance of lawful commerce, and of protection of lives and property of our citizens by all means guaranteed under extraterritorial treaty rights and by the law of nations. If wrong be done to our citizens we propose to hold the responsible authors to the uttermost accountability. We regard the condition at Pekin as one of virtual anarchy, whereby power and responsibility are practically devolved upon the local provincial authorities. So long as they are not in overt collusion with rebellion and use their power to protect foreign life and property we regard them as representing the Chinese people, with whom we seek to remain in peace and friendship. The purpose of the President is, as it has been heretofore, to act concurrently with the other powers, first, in opening up communication with Pekin and rescuing the American officials, missionaries, and other Americans who are in danger; secondly, in affording all possible protection everywhere in China to American life and property; thirdly, in guarding and protecting all legitimate American interests; and fourthly, in aiding to prevent a spread of the disorders to the other provinces of the Empire and a recurrence of such disasters. It is, of course, too early to forecast the means of attaining this last result; but the policy of the government of the United States is to seek a solution which may bring about permanent safety and peace to China, preserve Chinese territorial and administrative entity, protect all rights guaranteed to friendly powers by treaty and international law, and safeguard for the world the principle of equal and impartial trade with all parts of the Chinese Empire.

You will communicate the purport of this instruction to the minister for foreign affairs.

Hay.

Source: William M. Malloy, ed., *Treaties, Conventions, International Acts, Protocols, and Agreements between the United States and Other Powers, 1776–1909*, vol. 1 (Washington, DC: Government Printing Office, 1910), 244–59.

47. PLATT AMENDMENT
22 May 1903

The American occupation of Cuba was followed by efforts to reconstruct its government. Mentored by military governor Leonard Wood, a constitutional convention met in November 1900 to redraw Cuba's basic governmental blueprint. The document failed, however, to include provisions for future Cuban relations with the United States. To resolve this situation, a series of amendments by Senator Orville H. Platt were offered into a 1901 Army appropriations bill. These were later incorporated into the Cuban constitution and a 1903 treaty between Cuba and the United States.

ART. I. The Government of Cuba shall never enter into any treaty or other compact with any foreign power or powers which will impair or tend to impair the independence of Cuba, nor in any manner authorize or permit any foreign power or powers to obtain by colonization or for military or naval purposes, or otherwise, lodgement in or control over any portion of said island.

ART. II. The Government of Cuba shall not assume or contract any public debt to pay the interest upon which, and to make reasonable sinking-fund provision for the ultimate discharge of which, the ordinary revenues of the Island of Cuba, after defraying the current expenses of the Government, shall be inadequate.

ART. III. The Government of Cuba consents that the United States may exercise the right to intervene for the preservation of Cuban independence, the maintenance of a government adequate for the protection of life, property, and individual liberty, and for discharging the obligations with respect to Cuba imposed by the treaty of Paris on the United States, now to be assumed and undertaken by the government of Cuba.

ART. IV. All Acts of the United States in Cuba during its military occupancy thereof are ratified and validated, and all lawful rights acquired thereunder shall be maintained and protected.

ART. V. The Government of Cuba will execute, and as far as necessary extend, the plans already devised or other plans to be mutually agreed upon, for the sanitation of the cities of the island, to the end that a recurrence of epidemics and infectious diseases may be prevented thereby assuring protection to the people and commerce of Cuba, as well as to the commerce of the southern ports of the United States and the people residing therein.

ART. VI. The Isle of Pines shall be omitted from the boundaries of Cuba, specified in the Constitution, the title thereto being left to future adjustment by treaty.

ART. VII. To enable the United States to maintain the independence of Cuba, and to protect the people thereof, as well as for its own defense, the government of Cuba will sell or lease to the United States lands necessary for coaling or naval stations at certain specified points to be agreed upon with the President of the United States. . . .

Source: Henry Steele Commager, *Documents of American History*, vol. 2 (Englewood Cliffs, NJ: Prentice Hall, 1973), 28–29.

---

48. CONVENTION WITH PANAMA FOR THE CONSTRUCTION OF A CANAL
(Concluded 18 November 1903)

The inability of Theodore Roosevelt's administration to secure a treaty with Colombia for a trans-isthmian canal led it to support a Panamanian *rebellion and the creation of the Republic of Panama on 6 November 1903. Less than two weeks after the country was created, it concluded a canal treaty with the United States. Colombia later received $25 million for its lost territory.*

ART. I. The United States guarantees and will maintain the independence of the Republic of Panama.

ART. II. The Republic of Panama grants to the United States in perpetuity the use, occupation and control of a zone of land and land under water for the construction, maintenance, operation, sanitation and protection of said Canal of the width of ten miles extending to the distance of five miles on each side of the center line of the route of the canal to be constructed; the said zone beginning in the Caribbean Sea, three marine miles from mean low water mark, and extending to and across the Isthmus of Panama into the Pacific Ocean to a distance of three marine miles from mean low water mark, with the proviso that the cities of Panama and Colon and the harbors adjacent to said cities, which are included within the boundaries of the zone above described, shall not be included within this grant. The Republic of Panama further grants to the United States in perpetuity the use, occupation and control of any other lands and waters outside of the zone above described which may be necessary and convenient for the construction, maintenance, operation, sanitation and protection of the said Canal or of any auxiliary canals or other works necessary and convenient for the construction, maintenance, operation, sanitation and protection of the said enterprise. The Republic of Panama further grants in like manner to the United States in perpetuity all islands within the limits of the zone above described and in addition thereto the group of small islands in the Bay of Panama, named Perico, Naos, Culebra and Flamenco.

ART. III. The Republic of Panama grants to the United States all the rights, power and authority within the zone mentioned and described in Article II of this agreement and within the limits of all auxiliary lands and waters mentioned and described in said Article II which the United States would possess and exercise if it were the sovereign of the territory within which said lands and waters are located to the entire exclusion of the exercise by the Republic of Panama of any such sovereign rights, power or authority. . . .

ART. V. The Republic of Panama grants to the United States in perpetuity a monopoly for the construction, maintenance and operation of any system of communication by means of canal or railroad across its territory between the Caribbean Sea and the Pacific Ocean. . . .

ART. VII. The Republic of Panama grants to the United States within the limits of the cities of Panama and Colon and their adjacent harbors and within the territory adjacent thereto the right to acquire by purchase or by the exercise of the right of eminent domain, any lands, buildings, water rights or other properties necessary and convenient for the construction, maintenance, operation and protection of the Canal and of any works of sanitation, such as the collection and disposition of sewage and the distribution of water in the said cities of Panama and Colon, which, in the discretion of the United States may be necessary and convenient for the construction, maintenance, operation, sanitation and protection of the said Canal and railroad.

The Republic of Panama agrees that the cities of Panama and Colon shall comply in perpetuity with the sanitary ordinances whether of a preventive or curative character prescribed by the United States and in case the Government of Panama is unable or fails in its duty to enforce this compliance by the cities of Panama and Colon with the sanitary ordinances of the United States the Republic of Panama grants to the United States the right and authority to enforce the same.

The same right and authority are granted to the United States for the maintenance of public order in the cities of Panama and Colon and the territories and harbors adjacent thereto in case the Republic of Panama should not be, in the judgment of the United States, able to maintain such order.

ART. VIII. The Republic of Panama grants to the United States all rights which it now has or hereafter may acquire to the property of the New Panama Canal Company and the Panama Railroad Company as a result of the transfer of sovereignty from the Republic of Colombia to the Republic of Panama over the Isthmus of Panama and authorizes the New Panama Canal Company to sell and transfer to the United States its rights, privileges, properties and concessions as well as the Panama Railroad and all the shares or part of the shares of that company.

ART. IX. The United States agrees that the ports at either entrance of the Canal and the waters thereof and the Republic of Panama agrees that the towns of Panama and Colon shall be free for all time so that there shall not be imposed or collected custom house tolls, tonnage, anchorage, lighthouse, wharf, pilot or quarantine dues or any other charges or taxes of any kind upon any vessel using or passing through the Canal or belonging to or employed by the United States, directly or indirectly, in connection with the construction, maintenance, operation, sanitation and protection of the main Canal, or auxiliary works, or upon the cargo, officers, crew or passengers of any such vessels, except such tolls and charges as may be imposed by the United States for the use of the Canal and other works, and except tolls and charges imposed by the Republic of Panama upon merchandise destined to be introduced for the consumption of the rest of the Republic of Panama, and upon vessels touching at the ports of Colon and Panama and which do not cross the Canal. The Government of the Republic of Panama shall have the right to establish in such ports and in the towns of Panama and Colon such houses and guards as it may deem necessary to collect duties on importations destined to other portions of Panama and to prevent contraband trade. The United States shall have the right to make use of the towns and harbors of Panama and Colon as places of anchorage, and for making repairs, for loading, unloading, depositing or trans-shipping cargoes either in transit or destined for the service of the canal and for other works pertaining to the canal.

ART. X. The Republic of Panama agrees that there shall not be imposed any taxes, national, municipal, departmental or of any other class upon the Canal, the railways and auxiliary works, tugs and other vessels employed in the service of the canal, storehouse, workshops, offices, quarters for laborers, factories of all kinds, warehouses, wharves, machinery and other works, property, and effects appertaining to the Canal or railroad and auxiliary works, or their officers or employees, situated within the cities of Panama and Colon, and that there shall not be imposed contributions or charges of a personal character of any kind upon officers, employees, laborers and other individuals in the service of the Canal and railroad and auxiliary works. . . .

ART. XIV. As the price or compensation for the rights, powers and privileges granted in this convention by the Republic of Panama to the United States, the Government of the United States agrees to pay to the Republic of Panama the sum of ten million dollars ($10,000,000) in gold coin of the United States on the exchange of the ratification of this convention and also an annual payment during the life of this convention of two hundred and fifty thousand dollars ($250,000) in like gold coin, beginning nine years after the date aforesaid.

The provisions of this article shall be in addition to all other benefits assured to the Republic of Panama under this convention.

But no delay or difference of opinion under this article or any other provisions of this treaty shall affect or interrupt the full operation and effect of this convention in all other respects. . . .

ART. XVIII. The Canal, when constructed, and the entrances thereto shall be neutral in perpetuity, and shall be opened upon the terms provided for by Section I of Article III of, and in conformity with all the stipulations of, the treaty entered into by the Governments of the United States and Great Britain on November 18, 1901.

ART. XIX. The Government of the Republic of Panama shall have the right to transport over the Canal its vessels and its troops and munitions of war in such vessels at all times without paying charges of any kind. The exemption is to be extended to the auxiliary railway for the transportation of persons in the service of the Republic of Panama, or of the police force charged with the preservation of public order outside of said zone, as well as to their baggage, munitions of war and supplies.

ART. XX. If by virtue of any existing treaty in relation to the territory of the Isthmus of Panama, whereof the obligations shall descend or be assumed by the Republic of Panama, there may be any privilege or concession in favor of the Government or the citizens and subjects of a third power relative to an interoceanic means of communication which in any of its terms may be incompatible with the terms of the present convention, the Republic of Panama agrees to cancel or modify such treaty in due form, for which purpose it shall give to the said third power the requisite notification within the term of four months from the date of the present convention, and in case the existing treaty contains no clause permitting its modifications or annulment, the Republic of Panama agrees to procure its modifications or annulment in such form that there shall not exist any conflict with the stipulations of the present convention. . . .

ART. XXII. The Republic of Panama renounces and grants to the United States the participation to which it might be entitled in the future earnings of the Canal under Article XV of the concessionary contract with Lucien N. B. Wyse, now owned by the New Panama Canal Company, and any and all other rights or claims of a pecuniary nature arising under or relating to said concession, or arising under or relating to the concessions to the Panama Railroad Company or any extension or modification thereof; and it likewise renounces, confirms and grants to the United States, now and hereafter, all the rights and property reserved in the said concessions which otherwise would belong to Panama at or before the expiration of the terms of ninety-nine years of the concessions granted to or held by the above-mentioned party and companies, and all right, title and interest which it now has or may hereafter have, in and to the lands, canal, works, property and rights held by the said companies under said concessions or otherwise, and acquired or to be acquired by the United States from or through the New Panama Canal Company, including any property and rights which might or may in the future either by lapse of time, forfeiture or otherwise, revert to the Republic of Panama under any contracts or concessions, with said Wyse, the Universal Panama Canal Company, the Panama Railroad Company and the new Panama Canal Company.

The aforesaid rights and property shall be and are free and released from any present or reversionary interest in or claims of Panama and the title of the United States thereto upon consummation of the contemplated purchase by the United States from the New Panama Canal Company shall be absolute, so far as concerns the Republic of Panama, excepting always the rights of the Republic specifically secured under this treaty.

ART. XXIII. If it should become necessary at any time to employ armed forces for the safety or protection of the Canal, or of the ships that make use of the same, or the railways and auxiliary works, the United States shall have the right, at all times and in its discretion, to use its police and its land and naval forces or to establish fortifications for these purposes.

ART. XXIV. No change either in the Government or in the laws and treaties of the Republic of Panama shall, without the consent of the United States, affect any rights of the United States under the present convention, or under any treaty stipulation between the two countries that now exists or may hereafter exist touching the subject material of this convention.

If the Republic of Panama shall hereafter enter as a constituent into any other Government or into any union or confederation of States, so as to merge her sovereign or independence in such Government, union or confederation, the rights of the United States under this convention shall not be in any respect lessened or impaired.

ART. XXV. For the better performance of the engagements of this convention and to the end of the efficient protection of the Canal and the preservation of its neutrality, the Government of the Republic of Panama will sell or lease to the United States lands adequate and necessary for naval or coaling stations on the Pacific coast and on the western Caribbean coast of the Republic at certain points to be agreed upon with the President of the United States. . . .

JOHN HAY-BUNAU-VARILLA

Source: William M. Malloy, ed., *Treaties, Conventions, International Acts, Protocols, and Agreements between the United States and Other Powers, 1776–1909*, vol. 2 (Washington, DC: Government Printing Office, 1910), 1349–56.

49. ROOSEVELT COROLLARY TO THE MONROE DOCTRINE
1904 and 1905

When the Dominican Republic appealed to the United States for protection against European creditors, Theodore Roosevelt used the moment to artic-ulate his own corollary to the Monroe Doctrine. *He declared that it was America's sole duty to protect life and property in the Western Hemi-sphere. His statement of policy eventually led to American interventions in Haiti, Nicaragua, and Cuba.*

ROOSEVELT'S ANNUAL MESSAGE
6 December 1904

. . . It is not true that the United States feels any land hunger or entertains any projects as regards the other nations of the Western Hemisphere save such as are for their welfare. All that this country desires is to see the neighboring countries stable, orderly, and prosperous. Any country whose people conduct themselves well can count upon our hearty friendship. If a nation shows that it knows how to act with reasonable efficiency and decency in social and political matters, if it keeps order and pays its obligations, it need fear no interference from the United States. Chronic wrongdoing, or an impotence which results in a general loosening of the ties of civilized society, may in America, as else-where, ultimately require intervention by some civilized nation, and in the West-ern Hemisphere the adherence of the United States to the Monroe Doctrine may force the United States, however reluctantly, in flagrant cases of such wrong-doing or impotence, to the exercise of an international police power. If every country washed by the Caribbean Sea would show the progress in stable and just civilization which with the aid of the Platt amendment Cuba has shown since our troops left the island, and which so many of the republics in both

Americas are constantly and brilliantly showing, all question of interference by this Nation with their affairs would be at an end. Our interests and those of our southern neighbors are in reality identical. They have great natural riches, and if within their borders the reign of law and justice obtains, prosperity is sure to come to them. While they thus obey the primary laws of civilized society they may rest assured that they will be treated by us in a spirit of cordial and helpful sympathy. We would interfere with them only in the last resort, and then only if it became evident that their inability or unwillingness to do justice at home and abroad had violated the rights of the United States or had invited foreign aggression to the detriment of the entire body of American nations. It is a mere truism to say that every nation, whether in America or anywhere else, which desires to maintain its freedom, its independence, must ultimately realize that the right of such independence can not be separated from the responsibility of making good use of it.

In asserting the Monroe Doctrine, in taking such steps as we have taken in regard to Cuba, Venezuela, and Panama, and in endeavoring to circumscribe the theater of war in the Far Fast, and to secure the open door in China, we have acted in our own interest as well as in the interest of humanity at large. There are, however, cases in which, while our own interests are not greatly involved, strong appeal is made to our sympathies. . . . But in extreme cases action may be justifiable and proper. What form the action shall take must depend upon the circumstances of the case; that is, upon the degree of the atrocity and upon our power to remedy it. The cases in which we could interfere by force of arms as we interfered to put a stop to intolerable conditions in Cuba are necessarily very few . . .

ROOSEVELT'S ANNUAL MESSAGE
5 December 1905

. . . It must be understood that under no circumstances will the United States use the Monroe Doctrine as a cloak for territorial aggression. We desire peace with all the world, but perhaps most of all with the other peoples of the American Continent. There are, of course, limits to the wrongs which any self-respecting nation can endure. It is always possible that wrong actions toward this Nation, or toward citizens of this Nation, in some State unable to keep order among its own people, unable to secure justice from outsiders, and unwilling to do justice to those outsiders who treat it well, may result in our having to take action to protect our rights; but such action will not be taken with a view to territorial aggression, and it will be taken at all only with extreme reluctance and when it has become evident that every other resource has been exhausted.

Moreover, we must make it evident that we do not intend to permit the Monroe Doctrine to be used by any nation on this Continent as a shield to protect it from the consequences of its own misdeeds against foreign nations. If a republic to the south of us commits a tort against a foreign nation, such as an outrage against a citizen of that nation, then the Monroe Doctrine does not force us to interfere to prevent punishment of the tort, save to see that the punishment does not assume the form of territorial occupation in any shape. The case is more difficult when it refers to a contractual obligation. Our own Government has always refused to enforce such contractual obligations on behalf of its citizens by an appeal to arms. It is much to be wished that all foreign governments would take the same view. But they do not: and in consequence we are liable at any time to be brought face to face with disagreeable alternatives. On the one hand, this country would certainly decline to go to war to prevent a foreign government from collecting a just debt; on the other hand, it is very inadvisable to permit any foreign power to take possession, even temporarily, of the custom houses of an American Republic in order to enforce the payment of its obligations; for such temporary occupation might turn into a permanent occupation. The only escape from these alternatives may at any time be that we must ourselves undertake to bring about some arrangement by which so much as possible of a just obligation shall be paid. It is far better that this country should put through such an arrangement, rather than allow any foreign country to undertake it. To do so insures the defaulting republic from having to pay debt of an improper character under duress, while it also insures honest creditors of the republic from being passed by in the interest of dishonest or grasping creditors. Moreover, for the United States to take such a position offers the only possible way of insuring us against a clash with some foreign power. The position is, therefor in the interest of peace as well as in the interest of justice. It is of benefit to our people; it is of benefit to foreign peoples; and most of all it is really of benefit to people of the country concerned. . . .

Source: James D. Richardson, ed., *A Compilation of the Messages and Papers of the Presidents*, vol. 15 (New York: Bureau of National Literature, 1917), 6923–24, 6995–96.

---

50. THE "GENTLEMEN'S AGREEMENT" ON JAPANESE IMMIGRATION
1908

After the turn of the century, anti-immigration sentiment in California was on the rise, particularly with respect to Japanese residing in the state. By 1906, the city of San Francisco had initiated measures to segregate Japanese schoolchildren from their white counterparts. Theodore Roosevelt intervened two years later in an attempt to broker an informal solution to the conflict before it could escalate into an international crisis.

In order that the best results might follow from an enforcement of the regulations, an understanding was reached with Japan that the existing policy of discouraging emigration of its subjects of the laboring classes to continental United States should be continued, and should, by co-operation with the governments, be made as effective as possible. This understanding contemplates that the Japanese government shall issue passports to continental United States only to such of its subjects as are non-laborers or are laborers who, in coming to the continent, seek to resume a formerly acquired domicile, to join a parent, wife, or children residing there, or to assume active control of an already possessed interest in a farming enterprise in this country, so that the three classes of laborers entitled to receive passports have come to be designated "former residents," "parents, wives, or children of residents," and "settled agriculturists."

With respect to Hawaii, the Japanese government of its own volition stated that, experimentally at least, the issuance of passports to members of the laboring classes proceeding thence would be limited to "former residents" and "parents, wives, or children of residents." The said government has also been exercising a careful supervision over the subject of emigration of its laboring class to foreign contiguous territory.

Source: Henry Steele Commager, *Documents of American History*, vol. 2 (Englewood Cliffs, NJ: Prentice Hall, 1973), 45.

---

51.   ROOT-TAKAHIRA AGREEMENT
30 November 1908

Theodore Roosevelt's successful arbitration of the Russo-Japanese War (1904–1905) marked a decline of U.S. influence in Asian and Japanese ascendancy. A 1905 agreement recognized American and Japanese interests, respectively, in the Philippines and Korea. A 1908 exchange of notes between the Japanese ambassador and Secretary of State Elihu Root committed America and Japan to the Open Door Policy and the existing status quo in the Pacific.

The Japanese Ambassador to the Secretary of State
Imperial Japanese Embassy
Washington, November 30, 1908

SIR: The exchange of views between us, which has taken place at the several interviews which I have recently had the honor of holding with you, has shown that Japan and the United States holding important outlying insular possessions in the region of the Pacific Ocean, the Governments of the two countries are animated by a common aim, policy, and intention in that region.

Believing that a frank avowal of that aim, policy, and intention would not only tend to strengthen the relations of friendship and good neighborhood, which have immemorially existed between Japan and the United States, but would materially contribute to the preservation of the general peace, the Imperial Government have authorized me to present to you an outline of their understanding of that common aim, policy and intention.

1. It is the wish of the two Governments to encourage the free and peaceful development of their commerce on the Pacific Ocean.

2. The policy of both Governments, uninfluenced by any aggressive tendencies, is directed to the maintenance of the existing status quo in the region above mentioned and to the defense of the principle of equal opportunity for commerce and industry in China.

3. They are accordingly firmly resolved reciprocally to respect the territorial possessions belonging to each other in said region.

4. They are also determined to preserve the common interest of all powers in China by supporting by all pacific means at their disposal the independence and integrity of China and the principle of equal opportunity for commerce and industry of all nations in that Empire.

5. Should any event occur threatening the status quo as above described or the principle of equal opportunity as above defined, it remains for the two Governments to communicate with each other in order to arrive at an understanding as to what measures they may consider it useful to take.

If the foregoing outline accords with the view of the Government of the United States, I shall be gratified to receive your confirmation.

I take this opportunity to renew to your excellency the assurance of my highest consideration.

K. Takahira.

Source: William M. Malloy, ed., *Treaties, Conventions, International Acts, Protocols, and Agreements between the United States and Other Powers, 1776–1909*, vol. 1 (Washington, DC: Government Printing Office, 1910), 1045–47.

52.   TAFT ON "DOLLAR DIPLOMACY"
3 December 1912

Prior to the Taft administration, American overseas investments had largely gravitated to Latin America. After 1909, the United States began to pursue more aggressive support of American capital abroad. This was the case in China, where American bankers had made inroads in railroad investments, and Central America, the location of new U.S. investments in mining, cattle, and export agriculture.

CHINA

In China the policy of encouraging financial investment to enable that country to help itself has had the result of giving new life and practical application to the open-door policy. The consistent purpose of the present administration has been to encourage the use of American capital in the development of China by the promotion of those essential reforms to which China is pledged by treaties with the United States and other powers. The hypothecation to foreign bankers in connection with certain industrial enterprises, such as the Hukuang railways, of the national revenues upon which these reforms depended, led the Department of State early in the administration to demand for American citizens participation in such enterprises, in order that the United States might have equal rights and an equal voice in all questions pertaining to the disposition of the public revenues concerned. The same policy of promoting international accord among the powers having similar treaty rights as ourselves in the matters of reform, which could not be put into practical effect without the common consent of all, was likewise adopted in the case of the loan desired by China for the reform of its currency. The principle of international cooperation in matters of common interest upon which our policy had already been based in all of the above instances has admittedly been a great factor in that concert of the powers which has been so happily conspicuous during the perilous period of transition through which the great Chinese nation has been passing.

CENTRAL AMERICA NEEDS OUR HELP IN DEBT ADJUSTMENT

In Central America the aim has been to help such countries as Nicaragua and Honduras to help themselves. They are the immediate beneficiaries. The national benefit to the United States is twofold. First, it is obvious that the Monroe doctrine is more vital in the neighborhood of the Panama Canal and the zone of the Caribbean than anywhere else. There, too, the maintenance of that doctrine falls most heavily upon the United States. It is therefore essential that the countries within that sphere shall be removed from the jeopardy involved by heavy foreign debt and chaotic national finances and from the ever-present danger of international complications due to disorder at home. Hence the United States has been glad to encourage and support American bankers who were willing to lend a helping hand to the financial rehabilitation of such countries because this financial rehabilitation and the protection of their customhouses from being the prey of would-be dictators would remove at one stroke the menace of foreign creditors and the menace of revolutionary disorder.

The second advantage of the United States is one affecting chiefly all the southern and Gulf ports and the business and industry of the South. The Republics of Central America and the Caribbean possess great natural wealth. They need only a measure of stability and the means of financial regeneration to enter upon an era of peace and prosperity, bringing profit and happiness to themselves and at the same time creating conditions sure to lead to a flourishing interchange of trade with this country.

I wish to call your especial attention to the recent occurrences in Nicaragua, for I believe the terrible events recorded there during the revolution of the past summer—the useless loss of life, the devastation of property, the bombardment of defenseless cities, the killing and wounding of women and children, the torturing of noncombatants to exact contributions, and the suffering of thousands of human beings—might have been averted had the Department of State, through approval of the loan convention by the Senate, been permitted to carry out its now well-developed policy of encouraging the extending of financial aid to weak Central American States with the primary objects of avoiding just such revolutions by assisting those Republics to rehabilitate their finances, to establish their currency on a stable basis, to remove the customhouses from the danger of revolutions by arranging for their secure administration, and to establish reliable banks.

Source: James D. Richardson, ed., *A Compilation of the Messages and Papers of the Presidents*, vol. 16 (New York: Bureau of National Literature, 1917), 7772–90.

53. WILSON'S REPUDIATION OF "DOLLAR DIPLOMACY" 19 March 1913

Taft's emphasis on supporting American overseas investment did not survive his departure from office. Secretary of State Philander C. Knox's treaties with Nicaragua and Honduras for loans in exchange for stability were rejected by the Senate. Woodrow Wilson capped this reaction by repudiating the close relationship between American investments and official U.S. policy decisions.

We are informed that at the request of the last administration a certain group of American bankers undertook to participate in the loan now desired by the Government of China (approximately $125,000,000). Our government wished American bankers to participate along with the bankers of other nations, because it desired that the good will of the United States towards China should be exhibited in this practical way, that American capital should have access to that great country, and that the United States should be in a position to share with the other Powers any political responsibilities that might be associated with the development of the foreign relations of China in connection with her industrial and commercial enterprises. The present administration has been asked by this group of bankers whether it would also request them to participate in the loan. The representatives of the bankers through whom the administration was approached declared that they would continue to seek their share of the loan under the proposed agreements only if expressly requested to do so by the government. The administration has declined to make such request because it did not approve the conditions of the loan or the implications of responsibility on its own part which it was plainly told would be involved in the request.

The conditions of the loan seem to us to touch very nearly the administrative independence of China itself; and this administration does not feel that it ought, even by implication, to be a party to those conditions. The responsibility on its part which would be implied in requesting the bankers to undertake the loan might conceivably go to the length in some unhappy contingency of forcible interference in the financial, and even the political, affairs of that great oriental state, just now awakening to a consciousness of its power and its obligations to its people. The conditions include not only the pledging of particular taxes, some of them antiquated and burdensome, to secure the loan, but also the administration of those taxes by foreign agents. The responsibility on the part of our government implied in the encouragement of a loan thus secured and administered is plain enough and is obnoxious to the principles upon which the government of our people rests.

The Government of the United States is not only willing, but earnestly desirous, of aiding the great Chinese people in every way that is consistent with their untrammeled development and its own immemorial principles. The awakening of the people of China to a consciousness of their possibilities under free government is the most significant, if not the most momentous event of our generation. With this movement and aspiration the American people are in profound sympathy. They certainly wish to participate, and participate very generously, in opening to the Chinese and to the use of the world the almost untouched and perhaps unrivaled resources of China.

The Government of the United States is earnestly desirous of promoting the most extended and intimate trade relationships between this country and the Chinese Republic. . . . This is the main material interest of its citizens in the development of China. Our interests are those of the open door—a door of friendship and mutual advantage. This is the only door we care to enter.

Source: Henry Steele Commager, *Documents of American History*, vol. 2 (Englewood Cliffs, NJ: Prentice Hall, 1973), 85.

---

54. WILSON'S SPECIAL MESSAGE ON MEXICAN RELATIONS
27 August 1913

The collapse of Mexico into revolution and civil war was cause for great concern during the Wilson administration. In particular, Americans openly worried what stance a newly constituted government might adopt toward the United States and its extensive investments in Mexico. Wilson addressed the Congress during the summer of 1913 as General Victoriano Huerta consolidated his control of the country.

Gentlemen of the Congress: It is clearly my duty to lay before you, very fully and without reservation, the facts concerning our present relations with the Republic of Mexico. The deplorable posture of affairs in Mexico I need not describe, but I deem it my duty to speak very frankly of what this Government has done and should seek to do in fulfillment of its obligation to Mexico herself, as a friend and neighbor, and to American citizens whose lives and vital interests are daily affected by the distressing conditions which now obtain beyond our southern border. . . .

The peace, prosperity and contentment of Mexico mean more, much more, to us than merely an enlarged field for our commerce and enterprise. They mean an enlargement of the field of self-government and the realization of the hopes and rights of a nation with whose best aspirations, so long suppressed and disappointed, we deeply sympathize. We shall yet prove to the Mexican people that we know how to serve them without first thinking how we shall serve ourselves. . . .

Mexico has a great and enviable future before her, if only she choose and attain the paths of honest constitutional government.

The present circumstances of the Republic, I deeply regret to say, do not seem to promise even the foundations of such a peace. We have waited many months, months full of peril and anxiety for the conditions there to improve, and they have not improved. They have grown worse, rather. . . . War and disorder, devastation and confusion, seem to threaten to become the settled fortune of the distracted country. As friends we could wait no longer for a solution which every week seemed further away. It was our duty at least to volunteer our good offices—to offer to assist, if we might, in effecting some arrangement which would bring relief and peace and set up a universally acknowledged political authority there.

Accordingly, I took the liberty of sending the Hon. John Lind, formerly governor of Minnesota, as my personal spokesman and representative, to the City of Mexico, with the following instructions:
[Instructions follow]. . . .

Mr. Lind executed his delicate and difficult mission with singular tact, firmness, and good judgment, and made clear to the authorities at the City of Mexico not only the purpose of his visit but also the spirit in which it had been undertaken. But the proposals he submitted were rejected. . . .

I am led to believe that they were rejected partly because the authorities at Mexico City had been grossly misinformed and misled upon two points. They did not realize the spirit of the American people in this matter, their earnest friendliness and yet sober determination that some just solution be found for the Mexican difficulties; and they did not believe that the present administration spoke through Mr. Lind for the people of United States. The effect of this unfortunate misunderstanding on their part is to leave them singularly isolated and without friends who can effectually aid them. So long as the misunderstanding continues we can only await the time of their awakening to a realization of the actual facts. We can not thrust our good offices upon them. The situation must be given a little more time to work itself out in the new circumstances; and I believe that only a little more will be necessary. For the circumstances are new. The rejection of our friendship makes them new and will inevitably bring its own alterations in the whole aspect of affairs. The actual situation of the authorities at Mexico City will presently be revealed.

Meanwhile what is it our duty to do? Clearly everything that we do must be rooted in patience and done with calm and disinterested deliberation. Impatience on our part would be childish, and would be fraught with every risk of wrong and folly. We can afford to exercise the self-restraint of a really great nation which realizes its own strength and scorns to misuse it. It was our duty to offer our active assistance. It is now our duty to show what true neutrality will do to enable the people of Mexico to set their affairs in order again, and wait for a further opportunity to offer our friendly counsels. The door is not closed against the resumption, either upon the initiative of Mexico or upon our own, of the effort to bring order out of the confusion by friendly cooperative action, should fortunate occasion offer.

While we wait, the contest of the rival forces will undoubtedly for a little while be sharper than ever, just because it will be plain that an end must be made of the existing situation, and that very promptly; and with the increased activity of the contending factions will come, it is to be feared, increased danger to the non-combatants in Mexico, as well as to those actually in the field of battle. The position of outsiders is always particularly trying and full of hazard where there is civil strife and a whole country is upset. We should earnestly urge all Americans to leave Mexico at once, and should assist them to get away in every way possible—not because we would mean to slacken in the least our efforts to safeguard their lives and their interests, but because it is imperative that they should take no unnecessary risks when it is physically possible for them to leave the country. We should let every one who assumes to exercise authority in any part of Mexico know in the most unequivocal way that we shall vigilantly watch the fortunes of those Americans who can not get away, and shall hold those responsible for their sufferings and losses to a definite reckoning. That can be and will be made plain beyond the possibility of a misunderstanding.

For the rest, I deem it my duty to exercise the authority conferred upon me by the law of March 14, 1912, to see to it that neither side of the struggle now going on in Mexico receive any assistance from this side the border. I shall follow the best practice of nations in the matter of neutrality by forbidding the exportation of arms or munitions of war of any kind from the United States to any part of the Republic of Mexico—a policy suggested by several interesting precedents and certainly dictated by many manifest considerations of practical expediency. We can not in the circumstances be partisans of either party to the contest that now distracts Mexico, or constitute ourselves the virtual umpire between them.

I am happy to say that several of the great Governments of the world have given this Government their generous moral support in urging upon the provisional authorities at the City of Mexico the acceptance of our proffered offices in the spirit in which they were made. . . .

Source: James D. Richardson, ed., *Compilation of the Messages and Papers of the Presidents*, vol. 17 (New York: Bureau of National Literature, 1917), 6884–88.

55. THE TAMPICO INCIDENT
20 April 1914

Although Victoriano Huerta was able to arrange his election as president of Mexico in October 1913, the United States refused to recognize him in that capacity. Subsequently, relations between the two countries deteriorated, reaching a flash point the following April when several sailors assigned to the U.S.S. Dolphin *were arrested at Tampico by Mexican authorities. The U.S. naval commander demanded their return, an apology, and a twenty-one gun salute to the American flag. Huerta's refusal prompted Wilson to request Congressional support to take action to resolve the situation.*

Gentlemen of the Congress:

It is my duty to call your attention to a situation which has arisen in our dealings with General Victoriano Huerta at Mexico City which calls for action, and to ask your advice and cooperation in acting upon it. On the 9th of April a paymaster of the U.S.S. *Dolphin* landed at the Iturbide Bridge landing at Tampico with a whaleboat and boat's crew to take off certain supplies needed by his ship, and while engaged in loading the boat was arrested by an officer and squad of men of the army of General Huerta. . . . Admiral Mayo regarded the arrest as so serious an affront that he was not satisfied with the apologies offered, but demanded that the flag of the United States be saluted with special ceremony by the military commander of the port.

The incident can not be regarded as a trivial one, especially as two of the men arrested were taken from the boat itself—that is to say, from the territory of the United States—but had it stood by itself it might have been attributed to the ignorance or arrogance of a single officer. Unfortunately, it was not an isolated case. A series of incidents have recently occurred which can not but create the impression that the representatives of General Huerta were willing to go out of their way to show disregard for the dignity and rights of this Government and felt perfectly safe in doing what they pleased, making free to show in many ways their irritation and contempt. . . .

The manifest danger of such a situation was that such offenses might grow from bad to worse until something happened of so gross and intolerable a sort as to lead directly and inevitably to armed conflict. It was necessary that the apologies of General Huerta and his representatives should go much further, that they should be such as to attract the attention of the whole population to their significance, and such as to impress upon General Huerta himself the necessity of seeing to it that no further occasion for explanations and professed regrets should arise. I, therefore, felt it my duty to sustain Admiral Mayo in the whole of his demand and to insist that the flag of the United States should be saluted in such a way as to indicate a new spirit and attitude on the part of the Huertistas.

Such a salute, General Huerta has refused, and I have come to ask your approval and support in the course I now propose to pursue.

This Government can, I earnestly hope, in no circumstances be forced into war with the people of Mexico. Mexico is torn by civil strife. If we are to accept the tests of its own constitution, it has no government. General Huerta has set his power up in the City of Mexico, such as it is, without right and by methods for which there can be no justification. Only part of the country is under his control. If armed conflict should unhappily come as a result of his attitude of personal resentment toward this Government, we should be fighting only General Huerta and those who adhere to him and give him their support, and our object would be only to restore to the people of the distracted Republic the opportunity to set up again their own laws and their own government.

But I earnestly hope that war is not now in question. I believe I speak for the American people when I say that we do not desire to control in any degree the affairs of our sister Republic. Our feeling for the people of Mexico is one of deep and genuine friendship, and every thing that we have so far done or refrained from doing has proceeded from our desire to help them, not to hinder or embarrass them. We would not wish even to exercise the good offices of friendship without their welcome and consent. The people of Mexico are entitled to settle their own domestic affairs in their own way, and we sincerely desire to respect their right. The present situation need have none of the grave implications of interference if we deal with it promptly, firmly, and wisely.

No doubt I could do what is necessary in the circumstances to enforce respect for our Government without recourse to the Congress, and yet not exceed my constitutional powers as President; but I do not wish to act in a manner possibly of so grave consequence except in close conference and cooperation with both the Senate and House. I, therefore, come to ask your approval that I should use the armed forces of the United States in such ways and to such an extent as may be necessary to obtain from General Huerta and his adherents the fullest recognition of the rights and dignity of the United States, even amidst the distressing conditions now unhappily obtaining in Mexico.

There can in what we do be no thought of aggression or of selfish aggrandizement. We seek to maintain the dignity and authority of the United States only because we wish always to keep our great influence unimpaired for the uses of liberty, both in the United States and wherever else it may be employed for the benefit of mankind.

Source: James D. Richardson, ed., *Compilation of the Messages and Papers of the Presidents*, vol. 17 (New York: Bureau of National Literature, 1917), 7934–36.

56. THE BRYAN-CHAMORRO CONVENTION
5 August 1914

Upon the completion of its canal in Panama, the United States pursued a policy designed to acquire other potential sites for trans-isthmian crossing. The Bryan-Chamorro Convention secured an American lease to Nicaragua's Great Corn and Little Corn Islands and the Gulf of Fonseca. It was challenged by Costa Rica and El Salvador in the Central American Court of Justice as an American violation of Nicaraguan sovereignty. Although the court upheld the objection, the United States and Nicaragua ignored the judgment.

ART. I. The Government of Nicaragua grants in perpetuity to the Government of the United States, forever free from all taxation or other public charge, the exclusive proprietary rights necessary and convenient for the construction, operation and maintenance of an inter-oceanic canal by way of the San Juan River and the great Lake of Nicaragua or by way of any route over Nicaraguan territory, the details of the terms upon which such canal shall be constructed, operated and maintained to be agreed to by the two governments whenever the Government of the United States shall notify the Government of Nicaragua of its desire or intention to construct such canal.

ART. II. To enable the Government of the United States to protect the Panama Canal and the proprietary rights granted to the Government of the United States by the foregoing article, and also to enable the Government of the United States to take any measure necessary to the ends contemplated herein, the Government of Nicaragua hereby leases for a term of ninety-nine years to the Government of the United States the islands in the Caribbean Sea known as Great Corn Island and Little Corn Island; and the Government of Nicaragua further grants to the Government of the United States for a like period of ninety-nine years the right to establish, operate and maintain a naval base at such place on the territory of Nicaragua bordering upon the Gulf of Fonseca as the Government of the United States may select. The Government of the United States shall have the option of renewing for a further term of ninety-nine years the above leases and grants upon the expiration of their respective terms, it being expressly agreed that the territory hereby leased and the naval base which may be maintained under the grant aforesaid shall be subject exclusively to the laws and sovereign authority of the United States during the terms of such lease and grant and of any renewal or renewals thereof.

ART. III. In consideration of the foregoing stipulations and for the purposes contemplated by this Convention and for the purpose of reducing the present indebtedness of Nicaragua, the Government of the United States shall, upon the date of the exchange of ratification of this Convention, pay for the benefit of the Republic of Nicaragua the sum of three million dollars United States gold coin, of the present weight and fineness, to be deposited to the order of the Government of Nicaragua in such bank or banks or with such banking corporation as the Government of the United States may determine to be applied by Nicaragua upon its indebtedness or other public purposes for the advancement of the welfare of Nicaragua in a manner to be determined by the two High Contracting Parties, all such disbursements to be made by orders drawn by the Minister of Finance of the Republic of Nicaragua and approved by the Secretary of State of the United States or by such person as he may designate.

This Convention shall be ratified by the High Contracting Parties in accordance with their respective laws, and the ratification thereof shall be exchanged at Washington as soon as possible. . . .

WILLIAM JENNINGS BRYAN.
EMILIANO CHAMORRO.

Source: William M. Malloy, ed., *Treaties, Conventions, International Acts, Protocols, and Agreements between the United States and Other Powers, 1776–1909*, vol. 3 (Washington, DC: Government Printing Office, 1923), 2740–43.

Part Six

The First World War

The First World War shattered the conventions that had guided western thought since the Age of Reason. The rationalism that had served the industrial age and produced and fostered a sense of confidence in the utility of science had led a generation. The major powers that were locked in combat in 1914 came to the tragic realization that power could also turn against the hands that wielded it. Sir Edward Grey captured the moment that year when he sadly remarked that "The lamps are going out all over Europe; we shall not see them lit again in our lifetime."[1]

The conduct of this war horrified Americans. The sheer scale of the conflict in Belgium, France, and Russia staggered contemporary observers. The prospect of losing, in one battle, casualties comparable to the entire American Civil War was something beyond the imagination of U.S. leaders and the public at large.[2] More to the point, the havoc it created among the European combatants led many outside observers to openly question whether they or their system of foreign affairs could or should survive the war. The balance of power paradigm embraced by the capitals of Europe had led them from a small flash point in the Balkans to a world war. The stakes involved in forging a new peace were enormous. Postwar diplomacy would not be a simple matter of discovering an alternative to the old European order, but finding a means adequate to ensure human survival from a man-made disaster.

Initially, the United States enveloped itself in neutrality as it sought out an alternative to the way it dealt with international affairs. Part of this decision was a matter of practicality. In 1914, the country had neither the will nor any intention of intervening in the war. Opposition to the war, from leaders as diverse as Samuel L. Gompers, Jane Addams, and Woodrow Wilson, reflected a nation anxious to avoid the bloodbath unfolding on the western front.[3] So the country reverted to a position reminiscent of the America of George Washington and John Adams. For three years, the United States attempted to establish itself as an absolute neutral. It embraced the principles of freedom of the seas and open commerce with all belligerents. In doing so, America reaffirmed the traditional facets of its diplomacy; a stance that was a dramatic departure from the past. From the diplomatic perspective of Woodrow Wilson, neutrality was a position through which the United States might successfully mediate an end to the war. By retaining its neutral status, the United States could sponsor a global return to civilization.[4]

Ultimately, Wilson's neutral strategy failed. In part, its downfall was the result of the strong links that existed between the United States and the Allied nations of France and England. The desperate defense of Paris captured the imagination of the American public as did the exploits of American volunteers in the *Lafayette Escadrille*. Anglophiles populated the upper echelons of the Wilson administration. Key policy advisors, such as Colonel Edward M. House and Secretary of State Robert Lansing, offered little apology for their pro-British sympathies. Explicit ties with England, which had evolved considerably in the long history following the American Revolution, seemed eminently preferable to the brutal militarism that Germany represented in 1914. The close economic ties between America and the Allied countries embellished this attitude. American trade with England and France stood at $3.2 billion in 1916, with more than $1.2 billion of the total comprised of American munitions exports.[5]

Germany's naval campaign to break this economic link ultimately pushed the United States into the war. Lacking a surface fleet adequate to challenge the Royal Navy, Germany unleashed an innovation new in modern warfare, the U-Boat, on the Sea-lanes of the northern Atlantic. The impact on the United States was almost immediate. The loss of life on the *Lusitania* in 1915 and the *Sussex* the following year brought the war home to the United States and provoked public outrage. More pointedly, the U-Boat assault on Allied shipping proved not only a devastating challenge to the principle of free commerce but an extremely effective military tactic against the Atlantic sea link. During the month of April 1917 alone, following the reimposition of unrestricted submarine warfare, more than 881,000 tons of Allied shipping were lost.[6]

The final decision to join in the war against Germany opened the door to a whole new array of foreign policy decisions for the United States. The first dealt with the actual conduct of the war. When General John J. Pershing deployed to western Europe with the American expeditionary force, he did so with the mandate that it remain under American command. Pershing's ultimate success in this one important task was a testament to both his own tenacity as a diplomat and the fact that neither he nor Wilson was willing to sacrifice sovereignty for the sake of diplomacy. It signaled as well a tangible American desire to be treated as a peer by the Allies during the conduct of the war.

America was less successful in influencing the peace. As the hostilities raged, Wilson made his case for a new, more liberal international order. He called for a new world built upon principles that transcended the priorities of individual nations. As early as January 1917, portions of this proposal had appeared in his "peace without victory" speech:

It will be absolutely necessary that a force be created as a guarantor of the permanency of the settlement so much greater than the force of any nation now engaged or any alliance hitherto formed or projected that no nation, no probable combination of nations could face or withstand it. If the peace presently to be made is to endure, it must be a peace made secure by the organized major force of mankind.[7]

One year later, Wilson offered more specific guidelines in an address to Congress. His famous "fourteen points" called for significant alterations in the conduct of international affairs. In them, he preached the constructive value of disarmament, free trade, an end to secret diplomacy, and an end to imperial competition. To hammer home his commitment, Wilson took the unprecedented step of departing America to act as the chief negotiator for the United States during final peace negotiations with Germany.

Wilson soon discovered that his principles of a new international system could not overcome the animosities among the other allies that eventually dominated the Versailles Treaty. The final document presented to the German delegation represented a pure exercise in power politics. It stripped the country of territory and most of its military might. More crippling was the $33 billion in reparations assigned to Germany as part of Article 231, the so-called "war guilt clause," for all the damage created by the war. The overall intent of the Versailles Treaty, in the words of British economist John Maynard Keynes, was a "Carthaginian peace which aimed to reduce Germany to a second rate power and led to the impoverishment of the German people."[8]

Wilson's effort to promote the League of Nations fared little better but for much different reasons. His intent was to construct an agency that would promote collective global security. The foundation of this idea was that league members would be pledged to come to the aid of each other in cases of overt aggression. This one point, contained in Article 10 of the League Covenant, proved an insurmountable barrier to the American Senate, led by Senate Foreign Relations Committee Chairman Henry Cabot Lodge. Lodge questioned both the extensiveness and the cost of Article 10 in an argument that was reminiscent of past debates over European entanglements. In the larger domain of public opinion, Wilson's case also suffered because most Americans assumed that the demon of German militarism had been exorcised by the expedition to France. The more abstract principle of collective security against some unnamed future adversary failed to resonate with the American people.[9]

In the end, the Senate refused to ratify U.S. membership in the League. The vote, for all appearances, was a reflection of the declining fortunes of Wilsonian internationalism. Incapacitated by a stroke in 1919, Wilson was unable to provide the mentorship necessary to carry it into the next decade. The American public, reeling from the outbreak of the "Spanish Flu" epidemic of 1918–1919, seemed little interested in a new foreign crusade.[10]

However, America did not turn its back on the world at the beginning of the 1920s. As the sole major nation left relatively undamaged by the Great War, the vacuum presented by the new reordering of world power proved an irresistible attraction to American capital and American leadership. Reconciling this attraction with the increasingly insular nature of the home front would prove to be one of the most important challenges to the country in the postwar period.

NOTES

1. William Laird Kleine-Ahlbrandt, *Twentieth-Century European History* (New York: West Publishing, 1993), 11.

2. John Ellis, *Eye-Deep in Hell: Trench Warfare in World War I* (Baltimore: Johns Hopkins University Press, 1976), 80–104.

3. See David Kennedy, *Over Here: The First World War and American Society* (New York: Oxford University Press, 1980).

4. Frank Ninkovich, *The Wilsonian Century: U.S. Foreign Policy since 1900* (Chicago: University of Chicago Press, 1999), 48–77.

5. Samuel Eliot Morison, Henry Steele Commager, and William E. Leuchtenburg, *The Growth of the American Republic*, vol. 2 (New York: Oxford University Press, 1969), 362.

6. Warren W. Hassler, *With Shield and Sword: American Military Affairs, Colonial Times to the Present* (Ames: Iowa State University Press, 1982), 266–69.

7. Henry Steele Commager, *Documents of American History*, vol. 2 (Englewood Cliffs, NJ: Prentice Hall, 1973), 125–28.

8. Paul Bookbinder, *Weimar Germany: The Republic of the Reasonable* (New York: Manchester University Press, 1996), 35.

9. See Frederick S. Calhoun, *Power and Principle: Armed Intervention in Wilsonian Foreign Policy* (Kent, OH: Kent State University Press, 1986).

10. Gina Kolata, *Flu: The Story of the Great Influenza Pandemic of 1918 and the Search for the Virus That Caused It* (New York: Farrar, Straus & Giroux, 1999), 3–34.

57. WILSON'S APPEAL FOR NEUTRALITY
19 August 1914

Upon the outbreak of general war in Europe, Woodrow Wilson immediately issued a proclamation of neutrality. He asserted a traditional American policy to avoid the bloody and indecisive conflict unfolding before the world. The president was, however, cognizant of the sentiments among many Americans who pressed for intervention. The 19 August appeal was an attempt to address this significant portion of U.S. society.

My fellow countrymen: I suppose that every thoughtful man in America has asked himself, during these last troubled weeks, what influence the European war may exert upon the United States, and I take the liberty of addressing a few words to you in order to point out that it is entirely within our own choice what its effects upon us will be and to urge very earnestly upon you the sort of speech and conduct which will best safeguard the Nation against distress and disaster.

The effect of the war upon the United States will depend upon what American citizens say and do. Every man who really loves America will act and speak in the true spirit of neutrality, which is the spirit of impartiality and fairness and friendliness to all concerned. The spirit of the Nation in this critical matter will be determined largely by what individuals and society and those gathered in public meetings do and say, upon what newspapers and magazines contain, upon what ministers utter in their pulpits, and men proclaim as their opinions on the street.

The people of the United States are drawn from many nations, and chiefly from the nations now at war. It is natural and inevitable that there should be the utmost variety of sympathy and desire among them with regard to the issues and circumstances of the conflict. Some will wish one nation, others another, to succeed in the momentous struggle. It will be easy to excite passion and difficult to allay it. Those responsible for exciting it will assume a heavy responsibility, responsibility for no less a thing than that the people of the United States, whose love of their country and whose loyalty to its Government should unite them as Americans all, bound in honor and affection to think first of her and her interests, may be divided in camps of hostile opinion, hot against each other, involved in the war itself in impulse and opinion if not in action.

Such divisions amongst us would be fatal to our peace of mind and might seriously stand in the way of the proper performance of our duty as the one great nation at peace, the one people holding itself ready to play a part of impartial mediation and speak the counsels of peace and accommodation, not as a partisan, but as a friend.

I venture, therefore, my fellow countrymen, to speak a solemn word of warning to you against that deepest, most subtle, most essential breach of neutrality which may spring out of partisanship, out of passionately taking sides. The United States must be neutral in fact as well as in name during these days that are to try men's souls. We must be impartial in thought as well as in action, must put a curb upon our sentiments as well as upon every transaction that might be construed as a preference of one party to the struggle before another.

My thought is of America. I am speaking, I feel sure, the earnest wish and purpose of every thoughtful American that this great country of ours, which is, of course, the first in our thoughts and in our hearts, should show herself in this time of peculiar trial a Nation fit beyond others to exhibit the fine poise of undisturbed judgment, the dignity of self-control, the efficiency of dispassionate action; a Nation that neither sits in judgment upon others nor is disturbed in her own counsels and which keeps herself fit and free to do what is honest and disinterested and truly serviceable for the peace of the world.

Shall we not resolve to put upon ourselves the restraints which will bring to our people the happiness and the great and lasting influence for peace we covet for them?

Source: James D. Richardson, ed., *A Compilation of the Messages and Papers of the Presidents*, vol. 17 (New York: Bureau of National Literature, 1917), 7978–79.

---

58. THE FIRST *LUSITANIA* NOTE
13 May 1915

A general assumption of American neutrality was that commerce and individual citizens would be unmolested by either side in the war. This was challenged on 7 May 1915 when the British liner Lusitania *was sunk with the loss of over eleven hundred passengers and crew. One hundred and twenty-four Americans died in what many Americans considered a German act of war.*

The Secretary of State to Ambassador
Gerard.
DEPARTMENT OF STATE
Washington, May 13, 1915.

Please call on the Minister of Foreign Affairs and after reading to him this communication leave with him a copy.

In view of recent acts of the German authorities in violation of American rights on the high seas which culminated in the torpedoing and sinking of the British steamship *Lusitania* on May 7, 1915, by which over 100 American citizens lost their lives, it is clearly wise and desirable that the Government of the United States and the Imperial German Government should come to a clear and full understanding as to the grave situation which has resulted.

The sinking of the British passenger steamer *Falaba* by a German submarine on March 28, through which Leon C. Thrasher, an American citizen, was drowned; the attack on April 28 on the American vessel *Cushing* by a German aeroplane; the torpedoing on May 1, of the American vessel *Gulflight* by a German submarine, as a result of which two or more American citizens met their death; and, finally, the torpedoing and sinking of the steamship *Lusitania*, constitute a series of events which the Government of the United States has observed with growing concern, distress, and amazement.

Recalling the humane and enlightened attitude hitherto assumed by the Imperial German Government in matters of international right, and particularly with regard to the freedom of the seas; having learned to recognize the German views and the German influence in the field of international obligation as always engaged upon the side of justice and humanity; and having understood the instructions of the Imperial German Government to its naval commanders to be upon the same plane of humane action prescribed by the naval codes of other nations, the Government of the United States was loath to believe—it can not now bring itself to believe—that these acts, so absolutely contrary to the rules, the practices, and the spirit of modern warfare, could have the countenance or sanction of that great Government. It feels it to be its duty, therefore, to address the Imperial German Government concerning them with the utmost frankness and in the earnest hope that it is not mistaken in expecting action on the part of the Imperial German Government which will correct the unfortunate impressions which have been created and vindicate once more the position of that Government with regard to the sacred freedom of the seas.

The Government of the United States has been apprised that the Imperial German Government considered themselves obliged by the extraordinary circumstances of the present war and the measures adopted by their adversaries in seeking to cut Germany off from all commerce, to adopt methods of retaliation which go much beyond the ordinary methods of warfare at sea, in the proclamation of a war zone from which they have warned neutral ships to keep away. This Government has already taken occasion to inform the Imperial German Government that it can not admit the adoption of such measures or such a warning of danger to operate as in any degree an abbreviation of the rights of American shipmasters or of American citizens bound on lawful errands as passengers on merchant ships of belligerent nationality; and that it must hold the Imperial German Government to a strict accountability for any infringement of those rights, intentional or incidental. It does not understand the Imperial German Government to question those rights. It assumes, on the contrary, that the Imperial Government accept, as of course, the rule that the lives of noncombatants, whether they be of neutral citizenship or citizens of one of the nations at war, can not lawfully or rightfully be put in jeopardy by the capture or destruction of an unarmed merchantman, and recognize also, as all other nations do, the obligation to take the usual precaution of visit and search to ascertain whether a suspected merchantman is in fact of belligerent nationality or is in fact carrying contraband of war under a neutral flag.

The Government of the United States, therefore, desires to call the attention of the Imperial German Government with the utmost earnestness to the fact that the objection to their present method of attack against the trade of their enemies lies in the practical impossibility of employing submarines in the destruction of commerce without disregarding those rules of fairness, reason, justice, and humanity which all modern opinion regards as imperative. It is practically impossible for the officers of a submarine to visit a merchantman at sea and examine her papers and cargo. It is practically impossible for them to make a prize of her; and, if they can not put a prize crew on board of her, they can not sink her without leaving her crew and all on board of her to the mercy of the sea in her small boats. These facts it is understood the Imperial German Government frankly admit. We are informed that in the instances of which we have spoken time enough for even that poor measure of safety was not given, and in at least two of the cases cited not so much as a warning was received. Manifestly submarines can not be used against merchantmen, as the last few weeks have shown, without an inevitable violation of many sacred principles of justice and humanity.

American citizens act within their indisputable rights in taking their ships and in traveling wherever their legitimate business calls them upon the high seas, and exercise those rights in what should be the well-justified confidence that their lives will not be endangered by acts done in clear violation of universally acknowledged international obligations, and certainly in the confidence that their own Government will sustain them in the exercise of their rights.

There was recently published in the newspapers of the United States, I regret to inform the Imperial German Government, a formal warning, purporting to come from the Imperial German Embassy at Washington, addressed to the people of the United States and stating, in effect, that any citizen of the United States who exercised his right of free travel upon the seas would do so at his peril if his journey should take him within the zone of waters within which the Imperial German Navy was using submarines against the commerce of Great Britain and France, notwithstanding the respectful but very earnest protest of his Government, the Government of the United States. I do not refer to this for the purpose of calling the attention of the Imperial German Government at this time to the surprising irregularity of a communication from the Imperial German Embassy at Washington addressed to the people of the United States through the newspapers, but only for the purpose of pointing out that no warning that an unlawful and inhumane act will be committed can possibly be accepted as an excuse palliation for that act or as an abatement of the responsibility for its commission.

Long acquainted as this Government has been with the character of the Imperial German Government and with the high principles of equity by which they have in the past been actuated and guided, the Government of the United States can not believe that the commanders of the vessels which committed these acts of lawlessness did so except under a misapprehension of the orders issued by the Imperial German naval authorities. It takes it for granted that, at least within the practical possibilities every such case, the commanders even of submarines were expected to do nothing that would involve the lives of non-combatants or the safety of neutral ships, even at the cost of failing of their object of capture or destruction. It confidently expects, therefore, that the Imperial German Government will disavow the acts of which the Government of the United States complains, that they will make reparation so far as reparation is possible for injuries which are without measure, and that they will take immediate steps to prevent the recurrence of anything so obviously subversive of the principles of warfare for which the Imperial German Government have in the past so wisely and so firmly contended.

The Government and people of the United States look to the Imperial German Government for just, prompt, and enlightened action in this vital matter with the greater confidence because the United States and Germany are bound together not only by special ties of friendship but also by the explicit stipulations of the treaty of 1828 between the United States and the Kingdom of Prussia.

Expressions of regret and offers of reparation in the case of the destruction of neutral ships sunk by mistake, while they may satisfy international obligations, if no loss of life results, can not justify or excuse a practice, the natural and necessary effect of which is to subject neutral nations and neutral persons to new and immeasurable risks.

The Imperial German Government will not expect the Government of the United States to omit any word or any act necessary to the performance of its sacred duty of maintaining the rights of the United States and its citizens and of safeguarding their free exercise and enjoyment.

BRYAN

Source: James D. Richardson, ed., *A Compilation of the Messages and Papers of the Presidents*, vol. 17 (New York: Bureau of National Literature, 1917), 8062–64.

59. THE SUSSEX AFFAIR
19 April 1916

After the uproar that followed the destruction of the Lusitania, *Germany gave assurances that attacks on shipping would be preceded by a warning and consideration for noncombatants. This pledge ended in April 1916 with the sinking of the French ship* Sussex *on 24 April 1916. Wilson subsequently warned that unless this policy of unrestricted submarine warfare was discontinued, the United States would formally break off diplomatic relations. Germany complied until January 1917.*

GENTLEMEN OF THE CONGRESS: A situation has arisen in the foreign relations of the country of which it is my plain duty to inform you very frankly. . . .

In February of the present year the Imperial German Government informed this Government . . . that the Imperial German Government felt justified in the circumstances in treating all armed merchantmen of belligerent ownership as auxiliary vessels of war, which it would have the right to destroy without warning. . . .

One of the latest and most shocking instances of this method of warfare was that of the destruction of the French cross-channel steamer *Sussex*. It must stand forth, as the sinking of the *Lutsitania* did, as so singulary tragical and unjustifiable as to constitute a truly terrible example of the inhumanity of submarine warfare as the commanders of German vessels have for the past twelve months been conducting it. If this instance stood alone, some explanation, some disavowal by the German Government, some evidence of criminal mistake or willful disobedience on the part of the commander of the vessel that fired the torpedo might be sought or entertained; but unhappily it does not stand alone. . . .

The Government of the United States has been very patient. At every stage of this distressing experience of tragedy after tragedy in which its own citizens were involved, it has sought to be restrained from any extreme course of action or of protest by a thoughtful consideration of the extraordinary circumstances of this unprecedented war, and actuated in all that it said or did by the sentiments of genuine friendship which the people of the United States have always entertained and continue to entertain towards the German nation. It has of course accepted the successive explanations and assurances of the Imperial German Government as given in entire sincerity and good faith, and has hoped, even against hope, that it would prove to be possible for the German Government so to order and control the acts of its naval commanders as to square its policy with the principles of humanity as embodied in the law of nations. It has been willing to wait until the significance of the facts became absolutely unmistakable and susceptible of but one interpretation.

That point has now unhappily been reached. The facts are susceptible of but one interpretation. The Imperial German Government has been unable to put any limits or restraints upon its warfare against either freight or passenger ships. It has therefore become painfully evident that the position which this Government took at the very outset is inevitable, namely, that the use of submarines for the destruction of an enemy's commerce is, of necessity, because of the very character of the vessels employed and the very methods of attack which their employment of course involves, incompatible with the principles of humanity, the long established and incontrovertible rights of neutrals, and the sacred immunities of non-combatants.

I have deemed it my duty, therefore, to say to the Imperial German Government, that if it is still its purpose to prosecute relentless and indiscriminate warfare against vessels of commerce by the use of submarines, notwithstanding the now demonstrated impossibility of conducting that warfare in accordance with what the Government of the United States must consider the sacred and indisputable rules of international law and the universally recognized dictates of humanity, the Government of the United States is at last forced to the conclusion that there is but one course it can pursue; and that unless the Imperial German Government should now immediately declare and effect an abandonment of its present methods of warfare against passenger and freight carrying vessels this Government can have no choice but to sever diplomatic relations with the Government of the German Empire altogether.

This decision I have arrived at with the keenest regret; the possibility of the action contemplated I am sure all thoughtful Americans will look forward to with unaffected reluctance. But we cannot forget that we are in some sort and by the force of circumstances the responsible spokesmen of the rights of humanity, and that we cannot remain silent while those rights seem in process of being swept utterly away in the maelstrom of this terrible war. We owe it to a due regard for our own rights as a nation, to our sense of duty as a representative of the rights of neutrals the world over, and to a just conception of the rights of mankind to take this stand now with the utmost solemnity and firmness. . . .

Source: James D. Richardson, ed., *Compilation of the Messages and Papers of the Presidents*, vol. 17 (New York: Bureau of National Literature, 1917), 8121–24.

60. TREATY BETWEEN THE UNITED STATES AND HAITI
3 May 1916

Revolution in Haiti prompted American intervention in 1914. Continued violence caused the dispatch of U.S. Marines a year later where they oversaw finances, customs collections, and military affairs for fifteen years. The subsequent treaty between the United States and Haiti was designed to preserve order, protect American investments, and forestall any potential European intervention.

ART. I. The Government of the United States will, by its good offices, aid the Haitian Government in the proper and efficient development of its agricultural, mineral and commercial resources and in the establishment of the finances of Haiti on a firm and solid basis.

ART. II. The President of Haiti shall appoint, upon nomination by the President of the United States, a General Receiver and such aids and employees as may be necessary, who shall collect, receive and apply all customs duties on imports and exports accruing at the several custom houses and ports of entry of the Republic of Haiti.

The President of Haiti shall appoint, upon nomination by the President of the United States, a Financial Adviser, who shall be an officer attached to the Ministry of Finance, to give effect to whose proposals and labours the Minister will lend efficient aid. The Financial Adviser shall devise an adequate system of public accounting, aid in increasing the revenues and adjusting them to the expenses, inquire into the validity of the debts of the Republic, enlighten both Governments with reference to all eventual debts, recommend improved methods of collecting and applying the revenues, and make such other recommendations to the Minister of Finance as may be deemed necessary for the welfare and prosperity of Haiti.

ART. III. The Government of the Republic of Haiti will provide by law or appropriate decrees for the payment of all customs duties to the General Receiver, and will extend to the Receivership, and to the Financial Adviser, all needful aid and full protection in the execution of the powers conferred and duties imposed herein; and the United States on its part will extend like aid and protection.

ART. IV. Upon the appointment of the Financial Adviser, the Government of the Republic of Haiti, in co-operation with the Financial Adviser, shall collate, classify, arrange and make full statement of all the debts of the Republic, the amounts, character, maturity and condition thereof, and the interest accruing and the sinking fund requisite to their final discharge.

ART. V. All sums collected and received by the General Receiver shall be applied, first, to the payment of the salaries and allowances of the General Receiver, his assistants and employees and expenses of the Receivership, including the salary and expenses of the Financial Adviser, which salaries will be determined by previous agreement; second, to the interest and sinking fund of the public debt of the Republic of Haiti; and, third, to the maintenance of the constabulary referred to in Article X, and then the remainder to the Haitian Government for purposes of current expenses. . . .

ART. VI. The expenses of the Receivership, including salaries and allowances of the General Receiver, his assistants and employees, and the salary and expenses of the Financial Adviser, shall not exceed five per centum of the collections and receipts from customs duties, unless by agreement by the two Governments.

ART. VII. The General Receiver shall make monthly reports of all collections, receipts and disbursements to the appropriate officer of the Republic of Haiti and to the Department of State of the United States, which reports shall be open to inspection and verification at all times by the appropriate authorities of each of the said Governments.

The Republic of Haiti shall not increase its public debt except by previous agreement with the President of the United States, and shall not contract any debt or assume any financial obligation unless the ordinary revenues of the Republic available for that purpose, after defraying the expenses of the Government, shall be adequate to pay the interest and provide a sinking fund for the final discharge of such debt. . . .

ART. IX. The Republic of Haiti will not without a previous agreement with the President of the United States, modify the customs duties in a manner to reduce the revenues therefrom; and in order that the revenues of the Republic may be adequate to meet the public debt and the expenses of the Government, to preserve tranquility and to promote material prosperity, the Republic of Haiti will co-operate with the Financial Adviser in his recommendations for improvement in the methods of collecting and disbursing the revenues and for new sources of needed income.

ART. X. The Haitian Government obligates itself, for the preservation of domestic peace, the security of individual rights and full observance of the provisions of this treaty, to create without delay an efficient constabulary, urban and rural, composed of native Haitians. This constabulary shall be organized and officered by Americans, appointed by the President of Haiti, upon nomination by the President of the United States. . . . These officers will be replaced by Haitians as they, by examination, conducted under direction of a board to be selected by the senior American officer of this constabulary and in the presence of a representative of the Haitian Government, are found to be qualified to assume such duties. The constabulary herein provided for, shall, under the direction of the Haitian Government, have supervision and control of arms and ammunition, military supplies, and traffic therein, throughout the country. The high contracting parties agree that the stipulations in this Article are necessary to prevent factional strife and disturbances.

ART. XI. The Government of Haiti agrees not to surrender any of the territory of the Republic of Haiti by sale, lease or otherwise, or jurisdiction over such territory, to any foreign government or power, not to enter into any treaty or contract with any foreign power or powers that will impair or tend to impair the independence of Haiti.

ART. XII. The Haitian Government agrees to execute with the United States a protocol for the settlement, by arbitration or otherwise, of all pending pecuniary claims foreign corporations, companies, citizens or subjects against Haiti.

ART. XIII. The Republic of Haiti being desirous to further the development of its natural resources, agrees to undertake and execute such measures as in the opinion of the high contracting parties may be necessary for the sanitation and public improvement of the Republic, under the supervision and direction of an engineer or engineers, to be appointed by the President of Haiti upon nomination by the President of the United States, and authorized for that purpose by the Government of Haiti.

ART. XIV. The high contracting parties shall have authority to take such steps as may be necessary to insure the complete attainment of any of the objects comprehended in this treaty; and, should the necessity occur, the United States will lend an efficient aid for the preservation of Haitian Independence and the maintenance of a Government adequate for the protection of life, property and individual liberty. . . .

ART. XVI. The present treaty shall remain in full force and virtue for the term of ten years, to be counted from the day of exchange of ratifications, and further for another term of ten years if, for specific reasons presented by either of the high contracting parties, the purpose of this treaty has not been fully accomplished. . . .

Source: Henry Steele Commager, *Documents of American History*, vol. 2 (Englewood Cliffs, NJ: Prentice Hall, 1973), 113–14.

61. ORGANIC ACT OF THE PHILIPPINE ISLANDS
29 August 1916

Philippine independence became an election issue in 1912 when the Democratic Party pledged its support of the final separation of the territory from American control. The so-called "Jones Act" of 29 August 1916 improved the lawmaking capacity of the Philippine legislature and the government's authority to control its own finances. It reserved the right of the United States to appoint a Governor General and left judgments made by the Philippine Supreme Court open to review by the U.S. Supreme Court.

An Act to declare the purpose of the people of the United States as to the future political status of the people of the Philippine Islands, and to provide a more autonomous government for those islands.

Whereas it was never the intention of the People of the United States in the incipiency of the War with Spain to make it a war of conquest or for territorial aggrandizement; and

Whereas it is, as it has always been, the purpose of the people of the United States to withdraw their sovereignty over the Philippine Islands and to recognize their independence as soon as a stable government can be established therein; and

Whereas for the speedy accomplishment of such purpose it is desirable to place in the hands of the people of the Philippines as large a control of their domestic affairs as can be given them without, in the meantime, impairing the exercise of the rights, of sovereignty by the people of the United States, in order that, by the use and exercise of popular franchise and governmental powers, they may be the better prepared to fully assume the responsibilities and enjoy all the privileges of complete independence: Therefore

Be it enacted . . .

SEC. 2. That all inhabitants of the Philippine Islands who were Spanish subjects on [11 April 1899] and then resided in said islands, and their children born subsequent thereto, shall be deemed and held to be citizens of the Philippine Islands, except such as shall have elected to preserve their allegiance to the Crown of Spain in accordance with the provisions of the treaty of peace between the United States and Spain. . . . and except such others as have since become citizens of some other country:. . . .

SEC. 3. [Bill of rights for the Philippines]. . . .

SEC. 5. That the statutory laws of the United States hereafter enacted shall not apply to the Philippine Islands, except when they specifically so provide, or it is so provided in this Act.

SEC. 6. That the laws now in force in the Philippines shall continue in force and effect, except as altered, amended, or modified herein, until altered, amended or repealed by the legislative authority herein provided or by Act of Congress of the United States.

SEC. 7. That the legislative authority herein provided shall have power, when not inconsistent with this Act, by due enactment to amend, alter, modify, or repeal any law, civil or criminal, continued in force by this Act as it may from time to time see fit.

This power shall specifically extend with the limitation herein provided as to the tariff to all laws relating to revenue and taxation in effect in the Philippines.

SEC. 8. That general legislative power, except as otherwise herein provided, is hereby granted to the Philippine Legislature, authorized by this Act. . . .

SEC. 10. That while this Act provides that the Philippine government shall have the authority to enact a tariff law the trade relations between the islands and the United States shall continue to be governed exclusively by laws of the Congress of the United States: *Provided*, That tariff acts or acts amendatory to the tariff of the Philippine Islands shall not become law until they shall receive the approval of the President of the United States, nor shall any act of the Philippine Legislature affecting immigration or the currency or coinage laws of the Philippines become a law until it has been approved by the President of the United States: *Provided further*, That the President shall approve or disapprove any act mentioned in the foregoing proviso within six months from and after its enactment and submission for his approval, and if not disapproved within such time it shall become a law the same as if it had been specifically approved.

SEC. 11. . . . That the entire indebtedness of the Philippine government . . . shall not exceed at any one time the sum of $15,000,000. . . .

SEC. 12. That general legislative powers in the Philippines, except as herein otherwise provided, shall be vested in a legislature which shall consist of two houses, one the senate and the other the house of representatives, and the two houses shall be designated "The Philippine Legislature": . . .

SEC. 13. [The Senate]

SEC. 14. [The House of Representatives]

SEC. 15. . . . Until otherwise provided by the Philippine Legislature herein provided for the qualifications of voters for senators and representatives in the Philippines and all officers elected by the people shall be as follows:

Every male person who is not a citizen or subject of a foreign power twenty-one years of age or over . . . who shall have been a resident of the Philippines for one year and of the municipality in which he shall offer to vote for six months next preceding the day of voting, and who is comprised within one of the following classes:

(a) Those who under existing law are legal voters and have exercised the right of suffrage.

(b) Those who own real property to the value of 500 pesos, or who annually pay 30 pesos or more of the established taxes.

(c) Those who are able to read and write either Spanish, English or a native tongue.

... The first election under the provisions of this Act shall be held on the first Tuesday of October, nineteen hundred and sixteen. ... *Provided*, That the Governor General of the Philippine Islands shall appoint, without the consent of the senate and without restriction as to residence, senators and representatives who will, in his opinion, best represent the senate district and those representative districts which may be included in the territory not now represented in the Philippine Assembly:. ...

SEC. 19. ... Every bill and joint resolution which shall have passed both houses shall, before it becomes a law, be presented to the Governor General. If he approve the same, he shall sign it; but if not, he shall return it with his objections to that house in which it shall have originated, which shall enter the objections at large on its journal and proceed to reconsider it. If, after such reconsideration, two-thirds of the members elected to that house shall agree to pass the same, it shall be sent, together with the objections, to the other house, by which it shall likewise be reconsidered, and if approved by two-thirds of all the members elected to that house it shall be sent to the Governor General, who, in case he shall then not approve, shall transmit the same to the President of the United States. ... If the President of the United States approve the same, he shall sign it and it shall become a law. If he shall not approve same, he shall return it to the Governor General, so stating, and it shall not become a law; ...

All laws enacted by the Philippine Legislature shall be reported to the Congress of the United States, which hereby reserves the power and authority to annul the same. If at the termination of any fiscal year the appropriations necessary for the support of government for the ensuing fiscal year shall not have been made, the several sums appropriated in the last appropriation bills for the objects and purposes therein specified, so far as the same may be done, shall be deemed to be reappropriated for the several objects and purposes specified in said last appropriation bill; ...

SEC. 20. That at the first meeting of the Philippine Legislature created by this Act and triennially thereafter there shall be chosen by the legislature two Resident Commissioners to the United States, who shall hold their office for a term of three years beginning with the fourth day of March following their election, and which shall be entitled to an official recognition as such by all departments upon presentation to the President of a certificate of election by the Governor General of said islands. ...

SEC. 21. That the supreme executive power shall be vested in an executive officer, whose official title shall be "The Governor General of the Philippine Islands." He shall be appointed by the President, by and with the advice and consent of the Senate of the United States, and hold his office at the pleasure of the President and until his successor is chosen and qualified. The Governor General shall reside in the Philippine Islands during his official incumbency, and maintain his office at the seat of government. He shall unless otherwise herein provided, appoint by and with the consent of the Philippine Senate, such officers as may now be appointed by the Governor General, or such as he is authorized by this Act to appoint or whom he may hereafter be authorized by law to appoint; . . . He . . . shall be commander in chief of all locally created armed forces and militia. . . . He shall be responsible for the faithful execution of the laws of the Philippine Islands and of the United States operative within the Philippine Islands, and whenever it becomes necessary he may call upon the commanders of the military and naval forces of the United States in the islands, or summon the *posse comitatus*, or call out the militia or other locally created armed forces, to prevent or suppress lawless violence, invasion, insurrection, or rebellion; and he may, in case of rebellion or invasion, or imminent danger thereof, when the public safety requires it, suspend the privileges of the writ of habeas corpus, or place the islands, or any part thereof, under martial law. . . .

SEC. 26. . . . The chief justice and associate justices of the Supreme Court shall hereafter be appointed by the President, by and with the advice and consent of the Senate of the United States. The judges of the court of first instance shall be appointed by the Governor General by and with the advice and consent of the Philippine Senate. . . .

SEC. 27. That the Supreme Court of the United States shall have jurisdiction to review, revise, reverse, modify, or affirm the final judgments and decrees of the Supreme Court of the Philippine Islands in all actions, cases, causes, and proceedings now pending therein or hereafter determined thereby in which the Constitution or any statute, treaty, title, right, or privilege of the United States is involved, or in causes in which the value in controversy exceeds $25,000. . . .

SEC. 28. . . . It shall be unlawful for any corporation organized under this Act, or for any person, company, or corporation receiving any grant, franchise, or concession from the government of said islands, to use, employ, or contract for the labor of persons held in involuntary serviture; . . .

SEC. 29. That, except as in this Act otherwise provided, the salaries of all the officials of the Philippines not appointed by the President, including deputies, assistants, and other employees, shall be such and be so paid out of the revenues of the Philippines as shall from time to time be determined by the Philippine Legislature; and if the legislature shall fail to make an appropriation for such salaries, the salaries fixed shall be paid without the necessity of further appro-priations therefor. The salaries of all officers and all expenses of the offices of the various officials of the Philippines appointed as herein provided by the Pres-ident shall also be paid out of the revenues of the Philippines. . . .

Source: Henry Steele Commager, *Documents of American History*, vol. 2 (Englewood Cliffs, NJ: Prentice Hall, 1973), 116–19.

62.   WILSON'S "PEACE WITHOUT VICTORY" ADDRESS
22 January 1917

As the tenuous relationship between Germany and the United States con-
tinued to deteriorate, Woodrow Wilson made a late appeal for peace. In
January 1917 he asked the Senate to consider a conclusion to the First
World War without a clear or decisive victory for either side. Wilson
appealed to the same universal benefit of peace that would later character-
ize his campaign for a League of Nations.

To the Senate of the United States:

Gentlemen of the Senate . . .

. . . I have sought this opportunity to address you because I thought that I
owed it to you, as the counsel associated with me in the final determination of
our international obligations, to disclose to you without reserve the thought and
purpose that have been taking form in my mind in regard to the duty of our
Government in the days to come when it will be necessary to lay afresh and
upon a new plan the foundations of Peace among the nations.

It is inconceivable that the people of the United States should play no part in
that great enterprise. . . . They cannot in honor withhold the service to which
they are now about to be challenged. They do not wish to withhold it. But they
owe it to themselves and to the other nations of the world to state the conditions
under which they will feel free to render it.

That service is nothing less than this, to add their authority and their power
to the authority and force of other nations to guarantee peace and justice
throughout the world. Such a settlement cannot now be long postponed. It is
right that before it comes this Government should frankly formulate the conditions upon which it would feel justified in asking our people to approve its
formal and solemn adherence to a League for Peace. I am here to attempt to
state those conditions.

The present war must first be ended; but we owe it to candor and to a just
regard for the opinion of mankind to say that, so far as our participation in
guarantees of future peace is concerned, it makes a great deal of difference in
what way and upon what terms it is ended. The treaties and agreements which
bring it to an end must embody terms which will create a peace that is worth
guaranteeing and preserving, a peace that will win the approval of mankind, not
merely a peace that will serve the several interests and immediate aims of the
nations engaged. . . .

No covenant of co-operative peace that does not include the peoples of the
New World can suffice to keep the future safe against war; and yet there is only

one sort of peace that the peoples of America could join in guaranteeing. The elements of that peace must be elements that engage the confidence and satisfy the principles of the American governments, elements consistent with their political faith and with the practical convictions which the peoples of America have once for all embraced and undertaken to defend. . . .

It will be absolutely necessary that a force be created as a guarantor of the permanency of the settlement so much greater than the force of any nation now engaged or any alliance hitherto formed or projected that no nation, no probable combination of nations could face or withstand it. If the peace presently to be made is to endure, it must be a peace made secure by the organized major force of mankind.

The terms of the immediate peace agreed upon will determine whether it is a peace for which such a guarantee can be secured. The question upon which the whole future peace and policy of the world depends is this: Is the present war a struggle for a just and secure peace, or only for a new balance of power? If it be only a struggle for a new balance of power, who will guarantee, who can guarantee the stable equilibrium of the new arrangement? Only a tranquil Europe can be a stable Europe. There must be, not a balance of power, but a community of power; not organized rivalries, but an organized common peace. Fortunately we have received very explicit assurances on this point. . . . I think it will be serviceable if I attempt to set forth what we understand them to be.

They imply, first of all, that it must be a peace without victory. It is not pleasant to say this. I beg that I may be permitted to put my own interpretation upon it and that it may be understood that no other interpretation was in my thought. I am seeking only to face realities and to face them without soft concealments. Victory would mean peace forced upon the loser, a victor's terms imposed upon the vanquished. It would be accepted in humiliation, under duress, at an intolerable sacrifice, and would leave a sting, a resentment, a bitter memory upon which terms of peace would rest, not permanently but only as upon quicksand. Only a peace between equals can last. Only a peace the very principle of which is equality and a common participation in a common benefit. The right state of mind, the right feeling between nations, is as necessary for a lasting peace as is the just settlement of questions of territory or of racial and national allegiance.

The equality of nations upon which peace must be founded if it is to last must be an equality of rights; the guarantees exchanged must neither recognize nor imply a difference between big nations and small, between those that are powerful and those that are weak. Right must be based upon the common strength, not upon the individual strength, of the nations upon whose concert peace will depend. Equality of territory or of resources there of course cannot be; nor any sort of equality not gained in the ordinary peaceful and legitimate development of the peoples themselves. But no one asks or expects anything more than an equality of rights. Mankind is looking now for freedom of life, not for equipoises of power.

And there is a deeper thing involved than even equality of right among organized nations. No peace can last, or ought to last, which does not recognize and accept the principle that governments derive all their just powers from the consent of the governed, and that no right anywhere exists to hand peoples about from sovereignty to sovereignty as if they were property. I take it for granted, for instance, if I may venture upon a single example, that statesmen everywhere are agreed that there should be a united, independent, and autonomous Poland and that henceforth inviolable security of life, of worship, and of industrial and social development should be guarantee to all peoples who have lived hitherto under the power of governments devoted to a faith and purpose hostile to their own. . . .

So far as practicable, moreover, every great people now struggling towards a full development of its resources and of its powers should be assured a direct outlet to the great highways of the sea. Where this cannot be done by the cession of territory, it can no doubt be done by the neutralization of direct rights of way under the general guarantee which will assure the peace itself. With a right comity of arrangement no nation need be shut away from free access to the open paths of the world's commerce.

And the paths of the sea must alike in law and in fact be free. The freedom of the seas is the *sine qua non* of peace, equality, and cooperation. No doubt a somewhat radical reconsideration of many of the rules of international practice hitherto thought to be established may be necessary in order to make the seas indeed free and common in practically all circumstances for the use of mankind, but the motive for such changes is convincing and compelling. There can be no trust or intimacy between the peoples of the world without them. The free, constant, unthreatened intercourse of nations is an essential part of the process of peace and of development. It need not be difficult either to define or to secure the freedom of the seas if the governments of the world sincerely desire to come to an agreement concerning it.

It is a problem closely connected with the limitation of naval armaments and the co-operation of the navies of the world in keeping the seas at once free and safe. And the question of limiting naval armaments opens the wider and perhaps more difficult question of the limitation of armies and of all programs of military preparation. Difficult and delicate as these questions are, they must be faced with the utmost candor and decided in a spirit of real accommodation if peace is to come with healing in its wings, and come to stay. Peace cannot be had without concession and sacrifice. There can be no sense of safety and equality among the nations if great preponderating armaments are henceforth to continue here and there to be built up and maintained. The statesmen of the world must plan for peace and nations must adjust and accommodate their policy to it as they have planned for war and made ready for pitiless contest and rivalry. The question of armaments, whether on land or sea, is the most immediately and intensely practical question connected with the future fortunes of nations and of mankind.

I have spoken upon these great matters without reserve and with the utmost explicitness because it has seemed to me to be necessary if the world's yearning desire for peace was anywhere to find free voice and utterance. Perhaps I am the only person in high authority amongst all the peoples of the world who is at liberty to speak and hold nothing back. I am speaking as an individual, and yet I am speaking also, of course, as the responsible head of a great government, and I feel confident that I have said what the people of the United States would wish me to say. . . .

I am proposing, as it were, that the nations should with one accord adopt the doctrine of President Monroe as the doctrine of the world: that no nation should seek to extend its polity over any other nation or people, but that every people should be left free to determine its own polity, its own way of development, unhindered, unthreatened, unafraid, the little along with the great and powerful.

I am proposing that all nations henceforth avoid entangling alliances which would draw them into competitions of power; catch them in a net of intrigue and selfish rivalry, and disturb their own affairs with influences intruded from without. There is no entangling alliance in a concert of power. When all unite to act in the same sense and with the same purpose all act in the common interest and are free to live their own lives under a common protection.

I am proposing government by the consent of the governed; that freedom of the seas which in international conference after conference representatives of the United States have urged with the eloquence of those who are the convinced disciples of liberty; and that moderation of armaments which makes of armies and navies a power for order merely, not an instrument of aggression or of selfish violence.

These are American principles, American policies. We could stand for no others. And they are also the principles and policies of forward looking men and women everywhere, of every modern nation, of every enlightened community. They are the principles of mankind and must prevail.

Source: James D. Richardson, ed., *A Compilation of the Messages and Papers of the Presidents*, vol. 17 (New York: Bureau of National Literature, 1917), 8199–8204.

---

63. THE ZIMMERMAN NOTE
1917

In early 1917, the German Foreign Office telegraphed its embassy in Mexico instructing it to propose an alliance between the two countries. In exchange, it offered Mexico the prospect of recovering territories lost to the United States in 1848. Unfortunately for Berlin, the telegram was intercepted by British operatives and provided to the American press. The

message was a bombshell when released in 1917, inflaming an American
public already antagonized by mounting civilian losses at sea.

Berlin, January 19, 1917

On the first of February we intend to begin submarine warfare unrestricted.
In spite of this it is our intention to keep neutral the United States of America.

If this attempt is not successful we propose an alliance on the following basis
with Mexico: That we shall make war together and together make peace. We
shall give general financial support, and it is understood that Mexico is to re-
conquer the lost territory in New Mexico, Texas, and Arizona. The details are
left for your settlement.

You are instructed to inform the President of Mexico of the above in the great
confidence as soon as it is certain there will be an outbreak of war with the
United States, and we suggest that the President of Mexico on his own initiative
should communicate with Japan suggesting adherence at once to this plan; at
the same time offer to mediate between Germany and Japan.

Please call to the attention of the President of Mexico that the employment
of ruthless submarine warfare now promises to compel England to make peace
in a few months.

Zimmerman.

Source: Henry Steele Commager, *Documents of American History*, vol. 2 (Englewood
Cliffs, NJ: Prentice Hall, 1973), 128.

---

64. WILSON'S REQUEST FOR A DECLARATION OF WAR ON GERMANY
2 April 1917

Germany's announcement that it would resume unrestricted submarine
warfare in February 1917 was the final straw for the Wilson administra-
tion. The United States formally severed diplomatic relations that month.
Faced with record shipping losses, Wilson called Congress into extraor-
dinary session to request a declaration of war.

I have called the Congress into extraordinary session because there are serious, very serious choices of policy to be made, and made immediately, which
it was neither right nor constitutionally permissible that I should assume the
responsibility of making.

On the third of February last I officially laid before you the extraordinary
announcement of the Imperial German Government that on and after the first
day of February it was its purpose to put aside all restraints of law or of hu-

manity and use its submarines to sink every vessel that sought to approach either the ports of Great Britain and Ireland or the western coasts of Europe or any of the ports controlled by the enemies of Germany within the Mediterranean. That had seemed to be the object of the German submarine warfare earlier in the war, but since April of last year the Imperial Government had somewhat restrained the commanders of its undersea craft in conformity with its promise then given to us that passenger boats should not be sunk and that due warning would be given to all other vessels which its submarines might seek to destroy, when no resistance was offered or escape attempted, and care taken that their crews were given at least a fair chance to save their lives in their open boats. The precautions taken were meager and haphazard enough, as was proved in distressing instance after instance in the progress of the cruel and unmanly business, but a certain degree of restraint was observed. The new policy has swept every restriction aside. Vessels of every kind, whatever their flag, their character, their cargo, their destination, their errand, have been ruthlessly sent to the bottom without warning and without thought of help or mercy for those on board, the vessels of friendly neutrals along with those of belligerents. Even hospital ships and ships carrying relief to the sorely bereaved and stricken people of Belgium, though the latter were provided with safe conduct through the proscribed areas by the German Government itself and were distinguished by unmistakable marks of identity, have been sunk with the same reckless lack of compassion or of principle.

I was for a little while unable to believe that such things would in fact be done by any government that had hitherto subscribed to the humane practices of civilized nations. International law had its origin in the attempt to set up some law which would be respected and observed upon the seas, where no nation had right of dominion and where lay the free highways of the world. . . . This minimum of right the German Government has swept aside under the plea of retaliation and necessity and because it had no weapons, which it could use at sea except these [U-Boats] which it is impossible to employ as it is employing them without throwing to the winds all scruples of humanity or of respect for the understandings that were supposed to underlie the intercourse of the world. I am not now thinking of the loss of property involved, immense and serious as that is, but only of the wanton and wholesale destruction of the lives of noncombatants, men, women, and children, engaged in pursuits which have always, even in the darkest periods of modern history, been deemed innocent and legitimate. Property can be paid for; the lives of peaceful and innocent people cannot be. The present German submarine warfare against commerce is a warfare against mankind.

It is a war against all nations. American ships have been sunk, American lives taken, in ways which it has stirred us very deeply to learn of, but the ships and people of other neutral and friendly nations have been sunk and overwhelmed in the waters in the same way. There has been no discrimination. The challenge is to all mankind. Each nation must decide for itself how it will meet it. The choice we make for ourselves must be made with a moderation of counsel and a temperateness of judgment befitting our character and our motives as a nation. We must put excited feeling away. Our motive will not be revenge or the victorious assertion of the physical might of the nation, but only the vindication of right, of human right, of which we are only a single champion.

When I addressed the Congress on the twenty-sixth of February last I thought that it would suffice to assert our neutral rights with arms, our right to use the seas against unlawful interference, our right to keep our people safe against unlawful violence. But armed neutrality, it now appears, is impracticable. Because submarines are in effect outlaws when used as the German submarines have been used against merchant shipping, it is impossible to defend ships against their attacks as the law of nations has assumed that merchantmen would defend themselves against privateers or cruisers, visible craft giving chase upon the open sea. It is common prudence in such circumstances, grim necessity indeed, to endeavor to destroy them before they have shown their own intention. They must be dealt with upon sight, if dealt with at all. The German Government denies the right of neutrals to use arms at all within the areas of the sea which it has proscribed, even in the defense of rights which no modern publicist has ever before questioned their right to defend. The intimation is conveyed that the armed guards which we have placed on our merchant ships will be treated as beyond the pale of law and subject to be dealt with as pirates would be. Armed neutrality is ineffectual enough at best; in such circumstances and in the face of such pretensions it is worse than ineffectual: it is likely only to produce what it was meant to prevent; it is practically certain to draw us into the war without either the rights or the effectiveness of belligerents. There is one choice we cannot make, we are incapable of making: we will not choose the path of submission and suffer the most sacred rights of our Nation and our people to be ignored or violated. The wrongs against which we now array ourselves are no common wrongs; they cut to the very roots of human life.

With a profound sense of the solemn and even tragical character of the step I am taking and of the grave responsibilities which it involves, but in unhesitating obedience to what I deem my constitutional duty, I advise that the Congress declare the recent course of the Imperial German Government to be in fact nothing less than war against the government and people of the United States; that it formally accept the status of belligerent which has thus been thrust upon it; and that it take immediate steps not only to put the country in a more thorough state of defense but also to exert all its power and employ all its resources to bring the Government of the German Empire to terms and end the war.

What this will involve is clear. It will involve the utmost practicable cooperation in counsel and action with the governments now at war with Germany, and, as incident to that, the extension to those governments of the most liberal financial credits, in order that our resources may so far as possible be added to theirs. It will involve the organization and mobilization of all the material resources of the country to supply the materials of war and serve the incidental needs of the Nation in the most abundant and yet the most economical and efficient way possible. It will involve the immediate full equipment of the navy in all respects but particularly in supplying it with the best means of dealing with the enemy's submarines. It will involve the immediate addition to the armed forces of the United States already provided for by law in case of war at least five hundred thousand men, who should, in my opinion, be chosen upon the principle of universal liability to service, and also the authorization of subsequent additional increments of equal force so soon as they may be needed and can be handled in training. It will involve also, of course, the granting of adequate credits to the Government, sustained, I hope, so far as they can equitably be sustained by the present generation, by well conceived taxation. . . .

While we do these things, these deeply momentous things, let us be very clear, and make very clear to all the world what our motives and our objects are. My own thought has not been driven from its habitual and normal course by the unhappy events of the last two months, and I do not believe the thought of the Nation has been altered or clouded by them. I have exactly the same things in mind now that I had in mind when I addressed the Senate on the twenty-second of January last; the same that I had in mind when I addressed the Congress on the third of February and on the twenty-sixth February. Our object now, as then, is to vindicate the principles of peace and justice in the life of the world as against selfish and autocratic power and to set up amongst the really free and self-governed peoples of the world such a concert of purpose and of action as will henceforth insure the observance of those principles. Neutrality is no longer feasible or desirable where the peace of the world is involved and the freedom of its peoples, and the menace to that peace and freedom lies in the existence of autocratic governments backed by organized force which is controlled wholly by their will, not by the will of their people. We have seen the last of neutrality in such circumstances. We are at the beginning of an age in which it will be insisted that the same standards of conduct and of responsibility for wrong done shall be observed among nations and their governments that are observed among the individual citizens of civilized states.

We have no quarrel with the German people. We have no feeling towards them but one of sympathy and friendship. It was not upon their impulse that their government acted in entering this war. It was not with their previous knowledge or approval. It was a war determined upon as wars used to be determined upon in the old, unhappy days when peoples were nowhere consulted by their rulers and wars were provoked and waged in the interest of dynasties or of little groups of ambitious men who were accustomed to use their fellow men as pawns and tools. . . .

We are accepting this challenge of hostile purpose because we know that in such a Government, following such methods, we can never have a friend; and that in the presence of its organized power, always lying in wait to accomplish we know not what purpose, there can be no assured security for the democratic

Governments of the world. We are now about to accept gauge of battle with this natural foe to liberty and shall, if necessary, spend the whole force of the nation to check and nullify its pretensions and its power. We are glad, now that we see the facts with no veil of false pretense about them, to fight thus for the ultimate peace of the world and for the liberation of its peoples, the German peoples included: for the rights of nations great and small and the privilege of men everywhere to choose their way of life and of obedience. The world must be made safe for democracy. Its peace must be planted upon the tested foundations of political liberty. We have no selfish ends to serve. We desire no conquest, no dominion. We seek no indemnities for ourselves, no material compensation for the sacrifices we shall freely make. We are but one of the champions of the rights of mankind. We shall be satisfied when those rights have been made as secure as the faith and the freedom of nations can make them.

Just because we fight without rancor and without selfish object, seeking nothing for ourselves but what we shall wish to share with all free peoples, we shall, I feel confident, conduct our operations as belligerents without passion and ourselves observe with proud punctilio the principles of right and of fair play we profess to be fighting for.

I have said nothing of the Governments allied with the Imperial Government of Germany because they have not made war upon us or challenged us to defend our right and our honor. The Austro-Hungarian Government has, indeed, avowed its unqualified indorsement and acceptance of the reckless and lawless submarine warfare adopted now without disguise by the Imperial German Government, and it has therefore not been possible for this Government to receive Count Tarnowski, the Ambassador recently accredited to this Government by the Imperial and Royal Government of Austria-Hungary; but that Government has not actually engaged in warfare against citizens of the United States on the seas, and I take the liberty, for the present at least, of postponing a discussion of our relations with the authorities at Vienna. We enter this war only where we are clearly forced into it because there are no other means of defending our rights.

It will be all the easier for us to conduct ourselves as belligerents in a high spirit of right and fairness because we act without animus, not in enmity towards a people or with the desire to bring any injury or disadvantage upon them, but only in armed opposition to an irresponsible government which has thrown aside all considerations of humanity and of right and is running amuck. We are, let me say again, the sincere friends of the German people, and shall desire nothing so much as the early reestablishment of intimate relations of mutual advantage between us—however hard it may be for them, for the time being, to believe that this is spoken from—our hearts. We have borne with their present Government through all these bitter months because of that friendship,—exercising a patience and forbearance which would otherwise have been impossible. We shall, happily, still have an opportunity to prove that friendship in our daily attitude and actions towards the millions of men and women of German birth and native sympathy who live amongst us and share our life, and we shall be proud to prove it towards all who are in fact loyal to their neighbors and to the Government in the hour of test. They are, most of them, as true and loyal Americans as if they had never known any other fealty or allegiance. They will be prompt to stand with us in rebuking and restraining the few who may be of a different mind and purpose. If there should be disloyalty, it will be dealt with with a firm hand of stern repression; but, if it lifts its head at all, it will lift it only here and there and without countenance except from a lawless and malignant few.

It is a distressing and oppressive duty, Gentlemen of the Congress, which I have performed in thus addressing you. There are, it may be, many months of fiery trial and sacrifice ahead of us. It is a fearful thing to lead this great peaceful people into war, into the most terrible and disastrous of all wars, civilization itself seeming to be in the balance. But the right is more precious than peace, and we shall fight for the things which we have always carried nearest our hearts,—for democracy, for the right of those who submit to authority to have a voice in their own Governments, for the rights and liberties of small nations, for a universal dominion of right by such a concert of free peoples as shall bring peace and safety to all nations and make the world itself at last free. To such a task we can dedicate our lives and our fortunes, everything that we are and everything that we have, with the pride of those who know that the day has come when America is privileged to spend her blood and her might for the principles that gave her birth and happiness and the peace which she has treasured. God helping her, she can do no other.

Source: James D. Richardson, ed., *A Compilation of the Messages and Papers of the Presidents*, vol. 17 (New York: Bureau of National Literature, 1917), 8226–33.

65. THE LANSING-ISHII AGREEMENT
1917

In 1915 Japan announced to the world that she would not be bound by the Open Door policy. Two years later, the Viscount Ishii traveled to the United States to negotiate a modification of its China policy. The subsequent agreement signed in November reaffirmed the Open Door notes, but recognized Japan's special interests in China.

Department of State
Washington, November 2, 1917

Excellency: I have the honor to communicate herein my understanding of the agreement reached by us in our recent conversations touching the questions of mutual interest to our Governments relating to the Republic of China.

In order to silence mischievous reports that have from time to time been circulated, it is believed by us that a public announcement once more of the desires and intentions shared by our two Governments with regard to China is advisable.

The Governments of the United States and Japan recognize that territorial propinquity creates special relations between countries, and consequently the Government of the United States recognizes that Japan has special interests in China, particularly in that part to which her possessions are contiguous.

The territorial sovereignty of China, nevertheless, remains unimpaired, and the Government of the United States has every confidence in the repeated assurances of the Imperial Japanese Government that while geographical position gives Japan such special interests, they have no desire to discriminate against the trade of other nations or to disregard the commercial rights heretofore granted by China in treaties with other powers.

The Governments of the United States and Japan deny that they have any purpose to infringe in any way the independence territorial integrity of China, and they declare furthermore, that they always adhere to the principle of the so-called "open-door" or equal opportunity for commerce and industry in China.

Moreover, they mutually declare that they are opposed to the acquisition by any government of any special rights or privileges that would affect the independence or territorial integrity of China, or that would deny to the subjects or citizens of any country the full enjoyment of equal opportunity in the commerce and industry of China.

I shall be glad to have Your Excellency confirm this understanding of the agreement reached by us.

Accept, Excellency, the renewed assurance of my highest consideration.

Robert Lansing.

His Excellency
    Viscount Kikujiro Ishii
        Ambassador Extraordinary and Plenipotentiary of Japan, on Special Mission.

Source: William M. Malloy, ed., *Treaties, Conventions, International Acts, Protocols, and Agreements between the United States and Other Powers, 1910–1923*, vol. 3 (Washington, DC: Government Printing Office, 1923), 2720–22.

66. WILSON'S FOURTEEN POINTS
8 January 1918

Woodrow Wilson's address to Congress in January 1918 was a basic statement of his wartime goals. In the short term, the president hoped to bolster flagging Allied morale. More important, the fourteen points offered the basic template for Wilson's vision of the post-war international order.

Gentlemen of the Congress:

... It will be our wish and purpose that the processes of peace, when they are begun, shall be absolutely open and that they shall involve and permit henceforth no secret understandings of any kind. The day of conquest and aggrandizement is gone by; so is also the day of secret covenants entered into in the interest of particular governments and likely at some unlooked-for moment to upset the peace of the world. It is this happy fact, now clear to the view of every public man whose thoughts do not still linger in an age that is dead and gone, which makes it possible for every nation whose purposes are consistent with justice and the peace of the world to avow now or at any other time the objects it has in view.

We entered this war because violations of right had occurred which touched us to the quick and made the life of our own people impossible unless they were corrected and the world secured once for all against their recurrence. What we demand in this war, therefore, is nothing peculiar to ourselves. It is that the world be made fit and safe to live in; and particularly that it be made safe for every peace-loving nation which, like our own, wishes to live its own life, determine its own institutions, be assured of justice and fair dealing by the other peoples of the world as against force and selfish aggression. All the peoples of the world are in effect partners in this interest, and for our own part we see very clearly that unless justice be done to others it will not be done to us. The program of the world's peace, therefore, is our program; and that program, the only possible program, as we see it, is this:

I. Open covenants of peace, openly arrived at, after which there shall be no private international understandings of any kind but diplomacy shall proceed always frankly and in the public view.

II. Absolute freedom of navigation upon the seas, outside territorial waters, alike in peace and in war, except as the seas may be closed in whole or in part by international action for the enforcement of international covenants.

III. The removal, so far as possible, of all economic barriers and the establishment of an equality of trade conditions among all the nations consenting to the peace and associating themselves for its maintenance.

IV. Adequate guarantees given and taken that national armaments will be reduced to the lowest point consistent with domestic safety.

V. A free, open-minded, and absolutely impartial adjustment of all colonial claims, based upon a strict observance of the principle that in determining all such questions of sovereignty the interests of the populations concerned must have equal weight with the equitable claims of the government whose title is to be determined.

VI. The evacuation of all Russian territory and such a settlement of all questions affecting Russia as will secure the best and freest cooperation of the other nations of the world in obtaining for her an unhampered and unembarrassed opportunity for the independent determination of her own political development and national policy and assure her of a sincere welcome into the society of free nations under institutions of her own choosing; and, more than a welcome, assistance also of every kind that she may need and may herself desire. The treatment accorded Russia by her sister nations in the months to come will be the acid test of their good will, of their comprehension of her needs as distinguished from their own interests, and of their intelligent and unselfish sympathy.

VII. Belgium, the whole world will agree, must be evacuated and restored, without any attempt to limit the sovereignty which she enjoys in common with all other free nations. No other single act will serve as this will serve to restore confidence among the nations in the laws which they have themselves set and determined for the government of their relations with one another. Without this healing act the whole structure and validity of international law is forever impaired.

VIII. All French territory should be freed and the invaded portions restored, and the wrong done to France by Prussia in 1871 in the matter of Alsace-Lorraine, which has unsettled the peace of the world for nearly fifty years, should be righted, in order that peace may once more be made secure in the interest of all.

IX. A readjustment of the frontiers of Italy should be effected along clearly recognizable lines of nationality.

X. The peoples of Austria-Hungary, whose place among the nations we wish to see safe-guarded and assured, should be accorded the freest opportunity of autonomous development.

XI. Rumania, Serbia, and Montenegro should be evacuated; occupied territories restored; Serbia accorded free and secure access to the sea; and the relations of the several Balkan states to one another determined by friendly counsel along historically established lines of allegiance and nationality; and international guarantees of the political and economic independence and territorial integrity of the several Balkan states should be entered into.

XII. The Turkish portions of the present Ottoman Empire should be assured a secure sovereignty, but the other nationalities which are now under Turkish rule should be assured an undoubted security of life and an absolutely unmolested opportunity of autonomous development, and the Dardanelles should be permanently opened as a free passage to the ships and commerce of all nations under international guarantees.

XIII. An independent Polish state should be erected which should include the territories inhabited by indisputably Polish populations, which should be assured a free and secure access to the sea, and whose political and economic independence and territorial integrity should be guaranteed by international covenant.

XIV. A general association of nations must be formed under specific covenants for the purpose of affording mutual guarantees of political independence and territorial integrity to great and small states alike.

In regard to these essential rectifications of wrong and assertions of right we feel ourselves to be intimate partners of all the governments and peoples associated together against the Imperialists. We cannot be separated in interest or divided in purpose. We stand together until the end.

For such arrangements and covenants we are willing to fight and to continue to fight until they are achieved; but only because we wish the right to prevail and desire a just and stable peace such as can be secured only by removing the chief provocations to war, which this program does not remove. We have no jealousy of German greatness, and there is nothing in this program that impairs it. We grudge her no achievement or distinction of learning or of pacific enterprise such as have made her record very bright and very enviable. We do not wish to injure her or to block in any way her legitimate influence or power. We do not wish to fight her either with arms or with hostile arrangements of trade if she is willing to associate herself with us and the other peace-loving nations of the world in covenants of justice and law and fair dealing. We wish her only to accept a place of equality among the peoples of the world—the new world in which we now live—instead of a place of mastery.

Neither do we presume to suggest to her any alteration or modification of her institutions. But it is necessary, we must frankly say, and necessary as a preliminary to any intelligent dealings with her on our part, that we should know whom her spokesmen speak for when they speak to us, whether for the Reichstag majority or for the military party and the men whose creed is imperial domination.

We have spoken now, surely, in terms too concrete to admit of any further doubt or question. An evident principle runs through the whole program I have outlined. It is the principle of justice to all peoples and nationalities, and their right to live on equal terms of liberty and safety with one another, whether they be strong or weak. Unless this principle be made its foundation no part of the structure of international justice can stand. The people of the United States could act upon no other principle; and to the vindication of this principle they are ready to devote their lives, their honor, and everything that they possess. The moral climax of this the culminating and final war for human liberty has come, and they are ready to put their own strength, their own highest purpose, their own integrity and devotion to the test.

Source: Henry Steele Commager, *Documents of American History*, vol. 2 (Englewood Cliffs, NJ: Prentice Hall, 1973), 137–39.

67. WILSON'S EXPOSITION OF THE LEAGUE OF NATIONS TO THE SENATE FOREIGN RELATIONS COMMITTEE
19 August 1919

The Senate received both the Treaty of Versailles and the Covenant of the League of Nations in July 1919. Wilson subsequently provided legislators with a letter to assuage concerns regarding the Covenant's jurisdiction over the domestic affairs of member nations and the obligations it required for mutual security.

MR. CHAIRMAN:

I have taken the liberty of writing out a little statement in the hope that it might faciliate discussion by speaking directly on some points that I know have been points of controversy and upon which I thought an expression of opinion would not be unwelcome. . . .

Nothing, I am led to believe, stands in the way of ratification of the treaty except certain doubts with regard to the meaning and implication of certain articles of the Covenant of the League of Nations; and I must frankly say that I am unable to understand why such doubts should be entertained. You will recall that when I had the pleasure of a conference with your committee and with the committee of the House of Representatives on Foreign Affairs at the White House in March last the questions now most frequently asked about the League of Nations were all canvassed with a view to their immediate clarification. The Covenant of the League was then in its first draft and subject to revision. It was pointed out that no express recognition was given to the Monroe Doctrine; that it was not expressly provided that the League should have no authority to act or to express a judgment on matters of domestic policy; that the right to withdraw from the League was not expressly recognized; and that the constitutional right of the Congress to determine all questions of peace and war was not sufficiently safeguarded. On my return to Paris all these matters were taken up again by the Commission on the League of Nations and every suggestion of the United States was accepted.

The views of the United States with regard to the questions I have mentioned had, in fact, already been accepted by the commission and there was supposed to be nothing inconsistent with them in the draft of the Covenant first adopted—the draft which was the subject of our discussion in March—but no objection was made to saying explicitly in the text what all had supposed to be implicit in it. There was absolutely no doubt as to the meaning of any one of the resulting provisions of the Covenant in the minds of those who participated in drafting them, and I respectfully submit that there is nothing vague or doubtful in their wording.

The Monroe Doctrine is expressly mentioned as an understanding which is in no way to be impaired or interfered with by anything contained in the covenant and the expression "regional understandings like the Monroe Doctrine" was used, not because any one of the conferees thought there was any comparable agreement anywhere else in existence or in contemplation, but only because it was thought best to avoid the appearance of dealing in such a document with the policy of a single nation. Absolutely nothing is concealed in the phrase.

With regard to domestic questions Article 16 of the Covenant expressly provides that, if in case of any dispute arising between members of the League the matter involved is claimed by one of the parties "and is found by the council to arise out of a matter which by international law is solely within the domestic jurisdiction of that party, the council shall so report, and shall make no recommendation as to its settlement." The United States was by no means the only Government interested in the explicit adoption of this provision, and there is no doubt in the mind of any authoritative student of international law that such matters as immigration, tariffs, and naturalization are incontestably domestic questions with which no international body could deal without express authority to do so. No enumeration of domestic questions was undertaken because to undertake it, even by sample, would have involved the danger of seeming to exclude those not mentioned.

The right of any sovereign State to withdraw had been taken for granted, but no objection was made to making it explicit. Indeed, so soon as the views expressed at the White House conference were laid before the commission it was at once conceded that it was best not to leave the answer to so important a question to inference. No proposal was made to set up any tribunal to pass judgment upon the question whether a withdrawing nation had in fact fulfilled "all its international obligations and all its obligations under the covenant." It was recognized that that question must be left to be resolved by the conscience of the Nation proposing to withdraw; and I must say that it did not seem to me worth while to propose that the article be made more explicit, because I knew that the United States would never itself propose to withdraw from the League if its conscience was not entirely clear as to the fulfillment of all its international obligations. It has never failed to fulfill them and never will.

Article 10 is in no respect of doubtful meaning when read in the light of the covenant as a whole. The council of the League can only "advise upon" the means by which the obligations of that great article are to be given effect to. Unless the United States is a party to the policy or action in question, her own affirmative vote in the council is necessary before any advice can be given, for a unanimous vote of the council is required. If she is a party, the trouble is hers anyhow. And the unanimous vote of the council is only advice in any case. Each Government is free to reject it if it pleases. Nothing could have been made more clear to the conference than the right of our Congress under our Constitution to exercise its independent judgment in all matters of peace and war. No attempt was made to question or limit that right.

The United States will, indeed, undertake under Article 10 to "respect and preserve as against external aggression the territorial integrity and existing political independence of all members of the League," and that engagement constitutes a very grave and solemn moral obligation. But it is a moral, not a legal, obligation, and leaves our Congress absolutely free to put its own interpretation upon it in all cases that call for action. It is binding in conscience only, not in law.

Article 10 seems to me to constitute the very backbone of the whole covenant. Without it the League would be hardly more than an influential debating society.

It has several times been suggested, in public debate and in private conference, that interpretations of the sense in which the United States accepts the engagements of the covenant should be embodied in the instrument of ratification. There can be no reasonable objection to such interpretations accompanying the act of ratification provided they do not form a part of the formal ratification itself. Most of the interpretations which have been suggested to me embody what seems to me the plain meaning of the instrument itself. But if such interpretations should constitute a part of the formal resolution of ratification, long delays would be the inevitable consequence, inasmuch as all the many Governments concerned would have to accept, in effect, the language of the Senate as the language of the treaty before ratification would be complete. The assent of the German Assembly at Weimar would have to be obtained, among the rest, and I must frankly say that I could only with the greatest reluctance approach that Assembly for permission to read the treaty as we understand it and as those who framed it quite certainly understood it. If the United States were to qualify the document in any way moreover, I am confident from what I know of the many conferences and debates which accompanied the formulation of the treaty that our example would immediately be followed in many quarters, in some instances with very serious reservations, and that the meaning and operative force of the treaty would presently be clouded from one end of its clauses to the other.

Pardon me, Mr. Chairman, if I have been entirely unreserved and plain-spoken in speaking of the great matters we all have so much at heart. If excuse is needed, I trust that the critical situation of affairs may serve as my justification. The issues that manifestly hang upon the conclusions of the Senate with regard to peace and upon the time of its action are so grave and so clearly insusceptible of being thrust on one side or postponed that I have felt it necessary in the public interest to make this urgent plea, and to make it as simply and as unreservedly as possible.

I thought that the simplest way, Mr. Chairman, to cover the points that I knew to be points of interest.

Source: Henry Steele Commager, *Documents of American History*, vol. 2 (Englewood Cliffs, NJ: Prentice Hall, 1973), 158–60.

---

68. DEFEAT OF THE LEAGUE OF NATIONS
19 March 1920

The debate over the League of Nations raged throughout the summer of 1919 and well into the following year. Woodrow Wilson pressed for its acceptance and found that he was opposed by senators clustered around Henry Cabot Lodge. Lodge's primary objection was to Article 10, which required League members to defend each other against external aggression. An initial vote, held on November 19, failed to pass the League of Nations. A final vote on 19 March 1920 lacked the two-thirds votes necessary for ratification.

The PRESIDENT pro tempore. Upon agreeing to the resolution of ratification the yeas are 49 and the nays are 35. Not having received the affirmative votes of two-thirds of the Senators present and voting, the resolution is not agreed to, and the Senate does not advise and consent to the ratification of the treaty of peace with Germany.

The resolution of ratification voted upon and rejected is as follows:

Resolution of ratification.

Resolved (two-thirds of the Senators present concurring therein), That the Senate advise and consent to the ratification of the treaty of peace with Germany concluded at Versailles on the 28th day of June, 1919, subject to the following reservations and understandings, which are hereby made a part and condition of this resolution of ratification, which ratification is not to take effect or bind the United States until the said reservations and understandings adopted by the Senate have been accepted as a part and a condition of this resolution of ratification by the allied and associated powers and a failure on the part of the allied and associated powers to make objection to said reservations and understandings prior to the deposit of ratification by the United States shall be taken as a full and final acceptance of such reservations and understandings by said powers:

1. The United States so understands and construes article 1 that in case of notice of withdrawal from the League of Nations, as provided in said article, the United States shall be the sole judge as to whether all its international obligations and all its obligations under the said covenant have been fulfilled, and notice of withdrawal by the United States may be given by a concurrent resolution of the Congress of the United States.

2. The United States assumes no obligation to preserve the territorial integrity or political independence of any other country by the employment of its military or naval forces, its resources, or any form of economic discrimination, or to interfere in any way in controversies between nations, including all controversies relating to territorial integrity or political independence, whether members of the league or not, under the provisions of article 10, or to employ the military or naval forces of the United States, under any article of the treaty for any purpose, unless in any particular case the Congress, which, under the Constitution, has the sole power to declare war or authorize the employment of the military or naval forces of the United States, shall, in the exercise of full liberty of action, by act or joint resolution so provide.

3. No mandate shall be accepted by the United States under article 22, part 1, or any other provision on the treaty of peace with Germany, except by action of the Congress of the United States.

4. The United States reserves to itself exclusively the right to decide what questions are within its domestic jurisdiction and declares that all domestic and political questions relating wholly or in part to its internal affairs, including immigration, labor, coastwise traffic, the tariff, commerce, the suppression of traffic in women and children and in opium and other dangerous drugs, and all other domestic questions, are solely within the jurisdiction of the United States and are not under this treaty to be submitted in any way either to arbitration or to the consideration of the council or of the assembly of the League of Nations, or any agency thereof, or to the decision or recommendation of any other power.

5. The United States will not submit to arbitration or to inquiry by the assembly or by the council of the League of Nations, provided for in said treaty of peace, any questions which in the judgment of the United States depend upon or relate to its long-established policy, commonly known as the Monroe doctrine; said doctrine is to be interpreted by the United States alone and is hereby declared to be wholly outside the jurisdiction of said League of Nations and entirely unaffected by any provision contained in the said treaty of peace with Germany.

6. The United States withholds its assent to articles 156, 157, and 158, and reserves full liberty of action with respect to any controversy which may arise under said articles.

7. No person is or shall be authorized to represent the United States, nor shall any citizen of the United States be eligible, as a member of any body or agency established or authorized by said treaty of peace with Germany, except pursuant to an act of the Congress of the United States providing for his appointment and defining his powers and duties.

8. The United States understands that the reparation commission will regulate or interfere with exports from the United States to Germany, or from Germany to the United States, only when the United States by act or joint resolution of Congress approves such regulation or interference.

9. The United States shall not be obligated to contribute to any expenses of the League of Nations, or of the secretariat, or of any commission, or committee, or conference, or other agency, organized under the League of Nations or under the treaty or for the purpose of carrying out the treaty provisions, unless and until an appropriation of funds available for such expenses shall have been made by the Congress of the United States: *Provided,* That the foregoing limitation shall not apply to the United States' proportionate share of the expense of the office force and salary of the secretary general.

10. No plan for the limitation of armaments proposed by the council of the League of Nations under the provisions of article 8 shall be held as binding the United States until the same shall have been accepted by Congress, and the United States reserves the right to increase its armament without the consent of the council whenever the United States is threatened with invasion or engaged in war.

11. The United States reserves the right to permit, in its discretion, the na-

tionals of a covenant-breaking State, as defined in article 16 of the covenant of the League of Nations, residing within the United States or in countries other than such covenant-breaking State, to continue their commercial, financial, and personal relations with the nationals of the United States.

12. Nothing in articles 296, 297, or in any of the annexes thereto or in any other article, section, or annex of the treaty of peace with Germany shall, as against citizens of United States, be taken to mean any confirmation, ratification, or approval of any act otherwise illegal or in contravention of the rights of citizens of the United States.

13. The United States withholds its assent to Part XIII (articles 387 to 427, inclusive) unless Congress by act or joint resolution shall hereafter make provision for representation in the organization established by said Part XIII, and in such event the participation of the United States will be governed and conditioned by the provisions of such act or joint resolution.

14. Until Part 1, being the covenant of the League of Nations, shall be so amended as to provide that the United States shall be entitled to cast a number of votes equal to that which any member of the league and its self-governing dominions, colonies, or parts of empire, in the aggregate shall be entitled to cast, the United States assumes no obligation to be bound, except in cases where Congress has previously given its consent, by any election, decision, report, or finding of the council or assembly in which any member of the league and its self-governing dominions, colonies, or parts of empire, in the aggregate have cast more than one vote.

The United States assumes no obligation to be bound by any decision, report, or finding of the council or assembly arising out of any dispute between the United States and any member of the league if such member, or any self-governing dominion, colony, empire, or part of empire united with it politically has voted.

15. In consenting to the ratification of the treaty with Germany the United States adheres to the principle of self-determination and to the resolution of sympathy with the aspirations of the Irish people for a government of their own choice adopted by the Senate June 6, 1919, and declares that when such government is attained by Ireland, a consummation it is hoped is at hand, it should promptly be admitted as a member of the League of Nations.

Source: Henry Steele Commager, *Documents of American History*, vol. 2 (Englewood Cliffs, NJ: Prentice Hall, 1973), 161–62.

Part Seven

The Interwar Period

America exited the Great War with a grand celebration of victory, but also with a broadly held understanding of its substantial cost. In little more than a year, 116,516 Americans died in the conflict. Another 204,002 were wounded. Few communities were left untouched by the sacrifice of so many young men.[1] Few also escaped the public passions uncapped by the domestic mobilization for the war. Wartime patriotism had illustrated a remarkable degree of national unity in a time of crisis. But it had also revealed a disturbing streak of intolerance deep within the recesses of American society. Many of the wounds suffered by the United States were self-inflicted, through its jingoism and nativism. Many of these problems were compounded by a wartime government intent on enforcing a national consensus at times without regard for the rule of law.[2] The hysteria that surrounded the Red Scare of 1919–1920 seemed to promise more of the same in the postwar.[3]

America therefore exited the Great War occupied by an interesting paradox. For the most part, the country wanted to leave the war behind and discount it as a brief, albeit necessary, exposure to the problems of the Old World. Americans seemed little interested in the jobs left unfinished by the war: the reconstruction of Europe and the nurturing of a new democracy in Weimar Germany. Instead, the general public focused on a new presidential election, the question of universal suffrage, and the prosperity beginning to take hold in a peacetime nation. Conversely, the United States stood poised in 1920 to assume an unprecedented role in world affairs. America began the new peace a creditor nation, one which controlled a major share of global capital and investment. After the First World War, the United States produced 70 percent of the world's oil and 40 percent of its coal. Between 1914 and 1930, American private investments abroad would grow from $3.5 billion to $17.2 billion. Between 1925 and 1929, 46 percent of the world's industrial goods came from the United States. New York would displace London as the world's financial capital.[4] The extensive war debt of more than $10–12 billion owed to Washington by its allies made American leverage overseas significant.[5]

The dilemma for American policy makers was reconciling entrenched domestic isolationism with a global vacuum that invited American power at almost every turn. Initially, their response was to take incremental steps toward securing some of the principles of Wilsonian internationalism. In the new decade, the United States would sponsor the cause of disarmament, particularly among the naval forces of the world's major nations. At the 1921 Washington Conference, American diplomats were able to win agreements from England, France, Italy, and Japan to restore a semblance of strategic military balance by introducing national quotas into naval construction. During negotiations over the Four Power Treaty, the signatories (the United States, Japan, Britain, and France) endorsed the Wilsonian principle of collective security in the Pacific, agreeing to "communicate with one another fully and frankly" in order to present a united front against aggression.[6] The apex of the effort to refashion international relations was the 1928 Kellogg-Briand Pact. Initially, the product of French entreaties to the United States for an alliance, the discussions between Secretary of State Frank Kellogg and French Foreign Minister Aristide Briand grew into a declaration by sixty-two nations that "outlawed" war as an instrument of national policy. The aim of the pact was to take away the legal justification for war. It was a tentative step toward the type of global collective action that Wilsonians craved. However, most of the signatories made only conditional commitments, reserving the right to defend their country in the case of conflict.

American policy in Central America and the Caribbean clearly violated the spirit of the Kellogg-Briand Pact. The American occupation and administration of the Dominican Republic (1916–1924), Haiti (1915–1934), and Nicaragua (1912–1925 and 1926–1933) reflected a desire to both protect U.S. private investments and reconstruct client nations in more stable, productive forms. The difficulty of this arrangement, particularly in the protracted and unsuccessful American campaigns against Augusto César Sandino in Nicaragua, eventually soured the public and policy makers alike to the future prospects of intervention. When Henry Stimson announced in 1931 that the United States would revert back to traditional American policy—allowing nations to regulate their own internal affairs as long as they could fulfill their obligations as a member of the family of nations—it became clear that an era of U.S. intervention in Latin America had come to a close.[7]

As official diplomacy directed its energies to arms reduction and collective security concerns, the American private sector was encouraged to assert the nation's prerogatives around the world. In one important sense, this approach harkened back to the age of Thomas Jefferson and the belief that commercial relations could be a balm for international affairs. For contemporary Americans in the 1920s the introduction of the private sector into diplomacy reflected the faith that the modernization of economic processes would make politics obsolete. In this context, Henry Ford could win agreement from former foes in the

Great War by introducing them to the techniques of mass production.[8] More important, by emphasizing the economic element in foreign policy, American leaders were able to proceed in international relations from a position of relative strength.

Consequently, private businessmen often became critical actors in American diplomacy. One such intervention occurred in 1924 when Chicago banker Charles M. Dawes arranged a $200 million bond issues loan that allowed a destitute Weimar government to start its reparations and make payments at reduced rates. With Germany solvent, billions in additional American capital flowed into the country, sustaining its national recovery for the remainder of the decade. The so-called Young Plan of 1929 took the process of privatization a step further. The brainchild of industrialist Owen D. Young, the plan reduced the total sum of German reparations to $9 billion, thus reducing the country's annual payments. The subsequent repayment amounts closely mirrored those owed the United States for its First World War loans.[9]

The commercial alternative to official policy was severely handicapped by protectionism at home. Tariff walls against foreign imports grew throughout the 1920s despite American invocations of the free-market creed. The Fordney McCumber Tariff (1922) and the Smoot-Hawley Tariff (1930) significantly raised the protective barriers against foreign products and allowed the United States to record consistent annual trade surpluses. The concurrent balance of payments problem this relationship caused placed a premium on the capital available in Europe for investment. American banks, although prodded by the Hoover administration at the end of the decade, were reluctant to make up the difference with additional loans, seeking instead higher rates of return in Latin America and Asia.[10]

The global depression of 1929 ripped away the veneer of international cooperation and exposed the weakness of cooperative diplomacy. Individual nations struggled to contend with the socioeconomic chaos that traveled in the wake of the American stock market crash. Populations desperate to regain order granted traction to totalitarian movements bent on national self-aggrandizement. The times smoothed the path for Adolf Hitler's rise to power, gave credence to Stalin's Soviet Union, and emboldened Imperial Japan to pursue territorial expansion in Asia.[11]

Faced with the devastating impact of depression at home, the United States chose neutrality as the guiding principle of its foreign policy. Franklin D. Roosevelt's dilemma was not whether the United States should involve itself in foreign affairs but when and how. In his first inaugural address Roosevelt described America as a "good neighbor" with respect to international affairs:

In the field of world policy I would dedicate this nation to the policy of the good neighbor—the neighbor who resolutely respects himself and, because he does so, respects the rights of others—the neighbor who respects the sanctity of his agreements in and with a world of neighbors.[12]

Contemporaries interpreted this as a statement of retrenchment and a recognition of the need to focus on the myriad programs contained within the confines of the New Deal. Americans accepted the new president's pledge to attend to the "evils of the old order" rather than strike out upon new paths of overseas entanglements.[13] In his first major foreign policy initiative, taken at the London Economic Conference of 1933, Roosevelt removed the United States from the gold standard and severed the country from the keystone of the global economy, bowing to domestic pressures instead of the international furor that followed his announcement.

Roosevelt, however, was not intent on indefinitely preserving American isolationism. His first two terms represented an ongoing struggle to reintroduce the United States back into the world system. His administration maintained a constant drumbeat in the public forum, depicting the darkening world situation as a threat to the average citizen and conflating the problems many Americans associated with the stock market crash with overseas affairs. Roosevelt's references to the "world of neighbors" was an echo of Wilsonianism and a call for the collective need to defend against aggression.[14]

This vision failed to resonate with the country for most of the 1930s. For much of the decade, the public mood was encapsulated in committee hearings conducted by Senator Gerald Nye in 1934. The Nye Committee condemned American entry into the First World War, in particular, and international affairs, in general. Its damning depiction of industrialists and bankers leading the nation to bloodshed involved significant speculation, but caught the imagination of an America mired in the fifth year of a depression and eager to find scapegoats for its predicament.

Public sentiments quickly coalesced into law. In 1935, Congress established basic parameters for executive authority in international relations and the definition of neutrality. The initial Neutrality Act prohibited the United States from supplying arms to any party at war. Subsequent versions of the act would include a ban on loans to belligerents. To hammer home the isolationist sentiment present in the national legislature, the Senate also decisively rejected American participation in the World Court.

As the United States constructed barriers against international intervention, the world situation worsened. On 3 October 1935, Italy marched on Ethiopia with 250,000 men. On 7 March 1936, German military forces remilitarized the Rhineland, defying the nations of western Europe to stop them. That July, an uprising of the garrison in the port of Cueta, Spanish Morocco, marked the start of the Spanish Civil War. In 1937, Roosevelt wrote Ambassador Jesse Strauss: "One cannot help feeling that the whole European panorama is fundamentally blacker than at any time in your life time or mine."[15] Japan's war in China in 1937 was a bleak accompaniment to fascism's emerging influence in Europe. As the Japanese mobilized for the war, Japanese diplomats denounced the Washington Naval Treaty and signed the Anti-Comintern Pact with Nazi Germany.[16]

As global stability deteriorated, Roosevelt initiated some limited measures to restore the United States' participation in foreign affairs. In June 1937, he invited British Prime Minister Neville Chamberlain to Washington to discuss measures necessary to repair Anglo-American relations. In an October 1937 speech in Chicago, Roosevelt tested public tolerance of a more aggressive American diplomacy. Noting the spreading "epidemic of world lawlessness," he warned that it was unlikely the United States would be able to maintain its isolationism. The president noted further: "The peace-loving nations must make a concerted effort in opposition to those violations of treaties and those ignorings of humane instincts which today are creating a state of international anarchy and instability from which there is no escape through mere isolation or neutrality."[17] However, despite careful qualifications that the United States would not directly involve itself in world conflicts, the response to Roosevelt's "quarantine" speech was almost overwhelmingly negative.

The progressive collapse of European peace allowed Roosevelt to shift American policy from neutrality to more overt sympathy and support for nations arrayed against Hitler and Mussolini. The failure of the Munich Pact to assuage German territorial demands alarmed Americans and made it possible for the White House to win back some latitude in foreign affairs. Appropriations for the military increased from $1 billion in 1938 to $1.6 billion in 1939.[18] Two months after the German invasion of Poland, Congress repealed the arms embargo provision of the Neutrality Act and introduced the "cash and carry" provision on weapons and materiel transfers; a measure deliberately designed to favor a mercantile nation such as England.

France's rapid defeat shocked America into even more drastic action. Peacetime conscription became the law of the land in September 1940. An initial draft call brought 630,000 men into active service.[19] That same month Roosevelt promised Churchill fifty obsolete destroyers in exchange for base rights in the British West Indies. In December 1940, with American public opinion apparently prepared to contemplate open intervention, the president argued that America should become the "arsenal of democracy" for the remaining free nations of the world. In March 1941, Congress agreed, passing the Lend-Lease Act which provided for the sale, lease, or loan of war materials to nations allied with the United States. Additional military measures soon followed. On 27 March 1941, as part of the American British Conference (ABC-1) Staff Agreement, the United States agreed to provide convoy escorts for foreign shipping. By the spring of 1941, American naval patrols periodically clashed with German submarines in the North Atlantic.

The event that triggered the formal entry of the United States into the Second World War occurred on the other side of the world. In Asia, the United States adopted a more direct and confrontational policy against Japanese expansion. In 1939, faced with the continuing war against China, America canceled its commercial treaty with Japan and initiated an embargo of fuel and scrap metal. When Japan invaded and occupied French Indochina in July 1941, the United States froze all Japanese monetary assets in American banks.[20] Collectively, these pressures moved Tokyo to a preemptive strike against the United States. The December 17, 1941 attack on Pearl Harbor was an enormous military success, one that crippled the American Pacific fleet. However, the attack proved to be an incredible miscalculation. One day after the disaster, Franklin D. Roosevelt stood before the Congress and requested a declaration of war. Without one dissenting vote, the United States joined the conflict.

NOTES

1. Allan R. Millet and Peter Maslowski, *For the Common Defense: A Military History of the United States of America* (New York: Free Press, 1994), 653.

2. David M. Kennedy, *Over Here: The First World War and American Society* (New York: Oxford University Press, 1980), 287–95.

3. See Robert K. Murray, *Red Scare: A Study in National Hysteria, 1919–1920* (Minneapolis: University of Minnesota Press, 1955).

4. Thomas G. Paterson, J. Garry Clifford, and Kenneth J. Hagan, *American Foreign Relations: A History, since 1945*, vol. 2 (Boston: Houghton Mifflin, 2000), 117–18.

5. John M. Carroll, "American Diplomacy in the 1920's," in *Modern American Diplomacy*, ed. John M. Carroll and George C. Herring (Wilmington, DE: SR Books, 1996), 67.

6. Henry Steele Commager, *Documents of American History*, vol. 2 (Englewood Cliffs, NJ: Prentice Hall, 1973), 184.

7. Walter LaFeber, *Inevitable Revolutions: The United States in Central America* (New York: W. W. Norton, 1984), 42–84; Knut Walter, *The Regime of Anastasio Somoza, 1936–1956* (Chapel Hill: University of North Carolina Press, 1993), 1–66.

8. See Emily S. Rosenberg, *Spreading the American Dream: American Economic and Cultural Expansion, 1890–1945* (New York: Hill & Wang, 1982).

9. Frank Ninkovich, *The Wilsonian Century: U.S. Foreign Policy since 1900* (Chicago: University of Chicago Press, 1999), 94.

10. Ibid., 98–99.

11. See Saburo Ienaga, *The Pacific War, 1931–1945: A Critical Perspective on Japan's Role in World War II* (New York: Pantheon Books, 1978), 57–74; John Toland, *Adolf Hitler* (New York: Doubleday, 1976), 387–500; Roy Medvedev, *Let History Judge: The Origins and Consequences of Stalinism* (New York: Columbia University Press, 1989), 255–485.

12. Samuel I. Rosenman, ed., *The Public Papers and Addresses of Franklin D. Roosevelt*, vol. 2 (New York: Random House, 1938), 14.

13. Ibid.

14. Ninkovich, *The Wilsonian Century*, 111–13, 121–37.

15. Samuel Eliot Morison, Henry Steele Commager, and William E. Leuchtenburg, *The Growth of the American Republic*, vol. 2 (New York: Oxford University Press, 1969), 534.

16. W. G. Beasley, *The Rise of Modern Japan* (New York: St. Martin's Press, 1990), 193–207.

17. Rosenman, *The Public Papers and Addresses of Franklin D. Roosevelt*, 407–11.

18. Warren W. Hassler, *With Shield and Sword: American Military Affairs, Colonial Times to the Present* (Ames: Iowa State University Press, 1982), 298.

19. Ibid., 299.

20. Akira Iriye, *Power and Culture: The Japanese-American War, 1941–1945* (Cambridge: Harvard University Press, 1981), 1–35.

---

69. FOUR POWER TREATY
13 December 1921

After the First World War, the United States wanted to play a greater
role in Asia. The Four Power Treaty was designed to replace England as
the primary non-Asian power in the region. Both Japan and England
agreed to this new arrangement, recognizing America's newfound power
in the world. American diplomats, however, overestimated the consensus
at the beginning of the treaty and made few provisions to respond to any
one signatory who challenged Asian stability.

Treaty between the United States, the British Empire, France and Japan relating
to their Insular Possessions and Insular Dominions in the Region of the Pacific
Ocean

The United States of America, the British Empire, France and Japan,

With a view to the preservation of the general peace and the maintenance of their rights in relation to their insular possessions and insular dominions in the region of the Pacific Ocean,

Have determined to conclude a treaty to this effect and have appointed as their plenipotentiaries: . . .

Who, having communicated their full powers, found in good and due form, have agreed as follows:

I. The high contracting parties agree as between themselves to respect their rights in relation to their insular possessions and insular dominions in the region of the Pacific Ocean.

If there should develop between any of the high contracting parties a controversy arising out of any Pacific question and involving their said rights which is not satisfactorily settled by diplomacy and is likely to affect the harmonious accord now happily subsisting between them, they shall invite the other high contracting parties to a joint conference to which the whole subject will be referred for consideration and adjustment.

II. If the said rights are threatened by the aggressive action of any other power, the high contracting parties shall communicate with one another fully and frankly in order to arrive at an understanding as to the most efficient measures to be taken, jointly or separately, to meet the exigencies of the particular situation.

III. This treaty shall remain in force for 10 years from the time it shall take

effect and after the expiration of said period it shall continue to be in force
subject to the right of any of the high contracting parties to terminate it upon
12 months' notice.

IV. This treaty shall be ratified as soon as possible in accordance with the
constitutional methods of the high contracting parties and shall take effect on
the deposit of ratifications, which shall take place at Washington, and thereupon
the agreement between Great Britain and Japan, which was concluded at London
on July 13, 1911, shall terminate. . . .

Source: William M. Malloy, ed., *Treaties, Conventions, International Acts, Protocols,
and Agreements between the United States and Other Powers, 1910–1923*, vol. 3 (Washington, DC: Government Printing Office, 1923), 3094–96.

70. NAVAL LIMITATION TREATY
6 February 1922

*After the First World War, naval armaments were the bane of liberal
internationalists, who saw them as unnecessarily expensive threats to
global peace. After some prompting by Senator William Borah, in November 1922 the Harding administration convened a conference to discuss
naval disarmament and great power influence in the Pacific.*

The United States of America, the British Empire, France, Italy and Japan;
  Desiring to contribute to the maintenance of the general peace, and to reduce
the burdens of competition in armament;
  Have resolved, with a view to accomplish these purposes, to conclude a treaty
to limit their respective naval armament, and to that end have appointed their
Plenipotentiaries; . . .
  Who, have communicated to each other their respective full powers, found to
be in good and due form, have agreed as follows:

CHAPTER I

ART. I. The Contracting Powers agree to limit their respective naval armament as provided in the present Treaty.
  ART. II. The Contracting Powers may retain respectively the capital ships
which are specified in Chapter II, Part 1. On the coming into force of the present
Treaty, but subject to the following provisions of this Article, all other capital
ships, built or building, of the United States, the British Empire and Japan shall
be disposed of as prescribed in Chapter II, Part 2. In addition to the capital
ships specified in Chapter II, Part 1, the United States may complete and retain
two ships of the West Virginia class now under construction. On the completion

of these two ships the *North Dakota* and *Delaware* shall be disposed of as prescribed in Chapter II, Part 2.

The British Empire may, in accordance with the replacement table in Chapter II, Part 3, construct two new capital ships not exceeding 35,000 tons (35,560 metric tons) standard displacement each. On the completion of the said two ships the *Thunderer, King George V, Ajax* and *Centurion* shall be disposed of as prescribed in Chapter II, Part 2.

ART. III. Subject to the provisions of Article II, the Contracting Powers shall abandon their respective capital ship building programs, and no new capital ships shall be constructed or acquired by any of the Contracting Powers except replacement tonnage which may be constructed or acquired as specified in Chapter II, Part 3.

Ships which are replaced in accordance with Chapter II, Part 3, shall be disposed of as prescribed in Part 2 of that Chapter.

ART. IV. The total capital ship replacement tonnage of the Contracting Powers shall not exceed in standard displacement, for the United States 525,000 tons (533,400 metric tons); for the British Empire 525,000 tons (533,400 metric tons); for France 175,000 tons (177,800 metric tons); for Italy 175,000 tons (177,800 metric tons); for Japan 315,000 tons (320,040 metric tons).

ART. V. No capital ship exceeding 35,000 tons (35,560 metric tons) standard displacement shall be acquired by, or constructed by, for, or within the jurisdiction of, any of the Contracting Powers.

ART. VI. No capital ship of any of the Contracting Powers shall carry a gun with a calibre in excess of 16 inches (405 millimetres).

ART. VII. The total tonnage for aircraft carriers of each of the Contracting Powers shall not exceed in standard displacement, for the United States 135,000 tons (137,160 metric tons); for the British Empire 135,000 tons (137,160 metric tons); for France 60,000 tons (60,960 metric tons); for Italy 60,000 tons (60,960 metric tons); for Japan 81,000 tons (82,296 metric tons). . . .

ART. IX. No aircraft carrier exceeding 27,000 tons (27,432 metric tons) standard displacement shall be acquired by, or constructed by, for or within the jurisdiction of, any of the Contracting Powers. . . .

ART. XI. No vessel of war exceeding 10,000 tons (10,160 metric tons) standard displacement, other than a capital ship or aircraft carrier, shall be acquired by, or constructed by, for, or within the jurisdiction of, any of the Contracting Powers. Vessels not specifically built as fighting ships nor taken in time of peace under government control for fighting purposes, which are employed on fleet duties or as troop transports or in some other way for the purpose of assisting in the prosecution of hostilities otherwise than as fighting ships, shall not be within the limitations of this Article.

ART. XII. No vessel of war of any of the Contracting Powers, hereafter laid down, other than a capital ship, shall carry a gun with a calibre in excess of 8 inches (203 millimetres).

ART. XIII. Except as provided in Article IX, no ship designated in the present Treaty, to be scrapped may be reconverted into a vessel of war.

ART. XIV. No preparations shall be made in merchant ships in time of peace for the installation of warlike armaments for the purpose of converting such ships into vessels of war. . . .

ART. XIX. The United States, the British Empire and Japan agree that the status quo at the time of the signing of the present Treaty, with regard to fortifications and naval bases, shall be maintained in their respective territories and possessions specified hereunder:

(1) The insular possessions which the United States now holds or may hereafter acquire in the Pacific Ocean, except (a) those adjacent to the coast of the United States, Alaska and Panama Canal Zone, not including the Aleutian Islands, and (b) the Hawaiian Islands;

(2) Hongkong and the insular possessions, which the British Empire now holds or may hereafter acquire in the Pacific Ocean, east of the meridian of 110° east longitude except (a) those adjacent to the coast of Canada, (b) the Commonwealth of Australia and its Territories, and (c) New Zealand;

(3) The following insular territories and possessions of Japan in the Pacific Ocean, to wit: the Kurile Islands, the Bonin Islands Amami-Oshima, the Loochoo Islands, Formosa and the Pescadores, and any insular territories or possessions in the Pacific Ocean which Japan may hereafter acquire.

The maintenance of the status quo under the foregoing provisions implies that no new fortifications or naval bases shall be established in the territories and possessions specified; that no measures shall be taken to increase the existing naval facilities for the repair and maintenance of naval forces, and that no increase shall be made in the coast defences of the territories and possessions above specified. This restriction, however, does not preclude such repair and replacement of worn-out weapons and equipment as is customary in naval and military establishments in time of peace. . . .

CHAPTER II
PART 1.
CAPITAL SHIPS WHICH MAY BE RETAINED BY THE CONTRACTING POWERS

[Lists]

PART 2.
RULES FOR SCRAPPING VESSELS OF WAR.

The following rules shall be observed for the scrapping of vessels of war which are to be disposed of in accordance with Articles II and III.

I. A vessel to be scrapped must be placed in such condition that it cannot be put to combatant use.

II. This result must be finally effected in any one of the following ways:

(a) Permanent sinking of the vessel;

(b) Breaking the vessel up.

This shall always involve the destruction or removal of all machinery, boilers and armour, and all deck, side and bottom plating;

(c) Converting the vessel to target use exclusively. . . . Not more than one capital ship may be retained for this purpose at one time by any of the Contracting Powers. . . .

PART 3.
SEC. 1.
RULES FOR REPLACEMENT.

(a) Capital ships and aircraft carriers twenty years after the date of their completion may, except as otherwise provided in Article VIII and in the tables in Section II of this Part, be replaced by new construction, but within the limits prescribed in Article IV and Article VII. The keels of such new construction may, except as otherwise provided in Article VIII and in the tables in Section II of this Part, be laid down not earlier than seventeen years from the date of completion of the tonnage to be replaced, provided, however, that no capital ship tonnage, with the exception of the ships referred to in the third paragraph of Article II, and replacement tonnage specifically mentioned in Section II of this Part, shall be laid down until ten years from November 12, 1921. . . .

CHAPTER III

ART. XXIII. The present Treaty shall remain in force until December 31st, 1936, and in case none of the Contracting Powers shall have given notice two years before that date of its intention to terminate the Treaty, it shall continue in force until the expiration of two years from the date on which notice of termination shall be given by one of the Contracting Powers. . . .

Source: William M. Malloy, ed., *Treaties, Conventions, International Acts, Protocols, and Agreements between the United States and Other Powers, 1910–1923*, vol. 3 (Washington, DC: Government Printing Office, 1923), 3100–16.

---

71. NINE POWER TREATY
6 February 1922

One subject discussed at the 1921–1922 Washington Conference was the status of China. Until this point in time, the American Open Door Policy notes had been little more than a statement of principle, albeit one that most major powers did not openly challenge. Although it did little to incorporate contemporary Chinese sentiments, the Nine Power Treaty gave final legal definition to the Open Door Policy.

A Treaty Between the United States of America, Belgium, the British Empire, China, France, Italy, Japan, the Netherlands, and Portugal, Relating to Principles and Policies to be Followed in Matters Concerning China.

The United States of America, Belgium, the British Empire, China, France, Italy, Japan, the Netherlands and Portugal:

Desiring to adopt a policy designed to stabilize conditions in the Far East, to safeguard the rights and interests of China, and to promote intercourse between China and the other Powers upon the basis of equality of opportunity;

Have resolved to conclude a treaty for that purpose and to that end have appointed as their respective Plenipotentiaries: . . .

Who, having communicated to each other their full powers, found to be in good and due form, have agreed as follows:

I. The Contracting Powers, other than China agree:

(1) To respect the sovereignty, the independence, and the territorial and administrative integrity of China;

(2) To provide the fullest and most unembarrassed opportunity to China to develop and maintain for herself an effective and stable government;

(3) To use their influence for the purpose of effectually establishing and maintaining the principle of equal opportunity for the commerce and industry of all nations throughout the territory of China;

(4) To refrain from taking advantage of conditions in China in order to seek special rights or privileges which would abridge the rights of subjects or citizens of friendly States, and from countenancing action inimical to the security of such States.

II. The Contracting Powers agree not to enter into any treaty, agreement, arrangement or understanding, either with one another, or individually or collectively, with any Power or Powers, which would infringe or impair the principles stated in Article I.

III. With a view to applying more effectual the principles of the Open Door or equality of opportunity in China for the trade and industry of all nations, the Contracting Powers other than China, agree that they will not seek nor support their respective nationals, in seeking

(a) any arrangement which might purport to establish in favor of their interests any general superiority of rights with respect to commercial or economic development in any designated region of China.

(b) any such monopoly or preference as would deprive the nationals of any other Power of the right of undertaking any legitimate trade or industry in China, or of participating with the Chinese Government, or with any local authority, in any category of public enterprise, or which by reason of its scope, duration or geographical extent is calculated to frustrate the practical application of the principle of equal opportunity.

It is understood that the foregoing stipulations of this Article are not to be so construed as to prohibit the acquisitions of such properties or rights as may be necessary to the conduct of a particular commercial, industrial, or financial undertaking or to the encouragement of invention and research.

China undertakes to be guided by the principles stated in the foregoing stipulations of this Article in dealing with applications for economic rights and privileges from Governments and nationals of all foreign countries, whether parties to the present Treaty or not.

IV. The Contracting Powers agree not to support any agreements by their respective nationals with each other designed to create Spheres of Influence or to provide for the enjoyment of mutually exclusive opportunities in designated parts of Chinese territory.

V. China agrees that, throughout the whole of the railways in China, she will not exercise or permit unfair discrimination of any kind. In particular there shall be no discrimination whatever, direct or indirect, in respect of charges or of facilities on the ground of the nationality of passengers or the countries from which or to which they are proceeding, or the origin or ownership of goods or the country from which or to which they are consigned, or the nationality or ownership of the ship or other means of conveying such passengers or goods before or after their transport on the Chinese railways. The Contracting Powers, other than China, assume a corresponding obligation in respect of any of the aforesaid railways over which they or their nationals are in a position to exercise any control in virtue of any concession, special agreement or otherwise.

VI. The Contracting Powers, other than China, agree fully to respect China's rights as a neutral in time of war to which China is not a party; and China declares that when she is a neutral she will observe the obligations of neutrality.

VII. The Contracting Powers agree that, whenever a situation arises which in the opinion of any one of them involves the application of the stipulations of the present Treaty, and renders desirable discussion of such application, there shall be full and frank communication between the Contracting Powers concerned.

VIII. Powers not signatory to the present Treaty which have Governments recognized by the Signatory Powers and which have treaty relations with China, shall be invited to adhere to the present Treaty. To this end the Government of the United States will make the necessary communications to non-signatory Powers and will inform the Contracting Powers of the replies received. Adherence by any Power shall become effective on receipt of notice thereof by the Government of the United States.

IX. The present Treaty shall be ratified by the Contracting Powers in accordance with their respective constitutional methods and shall take effect on the date of the deposit of all the ratifications, which shall take place at Washington as soon as possible. The Government of the United States will transmit to the other Contracting Powers a certified copy of the procés-verbal of the deposit of ratifications.

The present Treaty, of which the French and English texts are both authentic, shall remain deposited in the archives of the Government of the United States, and duly certified copies thereof shall be transmitted by that Government to the other Contracting Powers.

In faith whereof the above-named Plenipotentiaries have signed the Present Treaty.

Done at the City of Washington the sixth day of February One Thousand Nine Hundred and Twenty-Two.

Source: William M. Malloy, ed., *Treaties, Conventions, International Acts, Protocols, and Agreements between the United States and Other Powers, 1910–1923*, vol. 3 (Washington, DC: Government Printing Office, 1923), 3120–25.

72. COOLIDGE'S MESSAGE ON NICARAGUAN INTERVENTION
10 January 1927

America's original occupation of Nicaragua (1912) failed to produce long-term stability. The collapse of the Nicaraguan national government in 1926 spurred the Coolidge administration to once again introduce U.S. military forces to restore order. American marines were accompanied by Henry L. Stimson, who was sent as a special commissioner to win some type of consensus from the warring Nicaraguan factions. The United States would remain in Nicaragua for an additional seven years in an attempt to reconstruct a stable country.

The White House

To the Congress of the United States:

. . . It is well known that in 1912 the United States intervened in Nicaragua with a large force and put down a revolution, and that from that time to 1925 a location guard of American marines was, with the consent of the Nicaraguan Government, kept in Managua to protect American lives and property. In 1923 representatives of the Central American countries, namely, Cost Rica, Guatemala, Honduras, Nicaragua and Salvador, at the invitation of the United States, met in Washington and entered into a series of treaties. These treaties dealt with limitation of armament, a Central American tribunal for arbitration, and the general subject of peace and amity. The treaty last referred to specifically provides in Article II that the Governments of the contracting parties will not recognize any other government which may come into power in any of the five Republics through a coup d'état, or revolution, and disqualifies the leaders of such coup d'état, or revolution, from assuming the presidency or vice presidency. . . .

The United States was not a party to this treaty, but it was made in Washington under the auspices of the Secretary of State, and this Government has felt a moral obligation to apply its principles in order to encourage the Central American States in their efforts to prevent revolution and disorder. . . .

The Nicaraguan constitution provides in article 106 that in the absence of the President and Vice President the Congress shall designate one of its members to complete the unexpired term of President . . . the action of Congress in designating Senor Diaz was perfectly legal and in accordance with the constitution. Therefore the United States Government on November 17 extended recognition to Senor Diaz. . . .

Immediately following the inauguration of President Diaz and frequently since that date he has appealed to the United States for support, has informed this Government of the aid which Mexico is giving to the revolutionists, and has stated that he is unable solely because of the aid given by Mexico to the revolutionists to protect the lives and property of American citizens and other foreigners. When negotiations leading up to the Corinto conferences began, I immediately placed an embargo on the shipment of arms and ammunition to Nicaragua. . . .

. . . At the end of November, after spending some time in Mexico City, Doctor Sacasa went back to Nicaragua, landing at Puerto Cabezas, near Bragmans Bluff. He immediately placed himself at the head of the insurrection and declared himself President of Nicaragua. He has never been recognized by any of the Central American Republics nor by any other government, with the exception of Mexico, which recognized him immediately. As arms and munitions in large quantities were reaching the revolutionists, I deemed it unfair to prevent the recognized government from purchasing arms abroad, and, accordingly, the Secretary of State has notified the Diaz Government that licenses would be issued for the export of arms and munitions purchased in this country. It would be thoroughly inconsistent for this country not to support the government recognized by it while the revolutionists were receiving arms and munitions from abroad. . . .

For many years numerous Americans have been living in Nicaragua, developing its industries and carrying on business. At the present time there are large investments in lumbering, mining, coffee growing, banana culture, shipping, and also in general mercantile and other collateral business.

In addition to these industries now in existence, the Government of Nicaragua, by a treaty entered into on the 5th day of August, 1914, granted in perpetuity to the United States the exclusive proprietary rights necessary and convenient for the construction, operation, and maintenance of an oceanic canal. . . .

There is no question that if the revolution continues American investments and business interests in Nicaragua will be very seriously affected, if not destroyed.

Manifestly the relation of this Government to the Nicaraguan situation and its policy in the existing emergency, are determined by the facts which I have described. The proprietary rights of the United States in the Nicaraguan canal route, with the necessary implications growing out of it affecting the Panama

Canal, together with the obligations flowing from the investments of all classes of our citizens in Nicaragua, place us in a position of peculiar responsibility. I am sure it is not the desire of the United States to intervene in the internal affairs of Nicaragua or of any other Central American Republic. Nevertheless it must be said that we have a very definite and special interest in the maintenance of order and good government in Nicaragua at the present time, and that the stability, prosperity, and independence of all Central American countries can never be a matter of indifference to us. The United States can not, therefore, fail to view with deep concern any serious threat to stability and constitutional government in Nicaragua tending toward anarchy and jeopardizing American interests, especially if such state of affairs is contributed to or brought about by outside influences or by any foreign power. It has always been and remains the policy of the United States in such circumstances to take the steps that may be necessary for the preservation and protection of the lives, property, and the interests of its citizens and of the Government itself. In this respect I propose to follow the path of my predecessors.

Consequently, I have deemed it my duty to use the powers committed to me to insure the adequate protection of all American interests in Nicaragua, whether they be endangered by internal strife or by outside interference in the affairs of that Republic.

Source: Henry Steele Commager, *Documents of American History*, vol. 2 (Englewood Cliffs, NJ: Prentice Hall, 1973), 208–10.

73. TREATIES OF ARBITRATION AND CONCILIATION WITH GERMANY
5 May 1928

In the late 1920s, the United States, like its counterparts in western Europe, embraced the concept that war could be avoided through the constant application of diplomacy to international problems. The treaties arranged with Weimar Germany in 1928 were intended to avoid open conflict as well as secure the hundreds of millions of dollars in American loans and investments provided after the conclusion of the First World War.

TREATY OF ARBITRATION

The President of the United States of America and the President of the German Reich

Determined to prevent so far as in their power lies any interruption in the peaceful relations now happily existing between the two nations; Desirous of reaffirming their adherence to the policy of submitting to impartial decision all justiciable controversies that may arise between them; and

Eager by their example not only to demonstrate their condemnation of war as an instrument of national policy in their mutual relations, but also to hasten the time when the perfection of international arrangements for the pacific settlement of international disputes shall have eliminated forever the possibility of war among any of the powers of the world;

Have decided to conclude a treaty of arbitration and for that purpose they have appointed as their respective plenipotentiaries

The President of the United States of America, Frank B. Kellogg, Secretary of State of the United States, and

The President of the German Reich, Herr Friedrich von Prittwitz und Gaffron, German Ambassador to the United States of America:

Who, having communicated to one another their full powers found in good and due form, have agreed upon the following articles:

ART. I. All differences relating to international matters in which the high contracting parties are concerned by virtue of a claim of right made by one against the other under treaty or otherwise, which it has not been possible to adjust by diplomacy, which have not been adjusted as a result of reference to an appropriate commission of conciliation, and which are justiciable in their nature by reason of being susceptible of decision by the application of the principles of law or equity, shall be submitted to the Permanent Court of Arbitration established at The Hague by the convention of October 18, 1907, or to some other competent tribunal, as shall be decided in each case by special agreement, which special agreement shall provide for the organization of such tribunal if necessary, define its powers, state the question or questions at issue, and settle the terms of reference.

The special agreement in each case shall be made on the part of the United States of America by the President of the United States of America by and with the advice and consent of the Senate thereof, and on the part of Germany in accordance with its constitutional laws.

ART. II. The provisions of this treaty shall not be invoked in respect of any dispute the subject matter of which

(a) is within the domestic jurisdiction of either of the high contracting parties,

(b) involves the interests of third parties.

(c) depends upon or involves the maintenance of the traditional attitude of the United States concerning American questions, commonly described as the Monroe doctrine,

(d) depends upon or involves the observance of the obligations of Germany in accordance with the Covenant of the League of Nations.

ART. III. The present treaty shall be ratified by the President of the United States of America by and with the advice and consent of the Senate thereof and by the President of the German Reich in accordance with German constitutional laws.

The ratifications shall be exchanged at Washington as soon as possible, and the treaty shall take effect on the date of the exchange of the ratifications. It shall thereafter remain in force continuously unless and until terminated by one year's written notice given by either high contracting party to the other.

In faith whereof the respective plenipotentiaries have signed this treaty in duplicate in the English and German languages, both texts having equal force, and hereunto affix their seals.

Done at Washington the fifth day of May in the year of our Lord one thousand nine hundred and twenty-eight.

FRANK B. KELLOGG,
F. VON PRITTWITZ.

TREATY OF CONCILIATION

The President of the United States of America and the President of the German Reich, being desirous to strengthen the bonds of amity that bind them together and also to advance the cause of general peace, have resolved to enter into a treaty for that purpose, and have agreed upon and concluded the following articles:

ART. I. Any disputes arising between the Government of the United States of America and the Government of Germany, of whatever nature they may be, shall, when ordinary diplomatic proceedings have failed and the high contracting parties do not have recourse to adjudication by a competent tribunal, be submitted for investigation and report to a permanent International Commission constituted in the manner prescribed in the next succeeding article; the high contracting parties agree not to declare war or begin hostilities during such investigation and before the report is submitted.

ART. II. The International Commission shall be composed of five members, to be appointed as follows: One member shall be chosen from each country, by the Government thereof; one member shall be chosen by each Government from some third country; the fifth member shall be chosen by common agreement between the two Governments, it being understood that he shall not be a citizen of either country. The expenses of the Commission shall be paid by the two Governments in equal proportions.

The International Commission shall be appointed within six months after the exchange of ratifications of this treaty; and vacancies shall be filled according to the manner of the original appointment.

ART. III. In case the high contracting parties shall have failed to adjust a dispute by diplomatic methods, and they do not have recourse to adjudication by a competent tribunal, they shall at once refer it to the International Commission for investigation and report. The International Commission may, however, spontaneously by unanimous agreement offer its services to that effect, and in such case it shall notify both Governments and request their cooperation in the investigation.

The high contracting parties agree to furnish the Permanent International Commission with all the means and facilities required for its investigation and report.

The report of the commission shall be completed within one year after the date on which it shall declare its investigation to have begun, unless the high contracting parties shall shorten or extend the time by mutual agreement. The report shall be prepared in triplicate; one copy shall be presented to each Government, and the third retained by the commission for its files.

The high contracting parties reserve the right to act independently on the subject matter of the dispute after the report of the commission shall have been submitted. . . .

Washington the fifth of May one thousand nine hundred and twenty-eight.

FRANK B. KELLOGG.

F. VON PRITTWITZ.

Source: William M. Malloy, ed., *Treaties, Conventions, International Acts, Protocols, and Agreements between the United States and Other Powers, 1923–1937*, vol. 4 (Washington, DC: Government Printing Office, 1938), 4210–13.

74. THE KELLOGG-BRIAND PEACE PACT
27 August 1928

America was a much sought after ally in the years following the First World War. France in particular devoted considerable efforts to gain an alliance with America. In 1928, French minister Aristide Briand suggested that the two nations jointly pledge to remain at peace with each other. Secretary of State Frank Kellogg's response was to call for an international renunciation of war. The resulting peace pact, signed by sixty-two nations, outlawed "war as an instrument of national policy."

The President of the German Reich, the President of the United States of America, His Majesty the King of the Belgians, the President of the French Republic, His Majesty the King of Great Britain, Ireland and the British Dominions beyond the Seas, Emperor of India, His Majesty the King of Italy, His Majesty the Emperor of Japan, the President of the Republic of Poland, the President of the Czechoslovak Republic,

Deeply sensible of their solemn duty to promote the welfare of mankind;

Persuaded that the time has come when a frank renunciation of war as an instrument of national policy should be made to the end that the peaceful and friendly relations now existing between their peoples may be perpetuated;

Convinced that all changes in their relations with one another should be sought only by pacific means and be the result of a peaceful and orderly process, and that any signatory power which shall hereafter seek to promote its national interests by resort to war should be denied the benefits furnished by this treaty;

Hopeful that encouraged by their example, all the other nations of the world will join in this humane endeavor and by adhering to the present treaty as soon as it comes into force bring their peoples within the scope of its beneficent provision, thus uniting the civilized nations of the world in a common renunciation of war as an instrument of their national policy;

Have decided to conclude a treaty and for that purpose have appointed as their respective plenipotentiaries: . . .

Who, having communicated to one another their full powers found in good and due form have agreed upon the following articles:

ART. 1. The high contracting parties solemnly declare in the names of their respective peoples that they condemn recourse to war for the solution of international controversies, and renounce it as an instrument of national policy in their relations with one another.

ART. 2. The high contracting parties agree that the settlement or solution of all disputes or conflicts of whatever nature or of whatever origin they may be, which may arise among them, shall never be sought except by pacific means.

ART. 3. The present treaty shall be ratified by the high contracting parties named in the preamble in accordance with their respective constitutional requirements, and shall take effect as between them as soon as all their several instruments of ratification shall have been deposited at Washington.

This treaty shall, when it has come into effect as prescribed in the preceding paragraph, remain open as long as may be necessary for adherence by all the other powers of the world. Every instrument evidencing, the adherence of a power shall be deposited at Washington and the treaty shall immediately upon such deposit become effective as between the power thus adhering and the other powers parties hereto. . . .

Source: William M. Malloy, ed., *Treaties, Conventions, International Acts, Protocols, and Agreements between the United States and Other Powers, 1923–1937*, vol. 4 (Washington, DC: Government Printing Office, 1938), 5130–34.

---

75.   STIMSON DOCTRINE
6 February 1931

From a very early point in his presidency, Woodrow Wilson attempted to link the legitimacy of a standing government with the United States' willingness to officially recognize it. His refusal to recognize the Mexican government of Victoriano Huerta in 1913 revoked previous American policy to acknowledge any government holding de facto *control over a country. Stimson's intent in 1931 was to reverse Wilson's standard and revert back to traditional American policy.*

... The practice of this country as to the recognition of new governments has been substantially uniform from the days of the administration of Secretary of State Jefferson in 1792 to the days of Secretary of State Bryan in 1913. There were certain slight departures from this policy during the Civil War, but they were manifestly due to the exigencies of warfare and were abandoned immediately afterwards. This general policy, as thus observed, was to base the act of recognition not upon the question of the constitutional legitimacy of the new government but upon its *de facto* capacity to fulfill its obligations as a member of the family of nations. This country recognized the right of other nations to regulate their own internal affairs of government and disclaimed any attempt to base its recognition upon the correctness of their constitutional action.

Said Mr. Jefferson in 1792:

We certainly cannot deny to other nations that principle whereon our own Government is founded, that every nation has a right to govern itself internally under what forms it pleases, and to change these forms at its own will; and externally to transact business with other nations through whatever organ it chooses, whether that be a king, convention, assembly, committee, president, or whatever it be.

In these essentials our practice corresponded with the practice of the other nations of the world.

The particular considerations upon which our action was regularly based were well stated by Mr. Adee, long the trusted Assistant Secretary of State of this Government, as follows:

Ever since the American Revolution entrance upon diplomatic intercourse with foreign states has been *de facto*, dependent upon the existence of three conditions of fact: the control of the administrative machinery of the state; the general acquiescence of its people; and the ability and willingness of their government to discharge international and conventional obligations. The form of government has not been a conditional factor in such recognition; in other words, the *de jure* element of legitimacy of title has been left aside.

With the advent of President Wilson's administration this policy of over a century was radically departed from in respect to the Republic of Mexico, and, by a public declaration on March 11, 1913, it was announced that

Cooperation (with our sister republics of Central and South America) is possible only when supported at every turn by the orderly processes of just government based upon law, not upon arbitrary or irregular force. We hold, as I am sure that all thoughtful leaders of republican government everywhere hold, that just government rests always upon the consent of the governed, and that there can be no freedom without order based upon law and upon the public conscience and approval. We shall look to make these principles the basis of mutual intercourse, respect, and helpfulness between our sister republics and ourselves.

Mr. Wilson's government sought to put this new policy into effect in respect to the recognition of the then Government of Mexico held by President Victoriano Huerta. Although Huerta's government was in *de facto* possession, Mr.

Wilson refused to recognize it, and he sought through the influence and pressure of his great office to force it from power. Armed conflict followed with the forces of Mexico, and disturbed relations between us and that republic lasted until a comparatively few years ago.

In his sympathy for the development of free constitutional institutions among the people of our Latin American neighbors, Mr. Wilson did not differ from the feelings of the great mass of his countrymen in the United States . . . but he differed from the practice of his predecessors in seeking actively to propagate these institutions in a foreign country by the direct influence of this Government and to do this against the desires of the authorities and people of Mexico.

The present administration has declined to follow the policy of Mr. Wilson and has followed consistently the former practice of this Government since the days of Jefferson. As soon as it was reported to us, through our diplomatic representatives, that the new governments in Bolivia, Peru, Argentina, Brazil, and Panama were in control of the administrative machinery of the state, with the apparent general acquiescence of their people, and that they were willing and apparently able to discharge their international and conventional obligations, they were recognized by our Government. And, in view of the economic depression, with the consequent need for prompt measures of financial stabilization, we did this with as little delay as possible in order to give those sorely pressed countries the quickest possible opportunities for recovering their economic poise.

Source: Henry Steele Commager, *Documents of American History*, vol. 2 (Englewood Cliffs, NJ: Prentice Hall, 1973), 225–26.

---

76. ABANDONMENT OF THE GOLD STANDARD
5 June 1933

One of the major actions taken in Franklin D. Roosevelt's first one hundred days as president was the abandonment of the gold standard. It was intended to raise prices then suffering under the weight of the global economic collapse. The June 1933 joint congressional resolution canceled the gold clauses in private transactions and government obligations and made all debts payable in legal tender.

JOINT RESOLUTION to assure uniform value to the coins and currencies of the United States
Whereas the holding of or dealing in gold affect the public interest, and are therefore subject to proper regulation and restriction; and
Whereas the existing emergency has disclosed that provisions of obligations

which purport to give the obligee a right to require payment in gold or a particular kind of coin or currency of the United States, or in an amount of money of the United States measured thereby, obstruct the power of the Congress to regulate the value of the money of the United States, and are inconsistent with the declared policy of the Congress to maintain at all times the equal power of every dollar, coined or issued by the United States, in the markets and in the payment of debt. Now, therefore, be it

Resolved by the Senate and House of Representatives of the United States of America in Congress assembled, That (a) every provision contained in or made with respect to any obligation which purports to give the obligee a right to require payment in gold or a particular kind of coin or currency, or in an amount in money of the United States measured thereby, is declared to be against public policy; and no such provision shall be contained in or made with respect to any obligation hereafter incurred. Every obligation, heretofore or hereafter incurred, whether or not any such provision is contained therein or made with respect thereto, shall be discharged upon payment, dollar for dollar, in any coin or currency which at the time of payment is legal tender for public and private debts. Any such provision contained in any law authorizing obligations to be issued by or under authority of the United States, is hereby repealed, but the repeal of any such provision shall not invalidate any other provision or authority contained in such law. (b) As used in this resolution, the term "obligation" means an obligation (including every obligation of and to the United States, excepting currency) payable in money of the United States; and the term "coin or currency" means coin or currency of the United States, including Federal Reserve notes and circulating notes of Federal Reserve banks and national banking associations.

SEC. 2. The last sentence of paragraph (1) of subsection (b) of section 43 of the act entitled "An act to relieve the existing national economic emergency by increasing agricultural purchasing power, to raise revenue for extraordinary expenses incurred by reason of such emergency, to provide emergency relief with respect to agricultural indebtedness, to provide for the orderly liquidation of joint-stock land banks, and for other purposes," approved May 12, 1933, is amended to read as follows:

"All coins and currencies of the United States (including Federal Reserve notes and circulating notes of Federal Reserve banks and national banking associations) heretofore or hereafter coined or issued shall be legal tender for all debts, public and private, public charges, taxes, duties, and dues, except that gold coins, when below the standard weight and limit of tolerance provided by law for the single piece, shall be legal tender only at valuation in proportion to their actual weight."

Source: Henry Steele Commager, *Documents of American History*, vol. 2 (Englewood Cliffs, NJ: Prentice Hall, 1973), 262–63.

77. THE GOOD NEIGHBOR POLICY
4 March 1933

Beset by the domestic consequences of the Great Depression, Franklin D. Roosevelt lacked a mandate to pursue an aggressive foreign policy. His first inaugural address explicitly committed the United States to a more passive foreign policy as the government grappled with economic recovery. Roosevelt's statement was significant in the Western Hemisphere to the extent that the policy of U.S. intervention in Latin America was over.

Our international trade relations, though vastly important, are in point of time and necessity secondary to the establishment of a sound national economy. I favor as a practical policy the putting of first things first. I shall spare no effort to restore world trade by international economic readjustment, but the emergency at home cannot wait on that accomplishment.

The basic thought that guides these specific means of national recovery is not narrowly nationalistic. It is the insistence, as a first consideration, upon the interdependence of the various elements in, and parts of, the United States—a recognition of the old and permanently important manifestation of the American spirit of the pioneer. It is the way to recovery. It is the immediate way. It is the strongest assurance that the recovery will endure.

In the field of world policy I would dedicate this Nation to the policy of the good neighbor—the neighbor who resolutely respects himself and, because he does so, respects the rights of others—the neighbor who respects his obligations and respects the sanctity of his agreements in and with a world of neighbors.

If I read the temper of our people correctly, we now realize as we have never realized before our interdependence on each other; that we cannot merely take but we must give as well; that if we are to go forward, we must move as a trained and loyal army willing to sacrifice for the good of a common discipline, because without such discipline no progress is made, no leadership becomes effective. We are, I know, ready and willing to submit our lives and property to such discipline, because it makes possible a leadership which aims at a larger good. This I propose to offer, pledging that the larger purposes will bind upon us all as a sacred obligation with a unity of duty hitherto evoked only in time of armed strife.

With this pledge taken, I assume unhesitatingly the leadership of this great army of our people dedicated to a disciplined attack upon our common problems.

Source: Samuel I. Rosenman, ed., *The Public Papers and Addresses of Franklin D. Roosevelt*, vol. 2 (New York: Russell & Russell, 1969), 11–16.

78. THE RECOGNITION OF SOVIET RUSSIA
1933

The United States was hostile to Soviet Russia from the time of the 1917
Revolution to the advent of the Roosevelt presidency. By 1933, the need
for a trading partner and the more tolerant atmosphere within Washington
led to official diplomatic relations with Moscow.

The White House,
Washington November 16, 1933

My dear Mr. Litvinov:

I am very happy to inform you that as a result of our conversations the
Government of the United States has decided to establish normal diplomatic
relations with the Government of the Union of Soviet Socialist Republics and
to exchange ambassadors.

I trust that the relations now established between our peoples may forever
remain normal and friendly, and that our Nations henceforth may cooperate for
their mutual benefit and for the preservation of the peace of the world.

I am, my dear Mr. Litvinov,

Very sincerely yours,
FRANKLIN D. ROOSEVELT

The White House, Washington,
November 16, 1933

My dear Mr. Litvinov:

I am glad to have received the assurance expressed in your note to me of this
date that it will be the fixed policy of the Government of the Union of Soviet
Socialist Republics:

1. To respect scrupulously the indisputable right of the United States to order
its own life within its own jurisdiction in its own way and to refrain from
interfering in any manner in the internal affairs of the United States, its territories
or possessions.

2. To refrain, and to restrain all persons in Government service and all organizations of the Government or under its direct or indirect control, including organizations in receipt of any financial assistance from it, from any act overt or
covert liable in any way whatsoever to injure the tranquility, prosperity, order,
or security of the whole or any part of the United States, its territories or possessions, and, in particular, from any act tending to incite or encourage armed
intervention, or any agitation or propaganda having as an aim, the violation of

the territorial integrity of the United States, its territories or possessions, or the bringing about by force of a change in the political or social order of the whole or any part of the United States, its territories or possessions.

3. Not to permit the formation or residence on its territory of any organization or group—and to prevent the activity on its territory of any organization or group, or of representatives or officials of any organization or group—which makes claim to be the Government of, or makes attempt upon the territorial integrity of, the United States, its territories or possessions; not to form, subsidize, support or permit on its territory military organizations or groups having the aim of armed struggle against the United States, its territories or possessions, and to prevent any recruiting on behalf of such organizations and groups.

4. Not to permit the formation or residence on its territory of any organization or group—and to prevent the activity on its territory of any organization or group, or of representatives or officials of any organization or group—which has as an aim the overthrow or the preparation for the overthrow of, or the bringing about by force of a change in, the political or social order of the whole or any part of the United States, its territories or possessions.

It will be the fixed policy of the Executive of the United States within the limits of the powers conferred by the Constitution and the laws of the United States to adhere reciprocally to the engagements above expressed.

I am, my dear Mr. Litvinov,

Very sincerely yours,
FRANKLIN D. ROOSEVELT

Source: Samuel I. Rosenman, ed., *The Public Papers and Addresses of Franklin D. Roosevelt*, vol. 2 (New York: Russell & Russell, 1969), 471–86.

79. PHILIPPINE INDEPENDENCE ACT
24 March 1934

Motivated by the continuing economic costs of maintaining domain in the Philippine Islands, American legislators crafted a law that would allow for independence. The final law produced in 1934 was accepted by the Philippine legislature. Implementation was delayed, however, by Japanese aggression in Asia and the fear that it entertained designs on the Philippines proper.

An Act to provide for the complete independence to the Philippine Islands, to provide for the adoption of a constitution and a form of government for the Philippine Islands, and for other purposes.

CONVENTION TO FRAME CONSTITUTION FOR PHILIPPINE ISLANDS

SEC. 1. The Philippine Legislature is hereby authorized to provide for the election of delegates to a constitutional convention, which shall meet . . . at such time as the Philippine Legislature may fix, but not later than October 1, 1934, to formulate and draft a Constitution for the government of the Commonwealth of the Philippine Islands, subject to the conditions and qualifications prescribed in this Act, which shall exercise jurisdiction over all the territory ceded to the United States by the treaty of peace concluded between the United States and Spain on the 10th day of December 1898, . . .

CHARACTER OF CONSTITUTION-MANDATORY PROVISIONS

SEC. 2. (a) The constitution formulated and drafted shall be republican in form, shall contain a bill of rights, and shall, either as a part thereof or in an ordinance appended thereto, contain provisions to the effect that, pending the final and complete withdrawal of the sovereignty of the United States over the Philippine Islands—

(1) All citizens of the Philippine Islands shall owe allegiance to the United States.

(2) Every officer of the government of the Commonwealth of the Philippine Islands shall, before entering upon the discharge of his duties, take and subscribe an oath of office, declaring, among other things, that he recognizes and accepts the supreme authority of and will maintain true faith and allegiance to the United States.

(3) Absolute toleration of religious sentiment shall be secured and no inhabitant or religious organization shall be molested in person or property on account of religious belief or mode of worship.

(4) Property owned by the United States, cemeteries, churches, and parsonages or convents appurtenant thereto, and all lands, buildings, and improvements used exclusively for religious, charitable, or educational purposes shall be exempt from taxation.

(5) Trade relations between the Philippine Islands and the United States shall be upon the basis prescribed in section 6.

(6) The public debt of the Philippine Islands and its subordinate branches shall not exceed limits now or hereafter fixed by the Congress of the United States; and no loans shall be contracted in foreign countries without the approval of the President of the United States.

(7) The debts, liabilities, and obligations of the present Philippine government, its Provinces, municipalities, and instrumentalities, valid and subsisting at the time of the adoption of the constitution, shall be assumed and paid by the new government.

(8) Provision shall be made for the establishment and maintenance of an adequate system of public schools, primarily conducted in the English language.

(9) Acts affecting currency, coinage, imports, exports, and immigration shall not become law until approved by the President of the United States.

(10) Foreign affairs shall be under the direct supervision and control of the United States.

(11) All acts passed by the Legislature of the Commonwealth of the Philippine Islands shall be reported to the Congress of the United States.

(12) The Philippine Islands recognizes the right of the United States to expropriate property for public uses, to maintain military and other reservations and armed forces in the Philippines, and, upon order of the President, to call into the service of such armed forces all military forces organized by the Philippine government.

(13) The decisions of the courts of the Commonwealth of the Philippine Islands shall be subject to review by the Supreme Court of the United States as provided in paragraph (6) of section 7.

(14) The United States may, by Presidential proclamation, exercise the right to intervene for the preservation of the government of the Commonwealth of the Philippine Islands and for the maintenance of the government as provided in the constitution thereof, and for the protection of life, property, and individual liberty and for the discharge of government obligations under and in accordance with the provisions of the constitution.

(15) The authority of the United States High Commissioner to the government of the Commonwealth of the Philippine Islands, as provided in this Act, shall be recognized.

(16) Citizens and corporations of the United States shall enjoy in the commonwealth of the Philippine Islands all the civil rights of the citizens and corporations, respectively, thereof.

(b) The constitution shall also contain the following provisions, effective as of the date of the proclamation of the President recognizing the independence of the Philippine Islands, as hereinafter provided:

(1) That the property rights of the United States and the Philippine Islands shall be promptly adjusted and settled, and that all existing property rights of citizens or corporations of the United States shall be acknowledged, respected, and safeguarded to the same extent as property rights of citizens of the Philippine Islands.

(2) That the officials elected and serving under the constitution adopted pursuant to the provisions of this Act shall be constitutional officers of the free and independent government of the Philippine Islands and qualified to function in all respects as elected directly under such government, and shall serve their full terms of office as prescribed in the constitution.

(3) That the debts and liabilities of the Philippine Islands, its Provinces, cities, municipalities, and instrumentalities, which shall be valid and subsisting at the time of the final and complete withdrawal of the sovereignty of the United

States, shall be assumed by the free and independent government of the Philippine Islands; and that where bonds have been issued under authority of an Act of Congress of the United States by the Philippine Islands, or any Province, city, municipality therein, the Philippine government will make adequate provision for the necessary funds for the payment of interest and principal, and such obligations shall be first lien on the taxes collected in the Philippine Islands.

(4) That the government of the Philippine Islands, on becoming independent of the United States, will assume all continuing obligations assumed by the United States under the treaty of peace with Spain ceding said Philippine Islands to the United States. . . .

SUBMISSION OF CONSTITUTION TO THE PRESIDENT OF THE UNITED STATES

SEC. 3. Upon the drafting and approval of the constitution by the constitutional convention in the Philippine Islands, the constitution shall be submitted within two years after the enactment of this Act to the President of the United States, who shall determine whether or not it conforms with the provisions of this Act. . . .

SUBMISSION OF CONSTITUTION TO FILIPINO PEOPLE

SEC. 4. After the President of the United States has certified that the constitution conforms with the provisions of this Act, it shall be submitted to the people of the Philippine Islands for their ratification or rejection at an election to be held within four months after the date of such certification, on a date to be fixed by the Philippine Legislature, at which election the qualified voters of the Philippine Islands shall have an opportunity to vote directly for or against the proposed constitution and ordinances appended thereto. . . . If a majority of the votes cast shall be for the constitution, such vote shall be deemed an expression of the will of the people of the Philippine Islands in favor of Philippine independence. . . .

If a majority of the votes cast are against the constitution, the existing government of the Philippine Islands shall continue without regard to the provisions of this Act. . . .

RELATIONS WITH THE UNITED STATES PENDING COMPLETE INDEPENDENCE

SEC. 6. After the date of the inauguration of the government of the Commonwealth of the Philippine Islands trade relations between the United States and the Philippine Islands shall be as now provided by law, subject to the following exceptions:

(a) There shall be levied, collected, and paid on all refined sugars in excess of fifty thousand long tons, and on unrefined sugars in excess of eight hundred thousand long tons, coming into the United States from the Philippine Islands in any calendar year, the same rates of duty which are required by the laws of the United States to be levied, collected, and paid upon like articles imported from foreign countries. . . .

(d) In the event that in any year the limit in the case of any article which may be exported to the United States free of duty shall be reached by the Philippine Islands, the amount or quantity of such articles produced or manufactured in the Philippine Islands thereafter that may be so exported to the United States free of duty shall be allocated, under export permits issued by the government of the Commonwealth of the Philippine Islands, to the producers or manufacturers of such articles proportionately on the basis of their exportation to the United States in the preceding year; except that in the case of unrefined sugar the amount thereof to be exported annually to the United States free of duty shall be allocated to the sugar-producing mills of the islands proportionately on the basis of their average annual production for the calendar years 1931, 1932, and 1933, and the amount of sugar from each mill which may be so exported shall be allocated in each year between the mill and the planters on the basis of the proportion of sugar to which the mill and the planters are respectively entitled. The government of the Philippine Islands is authorized to adopt the necessary laws and regulations for putting into effect the allocation hereinbefore provided.

(e) The government of the Commonwealth of the Philippine Islands shall impose and collect an export tax on all articles that may be exported to the United States from the Philippine Islands free of duty under the provisions of existing law as modified by the foregoing provisions of this section, including the articles enumerated in subdivisions (a), (b), and (c), within the limitations therein specified, as follows:

(1) During the sixth year after the inauguration of the new government the export tax shall be 5 per centum of the rates of duty which are required by the laws of the United States to be levied, collected, and paid on like articles imported from foreign countries;

(2) During the seventh year after the inauguration of the new government the export tax shall be 10 per centum. . . .

(3) During the eighth year after the inauguration of the new government the export tax shall be 15 per centum. . . .

(4) During the ninth year after the inauguration of the new government the export tax shall be 20 per centum. . . .

(5) After the expiration of the ninth year after the inauguration of the new government the export tax shall be 25 per centum. . . .

The government of the Commonwealth of the Philippine Islands shall place all funds received from such export taxes in a sinking fund, and such funds shall, in addition to other moneys available for that purpose, be applied solely to the payment of the principal and interest on the bonded indebtedness of the Philippine Islands, its Provinces, municipalities, and instrumentalities, until such indebtedness has been fully discharged. . . .

SEC. 7. Until the final and complete withdrawal of American sovereignty over the Philippine Islands—. . . .

(4) The President shall appoint, by and with the advice and consent of the Senate, a United States High Commissioner to the government of the Commonwealth of the Philippine Islands who shall hold office at the pleasure of the President and until his successor is appointed and qualified. . . .

If the government of the Commonwealth of the Philippine Islands fails to pay any of its bonded or other indebtedness or the interest thereon when due or to fulfill any of its contracts, the United States High Commissioner shall immediately report the facts to the President, who may thereupon direct the High Commissioner to take over the customs offices and administration of the same, administer the same, and apply such part of the revenue received therefrom as may be necessary for the payment of such overdue indebtedness or for the fulfillment of such contracts. . . .

(6) Review by the Supreme Court of the United States of cases from the Philippine Islands shall be as now provided by law; and such review shall also extend to all cases involving the constitution of the Commonwealth of the Philippine Islands.

SEC. 8. (a) Effective upon the acceptance of this Act by concurrent resolution of the Philippine Legislature or by a convention called for that purpose, as provided in section 17—

(1) For the purposes of the Immigration Act of 1917, the Immigration Act of 1924 (except section 13 (c)), this section, and all other laws of the United States relating to the immigration, exclusion, or expulsion of aliens, citizens of the Philippine Islands who are not citizens of the United States shall be considered as if they were aliens. For such purposes the Philippine Islands shall be considered as a separate country and shall have for each fiscal year a quota of fifty.

RECOGNITION OF PHILIPPINE INDEPENDENCE AND WITHDRAWAL OF AMERICAN SOVEREIGNTY

SEC. 10. (a) On the 4th day of July immediately following the expiration of a period of ten years from the date of the inauguration of the new government under the constitution provided for in this Act the President of the United States shall by proclamation withdraw and surrender all right of possession, supervision, jurisdiction, control, or sovereignty then existing and exercised by the United States in and over the territory and people of the Philippine Islands, including all military and other reservations of the Government of the United States in the Philippines (except such naval reservations and fueling stations as are reserved under section 5), and, on behalf of the United States, shall recognize the independence of the Philippine Islands as a separate and self governing nation and acknowledge the authority and control over the same of the government instituted by the people thereof, under the constitution then in force. . . .

NEUTRALIZATION OF PHILIPPINE ISLANDS

SEC. 11. The President is requested, at the earliest practicable date, to enter into negotiations with foreign powers with a view to the conclusion of a treaty for the perpetual neutralization of the Philippine Islands, if and when Philippine independence shall have been achieved. . . .

TARIFF DUTIES AFTER INDEPENDENCE

SEC. 13. After the Philippine Islands have become a free and independent nation there shall be levied, collected, and paid upon all articles coming into the United States from the Philippine Islands the rates of duty which are required to be levied, collected, and paid upon like articles imported from other foreign countries: *Provided*, That at least one year prior to the date fixed in this Act for the independence of the Philippine Islands, there shall be held a conference of representatives of the Government of the United States and the government of the Commonwealth of the Philippine Islands . . . for the purpose of formulating recommendations as to future trade relations between the Government of the United States and the independent government of the Philippine Islands. . . .

IMMIGRATION AFTER INDEPENDENCE

SEC. 14. Upon the final and complete withdrawal of American sovereignty over the Philippine Islands the immigration laws of the United States . . . shall apply to persons who were born in the Philippine Islands to the same extent as in the case of other foreign countries. . . .

EFFECTIVE DATE

SEC. 17. The foregoing provisions of this Act shall not take effect until accepted by concurrent resolution of the Philippine Legislature or by a convention called for the purpose of passing upon that question as may be provided by the Philippine Legislature.

Source: Henry Steele Commager, *Documents of American History*, vol. 2 (Englewood Cliffs, NJ: Prentice Hall, 1973), 287–91.

---

80. ABROGATION OF THE PLATT AMENDMENT
29 May 1934

In September 1933, a revolutionary junta took control of Cuba. One of its first acts was to abrogate the Platt Amendment to the Cuban constitution. With the Stimson Doctrine in place and Roosevelt's commitment to the Good Neighbor Policy part of the public record, the United States took the step of officially revoking the Platt Amendment as well.

The United States of America and the Republic of Cuba, being animated by the desire to fortify the relations of friendship between the two countries, and to modify, with this purpose, the relations established between them by the Treaty of Relations signed at Havana, May 22, 1903, have appointed, with this intention, as their plenipotentiaries: . . .

Who, after having communicated to each other their full powers, which were found to be in good and due form, have agreed upon the following articles:

ART. I. The Treaty of Relations which was concluded between the two contracting parties on May 22, 1903, shall cease to be in force, and is abrogated, from the date on which the present treaty goes into effect.

ART. II. All the acts effected in Cuba by the United States of America during its military occupation of the island, up to May 20, 1902, the date on which the Republic of Cuba was established, have been ratified and held as valid; and all rights legally acquired by virtue of those acts shall be maintained and protected.

ART. III. Until the two contracting parties agree to the modification or abrogation of the stipulations of the agreement in regard to the lease to the United States of America of lands in Cuba for coaling and naval stations signed by the President of the Republic of Cuba on February 16, 1903, and by the President of the United States of America on the 23rd day of the same month and year, the stipulations of that agreement with regard to the naval station of Guantanamo shall continue in effect. The supplementary agreement in regard to naval or coating stations signed between the two governments on July 2, 1903, shall continue in effect in the same form and on the same conditions with respect to the naval station at Guantanamo. So long as the United States of America shall not abandon the said naval station of Guantanamo or the two governments shall not agree to a modification of its present limits, the station shall continue to have the territorial area that it now has, with the limits that it has on the date of the signature of the present treaty.

ART. IV. If at any time in the future a situation should arise that appears to point to an outbreak of contagious disease in the territory of either of the contracting parties, either of the two governments shall, for its own protection, and without its act being considered unfriendly, exercise freely and at its discretion the right to suspend communications between those of its ports that it may designate and all or part of the territory of the other party, and for the period that it may consider to be advisable.

ART. V. The present Treaty shall be ratified by the contracting parties in accordance with their respective Constitutional methods; and shall go into effect on the date of the exchange of their ratifications, which shall take place in the city of Washington as soon as possible.

Source: William M. Malloy, ed., *Treaties, Conventions, International Acts, Protocols, and Agreements between the United States and Other Powers, 1923–1937*, vol. 4 (Washington, DC: Government Printing Office, 1938), 4054–55.

81. THE NEUTRALITY ACT OF 1937
1 May 1937

Throughout his two terms before the Second World War, Roosevelt en-
gaged in a protracted struggle with Congress and the public over his
ability to involve America in foreign conflicts. Starting in 1935, American
legislators passed a series of joint resolutions prohibiting U.S. intervention
in wars abroad. In subsequent years, these provisions would be strength-
ened and articulated as aggression in Europe and Asia spread.

JOINT RESOLUTION

To amend the joint resolution, approved August 31, 1935, as amended.
Resolved . . .

EXPORT OF ARMS, AMMUNITION, AND IMPLEMENTS OF WAR

Section 1. (a) Whenever the President, shall find that there exists a state of
war between, or among, two or more foreign states, the President shall proclaim
such fact, and, it shall thereafter be unlawful to export, or, attempt to export, or
cause to be exported, arms, ammunition, or implements of war from any place
in the United States to any belligerent state named in such proclamation, or any
neutral state for transshipment to, or for the use of, any such belligerent state.

(b) The President shall, from time to time, by proclamation, extend such
embargo upon the export of arms, ammunition, or implements of war to other
states as and when they may become involved in such war.

(c) Whenever the President shall find that a state of civil strife exists in a
foreign state and that such civil strife is of a magnitude or is being conducted
under such conditions that the export of arms, ammunition or implements of
war from the United States the President shall proclaim such fact and it shall
thereafter be unlawful to export, or attempt to export, or cause to be exported,
arms, ammunition, or implements of war from any place in the United States
to such foreign state, or to any neutral state for transshipment to, or for the use
of, such foreign state.

(d) The President shall, from time to time by proclamation, definitely enumerate the arms, ammunition, and implements of war, the export of which is
prohibited by this section. The arms, ammunition, and implements of war so
enumerated shall include those enumerated in the President's proclamation
Numbered 2163, of April 10, 1936, but shall not include raw materials or any
other articles or materials not of the same general character as those enumerated
in the said proclamation, and in the Convention for the Supervision of the In-

ternational Trade in Arms and Ammunition and in Implements of War, signed at Geneva June 17, 1925.

(e) Whoever, in violation of any of the provisions of this Act, shall export, or attempt to export, or cause to be exported, arms, ammunition, or implements of war from the United States shall be fined not more than $10,000, or imprisoned not more than five years, or both. . . .

(f) In the case of the forfeiture of any arms, ammunition, or implements of war by reason of a violation of this Act . . . such arms, ammunition, or implements of war shall be delivered to the Secretary of War for such use or disposal thereof as shall be approved by the President of the United States.

(g) Whenever, in the judgment of the President, the conditions which have caused him to issue any proclamation under the authority of this section have ceased to exist, he shall revoke the same, and the provisions of this section shall thereupon cease to apply with respect to the state or states named in such proclamation, except with respect to offenses committed, or forfeitures incurred, prior to such revocation.

EXPORT OF OTHER ARTICLES AND MATERIALS

SEC. 2. (a) Whenever the President shall have issued a proclamation under the authority of section 1 of this Act and he shall thereafter find that the placing of restrictions on the shipment of certain articles or materials in addition to arms, ammunition, and implements of war from the United States to belligerent states, or to a state wherein civil strife exists, is necessary to promote the security or preserve the peace of the United States or to protect the lives of citizens of the United States, he shall so proclaim, and it shall thereafter be unlawful, for any American vessel to carry such articles or materials to any belligerent state, or to any state wherein civil strife exists, named in such proclamation issued under the authority of section 1 of this Act, or to any neutral state for transshipment to, or for the use of, any such belligerent state or any such state wherein civil strife exists. The President shall by proclamation from time to time definitely enumerate the article and materials which it shall be unlawful for American vessels to so transport. . . .

(c) The President shall from time to time by proclamation extend such restrictions as are imposed under the authority of this section to other states as and when they may be declared to become belligerent states under proclamations issued under the authority of section 1 of this Act.

(d) The President may from time to time change, modify, or revoke in whole or in part any proclamations issued by him under the authority of this section.

(e) Except with respect to offenses committed, or forfeitures incurred, prior to May 1, 1939, this section and all proclamations issued thereunder shall not be effective after May 1, 1939.

FINANCIAL TRANSACTIONS

SEC. 3 (a) Whenever the President shall have issued a proclamation under the authority of section 1 of this Act, it shall thereafter be unlawful for any person within the United States to purchase, sell, or exchange bonds, securities, or other obligations of the government of any belligerent state or of any state wherein civil strife exists, named in such proclamation, or of any political subdivision of any such state, or of any person acting for or on behalf of the government of any such state, or of any such faction or asserted government within any such state wherein civil strife exists, or of any person acting for or on behalf of any faction or asserted government within any such state wherein civil strife exists, issued after the date of such proclamation, or to make any loan or extend any credit to any such government, political subdivision, faction, asserted government, or person, or to solicit or receive any contribution for any such government, political subdivision, faction, asserted government, or person: *Provided*, That if the President shall find that such action will serve to protect the commercial or other interests of the United States or its citizens, he may, in his discretion, and to such extent and under such regulations as he may prescribe, except from the operation of this section ordinary commercial credits and short-time obligations in aid of legal transactions and of a character customarily used in normal peacetime commercial transactions. Nothing in this subsection shall be construed to prohibit the solicitation or collection of funds to be used for medical aid and assistance, or for food and clothing to relieve human suffering, when such solicitation or collection of funds is made on behalf of and for use by any person or organization which is not acting for or on behalf of any such government, political subdivision, faction, or asserted government, but all such solicitations and collections of funds shall be subject to the approval of the President and shall be made under such rules and regulations as he shall prescribe. . . .

(c) Whoever shall violate the provisions of this section or of any regulations issued hereunder shall, upon conviction thereof, be fined not more than $50,000 or imprisoned for not more than five years, or both. Should the violation be by a corporation, organization, or association, each officer or agent thereof participating in the violation may be liable to the penalty herein prescribed. . . .

EXCEPTIONS—AMERICAN REPUBLICS

SEC. 4. This Act shall not apply to an American republic or republics engaged in war against a non-American state or states, provided the American republic is not cooperating with a non-American state or states in such war.

NATIONAL MUNITIONS CONTROL BOARD

SEC. 5 (a) There is hereby established a National Munitions Control Board (hereinafter referred to as the 'Board') to carry out the provisions of this Act. The Board shall consist of the Secretary of State, who shall be chairman and executive officer of the Board, the Secretary of the Treasury, the Secretary of War, the Secretary of the Navy, and the Secretary of Commerce. Except as otherwise provided in this Act, or by other law, the administration of this Act is vested in the Department of State. The Secretary of State shall promulgate such rules and regulations with regard to the enforcement of this section as he may deem necessary to carry out its provisions. The Board shall be convened by the chairman and shall hold at least one meeting a year.

(b) Every person who engages in the business of manufacturing, exporting, or importing any of the arms, ammunition, or implements of war referred to in this Act, whether as an exporter, importer, manufacturer, or dealer, shall register with the Secretary of State his name, or business name, principal place of business, and places of business in the United States, and a list of the arms, ammunition, and implements of war which he manufactures, imports, or exports.

(c) Every person required to register under this section shall notify the Secretary of State of any change in the arms, ammunition, or implements of war which he exports, imports, or manufactures; . . .

(d) It shall be unlawful for any person to export, or attempt to export, from the United States to any other state, any of the arms, ammunition, or implements of war referred to in this Act, or to import, or attempt to import, to the United States from any other state, any of the arms, ammunition, or implements of war referred to in this Act, without first having obtained a license therefor. . . .

(k) The President is hereby authorized to proclaim upon recommendation of the Board from time to time a list of articles which shall be considered arms, ammunition, and implements of war for the purposes of this section.

AMERICAN VESSELS PROHIBITED FROM CARRYING ARMS TO BELLIGERENT STATES

SEC. 6. (a) Whenever the President shall have issued a proclamation under the authority of section 1 of this Act, it shall thereafter be unlawful, until such proclamation is revoked, for any American vessel to carry any arms, ammunition, or implements of war to any belligerent state, or to any state wherein civil strife exists, named in such proclamation, or to any neutral state for transshipment to, or for the use of, any such belligerent state or any such state wherein civil strife exists.

(b) Whoever, in violation of the provisions of this section, shall take, or attempt to take, or shall authorize, hire, or solicit another to take, any American vessel carrying such cargo out of port or from the jurisdiction of the United States shall be fined not more than $10,000, or imprisoned not more than five years, or both; and, in addition, such vessel, and her tackle, apparel, furniture, and equipment, and the arms, ammunition, and implements of war on board, shall be forfeited to the United States.

USE OF AMERICAN PORTS AS BASE OF SUPPLY

SEC. 7. (a) Whenever, during any war in which the United States is neutral, the President, or any person thereunto authorized by him, shall have cause to believe that any vessel, domestic or foreign, whether requiring clearance or not, is about to carry out of a port of the United States, fuel, men, arms, ammunition, implements of war, or other supplies to any warship, tender, or supply ship of a belligerent state, but the evidence is not deemed sufficient to justify forbidding the departure of the vessel as provided for by section 1, title V, chapter 30, of the Act approved June 15, 1917, and if, in the President's judgment, such action will serve to maintain peace between the United States and foreign states, or to protect the commercial interests of the United States and its citizens, or to promote the security or neutrality of the United States, he shall have the power and it shall be his duty to require the owner, master, or person in command thereof, before departing from a port of the United States, to give a bond to the United States, with sufficient sureties, in such amount as he shall deem proper, conditioned that the vessel will not deliver the men, or any part of the cargo, to any warship, tender, or supply ship of a belligerent state.

(b) If the President, or any person thereunto authorized by him, shall find that a vessel, domestic or foreign, in a port of the United States, has previously cleared from a port of the United States during such war and delivered its cargo or any part thereof to a warship, tender, or supply ship of a belligerent state, he may prohibit the departure of such vessel during the duration of the war.

SUBMARINES AND ARMED MERCHANT VESSELS

SEC. 8. Whenever, during any war in which the United States is neutral, the President shall find that special restrictions placed on the use of the ports and territorial waters of the United States by the submarines or armed merchant vessels of a foreign state, will serve to maintain peace between the United States and foreign states, or to protect the commercial interests of the United States and its citizens, or to promote the security of the United States, and shall make proclamation therefore, it shall thereafter be unlawful for any such submarine or armed merchant vessel to enter a port or the territorial waters of the United States or to depart therefrom, except under such conditions and subject to such limitations as the President may prescribe. Whenever, in his judgment, the conditions which have caused him to issue his proclamation have ceased to exist, he shall revoke his proclamation and the provisions of this section shall thereupon cease to apply.

TRAVEL ON VESSELS OF BELLIGERENT STATES

SEC. 9. Whenever the President shall have issued a proclamation under the authority of section 1 of this Act it shall thereafter be unlawful for any citizen of the United States to travel on any vessel of the state or states named in such proclamation, except in accordance with such rules and regulations as the President shall prescribe: . . .

ARMING OF AMERICAN MERCHANT VESSELS
PROHIBITED

SEC. 10. Whenever the President shall have issued a proclamation under the authority of section 1, it shall thereafter be unlawful, until such proclamation is revoked, for any American vessel engaged in commerce with any belligerent state, or any state wherein civil strife exists, named in such proclamation, to be armed or to carry any armament, arms, ammunition, or implements of war, except small arms and ammunition therefor which the President may deem necessary and shall publicly designate for the preservation of discipline aboard such vessels.

REGULATIONS

SEC. 11. The President may, from time to time, promulgate such rules and regulations not inconsistent with law, as may be necessary and proper to carry out any of the provisions of this Act; and he may exercise any power or authority conferred on him by this Act through such officer or officers, or agency or agencies, as he shall direct. . . .

Source: Congressional Record, vol. 81, pt. 2 (Washington, DC: Government Printing Office, 1937), 1650–52.

82. ROOSEVELT'S "QUARANTINE" SPEECH
5 October 1937

Faced with evidence of Japanese imperial designs in China, Roosevelt gave a speech in October 1937 designed to condemn Tokyo and also test the American public's tolerance of a more proactive U.S. role in international affairs. The speech failed on both counts. Japanese expansion in China continued unabated, and the president was roundly criticized for suggesting American intervention against it.

. . . The political situation in the world, which of late has been growing progressively worse, is such as to cause grave concern and anxiety to all the peoples and nations who wish to live in peace and amity with their neighbors. . . . Without a declaration of war and without warning or justification of any kind, civilians, including vast numbers of women and children, are being ruthlessly murdered with bombs from the air. In times of so-called peace, ships are being attacked and sunk by submarines without cause or notice. Nations are fomenting and taking sides in civil warfare in nations that have never done them any harm. Nations claiming freedom for themselves deny it to others.

Innocent peoples, innocent nations, are being cruelly sacrificed to a greed for power and supremacy which is devoid of all sense of justice and humane considerations. . . .

The peace-loving nations must make a concerted effort in opposition to those violations of treaties and those ignorings of humane instincts which today are creating a state of international anarchy and instability from which there is no escape through mere isolation or neutrality.

Those who cherish their freedom and recognize and respect the equal right of their neighbors to be free and live in peace, must work together for the triumph of law and moral principles in order that peace, justice and confidence may prevail in the world. There must be a return to a belief in the pledged word, in the value of a signed treaty. There must be recognition of the fact that national morality is as vital as private morality. . . .

It seems to be unfortunately true that the epidemic of world lawlessness is spreading.

When an epidemic of physical disease starts to spread, the community approves and joins in a quarantine of the patients in order to protect the health of the community against the spread of the disease.

It is my determination to pursue a policy of peace. It is my determination to adopt every practicable measure to avoid involvement in war. It ought to be inconceivable that in this modern era, and in the face of experience, any nation could be so foolish and ruthless as to run the risk of plunging the whole world into war by invading and violating, in contravention of solemn treaties, the territory of other nations that have done them no real harm and are too weak to protect themselves adequately. Yet the peace of the world and the welfare and security of every nation, including our own, is today being threatened by that very thing.

No nation which refuses to exercise forbearance and to respect the freedom and rights of others can long remain strong and retain the confidence and respect of other nations. No nation ever loses its dignity or its good standing by conciliating its differences, and by exercising great patience with, and consideration for, the rights of other nations.

War is a contagion, whether it be declared or undeclared. It can engulf states and peoples remote from the original scene of hostilities.

We are determined to keep out of war, yet we cannot insure ourselves against the disastrous effects of war and the dangers of involvement. We are adopting such measures as will minimize our risk of involvement, but we cannot have complete protection in a world of disorder in which confidence and security have broken down.

If civilization is to survive the principles of the Prince of Peace must be restored. Trust between nations must be revived.

Most important of all, the will for peace on the part of peace-loving nations must express itself to the end that nations that may be tempted to violate their agreements and the rights of others will desist from such a course. There must be positive endeavors to preserve peace.

America hates war. America hopes for peace. Therefore, America actively engages in the search for peace.

Source: Samuel I. Rosenman, ed., *The Public Papers and Addresses of Franklin D. Roosevelt*, vol. 6 (New York: Russell & Russell, 1969), 406–11.

83.   THE "NEW ORDER" IN THE FAR EAST
31 December 1938

*As it pursued a campaign of conquest against China, Japan rebuffed Amer-
ican protests that it was violating U.S. treaty rights and the Open Door
Policy. The note of 31 December comprises Washington's reaction to this
new situation. The following year, the United States would initiate the
abrogation of the 1911 Commercial Treaty with Japan.*

United States Note to Japan Regarding Violations of American
Rights in China
31 December 1938

The Government of the United States has received and has given full consideration to the reply of the Japanese Government of November 18 to this Government's note of October 6 on the subject of American rights and interests in
China.

In the light of facts and experience the Government of the United States is
impelled to reaffirm its previously expressed opinion that imposition of restrictions upon the movements and activities of American nationals who are engaged
in philanthropic, educational and commercial endeavors in China has placed and
will, if continued, increasingly place Japanese interests in a preferred position
and is, therefore, unquestionably discriminatory, in its effect, against legitimate
American interests. Further, with reference to such matters as exchange control,
compulsory currency circulation, tariff revision, and monopolistic promotion in
certain areas of China, the plans and practices of the Japanese authorities imply
an assumption on the part of those authorities that the Japanese Government or
the regimes established and maintained in China by Japanese armed forces are
entitled to act in China in a capacity such as flows from rights of sovereignty
and, further, in so acting to disregard and even to declare nonexistent or abrogated the established rights and interests of other countries, including the United
States.

The Government of the United States expresses its conviction that the restrictions and measures under reference not only are unjust and unwarranted but are
counter to the provisions of several binding international agreements, voluntarily
entered into, to which both Japan and the United States, and in some cases other
countries, are parties.

In the concluding portion of its note under reference, the Japanese Government states that it is firmly convinced that "in the face of the new situation, fast
developing in East Asia, any attempt to apply to the conditions of today and
tomorrow inapplicable ideas and principles of the past neither would contribute

toward the establishment of a real peace in East Asia nor solve the immediate issues," and that "as long as these points are understood, Japan has not the slightest inclination to oppose the participation of the United States and other powers in the great work of reconstructing East Asia along all lines of industry and trade."

The Government of the United States in its note of October 6 requested, in view of the oft-reiterated assurances proffered by the Government of Japan of its intention to observe the principle of equality of opportunity in its relations with China, and in view of Japan's treaty obligations so to do, that the Government of Japan abide by these obligations and carry out these assurances in practice. The Japanese Government in its reply appears to affirm that it is its intention to make its observance of that principle conditional upon an understanding by the American Government and by other governments of a "new situation" and a "new order" in the Far Fast as envisaged and fostered by Japanese authorities.

Treaties which bear upon the situation in the Far East have within them provisions relating to a number of subjects. . . . The various provisions agreed upon may be said to have constituted collectively an arrangement for safeguarding, for the benefit of all, the correlated principles on the one hand of national integrity and on the other hand of equality of economic opportunity. Experience has shown that impairment of the former of these principles is followed almost invariably by disregard of the latter. Whenever any government begins to exercise political authority in areas beyond the limits of its lawful jurisdiction there develops inevitably a situation in which the nationals of that government demand and are accorded, at the hands of their government, preferred treatment, whereupon equality of opportunity ceases to exist and discriminatory practices, productive of friction, prevail.

The admonition that enjoyment by the nationals of the United States of non-discriminatory treatment in China—a general and well-established right—is henceforth to be contingent upon an admission by the Government of the United States of the validity of the conception of Japanese authorities of a "new situation" and a "new order" in East Asia, is, in the opinion of this Government, highly paradoxical.

This country's adherence to and its advocacy of the principle of equality of opportunity do not flow solely from a desire to obtain the commercial benefits which naturally result from the carrying out of that principle. They flow from a firm conviction that observance of that principle leads to economic and political stability, which are conducive both to the internal well-being of nations and to mutually beneficial and peaceful relationships between and among nations; from a firm conviction that failure to observe that principle breeds international friction and ill-will, with consequences injurious to all countries, including in particular those countries which fail to observe it; and from an equally firm conviction that observance of that principle promotes the opening of trade channels thereby making available the markets, the raw materials and the manufactured products of the community of nations on a mutually and reciprocally beneficial basis.

The principle of equality of economic opportunity is, moreover, one to which over a long period and on many occasions the Japanese Government has given definite approval. It is one to the observance of which the Japanese Government has committed itself in various international agreements and understandings. It is one upon observance of which by other nations the Japanese Government has of its own accord and upon its own initiative frequently insisted. It is one to which the Japanese Government has repeatedly during recent months declared itself committed.

The people and the Government of the United States could not assent to the establishment, at the instance of and for the special purposes of any third country, of a regime which would arbitrarily deprive them of the long-established rights of equal opportunity and fair treatment which are legally and justly theirs along with those of other nations.

Fundamental principles, such as the principle of equality of opportunity, which have long been regarded as inherently wise and just, which have been widely adopted and adhered to, and which are general in their application, are not subject to nullification by a unilateral affirmation.

With regard to the implication in the Japanese Government's note that the "conditions of today and tomorrow" in the Far East call for a revision of the ideas and principles of the past, this Government desires to recall to the Japanese Government its position on the subject of revision of agreements.

This Government had occasion in the course of a communication delivered to the Japanese Government on April 29, 1934, to express its opinion that "treaties can lawfully be modified or be terminated, but only by processes prescribed or recognized or agreed upon by the parties to them."

In the same communication this Government also said, "In the opinion of the American people and the American Government no nation can, without the assent of the other nations concerned, rightfully endeavor to make conclusive its will in situations where there are involved the rights, the obligations and the legitimate interests of other sovereign states." . . .

At various times during recent decades various powers, among which have been Japan and the United States, have had occasion to communicate and to confer with regard to situations and problems in the Far East. In the conducting of correspondence and of conferences relating to these matters, the parties involved have invariably taken into consideration past and present facts and they have not failed to perceive the possibility and the desirability of changes in the situation. In the making of treaties they have drawn up and have agreed upon provisions intended to facilitate advantageous developments and at the same time to obviate and avert the arising of friction between and among the various powers which, having interests in the region or regions under reference, were and would be concerned.

In the light of these facts, and with reference especially to the purpose and the character of the treaty provisions from time to time solemnly agreed upon for the very definite purposes indicated, the Government of the United States deprecates the fact that one of the parties to these agreements has chosen to embark—as indicated both by action of its agents and by official statements of its authorities—upon a course directed toward the arbitrary creation by that power by methods of its own selection, regardless of treaty pledges and the established rights of other powers concerned, of a "new order" in the Far East. Whatever may be the changes which have taken place in the situation in the Far East and whatever may be the situation now, these matters are of no less interest and concern to the American Government than have been the situations which have prevailed there in the past, and such changes as may henceforth take place there, changes which may enter into the producing of a "new situation" and a "new order," are and will be of like concern to this Government. This Government is well aware that the situation has changed. This Government is also well aware that many of the changes have been brought about by action of Japan. This Government does not admit, however, that there is need or warrant for any one power to take upon itself to prescribe what shall be the terms and conditions of a "new order" in areas not under its sovereignty and to constitute itself the repository of authority and the agent of destiny in regard thereto. . . .

The United States has in its international relations rights and obligations which derive from international law and rights and obligations which rest upon treaty provisions. Of those which rest on treaty provisions, its rights and obligations in and with regard to China rest in part upon provisions in treaties between the United States and China, and in part upon provisions in treaties between the United States and several other powers, including both China and Japan. These treaties were concluded in good faith for the purpose of safeguarding and promoting the interests not of one only but of all their signatories. The people and the Government of the United States cannot assent to the abrogation of any of this country's rights or obligations by the arbitrary action of agents or authorities of any other country.

The Government of the United States has, however, always been prepared, and is now, to give due and ample consideration to any proposals based on justice and reason which envisage the resolving of problems in a manner duly considerate of the rights and obligations of all parties directly concerned by processes of free negotiation and new commitment by and among all of the parties so concerned. There has been and there continues to be opportunity for the Japanese Government to put forward such proposals. This Government has been and it continues to be willing to discuss such proposals, if and when put forward, with representatives of the other powers, including Japan and China, whose rights and interests are involved, at whatever time and in whatever place may be commonly agreed upon.

Meanwhile, this Government reserves all rights of the United States as they exist and does not give assent to any impairment of any of those rights.

Source: Henry Steele Commager, *Documents of American History*, vol. 2 (Englewood Cliffs, NJ: Prentice Hall, 1973), 411–15.

84. ROOSEVELT'S APPEAL FOR PEACE IN EUROPE
1939

As Hitler escalated his demands for the secession of the Danzig Corridor from Poland, Europe began final preparations for war. In the United States, Roosevelt engaged in a last-ditch effort to convince the belligerent parties that a peaceful resolution of the deteriorating situation was still preferable to the outbreak of hostilities

THE WHITE HOUSE

April 14, 1939

HIS EXCELLENCY
ADOLF HITLER,
CHANCELLOR OF THE GERMAN REICH,
BERLIN, GERMANY

You realize I am sure that throughout the world hundreds of millions of human beings are living today in constant fear of a new war or even a series of wars.

The existence of this fear—and the possibility of such a conflict—is of definite concern to the people of the United States for whom I speak, as it must also be to the peoples of the other nations of the entire Western Hemisphere. All of them know that any major war, even if it were to be confined to other continents, must bear heavily on them during its continuance and also for generations to come.

Because of the fact that after acute tension in which during the past few weeks there would seem to be at least a momentary relaxation—because no troops are at this moment on the march—this may be an opportune moment for me to send you this message.

On a previous occasion I have addressed you in behalf of the settlement of political, economic, and social problems by peaceful methods and without resort to arms.

But the tide of events seems to have reverted to the threat of arms. If such threats continue, it seems inevitable that much of the world must become involved in common ruin. All the world, victor nations, vanquished nations, and neutral nations will suffer. I refuse to believe that the world is, of necessity, such a prisoner of destiny. On the contrary, it is clear that the leaders of great nations have it in their power to liberate their peoples from the disaster that impends. It is equally clear that in their own minds and in their hearts the peoples themselves desire that their fears be ended.

It is, however, unfortunately necessary to take cognizance of recent facts.

Three nations in Europe and one in Africa have seen their independent existence terminated. A vast territory in another independent nation of the Far East has been occupied by a neighboring state. Reports, which we trust are not true, insist that further acts of aggression are contemplated against still other independent nations. Plainly the world is moving toward the moment when this situation must end in catastrophe unless a more rational way of guiding events is found.

You have repeatedly asserted that you and the German people have no desire for war. If this is true there need be no war.

Nothing can persuade the peoples of the earth that any governing power has any right or need to inflict the consequences of war on its own or any other people save in the cause of self-evident home defense.

In making this statement we as Americans speak not through selfishness or fear or weakness. If we speak now it is with the voice of strength and with friendship for mankind. It is still clear to me that international problems can be solved at the council table.

It is therefore no answer to the plea for peaceful discussion for one side to plead that unless they receive assurances beforehand that the verdict will be theirs, they will not lay aside their arms. In conference rooms, as in courts, it is necessary that both sides enter upon the discussion in good faith, assuming that substantial justice will accrue to both; and it is customary that they leave their arms outside the room where they confer.

I am convinced that the cause of world peace would be greatly advanced if the nations of the world were to obtain a frank statement relating to the present and future policy of governments.

Because the United States, as one of the nations of the Western Hemisphere, is not involved in the immediate controversies which have arisen in Europe, I trust that you may be willing to make such a statement of policy to me as the head of a nation far removed from Europe in order that I, acting only with the responsibility and obligation of a friendly intermediary, may communicate such declaration to other nations now apprehensive as to the course which the policy of your Government may take.

Are you willing to give assurance that your armed forces will not attack or invade the territory or possessions of the following independent nations: Finland, Estonia, Latvia, Lithuania, Sweden, Norway, Denmark, The Netherlands, Belgium, Great Britain and Ireland, France, Portugal, Spain, Switzerland, Liechtenstein, Luxemburg, Poland, Hungary, Rumania, Yugoslavia, Russia, Bulgaria, Greece, Turkey, Iraq, the Arabias, Syria, Palestine, Egypt and Iran.

Such an assurance clearly must apply not only to the present day but also to a future sufficiently long to give every opportunity to work by peaceful methods for a more permanent peace. I therefore suggest that you construe the word "future" to apply to a minimum period of assured non-aggression—ten years at the least—a quarter of a century, if we dare look that far ahead.

If such assurance is given by your Government, I will immediately transmit it to the governments of the nations I have named and I will simultaneously inquire whether I am reasonably sure, each of the nations enumerated above will in turn give like assurance for transmission to you. Reciprocal assurances such as I have outlined will bring to the world an immediate measure of relief.

I propose that if it is given, two essential problems shall promptly be discussed in the resulting peaceful surroundings, and in those discussions the Government of the United States will gladly take part.

The discussions which I have in mind relate to the most effective and immediate manner through which the peoples of the world can obtain progressive relief from the crushing burden of armament which is each day bringing them more closely to the brink of economic disaster. Simultaneously the Government of the United States would be prepared to take part in discussions looking towards the most practical manner of opening up avenues of international trade to the end that every nation of the earth may be enabled to buy and sell on equal terms in the world market as well as to possess assurance of obtaining the materials and products of peaceful economic life.

At the same time, those governments other than the United States which are directly interested could undertake such political discussions as they may consider necessary or desirable.

We recognize complex world problems which affect all humanity but we know that study and discussion of them must be held in an atmosphere of peace. Such an atmosphere of peace cannot exist if negotiations are overshadowed by the threat of force or by the fear of war.

I think you will not misunderstand the spirit of frankness in which I send you this message. Heads of great governments in this hour are literally responsible for the fate of humanity in the coming years. They cannot fail to hear the prayers of their peoples to be protected from the foreseeable chaos of war. History will hold them accountable for the lives and the happiness of all—even unto the least.

I hope that your answer will make it possible for humanity to lose fear and regain security for many years to come.

A similar message is being addressed to the Chief of the Italian Government.

FRANKLIN D. ROOSEVELT

August 24, 1939

The following is the text of a communication, dispatched yesterday by the President and delivered today to the King of Italy by Ambassador Phillips:

Again a crisis in world affairs makes clear the responsibility of heads of nations for the fate of their own people and indeed of humanity itself. It is because of traditional accord between Italy and the United States and the ties of consanguinity between millions of our citizens that I feel that I can address Your Majesty in behalf of the maintenance of world peace.

It is my belief and that of the American People that Your Majesty and Your Majesty's Government can greatly influence the averting of an outbreak of war. Any general war would cause to suffer all nations whether belligerent or neutral, whether victors or vanquished, and would clearly bring devastation to the peoples and perhaps to the governments of some nations most directly concerned.

The friends of the Italian people and among them the American people could only regard with grief the destruction of great achievements which European nations and the Italian nation in particular have attained during the past generation.

We in America having welded a homogeneous nation out of many nationalities, often find it difficult to visualize the animosities which so often have created crises among nations of Europe which are smaller than ours in population and in territory, but we accept the fact that these nations have an absolute right to maintain their national independence if they so desire. If that be sound doctrine then it must apply to the weaker nations as well as to the stronger.

Acceptance of this means peace, because fear of aggression ends. The alternative, which means of necessity efforts by the strong to dominate the weak, will lead not only to war, but to long future years of oppression on the part of victors and to rebellion on the part of the vanquished. So history teaches us.

On April fourteenth last I suggested in essence an understanding that no armed forces should attack or invade the territory of any other independent nation, and that this being assured, discussions be undertaken to seek progressive relief from the burden of armaments and to open avenues of international trade including sources of raw materials necessary to the peaceful economic life of each nation.

I said that in these discussions the United States would gladly take part. And such peaceful conversations would make it wholly possible for governments other than the United States to enter into peaceful discussions of political or territorial problems in which they were directly concerned.

Were it possible for Your Majesty's Government to formulate proposals for a pacific solution of the present crisis along these lines you are assured of the earnest sympathy of the United States.

The Government of Italy and the United States can today advance those ideals of Christianity which of late seems so often to have been obscured.

The unheard voices of countless millions of human beings ask that they shall not be vainly sacrificed again.

Source: Samuel I. Rosenman, ed., *The Public Papers and Addresses of Franklin D. Roosevelt*, vol. 8 (New York: Russell & Russell, 1969), 201–5, 444–49.

85. DECLARATION OF PANAMA
2 October 1939

*After the outbreak of war in September 1939, the United States and its
Latin American allies announced the creation of a three-hundred-mile neutral zone around the Western Hemisphere, with the exception of Canada.
The Panama Declaration was routinely ignored by both sides in the unfolding naval war in the Atlantic.*

The republics of America, meeting in Panama, have solemnly ratified their
position as neutrals in the conflict which disturbs the Peace of Europe. But as
the present war may reach unexpected derivations, which by their gravitation
may affect the fundamental interests of America, it is hereby declared that nothing can justify that the interests of belligerents prevail over the rights of neutrals,
causing upsets and sufferings of peoples who, by their neutrality in the conflict
and their distance from the scene of the happenings, should not suffer its fatal
dolorous consequences.

During the World War of 1914–1918, the Governments of Argentina, Brazil,
Chile, Colombia and Ecuador presented or supported individual proposals seeking in principle a declaration of American republics which entreated the belligerent nations to abstain from engaging in bellicose activities within a prudent
distance from the American coasts.

Therefore, it is imperative as a formula of immediate necessity to adopt urgent
dispositions based on such precedents, and in guarantee of these interests to
avoid a repetition of the damages and sufferings experienced by the American
nations and their citizens in the 1914–1918 war.

There is no doubt that the governments of the American republics ought to
foresee these dangers as a means of self-protection and to insist upon the determination that in their waters and up to a reasonable distance from their coasts
no hostile acts may be engaged in or bellicose activities carried out by participants in a war in which the said [American] governments do not participate.

For these considerations the governments of the American republics resolve
and herewith declare:

1. As a measure of continental protection, the American republics, as long as
they maintain their neutrality, have the undisputed right to conserve free from
all hostile acts by any belligerent non-American nation those waters adjacent to
the American continents which they consider of primordial interest and direct
utility for their relations, whether such hostile act is attempted or carried out by
land, sea or air.

These waters described will be determined in the following manner:

All waters within the limits herewith specified, except the territorial waters of Canada, and of colonies and undisputed possessions of European countries within these limits.

Beginning at a point on the frontier between the United States and Canada at Passamaquoddy Bay, where the 44th degree 46 minutes and 36 seconds of North Latitude crosses the 66th degree 44 minutes and 11 seconds of West Longitude; from there, directly along parallel 44 degrees 46 minutes and 36 seconds to a point crossing 60 degrees West Longitude; from there directly southward to a point at 20 degrees North Latitude; from there by loxodromical line to a point at 5 degrees North Latitude and 24 degrees West Longitude; from there directly south to a point at 20 degrees South Latitude; from there by loxodromical line to a point at 58 degrees South Latitude and 57 degrees West Longitude; thence westward to a point at 80 degrees West Longitude; thence by loxodromical line to a point where the Equator crosses 97 degrees West Longitude; thence by loxodromical line to a point 15 degrees North Latitude and 120 degrees West Longitude thence by loxodromical line to a point at 48 degrees 29 minutes and 38 seconds North Latitude and 136 degrees West Longitude; thence directly east to the termination in the Pacific Ocean, at Jean de Fuqua Strait, on the frontier between the United States and Canada.

2. The governments of the American republics agree to make an effort to seek observance by the belligerents of the dispositions contained in this declaration through joint representations to the governments actually participating in hostilities or those that may participate in the future.

This procedure will in no wise affect the exercise of the individual rights of each State inherent in its sovereignty.

3. The governments of the American republics further declare that, whenever they consider it necessary, they will consult among themselves to determine what measures they can take individually or collectively for the purpose of obtaining fulfillment of the dispositions of this declaration.

4. The American republic, as long as there exists a state of war in which they themselves are not participating and whenever they consider it necessary, may carry out individual or collective patrols, whichever they may decide through mutual agreement or as far as the elements and resources of each one permit, in waters adjacent to their coasts within the zone already defined.

Source: Henry Steele Commager, *Documents of American History*, vol. 2 (Englewood Cliffs, NJ: Prentice Hall, 1973), 419–20.

---

86.   THE NEUTRALITY ACT OF 1939
4 November 1939

Once war became a fact, American sympathies gravitated toward England, France, and the nations allied against Nazi Germany. In September, Roo-

sevelt asked the Congress to consider amending the existing Neutrality Act to include a "cash and carry" provision, one that allowed the combatants to acquire and transport war materials with their own shipping. The provision clearly favored England, whose surface fleet was superior to that of Germany. Congress agreed, but kept many of the restrictions contained in previous legislation.

JOINT RESOLUTION

To preserve the neutrality and the peace of the United States and to secure the safety of its citizens and their interests.

Whereas the United States, desiring to preserve its neutrality in wars between foreign states and desiring also to avoid involvement therein, voluntarily imposes upon its nationals by domestic legislation the restrictions set out in this joint resolution; and

Whereas by so doing the United States waives none of its own rights or privileges, or those of any of its nationals, under international law, and expressly reserves all the rights and privileges to which it and its nationals are entitled under the law of nations; and

Whereas the United States hereby expressly reserves the right to repeal, change or modify this joint resolution or any other domestic legislation in the interests of the peace, security or welfare of the United States and its people:

Therefore be it *Resolved,*

PROCLAMATION OF A STATE OF WAR BETWEEN FOREIGN STATES

SEC. 1. (a) That whenever the President, or the Congress by concurrent resolution, shall find that there exists a state of war between foreign states, and that it is necessary to promote the security or preserve the peace of the United States or to protect the lives of citizens of the United States, the President shall issue a proclamation naming the states involved; and he shall, from time to time, by proclamation, name other states as and when they may become involved in the war.

(b) Whenever the state of war which shall have caused the President to issue any proclamation under the authority of this section shall have ceased to exist with respect to any state named in such proclamation, he shall revoke such proclamation with respect to such state.

COMMERCE WITH STATES ENGAGED IN ARMED CONFLICT

SEC. 2. (a) Whenever the President shall have issued a proclamation under the authority of section 1 (a) it shall thereafter be unlawful for any American vessel to carry any passengers or any articles or materials to any state named in such proclamation.

(b) Whoever shall violate any of the provisions of subsection (a) of this section or of any regulations issued thereunder shall, upon conviction thereof, be fined not more than $50,000 or imprisoned for not more than five years, or both. Should the violation be by a corporation, organization, or association, each officer or director thereof participating in the violation shall be liable to the penalty herein prescribed.

(c) Whenever the President shall have issued a proclamation under the authority of section 1 (a) it shall thereafter be unlawful to export or transport, or attempt to export or transport, or cause to be exported or transported, from the United States to any state named in such proclamation, any articles or materials (except copyrighted articles or materials) until all right, title, and interest therein shall have been transferred to some foreign government, agency, institution, association, partnership, corporation, or national. . . .

(g) The provisions of subsections (a) and (c) of this section shall not apply to transportation by American vessels (other than aircraft) of mail, passengers, or any articles or materials (except articles or materials listed in a proclamation referred to in or issued under the authority of section 12 (i)) (1) to any port in the Western Hemisphere south of thirty-five degrees north latitude, (2) to any port in the Western Hemisphere north of thirty-five degrees north latitude and west of sixty-six degrees west longitude, (3) to any port on the Pacific or Indian Oceans, including the China Sea the Tasman Sea, the Bay of Bengal, and the Arabian Sea, and any other dependent waters of either of such oceans, seas, or bays, or (4) to any port on the Atlantic Ocean or its dependent waters south of thirty degrees north latitude. The exceptions contained in this subsection shall not apply to any such port which is included within a combat area as defined in section 3 which applies to such vessels. . . .

(i) Every American vessel to which the provisions of subsections (g) and (h) apply, and every neutral vessel to which the provisions of subsection (1) apply, shall, before departing from a port or from the jurisdiction of the United States, file with the collector of customs of the port of departure, or if there is no such collector at such port then with the nearest collector of customs, a sworn statement (1) containing a complete list of all the articles and materials carried as cargo by such vessel, and the names and addresses of the consignees of all such articles and materials, and (2) stating the ports at which such articles and materials are to be unloaded and the ports of call of such vessel. All transportation referred to in subsections (f), (g), (h), and (1) of this section shall be subject to such restrictions, rules, and regulations as the President shall prescribe; but no loss incurred in connection with any transportation excepted under the provisions of subsections (g), (h), and (1) of this section shall be made the basis of any claim put forward by the Government of the United States. . . .

(1) The provisions of subsection (c) of this section shall not apply to the transportation by a neutral vessel to any port referred to in subsection (g) of this section of any articles or materials (except articles or materials listed in a proclamation referred to in or issued under the authority of section 12 (i)) so long

as such port is not included within a combat area as defined in section 3 which applies to American vessels.

COMBAT AREAS

SEC. 3. (a) Whenever the President shall have issued a proclamation under the authority of section 1 (a), and he shall thereafter find that the protection of citizens of the United States so requires, he shall, by proclamation, define combat areas, and thereafter it shall be unlawful, except under such rules and regulations as may be prescribed, for any citizen of the United States or any American vessel to proceed into or through any such combat area. The combat areas so defined may be made to apply to surface vessels or aircraft, or both.

(b) In case of the violation of any of the provisions of this section by any American vessel, or any owner or officer thereof, such vessel, owner, or officer shall be fined not more than $50,000 or imprisoned for not more than five years, or both. Should the owner of such vessel be a corporation, organization, or association, each officer or director participating in the violation shall be liable to the penalty hereinabove prescribed. In case of the violation of this section by any citizen traveling as a passenger, such passenger may be fined not more than $10,000 or imprisoned for not more than two years, or both.

(c) The President may from time to time modify or extend any proclamation issued under the authority of this section, and when the conditions which shall have caused him to issue any such proclamation shall have ceased to exist he shall revoke such proclamation and the provisions of this section shall thereupon cease to apply, except as to offenses committed prior to such revocation. . . .

TRAVEL ON VESSELS OF BELLIGERENT STATES

SEC. 5. (a) Whenever the President shall have issued a proclamation under the authority of section 1 (a) it shall thereafter be unlawful for any citizen of the United States to travel on any vessel of any state named in such proclamation, except in accordance with such rules and regulations as may be prescribed.

(b) Whenever any proclamation issued under the authority of section 1 (a) shall have been revoked with respect to any state the provisions of this section shall thereupon cease to apply with respect to such state, except as to offenses committed prior to such revocation.

ARMING OF AMERICAN MERCHANT VESSELS PROHIBITED

SEC. 6. Whenever the President shall have issued a proclamation under the authority of section 1 (a), it shall thereafter be unlawful, until such proclamation is revoked, for any American vessel, engaged in commerce with any foreign state to be armed, except with small arms and ammunition therefor, which the President may deem necessary and shall publicly designate for the preservation of discipline aboard any such vessel.

FINANCIAL TRANSACTIONS

SEC. 7. (a) Whenever the President shall have issued a proclamation under the authority of section 1 (a), it shall thereafter be unlawful for any person within the United States to purchase, sell, or exchange bonds, securities, or other obligations of the government of any state named in such proclamation, or of any political subdivision of any such state, or of any person acting for or on behalf of the government of any such state, or political subdivision thereof, issued after the date of such proclamation, or to make any loan or extend any credit (other than necessary credits accruing in connection with the transmission of telegraph, cable, wireless and telephone services) to any such government, political subdivision, or person. The provisions of this subsection shall also apply to the sale by any person within the United States to any person in a state named in any such proclamation of any articles or materials listed in a proclamation referred to in or issued under the authority of section 12 (i) . . .

SOLICITATION AND COLLECTION OF FUNDS AND CONTRIBUTIONS

SEC. 8. (a) Whenever the President shall have issued a proclamation under the authority of section 1 (a), it shall thereafter be unlawful for any person within the United States to solicit or receive any contribution for or on behalf of the government of any state named in such proclamation or for or on, behalf of any agent or instrumentality of any such state. . . .

AMERICAN REPUBLICS

SEC. 9. This joint resolution (except section 12) shall not apply to any American republic engaged in war against a non-American state or states, provided the American republic is not cooperating with a non-American state or states in such war. . . .

NATIONAL MUNITIONS CONTROL BOARD

SEC. 12. (c) Every person required to register under this section shall notify the Secretary of State of any change in the arms, ammunition, or implements of war which he exports, imports, or manufactures; and upon such notification the Secretary of State shall issue to such person an amended certificate of registration, free of charge, which shall remain valid until the date of expiration of the original certificate. Every person required to register under the provisions of this section shall pay a registration fee of $100. Upon receipt of the required registration fee, the Secretary of State shall issue a registration certificate valid for five years, which shall be renewable for further periods of five years upon the payment for each renewal of a fee of $100; but valid certificates of registration (including amended certificates) issued under the authority of section 2 of the joint resolution of August 31, 1935, or section 5 of the joint resolution of August 31, 1935, as amended, shall, without payment of any additional registration fee, be considered to be valid certificates of registration issued under this subsection, and shall remain valid for the same period as if this joint resolution had not been enacted.

(d) It shall be unlawful for any person to export, or attempt to export, from the United States to any other state, any arms, ammunition, or implements of war listed in a proclamation referred to in or issued under the authority of subsection (i) of this section, or to import, or attempt to import, to the United States from any other state, any of the arms, ammunition, or implements of war listed in any such proclamation, without first having submitted to the Secretary of State the name of the purchaser and the terms of sale and having obtained a license therefor. . . . (g) No purchase of arms, ammunition, or implements of war shall be made on behalf of the United States by any officer, executive department, or independent establishment of the Government from any person who shall have failed to register under the provisions of this joint resolution. . . .

(h) The Board shall make a report to Congress on January 3 and July 3 of each year, copies of which shall be distributed as are other reports transmitted to Congress. Such reports shall contain such information and data collected by the Board as may be considered of value in the determination of questions connected with the control of trade in arms, ammunition, and implements of war, including the name of the purchaser and the terms of sale made under any such license. The Board shall include in such reports a list of all persons required to register under the provisions of this joint resolution, and full information concerning the licenses issued hereunder, including the name of the purchaser and the terms of sale made under any such license.

(i) The President is hereby authorized to proclaim upon recommendation of the Board from time to time a list of articles which shall be considered arms, ammunition, and implements of war for the purposes of this section; but the proclamation Numbered 2237, of May 1, 1937 (50 Stat. 1834) defining the term "arms, ammunition, and implements of war" shall, until it is revoked, have full force and effect as if issued under the authority of this subsection. . . .

GENERAL PENALTY PROVISION

SEC. 15. In every case of the violation any of the provisions of this joint resolution or of any rule or regulation issued pursuant thereto where a specific penalty is not herein provided, such violator or violators, upon conviction, shall be fined not more than $10,000, or imprisoned not more than two years, or both. . . .

REPEALS

SEC. 19. The joint resolution of August 31, 1935, as amended, and the joint resolution of January 8, 1937, are hereby repealed; but offenses committed and penalties, forfeitures, or liabilities incurred under either of such joint resolutions prior to the date of enactment of this joint resolution may be prosecuted and punished, and suits and proceedings for violations of either of such joint resolutions or of any rule or regulation issued pursuant thereto may be commenced and prosecuted, in the same manner and with the same effect as if such joint resolutions had not been repealed.

Source: Congressional Record, vol. 85, pt. 1 (Washington, DC: Government Printing Office, 1939), 1024–27.

---

87. THE ACT OF HAVANA
29 July 1940

The collapse of France's and Japan's campaigns in Southeast Asia led American leaders to fear that intrusions upon the Western Hemisphere might follow. The Havana Conference was convened in July 1940 in order to forestall any Axis seizure of European territories in Latin America.

The text of the convention covering the legal phase of the plan to be acted upon regarding foreign possessions in the New World follows:

The governments represented in the second consultative meeting of American Foreign Ministers considering:

That, as a consequence of the acts which are developing on the European Continent, there might be produced in territories of possessions which some belligerent nations hold in America situations wherein that sovereignty may be extinguished or essentially affected, or the government suffers acephalism (becomes headless), generating peril for the peace of the Continent and creating a situation wherein the dominion of law and order and respect of life, liberty and property of the inhabitants disappears;

That the American republics would consider any transfer or attempt to transfer sovereignty, jurisdiction, possession or any interest or control in any of these regions to another non-American State as contrary to American sentiments, principles and rights of American States to maintain their security and political independence;

That the American republics would not recognize nor accept such transfer or intent to transfer or acquire interests or rights, direct or indirect, in any of these regions, whatever might be the form employed to realize it;

That the American republics reserve the right to judge through their respective organs of government if some transfer or intent to transfer sovereignty, jurisdiction, cession or incorporation of geographical regions in America owned by European countries until Sept. 1, 1939, may impair their political independence even though there has been no formal transfer or change in the status of the regions;

That for this reason it is necessary to establish for unforeseen cases as for any other which may produce acephalism of the government in the said regions a regime of provisional administration, while arriving at the objective for free determination of the peoples;

That the American republics, as an international community which acts integrally and forcefully, supporting itself on political and juridical principles which have been applied for more than a century, have the incontestable right, in order to preserve their unity and security, to take under their administration said regions and to deliberate over their destinies in accordance with their respective degrees of political and economic development;

That the provisional and transitory character of the measures agreed upon does not mean forgetfulness or abrogation of the principle of non-intervention, the regulator of inter-American life, a principle proclaimed by the American Institute, recognized by the celebrated committee of experts on international law which met at Rio de Janeiro and consecrated in all its amplitude in the seventh Pan-American conference held at Montevideo;

That this community, therefore, has the international juridical capacity to act in such matters;

That in such a case the most adequate regime is that of provisional administration.

Desiring to protect their peace and security and to promote the interests of any of the regions to which this (document) refers and which are understood to be within the foregoing consideration;

Have resolved to conclude the following convention:

First—If a non-American State attempts directly or indirectly to substitute for another non-American State in the sovereignty or control which that (other State) exerted over any territory situated in America, thereby threatening the peace of the continent, said territory automatically will be considered to be within the stipulations of this convention, and will be submitted to a regime of provisional administration.

Second—That administration shall be executed—as it is considered advisable in each case—by one or more American States by virtue of previous consent.

Third—When administration is established over a region it shall be executed in the interest of the security of America and to the benefit of the administered region looking toward its well-being and development, until the region is found to be in condition to administer itself or to return to its former status, so long as this is compatible with the security of the American republics.

Fourth—Administration of the territory shall operate under conditions which guarantee freedom of conscience and faith with the restrictions demanded by the maintenance of public order and good habits.

Fifth—The administration shall apply local laws, coordinating them with the objectives of this convention, but it may adopt in addition those decisions necessary to solve situations concerning which no such local laws exist.

Sixth—In all that concerns commerce and industry the American nations shall enjoy equal conditions and the same benefits, and the administrator never shall create a situation of privilege for himself or his compatriots or for any particular nations. Liberty of economic relations with all countries on a basis of reciprocity shall be maintained.

Seventh—The natives of the region shall participate as citizens in the public administration and tribunals of justice, with no other consideration than that of competence.

Eighth—In so far as possible rights of any kind shall be governed by local laws and customs, acquired to be protected in conformity with such laws.

Ninth—Forced labor shall be abolished in regions where it exists.

Tenth—The administration will provide means to diffuse public education in all grades, with the double aim of promoting the wealth of the region and better living conditions of the people, especially in regard to public and individual hygiene, and preparation of the exercise of political autonomy in the shortest time.

Eleventh—The natives of the region under administration shall have their own organic charter, which the administration shall establish, consulting the people in whatever way possible.

Twelfth—The administration shall submit an annual report to the inter-American organization charged with control of the administered regions, on the manner in which it carried out its mission, attaching accounts and measures adopted during the year in said region.

Thirteenth—The organization to which the preceding article refers shall be authorized to take cognizance of petitions which inhabitants of the region transmit through the intermediary of the administration with reference to the operation of the provisional administration. The administration shall remit, along with these petitions, such observations as it considers convenient.

Fourteenth—First the administration shall be authorized for a period of three years, at the termination of which, and in case of necessity, it shall be renewed for successive periods of not longer than a decade.

Fifteenth—Expenses incurred in the exercise of the administration shall be covered by revenues from the administered region, but in case these are insufficient the deficit shall be covered by the administering nation or nations.

Sixteenth—There shall be established a commission which shall be called the "InterAmerican Commission of Territorial Administration" and shall be composed of one representative for each of the States which ratify this convention, and it shall be the international organization to which the convention refers.

Any country which ratifies it (the convention) may call the first meeting, indicating the most convenient city. The commission shall elect a president, complete its organization and fix a definite headquarters. Two-thirds of its members shall constitute a quorum and two-thirds of the members present may adopt agreements.

Seventeenth—The commission is authorized to establish a provisional administration over regions to which the present convention applies; it also is authorized to install said administration so that it will be operated by the number of States which will be determined according to the case, and to legalize its execution in terms of the preceding articles.

Eighteenth—The present convention will be opened for signatures of the American republics in Havana and shall be ratified by the high contracting parties in accordance with their constitutional procedures. The Secretary of State of the Republic of Cuba shall transmit, as soon as possible, authentic copies certified to the various governments to obtain ratifications. Instruments of ratification shall be deposited in the archives of the Pan-American Union in Washington, which shall notify the signatory governments of said deposit; such notification shall be considered as exchange of ratifications.

Nineteenth—The present convention shall be effective when two-thirds of the American States shall have deposited their respective instruments of ratification.

Source: Henry Steele Commager, *Documents of American History*, vol. 2 (Englewood Cliffs, NJ: Prentice Hall, 1973), 442–44.

---

88. HEMISPHERIC DEFENSE
18 August 1940

Shortly after the Havana Conference, Franklin D. Roosevelt and Canadian Prime Minister William Lyon Mackenzie King met to discuss the subject of mutual security. Both countries agreed to begin joint defense planning for the northern portion of the hemisphere.

The Prime Minister and the President have discussed the mutual problems of defense in relation to the safety of Canada and the United States.

It has been agreed that a Permanent Joint Board on Defense shall be set up at once by the two countries.

The Permanent Joint Board on Defense shall commence immediate studies relating to sea, land and air problems including personnel and matériel.

It will consider in the broad sense the defense of the north half of the Western Hemisphere.

The Permanent Joint Board on Defense will consist of four or five members from each country, most of them from the services. It will meet shortly.

Source: Henry Steele Commager, *Documents of American History*, vol. 2 (Englewood Cliffs, NJ: Prentice Hall, 1973), 444.

---

89. THE DESTROYERS FOR BASES DECISION
1940

One year after the outbreak of the Second World War, Roosevelt openly considered policies that would supply England with the arms and matériel necessary to defend itself against an expected German invasion. Congres-sional leaders were less certain, voting for significant increases in the American defense budget, but demonstrating great reticence on the subject of foreign aid. Undeterred, Roosevelt arranged an exchange of fifty World War One era destroyers for 99-year leases on a number of naval and air bases in the British West Indies.

Washington, September 2, 1940

Sir:

I have the honor under instructions from His Majesty's Principal Secretary of State for Foreign Affairs to inform you that in view of the friendly and sympathetic interests of His Majesty's Government in the United Kingdom in the national security of the United States and their desire to strengthen the ability of the United States to cooperate effectively with the other nations of the Americas in the defense of the Western Hemisphere, His Majesty's Government will secure the grant to the Government of the United States, freely and without consideration, of the lease for immediate establishment and use of naval and air bases and facilities for entrance thereto and the operation and protection thereof, on the Avalon Peninsula and on the southern coast of Newfoundland, and on the east coast and on the Great Bay of Bermuda.

Furthermore, in view of the above and in view of the desire of the United States to acquire additional air and naval bases in the Caribbean and in British Guiana, and with endeavoring to place a monetary or commercial value upon the many tangible and intangible rights and properties involved, His Majesty's Government will make available to the United States for immediate establishment and use naval and air bases and facilities for entrance thereto and the operation and protection thereof, on the eastern side of the Bahamas, the southern coast of Jamaica, the western coast of St. Lucia, the west coast of Trinidad in the Gulf of Paria, in the island of Antigua and in British Guiana within fifty miles of Georgetown, in exchange for naval and military equipment and material which the United States Government will transfer to His Majesty's Government.

All the bases and facilities referred to in the preceding paragraphs will be leased to the United States for a period of ninety-nine years, free from all rent and charges other than such compensation to be mutually agreed on to be paid by the United States in order to compensate the owners of private property for loss by expropriation or damage arising out of the establishment of the bases and facilities in question.

His Majesty's Government, in the leases to be agreed upon, will grant to the United States for the period of the leases all the rights, power and authority within the bases leased, and within the limits of the territorial waters and air spaces adjacent to or in the vicinity of such bases, necessary to provide access to and defense of such bases, and appropriate provisions for their control.

Without prejudice to the above-mentioned rights of the United States authorities and their jurisdiction within the leased areas, the adjustment and reconciliation between the jurisdiction of the authorities of the United States within these areas and the jurisdiction of the authorities of the territories in which these areas are situated, shall be determined by common agreement.

The exact location and bounds of the aforesaid bases, the necessary seaward, coast and anti-aircraft defenses, the location of sufficient military garrisons, stores and other necessary auxiliary facilities shall be determined by common agreement.

His Majesty's Government are prepared to designate immediately experts to meet with experts of the United States for these purposes. Should these experts be unable to agree in any particular situation, except in the case of Newfoundland and Bermuda, the matter shall be settled by the Secretary of State of the United States and His Majesty's Secretary of State for Foreign Affairs.

I have the honor to be, with the highest consideration, sir,

Your most obedient, humble servant.

LOTHIAN.

DEPARTMENT OF STATE
Washington, September 2, 1940

EXCELLENCY:

I have received your note of September 2, 1940. . . .

I am directed by the President to reply to your note as follows:

The Government of the United States appreciates the declarations and the generous action of His Majesty's Government as contained in your communication which are destined to enhance the national security of the United States and greatly to strengthen its ability to cooperate effectively with the other nations of the Americas in the defense of the Western Hemisphere. It therefore gladly accepts the proposals.

The Government of the United States will immediately designate experts to meet with the experts designated by His Majesty's Government to determine upon the exact location of the naval and air bases mentioned in your communication under acknowledgement.

In consideration of the declarations above quoted, the Government of the United States will immediately transfer to His Majesty's Government fifty United States Navy destroyers generally referred to as the twelve hundred-ton type.

Accept, Excellency, the renewed assurances of my highest consideration.

CORDELL HULL.

Source: Samuel I. Rosenman, ed., *The Public Papers and Addresses of Franklin D. Roosevelt*, vol. 9 (New York: Russell & Russell, 1969), 391–4.

90.   THE "FOUR FREEDOMS" SPEECH
6 January 1941

As part of his annual address to Congress, Roosevelt articulated America's growing involvement in the war, citing the common cause shared by the United States with the countries fighting fascism.

TO THE CONGRESS OF THE UNITED STATES:

I address you, the Members of the Seventy-Seventh Congress, at a moment unprecedented in the history of the Union. I use the word "unprecedented," because at no previous time has American security been as seriously threatened from without as it is today. . . .

It is true that prior to 1914 the United States often had been disturbed by events in other Continents. We have engaged in two wars with European nations and in a number of undeclared wars in the West Indies, in the Mediterranean and in the Pacific for the maintenance of American rights and for the principles of peaceful commerce. In no case, however, had a serious threat been raised against our national safety or independence.

What I seek to convey is the historic truth that the United States as a nation has at all times maintained opposition to any attempt to lock us behind an ancient Chinese wall while the procession of civilization swept past. Today, thinking of our children and their children, we oppose enforced isolation for ourselves or for any part of the Americas.

Even when the World War broke out in 1914, it seemed to contain only small threat of danger to our American future. But, as time went on, the American people began to visualize what the downfall of democratic nations might mean to our own democracy.

We need not over-emphasize imperfections in the Peace of Versailles. We need not harp on failure of the democracies to deal with problems of world deconstruction. We should remember that the Peace of 1919 was far less unjust than the kind of "pacification" which began even before Munich, and which is being carried on under the new order of tyranny that seeks to spread over every continent today. The American people have unalterably set their faces against that tyranny.

Every realist knows that the democratic way of life is at this moment being directly assailed in every part of the world—assailed either by arms, or by secret spreading of propaganda by those who seek to destroy unity and promote discord in nations still at peace. During sixteen months this assault has blotted out the whole pattern of democratic life in an appalling number of independent nations, great and small. The assailants are still on the march, threatening other nations, great and small.

Therefore, as your President, performing my constitutional duty to "give to the Congress information on the state of the Union," I find it necessary to report that the future and the safety of our country and of our democracy are overwhelmingly involved in events far beyond our borders.

Armed defense of democratic existence is now being gallantly waged in four continents. If that defense fails, all the population and all the resources of Europe, Asia, Africa and Australasia will be dominated by the conquerors. The total of those populations and their resources greatly exceeds the sum total of the population and resources of the whole of the Western Hemisphere—many times over.

In times like these it is immature—and incidentally untrue—for anybody to brag that an unprepared America, single-handed, and with one hand tied behind its back, can hold off the whole world.

No realistic American can expect from a dictator's peace international generosity, or return of true independence, or world disarmament, or freedom of expression, or freedom of religion—or even good business. Such a peace would bring no security for us or for our neighbors. "Those, who would give up essential liberty to purchase a little temporary safety, deserve neither liberty nor safety." As a nation we may take pride in the fact that we are soft-hearted; but we cannot afford to be soft-hearted. We must always be wary of those who with sounding brass and a tinkling cymbal preach the "ism" of appeasement. We must especially beware of that small group of selfish men who would clip the wings of the American eagle in order to feather their own nests.

I have recently pointed out how quickly the tempo of modern warfare could bring into our very midst the physical attack which we must expect if the dictator nations win this war.

There is much loose talk of our immunity from immediate and direct invasion from across the seas. Obviously, as long as the British Navy retains its power, no such danger exists. Even if there were no British Navy, it is not probable that any enemy would be stupid enough to attack us by landing troops in the United States from across thousands of miles of ocean, until it had acquired strategic bases from which to operate. But we learn much from the lessons of past years in Europe—particularly the lesson of Norway, whose essential seaports were captured by treachery and surprise built up over a series of years. The first phase of the invasion of this Hemisphere would not be the landing of regular troops. The necessary strategic points would be occupied by secret agents and their dupes—and great numbers of them are already here, and in Latin America.

As long as the aggressor nations maintain the offensive, they—not we—will choose the time and the place and the method of their attack. That is why the future of all American Republics is today in serious danger. That is why this Annual Message to the Congress is unique in our history. That is why every member of the Executive branch of the government and every member of the Congress face great responsibility—and great accountability.

The need of the moment is that our actions and our policy should be devoted primarily—almost exclusively—to meeting this foreign peril. For all our domestic problems are now a part of the great emergency. Just as our national policy in internal affairs has been based upon a decent respect for the rights and dignity of all our fellow man within our gates, so our national policy in foreign affairs has been based on a decent respect for the rights and dignity of all nations, large and small. And the justice of morality must and will win in the end.

Our national policy is this.

First, by an impressive expression of the public will and without regard to partisanship, we are committed to all-inclusive national defense.

Second, by an impressive expression of the public will and without regard to partisanship, we are committed to full support of all those resolute peoples, everywhere, who are resisting aggression and are thereby keeping war away from our Hemisphere. By this support, we express our determination that the democratic cause shall prevail; and we strengthen the defense and security of our own nation.

Third, by an impressive expression of the public will and without regard to partisanship we are committed to the proposition that principles of morality and considerations for our own security will never permit us to acquiesce in a peace dictated by aggressors and sponsored by appeasers. We know that enduring peace cannot be bought at the cost of other people's freedom.

In the recent national election there was no substantial difference between the two great parties in respect to that national policy. No issue was fought out on this line before the American electorate. Today, it is abundantly evident that American citizens everywhere are demanding and supporting speedy and complete action in recognition of obvious danger. Therefore, the immediate need is a swift and driving increase in our armament production. . . .

Our most useful and immediate role is to act as an arsenal for them as well as for ourselves. They do not need man power. They do need billions of dollars worth of the weapons of defense. . . .

Let us say to the democracies: "We Americans are vitally concerned in your defense of freedom. We are putting forth our energies, our resources and our organizing powers to give you the strength to regain and maintain a free world. We shall send you, in ever-increasing numbers, ships, planes, tanks, guns. This is our purpose and our pledge." In fulfillment of this purpose we will not be intimidated by the threats of dictators that they will regard as a breach of international law and as an act of war our aid to the democracies which dare to resist their aggression. Such aid is not an act of war, even if a dictator should unilaterally proclaim it so to be. When the dictators are ready to make war upon us, they will not wait for an act of war on our part. They did not wait for Norway or Belgium or the Netherlands to commit an act of war. Their only interest is in a new one-way international law, which lacks mutuality in its observance, and, therefore, becomes an instrument of oppression.

The happiness of future generations of Americans may well depend upon how effective and how immediate we can make our aid felt. No one can tell the exact character of the emergency situations that we may be called upon to meet. The Nation's hands must not be tied when the Nation's life is in danger. We must all prepare to make the sacrifices that the emergency—as serious as war itself—demands. Whatever stands in the way of speed and efficiency in defense preparations must give way to the national need.

A free nation has the right to expect full cooperation from all groups. A free nation has the right to look to the leaders of business, of labor, and of agriculture to take the lead in stimulating effort, not among other groups but within their own groups. The best way of dealing with the few slackers or trouble makers in our midst is, first, to shame them by patriotic example, and, if that fails, to use the sovereignty of government to save government.

As men do not live by bread alone, they do not fight by armaments alone. Those who man our defenses, and those behind them who build our defenses, must have the stamina and courage which come from an unshakable belief in the manner of life which they are defending. The mighty action which we are calling for cannot be based on a disregard of all things worth fighting for.

The Nation takes great satisfaction and much strength from the things which have been done to make its people conscious of their individual stake in the preservation of democratic life in America. Those things have toughened the fibre of our people, have renewed their faith and strengthened their devotion to the institutions we make ready to protect. Certainly this is no time to stop thinking about the social and economic problems which are the root cause of the social revolution which is today a supreme factor in the world.

There is nothing mysterious about the foundations of a healthy and strong democracy. The basic things expected by our people of their political and economic systems are simple. They are: equality of opportunity for youth and for others; jobs for those who can work; security for those who need it; the ending of special privilege for the few; the preservation of civil liberties for all; the enjoyment of the fruits of scientific progress in a wider and constantly rising standard of living.

These are the simple and basic things that must never be lost sight of in the turmoil and unbelievable complexity of our modern world. The inner and abiding strength of our economic and political systems is dependent upon the degree to which they fulfill these expectations.

Many subjects connected with our social economy call for immediate improvement. As examples: We should bring more citizens under the coverage of old age pensions and unemployment insurance. We should widen the opportunities for adequate medical care. We should plan a better system by which persons deserving or needing gainful employment may obtain it.

I have called for personal sacrifice. I am assured of the willingness of almost all Americans to respond to that call. . . .

In the future days, which we seek to make secure, we look forward to a world founded upon four essential human freedoms.

The first is freedom of speech and expression—everywhere in the world.

The second is freedom of every person to worship God in his own way—everywhere in the world.

The third is freedom from want—which, translated into world terms, means economic understandings which will secure to every nation a healthy peace time life for its inhabitants—everywhere in the world.

The fourth is freedom from fear—which, translated into world terms, means a world-wide reduction of armaments to such a point and in such a thorough fashion that no nation will be in a position to commit an act of physical aggression against any neighbor—anywhere in the world.

That is no vision of a distant millennium. It is a definite basis for a kind of world attainable in our own time and generation. That kind of world is the very antithesis of the so-called new order of tyranny which the dictators seek to create with the crash of a bomb.

To that new order we oppose the greater conception—the moral order. A good society is able to face schemes of world domination and foreign revolutions alike without fear.

Since the beginning of our American history we have been engaged in change—in a perpetual peaceful revolution—a revolution which goes on steadily, quietly adjusting itself to changing conditions—without the concentration camp or the quick-lime in the ditch. The world order which we seek is the cooperation of free countries, working together in a friendly, civilized society.

This nation has placed its destiny in the hands and heads and hearts of its millions of free men and women; and its faith in freedom under the guidance of God. Freedom means the supremacy of human rights everywhere. Our support goes to those who struggle to gain those rights or keep them. Our strength is in our unity of purpose. To that high concept there can be no end save victory.

Source: Henry Steele Commager, *Documents of American History*, vol. 2 (Englewood Cliffs, NJ: Prentice Hall, 1973), 446–49.

91. THE LEND LEASE ACT
11 March 1941

In March 1941, Roosevelt asked Congress to forego previous legislation regulating American neutrality in favor of direct foreign aid to the Allies. Although bitterly opposed by isolationists such as Robert Taft and Burton K. Wheeler, the act passed both Houses. It allowed the president to authorize direct assistance to countries of his own choosing. The act also opened American shipyards to foreign nations.

Be it enacted. That this Act may be cited as "An Act to Promote the Defense of the United States."

SECTION 3.

(a) Notwithstanding the provisions of any other law, the President may, from time to time, when he deems it in the interest of national defense, authorize the Secretary of War, the Secretary of the Navy, or the head of any other department or agency of the Government—

(1) To manufacture in arsenals, factories, and shipyards under their jurisdiction, or otherwise procure, to the extent to which funds are made available therefor, or contracts are authorized from time to time by the Congress, or both, any defense article for the government of any country whose defense the President deems vital to the defense of the United States.

(2) To sell, transfer title to, exchange, lease, lend, or otherwise dispose of, to any such government any defense article, but no defense article not manufactured or procured under paragraph (1) shall in any way be disposed of under this paragraph, except after consultation with the Chief of Staff of the Army or the Chief of Naval Operations of the Navy, or both. The value of defense articles disposed of in any way under authority of this paragraph, and procured from funds heretofore appropriated, shall not exceed $1,300,000,000. The value of such defense articles shall be determined by the head of the department or agency concerned or such other department, agency or officer as shall be designated in the manner provided in the rules and regulations issued hereunder. Defense articles procured from funds hereafter appropriated to any department or agency of the Government, other than from funds authorized to be appropriated under this Act, shall not be disposed of in any way under authority of this paragraph except to the extent hereafter authorized by the Congress in the Acts appropriating such funds or otherwise.

(3) To test, inspect, prove, repair, outfit, recondition, or otherwise to place in good working order, to the extent to which funds are made available therefor, or contracts are authorized from time to time by the Congress, or both, any defense article for any such government, or to procure any or all such services by private contract.

(4) To communicate to any such government any defense information, pertaining to any defense article furnished to such government under paragraph (2) of this subsection.

(5) To release for export any defense article disposed of in any way under this subsection to any such government.

(b) The terms and conditions upon which any such foreign government receives any aid authorized under subsection (a) shall be those which the President deems satisfactory, and the benefit to the United States may be payment or repayment in kind or property or any other direct or indirect benefit which the President deems satisfactory.

(c) After June 30, 1943, or after the passage of a concurrent resolution by the Houses before June 30, 1943, which declares that the powers conferred by or pursuant to subsection (a) are no longer necessary to promote the defense of the United States, neither the President nor the head of any department or agency shall exercise any of the powers conferred by or pursuant to subsection (a); except that until July 1, 1946 any of such powers may be exercised to the extent necessary to carry out a contract or agreement with such a foreign government made before July 1, 1943, or before the passage of such concurrent resolution, whichever is the earlier.

(d) Nothing in this Act shall be construed to authorize or to permit the authorization of conveying vessels by naval vessels of the United States.

(e) Nothing in this Act shall be construed to authorize or to permit the authorization of the entry of any American vessel into a combat area in violation of section 3 of the Neutrality Act of 1939.

SECTION 8.

The Secretaries of War and of the Navy are hereby authorized to purchase or otherwise acquire arms, ammunition, and implements of war produced within the jurisdiction of any country to which section 3 is applicable, whenever the President deems such purchase or acquisition to be necessary in the interests of the defense of the United States.

SECTION 9.

The President may, from time to time, promulgate such rules and regulations as may be necessary and proper to carry out any of the provisions of this Act; and he may exercise any power or authority conferred on him by this Act through such department, agency, or officer as he shall direct.

Source: Henry Steele Commager, *Documents of American History*, vol. 2 (Englewood Cliffs, NJ: Prentice Hall, 1973), 449–50.

92.   THE ATLANTIC CHARTER
14 August 1941

In August 1941, Roosevelt and British Prime Minister Winston Churchill met in Argentia Bay, Newfoundland, to craft what they considered to be common aims for the future. The resulting Atlantic Charter restated the principles stated in the Four Freedoms and pledged both nations to the restoration of self-government to conquered nations.

The President of the United States of America and the Prime Minister, Mr. Churchill, representing His Majesty's Government in the United Kingdom, being met together, deem it right to make known certain common principles in the national policies of their respective countries on which they base their hopes for a better future for the world.

First, their countries seek no aggrandizement, territorial or other;

Second, they desire to see no territorial changes that do not accord with the freely expressed wishes of the peoples concerned;

Third, they respect the right of all peoples to choose the form of government under which they will live; and they wish to see sovereign rights and self government restored to those who have been forcibly deprived of them;

Fourth, they will endeavor, with due respect for their existing obligations, to further the enjoyment by all States, great or small, victor or vanquished, of access, on equal terms, to the trade and to the raw materials of the world which are needed for their economic prosperity;

Fifth, they desire to bring about the fullest collaboration between all nations in the economic field with the object of securing, for all, improved labor standards, economic advancement and social security;

Sixth, after the final destruction of the Nazi tyranny, they hope to see established a peace which will afford to all nations the means of dwelling in safety within their own boundaries, and which will afford assurance that all the men in all the lands may live out their lives in freedom from fear and want;

Seventh, such a peace should enable all men to traverse the high seas and oceans without hindrance;

Eighth, they believe that all of the nations of the world, for realistic as well as spiritual reasons must come to the abandonment of the use of force. Since no future peace can be maintained if land, sea or air armaments continue to be employed by nations which threaten, or may threaten, aggression outside of their frontiers, they believe, pending the establishment of a wider and permanent system of general security, that the disarmament of such nations is essential. They will likewise aid and encourage all other practicable measures which will lighten for peace-loving peoples the crushing burden of armaments.

FRANKLIN D. ROOSEVELT
WINSTON S. CHURCHILL

Source: Samuel I. Rosenman, ed., *The Public Papers and Addresses of Franklin D. Roosevelt*, vol. 10 (New York: Russell & Russell, 1969), 314–15.

Part Eight

The Second World War

The primary objective of American diplomacy during the Second World War was victory. This one goal allowed American leaders to focus on the task of amassing and maintaining Allied support in the war against Hitler and Imperial Japan. This one idea is what created the necessary blinders in an alliance of an unlikely trio of countries—a Soviet dictatorship, a democratic republic, and a constitutional monarchy—that carried the primary burdens of the war. The singular purpose also established the foundation for the many unresolved problems that would beleaguer the Allies once the war was over.

To accomplish the tasks necessary for victory, diplomats attempted to reconcile strategic planning with military realities. American, British, and Soviet officials argued, sometimes bitterly, over the creation of a "second front" in western Europe, balancing Stalin's relentless demands for help with the problems of mobilizing an invasion force on the British home island, and early tactical failures such as the Dieppe landings of August 1942.[1] It was not until the Teheran Summit of November 1943 that the Allies agreed on the creation of a second front by the spring of 1944.

Throughout the war, compromise defined the American approach to its relations with the Allies. Roosevelt's decision to include the Soviet Union in the March 1941 Lend Lease Act was an expedient to bolstering a potential ally in the war against fascism and an attempt to reconstruct a working relationship with Moscow, a path he pursued throughout his three terms. His first act as president in 1933 was to revoke the official U.S. policy of nonrecognition regarding the Soviet Union that had been in place since the first Russian Revolution.[2] Roosevelt clearly saw wartime diplomacy as an opportunity to construct additional bridges to his new partner against Hitler.

Compromise was equally apparent in Roosevelt's handling of policy regarding the status of European colonies. Initially, the president endorsed the idea of trusteeship as a means to encourage the separation of colonies from their European patron states. This idea was soon displaced by the exigencies of war. Faced with the necessity of French support for the 1942 invasion of northern Africa, Roosevelt shelved trusteeship. Later in the war, the subject of freedom for French Indochina came second to the cultivation of French cooperation for the D-Day invasion, and, later to the Dumbarton Oaks economic conference.[3]

Agreement on other collective policies proved equally elusive. The combined Allies at Casablanca agreed on the demand for unconditional surrender of all Axis powers in January 1943; but what the victors hoped to accomplish in the peace was another matter. At the November 1943 Teheran Summit, the concept of a world body designed to ensure stability remained vague. Roosevelt's concept of "four policemen" acting as a break against aggression offered very few specific proposals and was further quelled by his transparent inclusion of China as a peer of the United States and the Soviet Union. The post-war treatment of Germany also divided the Allies. Initially, the "Big Three" endorsed the principle of a harsh peace. At Teheran, Churchill, Stalin, and Roosevelt debated, with significantly different degrees of seriousness, the number of executions that should take place in order to purge the German *Wehrmacht* (Stalin favored at least 50,000). In the end, all three leaders agreed on a post-war division of Germany into occupation zones, but again specific details were absent.[4]

Some degree of clarity appeared at the Yalta Conference in February 1945, as the Allies were able to agree on the partitioning of occupied Germany into four military zones, the reconstruction of the western Polish border, and the recognition of a Soviet sphere of influence in Eastern Europe. Stalin kept the territory won in 1939 as a result of the Non-Aggression Pact with Nazi Germany, but assuaged Roosevelt and Churchill by signing the joint Declaration on Liberated Europe which endorsed the principle of reestablishing democracy on the continent at the conclusion of the war.[5]

Discussions related to the post-war economic system were more tangible in terms of content and also expressed Anglo-American preferences for the peace. At the Bretton Woods Conference (1944), representatives from forty-four nations discussed the fundamental reorganization of the the global economic structure. In an attempt to redress the protectionism of the 1920s and 1930s, they agreed to the establishment of the General Agreement on Trade and Tariffs (GATT). In order to foster monetary stability and post-war reconstruction efforts, the assembled delegates also consented to the creation of the International Monetary Fund (IMF) and the International Bank for Reconstruction and Development (IBRD). Explicit throughout these proceedings was the simple fact that the United States and, more specifically, the U.S. dollar would define the boundaries of post-war international commerce. By exercising influence through organizations such as the IMF, American leaders hoped to parlay the wartime economic recovery into a point of credible leverage in world affairs, capturing potential rivals (e.g., the Soviet Union) within a newly constituted economic system, while opening up new markets for American products.[6]

The United Nations was the final institution created to foster post-war stability. Conceived as a permanent means to encourage international discourse, the formation of the United Nations carried with it the assumption that the postwar order would be maintained by its permanent Security Council membership (i.e., the United States, China, Great Britain, France, and the Soviet Union) rather than the institution itself. Thus, while the United Nations could serve as a location for international dialogue its inherent weakness was that it could not mandate action by members. The institution was perceived as a type of international clearinghouse in which the Yalta powers could police their own respective spheres of influence.[7]

Maintaining a consensus among the great powers proved problematic at the conclusion of the war. Key changes in leadership significantly altered the spirit and the letter of Yalta. By the summer of 1945, following Roosevelt's death and Churchill's defeat in the British polls, Stalin remained as the only survivor of the wartime "Big Three." The change in American leadership was striking. Poorly versed in foreign affairs, Harry S. Truman reverted to the political instincts that had served him throughout his life; instincts that blended, according to historian Melvyn Leffler, "parochial nationalism with pragmatic internationalism."[8] The new president was not prepared to command the plethora of committees and agencies within the Joint Chiefs of Staff, the State Department, and the War Department that were responsible for constructing American foreign policy. Truman also proved to be erratic in his dealings with the Soviet Union. His famous initial clash with Vyacheslav Molotov over the composition of the Polish Lublin government was later tempered by more moderate discussions. However, Truman's confrontational style encouraged the increasing sense of distrust apparent within the upper echelons of the U.S. policy community over Soviet post-war intentions.[9]

Substantive issues also created fissures between the former allies. A key point of contention was the conduct of German reconstruction. Many issues demanded immediate attention. In the summer of 1945, occupation forces had to attend to the needs of millions of military prisoners, shortages of food and fuel, and an infrastructure in utter shambles. Accompanying these problems were longer term questions regarding German reparations, a final partition of the country, and the status of former Nazi officials. Within the framework of the 1943 Moscow Conference, the Allies had agreed on the creation of occupation zones and payment of reparations "to the greatest extent possible."[10] These were reaffirmed at Yalta two years later. At Potsdam in July 1945, the major powers agreed to treat Germany as a single economic unit for the purpose of reparations and also agreed that the Soviet Union would receive industrial equipment from the western zones in exchange for food from their occupied portion of Germany. The agreement broke down in relatively short order. After denuding eastern Germany of virtually every remaining vestige of machinery, equipment, and transportation, the Soviets began making similar demands on the western half of the country. Responding to what he considered to be an unreasonable series of demands, General Lucius Clay, the deputy American commander in Germany, announced a halt in deliveries to the Soviet zone on 3 May 1946.[11]

Other clashes concerning post-war policy accompanied the debate over Germany. The Western allies expressed growing dismay at the Soviet consolidation of control over Eastern Europe. They criticized the ongoing occupation of the Baltic states and the reconstruction of the western Polish border, following the Oder-Neisse line, that resulted in the forced emigration of some 10 million Germans. More disturbing was Soviet interference in the post-war composition of governments in Poland, Rumania, Bulgaria, Hungary, and Czechoslovakia.[12] For his own part, Stalin openly lambasted the United States for its tepid efforts at "de-Nazification." Of the nearly 900,000 Nazis identified by occupation forces, less than 0.1 percent were classified as major offenders. The vast majority were returned to their previous positions in the civilian police and administration.[13]

In the end, the grand alliance that defeated Germany and Tokyo succeeded, and, in the absence of any further utility, promptly collapsed. The old divisions, based on mutual strategic suspicions and absent the wartime patina of necessity, reappeared and deepened into open confrontation. New to the picture, however, was the United States, the only nation that had not suffered the same disastrous costs as the other allies during the war. The Truman administration found itself challenged with the need to lead its debilitated western allies in an emerging struggle with the Communist bloc. The open question was whether a country preparing to enjoy the newly won peace was ready to consider its responsibilities as a superpower.

NOTES

1. Peter Young, *Commando* (New York: Ballantine Books, 1972), 128–55.

2. John Lewis Gaddis, *The Long Peace: Inquiries into the History of the Cold War* (New York: Oxford University Press, 1987), 3–29.

3. See Robert Blum, *Drawing the Line: The Origin of the American Containment Policy in East Asia* (New York: W. W. Norton, 1982).

4. Herbert Feis, *Churchill, Roosevelt, and Stalin: The War They Waged and the Peace They Sought* (Princeton, NJ: Princeton University Press, 1957), 269–83.

5. Ibid., 489–560.

6. Seyom Brown, *The Faces of Power: United States Foreign Policy from Truman to Clinton* (New York: Columbia University Press, 1994), 3–16; Dean Acheson, *Present at the Creation: My Years in the State Department* (New York: W. W. Norton, 1969), 81–87, 139–48; Walt W. Rostow, *The United States in the World Arena: An Essay in Recent History* (New York: Harper & Brothers, 1960), 134–37.

7. Frank Ninkovich, *The Wilsonian Century: U.S. Foreign Policy since 1900* (Chicago: University of Chicago Press, 1999), 141–44.

8. Melvyn P. Leffler, *A Preponderance of Power: National Security, the Truman Administration, and the Cold War* (Stanford, CA: Stanford University Press, 1992), 26.

9. Ibid., 25–54.

10. Samuel Eliot Morison, Henry Steele Commager, and William E. Leuchtenburg, *The Growth of the American Republic*, vol. 2 (New York: Oxford University Press, 1969), 646.

11. Frank Ninkovich, *Germany and the United States: The Transformation of the German Question since 1945* (Boston: Twayne Publishers, 1988), 48–81.

12. William Laird Kleine-Ahlbrandt, *Twentieth-Century European History* (New York: West Publishing, 1993), 618–27.

13. Ninkovich, *Germany and the United States*, 34–37.

93. ROOSEVELT'S REQUEST FOR WAR AGAINST JAPAN
8 December 1941

On December 8, 1941, with the nation still reeling from the news of the attack on Pearl Harbor, Franklin D. Roosevelt stood before Congress and requested that it declare war against Japan. Roosevelt's request was unanimously approved by both Houses that same day.

Yesterday, December 7, 1941—a date which will live in infamy—the United States of America was suddenly and deliberately attacked by the naval and air forces of the Empire of Japan.

The United States was at peace with that nation and, at the solicitation of Japan, was still in conversation with its Government and its Emperor looking toward the maintenance of peace in the Pacific. Indeed, one hour after Japanese air squadrons had commenced bombing in Oahu, the Japanese Ambassador to the United States and his colleague delivered to the Secretary of State a formal reply to a recent American message. While this reply stated that it seemed useless to continue the existing diplomatic negotiations, it contained no threat or hint of war or armed attack.

It will be recorded that the distance of Hawaii from Japan makes it obvious that the attack was deliberately planned many days or even weeks ago. During the intervening time the Japanese Government has deliberately sought to deceive the United States by false statements and expressions of hope for continued peace.

The attack yesterday on the Hawaiian Islands has caused severe damage to American naval and military forces. Very many American lives have been lost. In addition American ships have been reported torpedoed on the high seas between San Francisco and Honolulu.

Yesterday the Japanese Government also launched an attack against Malaya. Last night Japanese forces attacked Hong Kong. Last night Japanese forces attacked Guam. Last night Japanese forces attacked the Philippine Islands. Last night the Japanese attacked Wake Island. This morning the Japanese attacked Midway Island.

Japan has, therefore, undertaken a surprise offensive extending throughout the Pacific area. The facts of yesterday speak for themselves. The people of the United States have already formed their opinions and well understand the implications to the very life and safety of our nation.

As Commander-in-Chief of the Army and Navy, I have directed that all measures be taken for our defense.

Always will we remember the character of the onslaught against us.

No matter how long it may take us to overcome this premeditated invasion, the American people in their righteous might will win through to absolute victory.

I believe I interpret the will of the Congress and of the people when I assert that we will not only defend ourselves to the uttermost but will make very certain that this form of treachery shall never endanger us again.

Hostilities exist. There is no blinking at the fact that our people, our territory and our interests are in grave danger.

With confidence in our armed forces—with the unbonded determination of our people—we will gain the inevitable triumph—so help us God.

I ask that the Congress declare that since the unprovoked and dastardly attack by Japan on Sunday, December seventh, a state of war has existed between the United States and the Japanese Empire.

Source: Samuel I. Rosenman, ed., *The Public Papers and Addresses of Franklin D. Roosevelt*, vol. 10 (New York: Russell & Russell, 1969), 514–16.

94. THE CASABLANCA CONFERENCE
12 February 1943

At the beginning of January 1943, it appeared that the tide of war had finally shifted in favor of the Allies. While at Casablanca, Roosevelt and Churchill initiated plans for military operations in Europe and the Pacific and restated their commitment to Allied unity. Their most important announcement was reserved for the statement that the Allies would end the war only upon the "Unconditional Surrender" of all Axis forces throughout the world.

The decisions reached and the actual plans made at Casablanca were not confined to any one theater of war or to any one continent or ocean or sea. Before this year is out, it will be made known to the world—in actions rather than in words—that the Casablanca Conference produced plenty of news; and it will be bad news for the Germans and Italians—and the Japanese.

We have lately concluded a long, hard battle in the Southwest Pacific and we have made notable gains. That battle started in the Solomons and New Guinea last summer. It has demonstrated our superior power in planes and, most importantly, in the fighting qualities of our individual soldiers and sailors.

American armed forces in the Southwest Pacific are receiving powerful aid from Australia and New Zealand and also directly from the British themselves.

We do not expect to spend the time it would take to bring Japan to final defeat merely by inching our way forward from island to island across the vast expanse of the Pacific.

Great and decisive actions against the Japanese will be taken to drive the invader from the soil of China. Important actions will be taken in the skies over China—and over Japan itself.

The discussions at Casablanca have been continued in Chungking with the Generalissimo by General Arnold and have resulted in definite plans for offensive operations.

There are many roads which lead right to Tokyo. We shall neglect none of them.

In an attempt to ward off the inevitable disaster, the Axis propagandists are trying all of their old tricks in order to divide the United Nations. They seek to create the idea that if we win this war, Russia, England, China, and the United States are going to get into a cat-and-dog fight.

This is their final effort to turn one nation against another, in the vain hope that they may settle with one or two at a time—that any of us may be so gullible and so forgetful as to be duped into making "deals" at the expense of our Allies.

To these panicky attempts to escape the consequences of their crimes we say—all the United Nations say—that the only terms on which we shall deal with an Axis government or any Axis factions are the terms proclaimed at Casablanca: "Unconditional Surrender." In our uncompromising policy we mean no harm to the common people of the Axis nations. But we do mean to impose punishment and retribution in full upon their guilty, barbaric leaders. . . .

In the years of the American and French revolutions the fundamental principle guiding our democracies was established. The cornerstone of our whole democratic edifice was the principle that from the people and the people alone flows the authority of government.

It is one of our war aims, as expressed in the Atlantic Charter, that the conquered populations of today be again the masters of their destiny. There must be no doubt anywhere that it is the unalterable purpose of the United Nations to restore to conquered peoples their sacred rights.

Source: Samuel I. Rosenman, ed., *The Public Papers and Addresses of Franklin D. Roosevelt*, vol. 12 (New York: Russell & Russell, 1969), 71.

95. THE MOSCOW CONFERENCE
October 1943

By the fall of 1943, Allied armies had dealt a series of devastating defeats to Axis forces in Europe. However, an important stumbling block re-mained—the final launching of the Anglo-American invasion of France. In October, delegates from the United States, the United Kingdom, and the Soviet Union met in Moscow to discuss the future conduct of the war and some aspects of the post-war status of Europe.

The conference of foreign secretaries of the United States of America, Mr. Cordell Hull; of the United Kingdom, Mr. Anthony Eden; and of the Soviet Union, Mr. V. M. Molotov; took place at Moscow from 19 to 30 October 1943. There were twelve meetings. In addition to the foreign secretaries, the following took part in the conference:

For the United States of America: Mr. W. Averell Harriman, Ambassador of the United States; Major General John R. Deane, United States Army; Mr. H. Hackworth, Mr. James C. Dunn and experts.

For the United Kingdom: Sir Archibald Clark Kerr, Ambassador; Mr. William Strang; Lieutenant General Sir Hastings Ismay and experts.

For the Soviet Union: Marshal K. E. Voroshilov, Marshal of the Soviet Union; Mr. A. Y. Vishinsky, Mr. M. M. Litvinov, Deputy People's Commissar for Foreign Affairs; Mr. V. Sergeyev, Deputy People's Commissar for Foreign Trade; Major General A. A. Gryslov, of the general staff; Mr. G. F. Saksin, senior official for People's Commissariat for Foreign Affairs, and experts.

The agenda included all questions submitted for discussion by the three governments. Some of the questions called for final decisions, and these were taken. On other questions, after discussion, decisions of principle were taken: These questions were referred for detailed consideration to commissions specially set up for the purpose, or reserved for treatment through diplomatic channels. Other questions again were disposed of by an exchange of views. The governments of the United States, the United Kingdom, and the Soviet Union have been in close cooperation in all matters concerning the common war effort, but this is the first time that the foreign secretaries of the three governments have been able to meet together in conference.

In the first place there were frank and exhaustive discussions of the measures to be taken to shorten the war against Germany and her satellites in Europe. Advantage was taken of the presence of military advisers representing the re-spective chiefs of staff in order to discuss definite military operations with regard to which decisions had been taken and which are already being prepared in order to create a basis for the closest military cooperation in the future between the three countries.

Second only to the importance of hastening the end of the war was the recognition by the three governments that it was essential in their own national interests and in the interest of all peace-loving nations to continue to present close collaboration and cooperation in the conduct of the war into the period following the end of hostilities, and that only in this way could peace be maintained and the political, economic, and social welfare of their people fully promoted.

This conviction is expressed in a declaration in which the Chinese Government joined during the conference and which was signed by the three Foreign Secretaries and the Chinese Ambassador at Moscow on behalf of their governments. This declaration provided for even closer collaboration in the prosecution of the war and in all matters pertaining to the surrender and disarmament of the enemies with which the four countries were respectively at war. It set forth the principles upon which the four governments agreed that a broad system of international cooperation and security should be based. Provision is made for the inclusion of all other peace-loving nations, great and small, in this system.

The conference agreed to set up machinery for insuring the closest cooperation between the three governments in the examination of European questions arising as the war developed. For this purpose the conference decided to establish in London a European advisory-commission to study these questions and to make joint recommendations to the three governments.

Provision was made for continuing when necessary the tri-partite consultations of representatives of the three governments in the respective capitals through the existing diplomatic channels.

The conference also agreed to establish an advisory council for matters relating to Italy, to be composed, in the first instance, of representatives of their three governments and of the French Committee of National Liberation. Provision is made for addition to this council of representatives of Greece and Yugoslavia in view of their special interests arising out of aggressions of Fascist Italy upon their territory during the present war. This council will deal with day to day questions other than military preparations and will make recommendations designed to coordinate allied policy with regard to Italy. The three foreign secretaries considered it appropriate to reaffirm, by a declaration published today, the attitude of the allied governments in favor of the restoration of democracy in Italy.

The three foreign secretaries declared it to be the purpose of their governments to restore the independence of Austria. At the same time they reminded Austria that in the final settlement account will be taken of efforts that Austria may make toward its own liberation.

The foreign secretaries issued at the conference a declaration by President Roosevelt, Prime Minister Churchill and Premier Stalin containing a solemn warning that at the time of granting any armistice to any German government, those German officers and men and members of the Nazi party who have had any connection with atrocities and executions in countries overrun by German forces, will be taken back to the countries in which their abominable crimes were committed to be charged and punished according to the laws of those countries.

In an an atmosphere of mutual confidence and understanding which characterized all the work of the conference, consideration was also given to other important questions. These included not only questions of a current nature, but also questions concerning treatment of Hitlerite Germany and its satellites, economic cooperation and assurance of general peace.

JOINT FOUR-NATION DECLARATION

The governments of the United States of America, United Kingdom, the Soviet Union and China;

United in their determination, in accordance with the declaration by the United Nations of January 1942, and subsequent declarations, to continue hostilities against those Axis powers with which they respectively are at war until such powers have laid down their arms on the basis of unconditional surrender;

Conscious of their responsibility to secure the liberation of themselves and the peoples allied with them from the menace of aggression;

Recognizing the necessity of insuring a rapid and orderly transition from war to peace and of establishing and maintaining international peace and security with the least diversion of the world's human and economic resources for armaments;

Jointly declare:

1. That their united action, pledged for the prosecution of the war against their respective enemies, will be continued for the organization and maintenance of peace and security.

2. That those of them at war with a common enemy will act together in all matters relating to the surrender and disarmament of that enemy.

3. That they will take all measures deemed by them to be necessary to provide against any violation of the terms imposed upon the enemy.

4. That they recognize the necessity of establishing at the earliest practicable date a general international organization, based on the principle of the sovereign equality of all peace-loving states, and open to membership by all such states, large and small, for the maintenance of international peace and security.

5. That for the purpose of maintaining international peace and security pending the re-establishment of law and order and the inauguration of a system of general security they will consult with one another and as occasion requires with other members of the United Nations, with a view to joint action on behalf of the community of nations.

6. That after the termination of hostilities they will not employ their military

forces within the territories of other states except for the purposes envisaged in this declaration and after joint consultation.

7. That they will confer and cooperate with one another and with other members of the United Nations to bring about a practicable general agreement with respect to the regulation of armaments in the post-war period.

DECLARATION REGARDING ITALY

The Foreign Secretaries of the United States, the United Kingdom and the Soviet Union have established that their three governments are in complete agreement that Allied policy toward Italy must be based upon the fundamental principle that Fascism and all its evil influence and configuration shall be completely destroyed and that the Italian people shall be given every opportunity to establish governmental and other institutions based upon democratic principles.

The Foreign Secretaries of the United States and United Kingdom declare that the action of their governments from the inception of the invasion of Italian territory so far as paramount military requirements have permitted, has been based upon this policy.

In furtherance of this policy in the future the Foreign Secretaries of the three governments are agreed that the following measures are important and should be put into effect:

1. It is essential that the Italian Government should be made more democratic by inclusion of representatives of those sections of the Italian people who have always opposed Fascism.

2. Freedom of speech, of religious worship, of political belief, of press and of public meeting shall be restored in full measure to the Italian people, who shall be entitled to form anti-Fascist political groups.

3. All institutions and organizations created by the Fascist regime shall be suppressed.

4. All Fascist or pro-Fascist elements shall be removed from the administration and from institutions and organizations of a public character.

5. All political prisoners of the Fascist regime shall be released and accorded full amnesty.

6. Democratic organs of local government shall be created.

7. Fascist chiefs and army generals known or suspected to be war criminals shall be arrested and handed over to justice. In making this declaration the three Foreign Secretaries recognize that so long as active military operations continue in Italy the time at which it is possible to give full effect to the principles stated above will be determined by the Commander-in-chief on the basis of instructions received through combined chiefs of staff.

The three governments, parties to this declaration, will, at the request of any one of them, consult on this matter. It is further understood that nothing in this resolution is to operate against the right of the Italian people ultimately to choose their own form of government.

DECLARATION ON AUSTRIA

The governments of the United Kingdom, the Soviet Union and the United States of America are agreed that Austria, the first free country to fall a victim to Hitlerite aggression, shall be liberated from German domination.

They regard the annexation imposed on Austria by Germany on March 15, 1938, as null and void. They consider themselves as in no way bound by any changes effected in Austria since that date. They declare that they wish to see re-established a free and independent Austria and thereby to open the way for the Austrian people themselves, as well as those neighboring States which will be faced with similar problems, to find that political and economic security which is the only basis for lasting peace.

Austria is reminded, however, that she has a responsibility, which she cannot evade, for participation in the war at the side of Hitlerite Germany, and that in the final settlement account will inevitably be taken of her own contribution to her liberation.

STATEMENT ON ATROCITIES
Signed by President Roosevelt, Prime Minister Churchill and Premier Stalin

The United Kingdom, the United States and the Soviet Union have received from many quarters evidence of atrocities, massacres and cold-blooded mass executions which are being perpetrated by Hitlerite forces in many of the countries they have overrun and from which they are now being steadily expelled. The brutalities of Nazi domination are no new thing, and all peoples or territories in their grip have suffered from the worst form of government by terror. What is new is that many of the territories are now being redeemed by the advancing armies of the liberating powers, and that in their desperation the recoiling Hitlerites and Huns are redoubling their ruthless cruelties. This is now evidenced with particular clearness by monstrous crimes on the territory of the Soviet Union which is being liberated from Hitlerites, and on French and Italian territory.

Accordingly, the aforesaid three Allied powers, speaking in the interest of the thirty-two United Nations, hereby solemnly declare and give full warning of their declaration as follows:

At the time of granting of any armistice to any government which may be set up in Germany, those German officers and men and members of the Nazi party who have been responsible for or have taken a consenting part in the above atrocities, massacres and executions will be sent back to the countries in which their abominable deeds were done in order that they may be judged and punished according to the laws of these liberated countries and of free governments which will be erected therein. Lists will be compiled in all possible detail from all these countries having regard especially to invaded parts of the Soviet Union, to Poland and Czechoslovakia, to Yugoslavia and Greece including Crete and other islands, to Norway, Denmark, Netherlands, Belgium, Luxemburg, France and Italy.

Thus, Germans who take part in wholesale shooting of Polish officers or in the execution of French, Dutch, Belgian or Norwegian hostages or Cretan peasants, or who have shared in slaughters inflicted on the people of Poland or in territories of the Soviet Union which are now being swept clear of the enemy, will know they will be brought back to the scene of their crimes and judged on the spot by the peoples whom they have outraged.

Let those who have hitherto not imbued their hands with innocent blood beware lest they join the ranks of the guilty, for most assuredly the three Allied powers will pursue them to the uttermost ends of the earth and will deliver them to their accusors in order that justice may be done.

The above declaration is without prejudice to the case of German criminals, whose offenses have no particular geographical localization and who will be punished by joint decision of the governments of the Allies.

Source: Henry Steele Commager, *Documents of American History*, vol. 2 (Englewood Cliffs, NJ: Prentice Hall, 1973), 476–80.

96. THE CAIRO CONFERENCE
1 December 1943

Near the conclusion of 1943, Roosevelt and Churchill turned their attention to the war effort in Asia. At Cairo, with Chiang Kai-shek in attendance, they fashioned a basic statement of purpose for the military campaign against Japan.

The several military missions have agreed upon future military operations against Japan. The Three Great Allies expressed their resolve to bring unrelenting pressure against their brutal enemies by sea, land, and air. This pressure is already rising.

The Three Great Allies are fighting this war to restrain and punish the aggression of Japan. They covet no gain for themselves and have no thought of territorial expansion. It is their purpose that Japan shall be stripped of all the islands in the Pacific which she has seized or occupied since the beginning of the first World War in 1914, and that all the territories Japan has stolen from the Chinese, such as Manchuria, Formosa, and the Pescadores, shall be restored to the Republic of China. Japan will also be expelled from all other territories which she has taken by violence and greed. The aforesaid three great powers, mindful of enslavement of the people of Korea, are determined that in due course Korea shall become free and independent.

With these objects in view the three Allies, in harmony with those of the

United Nations at war with Japan, will continue to persevere in the serious and prolonged operations necessary to procure the unconditional surrender of Japan.

Source: Henry Steele Commager, *Documents of American History*, vol. 2 (Englewood Cliffs, NJ: Prentice Hall, 1973), 480.

97. THE TEHERAN CONFERENCE
1 December 1943

Following the meeting in Moscow of their primary diplomatic advisors, Churchill, Roosevelt, and Stalin met for the first time in November 1943. The primary topic of discussion was the planned invasion of France, although the Allies also considered Soviet participation in the war against Japan and the post-war treatment of Germany.

We—The President of the United States, the Prime Minister of Great Britain, and the Premier of the Soviet Union, have met these four days past, in this, the Capital of our Ally, Iran, and have shaped and confirmed our common policy.

We express our determination that our nations shall work together in war and in the peace that will follow.

As to war—our military staffs have joined in our round table discussions, and we have concerted our plans for the destruction of the German forces. We have reached complete agreement as to the scope and timing of the operations to be undertaken from the east, west and south.

The common understanding which we have here reached guarantees that victory will be ours.

And as to peace—we are sure that our concord will win an enduring Peace. We recognize fully the supreme responsibility resting upon us and all the United Nations to make a peace which will command the goodwill of the overwhelming mass of the peoples of the world and banish the scourge and terror of war for many generations.

With our Diplomatic advisers we have surveyed the problems of the future. We shall seek the cooperation and active participation of all nations, large and small, whose peoples in heart and mind are dedicated, as are our own peoples, to the elimination of tyranny and slavery, oppression and intolerance. We will welcome them, as they may choose to come, into a world family of Democratic Nations.

No power on earth can prevent our destroying the German armies by land, their U Boats by sea, and their war plants from the air.

Our attack will be relentless and increasing.

Emerging from these cordial conferences we look with confidence to the day when all peoples of the world may live free lives, untouched by tyranny, and according to their varying desires and their own consciences.

We came here with hope and determination. We leave here, friends in fact, in spirit and in purpose.

ROOSEVELT, CHURCHILL and STALIN

Declaration of the Three Powers Regarding Iran
(This declaration was published Dec. 7, 1943.)

The President of the United States, the Premier of the U.S.S.R. and the Prime Minister of the United Kingdom, having consulted with each other and with the Prime Minister of Iran, desire to declare the mutual agreement of their three Governments regarding their relations with Iran.

The Governments of the United States, the U.S.S.R. and the United Kingdom recognize the assistance which Iran has given in the prosecution of the war against the common enemy, particularly by facilitating the transportation of supplies from overseas to the Soviet Union.

The three Governments realize that the war has caused special economic difficulties for Iran, and they are agreed that they will continue to make available to the Government of Iran such economic assistance as may be possible, having regard to the heavy demands made upon them by their worldwide military operations and to the worldwide shortage of transport, raw materials and supplies for civilian consumption.

With respect to the post-war period, the Governments of the United States, the U.S.S.R. and the United Kingdom are in accord with the Government of Iran that any economic problems confronting Iran at the close of hostilities should receive full consideration, along with those of other members of the United Nations, by conferences or international agencies held or created to deal with international economic matters.

The Governments of the United States, the U.S.S.R. and the United Kingdom are at one with the Government of Iran in their desire for the maintenance of the independence, sovereignty and territorial integrity of Iran. They count upon the participation of Iran, together with all other peace-loving nations, in the establishment of international peace, security and prosperity after the war, in accordance with the principles of the Atlantic Charter, to which all four Governments have subscribed.

WINSTON S. CHURCHILL
JOSEPH V. STALIN
FRANKLIN D. ROOSEVELT

Washington, March 24, 1947—The text of the military and other conclusions reached at the Teheran conference, as announced today by the State Department:

The conference:

(1) Agreed that the partisans in Yugoslavia should be supported by supplies and equipment to the greatest possible extent, and also by Commando operations;

(2) Agreed that, from the military point of view, it was most desirable that Turkey should come into the war on the side of the Allies before the end of the year;

(3) Took note of Marshal Stalin's statement that if Turkey found herself at war with Germany, and as a result Bulgaria declared war on Turkey or attacked her, the Soviet would immediately be at war with Bulgaria. The conference further took note that this fact could be explicitly stated in the forthcoming negotiations to bring Turkey into the war;

(4) Took note that Operation Overlord [the landings in Normandy] would be launched during May, 1944, in conjunction with an operation against southern France. The latter operation would be undertaken in as great a strength as availability of landing craft permitted. The conference further took note of Marshal Stalin's statement that the Soviet forces would launch an offensive at about the same time with the object of preventing the German forces from transferring from the eastern to the western front;

(5) Agreed that the military staffs of the three powers should hence forward keep in close touch with each other in regard to the impending operations in Europe. In particular it was agreed that a cover plan to mystify and mislead the enemy as regards these operations should be concerted between the staffs concerned.

> FRANKLIN D. ROOSEVELT
> JOSEPH V. STALIN
> WINSTON S. CHURCHILL
> Teheran, December 1, 1943.

Source: Henry Steele Commager, *Documents of American History*, vol. 2 (Englewood Cliffs, NJ: Prentice Hall, 1973), 481–83.

98. THE YALTA CONFERENCE
4–11 February 1945

In early 1945, Roosevelt, Churchill, and Stalin met to discuss the fate of the post-war world. During a series of meetings held in the Crimean town of Yalta, the "Big Three" addressed the creation of a United Nations organization, provisions for governing the liberated territories of Europe, the status of Germany, and Soviet participation in the invasion of Japan. The unsettled nature of many agreements, particularly with respect to the status of liberated Europe, plagued Allied relations as the year progressed and provided the earliest points of controversy in the Cold War.

Washington, March 24—The text of the agreements reached at the Crimea (Yalta) Conference between President Roosevelt, Prime Minister Churchill and Generalissimo Stalin, as released by the State Department today, follows:

PROTOCOL OF PROCEEDINGS OF CRIMEA CONFERENCE

The Crimea Conference of the heads of the Governments of the United States of America, the United Kingdom, and the Union of Soviet Socialist Republics, which took place from Feb. 4 to 11, came to the following conclusions:

I. WORLD ORGANIZATION

It was decided:

1. That a United Nations conference on the proposed world organization should be summoned for Wednesday, 25 April, 1945, and should be held in the United States of America.

2. The nations to be invited to this conference should be:

(a) the United Nations as they existed on 8 Feb., 1945; and

(b) Such of the Associated Nations as have declared war on the common enemy by 1 March, 1945. (For this purpose, by the term "Associated Nations" was meant the eight Associated Nations and Turkey.) When the conference on world organization is held, the delegates of the United Kingdom and United States of America will support a proposal to admit to original membership two Soviet Socialist Republics, i.e., the Ukraine and White Russia.

3. That the United States Government, on behalf of the three powers, should consult the Government of China and the French Provisional Government in regard to decisions taken at the present conference concerning the proposed world organization.

4. That the text of the invitation to be issued to all the nations which would take part in the United Nations conference should be as follows:

"The Government of the United States of America, on behalf of itself and of the Governments of the United Kingdom, the Union of Soviet Socialistic Republics and the Republic of China and of the Provisional Government of the French Republic, invite the Government of ———— to send representatives to a conference to be held on 25 April, 1945, or soon thereafter, at San Francisco, in the United States of America, to prepare a charter for a general international organization for the maintenance of international peace and security.

"The above-named Governments suggest that the conference consider as affording a basis for such a Charter the proposals for the establishment of a general international organization which were made public last October as a result of the Dumbarton Oaks conference and which have now been supplemented by the following provisions for Section C of Chapter VI:

C. VOTING

"1. Each member of the Security Council should have one vote.

2. Decisions of the Security Council on procedural matters should be made by an affirmative vote of seven members.

3. Decisions of the Security Council on all matters should be made by an affirmative vote of seven members, including the concurring votes of the permanent members; provided that, in decisions under Chapter VIII, Section A and under the second sentence of Paragraph 1 of Chapter VIII, Section C, a party to a dispute should abstain from voting.

Further information as to arrangements will be transmitted subsequently.

In the event that the Government of ———— desires in advance of the conference to present views or comments concerning the proposals, the Government of the United States of America will be pleased to transmit such views and comments to the other participating Governments."

Territorial trusteeship:

It was agreed that the five nations which will have permanent seats on the Security Council should consult each other prior to the United Nations conference on the question of territorial trusteeship.

The acceptance of this recommendation is subject to its being made clear that territorial trusteeship will only apply to (a) existing mandates of the League of Nations; (b) territories detached from the enemy as a result of the present war; (c) any other territory which might voluntarily be placed under trusteeship; and (d) no discussion of actual territories is contemplated at the forthcoming United Nations conference or in the preliminary consultations, and it will be a matter for subsequent agreement which territories within the above categories will be placed under trusteeship.

[*The section from this point to the next italicized note was published Feb. 13, 1945.*]

II. DECLARATION ON LIBERATED EUROPE

The following declaration has been approved:

The Premier of the Union of Soviet Socialist Republics, the Prime Minister of the United Kingdom and the President of the United States of America have consulted with each other in the common interests of the peoples of their countries and those of liberated Europe. They jointly declare their mutual agreement to concert during the temporary period of instability in liberated Europe the policies of their three Governments in assisting the peoples liberated from the domination of Nazi Germany and the peoples of the former Axis satellite states of Europe to solve by democratic means their pressing political and economic problems.

The establishment of order in Europe and the rebuilding of national economic life must be achieved by processes which will enable the liberated peoples to destroy the last vestiges of nazism and fascism and to create democratic institutions of their own choice. This is a principle of the Atlantic Charter—the right of all peoples to choose the form of government under which they will live— the restoration of sovereign rights and self-government to those peoples who have been forcibly deprived of them by the aggressor nations.

To foster the conditions in which the liberated peoples may exercise these rights, the three Governments will jointly assist the people in any European liberated state or former Axis satellite state in Europe where, in their judgment conditions require, (a) to establish conditions of internal peace; (b) to carry out emergency measures for the relief of distressed peoples; (c) to form interim governmental authorities broadly representative of all democratic elements in the population and pledged to the earliest possible establishment through free elections of Governments responsive to the will of the people; and (d) to facilitate where necessary the holding of such elections.

The three Governments will consult the other United Nations and provisional authorities or other Governments in Europe when matters of direct interest to them are under consideration.

When, in the opinion of the three Governments, conditions in any European liberated state or any former Axis satellite state in Europe make such action necessary, they will immediately consult together on the measures necessary to discharge the joint responsibilities set forth in this declaration.

By this declaration we reaffirm our faith in the principles of the Atlantic Charter, our pledge in the Declaration by the United Nations and our determination to build in cooperation with other peace-loving nations world order, under law, dedicated to peace, security, freedom and general well-being of all mankind.

In issuing this declaration, the three powers express the hope that the Provisional Government of the French Republic may be associated with them in the procedure suggested.

III. DISMEMBERMENT OF GERMANY

It was agreed that Article 12 (a) of the Surrender Terms for Germany should be amended to read as follows:

"The United Kingdom, the United States of America and the Union of Soviet Socialist Republics shall possess supreme authority with respect to Germany. In the exercise of such authority they will take such steps, including the complete disarmament, demilitarization and dismemberment of Germany as they deem requisite for future peace and security."

The study of the procedure of the dismemberment of Germany was referred to a committee consisting of Mr. [Anthony] Eden [their Foreign Secretary] (chairman), Mr. [John] Winant [of the United States] and Mr. [Fedor T.] Gusev. This body would consider the desirability of associating with it a French representative.

IV. ZONE OF OCCUPATION FOR THE FRENCH AND CONTROL COUNCIL FOR GERMANY

It was agreed that a zone in Germany, to be occupied by the French forces, should be allocated to France. This zone would be formed out of the British and American zones and its extent would be settled by the British and Americans in consultation with the French Provisional Government.

It was also agreed that the French Provisional Government should be invited to become a member of the Allied Control Council for Germany.

V. REPARATION

The following protocol has been approved:

Protocol

On the Talks Between the Heads of Three Governments at the Crimean Conference on the Question of the German Reparations in Kind

1. Germany must pay in kind for the losses caused by her to the Allied nations in the course of the war. Reparations are to be received in the first instance by those countries which have borne the main burden of the war, have suffered the heaviest losses and have organized victory over the enemy.

2. Reparations in kind is to be exacted from Germany in three following forms:

(a) Removals within two years from the surrender of Germany or the cessation of organized resistance from the national wealth of Germany located on the territory of Germany herself as well as outside her territory (equipment, machine tools, ships, rolling stock, German investments abroad, shares of industrial, transport and other enterprises, in Germany, etc.), these removals to be carried out chiefly for the purpose of destroying the war potential of Germany.

(b) Annual deliveries of goods from current production for a period to be fixed.

(c) Use of German labor.

3. For the working out on the above principles of a detailed plan for exaction of reparation from Germany an Allied reparations commission will be set up in Moscow. It will consist of three representatives—one from the Union of Soviet Socialist Republics, one from the United Kingdom and one from the United States of America.

4. With regard to the fixing of the total sum of the reparation as well as the distribution of it among the countries which suffered from the German aggression, the Soviet and American delegations agreed as follows.

"The Moscow reparation commission should take in its initial studies as a basis for discussion the suggestion of the Soviet Government that the total sum of the reparation in accordance with the points (a) and (b) of the Paragraph 2 should be 20 billion dollars and that 50 per cent of it should go to the Union of Soviet Socialist Republics."

The British delegation was of the opinion that, pending consideration of the reparation question by the Moscow reparation commission, no figures of reparation should be mentioned.

The above Soviet-American proposal has been passed to the Moscow reparation commission as one of the proposals to be considered by the commission.

VI. MAJOR WAR CRIMINALS

The conference agreed that the question of the major war criminals should be the subject of inquiry by the three Foreign Secretaries for report in due course after the close of the conference.

[The section from this point to the next italicized note was published Feb. 13, 1945.]

VII. POLAND

The following declaration on Poland was agreed by the conference:

"A new situation has been created in Poland as a result of her complete liberation by the Red Army. This calls for the establishment of a Polish Provisional Government which can be more broadly based than was possible before the recent liberation of the western part of Poland. The Provisional Government which is now functioning in Poland should therefore be reorganized on a broader democratic basis with the inclusion of democratic leaders from Poland itself and from Poles abroad. This new Government should then be called the Polish Provisional Government of National Unity.

"M. Molotov, Mr. Harriman and Sir A. Clark Kerr are authorized as a commission to consult in the first instance in Moscow with members of the present Provisional Government and with other Polish democratic leaders from within Poland and from abroad, with a view to the reorganization of the present Government along the above lines. This Polish Provisional Government of National Unity shall be pledged to the holding of free and unfettered elections as soon as possible on the basis of universal suffrage and secret ballot. In these elections all democratic and anti-Nazi parties shall have the right to take part and to put forward candidates.

"When a Polish Provisional Government of National Unity has been properly formed in conformity with the above, the Government of the U.S.S.R., which now maintains diplomatic relations with the present Provisional Government of Poland, and the Government of the United Kingdom and the Government of the United States of America will establish diplomatic relations with the new Polish Provisional Government of National Unity, and will exchange Ambassadors by whose reports the respective Governments will be kept informed about the situation in Poland.

"The three heads of Government consider that the eastern frontier of Poland should follow the Curzon Line with digressions from it in some regions of five to eight kilometers in favor of Poland. They recognize that Poland must receive substantial accessions of territory in the north and west. They feel that the opinion of the new Polish Provisional Government of National Unity should be sought in due course of the extent of these accessions and that the final delimitation of the western frontier of Poland should thereafter await the peace conference."

VIII. YUGOSLAVIA

It was agreed to recommend to Marshal Tito and to Dr. [Ivan] Subasitch:

(a) That the Tito-Subasitch agreement should immediately be put into effect and a new Government formed on the basis of the agreement.

(b) That as soon as the new Government has been formed it should declare:

(I) That the Anti-Fascist Assembly of the National Liberation (AVNOJ) will be extended to include members of the last Yugoslav Skupstina who have not compromised themselves by collaboration with the enemy, thus forming a body to be known as a temporary Parliament and

(II) That legislative acts passed by the Anti-Fascist Assembly of National Liberation (AVNOJ) will be subject to subsequent ratification by a Constituent Assembly; and that this statement should be published in the communique of the conference.

[*Here ends the previously published section of the agreements.*]

IX. ITALO-YUGOSLAV FRONTIER—
ITALO-AUSTRIAN FRONTIER

Notes on these subjects were put in by the British delegation, and the American and Soviet delegations agreed to consider them and give their views later.

X. YUGOSLAV-BULGARIAN RELATIONS

There was an exchange of views between the Foreign Secretaries on the question of the desirability of a Yugoslav-Bulgarian pact of alliance. The question at issue was whether a state still under an armistice regime could be allowed to enter into a treaty with another state. Mr. Eden suggested that the Bulgarian and Yugoslav Governments should be informed that this could not be approved. Mr. Stettinius suggested that the British and American Ambassadors should discuss the matter further with Mr. Molotov in Moscow. Mr. Molotov agreed with the proposal of Mr. Stettinius.

XI. SOUTHEASTERN EUROPE

The British delegation put in notes for the consideration of their colleagues on the following subjects:

(a) The Control Commission in Bulgaria.

(b) Greek claims upon Bulgaria, more particularly with reference to reparations.

(c) Oil equipment in Rumania.

XII. IRAN

Mr. Eden, Mr. Stettinius and Mr. Molotov exchanged views on the situation in Iran. It was agreed that this matter should be pursued through the diplomatic channel.

[*The section from this point to the next italicized note was published Feb. 13, 1949.*]

XIII. MEETINGS OF THE THREE FOREIGN SECRETARIES

The conference agreed that permanent machinery should be set up for consultation between the three Foreign Secretaries; they should meet as often as necessary, probably about every three or four months.

These meetings will be held in rotation in the three capitals, the first meeting being held in London.

[*Here ends the previously published section of the agreements.*]

XIV. THE MONTREAUX CONVENTION AND THE STRAITS

It was agreed that at the next meeting of the three Foreign Secretaries to be held in London, they should consider proposals which it was understood the Soviet Government would put forward in relation to the Montreaux Convention, and report to their Governments. The Turkish Government should be informed at the appropriate moment.

The foregoing protocol was approved and signed by the three Foreign Secretaries at the Crimean Conference Feb. 11, 1945.

E. R. STETTINIUS JR.
M. MOLOTOV
ANTHONY EDEN

AGREEMENT REGARDING JAPAN

The leaders of the three great powers—the Soviet Union, the United States of America and Great Britain—have agreed that in two or three months after Germany has surrendered and the war in Europe has terminated, the Soviet Union shall enter into the war against Japan on the side of the Allies on condition that:

1. The status quo in Outer Mongolia (the Mongolian People's Republic) shall be preserved;

2. The former rights of Russia violated by the treacherous attack of Japan in 1904 shall be restored, viz.:

(a) The southern part of Sakhalin as well as the islands adjacent to it shall be returned to the Soviet Union;

(b) The commercial port of Dairen shall be internationalized, the pre-eminent interests of the Soviet Union in this port being safeguarded, and the lease of Port Arthur as a naval base of the U.S.S.R. restored;

(c) The Chinese-Eastern Railroad and the South Manchurian Railroad, which provide an outlet to Dairen, shall be jointly operated by the establishment of a joint Soviet-Chinese company, it being understood that the pre-eminent interests of the Soviet Union shall be safeguarded and that China shall retain full sovereignty in Manchuria;

3. The Kurile Islands shall be handed over to the Soviet Union.

It is understood that the agreement concerning Outer Mongolia and the ports and railroads referred to above will require concurrence of Generalissimo Chiang Kai-shek. The President will take measures in order to obtain this concurrence on advice from Marshal Stalin.

The heads of the three great powers have agreed that these claims of the Soviet Union shall be unquestionably fulfilled after Japan has been defeated.

For its part, the Soviet Union expresses its readiness to conclude with the National Government of China a pact of friendship and alliance between the U.S.S.R. and China in order to render assistance to China with its armed forces for the purpose of liberating China from the Japanese yoke.

> JOSEPH V. STALIN
> FRANKLIN D. ROOSEVELT
> WINSTON S. CHURCHILL
> February 11, 1945.

Source: Henry Steele Commager, *Documents of American History*, vol. 2 (Englewood Cliffs, NJ: Prentice Hall, 1973), 488–93.

---

99. THE SURRENDER OF GERMANY
7 May 1945

The final reduction of the last organized German resistance was largely completed by April 1945. In a schoolhouse in Rheims, on 7 May, Germany signed the document that formally ended hostilities in Europe.

Instrument of surrender of all German forces to General Dwight D. Eisenhower, Supreme Commander of the Allied Expeditionary Forces, and to the Soviet High Command

Rheims, May 7, 1945.

1. We the undersigned, acting by authority of the German High Command, hereby surrender unconditionally to the Supreme Commander, Allied Expeditionary Force and simultaneously to the Soviet High Command all forces on land, sea, and in the air who are at this date under German control.

2. The German High Command will at once issue orders to all German military, naval and air authorities and to all forces under German control to cease active operations at 2301 hours Central European time on 8 May and to remain in the positions occupied at that time. No ship, vessel, or aircraft is to be scuttled, or any damage done to their hull, machinery or equipment.

3. The German High Command will at once issue to the appropriate commanders, and ensure the carrying out of any further orders issued by the Supreme Commander, Allied Expeditionary Force and by the Soviet High Command.

4. This act of military surrender is without prejudice to, and will be superseded by any general instrument of surrender imposed by, or on behalf of the United Nations and applicable to Germany and the German armed forces as a whole.

5. In the event of the German High Command or any of the forces under their control failing to act in accordance with this Act of Surrender, the Supreme Commander, Allied Expeditionary Force and the Soviet High Command will take such punitive or, other action as they deem appropriate.

Signed at Rheims at 0241 on the 7th day of May, 1945.

Statement by the Governments of the United States of America, Union of Soviet Socialist Republics, the United Kingdom and the provisional Government of the French Republic on zones of occupation in Germany.

1. Germany, within her frontiers as they were on Dec. 31, 1937, will, for the purposes of occupation, be divided into four zones, one to be allotted to each power as follows:

An eastern zone to the Union of Soviet Socialist Republics;

A northwestern zone to the United Kingdom;

A southwestern zone to the United States of America;

A western zone to France.

The occupying forces in each zone will be under a commander in chief designated by the responsible power. Each of the four powers may, at its discretion, include among the forces assigned to occupation duties under the command of its commander in chief, auxiliary contingents from the forces of any other Allied power which has actively participated in military operations against Germany.

2. The area of "Greater Berlin" will be occupied by forces of each of the four powers. An inter-Allied governing authority (in Russian, Komendatura) consisting of four commandants, appointed by their respective commanders-in-chief, will be established to direct jointly its administration.

Statement by the Governments of the United States of America, Union of Soviet Socialist Republics, United Kingdom, and the Provisional Government of the French Republic on control of machinery in Germany.

1. In the period when Germany is carrying out the basic requirements of unconditional surrender, supreme authority in Germany will be exercised, on

instructions from their Governments, by the Soviet, British, United States and French commanders-in-chief, each in his own zone of occupation, and also jointly, in matters affecting Germany as a whole. The four commanders-in-chief will together constitute the Control Council. Each commander-in-chief will be assisted by a political adviser.

2. The Control Council, whose decisions shall be unanimous, will ensure appropriate uniformity of action by the commanders-in-chief in their respective zones of occupation and will reach agreed decisions on the chief questions affecting Germany as a whole.

3. Under the Control Council, there will be a permanent coordinating committee composed of one representative of each of the four commanders-in-chief and a control staff organized in the following divisions (which are subject to adjustment in the light of experience): Military; naval; air; transport; political; economic; finance; reparation, deliveries and restitution; internal affairs and communications; legal; prisoners of war and displaced persons; manpower. There will be four heads of each division, one designated by each power. . . .

Source: Henry Steele Commager, *Documents of American History*, vol. 2 (Englewood Cliffs, NJ: Prentice Hall, 1973), 500–501.

100. THE OCCUPATION OF JAPAN
4 October 1945

After the United States dropped two atomic bombs over Hiroshima and Nagasaki, Japan surrendered in August 1945. General Douglas MacArthur was placed in charge of the subsequent occupation and administration of the country. His mandate included the demilitarization of Japan, trials for war criminals, and the construction of democratic institutions, among many other reforms.

1. In order to remove restrictions on political, civil and religious liberties and discrimination on grounds of race, nationality, creed or political opinion, the Imperial Japanese Government will:

a. Abrogate and immediately suspend the operation of all provisions of all laws, decrees, orders, ordinances and regulations which:

(1) Establish or maintain restrictions on freedom of thought, of religion, of assembly and of speech, including the unrestricted discussion of the Emperor, the Imperial Institution and the Imperial Japanese Government.

(2) Establish or maintain restrictions on the collection and dissemination of information.

(3) By their terms or their applications, operate unequally in favor of or against any person by reason of race, nationality, creed or political opinion. . . .

c. Release immediately all persons now detained, imprisoned, under "protection or surveillance," or whose freedom is restricted in any other manner who have been placed in that state of detention, imprisonment, "protection and surveillance," or restriction of freedom:

(1) Under the enactments referred to in Para 1 a and b above.

(2) Without charge.

(3) By charging them technically with a minor offense, when, in reality, the reason for detention, imprisonment, "Protection and Surveillance," or restriction of freedom, was because of their thought, speech, religion, political beliefs, or assembly. The release of all such persons will be accomplished by 10 October 1945.

d. Abolish all organizations or agencies created to carry out the provisions of the enactments referred to in Para 1 a and b above and that part of, or functions of, other offices or sub divisions of other civil departments or organs which supplement or assist them in the execution of such provisions. These include, but are not limited to:

(1) All secret police organs.

(2) Those departments in the Ministry of Home Affairs, such as the Bureau of Police, charged with supervision of publications, supervision of public meetings and organizations, censorship of motion pictures, and such other departments concerned with the control of thought, speech, religion or assembly.

(3) Those departments, such as the special higher police (Tokubetsu, Koto, Keisatsu Bu), in the Tokyo Metropolitan Police, the Osaka Metropolitan Police, and other Metropolitan Police, the Police of the Territorial Administration of Hokkaido and the various prefectural police charged with supervision of publications, supervision of public meetings and organizations, censorship of motion pictures, and such other departments concerned with the control of thought, speech, religion or assembly.

(4) Those departments, such as the Protection and Surveillance Commission, and all Protection and Surveillance Stations responsible thereto, under the Ministry of Justice charged with protection and surveillance and control of thought, speech, religion, or assembly.

e. Remove from office and employment the Minister of Home Affairs, the Chief of the Bureau of Police of the Ministry of Home Affairs, the Chief of the Tokyo Metropolitan Police Board, the Chief of Osaka Metropolitan Police Board, the Chief of any other Metropolitan Police, the Chief of Police of the Territorial Administration of Hokkaido, the Chiefs of each prefectural police department, the entire personnel of the special higher police of all metropolitan, territorial and prefectural police departments, the guiding and protecting officials and all other personnel of the Protection and Surveillance Commission and of the Protection and Surveillance Stations. None of the above persons will be reappointed to any position under the Ministry of Home Affairs, the Ministry of Justice or any police organ in Japan. Any of the above persons whose assistance is required to accomplish the provisions of this directive will be retained until the directive is accomplished and then dismissed.

f. Prohibit any further activity of police officials, members of police forces, and other government, national or local, officials or employees which is related to the enactments referred to in Para 1 a and b above and to the organs and functions abolished by Para 1 d above.

g. Prohibit the physical punishment and mistreatment of all persons detained, imprisoned, or under protection and surveillance under any and all Japanese enactments, laws, decrees, orders, ordinances and regulations. All such persons will receive at all times ample sustenance.

h. Ensure the security and preservation of all records and any and all other materials of the organs abolished in Para 1 d. These records may be used to accomplish the provisions of this directive, but will not be destroyed, removed, or tampered with in any way.

i. Submit a comprehensive report to this Headquarters not later than 15 October 1945 describing in detail all action taken to comply with all provisions of this directive. This report will contain the following specific information prepared in the form of separate supplementary reports: . . .

2. All officials and subordinates of the Japanese Government affected by the terms of this directive will be held personally responsible and strictly accountable for compliance with and adherence to the spirit and letter of this directive.

Source: Henry Steele Commager, *Documents of American History*, vol. 2 (Englewood Cliffs, NJ: Prentice Hall, 1973), 501–3.

Part Nine

The Cold War

According to Gordon Craig and Alexander George:

Cold War is a descriptive term that was generally adopted in the late forties to characterize the hostile relationship that developed between the West and the Soviet Union. While loosely employed, the term had an exceedingly important connotation: it called attention to the fact that, however acute their rivalry and conflict, the two sides were pursuing it by means short of another war and that, it was hoped, they would continue to do so. As some commentators noted, however bad the Cold War was, it was better than a hot one, and few would deny that the Cold War was an acceptable substitute for a thermonuclear war with the Russians, if that indeed were the only alternative.[1]

For nearly half a century, the Cold War defined the parameters of international relations, in general, and American foreign policy, specifically. Rooted in the fissures that existed among the Allies during the Second World War, the Cold War matured and evolved to accommodate, among many new factors, nuclear weaponry, the rise of a distinct version of Communism in Asia, and the aspirations of a postcolonial generation of underdeveloped nations.

Initially, the Cold War reflected a number of important points of departure that defined the western alliance clustered around U.S. leadership and the Soviet-led Communist bloc. One of these points of departure involved the strategic shift in power that followed the Second World War. After 1945, the former great powers of the nineteenth century, particularly Great Britain, were in retreat throughout the world, creating significant power vacuums in their wake. In the postwar, these powers were progressively forced to surrender their former domains by default (e.g., in the case of Greece and Turkey) or as a result of war (e.g., in the case of French Indochina). In this context, the Cold War became a struggle over the population and resources of the de-evolving colonial periphery as well as the core nations formerly in possession of it.

In another sense, the Cold War was an ideological conflict. When describing the Soviet Union, George F. Kennan, one of the earliest framers of American Cold War policies, conflated contemporary Moscow's socialist doctrine with the xenophobia and imperialism associated with the old Russian empire. His explanation of what motivated the Communist threat was critical to the formation of "containment" policy in the 1940s. Equally important, Kennan's stark depiction of Soviet Communism established from a very early point the positive ideological alternatives offered by free market capitalists and western democracy.[2]

Finally, the Cold War also followed the lines of a profound moral struggle. Best expressed by Reinhold Niebuhr in his landmark work *Christian Realism and Political Problems*, the fight against Communism was a crusade against an essentially evil system. Niebuhr offered a warning to those "deluded spirits" who might consider Communism to be simply another form of democracy or, at the very least, consistent with an old form of Russian imperialism. The "dictatorship of the proletariate" was, in practice, a monopoly on power which had led to the current system under Stalin. Moreover, Communism was also evil in its final objective: the creation of a system of absolute power "immune to any moral or political suasion."[3] For many Americans, particularly Secretary of State John Foster Dulles, the moral challenge of Soviet Communism lent an important sense of urgency to American foreign policy after 1945.

The post-1945 reconstruction of international affairs turned on these points of departure. As British power retreated in the eastern Mediterranean and the Middle East, the Soviet Union attempted to fill the vacuum, sponsoring guerrilla insurgents in Greece and using conventional military forces in an attempt to win concession from Iran.[4] In Japan, the United States established a permanent military presence and immediately began the process of restructuring both the economic and political institutions of the country.[5] As military governor, General Douglas MacArthur was charged by Washington to "remove restrictions on political, civil and religious liberties and discrimination on grounds of race, nationality, creed or political opinion." Although some vestiges of the old imperial system remained, MacArthur's reforms to the constitution, civil-military relations, and police functions introduced profound change to Japan.[6]

As the 1940s proceeded, the United States devoted renewed energies to the construction of alliances against the Soviet threat. In 1947, recognizing that neither multilateral institutions such as the International Monetary Fund (IMF) nor individual nations could successfully initiate European reconstruction, Secretary of State George C. Marshall called for a $13 billion U.S. aid program to accomplish the task. Dubbed the "Marshall Plan," almost from the outset it explicitly endorsed the principle that free markets were a critical component to not only stable democracies but also a necessary support for long-term American prosperity.[7] American support for European economic integration immediately accompanied the Marshall Plan. In 1947, the Committee on European Economic Cooperation was created with the commitment to the mutual reduction of tariffs and the free convertability of currencies. Later plans focused on long-term industrial modernization. Over the next decade these initiatives collectively developed into the European Economic Community (EEC).[8]

Overshadowing economic assistance was a parallel effort to construct a series of collective defense organizations to protect western Europe and contain the Soviet Union. The creation of the North Atlantic Treaty Organization (NATO) reflected U.S. commitment to the collective defense of the region and its critical strategic resources. Moreover, it served as a response to the ongoing Soviet consolidation of Eastern Europe under the auspices of the Red Army. In later years, NATO would provide a model for additional American-sponsored treaties in Southeast Asia (SEATO, 1954) and the Middle East (CENTO) as well as a host of bilateral security agreements.[9]

Clashes of some type were almost inevitable under this system, but the first, Korea, took U.S. leaders largely by surprise. Prior to 1950, the Korean peninsula was a place that lay outside the core conflicts dominating the Cold War.[10] Yet, by the time an armistice ended the Korean War in 1953, it had fundamentally altered America's approach to international relations. The traditional concept of total war essentially died in Korea. When General MacArthur's determination to secure victory at any cost—a determination reflected in his willingness to use atomic weapons against China—resulted in his removal from command, it became clear that the days of armored columns dramatically converging on an enemy's capital were effectively over. As early as 1950, there was a tangible sense that a Cold War conflict like the one in Korea could easily escalate into a full-scale atomic exchange. During the 1952 American presidential election, Korea also demonstrated the political costs of a stalemate. While the public generally supported the deployment of troops to northeast Asia, the absolute cost of the war, both in lives and the federal budget, and its very inconclusiveness, paved the way to the White House for a novice political candidate such as Dwight D. Eisenhower. Eisenhower's subsequent embrace of the doctrine of "massive retaliation" was an ackowledgment of his faith in nuclear deterrence, but also an important indicator of his desire to not let national security policy interfere with the post-war economic boom, which was in full stride by the 1950s.

Korea, in fact, was a cautionary tale for both sides in the Cold War, one that transformed the very nature of conflict in the 1950s and 1960s. Realizing the absolute costs involved if the East-West conflict were to suddenly become "hot," the contending sides extended their efforts into new arenas. Nikita Khrushchev's announcement at the 20th Party Congress in 1956 that the Soviet Union would abandon confrontation in favor of "peaceful co-existence" and his promise to support "wars of national liberation" signaled a transition of the Cold War into the underdeveloped regions of the war.[11] In Africa, Latin America, and Asia, superpower rivalry translated into billions of dollars and rubles spent on economic and military aid packages. By 1960, literally thousands of Americans were scattered around the world managing economic development and training the armies of dozens of nations. Former backwaters in the Cold War, afterthoughts in the minds of the public and policy makers alike, soon occupied center stage in the lives of most Americans. When journalist Stanley Karnow asked Robert Kennedy about the new priority Vietnam had in the new administration, the Attorney General ruefully remarked, "Vietnam . . . We have thirty Vietnams a day here."[12]

Vietnam eventually came to define both the level of American commitment and its limitations. In Vietnam, the United States undertook a massive, overlapping series of efforts to construct a viable, sovereign nation. It would spend billions and countless thousands of lives in an attempt to protect South Vietnam from the threat of Communist expansion, while constructing institutions perceived necessary to a modern democratic nation. The ultimate failure of this commitment was a testament to both its conceptual flaws and its execution.[13]

Moreover, Vietnam offered a stark example of the limitations of military policy in the Cold War. Although American commanders enjoyed overwhelming advantages in mobility and firepower, they found themselves severely constrained by the geopolitical consequences of escalation. American tactical victories populated the landscape of South Vietnam. However, because civilian policy makers refused to sanction expansion of the war into Cambodia, Laos, and the entirety of North Vietnam, the United States was unable to capture a decisive strategic victory. As was the case in Korea, domestic support slipped away as the war in Vietnam dragged on without measurable progress. The Tet Offensive of January 1968 was less a single climactic event than the final accumulation of the systemic limits inherent in the American war effort.[14]

Recurrent war in the Middle East proved to be an even greater threat to global stability. During the course of three wars, America forged a link with the state of Israel, providing it with millions in economic and military assistance. The apex of this effort was in 1973 during the Yom Kippur War when the Nixon administration airlifted more than $2 billion in emergency aid to the besieged Israelis. In doing so, Washington risked provoking the Soviet Union, the primary patron of the Arab alliance aligned against Israel. During the Yom Kippur War, anticipating an escalation of U.S.–Soviet tensions, American nuclear forces were placed on their highest state of alert since the Cuban Missile Crisis.[15]

However, despite its willingness to wield strategic military power, a characteristic most apparent in the latter stages of the Vietnam War, the Nixon administration was a point of departure in that it was willing to recognize the limits of American power in the Cold War. With the assistance of National Security Advisor Henry Kissinger, Richard Nixon recrafted American foreign policy priorities, taking note of the relative increase in Soviet strategic nuclear power, the economic reconstruction of Asia and Western Europe, the growing geopolitical importance of China, and the debilitating commitment to Southeast Asian security. The "Nixon Doctrine" subsequently focused U.S. foreign policy on a new set of what the president and Kissinger considered to be more rational priorities. Nixon placed the primary area of American interests in what he described as the "northern tier," a geographic region that included the United

States, the Soviet Union, China, Japan, and the Western European community.[16] For all intents and purposes, this "pentagonal strategy" was essentially an adaptation of Kennan's theory regarding key strategic industrial areas of importance to American security twenty years earlier.

However, Nixon's important contribution to Kennan's old model was in his adapting it to fit new Cold War realities. Nixon was fully cognizant that Asia, particularly Communist China, had become a significantly important factor in the global balance of power.[17] Moreover, he was equally aware that Sino-Soviet relations had deteriorated substantially on his watch. Military skirmishes between the Soviet Union and China were commonplace along the Siberian border by the late 1960s. Understanding that a diplomatic accord was possible, both Kissinger and Nixon devoted considerable energy to forging a tie with Peking. Nixon's famous visit to China in 1972 was the ultimate product of this effort, and an event which redefined the parameters of the Cold War.[18] In possession of an open diplomatic relationship with mainland China, the United States broke apart the so-called "Communist monolith" and parlayed this new situation into leverage against the Soviet Union. It was not a coincidence that the first Strategic Arms Limitation Treaty (SALT I) with Moscow followed soon after Nixon's return from Peking.

Despite its commitment to a diplomatic rapprochement with the Soviet Union and China, many aspects of U.S. foreign policy did not depart the old Cold War model. While wedded to the "northern tier" of nations, the United States did not abandon intervention in the Third World. American covert intervention against Chilean leader Salvador Allende in 1973 was more reminiscent of the Eisenhower administration's intervention than a new era of detente between the superpowers.

Conversely, this new era of diplomacy did not protect the United States from major strategic reverses in the 1970s. An easing of superpower relations could not anticipate the rise of Islamic fundamentalism and a revolution against the Pavlevi regime in Iran. Nor were U.S. policy makers prepared for the collapse of the Somoza dynasty in Nicaragua at the end of the decade.[19] Renewed Soviet aggression abroad compounded these problems. A Marxist revolution in Angola was reinforced by Soviet aid and the introduction of Cuban ground forces in 1975 and 1976. Cuban proxies intervened in Ethiopia two years later, while the Soviet Union provided $11 billion worth of arms and assistance.[20] The Soviet invasion of Afghanistan in December 1979 cemented American suspicions that Moscow was prepared to exploit Middle East instability for its own strategic designs.

By 1980, detente had become the subject of open ridicule. During the presidential campaign that year, it was interpreted as sign of strategic weakness and military decline by candidate Ronald Reagan. In fact, Reagan had launched his critique of American foreign policy two years earlier as part of the debate over the Panama Canal Treaty, depicting it as a tangible sign of American retreat.[21]

Reagan explicitly promised a return to a more assertive American foreign policy once he became president.

Reagan kept his promise. American foreign policy in the 1980s was defined by the reconstruction of the old Cold War dichotomy portraying the Soviet Union as the central cause of global instability and the United States as the leader of free, democratic nations opposed to it.[22] More to the point, the Reagan administration was prepared to openly confront instances of Soviet aggression with a broad range of military responses. Additional nuclear forces were deployed to western Europe while, at the same time, the United States devoted increasing military assistance to guerrilla forces in Afghanistan and Central America.[23] A massive American military buildup punctuated this new trajectory. U.S. defense budgets consistently increased over a six-year period, from FY1980 to FY1985, peaking in FY1985 at $286 billion. Overall, an estimated $2.4 trillion was spent on defense during the two Reagan terms.[24] This formidable commitment of resources paid for new weapons, training, and force modernization throughout the 1980s.

Conversely, public concerns regarding the actual use of American forces in combat significantly limited the administration's military operations. Although Reagan was able to deploy U.S. military might to Lebanon, Grenada, and Libya, his administration refused to commit conventional forces for any long-term effort. Reagan's recognition of public skepticism and his subsequent aversion to prolonged and overt American military commitments (the conduct of the *contra* war against Nicaragua being one case in point) ultimately led U.S. policy makers to embrace the convoluted and quasi-legal alternative of covert warfare. The subsequent 1986 Iran-Contra scandal significantly crippled the administration's domestic credibility and impeded its conduct of American foreign policy.[25]

Despite this considerable distraction, the Reagan administration was able to preside over the final demise of Soviet Communism. Early signs of deterioration appeared in the internal power struggle that followed the death of Leonid Brezhnev in 1982. The issue of succession was not settled for nearly three years when Mikhail Gorbachev finally took power in March 1985. Gorbachev proved to be a pragmatist and was prepared to recognize the unsustainable costs that burdened the Soviet Union as a result of the Cold War. The new Soviet leader initiated a period of *glasnost* and encouraged an unprecedented period of foreign access to his country. Gorbachev also appeared prepared to resume arms reduction negotiations that had been proposed by the United States as early as 1982.[26] These negotiations eventually matured into the Intermediate-range Nuclear Forces (INF) Treaty five years later.

In the meantime, Soviet power retreated. In Eastern Europe, Gorbachev appeared much more flexible than his predecessors, tolerating the expansion of a Polish independence movement and the opening of the common border with the west. In 1988, he formally announced the withdrawal of Soviet military forces from the region, precipitating the collapse of regimes aligned with Moscow.[27]

The final fall of the Berlin Wall became the symbolic endpoint of nearly one-half century of conflict.

NOTES

1. Gordon A. Craig and Alexander L. George, *Force and Statecraft: Diplomatic Problems of Our Time* (New York: Oxford University Press, 1990), 119.

2. George F. Kennan, *American Diplomacy* (Chicago: University of Chicago Press, 1951), 107–30; George F. Kennan, *Realities of American Foreign Policy* (Princeton, NJ: Princeton University Press, 1954), 63–90.

3. Reinhold Niebuhr, *Christian Realism and Political Problems* (New York: Charles Scribner's Sons, 1953), 33–42.

4. Ronald E. Powaski, *The Cold War: The United States and the Soviet Union, 1917–1991* (New York: Oxford University Press, 1998), 65–96; Mary Ann Heiss, *Empire and Nationhood: The United States, Great Britain, and Iranian Oil, 1950–1954* (New York: Columbia University Press, 1997), 1–44.

5. Michael Schaller, *The American Occupation of Japan: The Origins of the Cold War in Asia* (New York: Oxford University Press, 1985), 3–140.

6. Henry Steele Commager, *Documents of American History*, vol. 2 (Englewood Cliffs, NJ: Prentice Hall, 1973), 501–3.

7. Ed Cray, *General of the Army: George C. Marshall, Soldier and Statesman* (New York: Simon & Schuster, 1990), 586–644.

8. Dean Acheson, *Present at the Creation: My Years in the State Department* (New York: W. W. Norton, 1960), 226–35. See also Diane Kunz, *Guns and Butter: America's Cold War Economic Diplomacy* (New York: Free Press, 1997).

9. John Lewis Gaddis, *Strategies of Containment: A Critical Appraisal of Postwar American National Security Policy* (New York: Oxford University Press, 1982), 127–63.

10. This issue remains hotly contested within the diplomatic history community. See Bruce Cumings, *The Origins of the Korean War*, vol. 2, *The Roaring of the Cataract, 1947–1950* (Princeton, NJ: Princeton University Press, 1990), 625–65.

11. Nicola Miller, *Soviet Relations with Latin America, 1959–1987* (New York: Cambridge University Press, 1989), 7; S. Neil MacFarlane, *Superpower Rivalry and Third World Radicalism: The Idea of National Liberation* (Baltimore: Johns Hopkins University Press, 1985), 141–42; U.S. President's Message to Congress on the Mutual Security Program, *The Mutual Security Program: Fiscal Year 1958, A Summary Presentation* (Washington, DC: Government Printing Office, 1957), 47.

12. David Halberstam, *The Best and the Brightest* (Greenwich, CT: Fawcett Publications, 1969), 76.

13. For examples of both, see Frances Fitzgerald, *Fire in the Lake: The Vietnamese and the Americans in Vietnam* (Boston: Little, Brown, & Company, 1972); Stanley Karnow, *Vietnam: A History* (New York: Viking Press, 1983); Neil Sheehan, *A Bright Shining Lie: John Paul Vann and America in Vietnam* (New York: Vintage Books, 1988).

14. Leslie Gelb and Richard K. Betts, *The Irony of Vietnam: The System Worked* (Washington, DC: Brookings Institution, 1979), 129–30, 156–78, 220, 225–26.

15. Walter LaFeber, *America, Russia, and the Cold War, 1945–1984* (New York: Knopf, 1985), 276–77.

16. Joan Hoff, *Nixon Reconsidered* (New York: Basic Books, 1994), 158.

17. Richard M. Nixon, "Asia after Vietnam," *Foreign Affairs* 46 (October 1967): 111–25.

18. John Robert Greene, *The Limits of Power: The Nixon and Ford Administrations* (Indianapolis: Indiana University Press, 1992), 106–27.

19. Barry Rubin, *Paved with Good Intentions: The American Experience and Iran* (New York: Penguin Books, 1981), 190–251. See also Mark Falcoff and Robert Royal, eds., *Crisis and Opportunity: U.S. Policy in Central America and the Caribbean* (Washington, DC: Ethics & Public Policy Center, 1984); Robert A. Pastor, *Whirlpool: U.S. Foreign Policy in Latin America and the Caribbean* (Princeton, NJ: Princeton University Press, 1992); John H. Coatsworth, *Central America and the United States: The Clients and the Colossus* (New York: Twayne Publishers, 1994).

20. Allan R. Millett and Peter Maslowski, *For the Common Defense: A Military History of the United States of America* (New York: Free Press, 1994), 609.

21. LaFeber, *America, Russia, and the Cold War*, 289; Zbigniew Brzezinski, *Power and Principle: Memoirs of the National Security Adviser, 1977–1981* (New York: Farrar, Straus & Giroux, 1983), 134–39, 144–45.

22. Alexander Haig, "A New Direction in U.S. Foreign Policy," *State Department Bulletin* 81 (June 1981): 6; Condoleezza Rice, "U.S.–Soviet Relations," in *Looking Back on the Reagan Presidency*, ed. Larry Berman (Baltimore: Johns Hopkins University Press, 1990), 33–49.

23. Michael C. Desch, "Turning the Caribbean Flank: Sea-lane Vulnerability during a European War," *Survival* 29 (November/December 1987): 528–50; Coatsworth, *Central America and the United States*, 163–206.

24. Millett and Maslowski, *For the Common Defense*, 616–17.

25. Eldon Kensworthy, "United States Policy towards Central America," *Current History* 86 (December 1987): 401–4.

26. Jerry F. Hough, "The Future of Soviet-American Relations," *Current History* 85 (October 1986): 305–8.

27. Lawrence T. Caldwell, "Soviet-American Relations: The Cold War Ends," *Current History* 89 (October 1990): 305–8; Thomas J. McCormick, *America's Half-Century: United States Foreign Policy in the Cold War and After*, 2d ed. (Baltimore: Johns Hopkins University Press, 1995), 237–58.

101. TRUMAN'S STATEMENT ON THE FUNDAMENTALS OF U.S. FOREIGN POLICY
27 October 1945

With the Second World War concluded, the Truman administration articulated the basic principles that would guide American post-war diplomacy. In particular, the statement endorsed the concept of collective action as applied to reconstruction and subsequent international relations.

. . . 1. We seek no territorial expansion or selfish advantage. We have no plans for aggression against any other state, large or small. We have no objective which need clash with the peaceful aims of any other nation.

2. We believe in the eventual return of sovereign rights and self-government to all peoples who have been deprived of them by force.

3. We shall approve no territorial changes in any friendly part of the world unless they accord with the freely expressed wishes of the people concerned.

4. We believe that all peoples who are prepared for self-government should be permitted to choose their own form of government by their own freely expressed choice, without interference from any foreign source. That is true in Europe, in Asia, in Africa, as well as in the Western Hemisphere.

5. By the combined and cooperative action of our war Allies, we shall help the defeated enemy states establish peaceful, democratic governments of their own free choice. And we shall try to attain a world in which Nazism, Fascism, and military aggression cannot exist.

6. We shall refuse to recognize any government imposed upon any nation by the force of any foreign power. In some cases it may be impossible to prevent forceful imposition of such a government. But the United States will not recognize any such government.

7. We believe that all nations should have the freedom of the seas and equal rights to the navigation of boundary rivers and waterways and of rivers and waterways which pass through more than one country.

8. We believe that all states which are accepted in the society of nations should have access on equal terms to the trade and the raw materials of the world.

9. We believe that the sovereign states of the Western Hemisphere, without interference from outside the Western Hemisphere, must work together as good neighbors in the solution of their common problems.

10. We believe that full economic collaboration between all nations, great and small, is essential to the improvement of living conditions all over the world, and to the establishment of freedom from fear and freedom from want.

11. We shall continue to strive to promote freedom of expression and freedom of religion throughout the peace-loving areas of the world.

12. We are convinced that the preservation of peace between nations requires a United Nations Organization composed of all the peace-loving nations of the world who are willing jointly to use force if necessary to insure peace.

That is the foreign policy which guides the United States now. That is the foreign policy with which it confidently faces the future.

It may not be put into effect tomorrow or the next day. But none the less, it is our policy; and we shall seek to achieve it. It may take a long time, but it is worth waiting for, and it is worth striving to attain. . . .

Source: Public Papers of the Presidents of the United States: Harry S. Truman, 1945 (Washington, DC: Government Printing Office, 1961), 431–38.

102.   THE UNITED NATIONS PARTICIPATION ACT
20 December 1945

At the end of 1945, both the Senate and the House of Representatives overwhelmingly approved a bill that made the United States an official member of the United Nations.

An act—To provide for the appointment of representatives of the United States in the organs and agencies of the United Nations, and to make other provision with respect to the participation of the United States in such organization.

Sec. 2. (a) The President, by and with the advice and consent of the Senate, shall appoint a representative of the United States at the seat of the United Nations who shall leave the rank and status of envoy extraordinary and ambassador plenipotentiary, shall receive annual compensation of $20,000, and shall hold office at the pleasure of the President. Such representative shall represent the United States in the Security Council of the United Nations and shall perform such other functions in connection with the participation of the United States in the United Nations as the President may from time to time direct.

(b) The President, by and with the advice and consent of the Senate, shall appoint a deputy representative of the United States to the Security Council who shall have the rank and status of envoy extraordinary and minister plenipotentiary, shall receive annual compensation of $12,000, and shall hold office at the pleasure of the President. Such deputy representative shall represent the United States in the Security Council of the United Nations in the event of the absence or disability of the representative.

(c) The President, by and with the advice and consent of the Senate, shall designate from time to time to attend a specified session or specified sessions of the General Assembly of the United Nations not to exceed five representatives of the United States and such number of alternates as he may determine consistent with the rules of procedure of the General Assembly. One of the representatives shall be designated as the senior representative. Such representatives and alternates shall each be entitled to receive compensation at the rate of $12,000 per annum for such period as the President may specify, except that no member of the Senate or House of Representatives or officer of the United States who is designated under this subsection as a representative of the United States or as an alternate to attend any specified session or specified sessions of the General Assembly shall be entitled to receive such compensation.

(d) The President may also appoint from time to time such other persons as he may deem necessary to represent the United States in the organs and agencies of the United Nations, but the representative of the United States in the Economic and Social Council and in the Trusteeship Council of the United Nations shall be appointed only by and with the advice and consent of the Senate.

(e) Nothing contained in this section shall preclude the President or the Secretary of State, at the direction of the President, from representing the United States at any meeting or session of any organ or agency of the United Nations.

Sec. 3. The representatives provided for in section 2 hereof, when representing the United States in the respective organs and agencies of the United Nations, shall, at all times, act in accordance with the instructions of the President transmitted by the Secretary of State.

Sec. 4. The President shall, from time to time as occasion may require, but not less than once a year, make reports to the Congress of the activities of the United Nations and of the participation of the United States therein.

Sec. 5. (a) Notwithstanding the provisions of any other law, whenever the United States is called upon by the Security Council to apply measures which said Council has decided, pursuant to article 41 of said Charter, are to be employed to give effect to its decisions under said Charter, the President may, to the extent necessary to apply such measures, through any agency which he may designate, and under such orders, rules, and regulations as may be prescribed by him, investigate, regulate, or prohibit, in whole or in part, economic relations or rail, sea, air, postal, telegraphic, radio, and other means of communication between any foreign country or any national thereof or any person therein and the United States or any person subject to the jurisdiction thereof, or involving any property subject to the jurisdiction of the United States.

Sec. 6. The President is authorized to negotiate a special agreement or agreements with the Security Council which shall be subject to the approval of the Congress by appropriate Act or joint resolution, providing for the numbers and types of armed forces, their degree of readiness and general location, and the nature of facilities and assistance, including rights of passage, to be made available to the Security Council on its call for the purpose of maintaining international peace and security in accordance with article 43 of said Charter. The President shall not be deemed to require the authorization of the Congress to make available to the Security Council on its call in order to take action under article 42 of said Charter and pursuant to such special agreement or agreements the armed forces, facilities, or assistance provided for therein: *Provided*, That nothing herein contained shall be construed as an authorization to the President by the Congress to make available to the Security Council for such purpose armed forces, facilities or assistance in addition to the forces, facilities, and assistance provided for in such special agreement or agreements.

Approved December 20, 1945.

Source: Henry Steele Commager, *Documents of American History*, vol. 2 (Englewood Cliffs, NJ: Prentice Hall, 1973), 504–5.

103. KENNAN'S "LONG TELEGRAM"
22 February 1946

George F. Kennan, the U.S. chargé d'affairs in Moscow and a recognized expert on the Soviet Union offered the first comprehensive analysis of Soviet behavior in the post-war period. His examination offered not only the prospective organizational structure of Communist activity, but an in-depth discussion of the motives behind Soviet behavior.

PART 1: BASIC FEATURES OF POST WAR SOVIET OUTLOOK, AS PUT FORWARD BY OFFICIAL PROPAGANDA MACHINE, ARE AS FOLLOWS:

a. USSR still lives in antagonistic "capitalistic encirclement" with which in the long run there can be no permanent peaceful coexistence. As stated by Stalin in 1927 to a delegation of American workers: In course of further development of international revolution there will emerge two centers of world significance: a socialist center, drawing to itself the countries which tend toward socialism, and a capitalist center, drawing to itself the countries that incline toward capitalism. Battle between these two centers for command of world economy will decide fate of capitalism and of communism in entire world.

b. Capitalist world is beset with internal conflicts, inherent in nature of capitalist society. These conflicts are insoluble by means of peaceful compromise. Greatest of them is that between England and US.

c. Internal conflicts of capitalism inevitably generate wars. Wars thus generated may be of two kinds: intra-capitalist wars between two capitalist states, and wars of intervention against socialist world. Smart capitalists, vainly seeking escape from inner conflicts of capitalism, incline toward latter.

d. Intervention against USSR, while it would be disastrous to those who undertook it, would cause renewed delay in progress of Soviet socialism and must therefore be forestalled at all costs.

e. Conflicts between capitalist states, though likewise fraught with danger for USSR, nevertheless hold out great possibilities for advancement of socialist cause, particularly if USSR remains militarily powerful, ideologically monolithic and faithful to its present brilliant leadership.

f. It must be borne in mind that capitalist world is not all bad. In addition to hopelessly reactionary and bourgeois elements, it includes 1. certain wholly enlightened and positive elements united in acceptable communistic parties and 2. certain other elements now described for tactical reasons as progressive or democratic, whose reactions, aspirations and activities happen to be "objectively" favorable to interests of USSR. These last must be encouraged and utilized for Soviet purposes.

g. Among negative elements of bourgeois-capitalist society, most dangerous of all are those whom Lenin called false friends of the people, namely the moderate-socialist or social-democratic leaders in other words, non-Communist left-wing. These are more dangerous than out-and-out reactionaries, for latter at least march under their true colors, whereas moderate left-wing leaders confuse people by employing devices of socialism to serve interests of reactionary capital. So much for premises. To what deductions do they lead from standpoint of Soviet policy? To following:

   a. Everything must be done to advance relative strength of USSR as factor in international society. Conversely, no opportunity must be missed to reduce strength and influence, collectively as well as individually, of capitalist powers.

   b. Soviet efforts, and those of Russia's friends abroad, must be directed toward deepening and exploiting of differences and conflicts between capitalist powers. If these eventually deepen into an "imperialist" war, this war must be turned into revolutionary upheavals within the various capitalist countries.

   c. "Democratic-progressive" elements abroad are to be utilized to maximum to bring pressure to bear on capitalist governments along lines agreeable to Soviet interests.

   d. Relentless battle must be waged against socialist and social-democratic leaders abroad.

PART 2:   BACKGROUND OF OUTLOOK

Before examining ramifications of this party line in practice there are certain aspects of it to which I wish to draw attention.

First, it does not represent natural outlook of Russian people. Latter are, by and large, friendly to outside world, eager for experience of it, eager to measure against it talents they are conscious of possessing, eager above all to live in peace and enjoy fruits of their own labor. Party line only represents thesis which official propaganda machine puts forward with great skill and persistence to a public often remarkably resistant in the stronghold of its innermost thoughts. But party line is binding for outlook and conduct of people who make up apparatus of power—party, secret police and Government—and it is exclusively with these that we have to deal. . . .

At bottom of Kremlin's neurotic view of world affairs is traditional and instinctive Russian sense of insecurity. Originally, this was insecurity of a peaceful agricultural people trying to live on vast exposed plain in neighborhood of fierce nomadic peoples. To this was added, as Russia came into contact with economically advanced West, fear of more competent, more powerful, more highly organized societies in that area. But this latter type of insecurity was one which afflicted rather Russian rulers than Russian people; for Russian rulers have invariably sensed that their rule was relatively archaic in form, fragile and artificial in its psychological foundation, unable to stand comparison or contact with political systems of Western countries. For this reason they have always feared foreign penetration, feared direct contact between Western world and their own, feared what would happen if Russians learned truth about world without or if foreigners learned truth about world within. And they have learned to seek security only in patient but deadly struggle for total destruction of rival power, never in compacts and compromises with it.

It was no coincidence that Marxism, which had smoldered ineffectively for half a century in Western Europe, caught hold and blazed for first time in Russia. Only in this land which had never known a friendly neighbor or indeed any tolerant equilibrium of separate powers, either internal or international, could a doctrine thrive which viewed economic conflicts of society as insoluble by peaceful means. After establishment of Bolshevist regime, Marxist dogma, rendered even more truculent and intolerant by Lenin's interpretation, became a perfect vehicle for sense of insecurity with which Bolsheviks, even more than previous Russian rulers, were afflicted. In this dogma, with its basic altruism of purpose, they found justification for their instinctive fear of outside world, for the dictatorship without which they did not know how to rule, for cruelties they did not dare not to inflict, for sacrifices they felt bound to demand. In the name of Marxism they sacrificed every single ethical value in their methods and tactics. Today they cannot dispense with it. It is fig leaf of their moral and intellectual respectability. Without it they would stand before history, at best, as only the last of that long succession of cruel and wasteful Russian rulers who have relentlessly forced country on to ever new heights of military power in order to guarantee external security of their internally weak regimes. This is why Soviet purposes must always be solemnly clothed in trappings of Marxism, and why no one should underrate importance of dogma in Soviet affairs. Thus Soviet leaders are driven [by?] necessities of their own past and present position to put forward a dogma which [apparent omission] outside world as evil, hostile and menacing, but as bearing within itself germs of creeping disease and destined to be wracked with growing internal convulsions until it is given final *coup de grace* by rising power of socialism and yields to new and better world. This thesis provides justification for that increase of military and police power of Russian state, for that isolation of Russian population from outside world, and for that fluid and constant pressure to extend limits of Russian police power which are together the natural and instinctive urges of Russian rulers. Basically this is only the steady advance of uneasy Russian nationalism, a centuries old movement in which conceptions of offense and defense are inextricably confused. But in new guise of international Marxism, with its honeyed promises to a desperate and war torn outside world, it is more dangerous and insidious than ever before. . . .

PART 3:   PROJECTION OF SOVIET OUTLOOK IN PRACTICAL POLICY ON OFFICIAL LEVEL

We have now seen nature and background of Soviet program. What may we expect by way of its practical implementation?

Soviet policy, as Department implies in its query under reference, is conducted on two planes: 1. official plane represented by actions undertaken officially in name of Soviet Government; and 2. subterranean plane of actions undertaken by agencies for which Soviet Government does not admit responsibility.

Policy promulgated on both planes will be calculated to serve basic policies a. to d. outlined in part 1. Actions taken on different planes will differ considerably, but will dovetail into each other in purpose, timing and effect.

On official plane we must look for following:

a. Internal policy devoted to increasing in every way strength and prestige of Soviet state: intensive military-industrialization; maximum development of armed forces; great displays to impress outsiders; continued secretiveness about internal matters, designed to conceal weaknesses and to keep opponents in dark.

b. Wherever it is considered timely and promising, efforts will be made to advance official limits of Soviet power. For the moment, these efforts are restricted to certain neighboring points conceived of here as being of immediate strategic necessity, such as Northern Iran, Turkey, possibly Bornholm. However, other points may at any time come into question, if and as concealed Soviet political power is extended to new areas. Thus a "friendly" Persian Government might be asked to grant Russia a port on Persian Gulf. Should Spain fall under Communist control, question of Soviet base at Gibraltar Strait might be activated. But such claims will appear on official level only when unofficial preparation is complete.

c. Russians will participate officially in international organizations where they see opportunity of extending Soviet power or of inhibiting or diluting power of others. Moscow sees in UNO [United Nations organization] not the mechanism for a permanent and stable world society founded on mutual interest and aims of all nations, but an arena in which aims just mentioned can be favorably pursued. As long as UNO is considered here to serve this purpose, Soviets will remain with it. But if at any time they come to conclusion that it is serving to embarrass or frustrate their aims for power expansion and if they see better prospects for pursuit of these aims along other lines, they will not hesitate to abandon UNO. . . .

d. Toward colonial areas and backward or dependent peoples, Soviet policy, even on official plane, will be directed toward weakening of power and influence and contacts of advanced Western nations, on theory that in so far as this policy is successful, there will be created a vacuum which will favor Communist-Soviet penetration. . . .

PART 4: FOLLOWING MAY BE SAID AS TO WHAT WE MAY EXPECT BY WAY OF IMPLEMENTATION OF BASIC SOVIET POLICIES ON UNOFFICIAL, OR SUBTERRANEAN PLANE, I.E. ON PLANE FOR WHICH SOVIET GOVERNMENT ACCEPTS NO RESPONSIBILITY

Agencies utilized for promulgation of policies on this plane are following:

1. Inner central core of Communist Parties in other countries. While many of persons who compose this category may also appear and act in unrelated public capacities, they are in reality working closely together as an underground operating directorate of world communism, a concealed Comintern tightly coordinated and directed by

Moscow. It is important to remember that this inner core is actually working on underground lines, despite legality of parties with which it is associated.

2. Rank and file of Communist Parties. Note distinction is drawn between these and persons defined in paragraph 1. This distinction has become much sharper in recent years. Whereas formerly foreign Communist Parties represented a curious and from Moscow's standpoint often inconvenient mixture of conspiracy and legitimate activity, now the conspiratorial element has been neatly concentrated in inner circle and ordered underground, while rank and file—no longer even taken into confidence about realities of movement—are thrust forward as bona fide internal partisans of certain political tendencies within their respective countries, genuinely innocent of conspiratorial connection with foreign states. Only in certain countries where communists are numerically strong do they now regularly appear and act as a body. . . .

3. A wide variety of national associations or bodies which can be dominated or influenced by such penetration. These include: labor unions, youth leagues, women's organizations, racial societies, religious societies, social organizations, cultural groups, liberal magazines, publishing houses, etc.

4. International organizations which can be similarly penetrated through influence over various national components. Labor, youth and women's organizations are prominent among them. Particular, almost vital, importance is attached in this connection to international labor movement. In this, Moscow sees possibility of sidetracking western governments in world affairs and building up international lobby capable of compelling governments to take actions favorable to Soviet interests in various countries and of paralyzing actions disagreeable to USSR. . . . It may be expected that component parts of this far-flung apparatus will be utilized, in accordance with their individual suitability, as follows:

   a. To undermine general political and strategic potential of major western powers. Efforts will be made in such countries to disrupt national self confidence, to hamstring measures of national defense, to increase social and industrial unrest, to stimulate all forms of disunity. All persons with grievances, whether economic or racial, will be urged to seek redress not in mediation and compromise, but in defiant violent struggle for destruction of other elements of society. Here poor will be set against rich, black against white, young against old, newcomers against established residents, etc.

   b. On unofficial plane particularly violent efforts will be made to weaken power and influence of Western Powers of [on] colonial backward, or dependent peoples. On this level, no holds will be barred. Mistakes and weaknesses of western colonial administration will be mercilessly exposed and exploited. Liberal opinion in Western countries will be mobilized to weaken colonial policies. Resentment among dependent peoples will be stimulated. And while latter are being encouraged to seek independence of Western Powers, Soviet dominated puppet political machines will be undergoing preparation to take over domestic power in respective colonial areas when independence is achieved.

   c. Where individual governments stand in path of Soviet purposes pressure will be brought for their removal from office. This can happen where governments directly oppose Soviet foreign policy aims Turkey, Iran, where they seal their territories off against Communist penetration Switzerland, Portugal, or where they compete too strongly, like Labor Government in England, for moral domination among elements which it is important for Communists to dominate. . . .

d. In foreign countries Communists will, as a rule, work toward destruction of all forms of personal independence, economic, political or moral. Their system can handle only individuals who have been brought into complete dependence on higher power. Thus, persons who are financially independent—such as individual businessmen, estate owners, successful farmers, artisans and all those who exercise local leadership or have local prestige, such as popular local clergymen or political figures, are anathema. . . .

e. Everything possible will be done to set major Western Powers against each other. Anti-British talk will be plugged among Americans, anti-American talk among British. Continentals, including Germans, will be taught to abhor both Anglo-Saxon powers. Where suspicions exist, they will be fanned; where not, ignited. . . .

f. In general, all Soviet efforts on unofficial international plane will be negative and destructive in character, designed to tear down sources of strength beyond reach of Soviet control. This is only in line with basic Soviet instinct that there can be no compromise with rival power and that constructive work can start only when Communist power is dominant. But behind all this will be applied insistent unceasing pressure for penetration and command of key positions in administration and especially in police apparatus of foreign countries. The Soviet regime is a police regime par excellence, reared in the dim half world of Tsarist police intrigue, accustomed to think primarily in terms of police power. This should never be lost sight of in gauging Soviet motives.

PART 5: [PRACTICAL DEDUCTIONS FROM STANDPOINT OF US POLICY]

In summary, we have here a political force committed fanatically to the belief that with US there can be no permanent *modus vivendi*, that it is desirable and necessary that the internal harmony of our society be disrupted, our traditional way of life be destroyed, the international authority of our state be broken, if Soviet power is to be secure. This political force has complete power of disposition over energies of one of the world's greatest peoples and resources of world's richest national territory, and is borne along by deep and powerful currents of Russian nationalism. . . . This is admittedly not a pleasant picture. Problem of how to cope with this force in [is] undoubtedly greatest task our diplomacy has ever faced and probably greatest it will ever have to face. It should be point of departure from which our political general staff work at present juncture should proceed. It should be approached with same thoroughness and care as solution of major strategic problem in war, and if necessary, with no smaller outlay in planning effort. I cannot attempt to suggest all answers here. But I would like to record my conviction that problem is within our power to solve—and that without recourse to any general military conflict. And in support of this conviction there are certain observations of a more encouraging nature I should like to make:

1. Soviet power, unlike that of Hitlerite Germany, is neither schematic nor adventuristic. It does not work by fixed plans. It does not take unnecessary risks. Impervious to logic of reason, and it is highly sensitive to logic of force. For this reason it can easily withdraw—and usually does—when strong resistance is encountered at any point. Thus, if the adversary has sufficient force and makes clear his readiness to use it, he rarely has to do so. If situations are properly handled there need be no prestige-engaging showdowns.

2. Gauged against Western World as a whole, Soviets are still by far the weaker force. Thus, their success will really depend on degree of cohesion, firmness and vigor which Western World can muster. And this is factor which it is within our power to influence.

3. Success of Soviet system, as form of international power, is not yet finally proven. . . .

For these reasons I think we may approach calmly and with good heart problem of how to deal with Russia. As to how this approach should be made, I only wish to advance, by way of conclusion, following comments:

1. Our first step must be to apprehend, and recognize for what it is, the nature of the movement with which we are dealing. We must study it with same courage, detachment, objectivity, and same determination not to be emotionally provoked or unseated by it, with which doctor studies unruly and unreasonable individual.

2. We must see that our public is educated to realities of Russian situation. I cannot over-emphasize importance of this. Press cannot do this alone. It must be done mainly by Government, which is necessarily more experienced and better informed on practical problems involved. In this we need not be deterred by [ugliness?] of picture. I am convinced that there would be far less hysterical anti-Sovietism in our country today if realities of this situation were better understood by our people. There is nothing as dangerous or as terrifying as the unknown. It may also be argued that to reveal more information on our difficulties with Russia would reflect unfavorably on Russian-American relations. I feel that if there is any real risk here involved, it is one which we should have courage to face, and sooner the better. But I cannot see what we would be risking. Our stake in this country, even coming on heels of tremendous demonstrations of our friendship for Russian people, is remarkably small. We have here no investments to guard, no actual trade to lose, virtually no citizens to protect, few cultural contacts to preserve. Our only stake lies in what we hope rather than what we have; and I am convinced we have better chance of realizing those hopes if our public is enlightened and if our dealings with Russians are placed entirely on realistic and matter-of-fact basis.

3. Much depends on health and vigor of our own society. World communism is like malignant parasite which feeds only on diseased tissue. This is point at which domestic and foreign policies meet. Every courageous and incisive measure to solve internal problems of our own society, to improve self-confidence, discipline, morale and community spirit of our own people, is a diplomatic victory over Moscow worth a thousand diplomatic notes and joint communiqués. If we cannot abandon fatalism and indifference in face of deficiencies of our own society, Moscow will profit— Moscow cannot help profiting by them in its foreign policies.

4. We must formulate and put forward for other nations a much more positive and constructive picture of sort of world we would like to see than we have put forward in past. It is not enough to urge people to develop political processes similar to our own. Many foreign peoples, in Europe at least, are tired and frightened by experiences of past, and are less interested in abstract freedom than in security. They are seeking guidance rather than responsibilities. We should be better able than Russians to give them this. And unless we do, Russians certainly will.

5. Finally we must have courage and self-confidence to cling to our own methods and conceptions of human society. After all, the greatest danger that can befall us in coping with this problem of Soviet communism, is that we shall allow ourselves to become like those with whom we are coping.

Kennan

Source: U.S. Department of State, Papers Relating to the Foreign Relations of the United States, 1946, vol. 6 (Washington, DC: Government Printing Office, 1969), 697–709.

104. TRUMAN DOCTRINE
12 March 1947

In February 1947, England abruptly announced in a communication to the State Department that it could no longer sustain financial or economic aid in the eastern Mediterranean, specifically in Greece and Turkey. The message forced American leaders to reconsider their basic approach to nations threatened by external aggression and the parameters of U.S. foreign assistance.

The gravity of the situation which confronts the world today necessitates my appearance before a joint session of Congress. The foreign policy and the national security of this country are involved.

One aspect of the present situation, which I wish to present to you at this time for your consideration and decision, concerns Greece and Turkey.

The United States has received from the Greek Government an urgent appeal for financial and economic assistance. Preliminary reports from the American Economic Mission now in Greece and reports from the American Ambassador in Greece corroborate the statement of the Greek Government that assistance is imperative if Greece is to survive as a free nation.

I do not believe that the American people and the Congress wish to turn a deaf ear to the appeal of the Greek Government.

The very existence of the Greek state is today threatened by the terrorist activities of several thousand armed men, led by Communists, who defy the Government's authority at a number of points, particularly along the northern boundaries. A commission appointed by the United Nations Security Council is at present investigating disturbed conditions in Northern Greece and alleged border violations along the frontiers between Greece on the one hand and Albania, Bulgaria and Yugoslavia on the other.

Meanwhile, the Greek Government is unable to cope with the situation. The Greek Army is small and poorly equipped. It needs supplies and equipment if it is to restore the authority to the Government throughout Greek territory.

Greece must have assistance if it is to become a self-supporting and self-respecting democracy. The United States must supply this assistance. We have already extended to Greece certain types of relief and economic aid but these are inadequate. There is no other country to which democratic Greece can turn. No other nation is willing and able to provide the necessary support for a democratic Greek Government.

The British Government, which has been helping Greece, can give no further financial or economic aid after March 31. Great Britain finds itself under the necessity of reducing or liquidating its commitments in several parts of the world, including Greece.

We have considered how the United Nations might assist in this crisis. But the situation is an urgent one requiring immediate action, and the United Nations and its related organizations are not in a position to extend help of the kind that is required. . . .

Greece's neighbor, Turkey, also deserves our attention. The future of Turkey as an independent and economically sound state is clearly no less important to the freedom-loving peoples of the world than the future of Greece. The circumstances in which Turkey finds itself today are considerably different from those of Greece. Turkey has been spared the disasters that have beset Greece. And during the war, the United States and Great Britain furnished Turkey with material aid. Nevertheless, Turkey now needs support.

Since the war Turkey has sought additional financial assistance from Great Britain and the United States for the purpose of effecting the modernization necessary for the maintenance of its national integrity. That integrity is essential to the preservation of order in the Middle East.

The British Government has informed us that, owing to its own difficulties, it can no longer extend financial or economic aid to Turkey. As in the case of Greece, if Turkey is to have the assistance it needs, the United States must supply it. We are the only country able to provide that help.

I am fully aware of the broad implications involved if the United States extends assistance to Greece and Turkey, and I shall discuss these implications with you at this time.

One of the primary objectives of the foreign policy of the United States is the creation of conditions in which we and other nations will be able to work out a way of life free from coercion. This was a fundamental issue in the war with Germany and Japan. Our victory was won over countries which sought to impose their will, and their way of life, upon other nations.

To ensure the peaceful development of nations, free from coercion, the United

States has taken a leading part in establishing the United Nations. The United Nations is designed to make possible lasting freedom and independence for all its members. We shall not realize our objectives, however, unless we are willing to help free peoples to maintain their free institutions and their national integrity against aggressive movements that seek to impose on them totalitarian regimes. This is no more than a frank recognition that totalitarian regimes imposed on free peoples, by direct or indirect aggression, undermine the foundations of international peace and hence the security of the United States.

The peoples of a number of countries of the world have recently had totalitarian regimes forced upon them against their will. The Government of the United States has made frequent protests against coercion and intimidation, in violation of the Yalta Agreement, in Poland, Rumania and Bulgaria. I must also state that in a number of other countries there have been similar developments.

At the present moment in world history nearly every nation must choose between alternative ways of life. The choice is too often not a free one.

One way of life is based upon the will of the majority, and is distinguished by free institutions, representative government, free elections, guarantees of individual liberty, freedom of speech and religion, and freedom from political oppression.

The second way of life is based upon the will of the minority forcibly imposed upon the majority. It relies upon terror and oppression, a controlled press and radio, fixed elections, and the suppression of personal freedoms.

I believe that it must be the policy of the United States to support free peoples who are resisting attempted subjugation by armed minorities or by outside pressures.

I believe that we must assist free peoples to work out their own destinies in their own way.

I believe that our help should be primarily through economic and financial aid which is essential to economic stability and orderly political processes.

The world is not static, and the status quo is not sacred. But we cannot allow changes in the status quo in violation of the charter of the United Nations by such methods as coercion, or by such subterfuges as political infiltration. In helping free and independent nations to maintain their freedom, the United States will be giving effect to the principles of the charter of the United Nations.

It is necessary only to glance at a map to realize that the survival and integrity of the Greek nation are of grave importance in a much wider situation. If Greece should fall under the control of an armed minority, the effect upon its neighbor, Turkey, would be immediate and serious. Confusion and disorder might well spread throughout the entire Middle East.

Moreover, the disappearance of Greece as an independent state would have a profound effect upon those countries in Europe whose peoples are struggling against great difficulties to maintain their freedoms and their independence while they repair the damages of war.

It would be an unspeakable tragedy if these countries, which have struggled so long against overwhelming odds, should lose that victory for which they sacrificed so much. Collapse of free institutions and loss of independence would be disastrous not only for them but for the world. Discouragement and possibly failure would quickly be the lot of neighboring peoples striving to maintain their freedom and independence.

Should we fail to aid Greece and Turkey in this fateful hour, the effect will be far reaching to the west as well as to the east. We must take immediate and resolute action.

I therefore ask the Congress to provide authority for assistance to Greece and Turkey in the amount of $400,000,000 for the period ending June 30, 1948.

In addition to funds, I ask the Congress to authorize the detail of American civilian and military personnel to Greece and Turkey, at the request of those countries, to assist in the tasks of reconstruction, and for the purpose of supervising the use of such financial and material assistance as may be furnished. I recommend that authority also be provided for the instruction and training of selected Greek and Turkish personnel.

Finally, I ask that the Congress provide authority which will permit the speediest and most effective use, in terms of needed commodities, supplies, and equipment, of such funds as may be authorized. . . .

The seeds of totalitarian realms are nurtured by misery and want. They spread and grow in the evil soil of poverty and strife. They reach their full growth when the hope of a people for a better life has died. We must keep that hope alive. The free peoples of the world look to us for support in maintaining their freedoms.

If we falter in our leadership, we may endanger the peace of the world—and we shall surely endanger the welfare of this nation.

Great responsibilities have been placed upon us by the swift movement of events. I am confident that the Congress will face these responsibilities squarely.

Source: Public Papers of the Presidents, Harry Truman, 1947 (Washington, DC: Government Printing Office, 1963), 176–80.

105. THE MARSHALL PLAN
5 June 1947

On 5 June 1947, General George C. Marshall delivered the commencement address at Harvard University. The event served as an opportunity for the Truman administration to establish a case for a comprehensive assistance program for the reconstruction of Europe.

Remarks by the Honorable George C. Marshall, Secretary of State, at Harvard University on June 5, 1947.

I need not tell you gentlemen that the world situation is very serious. That must be apparent to all intelligent people. I think one difficulty is that the problem is one of such enormous complexity that the very mass of facts presented to the public by press and radio make it exceedingly difficult for the man in the street to reach a clear appraisement of the situation. Furthermore, the people of this country are distant from the troubled areas of the earth and it is hard for them to comprehend the plight and consequent reactions of the long-suffering peoples, and the effect of those reactions on their governments in connection with our efforts to promote peace in the world.

In considering the requirements for the rehabilitation of Europe the physical loss of life, the visible destruction of cities, factories, mines and railroads was correctly estimated, but it has become obvious during recent months that this visible destruction was probably less serious than the dislocation of the entire fabric of European economy. For the past 10 years conditions have been highly abnormal. The feverish preparation for war and the more feverish maintenance of the war effort engulfed all aspects of national economics. Machinery has fallen into disrepair or is entirely obsolete. Under the arbitrary and destructive Nazi rule, virtually every possible enterprise was geared into the German war machine. Long-standing commercial ties, private institutions, banks, insurance companies and shipping companies disappeared, through loss of capital, absorption through nationalization or by simple destruction. In many countries, confidence in the local currency has been severely shaken. The breakdown of the business structure of Europe during the war was complete. Recovery has been seriously retarded by the fact that 2 years after the close of hostilities a peace settlement with Germany and Austria has not been agreed upon. But even given a more prompt solution of these difficult problems, the rehabilitation of the economic structure of Europe quite evidently will require a much longer time and greater effort than had been foreseen.

There is a phase of this matter which is both interesting and serious. The farmer has always produced the foodstuffs to exchange with the city dweller for the other necessities of life. This division of labor is the basis of modern civilization. At the present time it is threatened with breakdown. The town and city industries are not producing adequate goods to exchange with the food-producing farmer. Raw materials and fuel are in short supply. Machinery is lacking or worn out. The farmer or the peasant cannot find the goods for sale which he desires to purchase. So the sale of his farm produce for money which he cannot use seems to him an unprofitable transaction. He, therefore, has withdrawn many fields from crop cultivation and is using them for grazing. He feeds more grain to stock and finds for himself and his family an ample supply of food, however short he may be on clothing and the other ordinary gadgets of civilization. Meanwhile people in the cities are short of food and fuel. So the governments are forced to use their foreign money and credits to procure these necessities abroad. This process exhausts funds which are urgently needed for reconstruction. Thus a very serious situation is rapidly developing which bodes no good for the world. The modern system of the division of labor upon which the exchange of products is based is in danger of breaking down.

The truth of the matter is that Europe's requirements for the next 3 or 4 years of foreign food and other essential products—principally from America—are so much greater than her present ability to pay that she must have substantial additional help, or face economic, social, and political deterioration of a very grave character.

The remedy lies in breaking the vicious circle and restoring the confidence of the European people in the economic future of their own countries and of Europe as a whole. The manufacturer and the farmer throughout wide areas must be able and willing to exchange their products for currencies the continuing value of which is not open to question.

Aside from the demoralizing effect on the world at large and the possibilities of disturbances arising as a result of the desperation of the people concerned, the consequences to the economy of the United States should be apparent to all. It is logical that the United States should do whatever it is able to do to assist in the return of normal economic health in the world, without which there can be no political stability and no assured peace. Our policy is directed not against any county or doctrine but against hunger, poverty, desperation, and chaos. Its purpose should be the revival of a working economy in the world so as to permit the emergence of political and social conditions in which free institutions can exist. Such assistance, I am convinced, must not be on a piecemeal basis as various crises develop. Any assistance that this Government may render in the future should provide a cure rather than a mere palliative. Any government that is willing to assist in the task of recovery will find full cooperation, I am sure, on the part of the United States Government. Any government which maneuvers to block the recovery of other countries cannot expect help from us. Furthermore, governments, political parties, or groups which seek to perpetuate human misery in order to profit therefrom politically or otherwise will encounter the opposition of the United States.

It is already evident that, before the United States Government can proceed much further in its efforts to alleviate the situation and help start the European world on its way to recovery, there must be some agreement among the countries of Europe as to the requirements of the situation and the part those countries themselves will take in order to give proper effect to whatever action might be undertaken by this Government. It would be neither fitting nor efficacious for this Government to undertake to draw up unilaterally a program designed to place Europe on its feet economically. This is the business of the Europeans. The initiative, I think, must come from Europe. The role of this country should consist of friendly aid in the drafting of a European program and of later support of such a program so far as it may be practical for us to do so. The program should be a joint one, agreed to by a number, if not all European nations.

An essential part of any successful action on the part of the United States is an understanding on the part of the people of America of the character of the problem and the remedies to be applied. Political passion and prejudice should have no part. With foresight, and a willingness on the part of our people to face up to the vast responsibility which history has clearly placed upon our country, the difficulties I have outlined can and will be overcome.

Source: U.S. Department of State, *Papers Relating to the Foreign Relations of the United States, 1947*, vol. 3 (Washington, DC: Government Printing Office, 1972), 237–39.

106. THE NATIONAL SECURITY ACT
26 July 1947

The unfolding confrontation with the Soviet Union starkly illustrated the obsolescence of American national security policy. The National Security Act provided for the reorganization of American strategic planning, military operations, and intelligence collection. It served as the framework for American strategic activity for the remainder of the Cold War.

An Act to promote the national security by providing for a Secretary of Defense; for a National Military Establishment; for a Department of the Army, a Department of the Navy, and a Department of the Air Force; and for the coordination of the activities of the National Military Establishment with other departments and agencies of the Government concerned with the national security.

Sec. 101. (a) There is hereby established a council to be known as the National Security Council (hereinafter in this section referred to as the "Council").

The President of the United States shall preside over meetings of the Council: *Provided*, That in his absence he may designate a member of the Council to preside in his Place.

The function of the Council shall be to advise the President with respect to the integration of domestic, foreign, and military policies relating to the national security so as to enable the military services and the other departments and agencies of the Government to cooperate more effectively in matters involving the national security.

The Council shall be composed of the President; the Secretary of State; the Secretary of Defense; the Secretary of the Army; the Secretary of the Navy; the Secretary of the Air Force; the Chairman of the National Security Resources Board; and such of the following named officers as the President may designate from time to time: The Secretaries of the executive departments, the Chairman of the Munitions Board, and the Chairman of the Research and Development Board; but no such additional member shall be designated until the advice and consent of the Senate has been given to his appointment to the office the holding of which authorizes his designation as a member of the Council.

(b) In addition to performing such other functions as the President may direct, for the purpose of more effectively coordinating the policies and functions of the departments and agencies of the Government relating to the national security, it shall, subject to the direction of the President, be the duty of the Council—

(1) to assess and appraise the objectives, commitments, and risks of the United States in relation to our actual and potential military power in the interest of national security, for the purpose of making recommendations to the President in connection therewith; and

(2) to consider policies on matters of common interest to the departments and agencies of the Government concerned with the national security, and to make recommendations to the President in connection therewith. . . .

(d) The Council shall, from time to time, make such recommendations, and such other reports to the President as it deems appropriate or as the President may require.

Sec. 102. (a) There is hereby established under the National Security Council a Central Intelligence Agency with a Director of Central Intelligence, who shall be the head thereof. . . .

(d) For the purpose of coordinating the Intelligence activities of the several Government departments and agencies in the interest of national security, it shall be the duty of the Agency, under the direction of the National Security Council—. . . .

(3) to correlate and evaluate intelligence relating to the national security, and provide for the appropriate dissemination of such intelligence within the Government using where appropriate existing agencies and facilities. . . .

Sec. 103. (a) There is hereby established a National Security Resources Board (hereinafter in this section referred to as the "Board") to be composed of the Chairman of the Board and such heads or representatives of the various executive departments and independent agencies as may from time to time be designated by the President to be members of the Board. . . .

(c) It shall be the function of the Board to advise the President concerning the coordination of military, industrial, and civilian mobilization, including—

(1) policies concerning industrial and civilian mobilization in order to assure the most effective mobilization and maximum utilization of the Nation's manpower in the event of war;

(2) programs for the effective use in time of war of the Nation's natural and industrial resources for military and civilian needs, for the maintenance and stabilization of the civilian economy in time of war, and for the adjustment of such economy to war needs and conditions;. . . .

Sec. 201. (a) There is hereby established the National Military Establishment, and the Secretary of Defense shall be the head thereof.

(b) The National Military Establishment shall consist of the Department of the Army, the Department of the Navy, and the Department of the Air Force, together with all other agencies created under title II of this Act.

Sec. 202. (a) There shall be a Secretary of Defense, who shall be appointed from civilian life by the President, by and with the advice and consent of the Senate: *Provided*, That a person who has within ten years been on active duty as a commissioned officer in a Regular component of the armed services shall not be eligible for appointment as Secretary of Defense. The Secretary of Defense shall be the principle assistant to the President in all matters relating to the national security. Under the direction of the President and subject to the provisions of this Act he shall perform the following duties:

(1) Establish general policies and programs for the National Military Establishment and for all of the departments and agencies therein;

(2) Exercise general direction, authority, and control over such departments and agencies;

(3) Take appropriate steps to eliminate unnecessary duplication or overlapping in the fields of procurement, supply, transportation, storage, health, and research;

(4) supervise and coordinate the preparation of the budget estimates of the departments and agencies comprising the National Military Establishment; formulate and determine the budget estimates for submittal to the Bureau of the Budget; and supervise the budget programs of such departments and agencies under the applicable appropriation Act:. . . .

Sec. 210. There shall be within the National Military Establishment a War Council composed of the Secretary of Defense, as Chairman, who shall have power of decision; the Secretary of the Army; the Secretary of the Navy; the Secretary of the Air Force; the Chief of Staff, United States Army; the Chief of Naval Operations; and the Chief of Staff, United States Air Force. The War Council shall advise the Secretary of Defense on matters of broad policy relating to the armed forces, and shall consider and report on such other matters as the Secretary of Defense may direct.

Sec. 211. (a) There is hereby established within the National Military Establishment the Joint Chiefs of Staff, which shall consist of the Chief of Staff, United States Army; the Chief of Naval Operations; the Chief of Staff, United States Air Force; and the Chief of Staff to the Commander in Chief, if there be one.

(b) Subject to the authority and direction of the President and the Secretary of Defense, it shall be the duty of the joint Chiefs of Staff—

(1) to prepare strategic plans and to provide for the strategic direction of the military forces;

(2) to prepare joint logistic plans and to assign to the military services logistic responsibilities in accordance with such plans;

(3) to establish unified commands in strategic areas when such unified commands are in the interest of national security;

(4) to formulate policies for joint training of the military forces;. . . .

(c) The Joint Chiefs of Staff shall act as the principal military advisers to the President and the Secretary of Defense and shall perform such other duties as the President and the Secretary of Defense may direct or as may be prescribed by law. . . .

Source: Henry Steele Commager, Documents of American History, vol. 2 (Englewood Cliffs, NJ: Prentice Hall, 1973), 541–43.

107. THE UNITED STATES' NOTE ON THE BERLIN BLOCKADE AND AIRLIFT
6 July 1948

The final status of Germany evolved as a significant point of friction between the former Allies. Nowhere was this more true than in the debate over the status of Berlin, occupied by the United States, France, England, and the Soviet Union, but firmly ensconced within the Soviet occupation zone of eastern Germany. On 20 June 1948, the Soviet Union unilaterally declared that all of Berlin was a part of the Soviet zone. Four days later, it cut all land and water access to the city.

The United States Government wishes to call to the attention of the Soviet Government the extremely serious international situation which has been brought about by the actions of the Soviet Government in imposing restrictive measures on transport which amount now to a blockade against the sectors of Berlin occupied by the United States, United Kingdom and France. The United States Government regards these measures of blockade as a clear violation of existing agreements concerning the administration of the four occupying powers.

The rights of the United States as a joint occupying power in Berlin derive from the total defeat and unconditional surrender of Germany. The international agreements undertaken in connection therewith by the Governments of the United States, United Kingdom, France and the Soviet Union defined the zones in Germany and the sectors in Berlin which are occupied by these powers. They established the quadripartite control of Berlin on a basis of friendly cooperation which the Government of the United States earnestly desires to continue to pursue.

These agreements implied the right of free access to Berlin. This right has long been confirmed by usage. It was directly specified in a message sent by President Truman to Premier Stalin on June 14, 1945, which agreed to the withdrawal of United States forces to the zonal boundaries provided satisfactory arrangements could be entered into between the military commanders which would give access by rail, road and air to United States forces in Berlin. Premier Stalin replied on June 16 suggesting a change in date but no other alteration in the plan proposed by the President. Premier Stalin then gave assurances that all necessary measures would be taken in accordance with the plan. Correspondence in a similar sense took place between Premier Stalin and Mr. Churchill. In accordance with this understanding, the United States, whose armies had penetrated deep into Saxony and Thuringia, parts of the Soviet zone, withdrew its forces to its own area of occupation in Germany and took up its position in its own sector of Berlin. Thereupon the agreements in regard to the occupation of Germany and Berlin went into effect. The United States would not have so withdrawn its troops from a large area now occupied by the Soviet Union had there been any doubt whatsoever about the observance of its right and free access to its sector of Berlin. The right of the United States to its position in Berlin thus stems from precisely the same source as the right of the Soviet Union. It is impossible to assert the latter and deny the former.

It clearly results from these undertakings that Berlin is not a part of the Soviet zone, but is an international zone of occupation. Commitments entered into in good faith by the zone commanders and subsequently confirmed by the Allied Control Authority, as well as practices sanctioned by usage, guarantee the United States together with other powers, free access to Berlin for the purpose of fulfilling its responsibilities as an occupying power. The facts are plain. Their meaning is clear. Any other interpretation would offend all the rules of comity and reason.

In order that there should be no misunderstanding whatsoever on this point, the United States Government categorically asserts that it is in occupation of its sector in Berlin with free access thereto as a matter of established right deriving from the defeat and surrender of Germany and confirmed by formal agreements among the principal Allies. It further declares that it will not be induced by threats, pressures or other actions to abandon these rights. It is hoped that the Soviet Government entertains no doubts whatsoever on this point. . . .

The responsibility which this Government bears for the physical well-being and the safety of the German population in its sector of Berlin is outstandingly humanitarian in character. This population includes hundreds of thousands of women and children whose health and safety are dependent on the continued use of adequate facilities for moving food, medical supplies and other items indispensable to the maintenance of human life in the western sectors of Berlin. The most elemental of these human rights which both our Governments are solemnly pledged to protect are thus placed in jeopardy by these restrictions. It is intolerable that any one of the occupying authorities should attempt to impose a blockade upon the people of Berlin.

The United States Government is therefore obliged to insist that in accordance with existing agreements the arrangements for the movement of freight and passenger traffic between the western zones and Berlin be fully restored. There can be no question of delay in the restoration of these essential services since the needs of the civilian population in the Berlin area are imperative. . . .

Source: U.S. Department of State, *Department of State Bulletin*, vol. 19, no. 472 (18 July 1948): 85–86.

108. THE NORTH ATLANTIC TREATY
4 April 1949

*In April 1949, the United States agreed to join a collective security or-
ganization designed to protect Western Europe from Soviet attack. Based
upon the principles of the Treaty of Rio de Janeiro (1947), the North
Atlantic Treaty served as a model for similar agreements in Southeast
Asia and Central Asia.*

The Parties to this Treaty reaffirm their faith in the purposes and principles
of the Charter of the United Nations and their desire to live in peace with all
peoples and all governments.

They are determined to safeguard the freedom, common heritage and civilization of their peoples, founded on the principles of democracy, individual liberty and the rule of law.

They seek to promote stability and well-being in the North Atlantic area.

They are resolved to unite their efforts for collective defense and for the
preservation of peace and security.

They therefore agree to this North Atlantic Treaty:

ART. 1. The Parties undertake, as set forth in the Charter of the United
Nations, to settle any international disputes in which they may be involved by
peaceful means in such a manner that international peace and security, and
justice, are not endangered, and to refrain in their international relations from
the threat or use of force in any manner inconsistent with the purposes of the
United Nations.

ART. 2. The Parties will contribute toward the further development of peaceful and friendly international relations by strengthening their free institutions,
by bringing about a better understanding of the principles upon which these
institutions are founded, and by promoting conditions of stability and well-being.
They will seek to eliminate conflict in their international economic policies and
will encourage economic collaboration between any or all of them.

ART. 3. In order more effectively to achieve the objectives of this Treaty,
the Parties, separately and jointly, by means of continuous and effective self-
help and mutual aid, will maintain and develop their individual and collective
capacity to resist armed attack.

ART. 4. The Parties will consult together whenever, in the opinion of any of
them, the territorial integrity, political independence or security of any of the
Parties is threatened.

ART. 5. The Parties agree that an armed attack against one or more of them in Europe or North America shall be considered an attack against them all; and consequently they agree that, if such an armed attack occurs, each of them, in exercise of the right of individual or collective self-defense recognized by Article 51 of the Charter of the United Nations, will assist the Party or Parties so attacked by taking forthwith, individually and in concert with the other Parties, such action as it deems necessary, including the use of armed force, to restore and maintain the security of the North Atlantic area.

Any such armed attack and all measures taken as a result thereof shall immediately be reported to the Security Council. Such measures shall be terminated when the Security Council has taken the measures necessary to restore and maintain international peace and security.

ART. 6. For the purpose of Article 5 an armed attack on one or more of the Parties is deemed to include an armed attack on the territory of any of the Parties in Europe or North America, on the Algerian departments of France, on the occupation forces of any Party in Europe, on the islands under the jurisdiction of any Party in the North Atlantic area north of the Tropic of Cancer or on the vessels or aircraft in this area of any of the Parties.

ART. 7. This Treaty does not affect, and shall not be interpreted as affecting, in any way the rights and obligations under the Charter of the Parties which are members of the United Nations, or the primary responsibility of the Security Council for the maintenance of international peace and security.

ART. 8. Each Party declares that none of the international engagements now in force between it and any other of the Parties or any third state is in conflict with the provisions of this Treaty, and undertakes not to enter into any international engagement in conflict with this Treaty.

ART. 9. The Parties hereby establish a council, on which each of them shall be represented, to consider matters concerning the implementation of this Treaty. The council shall be so organized as to be able to meet promptly at any time. The council shall set up such subsidiary bodies as may be necessary; in particular it shall establish immediately a defense committee which shall recommend measures for the implementation of Articles 3 and 5.

ART. 10. The Parties may, by unanimous agreement, invite any other European state in a position to further the principles of this Treaty and to contribute to the security of the North Atlantic area to accede to this Treaty. Any state so invited may become a party to the Treaty by depositing its instrument of accession with the Government of the United States of America. The Government of the United States of America will inform each of the Parties of the deposit of each such instrument of accession.

ART. 11. . . . . The Treaty shall enter into force between the states which have ratified it as soon as the ratifications of the majority of the signatories, including the ratifications of Belgium, Canada, France, Luxembourg, the Netherlands, the United Kingdom and the United States, have been deposited and shall come into effect with respect to other states on the date of the deposit of their ratifications.

ART. 12. After the Treaty has been in force for ten years, or at any time thereafter, the Parties shall, if any of them so requests, consult together for the purpose of reviewing the Treaty, having regard for the factors then affecting peace and security in the North Atlantic area, including the development of universal as well as regional arrangements under the Charter of the United Nations for the maintenance of international peace and security.

ART. 13. After the Treaty has been in force for twenty years, any Party may cease to be a party one year after its notice of denunciation has been given to the Government of the United States of America, which will inform the Governments of the other Parties of the deposit of each notice of denunciation.

Source: Henry Steele Commager, *Documents of American History*, vol. 2 (Englewood Cliffs, NJ: Prentice Hall, 1973), 548–50.

109. THE RECOGNITION OF ISRAEL
1948–49

On 14 May 1948, the Jewish community of Palestine declared the independent state of Israel. American recognition soon followed, providing the soon beleaguered nation with a powerful patron in the United Nations.

1. Statement by President Truman
May 14, 1948

This Government has been informed that a Jewish state has been proclaimed in Palestine, and recognition has been requested by the provisional government thereof.

The United States recognizes the provisional government as the *de facto* authority of the new State of Israel.

2. Statement by President Truman
January 31, 1949

On October 24, 1948, the President stated that when a permanent government was elected in Israel, it would promptly be given *de jure* recognition. Elections for such a government were held on January 25th. The votes have now been counted, and this Government has now been officially informed of the results. The United States Government is therefore pleased to extend *de jure* recognition to the Government of Israel as of this date.

Source: Public Papers of the Presidents of the United States, Harry S. Truman, 1949 (Washington, DC: Government Printing Office, 1964), 121.

110.   THE CHINA WHITE PAPER
1949

*During the summer of 1949, Secretary of State Dean Acheson offered a
postmortem on the collapse of China's Nationalist government. Although
Acheson placed most of the responsibility for the Communist victory in
China squarely on the Nationalist's shoulders, he, George C. Marshall,
and the Truman administration garnered a barrage of criticism from the
Republican Party.*

LETTER OF TRANSMITTAL

Department of State
Washington, July 30, 1949

THE PRESIDENT: In accordance with your wish, I have had compiled a record
of our relations with China, special emphasis being placed on the last five years.
This record is being published and will therefore be available to the Congress
and to the people of the United States. . . .

The interest of the people and the Government of the United States in China
goes far back into our history. Despite the distance and broad differences in
background which separate China and the United States, our friendship for that
country has always been intensified by the religious, philanthropic and cultural
ties which have united the two peoples, and has been attested by many acts of
good will over a period of many years, including the use of the Boxer indemnity
for the education of Chinese students, the abolition of extraterritoriality during
the Second World War, and our extensive aid to China during and since the
close of the war. The record shows that the United States has consistently maintained and still maintains those fundamental principles of our foreign policy
toward China which include the doctrine of the Open Door, respect for the
administrative and territorial integrity of China, and opposition to any foreign
domination of China. . . .

From the wartime cooperation with the Soviet Union and from the costly
campaigns against the Japanese came the Yalta Agreement. The American Government and people awaited with intense anxiety the assault on the main islands
of Japan which it was feared would cost up to a million American casualties
before Japan was conquered. The atomic bomb was not then a reality and it
seemed impossible that the war in the Far East could be ended without this
assault. It thus became a primary concern of the American Government to see
to it that the Soviet Union enter the war against Japan at the earliest possible
date in order that the Japanese Army in Manchuria might not be returned to the

homeland at the critical moment. It was considered vital not only that the Soviet Union enter the war but that she do so before our invasion of Japan, which already had been set for the autumn of 1945.

At Yalta Marshal Stalin not only agreed to attack Japan within two or three months after V-E Day but limited his "price" with reference to Manchuria substantially to the position which Russia had occupied there prior to 1904. We for our part, in order to obtain this commitment and thus to bring the war to a close with a consequent saving of American, Chinese and other Allied lives, were prepared to and did pay the requisite price. Two facts must not, however, be lost sight of in this connection. First, the Soviet Union when she finally did enter the war against Japan, could in any case have seized all the territories in question and considerably more regardless of what our attitude might have been. Second, the Soviets on their side in the Sino-Soviet Treaty arising from the Yalta Agreement, agreed to give the National Government of China moral and material support and moreover formalized their assurances of noninterference in China's internal affairs. Although the unexpectedly early collapse of Japanese resistance later made some of the provisions of the Yalta Agreement seem unnecessary, in the light of the predicted course of the war at that time they were considered to be not only justified but clearly advantageous. Although dictated by military necessity, the Agreement and the subsequent Sino-Soviet Treaty in fact imposed limitations on the action which Russia would, in any case, have been in a position to take. . . .

When peace came the United States was confronted with three possible alternatives in China: 1. it could have pulled out lock, stock and barrel; 2. it could have intervened militarily on a major scale to assist the Nationalists to destroy the Communists; 3. it could, while assisting the Nationalists to assert their authority over as much of China as possible, endeavor to avoid a civil war by working for a compromise between the two sides.

The first alternative would, and I believe American public opinion at the time so felt, have represented an abandonment of our international responsibilities and of our traditional policy of friendship for China before we had made a determined effort to be of assistance. The second alternative policy, while it may look attractive theoretically and in retrospect, was wholly impracticable. The Nationalists had been unable to destroy the Communists during the 10 years before the war. Now after the war the Nationalists were, as indicated above, weakened, demoralized, and unpopular. They had quickly dissipated their popular support and prestige in the areas liberated from the Japanese by the conduct of their civil and military officials. The Communists on the other hand were much stronger than they had ever been and were in control of most of North China. Because of the ineffectiveness of the Nationalist forces which was later to be tragically demonstrated, the Communists probably could have been dislodged only by American arms. It is obvious that the American people would not have sanctioned such a colossal commitment of our armies in 1945 or later. We therefore came to the third alternative policy whereunder we faced the facts of the situation and attempted to assist in working out a *modus vivendi* which would avert civil war but nevertheless preserve and even increase the influence of the National Government. . . .

The reasons for the failures of the Chinese National Government appear in some detail in the attached record. They do not stem from any inadequacy of American aid. Our military observers on the spot have reported that the Nationalist armies did not lose a single battle during the crucial year of 1948 through lack of arms or ammunition. The fact was that the decay which our observers had detected in Chungking early in the war had fatally sapped the powers of resistance of the Kuomintang. Its leaders had proved incapable of meeting the crisis confronting them, its troops had lost the will to fight, and its Government had lost popular support. The Communists, on the other hand, through a ruthless discipline and fanatical zeal, attempted to sell themselves as guardians and liberators of the people. The Nationalist armies did not have to be defeated; they disintegrated. History has proved again and again that a regime without faith in itself and an army without morale cannot survive the test of battle. . . .

The historic policy of the United States of friendship and aid toward the people of China was, however, maintained in both peace and war. Since V-J Day, the United States Government has authorized aid to Nationalist China in the form of grants and credits totaling approximately 2 billion dollars, an amount equivalent in value to more than 50 percent of the monetary expenditures of the Chinese Government and of proportionately greater magnitude in relation to the budget of that Government than the United States has provided to any nation of Western Europe since the end of the war. In addition to these grants and credits, the United States Government has sold the Chinese Government large quantities of military and civilian war surplus property with a total procurement cost of over 1 billion dollars, for which the agreed realization to the United States was 232 million dollars. A large proportion of the military supplies furnished the Chinese armies by the United States since V-J Day has, however, fallen into the hands of the Chinese Communists through the military ineptitude of the Nationalist leaders, their defections and surrenders, and the absence among their forces of the will to fight.

It has been urged that relatively small amounts of additional aid—military and economic—to the National Government would have enabled it to destroy communism in China. The most trustworthy military, economic, and political information available to our Government does not bear out this view.

A realistic appraisal of conditions in China past and present, leads to the conclusion that the only alternative open to the United States was full-scale intervention on behalf of a Government which had lost the confidence of its own troops and its own people. Such intervention would have required the expenditure of even greater sums than have been fruitlessly spent thus far, the command of Nationalist armies by American officers, and the probable participation of American armed forces—land, sea, and air—in the resulting war.

Documents of American Diplomacy

Intervention of such a scope and magnitude would have been resented by the mass of the Chinese people, would have diametrically reversed our historic policy, and would have been condemned by the American people.

It must be admitted frankly that the American policy of assisting the Chinese people in resisting domination by any foreign power or powers is now confronted with the gravest difficulties. The heart of China is in Communist hands. The Communist leaders have foresworn their Chinese heritage and have publicly announced their subservience to a foreign power, Russia, which during the last 50 years, under czars and Communists alike, has been most assiduous in its efforts to extend its control in the Far East. In the recent past attempts at foreign domination have appeared quite clearly to the Chinese people as external aggression and as such have been bitterly and in the long run successfully resisted. Our aid and encouragement have helped them to resist. In this case, however, the foreign domination has been masked behind the facade of a vast crusading movement which apparently has seemed to many Chinese to be wholly indigenous and national. Under these circumstances, our aid has been unavailing.

The unfortunate but inescapable fact is that the ominous result of the civil war in China was beyond the control of the government of the United States. Nothing that this country did or could have done within the reasonable limits of its capabilities could have changed that result; nothing that was left undone by this country has contributed to it. It was the product of internal Chinese forces, forces which this country tried to influence but could not. A decision was arrived at within China, if only a decision by default.

And now it is abundantly clear that we must face the situation as it exists in fact. We will not help the Chinese or ourselves by basing our policy on wishful thinking. We continue to believe that, however tragic may be the immediate future of China and however ruthlessly a major portion of this great people may be exploited by a party in the interest of a foreign imperialism, ultimately the profound civilization and the democratic individualism of China will reassert themselves and she will throw off the foreign yoke. I consider that we should encourage all developments in China which now and in the future work toward this end.

In the immediate future, however, the implementation of our historic policy of friendship for China must be profoundly affected by current developments. It will necessarily be influenced by the degree to which the Chinese people come to recognize that the Communist regime serves not their interests but those of Soviet Russia and the manner in which, having become aware of the facts, they react to this foreign domination. One point, however, is clear. Should the Communist regime lend itself to the aims of Soviet Russian imperialism and attempt to engage in aggression against China's neighbors, we and the other members of the United Nations would be confronted by a situation violative of the principles of the United Nations Charter and threatening international peace and security.

Meanwhile our policy will continue to be based upon our own respect for the

Charter, our friendship for China, and our traditional support for the Open Door and for China's independence and administrative and territorial integrity.

Respectfully yours,

Dean Acheson

Source: The China White Paper (Stanford, CA: Stanford University Press, 1967), iii–xvii.

---

111.   THE POINT FOUR PROGRAM
24 June 1949

As the Marshall Plan began to take hold in Western Europe, Truman contemplated additional American assistance in other parts of the world. In June 1949, he requested funding for technical assistance to the underdeveloped world. The Point Four Program became the first stage in future aid programs in Africa, Asia, and Latin America.

To the Congress of the United States:

In order to enable the United States, in cooperation with other countries, to assist the peoples of economically underdeveloped areas to raise their standards of living, I recommend the enactment of legislation to authorize an expanded program of technical assistance for such areas, and an experimental program for encouraging the outflow of private investment beneficial to their economic development. These measures are the essential first steps in an undertaking which will call upon private enterprise and voluntary organizations in the United States, as well as the government, to take part in a constantly growing effort to improve economic conditions in the less developed regions of the world.

The grinding poverty and the lack of economic opportunity for many millions of people in the economically underdeveloped parts of Africa, the Near and Far East, and certain regions of Central and South America, constitute one of the greatest challenges of the world today. In spite of their age-old economic and social handicaps, the peoples in these areas have, in recent decades, been stirred and awakened. The spread of industrial civilization, the growing understanding of modern concepts of government, and the impact of two World Wars have changed their lives and their outlook. They are eager to play a greater part in the community of nations.

All these areas have a common problem. They must create a firm economic base for the democratic aspirations of their citizens. Without such an economic base, they will be unable to meet the expectations which the modern world has aroused in their peoples. If they are frustrated and disappointed, they may turn to false doctrines which hold that the way of progress lies through tyranny. . . .

For these various reasons, assistance in the development of the economically underdeveloped areas has become one of the major elements of our foreign policy. In my inaugural address, I outlined a program to help the peoples of these areas to attain greater production as a way to prosperity and peace.

The major effort in such a program must be local in character; it must be made by the people of the underdeveloped areas themselves. It is essential, however, to the success of their effort that there be help from abroad. In such cases, the peoples of these areas will be unable to begin their part of this great enterprise without initial aid from other countries.

The aid that is needed falls roughly into two categories. The first is the technical, scientific, and managerial knowledge necessary to economic development. This category includes not only medical and educational knowledge, and assistance and advice in such basic fields as sanitation, communications, road building, and governmental services, but also, and perhaps most important, assistance in the survey of resources and in planning for long-range economic development.

The second category is production goods—machinery and equipment—and financial assistance in the creation of productive enterprises. The underdeveloped areas need capital for port and harbor development, roads and communications, irrigation and drainage projects, as well as for public utilities and the whole range of extractive, processing, and manufacturing industries. Much of the capital required can be provided by these areas themselves, in spite of their low standards of living. But much must come from abroad.

The two categories of aid are closely related. Technical assistance is necessary to lay the ground-work for productive investment. Investment, in turn, brings with it technical assistance. In general, however, technical surveys of resources and of the possibilities of economic development must precede substantial capital investment. Furthermore, in many of the areas concerned, technical assistance in improving sanitation, communications, or education is required to create conditions in which capital investment can be fruitful. . . .

It has already been shown that experts in these fields can bring about tremendous improvements. For example, the health of the people of many foreign communities has been greatly improved by the work of United States sanitary engineers in setting up modern water supply systems. The food supply of many areas has been increased as the result of the advice of United States agricultural experts in the control of animal diseases and the improvement of crops. These are only examples of the wide range of benefits resulting from the careful application of modern techniques to local problems. The benefits which a comprehensive program of expert assistance will make possible can only be revealed by studies and surveys undertaken as a part of the program itself.

To inaugurate the program, I recommend a first year appropriation of not to exceed 45 million dollars. This includes 10 million dollars already requested in the 1950 Budget for activities of this character. The sum recommended will cover both our participation in the programs of the international agencies and the assistance to be provided directly by the United States.

In every case, whether the operation is conducted through the United Nations, the other international agencies, or directly by the United States, the country receiving the benefit of the aid will be required to bear a substantial portion of the expense.

Source: Public Papers of the Presidents of the United States, Harry S. Truman, 1949 (Washington, DC: Government Printing Office, 1964), 329–33.

112. ANNOUNCEMENT OF THE HYDROGEN BOMB PROGRAM
31 January 1950

In 1945, most American scientists had predicted that the Soviet Union would take at least ten years to develop an atomic bomb. Thus, the announcement of a successful Soviet atomic test in 1949 came as a surprise to the United States and prompted officials to pursue the next stage in nuclear weaponry.

It is part of my responsibility as Commander-in-Chief of the armed forces to see to it that our country is able to defend itself against any possible aggressor. Accordingly, I have directed the Atomic Energy Commission to continue its work on all forms of atomic weapons, including the so-called hydrogen or super-bomb. Like all other work in the field of atomic weapons, it is being and will be carried forward on a basis consistent with the over-all objectives of our program for peace and security.

This we shall continue to do until a satisfactory plan for international control of atomic energy is achieved. We shall also continue to examine all those factors that affect our program for peace and this country's security.

Source: Public Papers of the Presidents of the United States, Harry S. Truman, 1950 (Washington, DC: Government Printing Office, 1965), 138.

113. NSC-68
31 January 1950

At the start of 1950, President Harry Truman ordered a fundamental review of American national security policy. The resulting study recommended an increased American commitment to containing Communism at all points throughout the world and endorsed larger defense budgets to accomplish this task. The outbreak of the Korean War would usher in the policy recommendations made by the document.

ANALYSIS

I. BACKGROUND OF THE PRESENT CRISIS

Within the past thirty-five years the world has experienced two global wars of tremendous violence. It has witnessed two revolutions—the Russian and the Chinese—of extreme scope and intensity. It has also seen the collapse of five empires—the Ottoman, the Austro-Hungarian, German, Italian and Japanese— and the drastic decline of two major imperial systems, the British and the French. During the span of one generation, the international distribution of power has been fundamentally altered. For several centuries it had proved impossible for any one nation to gain such preponderant strength that a coalition of other nations could not in time face it with greater strength. The international scene was marked by recurring periods of violence and war, but a system of sovereign and independent states was maintained, over which no state was able to achieve hegemony.

Two complex sets of factors have now basically altered this historical distribution of power. First, the defeat of Germany and Japan and the decline of the British and French Empires have interacted with the development of the United States and the Soviet Union in such a way that power has increasingly gravitated to these two centers. Second, the Soviet Union, unlike previous aspirants to hegemony, is animated by a new fanatic faith, antithetical to our own, and seeks to impose its absolute authority over the rest of the world. Conflict has, therefore, become endemic and is waged, on the part of the Soviet Union, by violent or non-violent methods in accordance with the dictates of expediency. With the development of increasingly terrifying weapons of mass destruction, every individual faces the ever-present possibility of annihilation should the conflict enter the phase of total war.

On the one hand, the people of the world yearn for relief from the anxiety arising from the risk of atomic war. On the other hand, any substantial further extension of the area under the domination of the Kremlin would raise the possibility that no coalition adequate to confront the Kremlin with greater strength could be assembled. It is in this context that this Republic and its citizens in the ascendancy of their strength stand in their deepest peril. The issues that face us are momentous, involving the fulfillment or destruction not only of this Republic but of civilization itself. They are issues which will not await our deliberations. With conscience and resolution this Government and the people it represents must now take new and fateful decisions.

II. FUNDAMENTAL PURPOSE OF THE UNITED STATES

The fundamental purpose of the United States is laid down in the Preamble to the Constitution: ". . . to form a more perfect Union, establish Justice, insure domestic Tranquility, provide for the common defence, promote the general Welfare, and secure the Blessings of Liberty to ourselves and our Posterity." In essence, the fundamental purpose is to assure the integrity and vitality of our free society, which is founded upon the dignity and worth of the individual.

Three realities emerge as a consequence of this purpose: Our determination to maintain the essential elements of individual freedom, as set forth in the Constitution and Bill of Rights; our determination to create conditions under which our free and democratic system can live and prosper; and our determination to fight if necessary to defend our way of life, for which as in the Declaration of Independence, "with a firm reliance on the protection of Divine Providence, we mutually pledge to each other our lives, our Fortunes and our sacred Honor."

III. FUNDAMENTAL DESIGN OF THE KREMLIN

The fundamental design of those who control the Soviet Union and the international communist movement is to retain and solidify their absolute power, first in the Soviet Union and second in the areas now under their control. In the minds of the Soviet leaders, however, achievement of this design requires the dynamic extension of their authority and the ultimate elimination of any effective opposition to their authority.

The design, therefore, calls for the complete subversion or forcible destruction of the machinery of government and structure of society in the countries of the non-Soviet world and their replacement by an apparatus and structure subservient to and controlled from the Kremlin. To that end Soviet efforts are now directed toward the domination of the Eurasian land mass. The United States, as the principal center of power in the non-Soviet world and the bulwark of opposition to Soviet expansion, is the principal enemy whose integrity and vitality must be subverted or destroyed by one means or another if the Kremlin is to achieve its fundamental design. . . .

V.   SOVIET INTENTIONS AND CAPABILITIES

A. Political and Psychological

The Kremlin's design for world domination begins at home. The first concern of a despotic oligarchy is that the local base of its power and authority be secure. The massive fact of the iron curtain isolating the Soviet peoples from the outside world, the repeated political purges within the U.S.S.R. and the institutionalized crimes of the MVD are evidence that the Kremlin does not feel secure at home and that "the entire coercive force of the socialist state" is more than ever one of seeking to impose its absolute authority over "the economy, manner of life, and consciousness of people" (Vyshinski, "The Law of the Soviet State", [sic] p. 74). Similar evidence in the satellite states of Eastern Europe leads to the conclusion that this same policy, in less advanced phases, is being applied to the Kremlin's colonial areas.

Being a totalitarian dictatorship, the Kremlin's objectives in these policies, is the total subjective submission of the peoples now under its control. The concentration camp is the prototype of the society, which these policies are designed to achieve, a society in which the personality of the individual is so broken and perverted that he participates affirmatively in his own degradation.

The Kremlin's policy toward areas not under its control is the elimination of resistance to its will and the extension of its influence, and control. It is driven to follow this policy because it cannot, for the reasons set forth in Chapter IV, tolerate the existence of free societies; to the Kremlin the most mild and inoffensive free society is an affront, a challenge and a subversive influence. Given the nature of the Kremlin, and the evidence at hand, it seems clear that the ends toward which this policy is directed are the same as those where its control has already been established.

The means employed by the Kremlin in pursuit of this policy are limited only by considerations of expediency. Doctrine is not a limiting factor; rather it dictates the employment of violence, subversion and deceit, and rejects moral considerations. In any event, the Kremlin's conviction of its own infallibility has made its devotion to theory so subjective that past or present pronouncements as to doctrine offer no reliable guide to future actions. The only apparent restraints on resort to war are, therefore, calculations of practicality.

With particular reference to the United States, the Kremlin's strategic and tactical policy is affected by its estimate that we are not only the greatest immediate obstacle which stands between it and world domination, we are also the only power which could release forces in the free and Soviet worlds which could destroy it. The Kremlin's policy toward us is consequently animated by a peculiarly virulent blend of hatred and fear. Its strategy has been one of attempting to undermine the complex of forces, in this country and in the rest of the free world, on which our power is based. In this it has both adhered to doctrine and followed the sound principle of seeking maximum results with minimum risks and commitments. The present application of this strategy is a new form of expression for traditional Russian caution. However, there is no justification in Soviet theory or practice for predicting that, should the Kremlin become convinced that it could cause our downfall by one conclusive blow, it would not seek that solution. . . .

B. Economic

The Kremlin has no economic intentions unrelated to its overall policies. Economics in the Soviet world is not an end in itself. The Kremlin's policy, in so far as it has to do with economics, is to utilize economic processes to contribute to the overall strength, particularly the war-making capacity of the Soviet system. The material welfare of the totalitariat is severely subordinated to the interest of the system. . . .

C. Military

The Soviet Union is developing the military capacity to support its design for world domination. The Soviet Union actually possesses armed forces far in excess of those necessary to defend its national territory. These armed forces are probably not yet considered by the Soviet Union to be sufficient to initiate a war which would involve the United States. This excessive strength, coupled now with an atomic capability, provides the Soviet Union with great coercive power for use in time of peace in furtherance of its objectives and serves as a deterrent to the victims of its aggression from taking any action in opposition to its tactics which would risk war.

Should a major war occur in 1950 the Soviet Union and its satellites are considered by the Joint Chiefs of Staff to be in a sufficiently advanced state of preparation immediately to undertake and carry out the following campaigns.

a. To overrun Western Europe, with the possible exception of the Iberian and Scandinavian Peninsulas; to drive toward the oil-bearing areas of the Near and Middle East; and to consolidate Communist gains in the Far East;

b. To launch air attacks against the British Isles and air and sea attacks against the lines of communications of the Western Powers in the Atlantic and Pacific;

c. To attack selected targets with atomic weapons, now including the likelihood of such attacks against targets in Alaska, Canada, and the United States. Alternatively, this capability, coupled with other actions open to the Soviet Union, might deny the United Kingdom as an effective base of operations for allied forces. It also should be possible for the Soviet Union to prevent any allied "Normandy" type amphibious operations intended to force a reentry into the continent of Europe.

After the Soviet Union completed its initial campaigns and consolidated its positions in the Western European area, it could simultaneously conduct:

a. Full-scale air and limited sea operations against the British Isles;

b. Invasions of the Iberian and Scandinavian Peninsulas,

c. Further operations in the Near and Middle East, continued air operations against the North American continent, and air and sea operations against Atlantic and Pacific lines of communication; and

d. Diversionary attacks in other areas.

During the course of the offensive operations listed in the second and third paragraphs above, the Soviet Union will have an air defense capability with respect to the vital areas of its own and its satellites' territories which can oppose but cannot prevent allied air operations against these areas.

It is not known whether the Soviet Union possesses war reserves and arsenal capabilities sufficient to supply its satellite armies or even its own forces throughout a long war. It might not be in the interest of the Soviet Union to equip fully its satellite armies, since the possibility of defections would exist.

It is not possible at this time to assess accurately the finite disadvantages to the Soviet Union which may accrue through the implementation of the Economic Cooperation Act of 1948, as amended, and the Mutual Defense Assistance Act of 1949. It should be expected that, as this implementation progresses, the internal security situation of the recipient nations should improve concurrently. In addition, a strong United States military position, plus increases in the armaments of the nations of Western Europe, should strengthen the determination of the recipient nations to counter Soviet moves and in event of war could be considered as likely to delay operations and increase the time required for the Soviet Union to overrun Western Europe. In all probability, although United States backing will stiffen their determination, the armaments increase under the present aid programs will not be of any major consequence prior to 1952. Unless the military strength of the Western European nations is increased on a much larger scale than under current programs and at an accelerated rate, it is more than likely that those nations will not be able to oppose even by 1960 the Soviet armed forces in war with any degree of effectiveness. Considering the Soviet Union military capability, the long-range allied military objective in Western Europe must envisage an increased military strength in that area sufficient possibly to deter the Soviet Union from a major war or, in any event, to delay materially the overrunning of Western Europe and, if feasible, to hold a bridgehead on the continent against Soviet Union offensives. . . .

VI. U.S. INTENTIONS AND CAPABILITIES—ACTUAL AND POTENTIAL

A. Political and Psychological

Our overall policy at the present time may be described as one designed to foster a world environment in which the American system can survive and flourish. It therefore rejects the concept of isolation and affirms the necessity of our positive participation in the world community.

This broad intention embraces two subsidiary policies. One is a policy which we would probably pursue even if there were no Soviet threat. It is a policy of attempting to develop a healthy international community. The other is the policy of "containing" the Soviet system. These two policies are closely interrelated and interact on one another. Nevertheless, the distinction between them is basically valid and contributes to a clearer understanding of what we are trying to do.

The policy of striving to develop a healthy international community is the long-term constructive effort which we are engaged in. It was this policy which gave rise to our vigorous sponsorship of the United Nations. It is of course the principal reason for our long continuing endeavors to create and now develop the Inter-American system. It, as much as containment, underlay our efforts to rehabilitate Western Europe. Most of our international economic activities can likewise be explained in terms of this policy.

In a world of polarized power, the policies designed to develop a healthy international community are more than ever necessary to our own strength.

As for the policy of "containment," it is one which seeks by all means short of war to 1. block further expansion of Soviet power, 2. expose the falsities of Soviet pretensions, 3. induce a retraction of the Kremlin's control and influence and 4. in general, so foster the seeds of destruction within the Soviet system that the Kremlin is brought at least to the point of modifying its behavior to conform to generally accepted international standards.

It was and continues to be cardinal in this policy that we possess superior overall power in ourselves or in dependable combination with other like-minded nations. One of the most important ingredients of power is military strength. In the concept of "containment," the maintenance of a strong military posture is deemed to be essential for two reasons: 1. as an ultimate guarantee of our national security and 2. as an indispensable backdrop to the conduct of the policy of "containment." Without superior aggregate military strength, in being and readily mobilizable, a policy of "containment"—which is in effect a policy of calculated and gradual coercion—is no more than a policy of bluff.

At the same time, it is essential to the successful conduct of a policy of "containment" that we always leave open the possibility of negotiation with the U.S.S.R A diplomatic freeze—and we are in one now—tends to defeat the very purposes of "containment" because it raises tensions at the same time that it makes Soviet retractions and adjustments in the direction of moderated behavior more difficult. It also tends to inhibit our initiative and deprives us of opportunities for maintaining a moral ascendancy in our struggle with the Soviet system.

In "containment" it is desirable to exert pressure in a fashion which will avoid so far as possible directly challenging Soviet prestige, to keep open the possibility for the U.S.S.R to retreat before pressure with a minimum loss of face and to secure political advantage from the failure of the Kremlin to yield or take advantage of the openings we leave it.

We have failed to implement adequately these two fundamental aspects of "containment." In the face of obviously mounting Soviet military strength ours has declined relatively. Partly as a byproduct of this, but also for other reasons, we now find ourselves at a diplomatic impasse with the Soviet Union, with the Kremlin growing bolder, with both of us holding on grimly to what we have and with ourselves facing difficult decisions. . . .

C. Military

The United States now possesses the greatest military potential of any single nation in the world. The military weaknesses of the United States vis-a-vis the Soviet Union, however, include its numerical inferiority in forces in being and in total manpower. Coupled with the inferiority of forces in being, the United States also lacks tenable positions from which to employ its forces in event of war and munitions power in being and readily available.

It is true that the United States armed forces are now stronger than ever before in other times of apparent peace; it is also true that there exists a sharp disparity between our actual military strength and our commitments. The relationship of our strength to our present commitments, however, is not alone the governing factor. The world situation, as well as commitments, should govern; hence, our military strength more properly should be related to the world situation confronting us. When our military strength is related to the world situation and balanced against the likely exigencies of such a situation, it is clear that our military strength is becoming dangerously inadequate.

If war should begin in 1950, the United States and its allies will have the military capability of conducting defensive operations to provide a reasonable measure of protection to the Western Hemisphere, bases in the Western Pacific, and essential military lines of communication; and an inadequate measure of protection to vital military bases in the United Kingdom and in the Near and Middle East. We will have the capability of conducting powerful offensive air operations against vital elements of the Soviet war-making capacity.

The scale of the operations listed in the preceding paragraph is limited by the effective forces and material in being of the United States and its allies vis-a-vis the Soviet Union. Consistent with the aggressive threat facing us and in consonance with overall strategic plans, the United States must provide to its allies on a continuing basis as large amounts of military assistance as possible without serious detriment to the United States operational requirements.

If the potential military capabilities of the United States and its allies were rapidly and effectively developed, sufficient forces could be produced probably to deter war, or if the Soviet Union chooses war, to withstand the initial Soviet attacks, to stabilize supporting attacks, and to retaliate in turn with even greater impact on the Soviet capabilities. From the military point of view alone, however, this would require not only the generation of the necessary military forces but also the development and stockpiling of improved weapons of all types.

Under existing peacetime conditions, a period of from two to three years is required to produce a material increase in military power. Such increased power could be provided in a somewhat shorter period in a declared period of emergency or in wartime through a full-out national effort. . . .

IX. POSSIBLE COURSES OF ACTION

Introduction. Four possible courses of action by the United States in the present situation can be distinguished. They are:

a. Continuation of current policies, with current and currently projected programs for carrying out these policies;

b. Isolation;

c. War; and

d. A more rapid building up of the political, economic, and military strength of the free world than provided under a, with the purpose of reaching, if possible, a tolerable state of order among nations without war and of preparing to defend ourselves in the event that the free world is attacked. . . .

A. The First Course—Continuation of Current Policies, with Current and Currently Projected Programs for Carrying out These Policies

1. *Military aspects.* On the basis of current programs, the United States has a large potential military capability but an actual capability which, though improving, is declining relative to the U.S.S.R., particularly in light of its probable

fission bomb capability and possible thermonuclear bomb capability. The same holds true for the free world as a whole relative to the Soviet world as a whole. If war breaks out in 1950 or in the next few years, the United States and its allies, apart from a powerful atomic blow, will be compelled to conduct delaying actions, while building up their strength for a general offensive. A frank evaluation of the requirements, to defend the United States and its vital interests and to support a vigorous initiative in the cold war, on the one hand, and of present capabilities, on the other, indicates that there is a sharp and growing disparity between them. . . .

B. The Second Course—Isolation

Continuation of present trends, it has been shown above, will lead progressively to the withdrawal of the United States from most of its present commitments in Europe and Asia and to our isolation in the Western Hemisphere and its approaches. This would result not from a conscious decision but from a failure to take the actions necessary to bring our capabilities into line with our commitments and thus to a withdrawal under pressure. This pressure might come from our present Allies, who will tend to seek other "solutions" unless they have confidence in our determination to accelerate our efforts to build a successfully functioning political and economic system in the free world.

There are some who advocate a deliberate decision to isolate ourselves. Superficially, this has some attractiveness as a course of action, for it appears to bring our commitments and capabilities into harmony by reducing the former and by concentrating our present, or perhaps even reduced, military expenditures on the defense of the United States.

This argument overlooks the relativity of capabilities. With the United States in an isolated position, we would have to face the probability that the Soviet Union would quickly dominate most of Eurasia, probably without meeting armed resistance. It would thus acquire a potential far superior to our own, and would promptly proceed to develop this potential with the purpose of eliminating our power, which would, even in isolation, remain as a challenge to it and as an obstacle to the imposition of its kind of order in the world. . . .

C. The Third Course—War

Some Americans favor a deliberate decision to go to war against the Soviet Union in the near future. It goes without saying that the idea of "preventive" war—in the sense of a military attack not provoked by a military attack upon us or our allies—is generally unacceptable to Americans. Its supporters argue that since the Soviet Union is in fact at war with the free world now and that since the failure of the Soviet Union to use all-out military force is explainable on grounds of expediency, we are at war and should conduct ourselves accordingly. Some further argue that the free world is probably unable, except under the crisis of war, to mobilize and direct its resources to the checking and rolling back of the Kremlin's drive for world dominion. This is a powerful argument in the light of history, but the considerations against war are so compelling that the free world must demonstrate that this argument is wrong. The case for war is premised on the assumption that the United States could launch and sustain an attack of sufficient impact to gain a decisive advantage for the free world in a long war and perhaps to win an early decision.

The ability of the United States to launch effective offensive operations is now limited to attack with atomic weapons. A powerful blow could be delivered upon the Soviet Union, but it is estimated that these operations alone would not force or induce the Kremlin to capitulate and that the Kremlin would still be able to use the forces under its control to dominate most or all of Eurasia. This would probably mean a long and difficult struggle during which the free institutions of Western Europe and many freedom-loving people would be destroyed and the regenerative capacity of Western Europe dealt a crippling blow.

Apart from this, however, a surprise attack upon the Soviet Union, despite the provocativeness of recent Soviet behavior, would be repugnant to many Americans. Although the American people would probably rally in support of the war effort, the shock of responsibility for a surprise attack would be morally corrosive. . . .

D. The Remaining Course of Action—a Rapid Build-up of Political, Economic, and Military Strength in the Free World.

A more rapid build-up of political, economic, and military strength and thereby of confidence in the free world than is now contemplated is the only course which is consistent with progress toward achieving our fundamental purpose. The frustration of the Kremlin design requires the free world to develop a successfully functioning political and economic system and a vigorous political offensive against the Soviet Union. These, in turn, require an adequate military shield under which they can develop. It is necessary to have the military power to deter, if possible, Soviet expansion, and to defeat, if necessary aggressive Soviet or Soviet-directed actions of a limited or total character. The potential strength of the free world is great; its ability to develop these military capabilities and its will to resist Soviet expansion will be determined by the wisdom and will with which it undertakes to meet its political and economic problems. . . .

CONCLUSIONS

A continuation of present trends would result in a serious decline in the strength of the free world relative to the Soviet Union and its satellites. This unfavorable trend arises from the inadequacy of current programs and plans rather than from any error in our objectives and aims. These trends lead in the direction of isolation, not by deliberate decision but by lack of the necessary basis for a vigorous initiative in the conflict with the Soviet Union.

Our position as the center of power in the free world places a heavy responsibility upon the United States for leadership. We must organize and enlist the energies and resources of the free world in a positive program for peace which will frustrate the Kremlin design for world domination by creating a situation in the free world to which the Kremlin will be compelled to adjust. Without such a cooperative effort led by the United States, we will have to make gradual withdrawals under pressure until we discover one day that we have sacrificed positions of vital interest.

It is imperative that this trend be reversed by a much more rapid and concerted build-up of the actual strength of both the United States and the other nations of the free world. The analysis shows that this will be costly and will involve significant domestic financial and economic adjustments. . . .

In summary, we must, by means of a rapid and sustained build-up of the political, economic, and military strength of the free world, and by means of an affirmative program intended to wrest the initiative from the Soviet Union, confront it with convincing evidence of the determination and ability of the free world to frustrate the Kremlin to the new situation. Failing that, the unwillingness of the determination and ability of the free world to frustrate the Kremlin design of a world dominated by its will. Such evidence is the only means short of war which eventually may force the Kremlin to abandon its present course of action and to negotiate acceptable agreements on issues of major importance.

The whole success of the proposed program hangs ultimately on recognition by this Government, the American people, and all free peoples, that the cold war is in fact a real war in which the survival of the free world is at stake. Essential prerequisites to success are consultations with Congressional leaders designed to make the program the object of non-partisan legislative support, and a presentation to the public of a full explanation of the facts and implications of the present international situation. The prosecution of the program will require of us all the ingenuity, sacrifice, and unity demanded by the vital importance of the issue and the tenacity to persevere until our national objectives have been attained.

Source: U.S. Department of State, *Papers Relating to the Foreign Relations of the United States, 1950*, vol.1 (Washington, DC: Government Printing Office, 1977), 235–92.

---

114. TRUMAN'S STATEMENT ON THE KOREAN WAR
27 June 1950

On 25 June 1950, North Korea conducted a massive military offensive against South Korea. On 27 June, the United Nations Security Council, with the Soviet Union not present, voted nine to zero to assist South Korea in its defense against the invasion. That same day, President Truman described the actions taken by the United States.

In Korea the Government forces, which were armed to prevent border raids and to preserve internal security, were attacked by invading forces from North Korea. The Security Council of the United Nations called upon the invading troops to cease hostilities and to withdraw to the 38th parallel. This they have not done, but on the contrary have pressed the attack. The Security Council called upon all members of the United Nations to render every assistance to the United Nations in the execution of this resolution. In these circumstances I have ordered United States air and sea forces to give the Korean Government troops cover and support.

The attack upon Korea makes it plain beyond all doubt that Communism has passed beyond the use of subversion to conquer independent nations and will now use armed invasion and war. It has defied the orders of the Security Council of the United Nations issued to preserve international peace and security. In these circumstances the occupation of Formosa by Communist forces would be a direct threat to the security of the Pacific area and to the United States forces performing their lawful and necessary functions in that area. Accordingly I have ordered the Seventh Fleet to prevent any attack on Formosa. As a corollary of this action I am calling upon the Chinese Government on Formosa to cease all air and sea operations against the mainland. The Seventh Fleet will see that this is done. The determination of the future status of Formosa must await the restoration of security in the Pacific, a peace settlement with Japan, or consideration by the United Nations.

I have also directed that United States Forces in the Philippines be strengthened and that military assistance to the Philippine Government be accelerated.

I have similarly directed acceleration in the furnishing of military assistance to the forces of France and the Associated States in Indo-China and the dispatch of a military mission to provide close working relations with those forces.

I know that all members of the United Nations will consider carefully the consequences of this latest aggression in Korea in defiance of the Charter of the United Nations. A return to the rule of force in international affairs would have far reaching effects. The United States will continue to uphold the rule of law.

I have instructed Ambassador Austin, as the representative of the United States to the Security Council, to report these steps to the Council.

Source: Public Papers of the Presidents of the United States, Harry S. Truman, 1950 (Washington, DC: Government Printing Office, 1965), 492.

---

115. THE RECALL OF GENERAL DOUGLAS MacARTHUR
11 April 1951

During the winter of 1950–1951, the war in Korea escalated when Communist China deployed 260,000 soldiers against United Nations forces driving northward toward the Yalu River. In the aftermath, President Truman engaged in a debate with General Douglas MacArthur over the prospect of widening the war by attacking China. When MacArthur refused to accept Truman's order to limit combat operations to Korea, he was relieved of command in April 1951.

I want to talk plainly to you tonight about what we are doing in Korea and about our policy in the Far East.

In the simplest terms, what we are doing in Korea is this: We are trying to prevent a third world war.

I think most people in this country recognized that fact last June. And they warmly supported the decision of the Government to help the Republic of Korea against the Communist aggressors. Now, many persons, even some who applauded our decision to defend Korea, have forgotten the basic reason for our action. It is right for us to be in Korea. It was right last June. It is right today.

I want to remind you why this is true.

The Communists in the Kremlin are engaged in a monstrous conspiracy to stamp out freedom all over the world. If they were to succeed, the United States would be numbered among their principal victims. It must be clear to everyone that the United States cannot—and will not—sit idly by and await foreign conquest. The only question is: When is the best time to meet the threat and how?

The best time to meet the threat is in the beginning. It is easier to put out a fire in the beginning when it is small than after it has become a roaring blaze.

And the best way to meet the threat of aggression is for the peace-loving nations to act together. If they don't act together, they are likely to be picked off, one by one. . . .

This is the basic reason why we joined in creating the United Nations. And since the end of World War II we have been putting that lesson into practice— we have been working with other free nations to check the aggressive designs of the Soviet Union before they can result in a third world war.

That is what we did in Greece, when that nation was threatened by the aggression of international communism.

The attack against Greece could have led to general war. But this country came to the aid of Greece. The United Nations supported Greek resistance. With our help, the determination and efforts of the Greek people defeated the attack on the spot.

Another big Communist threat to peace was the Berlin blockade. That too could have led to war. But again it was settled because free men would not back down in an emergency. . . .

The question we have had to face is whether the Communist plan of conquest can be stopped without general war. Our Government and other countries associated with us in the United Nations believe that the best chance of stopping it without general war is to meet the attack in Korea and defeat it there.

That is what we have been doing. It is a difficult and bitter task.

But so far it has been successful.

So far, we have prevented World War III.

So far, by fighting a limited war in Korea, we have prevented aggression from succeeding and bringing on a general war. And the ability of the whole free world to resist Communist aggression has been greatly improved.

We have taught the enemy a lesson. He has found out that aggression is not cheap or easy. Moreover, men all over the world who want to remain free have been given new courage and new hope. They know now that the champions of freedom can stand up and fight and that they will stand up and fight.

Our resolute stand in Korea is helping the forces of freedom now fighting in Indochina and other countries in that part of the world. It has already slowed down the timetable of conquest. . . .

We do not want to see the conflict in Korea extended. We are trying to prevent a world war—not to start one. The best way to do this is to make plain that we and the other free countries will continue to resist the attack.

But you may ask: Why can't we take other steps to punish the aggressor? Why don't we bomb Manchuria and China itself? Why don't we assist Chinese Nationalist troops to land on the mainland of China?

If we were to do these things we would be running a very grave risk of starting a general war. If that were to happen, we would have brought about the exact situation we are trying to prevent.

If we were to do these things, we would become entangled in a vast conflict on the continent of Asia and our task would become immeasurably more difficult all over the world.

What would suit the ambitions of the Kremlin better than for our military forces to be committed to a full-scale war with Red China? . . .

The course we have been following is the one best calculated to avoid an all-out war. It is the course consistent with our obligation to do all we can to maintain international peace and security. Our experience in Greece and Berlin shows that it is the most effective course of action we can follow. . . .

If the Communist authorities realize that they cannot defeat us in Korea, if they realize it would be foolhardy to widen the hostilities beyond Korea, then they may recognize the folly of continuing their aggression. A peaceful settlement may then be possible. The door is always open.

Then we may achieve a settlement in Korea which will not compromise the principles and purposes of the United Nations.

I have thought long and hard about this question of extending the war in Asia. I have discussed it many times with the ablest military advisers in the country. I believe with all my heart that the course we are following is the best course.

I believe that we must try to limit war to Korea for these vital reasons: to make sure that the precious lives of our fighting men are not wasted; to see that the security of our country and the free world is not needlessly jeopardized; and to prevent a third world war.

A number of events have made it evident that General MacArthur did not agree with that policy. I have therefore considered it essential to relieve General MacArthur so that there would be no doubt or confusion as to the real purpose and aim of our policy.

It was with the deepest personal regret that I found myself compelled to take this action. General MacArthur is one of our greatest military commanders. But the cause of world peace is more important than any individual.

The change in commands in the Far East means no change whatever in the policy of the United States. We will carry on the fight in Korea with vigor and determination in an effort to bring the war to a speedy and successful conclusion.

The new commander, Lt. Gen. Matthew Ridgway, has already demonstrated that he has the great qualities of military leadership needed for this task.

We are ready, at any time, to negotiate for a restoration of peace in the area. But we will not engage in appeasement. We are only interested in real peace.

Real peace can be achieved through a settlement based on the following factors:

One: the fighting must stop.

Two: concrete steps must be taken to insure that the fighting will not break out again.

Three: there must be an end to the aggression.

A settlement founded upon these elements would open the way for the unification of Korea and the withdrawal of all foreign forces.

In the meantime, I want to be clear about our military objective. We are fighting to resist an outrageous aggression in Korea. We are trying to keep the Korean conflict from spreading to other areas. But at the same time we must conduct our military activities so as to insure the security of our forces. This is essential if they are to continue the fight until the enemy abandons its ruthless attempt to destroy the Republic of Korea.

That is our military objective—to repel attack and to restore peace.

In the hard fighting in Korea, we are proving that collective action among nations is not only a high principle but a workable means of resisting aggression. Defeat of aggression in Korea may be the turning point in the world's search for a practical way of achieving peace and security.

The struggle of the United Nations in Korea is a struggle for peace.

The free nations have united their strength in an effort to prevent a third world war.

That war can come if the Communist rulers want it to come. But this Nation and its allies will not be responsible for its coming.

We do not want to widen the conflict. We will use every effort to prevent that disaster. And in so doing we know that we are following the great principles of peace, freedom, and justice.

Source: *Public Papers of the Presidents of the United States, Harry S. Truman, 1951* (Washington, DC: Government Printing Office, 1965), 223–27.

116.   THE EUROPEAN RECOVERY PROGRAM
30 December 1951

Three years after the initiation of the Marshall Plan, the Truman admin-
istration issued a report listing the impressive achievements of the nations
involved in European recovery and the Economic Cooperation Adminis-
tration, the agency charged with administering assistance.

The recovery of Europe from the chaos of 1947, when it was hungry, cold, disorderly, and frightened, can be measured in cold statistics: Industrial production, 64 percent above 1947 and 41 percent above prewar; steel production, nearly doubled in less than 4 years; coal production, slightly below prewar but still 27 percent higher than in 1947; aluminum, copper, and cement production, up respectively 69, 31, and 90 percent from 1947; food production, 24 percent above 1947 and 9 percent above prewar levels.

The Economic Cooperation Administration has expended nearly 12 billion dollars in grants and loans in carrying out the European Recovery Program—equal to nearly 80 dollars for every man, woman, and child in the United States. To this, the countries of Europe have added the equivalent of another 9 billion dollars in its own currencies to match the American grant-aid dollars. Of the U.S. funds, about 5.5 billion dollars have been used to purchase industrial commodities, mostly from the United States, and another 5.2 billion dollars for the purchase of food and other agricultural commodities such as cotton. Over 800 million dollars has alone gone into the cost of ocean freight for goods sent to Europe. The U.S. contribution to the setting up of the EPU was 350 million dollars and another 100 million dollars has been used since then to help the payments union over rough spots.

In their turn, the Marshall Plan countries in the past 3 years completed or are pushing to completion a total of 27 major projects for the increase of power and 32 major projects for modernizing and expanding the production of iron and steel. Major petroleum refining works number 11 and the volume of refining has quadrupled over prewar. Other industrial projects costing the equivalent of a million dollars or more bring the total of such projects to 132, costing the equivalent of over two billion dollars. About half a billion dollars of the U.S. commodity and technical aid has gone into these projects.

Into other major recovery projects have gone also the equivalent of billions of dollars of the counterpart currencies generated in the Marshall Plan countries to match American dollar aid. Such counterpart funds are used by the respective countries for recovery projects approved by the ECA. Biggest single use—equivalent to more than a billion dollars—has been for the improvement of electric, gas, and power facilities, an improvement that is helping to make possible Europe's rearmament program today.

Similarly vital to Europe's defense has been the rehabilitation of the continent's run-down and war-smashed railway network, with approved projects for use of counterpart funds totaling more than the equivalent of half a billion dollars. Similarly, counterpart projects for the reconstruction of merchant fleets, port and shipping facilities, and inland waterways have been completed or are in the process of completion in the Marshall Plan countries. Airports, too, have been built or improved with ECA-generated local currencies.

Through such double-barreled use of dollar aid and local funds, Marshall Plan nations, in less than 4 years, have rebuilt their economies to a point that could well persuade the Kremlin that the Europe which looked like such easy pickings in 1946 and 1947 is indeed a formidable bastion today.

Steel production, for example, so necessary to a strong peace or war economy, has risen from less than 31 million tons in 1947 to nearly 60 million tons in 1951. Soviet Russia and her satellites combined have a steel production rate of about 35 million tons.

The average volume of crude oil refined in Europe in prewar years was 12 million tons annually. In 1950–51 the volume of refined products reached 46.8 million tons, or nearly four times prewar.

In 1947, Europe's average monthly electrical production was 13½ million kilowatt hours. In mid-1951 the wheels of Europe's industry were being turned with 20 ½ million kilowatt hours per month. From a monthly cement production average of less than 2 million metric tons in 1947, Europe's production rose to 4 million tons monthly during the first half of 1951.

Cotton-yarn production in free Europe has risen from a monthly average of 82,000 metric tons in 1947 to 125,000 tons in 1951; wool yarn production is up from 33,000 tons monthly in 1947 to 44,000 tons in 1951.

One of the most dramatic improvements, and one closely tied to Europe's defense capabilities, is in the production of motor vehicles. Monthly production, running at the rate of 54,000 vehicles in 1947, is up to 145,000 vehicles in 1951.

Agricultural production is up 9 percent over prewar and 24 percent over 1947–48, but at the same time there are many more mouths to feed (population is up from 250 million in 1938 to over 275 million in 1951) and Europe is not yet self-sufficient in food production.

Overall, Europe's gross national product—the total sum of its production of goods and services—rose by nearly 25 percent in the less than 4 years of Marshall Plan aid to over 125 billion dollars in 1950. This is a 15 percent increase over prewar levels.

But Europe by no means considers its job finished. Member countries of the OEEC recently issued a manifesto declaring their intention to work for an expansion of total production in Western Europe by 25 percent over the next 5 years.

With her industrial plant rebuilt to better than prewar years, Europe's hope for meeting or surpassing this goal must rest on improved production methods and greater productivity—increased output of goods with the same amount of manpower, machines, and management.

Source: U.S. Department of State, *Department of State Bulletin*, vol. 26, no. 655 (14 January 1952): 43–45.

117. THE MUTUAL SECURITY ACT
10 October 1951

In 1951, Congress created the Mutual Security Administration to coordinate American military and economic assistance throughout the world. With the Korean War as a backdrop, American attention focused in particular on military aid. By the end of 1954, the United States was responsible for the logistical support and training of forces equivalent to more than 200 American divisions.

An Act to maintain the security and promote the foreign policy and provide for the general welfare of the United States by furnishing assistance to friendly nations in the interest of international peace and security.

SEC. 2. The Congress declares it to be the purpose of this Act to maintain the security and to promote the foreign policy of the United States by authorizing military, economic, and technical assistance to friendly countries to strengthen the mutual security and individual and collective defenses of the free world, to develop their resources in the interest of their security and independence and the national interest of the United States and to facilitate the effective participation of those countries in the United Nations system for collective security. The purposes of the Mutual Defense Assistance Act of 1949, as amended (22 U.S.C. 1571–1604), the Economic Cooperation Act of 1948, as amended, and the Act for International Development (22 U.S.C. 1557) shall hereafter be deemed to include this purpose.

TITLE I
EUROPE

SEC. 101. (a) In order to support the freedom of Europe through assistance which will further the carrying out of the plans for defense of the North Atlantic area, while at the same time maintaining the economic stability of the countries of the area so that they may meet their responsibilities for defense, and to further encourage the economic unification and the political federation of Europe, there are hereby authorized to be appropriated to the President for the fiscal year 1952 for carrying out the provisions and accomplishing the policies and purpose of this Act—

(1) not to exceed $5,028,000,000 for assistance pursuant to the provisions of the Mutual Defense Assistance Act of 1949, as amended, for countries which are parties to the North Atlantic Treaty and for any country of Europe (other than a country covered by another title of this Act), which the President determines to be of direct importance to the defense of the North Atlantic area and whose increased ability to defend itself, the President determines is, important to the preservation of the peace and security of the North Atlantic area and to the security of the United States. . . .

(2) not to exceed $1,022,000,000 for assistance pursuant to the provisions of the Economic Cooperation Act of 1948, as amended (including assistance to further European military production), for any country of Europe covered by paragraph (1) of this subsection and for any other country covered by section 103 (a) of the said Economic Cooperation Act of 1948, as amended. . . .

TITLE II
NEAR EAST AND AFRICA

SEC. 201. In order to further the purpose of this Act by continuing to provide military assistance to Greece, Turkey, and Iran, there are hereby authorized to be appropriated to the President for the fiscal year 1952, not to exceed $396,250,000 for furnishing assistance to Greece and Turkey pursuant to the provisions of the Act of May 22, 1947, as amended, and for furnishing assistance to Iran pursuant to the provisions of the Mutual Defense Assistance Act of 1949, as amended (22 U.S.C. 1571–1604). In addition, unexpected balances of appropriations heretofore made for assistance to Greece and Turkey, available for the fiscal year 1951, pursuant to the Act of May 22, 1947, as amended, and for assistance to Iran pursuant to the Mutual Defense Assistance Act of 1949, as amended, are hereby authorized to be continued available through June 30, 1952, and to be consolidated with the appropriation authorized by this section.

SEC. 202. Whenever the President determines that such action is essential for the purpose of this Act, he may provide assistance, pursuant to the provisions of the Mutual Defense Assistance Act of 1949, as amended, to any country of the Near East area (other than those covered by section 201) and may utilize not to exceed 10 per centum of the amount made available (excluding balances of prior appropriations continued available) pursuant to section 201 of this Act: *Provided*, That any such assistance may be furnished only upon determination by the President that (1) the strategic location of the recipient country makes it of direct importance to the defense of the Near East area, (2) such assistance is of critical importance to the defense of the free nations, and (3) the immediately increased ability of the recipient country to defend itself is important to the preservation of the peace and security of the area and to the security of the United States.

SEC. 203. In order to further the purpose of this Act in Africa and the Near

East, there are hereby authorized to be appropriated to the President, for the fiscal year 1952, not to exceed $160,000,000 for economic and technical assistance in Africa and the Near East in areas other than those covered by section 103 (a) of the Economic Cooperation Act of 1948, as amended. . . .

TITLE III
ASIA AND PACIFIC

SEC. 301. In order to carry out in general area of China (including the Republic of the Philippines and the Republic of Korea) the provisions of subsection (a) of section 303 of the Mutual Defense Assistance Act of 1949, as amended, there are hereby authorized to be appropriated to the President for the fiscal year 1952, not to exceed $535,250,000. . . .

SEC 302. (a) In order to further the purpose of this Act through the strengthening of the area covered in section 301 of this Act (but not including the Republic of Korea), there are hereby authorized to be appropriated to the President, for the fiscal year 1952, not to exceed $237,500,000 for economic and technical assistance in those portions of such area which the President deems to be not under Communist control. Funds appropriated pursuant to authority of this section shall be available under the applicable provisions of the Economic Cooperation Act of 1948, as amended, and of the Act for International Development. . . .

TITLE IV
AMERICAN REPUBLICS

SEC. 401. In order to further the purpose of this Act through the furnishing of military assistance to the other American Republics, there are hereby authorized to be appropriated to the President, for the fiscal year 1952, not to exceed $38,150,000 for carrying out the purposes of this section under the provisions of the Mutual Defense Assistance Act of 1949, as amended. . . .

TITLE V
ORGANIZATION AND GENERAL PROVISIONS

SEC. 501. (a) In order that the programs of military, economic, and technical assistance authorized by this Act may be administered as parts of a unified program in accordance with the intent of Congress and to fix responsibility for the coordination and supervision of these programs in a single person, the President is authorized to appoint in the Executive Office of the President a Director for Mutual Security. The Director on behalf of the President and subject to his direction, shall have primary responsibility for—

(1) continuous supervision and general direction of the assistance programs under this Act to the end that such programs shall be (A) effectively integrated both at home and abroad, and (B) administered so as to assure that the defensive strength of the free nations of the world shall be built as quickly as possible on the basis of continuous and effective self-help and mutual aid;

(2) preparation and presentation to the Congress of such programs of foreign military, economic, and technical assistance as may be required in the interest of the security of the United States;

(3) preparation for the President of the report to the Congress required by section 518 of this Act. . . .

SEC. 502. (a) The Economic Cooperation Administration and the offices of Administrator for Economic Cooperation, Deputy Administrator, United States Special Representative in Europe, and Deputy Special Representative are hereby abolished.

(b) To assist in carrying out the purpose of this Act—

(1) there is hereby established, its principle office at the seat of the government, a Mutual Security Agency, hereinafter referred to as the Agency, which shall be headed by the Director for Mutual Security; and

(2) there shall be transferred to the Director the powers, functions, and responsibilities conferred upon the Administration for Economic Cooperation by the Economic Cooperation Act of 1948, as amended, and by any other law, but no such powers, functions, and responsibilities, shall be exercised after June 30, 1952, except as provided in subsection (c) of this section.

(c) Not later than April 1, 1952, the President shall inform the Committee on Foreign Relations of the Senate and the Committee on Foreign Affairs of the House of Representatives which of the powers, functions, and responsibilities transferred to the Director by subsection (b) (2) are found by the President to be necessary to enable the Director after June 30, 1952, to carry out the duties conferred upon him by section 503. The termination provisions of section 122 of the Economic Cooperation Act of 1948, as amended, shall come into effect on June 30, 1952, and none of the powers, functions, and responsibilities conferred by that Act shall be exercised after that date, except those powers, functions, and responsibilities found necessary to enable the Director to carry out the duties conferred on him by section 503 of this Act, which powers, functions, and responsibilities unless otherwise provided by law shall continue in effect until June 30, 1954. . . .

SEC. 503. After June 30, 1952, the Director, on behalf of the President and subject to his direction, shall, in consultation with the Secretaries of State and Defense, continue to have primary responsibility for—

(a) The development and administration of programs of assistance designed to sustain and increase military effort, including production, construction, equipment and materiel in each country or in groups of countries which receive United States military assistance;

(b) the provision of such equipment, materials, commodities, services, financial, or other assistance as he finds to be necessary for carrying out mutual defense programs; and

(c) the provision of limited economic assistance to foreign nations for which the United States has responsibility as a result of participation in joint control arrangements when the President finds that the provision of such economic assistance is in the interest of the security of the United States. . . .

SEC. 513. Whenever the President determines it to be necessary for the purpose of this Act, not to exceed 10 per centum of the funds made available under any title of this Act may be transferred to and consolidated with funds made available under any other title of this Act in order to furnish, to a different area, assistance of the kind for which such funds were available before transfer. Whenever the President makes any such determination, he shall forthwith notify the Committee on Foreign Relations of the Senate and the Committee on Foreign Affairs of the House of Representatives. In the case of the transfer of funds available for military purposes, he shall also forthwith notify the Committees on Armed Services of the Senate and House of Representatives. . . .

SEC. 516. It is hereby declared to be the policy of the Congress that this Act shall be administered in such a way as (1) to eliminate the barriers to, and provide the incentives for, a steadily increased participation of free private enterprise in developing the resources of foreign countries consistent with the policies of this Act, (2) to the extent that it is feasible and does not interfere with the achievement of the purposes set forth in this Act, to discourage the cartel and monopolistic business practices prevailing in certain countries receiving aid under this Act which result in restricting production and increasing prices, and to encourage where suitable competition and productivity, and (3) to encourage where suitable the development and strengthening of free labor union movements as the collective bargaining agencies of labor within such countries. . . .

SEC. 529. If the President determines that the furnishing of assistance to any nation—

(a) is no longer consistent with the national interest or security of the United States or the policies and purpose of this Act; or

(b) would contravene a decision of the Security Council of the United Nations; or

(c) would be inconsistent with the principle that members of the United Nations, should refrain from giving assistance to any nation against which the Security Council or the General Assembly has recommended, measures in case of a threat to, or breach of, the peace, or act of aggression, he shall terminate all or part of any assistance furnished pursuant to this Act. The function conferred herein shall be in addition to all other functions heretofore conferred with respect to the termination of military, economic, or technical assistance. . . .

Source: Henry Steele Commager, *Documents of American History*, vol. 2 (Englewood Cliffs, NJ: Prentice Hall, 1973), 71–74.

118. EISENHOWER'S "PEACE IN THE WORLD" SPEECH
16 April 1953

Newly arrived to the White House in 1953, Dwight D. Eisenhower gave an address to outline his perspectives on the Cold War. The speech was significant to the extent that he saw an important balance to be struck between the American commitment to world security and his own administration's continued cultivation of domestic prosperity.

. . . In this spring of 1953 the free world weighs one question above all others: The chance for a just peace—just peace—for all peoples.

To weigh this chance is to summon instantly to mind another recent moment of great decision. It came with that yet more hopeful Spring of 1945, bright with the promise of victory and of freedom. The hope of all just men in that moment too, was a just and lasting peace.

The eight years that have passed have seen that hope waver, grow dim, and almost die. And the shadow of fear again has lengthened across the world.

Today the hope of free men remains stubborn and brave but it is sternly disciplined by experience.

It shuns not only all crude counsel of despair, but also the self-deceit of easy illusion.

It weighs the chance for peace with sure, clear knowledge of what happened to the vain hope of 1945.

UNION AND DIVISION

In the spring of victory, the soldiers of the Western Allies met the soldiers of Russia in the center of Europe. They were triumphant comrades in arms. Their peoples shared the joyous prospect of building, in honor of their dead, the only fitting monument—an age of just peace.

All these war-weary peoples shared, too, this concrete, decent purpose: To guard vigilantly against the domination ever again of any part of the world by a single, unbridled aggressive power.

This common purpose lasted an instant—and perished. The nations of the world divided to follow two distinct roads.

The United States and our valued friends, the other free nations, chose one road.

The leaders of the Soviet Union chose another.

The way chosen by the United States was plainly marked by a few clear precepts which govern its conduct in world affairs.

FIRST—No people on earth can be held—as a people—to be an enemy, for all humanity shares the common hunger for peace and fellowship and justice.

SECOND—No nation's security and well-being can be lastingly achieved in isolation, but only in effective cooperation with fellow-nations.

THIRD—Any nation's right to a form of government and an economic system of its own choosing is inalienable.

FOURTH—Any nation's attempt to dictate to other nations their form of government is indefensible.

AND FIFTH—A nation's hope of a lasting peace cannot be firmly based upon any race in armaments, but rather upon just relations and honest understanding with all other nations.

THE WAY TO PEACE

In the light of these principles, the citizens of the United States defined the way they proposed to follow, through the aftermath of war, toward true peace.

This way was faithful to the spirit that inspired the United Nations: To prohibit strife, to relieve tensions, to banish fears. This way was to control and to reduce armaments. This way was to allow all nations to devote their energies and resources to the great and good tasks of healing the war's wounds, of clothing and feeding and housing the needy, of perfecting a just political life, of enjoying the fruits of their own free toil.

The Soviet Government held a vastly different vision of the future.

In the world of its design, security was to be found—not in mutual trust and mutual aid—but in force: Huge armies, subversion, rule of neighbor nations. The goal was power, superiority—at all cost. Security was to be sought by denying it to all others.

The result has been tragic for the world and, for the Soviet Union, it has also been ironic.

The amassing of Soviet power alerted free nations to a new danger of aggression. It compelled them in self-defense to spend unprecedented money and energy for armaments. It forced them to develop weapons of war now capable of inflicting instant and terrible punishment upon any aggressor.

It instilled in the free nations—and let none doubt this—the unshakable conviction that, as long as there persists a threat to freedom, they must, at any cost, remain armed, strong, and ready for any risk of war.

It inspired them—and let none doubt this—to attain a unity of purpose and will beyond the power of propaganda or pressure to break, now or ever.

There remained, however, one thing essentially unchanged and unaffected by Soviet conduct: This unchanged thing was the readiness of the free world to welcome sincerely any genuine evidence of peaceful purpose enabling all peoples again to resume their common quest of just peace. And the free world still holds to that purpose.

The free nations, most solemnly and repeatedly, have assured the Soviet Union that their firm association has never had any aggressive purpose whatsoever.

Soviet leaders, however, have seemed to persuade themselves—or tried to persuade their people—otherwise.

And so it came to pass that the Soviet Union itself has shared and suffered the very fears it has fostered in the rest of the world.

This has been the way of life forged by eight years of fear and force.

What can the world—or any nation in it—hope for if no turning is found on this dread road?

The worst to be feared and the best to be expected can be simply stated.

The worst is atomic war.

The best would be this: A life of perpetual fear and tension; a burden of arms draining the wealth and the labor of all peoples; a wasting of strength that defies the American system or the Soviet system or any system to achieve true abundance and happiness for the peoples of this earth.

Every gun that is made, every warship launched, every rocket fired signifies—in the final sense—a theft from those who hunger and are not fed, those who are cold and are not clothed.

This world in arms is not spending money alone. It is spending the sweat of its laborers, the genius of its scientists, the hopes of its children.

The cost of one modern heavy bomber is this: A modern brick school in more than 30 cities.

It is: Two electric power plants, each serving a town of 60,000 population.

It is: Two fine, fully equipped hospitals.

It is: Some 50 miles of concrete highway.

We pay for a single fighter plane with a half million bushels of wheat.

We pay for a single destroyer with new homes that could have housed more than 8,000 people.

NOT A WAY OF LIFE

This is—I repeat—the best way of life to be found on the road the world has been taking.

This is not a way of life at all, in any true sense. Under the cloud of threatening war, it is humanity hanging from a cross of iron.

These plain and cruel truths define the peril and point . . . the hope that come with Spring of 1953.

This is one of those times in the affairs of nations when the gravest choices must be made—if there is to be a turning toward a just and lasting peace.

It is a moment that calls upon the governments of the world to speak their intentions with simplicity and with honesty.

It calls upon them to answer the question that stirs the hearts of all sane men: Is there no other way the world may live?

The world knows that an era ended with the death of Joseph Stalin. The extraordinary thirty-year span of his rule saw the Soviet empire expand to reach from the Baltic Sea to the Sea of Japan, finally to dominate 800,000,000 souls.

The Soviet system shaped by Stalin and his predecessors was born of one world war. It survived with stubborn and often amazing courage a second world war. It has lived to threaten a third.

Source: Dwight D. Eisenhower, "Peace in the World: Acts, Not Rhetoric, Needed," *Vital Speeches* 19 (1 May 1953): 418–19.

119. THE DOMINO THEORY
7 April 1954

By 1954, the United States had become responsible for a large portion of the French war against Communism in Southeast Asia. When asked to explain the U.S. commitment, Eisenhower offered his version of the "domino theory" in an effort to explain his concern that the Communist threat would accumulate if the United States was not vigilant. This same model was later applied to other East-West confrontations during his two terms.

Q. Robert Richards, Copley Press: Mr. President, would you mind commenting on the strategic importance of Indochina to the free world? I think there has been, across the country, some lack of understanding on just what it means to us.

THE PRESIDENT. You have, of course, both the specific and the general when you talk about such things.

First of all, you have the specific value of a locality in its production of materials that the world needs.

Then you have the possibility that many human beings pass under a dictatorship that is inimical to the free world.

Finally, you have broader considerations that might follow what you would call the "falling domino" principle. You have a row of dominoes set up, you knock over the first one, and what will happen to the last one is the certainty that it will go over very quickly. So you could have a beginning of a disintegration that would have the most profound influences.

Now, with respect to the first one, two of the items from this particular area that the world uses are tin and tungsten. They are very important. There are others, of course, the rubber plantations and so on.

Then with respect to more people passing under this domination. Asia, after all, has already lost some 450 million of its peoples to the Communist dictatorship, and we simply can't afford greater losses.

But when we come to the possible sequence of events, the loss of Indochina, of Burma, of Thailand, of the Peninsula, and Indonesia following, now you begin to talk about areas that not only multiply the disadvantages that you would suffer through loss of materials, sources of materials, but now you are talking really about millions and millions and millions of people.

Finally, the geographical position achieved thereby does many things. It turns the so-called island defense chain of Japan, Formosa, of the Philippines and to the southward; it moves in to threaten Australia and New Zealand.

It takes away, in its economic aspects, that region that Japan must have as a trading area or Japan, in turn will have only one place in the world to go—that is, toward the Communist areas in order to live.

So, the possible consequences of the loss are just incalculable to the free world.

Source: Public Papers of the Presidents of the United States, Dwight D. Eisenhower, 1954 (Washington, DC: Government Printing Office, 1960), 382–83.

---

120. THE STRATEGY OF MASSIVE RETALIATION
12 January 1954

Eisenhower's desire to reconcile American security with American economic prosperity resulted in substantial reductions in conventional forces and a new emphasis on nuclear weapons. In January 1954, Secretary of State John Foster Dulles articulated this new emphasis on nuclear deterrence as the primary means to halt Communist aggression.

We live in a world where emergencies are always possible, and our survival may depend upon our capacity to meet emergencies. Let us pray that we shall always have that capacity. But, having said that, it is necessary also to say that emergency measures—however good for the emergency—do not necessarily make good permanent policies. Emergency measures are costly; they are superficial; and they imply that the enemy has the initiative. They cannot be depended on to serve our long-time interests.

This "long time" factor is of critical importance. The Soviet Communists are planning for what they call "an entire historical era," and we should do the same. They seek, through many types of maneuvers, gradually to divide and weaken the free nations by overextending them in efforts which, as Lenin put it, are "beyond their strength, so they come to practical bankruptcy." Then, said Lenin, "our victory is assured." Then, said Stalin, will be "the moment for the decisive blow."

In the face of this strategy, measures cannot be judged adequate merely because they ward off an immediate danger. It is essential to do this, but it is also essential to do so without exhausting ourselves.

When the Eisenhower administration applied this test, we felt that some transformations were needed. It is not sound military strategy permanently to commit U.S. land forces to Asia to a degree that leaves us no strategic reserves. It is not sound economics, or good foreign policy, to support permanently other countries; for in the long run, that creates as much ill will as good will. Also, it is not sound to become permanently committed to military expenditures so vast they lead to "practical bankruptcy."

Change was imperative to assure the stamina needed for permanent security. But it was equally imperative that change should be accompanied by understanding of our true purposes. Sudden and spectacular change had to be avoided. Otherwise, there might have been a panic among our friends and miscalculated aggression by our enemies. We can, I believe, make a good report in these respects.

We need allies and collective security. Our purpose is to make these relations more effective, less costly. This can be done by placing more reliance on deterrent power and less dependence on local defensive power.

This is accepted practice so far as local communities are concerned. We keep locks on our doors, but we do not have an armed guard in every home. We rely principally on a community security system so well equipped to punish any who break in and steal that, in fact, would-be aggressors are generally deterred. That is the modern way of getting maximum protection at a bearable cost. What the Eisenhower administration seeks is a similar international security system. We want, for ourselves and the other free nations, a maximum deterrent at a bearable cost.

Local defense will always be important. But there is no local defense which alone will contain the mighty land power of the Communist world. Local defenses must be reinforced by the further deterrent of massive retaliatory power. A potential aggressor must know that he cannot always prescribe battle conditions that suit him. Otherwise, for example, a potential aggressor, who is glutted with manpower, might be tempted to attack in confidence that resistance would be confined to manpower. He might be tempted to attack in places where his superiority was decisive.

The way to deter aggression is for the free community to be willing and able to respond vigorously at places and with means of its own choosing.

So long as our basic policy concepts were unclear, our military leaders could not be selective in building our military power. If an enemy could pick his time and place and method of warfare—and if our policy was to remain the traditional one of meeting aggression by direct and local opposition—then we needed to be ready to fight in the Arctic and in the Tropics; in Asia, the Near East, and in Europe; by sea, by land, and by air; with old weapons, and with new weapons. . . .

Before military planning could be changed, the President and his advisers, as represented by the National Security Council, had to make some basic policy decisions. This has been done. The basic decision was to depend primarily upon a great capacity to retaliate, instantly, by means and at places of our choosing. Now the Department of Defense and the Joint Chiefs of Staff can shape our military establishment to fit what is *our* policy, instead of having to try to be ready to meet the enemy's many choices. That permits of a selection of military means instead of a multiplication of means. As a result, it is now possible to get, and share, more basic security at less cost.

Let us now see how this concept has been applied to foreign policy, taking first the Far East.

In Korea this administration effected a major transformation. The fighting has been stopped on honorable terms. That was possible because the aggressor, already thrown back to and behind his place of beginning, was faced with the possibility that the fighting might, to his own great peril, soon spread beyond the limits and methods which he had selected.

The cruel toll of American youth and the nonproductive expenditure of many billions have been stopped. Also our armed forces are no longer largely committed to the Asian mainland. We can begin to create a strategic reserve which greatly improves our defensive posture.

This change gives added authority to the warning of the members of the United Nations which fought in Korea that, if the Communists renewed the aggression, the United Nations response would not necessarily be confined to Korea.

I have said in relation to Indochina that, if there were open Red Chinese army aggression there, that would have "grave consequences which might not be confined to Indochina." . . .

In the ways I outlined we gather strength for the long-term defense of freedom. We do not, of course, claim to have found some magic formula that insures against all forms of Communist successes. It is normal that at some times and at some places there may be setbacks to the cause of freedom. What we do expect to insure is that any setbacks will have only temporary and local significance, because they will leave unimpaired those free world assets which in the long run will prevail.

If we can deter such aggression as would mean general war, and that is our confident resolve, then we can let time and fundamentals work for us. . . .

Source: U.S. Department of State, *Department of State Bulletin*, vol. 30, no. 761 (25 January 1954): 107–10.

---

121. THE GUATEMALAN CRISIS
30 June 1954

Neglected for most of the decade following the Second World War, Central America became a focal point of the Eisenhower administration's anticommunist policy. The initial issue that drew American attention to Guatemala was the alleged degree of Communist influence within the government of Jacobo Arbenz and its ongoing conflict with the United Fruit Company. In 1954, an exile force led by Carlos Enrique Castillo

Armas and covertly supported by the Central Intelligence Agency suc-
cessfully triggered a military coup against the Arbenz government.

. . . In Guatemala, international Communism had an initial success. It began ten
years ago when a revolution occurred in Guatemala. The revolution was not
without justification. But the Communists seized on it, not as an opportunity for
real reforms, but as a chance to gain political power.

Communist agitators devoted themselves to infiltrating the public and private organizations of Guatemala. They sent recruits to Russia and other Communist countries for revolutionary training and indoctrination in such
institutions as the Lenin School in Moscow. Operating in the guise of "reformers" they organized the workers and peasants under Communist leadership. Having gained control of what they call "mass organizations" they
moved on to take over the official press and radio of the Guatemalan Government. They dominated the Social Security organization and ran the agrarian
reform program. Through the technique of the "popular front" they dictated to
the Congress and the President.

The judiciary made one valiant attempt to protect its integrity and independence. But the Communists, using their control of the legislative body, caused
the Supreme Court to be dissolved when it refused to give approval to a
Communist-contrived law. Arbenz, who until this week was President of Guatemala, was openly manipulated by the leaders of Communism.

Guatemala is a small country. But its power, standing alone, is not a measure
of the threat. The master plan of international Communism is to gain a solid
political base in this hemisphere, a base that can be used to extend Communist
penetration to the other peoples of the other American Governments. It was not
the power of the Arbenz Government that concerned us but the power behind
it.

If world Communism captures any American State, however small, a new
and perilous front is established which will increase the danger to the entire free
world and require even greater sacrifices from the American people.

This situation in Guatemala had become so dangerous that the American
States could not ignore it. At Caracas last March the American States held their
Tenth Inter-American Conference. They then adopted a momentous statement.
They declared that "the domination or control of the political institutions of any
American State by the international communist movement . . . would constitute
a threat to the sovereignty and political independence of the American States,
endangering the peace of America."

There was only one American State that voted against this Declaration. That
State was Guatemala.

This Caracas Declaration precipitated a dramatic chain of events. From their
European base the Communist leaders moved rapidly to build up the military
power of their agents in Guatemala. In May a large shipment of arms moved
from behind the Iron Curtain into Guatemala. The shipment was sought to be

secreted by false manifests and false clearances. Its ostensible destination was changed three times while en route.

At the same time, the agents of international Communism in Guatemala, intensified efforts to penetrate and subvert the neighboring Central American States. They attempted political assassinations and political strikes. They used consular agents for political warfare.

Many Guatemalan people protested against their being used by Communist dictatorship to serve the Communist's lust for power. The response was mass arrests, the suppression of constitutional guarantees, the killing of opposition leaders and other brutal tactics normally employed by Communism to secure the consolidation of its power.

In the face of these events and in accordance with the spirit of the Caracas Declaration, the nations of this hemisphere laid further plans to grapple with the danger. The Arbenz Government responded with an effort to disrupt the inter-American system. Because it enjoyed the full support of Soviet Russia, which is on the Security Council, it tried to bring the matter before the Security Council. It did so without first referring the matter to the American regional organization as is called for both by the United Nations Charter itself and by the treaty creating the American Organization.

The Foreign Minister of Guatemala openly connived in this matter with the Foreign Minister of the Soviet Union. The two were in open correspondence and ill-concealed privity. The Security Council at first voted overwhelmingly to refer the Guatemala matter to the Organization of American States. The vote was ten to one. But that one negative vote was a Soviet veto.

Then the Guatemalan Government, with a Soviet backing, redoubled its efforts to supplant the American States system by Security Council jurisdiction.

However, last Friday, the United Nations Security Council decided not to take up the Guatemalan matter, but to leave it in the first instance to the American States themselves. That was a triumph for the system of balance between regional organization and world organization, which the American States had fought for when the Charter was drawn up at San Francisco.

The American States then moved promptly to deal with the situation. Their "peace commission" left yesterday for Guatemala. Earlier the Organization of American States had voted overwhelmingly to call a meeting of their Foreign Ministers to consider the penetration of international Communism in Guatemala and the measures required to eliminate it. Never before has there been so clear a call uttered with such a sense of urgency and strong resolve.

Throughout the period I have outlined, the Guatemalan Government and Communist agents throughout the world have persistently attempted to obscure the real issue—that of Communist imperialism—by claiming that the United States is only interested in protecting American business. We regret that there have been disputes between the Guatemalan Government and the United Fruit Company. We have urged repeatedly that these disputes be submitted for settlement to an international tribunal or to international arbitration. That is the way to dispose of problems of this sort. But this issue is relatively unimportant. All who know the temper of the U.S. people and Government must realize that our overriding concern is that which, with others, we recorded at Caracas, namely the endangering by international Communism of the peace and security of this hemisphere.

The people of Guatemala have now been heard from. Despite the armaments piled up by the Arbenz Government, it was unable to enlist the spiritual cooperation of the people.

Led by Colonel Castillo Armas, patriots arose in Guatemala to challenge the Communist leadership—and to change it. Thus, the situation is being cured by the Guatemalans themselves.

Last Sunday, President Arbenz of Guatemala resigned and seeks asylum. Others are following his example.

Tonight, just as I speak, Colonel Castillo Armas is in conference in El Salvador with Colonel Monzon, the head of the Council which has taken over the power in Guatemala City. It was this power that the just wrath of the Guatemalan people wrested from President Arbenz who then took flight.

Now the future of Guatemala lies at the disposal of the Guatemalan people themselves. It lies also at the disposal of leaders loyal to Guatemala who have not treasonably become the agents of an alien despotism which sought to use Guatemala for its own evil ends.

Source: U.S. Department of State, *Papers Relating to the Foreign Policy of the United States, 1953–1954*, vol. 4 (Washington, DC: Government Printing Office, 1983), 1091–93.

122. CONGRESSIONAL RESOLUTION ON THE DEFENSE OF FORMOSA
29 January 1955

In 1954–1955, Communist China threatened the Nationalist government in Taiwan and began military operations against the islands of Quemoy and Matsu. The Eisenhower administration quickly responded to the action, threatening the use of nuclear weapons. To bolster this hard line, Eisenhower persuaded legislators to pass a resolution declaring the area to be of vital national interest. The presidential authority granted by the Congress provided interesting foreshadowing for the later Tonkin Gulf resolution.

Whereas the primary purpose of the United States, in its relations with all other nations, is to develop and sustain a just and enduring peace for all; and
Whereas certain territories in the West Pacific under the jurisdiction of the

Republic of China are now under armed attack, and threats and declarations have been and are being made by the Chinese Communists that such armed attack is in aid of and in preparation for armed attack on Formosa and the Pescadores;

Whereas such armed attack if continued would gravely endanger the peace and security of the West Pacific Area and particularly of Formosa and the Pescadores; and

Whereas the secure possession by friendly governments of the Western Pacific Island chain, of which Formosa is a part, is essential to the vital interests of the United States and all friendly nations in or bordering upon the Pacific Ocean; and

Whereas the President of the United States on January 6, 1955, submitted to the Senate for its advice and consent to ratification a Mutual Defense Treaty between the United States of America and the Republic of China, which recognizes that an armed attack in the West Pacific area directed against territories, therein described, in the region of Formosa and the Pescadores, would be dangerous to the peace and safety of the parties to the treaty: Therefore be it

Resolved by the Senate and House of Representatives of the United States of America in Congress assembled, That the President of the United States be and he hereby is authorized to employ the Armed Forces of the United States as he deems necessary for the specific purpose of securing and protecting Formosa and the Pescadores against armed attack, this authority to include the security and protection of such related positions and territories of that area now in friendly hands and the taking of such other measures as he judges to be required or appropriate in assuring the defense of Formosa and the Pescadores.

This resolution shall expire when the President shall determine that the peace and security of the area is reasonably assured by international conditions created by action of the United Nations or otherwise, and shall so report to the Congress.

Source: Henry Steele Commager, *Documents of American History*, vol. 2. (Englewood Cliffs, NJ: Prentice Hall, 1973), 605.

---

123. EISENHOWER'S ADDRESS ON THE MIDDLE EAST
20 February 1957

In 1956, a second Arab-Israeli war threatened the stability of the Middle East. The event marked a turning point in American relations with Europe when the United States successfully demanded the withdrawal of British and French forces from Egypt. The United States also committed itself to the preservation of Israel in exchange for the latter's agreement to return the Gaza Strip and the Gulf of Aqaba.

My Fellow Citizens:

May I first explain to you that for some days I have been experiencing a very stubborn cough, so if because of this I should have to interrupt myself this evening, I crave your indulgence in advance.

I come to you again to talk about the situation in the Middle East. The future of the United Nations and peace in the Middle East may be at stake.

In the four months since I talked to you about the crisis in that area, the United Nations has made considerable progress in resolving some of the difficult problems. We are now, however, faced with a fateful moment as the result of the failure of Israel to withdraw its forces behind the Armistice lines, as contemplated by the United Nations Resolutions on this subject. . . .

When I talked to you last October, I pointed out that the United States fully realized that military action against Egypt resulted from grave and repeated provocations. But also I said that the use of military force to solve international disputes could not be reconciled with the principles and purposes of the United Nations, to which we had all subscribed. I added that our country could not believe that resort to force and war would for long serve the permanent interests of the attacking nations, which were Britain, France and Israel.

So I pledged that the United States would seek through the United Nations to end the conflict and to bring about a recall of the forces of invasion, and then make a renewed and earnest effort through that organization to secure justice, under international law, for all of the parties concerned.

Since that time much has been achieved and many of the dangers implicit in the situation have been avoided. The governments of Britain and France have withdrawn their forces from Egypt. Thereby they showed respect for the opinions of mankind as expressed almost unanimously by the eighty-nation members of the United Nations General Assembly. . . .

The Prime Minister of Israel, in answer to a personal communication, assured me early in November that Israel would willingly withdraw its forces if and when there should be created a United Nations force to move into the Suez Canal area. This force was, in fact, created and has moved into the canal area.

Subsequently, Israeli forces were withdrawn from much of the territory of Egypt which they had occupied. However, Israeli forces still remain outside the armistice lines, notably at the mouth of the Gulf of Aqaba which is about 100 miles from the nearest Israeli territory and in the Gaza Strip which, by the armistice agreement, was to be occupied by Egypt. This fact creates the present crisis. . . .

In view of the valued friendly relations which the United States has always had with the state of Israel, I wrote to Prime Minister Ben-Gurion on Feb. 3. I recalled his statement to me of Nov. 8 to the effect that the Israeli forces would be withdrawn under certain conditions, and I urged that, in view of the General Assembly resolutions of Feb. 2, Israel should complete that withdrawal.

However, the Prime Minister, in his reply, took the position that Israel would not evacuate its military forces from the Gaza Strip unless Israel retained the civil administration and police. This would be in contradiction to the armistice agreement. Also, the reply said that Israel would not withdraw from the Straits of Aqaba unless freedom of passage through the straits was assured.

It was a matter of keen disappointment to us that the Government of Israel, despite the United Nations action, still felt unwilling to withdraw.

However, in a further effort to meet the views of Israel in these respects, Secretary of State Dulles, at my direction, gave to the Government of Israel on Feb. 11 a statement of United States policy. This has now been made public. It pointed out that neither the United States nor the United Nations had authority to impose upon the parties a substantial modification of the Armistice agreement which was freely signed by Israel and Egypt. Nevertheless, the statement said, the United States as a member of the United Nations would seek such disposition of the United Nations Emergency Force as would assure that the Gaza Strip could no longer be a source of armed infiltration and reprisals.

The Secretary of State orally informed the Israeli Ambassador that the United States would be glad to urge and support, also, some participation by the United Nations, with the approval of Egypt, in the administration of the Gaza Strip. The principal population of the strip consists of about 300,000 Arab refugees, who exist largely as a charge upon the benevolence of the United Nations and its members.

With reference to the passage into and through the Gulf of Aqaba, we expressed the conviction that the gulf constitutes international waters and that no nation has the right to prevent free and innocent passage in the gulf. We announced that the United States was prepared to exercise this right itself and to join with others to secure general recognition of this right. . . .

We should not assume that if Israel withdraws, Egypt will prevent Israeli shipping from using the Suez Canal or the Gulf of Aqaba. If, unhappily, Egypt does hereafter violate the Armistice agreement or other international obligation, then this should be dealt with firmly by the society of nations.

The present moment is a grave one, but we are hopeful that reason and right will prevail. Since the events of last October and November, solid progress has been made, in conformity with the Charter of the United Nations. There is the cease-fire, the forces of Britain and France have been withdrawn, the forces of Israel have been partially withdrawn, and the clearing of the Canal nears completion. When Israel completes its withdrawal, it will have removed a definite block to further progress.

Once this block is removed, there will be serious and creative tasks for the United Nations to perform. There needs to be respect for the right of Israel to national existence and to internal development. Complicated provisions insuring the effective international use of the Suez Canal will need to be worked out in detail. The Arab refugee problem must be solved. As I said in my special message to Congress on Jan. 5, it must be made certain that all the Middle East is kept free from aggression and infiltration.

Finally, all who cherish freedom, including ourselves, should help the nations of the Middle East achieve their just aspirations for improving the well-being of their peoples.

What I have spoken about tonight is only one step in a long process calling for patience and diligence, but at this moment it is the critical issue on which future progress depends.

It is an issue which can be solved if only we will apply the principles of the United Nations.

That is why, my fellow Americans, I know you want the United States to continue to use its maximum influence to sustain those principles as the world's best hope for peace.

Source: Public Papers of the Presidents of the United States, Dwight D. Eisenhower, 1957 (Washington, DC: Government Printing Office, 1958), 147–56.

124.   EISENHOWER DOCTRINE
9 March 1957

Only a few weeks after pledging that the United States would help preserve stability in the Middle East, Dwight D. Eisenhower committed American assistance to prevent Communist aggression in the region. Congress subsequently approved $200 million in military and economic aid to be utilized at the president's discretion.

Resolved, That the President be and hereby is authorized to cooperate with and assist any nation or group of nations in the general area of the Middle East desiring such assistance in the development of economic strength dedicated to the maintenance of national independence.

SEC. 2. The President is authorized to undertake, in the general area of the Middle East, military assistance programs with any nation or group of nations of that area desiring such assistance. Furthermore, the United States regards as vital to the national interest and world peace the preservation of the independence and integrity of the nations of the Middle East. To this end, if the President determines the necessity thereof, the United States is prepared to use armed force to assist any such nation or group of nations requesting assistance against armed aggression from any country controlled by international communism: *Provided*, That such employment shall be consonant with the treaty obligations of the United States and with the Constitution of the United States.

SEC. 3. The President is hereby authorized to use during the balance of the fiscal year 1957 for economic and military assistance under this joint resolution not to exceed $200,000,000 from any appropriation now available for carrying out the provisions of the Mutual Security Act of 1954. . . .

SEC. 4. The President should continue to furnish facilities and military assistance within the provisions of applicable law and established policies, to the United Nations Emergency Force in the Middle East, with a view to maintaining the truce in that region.

SEC. 5. The President shall within the months of January and July of each year report to the Congress his action hereunder.

SEC. 6. This joint resolution shall expire when the President shall determine that the peace and security of the nations in the general area of the Middle East are reasonably assured by international conditions created by action of the United Nations or otherwise except that it may be terminated earlier by a concurrent resolution of the two Houses of Congress.

Source: Public Papers of the Presidents of the United States, Dwight D. Eisenhower, 1957 (Washington, DC: Government Printing Office, 1958), 6–16.

---

125. NSAM 2
1961

One of the major points of contention regarding the Eisenhower administration's overt reliance on nuclear deterrence was its lack of flexibility. When John F. Kennedy became president in 1961, he almost immediately sought out additional elements for the United States' arsenal of responses to aggression and instability. Addressing the problem of "brushfire" wars was one of the administration's first priorities.

February 3, 1961

TOP SECRET
NATIONAL SECURITY ACTION MEMORANDUM NO. 2

TO: The Secretary of Defense
SUBJECT: Development of Counter-guerrilla Forces

At the National Security Council meeting on February 1, 1961, the President requested that the Secretary of Defense, in consultation with other interested agencies, should examine means for placing more emphasis on the development of counter-guerrilla forces.

Accordingly, it is requested that the Department of Defense take action on this request and inform this office promptly of the measures which it proposes to take.

McGeorge Bundy
Special Assistant to the President
for National Security Affairs

TOP SECRET

Source: National Archives and Records Administration, General Records of the Department of State, National Security Action Memoranda Files, 1961–1968, Box 1.

126. KENNEDY'S SPEECH ON THE ALLIANCE FOR PROGRESS
13 March 1961

Latin America became a showcase for the U.S. commitment to solving the problems of the underdeveloped world. Long neglected by policy makers since the Second World War, it drew significant attention after the collapse of the Batista government in Cuba. Kennedy's promise to reinforce the principle of collective security in Latin America was similar to the Truman Doctrine *and* Eisenhower Doctrine *that were announced in the wake of similar regional crises. It differed from the doctrines to the extent that the proposed Alliance promised an enormous amount of U.S. assistance for a broad array of social, economic, and political reforms.*

It is a great pleasure for Mrs. Kennedy and for me, for the Vice President and Mrs. Johnson, and for the Members of Congress, to welcome the Ambassadorial Corps of the Hemisphere, our long time friends, to the White House today. One hundred and thirty-nine years ago this week the United States—stirred by the heroic struggles of its fellow Americans—urged the independence and recognition of the new Latin American Republics. It was then, at the dawn of freedom throughout this hemisphere, that Bolivar spoke of his desire to see the Americas fashioned into the greatest region in the world, "greatest," he said, "not so much by virtue of her area and her wealth, as by her freedom and her glory."

Never—in the long history of our hemisphere—has this dream been nearer to fulfillment—and never has it been in greater danger.

The genius of our scientists has given us the tools to bring abundance to our land, strength to our industry, and knowledge to our people. For the first time we have the capacity to strike off the remaining bonds of poverty and ignorance—to free our people for the spiritual and intellectual fulfillment which has always been the goal of our civilization.

Yet at this very moment of maximum opportunity, we confront the same forces which have imperiled America throughout its history—the alien forces which once again seek to impose the despotisms of the old world on the people of the new.

I have asked you to come here today so that I might discuss these challenges and these dangers.

We meet together as firm and ancient friends—united by history and experience, and by our determination to advance the values of American civilization. For this new world of ours is not merely an accident of geography. Our continents are bound together by a common history—the endless exploration of new frontiers. Our nations are the product of a common struggle—the revolt from colonial rule. And our people share a common heritage—the quest for the dignity and freedom of man.

The revolutions which gave us birth ignited, in the words of Thomas Paine, "a spark never to be extinguished." And across vast, turbulent continents these American ideals still stir man's struggle for national independence and individual freedom. But as we welcome the spread of the American revolution to other lands, we must also remember that our own struggle—the revolution which began in Philadelphia in 1776, and in Caracas in 1811—is not yet finished. Our hemisphere's mission is not yet completed. For our unfulfilled task is to demonstrate to the entire world that man's unsatisfied aspiration for economic progress and social justice can best be achieved by free men working within a framework of democratic institutions. If we can do this in our own hemisphere, and for our own people, we may yet realize the prophecy of the great Mexican patriot, Benito Juarez, that "democracy is the destiny of future humanity."

As a citizen of the United States let me be the first to admit that we North Americans have not always grasped the significance of this common mission—just as it is also true that many in your own countries have not fully understood the urgency of the need to lift people from poverty and ignorance and despair. But we must turn from these mistakes—from the failures the misunderstandings of the past to a future full of peril, but bright with hope.

Throughout Latin America—a continent rich in resources and in the spiritual and culture achievements of its people—millions of men and women suffer the daily degradations of hunger and poverty. They lack decent shelter or protection from disease. Their children are deprived of the education or the jobs which are the gateway to a better life. And each day the problems grow more urgent. Population growth is outpacing economic growth—low living standards are even further endangered—and discontent—the discontent of a people who know that abundance and the tools of progress are at last within their reach—that discontent is growing. In the words of Jose Figueres, "once dormant peoples are struggling upward toward the sun, toward a better life."

If we are to meet a problem so staggering in its dimensions, our approach must itself be equally bold—an approach consistent with the majestic concept of Operation Pan America. Therefore I have called on all the people of the hemisphere to join in a new Alliance for Progress "Alianza para Progreso"—a vast cooperative effort, unparalleled in magnitude and nobility of purpose, to satisfy the basic needs of the American people for homes, work and land, health and schools—techo, trabajo y tierra, salud y escuela.

First, I propose that the American Republics begin on a vast new Ten Year

Plan for the Americas—a plan to transform the 1960s into an historic decade of democratic progress.

These ten years will be the years of maximum progress—maximum effort—the years when the greatest obstacles must be overcome—the years when the need for assistance will be the greatest.

And if we are successful—if our effort is bold enough and determined enough—then the close of this decade will mark the beginning of a new era in the American experience. The living standards of every American family will be on the rise—basic education will be available to all—hunger will be a forgotten experience—the need for massive outside help will have passed—most nations will have entered a period of self-sustaining growth—and—although there will be much to do—every American republic will be the master of its own revolution and its own hope of progress.

Let me stress that only the most determined efforts of the American nations themselves can bring success to this effort. They, and they alone, can mobilize their resources—enlist the energies of their people—and modify their social patterns so that all, and not just a privileged few, share in the fruits of growth. If this effort is made, then outside assistance will give a vital impetus to progress—without it, no amount of help will advance the welfare of the people.

Thus if the countries of Latin America are ready to do their part—and I am sure they are—then I believe the United States, for its part, should help provide resources of a scope and magnitude sufficient to make this bold development plan a success—just as we helped to provide, against equal odds nearly, the resources adequate to help rebuild the economies of Western Europe. For only an effort of towering dimensions can ensure fulfillment of our plan for a decade of progress.

Secondly, I will shortly request a ministerial meeting of the Inter-American Economic and Social Council—a meeting at which we can begin the massive planning effort which will be at the heart of the Alliance for Progress.

For if our Alliance is to succeed, each Latin nation must formulate long-range plans for its own development—plans which establish targets and priorities—ensure monetary stability—establish the machinery for vital social change—stimulate private activity and initiative—and provide for a maximum national effort. These plans will be the foundation of our development effort, and the basis for the allocation of outside resources.

A greatly strengthened IA-ECOSOC—working with the Economic Commission for Latin America and the Inter-American Development Bank—can assemble the leading economists and experts of the hemisphere to help each country develop its own development plan—and provide a continuing review of economic progress in this hemisphere.

Third, I have this evening signed a request to the Congress for 500 million dollars as a first step in fulfilling the Act of Bogota. This is the first large-scale Inter-American effort—instituted by my predecessor President Eisenhower—to attack the social barriers which block economic progress. The money will be used to combat illiteracy—improve the productivity and use of their land—wipe out disease—attack archaic tax and land tenure structures—provide educational opportunities—and offer a broad range of projects designed to make the benefits of increasing abundance available to all. We will begin to commit these funds as soon as they are appropriated.

Fourth, we must support all economic integration which is a genuine step toward larger markets and greater competitive opportunity. The fragmentation of Latin American economies is a serious barrier to industrial growth. Projects such as the Central American common market and free trade areas in South America can help to remove these obstacles.

Fifth, the United States is ready to cooperate in serious, case-by-case examinations of commodity market problems. Frequent changes in commodity prices seriously injure the economies of many Latin American countries—draining their resources, and stultifying their growth. Together we must find practical methods of bringing an end to this pattern.

Sixth, we will immediately step up our Food for Peace emergency program—help establish food reserves in areas of recurrent drought—and help provide school lunches for children and offer feed grains for use in rural development. For hungry men and women cannot wait for economic discussions or diplomatic meetings—their need is urgent—and their hunger rests heavily on the conscience of their fellow men.

Seventh, all the people of the hemisphere must be allowed to share in the expanding wonders of science—wonders which have captured man's imagination—challenged the powers of his mind and given him the tools for rapid progress. I invite Latin American scientists to work with us in new projects in fields such as medicine and agriculture, physics and astronomy and desalinization—and to help plan for regional research laboratories in these and other fields—and to strengthen cooperation between American universities and laboratories.

We also intend to expand our science teacher training programs to include Latin American Instructors—to assist in establishing such programs in other American countries—and translate and make available revolutionary new teaching materials in physics, chemistry, biology and mathematics—so that the young of all nations may contribute their skills to the advance of science.

Eighth, we must rapidly expand the training of those needed to man the economies of rapidly developing countries. This means expanded technical training programs—for which the Peace Corps, for example, will be available when needed. It also means assistance to Latin American universities, graduate schools and research institutes.

We welcome proposals in Central America for intimate cooperation in higher education—cooperation which can achieve a regional effort of increased effectiveness and excellence. We are ready to help fill the gap in trained manpower—realizing that our ultimate goal must be a basic education for all who wish to learn.

Ninth, we reaffirm our pledge to come to the defense of any American nation, whose independence is endangered. As its confidence in the collective security system of the OAS spreads, it will be possible to devote to constructive use a major share of those resources now spent on the instruments of war. Even now—as the government of Chile has said—the time has come to take the first steps toward sensible limitations of arms. And the new generation of military leaders has shown an increasing awareness that armies can not only defend their countries—they can, as we have learned through our own Corps of Engineers, they can help to build them.

Tenth, we invite our friends in Latin America to contribute to the enrichment of life and culture in the United States. We need teachers of your literature and history and tradition—opportunities for our young people to study, in your universities—access to your music, your art and the thought of your great philosophers. For we know we have much to learn.

In this way you can help bring a fuller spiritual and intellectual life to the people of the United States—and contribute to understanding and mutual respect among the nations of the hemisphere.

With steps such as these, we propose to complete the revolution of the Americas—to build a hemisphere where all men can hope for a suitable standard of living—and all can live out their lives in dignity and in freedom.

To achieve this goal political freedom must accompany material progress. Our Alliance for Progress is an alliance of free governments—and it must work to eliminate tyranny from a hemisphere in which it has no rightful place. Therefore let us express our special friendship to the people of Cuba and the Dominican Republic—and the hope they will soon rejoin the society of free men, uniting with us in our common effort.

This political freedom must be accompanied by social change. For unless necessary social reforms, including land and tax reform, are freely made—unless we broaden the opportunity of all of our people—unless the great mass of Americans share in increasing prosperity—then our alliance, our revolution, our dream and our freedom will fail. But we call for social change by free men—change in the spirit of Washington and Jefferson, of Bolivar and San Martin and Marti—not change which seeks to impose on men tyrannies which we cast out a century and a half ago. Our motto is what it has always been—progress yes, tyranny no—*progreso si, tirania no!*

But our greatest challenge comes from within—the task of creating an American civilization where spiritual and cultural values are strengthened by an ever-broadening base of material advance—where, within the rich diversity of its own traditions, each nation is free to follow its own path towards progress.

The completion of our task will, of course, require the efforts of all the governments of our hemisphere. But the efforts of governments alone will never be enough. In the end, the people must choose and the people must help themselves.

And so I say to the men and women of the Americas—to the campesino in the fields, to the obrero in the cities, to the estudiante in the schools—prepare your mind and heart for the task ahead—call forth your strength and let each devote his energies to the betterment of all, so that your children and our children in this hemisphere can find an ever richer and a freer life.

Let us once again transform the American continent into a vast crucible of revolutionary ideas and efforts—a tribute to the power of the creative energies of free men and women—an example to all the world that liberty and progress walk hand in hand. Let us once again awaken our American revolution until it guides the struggles of people everywhere—not with an imperialism of force or fear—but the rule of courage and freedom and hope for the future of man.

Source: John F. Kennedy Library, National Security File, Regional Security, Box 215.

127. KENNEDY'S ADDRESS ON THE CUBAN MISSILE CRISIS
22 October 1962

In October 1962, the United States and the Soviet Union were poised on the brink of thermonuclear war. The potential trigger was the deployment of Soviet interregional ballistic missiles to Cuba. On 23 October, the president appeared on national television to inform a world audience of the situation and some of the American demands necessary to resolve it.

Good evening, my fellow citizens:

This Government, as promised, has maintained the closest surveillance of the Soviet military buildup on the island of Cuba. Within the past week, unmistakable evidence has established the fact that a series of offensive missile sites is now in preparation on that imprisoned island. The purpose of these bases can be none other than to provide a nuclear strike capability against the Western Hemisphere.

Upon receiving the first preliminary hard information of this nature last Tuesday morning at 9 a.m., I directed that our surveillance be stepped up. And having now confirmed and completed our evaluation of the evidence and our decision on a course of action, this Government feels obliged to report this new crisis to you in fullest detail.

The characteristics of these new missile sites indicate two distinct types of installations. Several of them include medium range ballistic missiles, capable of carrying a nuclear warhead for a distance of more than 1000 nautical miles. Each of these missiles, in short, is capable of striking Washington, D.C., the Panama Canal, Cape Canaveral, Mexico City, or any other city in the southeastern part of the United States, in Central America, or in the Caribbean area.

Additional sites not yet completed appear to be designed for intermediate range ballistic missiles capable of traveling more than twice as far—and thus capable of striking most of the major cities in the Western Hemisphere, ranging as far north as Hudson Bay, Canada, and as far south as Lima, Peru. In addition, jet bombers, capable of carrying nuclear weapons, are now being uncrated and assembled in Cuba, while the necessary air bases are being prepared.

This urgent transformation of Cuba into an important strategic base by the presence of these large, long-range, and clearly offensive weapons of sudden mass destruction constitutes an explicit threat to the peace and security of all the Americas, in flagrant and deliberate defiance of the Rio Pact of 1947, the traditions of this Nation and hemisphere, the joint resolution of the 87th Congress, the Charter of the United Nations, and my own public warnings to the Soviets on September 4 and 13. This action also contradicts the repeated assurances of Soviet spokesmen, both publicly and privately delivered, that the arms buildup in Cuba would retain its original defensive character, and that the Soviet Union had no need or desire to station strategic missiles on the territory of any other nation.

The size of this undertaking makes clear that it has been planned for some months. Yet only last month, after I had made clear the distinction between any introduction of ground-to-ground missiles and the existence of defensive anti-aircraft missiles, the Soviet Government publicly stated on September 11th that, and I quote, "the armaments and military equipment sent to Cuba are designed exclusively for defensive purposes," that, and I quote the Soviet Government, "there is no need for the Soviet Government to shift its weapons . . . for a retaliatory blow to any other country, for instance Cuba," and that, and I quote their government, "the Soviet Union has so powerful rockets to carry these nuclear warheads that there is no need to search for sites for them beyond the boundaries of the Soviet Union." That statement was false.

Only last Thursday, as evidence of this rapid offensive buildup was already in my hand, Soviet Foreign Minister Gromyko told me in my office that he was instructed to make it clear once again, as he said his government had already done, that Soviet assistance to Cuba, and I quote, "pursued solely for the purpose of contributing to the defense capabilities of Cuba," that, and I quote him, "training by Soviet specialists of Cuban nationals in handling defensive armaments was by no means offensive, and if it were otherwise," Mr. Gromyko went on, "the Soviet Government would never become involved in rendering such assistance." That statement also was false.

Neither the United States of America nor the world community of nations can tolerate deliberate deception and offensive threats on the part of any nation, large or small. We no longer live in a world where only the actual firing of weapons represents an efficient challenge to a nation's security to constitute maximum peril. Nuclear weapons are so destructive and ballistic missiles are so swift, that any substantially increased possibility of their use or any sudden change in their deployment may well be regarded as a definite threat to peace.

For many years, both the Soviet Union and the United States, recognizing this fact, have deployed strategic nuclear weapons with great care, never upsetting the precarious status quo which insured that these weapons would not be used in the absence of some vital challenge. Our own strategic missiles have never been transferred to the territory of any other nation under a cloak of secrecy and deception; and our history—unlike that of the Soviets since the end of World War II—demonstrates that we have no desire to dominate or conquer any other nation or impose our system upon its people. Nevertheless, American citizens have become adjusted to living daily on the bull's-eye of Soviet missiles located inside the U.S.S.R. or in submarines.

In that sense, missiles in Cuba add to an already clear and present danger—although it should be noted the nations of Latin America have never previously been subjected to a potential nuclear threat.

But this secret, swift, and extraordinary buildup of Communist missiles—in an area well known to have a special and historical relationship to the United States and the nations of the Western Hemisphere, in violation of Soviet assurances, and in defiance of American and hemispheric policy—this sudden, clandestine decision to station strategic weapons for the first time outside of Soviet soil—is a deliberately provocative and unjustified change in the status quo which cannot be accepted by this country, if our courage and our commitments are ever to be trusted again by either friend or foe.

The 1930s taught us a clear lesson: aggressive conduct, if allowed to go unchecked and unchallenged, ultimately leads to war. This nation is opposed to war. We are also true to our word. Our unswerving objective, therefore, must be to prevent the use of these missiles against this or any other country, and to secure their withdrawal or elimination from the Western Hemisphere.

Our policy has been one of patience and restraint, as befits a peaceful and powerful nation, which leads a worldwide alliance. We have been determined not to be diverted from our central concerns by mere irritants and fanatics. But now further action is required—and it is under way, and these actions may only be the beginning. We will not prematurely or unnecessarily risk the costs of worldwide nuclear war in which even the fruits of victory would be ashes in our mouth—but neither will we shrink from that risk at any time it must be faced.

Acting, therefore, in the defense of our own security and of the entire Western Hemisphere, and under the authority entrusted to me by the Constitution as endorsed by the resolution of the Congress, I have directed that the following initial steps be taken immediately:

First: To halt this offensive buildup, a strict quarantine on all offensive military equipment under shipment to Cuba is being initiated. All ships of any kind bound for Cuba from whatever nation or port will, if found to contain cargoes of offensive weapons, be turned back. This quarantine will be extended, if needed, to other types of cargo and carriers. We are not at this time, however, denying the necessities of life as the Soviets attempted to do in their Berlin blockade of 1948.

Second: I have directed the continued and increased close surveillance of

Cuba and its military buildup. The foreign ministers of the OAS, in their communique of October 6th, rejected secrecy on such matters in this hemisphere. Should these offensive military preparations continue, thus increasing the threat to the hemisphere, further action will be justified. I have directed the Armed Forces to prepare for any eventualities; and I trust that in the interest of both the Cuban people and the Soviet technicians at the sites, the hazards to all concerned of continuing this threat will be recognized.

Third: It shall be the policy of this Nation to regard any nuclear missile launched from Cuba against any nation in the Western Hemisphere as an attack by the Soviet Union on the United States, requiring a full retaliatory response upon the Soviet Union.

Fourth: As a necessary military precaution, I have reinforced our base at Guantanamo, evacuated today the dependents of our personnel there, and ordered additional military units to be on a standby alert basis.

Fifth: We are calling tonight for an immediate meeting of the Organ of Consultation under the Organization of American States, to consider this threat to hemispheric security and to invoke articles 6 and 8 of the Rio Treaty in support of all necessary action. The United Nations Charter allows for regional security arrangements—and the nations of this hemisphere decided long ago against the military presence of outside powers. Our other allies around the world have also been alerted.

Sixth: Under the Charter of the United Nations, we are asking tonight that an emergency meeting of the Security Council be convoked without delay to take action against this latest Soviet threat to world peace. Our resolution will call for the prompt dismantling and withdrawal of all offensive weapons in Cuba, under the supervision of U.N. observers, before the quarantine can be lifted.

Seventh and finally: I call upon Chairman Khrushchev to halt and eliminate this clandestine, reckless, and provocative threat to world peace and to stable relations between our two nations. I call upon him further to abandon this course of world domination, and to join in an historic effort to end the perilous arms race and to transform the history of man. He has an opportunity now to move the world back from the abyss of destruction—by returning to his government's own words that it had no need to station missiles outside its own territory, and withdrawing these weapons from Cuba—by refraining from any action which will widen or deepen the present crisis—and then by participating in a search for peaceful and permanent solutions.

This Nation is prepared to present its case against the Soviet threat to peace, and our own proposals for a peaceful world, at any time and in any forum—in the OAS, in the United Nations, or in any other meeting that could be useful—without limiting our freedom of action. We have in the past made strenuous efforts to limit the spread of nuclear weapons. We have proposed the elimination of all arms and military bases in a fair and effective disarmament treaty. We are prepared to discuss new proposals for the removal of tensions on both sides—including the possibilities of a genuinely independent Cuba, free to determine its own destiny. We have no wish to war with the Soviet Union—for we are a peaceful people who desire to live in peace with all other peoples.

But it is difficult to settle or even discuss these problems in an atmosphere of intimidation. That is why this latest Soviet threat—or any other threat which is made either independently or in response to our actions this week—must and will be met with determination. Any hostile move anywhere in the world against the safety and freedom of peoples to whom we are committed—including in particular the brave people of West Berlin—will be met by whatever action is needed.

Finally, I want to say a few words to the captive people of Cuba, to whom this speech is being directly carried by special radio facilities. I speak to you as a friend, as one who knows of your deep attachment to your fatherland, as one who shares your aspirations for liberty and justice for all. And I have watched and the American people have watched with deep sorrow how your nationalist revolution was betrayed—and how your fatherland fell under foreign domination. Now your leaders are no longer Cuban leaders inspired by Cuban ideals. They are puppets and agents of an international conspiracy which has turned Cuba against your friends and neighbors in the Americas—and turned it into the first Latin American country to become a target for nuclear war—the first Latin American country to have these weapons on its soil.

These new weapons are not in your interest. They contribute nothing to your peace and well-being. They can only undermine it. But this country has no wish to cause you to suffer or to impose any system upon you. We know that your lives and land are being used as pawns by those who deny your freedom.

Many times in the past, the Cuban people have risen to throw out tyrants who destroyed their liberty. And I have no doubt that most Cubans today look forward to the time when they will be truly free—free from foreign domination, free to choose their own leaders, free to select their own system, free to own their own land, free to speak and write and worship without fear or degradation. And then shall Cuba be welcomed back to the society of free nations and to the association of nations of this hemisphere.

My fellow citizens: let no one doubt that this is a difficult and dangerous effort on which we have set out. No one can foresee precisely what course it will take or what costs or casualties will be incurred. Many months of sacrifice and self-discipline lie ahead—months in which both our patience and our will will be tested—months in which many threats and denunciations will keep us aware of our dangers. But the greatest danger of all would be to do nothing.

The path we have chosen for the present is full of hazards, as all paths are—but it is the one most consistent with our character and courage as a nation and our commitments around the world. The cost of freedom is always high—but Americans have always paid it. And one path we shall never choose, and that is the path of surrender or submission.

Our goal is not the victory of might, but the vindication of right—not peace at the expense of freedom, but both peace and freedom, here in this hemisphere, and, we hope, around the world. God willing, that goal will be achieved. Thank you and good night.

Source: Public Papers of the Presidents of the United States, John F. Kennedy, 1962 (Washington, DC: Government Printing Office, 1963), 806–9.

128. NSAM 288
17 March 1964

The November 1963 assassination of South Vietnamese president Ngo Dinh Diem further undercut an already unstable country. The death of John F. Kennedy only weeks later placed the burden of crafting a response to a likely South Vietnamese collapse in the hands of Lyndon Baines Johnson. While he preached nonintervention during the 1964 presidential election campaign, Johnson ordered preparations for an escalation of the U.S. role in Vietnam.

[The United States' policy is] to prepare immediately to be in a position on 72 hours' notice to initiate the full range of Laotian and Cambodian "Border Control actions" . . . and the "Retaliatory Actions" against North Vietnam, and to be in a position on 30 days' notice to initiate the program of "Graduated Overt Military Pressure" against North Vietnam. . . .

We seek an independent non-Communist South Vietnam. We do not require that it serve as a Western base or as a member of a Western Alliance. South Vietnam must be free, however, to accept outside assistance as required to maintain its security. This assistance should be able to take the form not only of economic and social measures but also police and military help to root out and control insurgent elements.

Unless we can achieve this objective in South Vietnam, almost all of Southeast Asia will probably fall under Communist dominance (all of Vietnam, Laos, and Cambodia), accommodate to Communism so as to remove effective U.S. and anti-Communist influence (Burma), or fall under the dominion of forces not now explicitly Communist but likely then to become so (Indonesia taking over Malaysia). Thailand might hold on for a period without help, but would be under grave pressure. Even the Philippines would become shaky, and the threat to India on the West, Australia and New Zealand to the South, and Taiwan, Korea, and Japan to the North and East would be greatly increased.

All of these consequences would probably have been true even if the U.S. had not since 1954, and especially since 1961, become so heavily engaged in South Vietnam. However, that fact accentuates the impact of a Communist South Vietnam not only in Asia but in the rest of the world, where the South Vietnam conflict is regarded as a test case of U.S. capacity to help a nation to meet the Communist "war of liberation."

Thus, purely in terms of foreign policy, the stakes are high. . . .

We are now trying to help South Vietnam defeat the Viet Cong, supported from the North, by means short of unqualified use of U.S. combat forces. We are not acting against North Vietnam except by a modest "covert" program operated by South Vietnamese (and a few Chinese Nationalists)—a program so limited that it is unlikely to have any significant effect. . . .

There were and are some sound reasons for the limits imposed by the present policy—the South Vietnamese must win their own fight; U.S. intervention on a larger scale, and/or GVN actions against the North, would disturb key allies and other nations; etc. In any case, it is vital that we continue to take every reasonable measure to assure success in South Vietnam. The policy choice is not an "either/or" between this course of action and possible pressure against the North: the former is essential and without regard to our decision with respect to the latter. The latter can, at best, only reinforce the former. . . .

Many of the actions described in the succeeding paragraphs fit right into the framework of the [pacification] plan announced by Khanh. Wherever possible, we should tie our urgings of such actions to Khanh's own formulation of them, so that he will be carrying out a Vietnamese plan and not one imposed by the United States. . . .

. . . the judgment of all senior people in Saigon, with which we concur, was that the possible military advantages of such action would be far outweighed by adverse psychological impact. It would cut across the whole basic picture of the Vietnamese winning their own war and lay us wide open to hostile propaganda both within South Vietnam and outside.

Source: Neil Sheehan, Hedrick Smith, E. W. Kenworthy, and Fox Butterfield, eds., *The Pentagon Papers* (New York: Bantam Books, 1971), 283–85.

---

129. GULF OF TONKIN RESOLUTION
7 August 1964

In early August 1964, the Johnson administration reported two unprovoked clashes between American naval units and North Vietnam in the Gulf of Tonkin. Although the second attack could not be verified, the administration pressed forward with a request for a congressional resolution that supported U.S. retaliation. The subsequent resolution later served as a legal justification for the escalation of American intervention in Vietnam.

THE RESOLUTION: Whereas naval units of the Communist regime in Vietnam, in violation of the principles of the Charter of the United Nations and of international law, have deliberately and repeatedly attacked United States naval vessels lawfully present in international waters, and have thereby created a serious threat to international peace;

Whereas these attacks are part of a deliberate and systematic campaign of aggression that the Communist regime in North Vietnam has been waging against its neighbors and the nations joined with them in the collective defense of their freedom;

Whereas the United States is assisting the peoples of southeast Asia to protect their freedom and has no territorial, military or political ambitions in that area, but desires only that these peoples should be left in peace to work out their own destinies in their own way: now, therefore, be it

Resolved by the Senate and House of Representatives of the United States of America in Congress assembled, That the Congress approves and supports the determination of the President, as Commander in Chief, to take all necessary measures to repel any armed attack against the forces of the United States and to prevent further aggression.

SEC. 2. The United States regards as vital to its national interest and to world peace the maintenance of international peace and security in southeast Asia. Consonant with the Constitution and the Charter of the United Nations and in accordance with its obligations under the Southeast Asia Collective Defense Treaty, the United States is, therefore, prepared, as the President determines, to take all necessary steps, including the use of armed force, to assist any member or protocol state of the Southeast Asia Collective Defense Treaty requesting assistance in defense of its freedom.

SEC. 3. This resolution shall expire when the President shall determine that the peace and security of the area is reasonably assured by international conditions created by action of the United Nations or otherwise, except that it may be terminated earlier by concurrent resolution of the Congress.

Source: U.S. *Congressional Record*, vol. 110, Part 14 (Washington, DC: Government Printing Office), 1847.

130. JOHNSON'S JOHNS HOPKINS ADDRESS ON VIETNAM
7 April 1965

One month after the first deployment of American marines to South Vietnam, President Johnson gave a speech at Johns Hopkins University that described the reasons for U.S. intervention. Although the president alluded to the possibility of a negotiated peace to end the conflict, his speech was also intended to express American resolve against the spread of Communism.

... Over this war, and all Asia, is the deepening shadow of Communist China. The rulers in Hanoi are urged on by Peking. This is a regime which has destroyed freedom in Tibet, attacked India, and been condemned by the United Nations for aggression in Korea. It is a nation which is helping the forces of violence in almost every continent. The contest in Vietnam is part of a wider pattern of aggressive purpose.

Why are these realities our concern? Why are we in South Vietnam? We are there because we have a promise to keep. Since 1954 every American President has offered support to the people of South Vietnam. We have helped to build, and we have helped to defend. Thus, over many years, we have made a national pledge to help South Vietnam defend its independence. And I intend to keep our promise.

To dishonor that pledge, to abandon this small and brave nation to its enemy, and to the terror that must follow, would be an unforgivable wrong.

We are also there to strengthen world order. Around the globe, from Berlin to Thailand, are people whose well-being rests, in part, on the belief that they can count on us if they are attacked. To leave Vietnam to its fate would shake the confidence of all these people in the value of American commitment, the value of America's word. The result would be increased unrest and instability, and even wider war.

We are also there because there are great stakes in the balance. Let no one think for a moment that retreat from Vietnam would bring an end to conflict. The battle would be renewed in one country and then another. The central lesson of our time is that the appetite of aggression is never satisfied. To withdraw from one battlefield means only to prepare for the next. We must say in Southeast Asia, as we did in Europe, in the words of the Bible: "Hitherto shalt thou come, but no further."

There are those who say that all our effort there will be futile, that China's power is such it is bound to dominate all Southeast Asia. But there is no end to that argument until all the nations of Asia are swallowed up.

There are those who wonder why we have a responsibility there. We have it for the same reason we have a responsibility for the defense of freedom in Europe. World War II was fought in both Europe and Asia, and when it ended we found ourselves with continued responsibility for the defense of freedom.

Our objective is the independence of South Vietnam, and its freedom from attack. We want nothing for ourselves, only that the people of South Vietnam be allowed to guide their own country in their own way.

We will do everything necessary to reach that objective. And we will do only what is absolutely necessary.

In recent months, attacks on South Vietnam were stepped up. Thus it became necessary to increase our response and to make attacks by air. This is not a change of purpose. It is a change in what we believe that purpose requires.

We do this in order to slow down aggression.

We do this to increase the confidence of the brave people of South Vietnam who have bravely borne this brutal battle for so many years and with so many casualties.

And we do this to convince the leaders of North Vietnam, and all who seek to share their conquest, of a very simple fact:

We will not be defeated.

We will not grow tired.

We will not withdraw, either openly or under the cloak of a meaningless agreement. . . .

Once this is clear, then it should also be clear that the only path for reasonable men is the path of peaceful settlement.

Such peace demands an independent South Vietnam securely guaranteed and able to shape its own relationships to all others, free from outside interference, tied to no alliance, a military base for no other country.

These are the essentials of any final settlement.

We will never be second in the search for such a peaceful settlement in Vietnam.

There may be many ways to this kind of peace: in discussion or negotiation with the governments concerned; in large groups or in small ones; in the reaffirmation of old agreements or their strengthening with new ones.

We have stated this position over and over again fifty times and more, to friend and foe alike. And we remain ready, with this purpose, for unconditional discussions.

And until that bright and necessary day of peace we will try to keep conflict from spreading. We have no desire to see thousands die in battle, Asians or Americans. We have no desire to devastate that which the people of North Vietnam have built with toil and sacrifice. We will use our power with restraint and with all the wisdom we can command. But we will use it. . . .

We will always oppose the effort of one nation to conquer another nation.

We will do this because our own security is at stake.

But there is more to it than that. For our generation has a dream. It is a very old dream. But we have the power and now we have the opportunity to make it come true.

For centuries, nations have struggled among each other. But we dream of a world where disputes are settled by law and reason. And we will try to make it so.

For most of history men have bated and killed one another in battle. But we dream of an end to war. And we will try to make it so.

For all existence most men have lived in poverty, threatened by hunger. But we dream of a world where all are fed and charged with hope. And we will help to make it so.

The ordinary men and women of North Vietnam and South Vietnam—of China and India—of Russia and America—are brave people. They are filled with the same proportions of hate and fear, of love and hope. Most of them want the same things for themselves and their families. Most of them do not want their sons ever to die in battle, or see the homes of others destroyed. . . .

Every night before I turn out the lights to sleep, I ask myself this question: Have I done everything that I can do to unite this country? Have I done everything I can to help unite the world, to try to bring peace and hope to all the peoples of the world? Have I done enough?

Ask yourselves that question in your homes and in this hall tonight. Have we done all we could? Have we done enough? . . .

Source: U.S. Department of State, *Department of State Bulletin*, vol. 52, no. 1348 (26 April 1965): 606–10.

131. WHEELER'S MEMORANDUM ON THE TET OFFENSIVE
27 February 1968

At the end of January 1968, Communist forces in South Vietnam launched a massive attack against nearly every major city, town, and military installation in the country. Although the offensive was successfully repelled by American and South Vietnamese forces, it prompted a major reevaluation of U.S. policy and the prospects for victory in Southeast Asia.

1. The Chairman, JCS and party visited SVN on 23, 24 and 25 February. This report summarizes the impressions and facts developed through conversations and briefings at MACV and with senior commanders throughout the country.

SUMMARY

—The current situation in Vietnam is still developing and fraught with opportunities as well as dangers.

—There is no question in the mind of MACV that the enemy went all out for a general offensive and general uprising and apparently believed that he would succeed in bringing the war to an early successful conclusion.

—The enemy failed to achieve his initial objective but is continuing his effort. Although many of his units were badly hurt, the judgment is that he has the will and the capability to continue.

—Enemy losses have been heavy; he has failed to achieve his prime objectives of mass uprisings and capture of a large number of the capital cities and towns. Morale in enemy units which were badly mauled or where the men were oversold the idea of a decisive victory at TET probably has suffered severely. However, with replacements, his indoctrination system would seem capable of maintaining morale at a generally adequate level. His determination appears to be unshaken.

—The enemy is operating with relative freedom in the countryside, probably recruiting heavily and no doubt infiltrating NVA units and personnel. His recovery is likely to be rapid; his supplies are adequate; and he is trying to maintain the momentum of his winter-spring offensive.

—The structure of the GVN held up but its effectiveness has suffered.

—The RVNAF held up against the initial assault with gratifying, and in a way, surprising strength and fortitude. However, RVNAF is now in a defensive posture around towns and cities and there is concern about how well they will bear up under sustained pressure.

—The initial attack nearly succeeded in a dozen places, and defeat in those places was only averted by the timely reaction of U.S. forces. In short, it was a very near thing.

—There is no doubt that the RD [Rural Development] Program has suffered a severe set back.

—RVNAF was not badly hurt physically—they should recover strength and equipment rather quickly (equipment in 2–3 months—strength in 3–6 months). Their problems are more psychological than physical.

—U.S. forces have lost none of their pre-TET capability. . . .

THE SITUATION AS IT STANDS TODAY:

a. Enemy capabilities.

(1) The enemy has been hurt badly in the populated lowlands, is practically intact elsewhere. He committed over 67,000 combat maneuver forces plus perhaps 25% or 17,000 more impressed men and boys, for a total of about 84,000. He lost 40,000 killed, at least 3,000 captured, and perhaps 5,000 disabled or died of wounds. He had peaked his force total to about 240,000 just before TET, by hard recruiting, infiltration, civilian impressment, and drawdowns on service and guerrilla personnel. So he has lost about one-fifth of his total strength. About two-thirds of his trained, organized unit strength can continue offensive action. He is probably infiltrating and recruiting heavily in the countryside while allied forces are securing the urban areas. . . . The enemy has adequate munitions, stockpiled in-country and available through the DMZ, Laos, and Cambodia, to support major attacks and countrywide pressure; food procurement may be a problem. . . . Besides strength losses, the enemy now has morale and training problems which currently limit combat effectiveness of VC guerrilla, main and local forces. . . .

d. GVN Strength and Effectiveness:

(1) Psychological—the people in South Vietnam were handed a psychological blow, particularly in the urban areas where the feeling of security had been strong. There is a fear of further attacks.

(2) The structure of the Government was not shattered and continues to function but at greatly reduced effectiveness.

(3) In many places, the RD program has been set back badly. In other places the program was untouched in the initial stage of the offensive. MACV reports that of the 555 RD cadre groups, 278 remain in hamlets, 245 are in district and province towns on security duty, while 32 are unaccounted for. It is not clear as to when, or even whether, it will be possible to return to the RD program in its earlier form. As long as the VC prowl the countryside it will be impossible, in many places, even to tell exactly what has happened to the program.

(4) Refugees—An additional 470,000 refugees were generated during the offensive. . . . It is anticipated that the care and reestablishment of the 250,000 persons or 50,000 family units who have lost their homes will require from GVN sources the expenditure of 500 million piasters for their temporary care and resettlement plus an estimated 30,000 metric tons of rice. . . .

WHAT DOES THE FUTURE HOLD

a. Probable enemy strategy. We see the enemy pursuing a reinforced offensive to enlarge his control throughout the country and keep pressure on the government and allies. We expect him to maintain strong threats in the DMZ areas, at Khe Sanh, in the highlands, and at Saigon, and to attack in force when conditions seem favorable. He is likely to try to gain control of the country's northern provinces. He will likely continue efforts to encircle cities and province capitals to isolate and disrupt normal activities, and infiltrate them to create chaos. He will seek maximum attrition of RVNAF elements. Against U.S. forces, he will emphasize attacks by fire on airfields and installations, using assaults and ambushes selectively. His central objective continues to be the destruction of the Government of SVN and its armed forces. As a minimum he hopes to seize sufficient territory and gain control of enough people to support establishment of the groups and committees he proposes for participation in an NLF dominated government.

Source: Neil Sheehan, Hedrick Smith, E. W. Kenworthy, and Fox Butterfield, eds., *The Pentagon Papers* (New York: Bantam Books, 1971), 615–21.

132. JOHNSON'S POST-TET ADDRESS TO THE NATION
31 March 1968

The Tet Offensive was a political disaster for Lyndon B. Johnson. It shattered previous administration claims that victory in Vietnam was at hand and demonstrated in the minds of many Americans that the war had reached a stalemate. Eugene McCarthy's near victory in the March 1968

*New Hampshire primary indicated to Johnson that he no longer possessed
the political credibility necessary for reelection. At the end of the month,
he concluded more than three decades of public service.*

Good evening my fellow Americans. Tonight I want to speak to you of peace
in Vietnam and Southeast Asia.

No other question so preoccupies our people. No other dream so absorbs the
250 million human beings who live in that part of the world. No other goal
motivates American policy in Southeast Asia.

For years, representatives of our Government and others have traveled the
world seeking to find a basis for peace talks.

Since last September, they have carried the offer that I made in San Antonio.

The offer was this: that the United States would stop its bombardment of
North Vietnam when that would lead promptly to productive discussions—and
that we would assume that North Vietnam would not take military advantage
of our restraint.

Hanoi denounced this offer, both privately and publicly. Even while the search
for peace was going on, North Vietnam rushed their preparations for a savage
assault on the people, the Government, and the allies of South Vietnam.

Their attack—during the Tet holidays—failed to achieve its principal objectives.

It did not collapse the elected governors of South Vietnam or shatter its army,
as the Communists had hoped.

It did not produce a "general uprising" among the people of the cities, as they
had predicted.

The Communists were unable to maintain control of any of the more than
thirty cities that they attacked. And they took very heavy casualties.

But they did compel the South Vietnamese and their allies to move certain
forces from the countryside into the cities. They caused widespread disruption
and suffering. Their attacks, and the battles that followed, made refugees of half
a million human beings.

The Communists may renew their attack any day. They are, it appears, trying
to make 1968 the year of decision in South Vietnam—the year that brings, if
not final victory or defeat, at least a turning point in the struggle.

This much is clear: If they do mount another round of heavy attacks, they
will not succeed in destroying the fighting power of South Vietnam and its allies.

But tragically, this is also clear: Many men—on both sides of the struggle—
will be lost. A nation that has already suffered twenty years of warfare will
suffer once again. Armies on both sides will take new casualties. And the war
will go on.

There is no need for this to be so.

There is no need to delay the talks that could bring an end to this long and
this bloody war.

Tonight I renew the offer I made last August—to stop the bombardment of

North Vietnam. We ask that talks begin promptly, that they be serious talks on the substance of peace. We assume that during those talks Hanoi will not take advantage of our restraint.

We are prepared to move immediately toward peace through negotiations.

So tonight, in the hope that this action will lead to early talks, I am taking the first step to deescalate the conflict. We are reducing—substantially reducing—the present level of hostilities. And we are doing so unilaterally and at once.

Tonight I have ordered our aircraft and our naval vessels to make no attacks on North Vietnam, except in the area north of the demilitarized zone where the continuing enemy buildup directly threatens Allied forward positions and where the movements of their troops and supplies are clearly related to that threat.

The area in which we are stopping our attacks includes almost 90 percent of North Vietnam's population and most of its territory. Thus there will be no attacks around the principal populated areas or in the food-producing areas of North Vietnam.

Even this very limited bombing of the North could come to an early end if our restraint is matched by restraint in Hanoi. But I cannot in good conscience stop all bombing so long as to do so would immediately and directly endanger the lives of our men and our allies. Whether a complete bombing halt becomes possible in the future will be determined by events.

Our purpose in this action is to bring about a reduction in the level of violence that now exists.

It is to save the lives of brave men and to save the lives of innocent women and children. It is to permit the contending forces to move closer to a political settlement.

And tonight I call upon the United Kingdom and I call upon the Soviet Union, as cochairmen of the Geneva conferences and as Permanent members of the United Nations Security Council, to do all they can to move from the unilateral act of deescalation that I have just announced toward genuine peace in Southeast Asia.

Now, as in the past, the United States is ready to send its representatives to any forum, at any time, to discuss the means of bringing this ugly war to an end.

I am designating one of our most distinguished Americans, Ambassador Averell Harriman, as my personal representative for such talks. In addition, I have asked Ambassador Llewellyn Thompson, who returned from Moscow for consultation, to be available to join Ambassador Harriman at Geneva or any other suitable place just as soon as Hanoi agrees to a conference.

I call upon President Ho Chi Minh to respond positively and favorably to this new step toward peace.

But if peace does not come now through negotiations, it will come when

Hanoi understands that our common resolve is unshakable and our common strength is invincible. . . .

We applaud this evidence of determination on the part of South Vietnam. Our first priority will be to support their effort.

We shall accelerate the reequipment of South Vietnam's armed forces in order to meet the enemy's increased firepower. This will enable them progressively to undertake a larger share of combat operations against the Communist invaders.

On many occasions I have told the American people that we would send to Vietnam those forces that are required to accomplish our mission there. So, with that as our guide, we have previously authorized a force level of approximately 525,000. . . .

. . . let it never be forgotten: Peace will come also because America sent her sons to help secure it.

It has not been easy—far from it. During the past four and a half years, it has been my fate and my responsibility to be Commander in Chief. I lived daily and nightly with the cost of this war. I know the pain that it has inflicted. I know perhaps better than anyone the misgivings that it has aroused.

Throughout this entire long period, I have been sustained by a single principle: that what we are doing now in Vietnam is vital not only to the security of Southeast Asia, but it is vital to the security of every American.

Surely we have treaties which we must respect. Surely we have commitments that we are going to keep. Resolutions of the Congress testify to the need to resist aggression in the world and in Southeast Asia.

But the heart of our involvement in South Vietnam—under three different Presidents, three separate administrations—has always been America's own security.

And the larger purpose of our involvement has always been to help the nations of Southeast Asia become independent and stand alone, self-sustaining as members of a great world community—at peace with themselves and at peace with all others.

With such an Asia, our country—and the world—will be far more secure than it is tonight.

I believe that a peaceful Asia is far nearer to reality because of what America has done in Vietnam. I believe that the men who endure the dangers of battle—fighting there for us tonight—are helping the entire world avoid far greater conflicts, far wider wars, far more destruction, than this one. . . .

Yet I believe that we must always be mindful of this one thing, whatever the trials and the tests ahead: The ultimate strength of our country and our cause will lie not in powerful weapons or infinite resources or boundless wealth but will lie in the unity of our people.

This I believe very deeply.

Throughout my entire public career I have followed the personal philosophy that I am a free man, an American, a public servant, and a member of my party, in that order always and only.

For thirty-seven years in the service of our nation, first as a Congressman, as a Senator and as Vice President and now as your President, I have put the unity of the people first. I have put it ahead of any divisive partisanship.

And in these times as in times before, it is true that a house divided against itself by the spirit of faction, of party, of region, of religion, of race, is a house that cannot stand.

There is division in the American house now. There is divisiveness among us all tonight. And holding the trust that is mine, as President of all the people, I cannot disregard the peril to the progress of the American people and the hope and the prospect of peace for all peoples.

So I would ask all Americans, whatever their personal interests or concern, to guard against divisiveness and all its ugly consequences.

Fifty-two months and ten days ago, in a moment of tragedy and trauma, the duties of this Office fell upon me. I asked then for your help and God's, that we might continue America on its course, binding up our wounds, healing our history, moving forward in new unity, to clear the American agenda and to keep the American commitment for all of our people.

United we have kept that commitment. United we have enlarged that commitment.

Through all time to come, I think America will be a stronger nation, a more just society, and a land of greater opportunity and fulfillment because of what we have all done together in these years of unparalleled achievement.

Our reward will come in the life of freedom, peace, and hope that our children will enjoy through ages ahead.

What we won when all of our people united just must not now be lost in suspicion, distrust, selfishness, and politics among any of our people.

Believing this as I do, I have concluded that I should not permit the Presidency to become involved in the partisan divisions that are developing in this political year.

With America's sons in the fields far away, with America's future under challenge right here at home, with our hopes and the world's hopes for peace in the balance every day, I do not believe that I should devote an hour or a day of my time to any personal partisan causes or to any duties other than the awesome duties of this Office—the Presidency of your country.

Accordingly, I shall not seek, and I will not accept, the nomination of my party for another term as your President.

But let men everywhere know, however, that a strong, a confident, and a vigilant America stands ready tonight to seek an honorable peace—and stands ready tonight to defend an honored cause—whatever the price, whatever the burden, whatever the sacrifices that duty may require.

Source: U.S. Department of State, *Department of State Bulletin*, vol. 58, no. 1503 (15 April 1968): 481–86.

133.   NIXON DOCTRINE
25 July 1969

The Nixon administration signaled a new era of retrenchment in American foreign policy. In 1969 Richard Nixon's intention was to set more realistic priorities for U.S. strategic commitments, with particular emphasis on Europe, China, and Japan. One of the first places that this new era of limits became apparent was in Southeast Asia.

[4.] Q. Mr. President, sir, on the question of U.S. military relationships in Asia, if I may ask a hypothetical question: If a leader of one of the countries with which we have had close military relationships, either through SEATO or in Vietnam, should say, "Well, you are pulling out of Vietnam with your troops, we can read in the newspapers. How can we know that you will remain to play a significant role as you say you wish to do in security arrangements in Asia?" What kind of an approach can you take to that question?

THE PRESIDENT. I have already indicated that the answer to that question is not an easy one—not easy because we will be greatly tempted when that question is put to us to indicate that if any nation desires the assistance of the United States militarily in order to meet an internal or external threat, we will provide it.

However, I believe that the time has come when the United States, in our relations with all of our Asian friends, be quite emphatic on two points: One, that we will keep our treaty commitments, our treaty commitments, for example, with Thailand under SEATO; but, two, that as far as the problems of internal security are concerned, as far as the problems of military defense, except for the threat of a major power involving nuclear weapons, that the United States is going to encourage and has a right to expect that this problem will be increasingly handled by, and the responsibility for it taken by, the Asian nations themselves.

I believe, incidentally, from my preliminary conversations with several Asian leaders over the past few months that they are going to be willing to undertake this responsibility. It will not be easy. But if the United States just continues down the road of responding to requests for assistance, of assuming the primary responsibility for defending these countries when they have internal problems or external problems, they are never going to take care of themselves.

I should add to that, too, that when we talk about collective security for Asia, I realize that at this time that looks like a weak reed. It actually is. But looking down the road—I am speaking now of 5 years from now, 10 years from now—I think collective security, insofar as it deals with internal threats to any one of the countries, or insofar as it deals with a threat other than that posed by a nuclear power, I believe that this is an objective which free Asian nations, independent Asian nations, can seek and which the United States should support.

[5.] Q. Mr. President, when you speak of internal threats, do you include threats internally assisted by a country from the outside, such as we have in Vietnam?

THE PRESIDENT. Generally speaking, that is the kind of internal threat that we do have in the Asian countries. For example, in Thailand the threat is one that is indigenous to a certain extent to the northeast and the north, but that would not be too serious if it were not getting the assistance that it was from the outside. The same is true in several of the other Asian countries.

Source: Public Papers of the Presidents of the United States, Richard Nixon, 1969 (Washington, DC: Government Printing Office, 1971), 548–49.

---

134. KISSINGER'S CONCEPT OF "LINKAGE"
4 February 1969

In 1969, President Nixon and National Security Advisor Henry Kissinger crafted the concept of "linkage" as a means to govern U.S.–Soviet relations. Linkage assumed that "the great issues are fundamentally interrelated," and should be advanced "on a front at least broad enough to make clear that we see some relationship between political and military issues." In practical terms, Nixon and Kissinger intended to link progress on arms control negotiations with Soviet cooperation in the Middle East and Vietnam.

I believe that the basis for a viable settlement is a mutual recognition of our vital interests. We must recognize that the Soviet Union has interests; in the present circumstances we cannot but take account of them in defining our own. We should leave the Soviet leadership in no doubt that we expect them to adopt a similar approach toward us. . . . In the past, we have often attempted to settle things in a fit of enthusiasm, relying on personal diplomacy. But the "spirit" that permeated various meetings lacked a solid basis of mutual interest, and therefore, every summit meeting was followed by a crisis in less than a year.

I am convinced that the great issues are fundamentally interrelated. I do not mean this to establish artificial linkages between specific elements of one or another issue or between tactical steps that we may elect to take. But I do believe that crisis or confrontation in one place and real cooperation in another cannot long be sustained simultaneously. I recognize that the previous Administration took the view that when we perceive a mutual interest on an issue with the USSR, we should pursue agreement and attempt to insulate it as much as possible from the ups and downs of conflicts elsewhere. This may well be sound on numerous bilateral and practical matters such as cultural or scientific exchanges. But, on the crucial issues of our day, I believe we must seek to advance on a front at least broad enough to make clear that we see some relationship between political and military issues. I believe that the Soviet leaders should be brought to understand that they cannot expect to reap the benefits of cooperation in one area while seeking to take advantage of tension or confrontation elsewhere. Such a course involves the danger that the Soviets will use talks on arms as a safety valve on intransigence elsewhere. . . .

I would like to illustrate what I have in mind in one case of immediate and widespread interest—the proposed talks on strategic weapons. I believe our decision on when and how to proceed does not depend exclusively on our review of the purely military and technical issues, although these are of key importance. This decision should also be taken in the light of the prevailing political context and, in particular, in light of progress toward stabilizing the explosive Middle East situation, and in light of the Paris talks [on Vietnam]. I believe I should retain the freedom to ensure, to the extent that we have control over it, that the timing of talks with the Soviet Union on strategic weapons is optimal. This may, in fact, mean delay beyond that required for our review of the technical issues. Indeed, it means that we should—at least in our public position—keep open the option that there may be no talks at all.

Source: Henry Kissinger, *White House Years* (New York: Little, Brown and Company, 1979), 135–36.

135. STRATEGIC ARMS LIMITATION TREATY I
26 May 1972

Following his historic visit to Communist China in February 1972, Nixon traveled to Moscow to sign an agreement that set limits on ground-and sea-launched nuclear weapons. The event marked one of the high points of Nixon's career as a diplomat and served as the foundation for subsequent arms negotiations with the Soviet Union.

ARTICLE I

The Parties undertake not to start construction of additional fixed land-based intercontinental ballistic missile (ICBM) launchers after July 1, 1972.

ARTICLE II

The Parties undertake not to convert land-based launchers for light ICBMs, or for ICBMs of older types deployed prior to 1964, into land-based launchers for heavy ICBMs of types deployed after that time.

ARTICLE III

The Parties undertake to limit submarine-launched ballistic missile (SLBM) launchers and modern ballistic missile submarines to the numbers operational and under construction on the date of the signature of this Interim Agreement, and in addition to launchers and submarines constructed under procedures established by the Parties as replacements for an equal number of ICBM launchers of older types deployed prior to 1964 or for launchers on older submarines.

ARTICLE IV

Subject to the provisions of this Interim Agreement, modernization and replacement of strategic offensive ballistic missiles and launchers covered by this Interim Agreement may be undertaken. . . .

ARTICLE VII

The Parties undertake to continue active negotiations for limitations on strategic offensive arms. The obligations provided for in this Interim Agreement shall not prejudice the scope or terms of the limitations on strategic offensive arms which may be worked out in the course of further negotiations. . . .

[Protocol]

The Parties understand that, under Article III of the Interim Agreement, for the period during which the Agreement remains in force:

The U.S. may have no more than 710 ballistic missile launchers on submarines (SLBM's) and no more than 44 modern ballistic missile submarines. The Soviet Union may have no more than 950 ballistic missile launchers on submarines and no more than 62 modern ballistic missile submarines.

Additional ballistic missile launchers on submarines up to the above mentioned levels, in the U.S.—over 656 ballistic missile launchers on nuclear-powered submarines, and in the U.S.S.R.—over 740 ballistic missile launchers on nuclear-powered submarines, operational and under construction, may become operational as replacements for equal numbers of ballistic missile launchers of older types deployed prior to 1964 or of ballistic missile launchers on older submarines.

The deployment of modern SLBM's on any submarine, regardless of type, will be counted against the total level of SLBM's permitted for the U.S. and the U.S.S.R.

This Protocol shall be considered an integral part of the Interim Agreement.

Source: U.S. Department of State, *Department of State Bulletin*, vol. 66, no. 1722 (26 June 1972): 920–21.

136.   VIETNAM PEACE AGREEMENT
24 January 1973

After years of negotiations in Paris, an agreement ending the war in Vietnam was announced in January 1973. It included provisions addressing the withdrawal of forces on both sides, the return of prisoners, and the composition of the post-war South Vietnamese government. Although Henry Kissinger and North Vietnamese negotiator Le Duc Tho jointly received the 1973 Nobel Peace Prize for their efforts, the agreement failed to prevent further conflict in South Vietnam.

CHAPTER I

THE VIETNAMESE PEOPLE'S FUNDAMENTAL NATIONAL RIGHTS

ARTICLE 1

The United States and all other countries respect the independence, sovereignty, unity, and territorial integrity of Vietnam as recognized by the 1954 Geneva Agreements on Vietnam.

CHAPTER II

CESSATION OF HOSTILITIES—WITHDRAWAL OF TROOPS

ARTICLE 2

A cease-fire shall be observed throughout South Vietnam as of 2400 hours G.M.T., on January 27, 1973.

At the same hour, the United States will stop all its military activities against the territory of the Democratic Republic of Vietnam by ground, air and naval forces, wherever they may be based, and end the mining of the territorial waters, ports, harbors, and waterways of the Democratic Republic of Vietnam. The United States will remove, permanently deactivate or destroy all the mines in the territorial waters, ports, harbors, and waterways of North Vietnam as soon as this Agreement goes into effect.

The complete cessation of hostilities mentioned in this Article shall be durable and without limit of time.

ARTICLE 3

The parties undertake to maintain the cease-fire and to ensure a lasting and stable peace.

As soon as the cease-fire goes into effect:

(a) The United States forces and those of the other foreign countries allied with the United States and the Republic of Vietnam shall remain in-place pending the implementation of the plan of troop withdrawal. The Four-Party joint Military Commission described in Article 16 shall determine the modalities.

(b) The armed forces of the two South Vietnamese parties shall remain in-place. The Two-Party joint Military Commission described by Article 17 shall determine the areas controlled by each party and the modalities of stationing.

(c) The regular forces of all services and arms and the irregular forces of the parties in South Vietnam shall stop all offensive activities against each other and shall strictly abide by the following stipulations:

—All acts of force on the ground, in the air, and on the sea shall be prohibited;

—All hostile acts, terrorism and reprisals by both sides will be banned.

ARTICLE 4

The United States will not continue its military involvement or intervene in the internal affairs of South Vietnam.

ARTICLE 5

Within sixty days of the signing of this Agreement, there will be a total withdrawal from South Vietnam of troops, military advisers, and military personnel, including technical military personnel and military personnel associated with the pacification program, armaments, munitions, and war material of the United States and those of the other foreign countries mentioned in Article 3 (a). Advisers from the above-mentioned countries to all paramilitary organizations and the police force will also be withdrawn within the same period of time.

ARTICLE 6

The dismantlement of all military bases in South Vietnam of the United States and of the other foreign countries mentioned in Article 3 (a) shall be completed within sixty days of the signing of this Agreement.

ARTICLE 7

From the enforcement of the cease-fire to the formation of the government provided for in Articles 9 (b) and 14 of this Agreement, the two South Vietnamese parties shall not accept the introduction of troops, military advisers, and military personnel including technical military personnel, armaments, munitions, and war material into South Vietnam.

The two South Vietnamese parties shall be permitted to make periodic replacement of armaments, munitions and war material which have been destroyed, damaged, worn out or used up after the cease-fire, on the basis of piece-for-piece, of the same characteristics and properties, under the supervision of the Joint Military Commission of the two South Vietnamese parties and of the International Commission of Control and Supervision.

CHAPTER III

THE RETURN OF CAPTURED MILITARY PERSONNEL AND FOREIGN CIVILIANS, AND CAPTURED AND DETAINED VIETNAMESE CIVILIAN PERSONNEL

ARTICLE 8

(a) The return of captured military personnel and foreign civilians of the parties shall be carried out simultaneously with and completed not later than the same day as the troop withdrawal mentioned in Article 5. The parties shall exchange complete lists of the above-mentioned captured military personnel and foreign civilians on the day of the signing of this Agreement.

(b) The parties shall help each other to get information about those military personnel and foreign civilians of the parties missing in action, to determine the location and take care of the graves of the dead so as to facilitate the exhumation and repatriation of the remains, and to take any such other measures as may be required to get information about those still considered missing in action.

(c) The question of the return of Vietnamese civilian personnel captured and detained in South Vietnam will be resolved by the two South Vietnamese parties on the basis of the principles of Article 21 (b) of the Agreement on the Cessation of Hostilities in Vietnam of July 20, 1954. The two South Vietnamese parties will do so in a spirit of national reconciliation and concord, with a view to ending hatred and enmity, in order to ease suffering and to reunite families. The two South Vietnamese parties will do their utmost to resolve this question within ninety days after the cease-fire comes into effect.

CHAPTER IV

THE EXERCISE OF THE SOUTH VIETNAMESE PEOPLE'S RIGHT TO SELF-DETERMINATION

ARTICLE 9

The Government of the United States of America and the Government of the Democratic Republic of Vietnam undertake to respect the following principles for the exercise of the South Vietnamese people's right to self-determination:

(a) The South Vietnamese people's right to self-determination is sacred, inalienable, and shall be respected by all countries.

CHAPTER VI

THE JOINT MILITARY COMMISSIONS, THE INTERNATIONAL COMMISSION OF CONTROL AND SUPERVISION, THE INTERNATIONAL CONFERENCE

ARTICLE 16

(a) The Parties participating in the Paris Conference on Vietnam shall immediately designate representatives to form a Four-Party Joint Military Commission with the task of ensuring joint action by the parties in implementing the . . . provisions of this Agreement. . . .

(c) The Four-Party joint Military Commission shall begin operating immediately after the signing of this Agreement and end its activities in sixty days, after the completion of the withdrawal of U.S. troops and those of the other foreign countries mentioned in Article 3 (a) and the completion of the return of captured military personnel and foreign civilians of the parties. . . .

ARTICLE 17

(a) The two South Vietnamese parties shall immediately designate representatives to form a Two-Party Joint Military Commission with the task of ensuring joint action by the two South Vietnamese parties in implementing the . . . provisions of this Agreement. . . .

(c) After the signing of this Agreement, the Two-Party Joint Military Commission shall agree immediately on the measures and organization aimed at enforcing the cease-fire and preserving peace in South Vietnam.

ARTICLE 18

(a) After the signing of this Agreement, an International Commission of Control and Supervision shall be established immediately.

(b) Until the International Conference provided for in Article 19 makes definitive arrangements, the International Commission of Control and Supervision will report to the four parties on matters concerning the control and supervision of the implementation . . . of this Agreement. . . .

(c) The International Commission of Control and Supervision shall form control teams for carrying out its tasks. The two South Vietnamese parties shall agree immediately on the location and operation of these teams. The two South Vietnamese parties will facilitate their operation.

(d) The International Commission of Control and Supervision shall be composed of representatives of four countries: Canada, Hungary, Indonesia and Poland. The chairmanship of this Commission will rotate among the members for specific periods to be determined by the Commission. . . .

ARTICLE 19

The parties agree on the convening of an International Conference within thirty days of the signing of this Agreement to acknowledge the signed agreements; to guarantee the ending of the war, the maintenance of peace in Vietnam, the respect of the Vietnamese people's fundamental national rights, and the South Vietnamese people's right to self-determination; and to contribute to and guarantee peace in Indochina.

The United States and the Democratic Republic of Vietnam, on behalf of the parties participating in the Paris Conference on Vietnam, will propose to the following parties that they participate in this International Conference: the People's Republic of China, the Republic of France, the Union of Soviet Socialist Republics, the United Kingdom, the four countries of the International Commission of Control and Supervision, and the Secretary General of the United Nations, together with the parties participating in the Paris Conference on Vietnam. . . .

CHAPTER VIII

THE RELATIONSHIP BETWEEN THE UNITED STATES AND THE DEMOCRATIC REPUBLIC OF VIETNAM

ARTICLE 21

The United States anticipates that this Agreement will usher in an era of reconciliation with the Democratic Republic of Vietnam as with all the peoples of Indochina. In pursuance of its traditional policy, the United States will contribute to healing the wounds of war and to postwar reconstruction of the Democratic Republic of Vietnam and throughout Indochina. . . .

DONE in Paris this 27th day of January, 1973, in Vietnamese and English. The Vietnamese and English texts are official and equally authentic.

PROTOCOL ON PRISONERS AND DETAINEES

PROTOCOL TO THE AGREEMENT ON ENDING THE WAR AND RESTORING PEACE IN VIETNAM CONCERNING THE RETURN OF CAPTURED MILITARY PERSONNEL AND FOREIGN CIVILIANS AND CAPTURED AND DETAINED VIETNAMESE CIVILIAN PERSONNEL

The Parties participating in the Paris Conference on Vietnam,

In implementation of Article 8 of the Agreement on Ending the War and Restoring Peace in Vietnam signed on this date providing for the return of captured military personnel and foreign civilians, and captured and detained Vietnamese civilian personnel,

Have agreed as follows:

THE RETURN OF CAPTURED MILITARY PERSONNEL AND FOREIGN CIVILIANS

ARTICLE 1

The parties signatory to the Agreement shall return the captured military personnel of the parties mentioned in Article 8 (a) of the Agreement as follows:

—all captured military personnel of the United States and those of the other foreign countries mentioned in Article 3 (a) of the Agreement shall be returned to United States authorities;

—all captured Vietnamese military personnel, whether belonging to regular or irregular armed forces, shall be returned to the two South Vietnamese parties; they shall be returned to that South Vietnamese party under whose command they served.

ARTICLE 2

All captured civilians who are nationals of the United States or of any other foreign countries mentioned in Article 3 (a) of the Agreement shall be returned to United States authorities. All other captured foreign civilians shall be returned to the authorities of their country of nationality by any one of the parties willing and able to do so. . . .

ARTICLE 6

Each party shall return all captured persons mentioned in Articles 1 and 2 of this Protocol without delay and shall facilitate their return and reception. The detaining parties shall not deny or delay their return for any reason, including the fact that captured persons may, on any grounds have been prosecuted or sentenced.

THE RETURN OF CAPTURED AND DETAINED VIETNAMESE CIVILIAN PERSONNEL
ARTICLE 7

(a) The question of the return of Vietnamese civilian personnel captured and detained in South Vietnam will be resolved by the two South Vietnamese parties on the basis of the principles of Article 21 (b) of the Agreement on the Cessation of Hostilities in Vietnam of July 20, 1954. . . .

TREATMENT OF CAPTURED PERSONS DURING DETENTION
ARTICLE 8

(a) All captured military personnel of the parties and captured foreign civilians of the parties shall be treated humanely at all times, and in accordance with international practice.

They shall be protected against all violence to life and person, in particular against murder in any form, mutilation, torture and cruel treatment, and outrages upon personal dignity. These persons shall not be forced to join the armed forces of the detaining party.

They shall be given adequate food, clothing, shelter, and the medical attention required for their state of health. They shall be allowed to exchange post cards and letters with their families and receive parcels.

(b) All Vietnamese civilian personnel captured and detained in South Vietnam shall be treated humanely at all times, and in accordance with international practice.

They shall be protected against all violence to life and person, in particular against murder in any form, mutilation, torture and cruel treatment, and outrages against personal dignity. The detaining parties shall not deny or delay their return for any reason, including the fact that captured persons may, on any grounds, have been prosecuted or sentenced. These persons shall not be forced to join the armed forces of the detaining party.

They shall be given adequate food, clothing, shelter, and the medical attention required for their state of health. They shall be allowed to exchange post cards and letters with their families and receive parcels. . . .

Source: U.S. Department of State, *Department of State Bulletin*, vol. 68, no. 1755 (12 February 1973): 169–88.

137. WAR POWERS ACT
7 November 1973

One of the end products of the Vietnam War was a reassertion of Congressional authority over the deployment of U.S. military forces abroad. The War Powers Act *limited combat deployments to sixty days unless the president received Congressional approval for the action.*

Public Law 93–148
93rd Congress, H. J. Res. 542
November 7, 1973

Joint Resolution

Concerning the war powers of Congress and the President.

Resolved by the Senate and the House of Representatives of the United States of America in Congress assembled,

SHORT TITLE

SECTION 1.
This joint resolution may be cited as the "War Powers Resolution."

PURPOSE AND POLICY

SECTION 2.
(a) It is the purpose of this joint resolution to fulfill the intent of the framers of the Constitution of the United States and insure that the collective judgment of both the Congress and the President will apply to the introduction of United

States Armed Forces into hostilities, or into situations where imminent involvement in hostilities is clearly indicated by the circumstances, and to the continued use of such forces in hostilities or in such situations.

(b) Under article 1, section 8, of the Constitution, it is specifically provided that the Congress shall have the power to make all laws necessary and proper for carrying into execution, not only its own powers but also all other powers vested by the Constitution in the Government of the United States, or in any department or officer thereof.

(c) The constitutional powers of the President as Commander-in-Chief to introduce United States Armed Forces into hostilities, or into situations where imminent involvement in hostilities is clearly indicated by the circumstances, are exercised only pursuant to (1) a declaration of war, (2) specific statutory authorization, or (3) a national emergency created by attack upon the United States, its territories or possessions, or its armed forces.

CONSULTATION

SECTION 3.

The President in every possible instance shall consult with Congress before introducing United States Armed Forces into hostilities or into situations where imminent involvement in hostilities is clearly indicated by the circumstances, and after every such introduction shall consult regularly with the Congress until United States Armed Forces are no longer engaged in hostilities or have been removed from such situations.

REPORTING

SECTION 4.

(1) into hostilities or into situations where imminent involvement in hostilities is clearly indicated by the circumstances;

(2) into the territory, airspace or waters of a foreign nation, while equipped for combat, except for deployments which relate solely to supply, replacement, repair, or training of such forces; or

(3) in numbers which substantially enlarge United States Armed Forces equipped for combat already located in a foreign nation; the president shall submit within 48 hours to the Speaker of the House of Representatives and to the President *pro tempore* of the Senate a report, in writing, setting forth—

(A) the circumstances necessitating the introduction of United States Armed Forces;

(B) the constitutional and legislative authority under which such introduction took place; and

(C) the estimated scope and duration of the hostilities or involvement.

(b) The President shall provide such other information as the Congress may request in the fulfillment of its constitutional responsibilities with respect to committing the Nation to war and to the use of United States Armed Forces abroad.

(c) Whenever United States Armed Forces are introduced into hostilities or into any situation described in sub section (a) of this section, the President shall, so long as such armed forces continue to be engaged in such hostilities or situation, report to the Congress periodically on the status of such hostilities or situation as well as on the scope and duration of such hostilities or situation, but in no event shall he report to the Congress less often than once every six months.

CONGRESSIONAL ACTION

SECTION 5.

(a) Each report submitted pursuant to section 4(a)(1) shall be transmitted to the Speaker of the House of Representatives and to the President *pro tempore* of the Senate on the same calendar day. Each report so transmitted shall be referred to the Committee on Foreign Affairs of the House of Representatives and to the Committee on Foreign Relations of the Senate for appropriate action. If, when the report is transmitted, the Congress has adjourned *sine die* or has adjourned for any period in excess of three calendar days, the Speaker of the House of Representatives and the President pro tempore of the Senate, if they deem it advisable (or if petitioned by at least 30 percent of the membership of their respective Houses) shall jointly request the President to convene Congress in order that it may consider the report and take appropriate action pursuant to this section.

(b) Within sixty calendar days after a report is submitted or is required to be submitted pursuant to section 4(a)(1), whichever is earlier, the President shall terminate any use of United States Armed Forces with respect to which such report was submitted (or required to be submitted), unless the Congress

(1) has declared war or has enacted a specific authorization for such use of United States Armed Forces,

(2) has extended by law such sixty-day period, or

(3) is physically unable to meet as a result of an armed attack upon the United States. Such sixty-day period shall be extended for not more than an additional thirty days if the President determines and certifies to the Congress in writing that unavoidable military necessity respecting the safety of United States Armed Forces requires the continued use of such armed forces in the course of bringing about a prompt removal of such forces.

(c) Notwithstanding subsection (b), at any time that United States Armed Forces are engaged in hostilities outside the territory of the United States, its posses-sions and territories without a declaration of war or specific statutory authori-zation, such forces shall be removed by the President if the Congress so directs by concurrent resolution.

CONGRESSIONAL PRIORITY PROCEDURES FOR JOINT RESOLUTION OR BILL

SECTION 6.

(a) Any joint resolution or bill introduced pursuant to section 5(b) at least thirty calendar days before the expiration of the sixty-day period specified in such section shall be referred to the Committee on Foreign Affairs of the House of Representatives or the Committee on Foreign Relations of the Senate, as the case may be, and such committee shall report one such joint resolution or bill, together with its recommendations, not later than twenty-four calendar days before the expiration of the sixty-day period specified in such section, unless such House shall otherwise determine by the yeas and nays.

(b) Any joint resolution or bill so reported shall become the pending business of the House in question (in the case of the Senate the time for debate shall be equally divided between the proponents and the opponents), and shall be voted on within three calendar days thereafter, unless such House shall otherwise determine by yeas and nays.

(c) Such a joint resolution or bill passed by one House shall be referred to the committee of the other House named in subsection (a) and shall be reported out not later than fourteen calendar days before the expiration of the sixty-day period specified in section 5(b). The joint resolution or bill so reported shall become the pending business of the House in question and shall be voted on within three calendar days after it has been reported, unless such House shall otherwise determine by yeas and nays.

(d) In the case of any disagreement between the two Houses of Congress with respect to a joint resolution or bill passed by both Houses, conferees shall be promptly appointed and the committee of conference shall make and file a report with respect to such resolution or bill not later than four calendar days before the expiration of the sixty-day period specified in section 5(b). In the event the conferees are unable to agree within 48 hours, they shall report back to their respective Houses in disagreement. Notwithstanding any rule in either House concerning the printing of conference reports in the Record or concerning any delay in the consideration of such reports, such report shall be acted on by both Houses not later than the expiration of such sixty-day period.

CONGRESSIONAL PRIORITY PROCEDURES FOR CONCURRENT RESOLUTION

SECTION 7.

(a) Any concurrent resolution introduced pursuant to section 5(b) at least thirty calendar days before the expiration of the sixty-day period specified in such section shall be referred to the Committee on Foreign Affairs of the House of Representatives or the Committee on Foreign Relations of the Senate, as the case may be, and one such concurrent resolution shall be reported out by such committee together with its recommendations within fifteen calendar days, unless such House shall otherwise determine by the yeas and nays.

(b) Any concurrent resolution so reported shall become the pending business of the House in question (in the case of the Senate the time for debate shall be equally divided between the proponents and the opponents), and shall be voted on within three calendar days thereafter, unless such House shall otherwise determine by yeas and nays.

(c) Such a concurrent resolution passed by one House shall be referred to the committee of the other House named in subsection (a) and shall be reported out by such committee together with its recommendations within fifteen calendar days and shall thereupon become the pending business of such House and shall be voted on within three calendar days after it has been reported, unless such House shall otherwise determine by yeas and nays.

(d) In the case of any disagreement between the two Houses of Congress with respect to a concurrent resolution passed by both Houses, conferees shall be promptly appointed and the committee of conference shall make and file a report with respect to such concurrent resolution within six calendar days after the legislation is referred to the committee of conference. Notwithstanding any rule in either House concerning the printing of conference reports in the Record or concerning any delay in the consideration of such reports, such report shall be acted on by both Houses not later than six calendar days after the conference report is filed. In the event the conferees are unable to agree within 48 hours, they shall report back to their respective Houses in disagreement.

INTERPRETATION OF JOINT RESOLUTION

SECTION 8.

(a) Authority to introduce United States Armed Forces into hostilities or into situations wherein involvement in hostilities is clearly indicated by the circumstances shall not be inferred—

(1) from any provision of law (whether or not in effect before the date of the enactment of this joint resolution), including any provision contained in any appropriation Act, unless such provision specifically authorizes the introduction of United States Armed Forces into hostilities or into such situations and stating that it is intended to constitute specific statutory authorization within the meaning of this joint resolution; or

(2) from any treaty heretofore or hereafter ratified unless such treaty is implemented by legislation specifically authorizing the introduction of United States Armed Forces into hostilities or into such situations and stating that it is intended to constitute specific statutory authorization within the meaning of this joint resolution.

(b) Nothing in this joint resolution shall be construed to require any further specific statutory authorization to permit members of United States Armed Forces to participate jointly with members of the armed forces of one or more foreign countries in the headquarters operations of high-level military commands which were established prior to the date of enactment of this joint resolution and pursuant to the United Nations Charter or any treaty ratified by the United States prior to such date.

(c) For purposes of this joint resolution, the term "introduction of United States Armed Forces" includes the assignment of a member of such armed forces to command, coordinate, participate in the movement of, or accompany the regular or irregular military forces of any foreign country or government when such military forces are engaged, or there exists an imminent threat that such forces will become engaged, in hostilities.

(d) Nothing in this joint resolution—

(1) is intended to alter the constitutional authority of the Congress or of the President, or the provision of existing treaties; or

(2) shall be construed as granting any authority to the President with respect to the introduction of United States Armed Forces into hostilities or into situations wherein involvement in hostilities is clearly indicated by the circumstances which authority he would not have had in the absence of this joint resolution.

SEPARABILITY CLAUSE

SECTION 9.

If any provision of this joint resolution or the application thereof to any person or circumstance is held invalid, the remainder of the joint resolution and the application of such provision to any other person or circumstance shall not be affected thereby.

EFFECTIVE DATE

SECTION 10.

This joint resolution shall take effect on the date of its enactment.

Source: Historic Documents, 1973 (Washington, DC: Congressional Quarterly, 1974), 923–30.

138. CARTER'S HUMAN RIGHTS FOREIGN POLICY
22 May 1977

An important legacy of the Vietnam era and contemporary criticism of the Nixon Doctrine was a dedicated American effort to reassert moral principles in U.S. foreign policy. President Jimmy Carter attempted to accomplish this by proclaiming human rights to be "a fundamental tenet of our foreign policy."

. . . But I want to speak to you today about the strands that connect our actions overseas with our essential character as a nation. I believe we can have a foreign policy that is democratic, that is based on fundamental values, and that uses power and influence, which we have, for humane purposes. We can also have a foreign policy that the American people both support and, for a change, know about and understand.

I have a quiet confidence in our own political system. Because we know that democracy works, we can reject the arguments of those rulers who deny human rights to their people.

We are confident that democracy's example will be compelling, and so we seek to bring that example closer to those from whom in the past few years we have been separated and who are not yet convinced about the advantages of our kind of life.

We are confident that the democratic methods are the most effective, and so we are not tempted to employ improper tactics here at home or abroad. . . .

For too many years, we've been willing to adopt the flawed and erroneous principles and tactics of our adversaries, sometimes abandoning our own values for theirs. We've fought fire with fire, never thinking that fire is better quenched with water. This approach failed, with Vietnam the best example of its intellectual and moral poverty. But through failure we have now found our way back to our own principles and values, and we have regained our lost confidence.

By the measure of history, our Nation's 200 years are very brief, and our rise to world eminence is briefer still. It dates from 1945, when Europe and the old international order lay in ruins. Before then, America was largely on the periphery of world affairs. But since then, we have inescapably been at the center of world affairs.

Our policy during this period was guided by two principles: a belief that Soviet expansion was almost inevitable but that it must be contained, and the corresponding belief in the importance of an almost exclusive alliance among non-Communist nations on both sides of the Atlantic. That system could not last forever unchanged. Historical trends have weakened its foundation. The unifying threat of conflict with the Soviet Union has become less intensive, even though the competition has become more extensive.

The Vietnamese war produced a profound moral crisis, sapping worldwide faith in our own policy and our system of life, a crisis of confidence made even more grave by the covert pessimism of some of our leaders.

In less than a generation, we've seen the world change dramatically. The daily lives and aspirations of most human beings have been transformed. Colonialism is nearly gone. A new sense of national identity now exists in almost 100 new countries that have been formed in the last generation. Knowledge has become more widespread. Aspirations are higher. As more people have been freed from traditional constraints, more have been determined to achieve, for the first time in their lives, social justice.

The world is still divided by ideological disputes, dominated by regional conflicts, and threatened by danger that we will not resolve the differences of race and wealth without violence or without drawing into combat the major military powers. We can no longer separate the traditional issues of war and peace from the new global questions of justice, equity, and human rights. . . .

First, we have reaffirmed America's commitment to human rights as a fundamental tenet of our foreign policy. In ancestry, religion, color, place of origin, and cultural background, we Americans are as diverse a nation as the world has ever seen. No common mystique of blood or soil unites us. What draws us together, perhaps more than anything else, is a belief in human freedom. We want the world to know that our Nation stands for more than financial prosperity.

This does not mean that we . . . conduct our foreign policy by rigid moral maxims. We live in a world that is imperfect and which will always be imperfect—a world that is complex and confused and which will always be complex and confused.

I understand fully the limits of moral suasion. We have no illusion that changes will come easily or soon. But I also believe that it is a mistake to undervalue the power of words and of the ideas that words embody. In our own history, that power has ranged from Thomas Paine's "Common Sense" to Martin Luther King, Jr.'s "I Have a Dream."

In the life of the human spirit, words *are* action, much more so than many of us may realize who live in countries where freedom of expression is taken for granted. The leaders of totalitarian nations understand this very well. The proof is that words are precisely the action for which dissidents in those countries are being persecuted.

Nonetheless, we can already see dramatic, worldwide advances in the protection of the individual from the arbitrary power of the state. For us to ignore this trend would be to lose influence and moral authority in the world. To lead it will be to regain the moral stature that we once had.

The great democracies are not free because we are strong and prosperous. I believe we are strong and influential and prosperous because we are free.

Throughout the world today, in free nations and in totalitarian countries as well, there is a preoccupation with the subject of human freedom, human rights. And I believe it is incumbent on us in this country to keep that discussion, that debate, that contention alive. No other country is as well-qualified as we to set an example. We have our own shortcomings and faults, and we should strive constantly and with courage to make sure that we are legitimately proud of what we have. . . .

Let me conclude by summarizing: Our policy is based on an historical vision of America's role. Our policy is derived from a larger view of global change. Our policy is rooted in our moral values, which never change. Our policy is reinforced by our material wealth and by our military power. Our policy is designed to serve mankind, And it is a policy that I hope will make you proud to be Americans.

Thank you.

Source: Public Papers of the Presidents of the United States, Jimmy Carter, 1977 (Washington, DC: Government Printing Office, 1977), 955–62.

139. THE PANAMA CANAL TREATY
7 September 1977

*The status of the Panama Canal had been a point of friction for U.S.–
Latin American relations for years when Jimmy Carter became president.
Realizing that a resolution of the conflict would help establish his credibility in foreign affairs, Carter focused on the issue, and in September
1977, the United States and Panama signed* The Panama Canal Treaty.
*The two nations agreed that Panama would assume legal control of the
canal from the United States in the year 2000, and that it would remain
a neutral territory thereafter. Despite his efforts, Republican leaders such
as presidential aspirant Ronald Reagan would heavily criticize Carter for
the treaty.*

THE UNITED STATES OF AMERICA AND THE REPUBLIC
OF PANAMA,

Acting in the spirit of the Joint Declaration of April 3, 1964, by the Representatives of the Governments of the United States of America and the Republic
of Panama, and of the Joint Statement of Principles of February 7, 1974, initialed
by the Secretary of State of the United States of America and the Foreign
Minister of the Republic of Panama, and

Acknowledging the Republic of Panama's sovereignty over its territory,

Have decided to terminate the prior Treaties pertaining to the Panama Canal
and to conclude a new Treaty to serve as the basis for a new relationship between them and, accordingly, have agreed upon the following:

ARTICLE I
ABROGATION OF PRIOR TREATIES AND ESTABLISHMENT
OF A NEW RELATIONSHIP

1. Upon its entry into force, this Treaty terminates and supersedes:

   a. The Isthmian Canal Convention between the United States of America and the
   Republic of Panama, signed at Washington, November 18, 1903;

   b. The Treaty of Friendship and Cooperation signed at Washington, March 2, 1936,
   and the Treaty of Mutual Understanding and Cooperation and the related Memorandum of Understandings Reached, signed at Panama, January 25, 1955, between the
   United States of America and the Republic of Panama;

   c. All other treaties, conventions, agreements and exchanges of notes between the
   United States of America and the Republic of Panama concerning the Panama Canal
   which were in force prior to the entry into force of this Treaty; and

   d. Provisions concerning the Panama Canal which appear in other treaties, conventions, agreements and exchanges of notes between the United States of America and

the Republic of Panama which were in force prior to the entry into force of this Treaty.

2. In accordance with the terms of this Treaty and related agreements, the Republic of Panama, as territorial sovereign, grants to the United States of America, for the duration of this Treaty, the rights necessary to regulate the transit of ships through the Panama Canal, and to manage, operate, maintain, improve, protect and defend the Canal. The Republic of Panama guarantees to the United States of America the peaceful use of the land and water area which it has been granted the rights to use for such purposes pursuant to this Treaty and related agreements.

3. The Republic of Panama shall participate increasingly in the management and protection and defense of the Canal, as provided in this Treaty.

4. In view of the special relationship established by this Treaty, the United States of America and the Republic of Panama shall cooperate to assure the uninterrupted and efficient operation of the Panama Canal.

ARTICLE II
RATIFICATION, ENTRY INTO FORCE, AND TERMINATION

1. This Treaty shall be subject to ratification in accordance with the constitutional procedures of the two Parties. The instruments of ratification of this Treaty shall be exchanged at Panama at the same time as the instruments of ratification of the Treaty Concerning the permanent Neutrality and Operation of the Panama Canal, signed this date, are exchanged. This treaty shall enter into force, simultaneously with the Treaty Concerning the Permanent Neutrality and Operation of the Panama Canal, six calendar months from the date of the exchange of the instruments of ratification.

2. This Treaty shall terminate at noon, Panama time, December 31, 1999.

ARTICLE III
CANAL OPERATION AND MANAGEMENT

1. The Republic of Panama, as territorial sovereign, grants to the United States of America the rights to manage, operate, and maintain the Panama Canal, its complementary works, installations and equipment and to provide for the orderly transit of vessels through the Panama Canal. The United States of America accepts the grant of such rights and undertakes to exercise them in accordance with this Treaty and related agreements. . . .

ARTICLE IV
PROTECTION AND DEFENSE

1. The United States of America and the Republic of Panama commit themselves to protect and defend the Panama Canal. Each Party shall act, in accordance with its constitutional processes, to meet the danger resulting from an armed attack or other actions which threaten the security of the Panama Canal or of ships transiting it.

2. For the duration of this Treaty, the United States of America shall have primary responsibility to protect and defend the Canal. The rights of the United States of America to station, train, and move military forces within the Republic of Panama are described in the Agreement in Implementation of this Article, signed this date. The use of areas and installations and the legal status of the armed forces of the

United States of America in the Republic of Panama shall be governed by the afore-said Agreement. . . .

ARTICLE XIII
PROPERTY TRANSFER AND ECONOMIC PARTICIPATION BY THE REPUBLIC OF PANAMA

1. Upon termination of this Treaty, the Republic of Panama shall assume total respon-sibility for the management, operation, and maintenance of the Panama Canal, which shall be turned over in operating condition and free of liens and debts, except as the two Parties may otherwise agree.

Source: U.S. Department of State, *Department of State Bulletin*, vol. 77, no. 1999 (17 October 1977): 483–501.

---

140.   CARTER'S SPEECH ON THE CAMP DAVID ACCORD
18 September 1978

The Camp David Accord was the diplomatic highlight of the Carter administration. After weeks of negotiations, Carter was able to broker an agreement between Egypt and Israel in which Israel consented to return territories seized during the 1967 war, particularly the Sinai Peninsula, and Egypt committed itself to full diplomatic recognition of Israel. The accord also won official Palestinian participation in subsequent negotia-tions over the final status of the West Bank and Gaza.

It's been more than 2,000 years since there was peace between Egypt and a free Jewish nation. If our present expectations are realized, this year we shall see such peace again.

The first thing I would like to do is to give tribute to the two men who made this impossible dream now become a real possibility, the two great leaders with whom I have met for the last 2 weeks at Camp David; first President Anwar Sadat of Egypt and the other, of course, is Prime Minister Menachem Begin of the nation of Israel.

I know that all of you would agree that these are two men of great personal courage, representing nations of peoples who are deeply grateful to them for the achievement which they have realized. And I am personally grateful to them for what they have done.

At Camp David, we sought a peace that is not only of vital importance to their own two nations but to all the people of the Middle East, to all the people of the United States, and, indeed, to all the world as well.

The world prayed for the success of our efforts, and I am glad to announce to you that these prayers have been answered.

I've come to discuss with you tonight what these two leaders have accomplished and what this means to all of us.

The United States has had no choice but to be deeply concerned about the Middle East and to try to use our influence and our efforts to advance the cause of peace. For the last 30 years, through four wars, the people of this troubled region have paid a terrible price in suffering and division and hatred and bloodshed. No two other nations have suffered more than Egypt and Israel. But the dangers and the costs of conflicts in this region for our own Nation have been great as well. We have longstanding friendships among the nations there and the peoples of the region, and we have profound moral commitments which are deeply rooted in our values as a people.

The strategic location of these countries and the resources that they possess mean that events in the Middle East directly affect people everywhere. We and our friends could not be indifferent if a hostile power were to establish domination there. In few areas of the world is there a greater risk that a local conflict could spread among other nations adjacent to them and then, perhaps, erupt into a tragic confrontation between us superpowers, ourselves.

Our people have come to understand that unfamiliar names like Sinai, Aqaba, Sharm el Sheikh, Ras en Naqb, Gaza, the West Bank of Jordan, can have a direct and immediate bearing on our own well-being as a nation and our hope for a peaceful world. That is why we in the United States cannot afford to be idle bystanders and why we have been full partners in the search for peace and why it is so vital to our Nation that these meetings at Camp David have been a success.

Through the long years of conflict, four main issues have divided the parties involved. One is the nature of peace—whether peace will simply mean that the guns are silenced, that the bombs no longer fall, that the tanks cease to roll, or whether it will mean that the nations of the Middle East can deal with each other as neighbors and as equals and as friends, with a full range of diplomatic and cultural and economic and human relations between them. That's been the basic question. The Camp David agreement has defined such relationships, I'm glad to announce to you between Israel and Egypt.

The second main issue is providing for the security of all parties involved, including, of course, our friends, the Israelis, so that none of them need fear attack or military threats from one another. When implemented, the Camp David agreement, I'm glad to announce to you, will provide for such mutual security.

Third is the question of agreement on secure and recognized boundaries, the end of military occupation, and the granting of self-government or else the return to other nations of territories which have been occupied by Israel since the 1967 conflict. The Camp David agreement, I'm glad to announce to you, provides for the realization of all these goals.

And finally, there is the painful human question of the fate of the Palestinians who live or who have lived in these disputed regions. The Camp David agreement guarantees that the Palestinian people may participate in the resolution of the Palestinian problem in all its aspects, a commitment that Israel has made in writing and which is supported and appreciated, I'm sure, by all the world.

Over the last 18 months, there has been, of course, some progress on these issues. Egypt and Israel came close to agreeing about the first issue, the nature of peace. They then saw that the second and third issues, that is withdrawal and security, were intimately connected, closely entwined. But fundamental divisions still remained in other areas—about the fate of the Palestinians, the future of the West Bank and Gaza, and the future of Israeli settlements in occupied Arab territories.

We all remember the hopes for peace that were inspired by President Sadat's initiative, that great and historic visit to Jerusalem last November that thrilled the world, and by the warm and genuine personal response of Prime Minister Begin and the Israeli people, and by the mutual promise between them, publicly made, that there would be no more war. These hopes were sustained when Prime Minister Begin reciprocated by visiting Ismailia on Christmas Day. That progress continued, but at a slower and slower pace through the early part of the year. And by early summer, the negotiations had come to a standstill once again.

It was this stalemate and the prospect for an even worse future that prompted me to invite both President Sadat and Prime Minister Begin to join me at Camp David. They accepted, as you know, instantly, without delay, without preconditions, without consultation even between them.

It's impossible to overstate the courage of these two men or the foresight they have shown. Only through high ideals, through compromises of words and not principle, and through a willingness to look deep into the human heart and to understand the problems and hopes and dreams of one another can progress in a difficult situation like this ever be made. That's what these men and their wise and diligent advisers who are here with us tonight have done during the last 13 days.

When this conference began, I said that the prospects for success were remote. Enormous barriers of ancient history and nationalism and suspicion would have to be overcome if we were to meet our objectives. But President Sadat and Prime Minister Begin have overcome these barriers, exceeded our fondest expectations, and have signed two agreements that hold out the possibility of resolving issues that history had taught us could not be resolved.

The first of these documents is entitled, "A Framework for Peace in the Middle East Agreed at Camp David." It deals with a comprehensive settlement, comprehensive agreement, between Israel and all her neighbors, as well as the difficult question of the Palestinian people and the future of the West Bank and the Gaza area.

The agreement provides a basis for the resolution of issues involving the West Bank and Gaza during the next 5 years. It outlines a process of change which is in keeping with Arab hopes, while also carefully respecting Israel's vital security.

The Israeli military government over these areas will be withdrawn and will be replaced with a self-government of the Palestinians who live there. And Israel has committed that this government will have full autonomy. Prime Minister Begin said to me several times, not partial autonomy, but full autonomy.

Israeli forces will be withdrawn and redeployed into specified locations to protect Israel's security. The Palestinians will further participate in determining their own future through talks in which their own elected representatives, the inhabitants of the West Bank and Gaza, will negotiate with Egypt and Israel and Jordan to determine the final status of the West Bank and Gaza.

Israel has agreed, has committed themselves, that the legitimate rights of the Palestinian people will be recognized. After the signing of this framework last night, and during the negotiations concerning the establishment of the Palestinian self-government, no new Israeli settlements will be established in this area. The future settlements issue will be decided among the negotiating parties.

The final status of the West Bank and Gaza will be decided before the end of the 5-year transitional period during which the Palestinian Arabs will have their own government, as part of a negotiation which will produce a peace treaty between Israel and Jordan specifying borders, withdrawal, all those very crucial issues.

These negotiations will be based on all the provisions and the principles of Security Council Resolution 242, with which you all are so familiar. The agreement on the final status of these areas will then be submitted to a vote by the representatives of the inhabitants of the West Bank and Gaza, and they will have the right for the first time in their history, the Palestinian people, to decide how they will govern themselves permanently.

We also believe, of course, all of us, that there should be a just settlement of the problems of displaced persons and refugees, which takes into account appropriate United Nations resolutions.

Finally, this document also outlines a variety of security arrangements to reinforce peace between Israel and her neighbors. This is, indeed, a comprehensive and fair framework for peace in the Middle East, and I'm glad to report this to you.

The second agreement is entitled, "A Framework for the Conclusion of a Peace Treaty Between Egypt and Israel." It returns to Egypt its full exercise of sovereignty over the Sinai Peninsula and establishes several security zones, recognizing carefully that sovereignty right for the protection of all parties. It also provides that Egypt will extend full diplomatic recognition to Israel at the time the Israelis complete an interim withdrawal from most of the Sinai, which will take place between 3 months and 9 months after the conclusion of the peace treaty. And the peace treaty is to be fully negotiated and signed no later than 3 months from last night.

I think I should also report that Prime Minister Begin and President Sadat have already challenged each other to conclude the treaty even earlier. And I hope they—[*applause*]. This final conclusion of a peace treaty will be completed late in December, and it would be a wonderful Christmas present for the world.

Final and complete withdrawal of all Israeli forces will take place between 2 and 3 years following the conclusion of the peace treaty.

While both parties are in total agreement on all the goals that I have just described to you, there is one issue on which agreement has not yet been reached. Egypt states that agreement to remove the Israeli settlements from Egyptian territory is a prerequisite to a peace treaty. Israel says that the issue of the Israeli settlements should be resolved during the peace negotiations themselves.

Now, within 2 weeks, with each member of the Knesset or the Israeli Parliament acting as individuals, not constrained by party loyalty, the Knesset will decide on the issue of the settlements. Our own Government's position, my own personal position is well known on this issue and has been consistent. It is my strong hope, my prayer, that the question of Israeli settlements on Egyptian territory will not be the final obstacle to peace.

None of us should underestimate the historic importance of what has already been done. This is the first time that an Arab and an Israeli leader have signed a comprehensive framework for peace. It contains the seeds of a time when the Middle East, with all its vast potential, may be a land of human richness and fulfillment, rather than a land of bitterness and continued conflict. No region in the world has greater natural and human resources than this one, and nowhere have they been more heavily weighed down by intense hatred and frequent war. These agreements hold out the real possibility that this burden might finally be lifted.

But we must also not forget the magnitude of the obstacles that still remain. The summit exceeded our highest expectations, but we know that it left many difficult issues which are still to be resolved. These issues will require careful negotiation in the months to come. The Egyptian and Israeli people must recognize the tangible benefits that peace will bring and support the decisions their leaders have made, so that a secure and a peaceful future can be achieved for them. The American public, you and I, must also offer our full support to those who have made decisions that are difficult and those who have very difficult decisions still to make.

What lies ahead for all of us is to recognize the statesmanship that President Sadat and Prime Minister Begin have shown and to invite others in that region to follow their example. I have already, last night, invited the other leaders of the Arab world to help sustain progress toward a comprehensive peace.

We must also join in an effort to bring an end to the conflict and the terrible suffering in Lebanon. This is a subject that President Sadat discussed with me many times while I was in Camp David with him. And the first time that the three of us met together, this was a subject of heated discussion. On the way to Washington last night in the helicopter we mutually committed ourselves to join with other nations with the Lebanese people themselves, all factions, with President Sarkis, with Syria and Saudi Arabia, perhaps the European countries like France, to try to move toward a solution of the problem in Lebanon which is so vital to us and to the poor people in Lebanon who have suffered so much.

We will want to consult on this matter and on these documents and their meaning with all of the leaders, particularly the Arab leaders. And I'm pleased to say to you tonight that just a few minutes ago, King Hussein of Jordan and King Khalid of Saudi Arabia, perhaps other leaders later, but these two have already agreed to receive Secretary Vance, who will be leaving tomorrow to explain to them the terms of the Camp David agreement. And we hope to secure their support for the realization of the new hopes and dreams of the people of the Middle East.

This is an important mission, and this responsibility, I can tell you, based on my last 2 weeks with him, could not possibly rest on the shoulders of a more able and dedicated and competent man than Secretary Cyrus Vance.

Finally, let me say that for many years the Middle East has been a textbook for pessimism, a demonstration that diplomatic ingenuity was no match for intractable human conflicts. Today we are privileged to see the chance for one of the sometimes rare, bright moments in human history—a chance that may offer the way to peace. We have a chance for peace because these two brave leaders found within themselves the willingness to work together to seek these lasting prospects for peace, which we all want so badly. And for that, I hope that you will share my prayer of thanks and my hope that the promise of this moment shall be fully realized.

The prayers at Camp David were the same as those of the shepherd King David, who prayed in the 85th Psalm, "Wilt thou not revive us again: that thy people may rejoice in thee? I will hear what God the Lord will speak: for he will speak peace unto his people, and unto his saints: but let them not return again unto folly."

And I would like to say, as a Christian, to these two friends of mine, the words of Jesus, "Blessed are the peacemakers, for they shall be the children of God."

Source: Jimmy Carter, "Camp David Meeting on the Middle East: The Possibility of Peace," *Vital Speeches* 45 (15 October 1978): 2–4.

141. CARTER'S SPEECH ON THE SALT II TREATY
25 April 1979

In 1979, Carter attempted to expand and refine the strategic arms limitation treaty signed by the United States and the Soviet Union seven years earlier. SALT II envisaged sharp reductions in strategic systems and the regulation of new weapons such as the cruise missile. However, with increased Soviet activity in the Middle East and Africa and Cuba prominent in the background of the treaty debate, Carter postponed ratification in January 1980.

President Al Neuharth, distinguished members of the American Newspaper Publishers Association, other guests and friends. I want first of all to commend and to endorse the theme of this convention, the defense of the First Amendment of our Constitution and the freedom of the press.

Liberty of expression is our most important civil right and freedom of the press is its most important bulwark. We can never afford to grow complacent about the First Amendment. On the contrary, you and I and others must actively protect it always.

The American press has grown enormously since the nation's early days not only in its size and breadth, but in its concepts of its own duties and its own responsibilities. The highest of these duties is to inform the public on the important issues of the day, and no issue is more important than the one I want to discuss with you today in a solemn and somber and sincere way: the control of nuclear arms.

Each generation of Americans faces a choice that defines our national character, a choice that is also important for what it says about our own nation's outlook toward the world.

In the coming months we will almost certainly be faced with such a choice, whether to accept or to reject a new strategic arms limitation treaty. The decision we make will profoundly affect our lives and the lives of people all over the world for years to come.

We face this choice from a position of strength as the strongest nation on earth, economically, militarily and politically. Our alliances are firm and reliable. Our military forces are strong and ready. Our economic power is unmatched.

Along with other industrial democracies who are our friends, we lead the way in technological innovation. Our combined economies are more than three times as productive as those of the Soviet Union and all its allies. Our political institutions are based on human freedom. Our open system encourages individual initiative and creativity, and that in turn strengthens our entire society.

Our values and our democratic way of life have a magnetic appeal for people all over the world which a materialistic and a totalitarian philosophy can never hope to challenge or to rival.

For all these reasons we have a capacity for leadership in the world that surpasses that of any other nation. That leadership imposes many responsibilities on us, on me, as President, and on you other leaders who shape opinion and the character of our country.

But our noblest duty is to use our strength to serve our highest interest: the building of a secure, stable and a peaceful world.

We perform that duty in the spirit proclaimed by John F. Kennedy in 1963, the year he died. "Confident and unafraid," he said, "we labor on not toward a strategy of annihilation but toward a strategy of peace."

In our relations with the Soviet Union the possibility of mutual annihilation makes a strategy of peace the only rational choice for both sides because our values are so different.

It is clear that the United States of America and the Soviet Union will be in competition as far ahead as we can imagine or see. Yet we have a common interest in survival and we share a common recognition that our survival depends in a real sense on each other.

The very competition between us makes it imperative that we bring under control its most dangerous aspect, the nuclear arms race.

That's why the strategic arms limitation talks are so very important. This effort by two great nations to limit vital security forces is unique in human history. None have ever done this before.

As the Congress and the American people consider the SALT treaty which is now nearly complete, the debate will center around four basic questions: Why do we need SALT? How is the treaty related to our overall defense strategy? Can Soviet compliance be verified? How does the treaty relate to Soviet activities which challenge us and challenge our interests?

Let me address each question in turn. First, why do we need a strategic arms limitation treaty? We need it because it will contribute to a more peaceful world and to our own national security.

Today we and the Soviet Union, with sharply different world outlooks and interests, both have the ominous destructive power literally to destroy each other as a functioning society, killing tens of millions of people in the process.

And common sense tells us as it tells the Soviet Union that we must work to make our competition less dangerous, less burdensome and less likely to bring the ultimate horror of nuclear war. Indeed the entire world has a vital interest in whether or not we control the strategic arms race.

We have consulted closely with our allies who count on us not only to maintain strong military forces to offset Soviet military power but also and equally important to manage successfully a stable East-West relationship. SALT is at the heart of both these crucial efforts.

That's why the leaders of France and Great Britain and Germany, England, Canada and other nations have voiced their full support for the emerging treaty.

Some nations which have so far held back from building their own nuclear weapons, and at least a dozen other nations on earth now have that capability, will be strongly influenced in their decision by whether the two nuclear superpowers will restrain our weapons.

Rejection of a new strategic arms limitation treaty would seriously undermine the effort to control proliferation of these deadly weapons and nothing—nothing—would more surely damage our other critical efforts in arms control from a ban on all nuclear testing to the prevention of dangerous satellite warfare in space, from equalizing NATO and Warsaw Pact forces to restraining the spread of sophisticated conventional weapons on earth.

Every President since the dawn of the nuclear age has pursued the effort to bring nuclear arms under control and this must be a continuing process.

President Kennedy, building on the efforts of Presidents Truman and Eisenhower, signed the first agreement with the Soviet Union in 1963 to stop the poisonous testing of nuclear explosives in the atmosphere.

In 1968, five years later under President Johnson the United States and the Soviet Union joined other nations throughout the world and signed a non-proliferation treaty, an important step in preventing the spread of nuclear explosives to other nations.

In 1972 under President Nixon the SALT I agreement placed the first agreed limits on the number of offensive weapons and the antiballistic missile treaty, the ABM treaty, made an enduring contribution to our own security.

President Ford continued in negotiations at Helsinki and at Vladivostok. Each negotiation builds on the accomplishments of the last. Each agreement provides a foundation for further progress toward a more stable nuclear relationship.

Three Presidents have now spent more than six years negotiating the next step in this process, SALT II. We have all negotiated carefully and deliberately every step of the way. We've worked with our military leaders and other experts and we've sought the advice and counsel of the members of Congress.

An overwhelming majority of the American people recognize the need for SALT II. Our people want and our people expect continued step-by-step progress toward bringing nuclear weapons under control. Americans will support a reasoned increase in our defense effort. But we do not want a wholly unnecessary return to the cold war and an all-out arms race with its vastly greater risks and costs.

Through strength we want world peace.

Let me turn to the second question: How is SALT II related to our overall defense strategy?

The strategic forces of the United States and the Soviet Union today are essentially equivalent. They have larger and more numerous land-based missiles; we have a larger number of warheads and, as you know, significant technological and geographical advantages.

Each side has the will and the means to prevent the other from achieving superiority. Neither side is in a position to exploit its nuclear weapons for political purposes nor to use strategic weapons without facing almost certain suicide.

What causes us concern is not the current balance but the momentum of the Soviet strategic buildup. Over the past decade the Soviets have steadily increased their real defense spending year by year, while our own defense spending over that decade has had a net decrease.

In areas not limited by SALT—SALT I—they have launched ambitious programs to strengthen their strategic forces. At some future point the Soviet Union could achieve a strategic advantage unless we alter these trends.

That is exactly what I want to do. With the support of the American people and the bipartisan support of Congress we must move on two fronts at the same time.

First, within mutually accepted limits we must modernize our own strategic forces. Along with the strengthening of NATO, that is a central purpose of the increased defense budget that I've submitted to Congress, improvements which are necessary even in a time of fiscal restraint.

And second, we must place more stringent limits on the arms race than are presently imposed by SALT I. That is the purpose of the SALT II treaty.

The defense budget I've submitted will insure that our nuclear force continues to be essentially equivalent to that of the Soviet Union. This year we've begun to equip our submarines with new, more powerful and longer range Trident I missiles. Next year the first of our new, even more secure Trident submarines will be going to sea. And we are working on a more powerful and accurate Trident II missile for these submarines.

Our cruise missile program will greatly enhance the effectiveness of our long-range bomber force. These missiles will be able to penetrate any air defense system which the Soviet Union could build in the foreseeable future.

We are substantially improving the accuracy and the power of our land-based Minuteman missiles. But in the coming decade missiles of this type, based in fixed silos, will become increasingly vulnerable to surprise attack.

The Soviets have three-quarters of their warheads in such fixed-base missiles, compared to one-quarter of ours. Nevertheless, this is a very serious problem and we must deal with it effectively and sensibly.

The Defense Department now has under consideration a number of options for responding to this program—this problem—including making some of our own ICBM's mobile.

I might add, and this is very important, that the options which we are evaluating would be far more costly and we would have far less confidence of their effectiveness in the absence of SALT II limits. For without these limits on the number of Soviet warheads, the Soviet Union could counter any effort we made simply by greatly increasing the number of warheads on their missiles.

Let me emphasize that the SALT II agreement preserves adequate flexibility for the United States in this important area. Our strategic forces must be able to survive any attack and to counterattack military and civilian targets in the aggressor nation. And the aggressor nation must know that we have the ability and the will to exercise this option if they should attack us.

We have had this capacity, which is the essence of deterrence, in the past; we have it today and SALT II plus the defense programs that I've described will insure that we have it for the future.

The SALT II agreement will slow the growth of Soviet arms and limit the strategic competition and by helping to define future threats that we might face. SALT II will make our defense planning much more effective.

Under the agreement the two sides will be limited to equal numbers of strategic launchers for the first time, ending the substantial Soviet numerical advantage which was permitted in the currently effective SALT I treaty.

To reach these new and lower levels the Soviets will have to reduce their overall number of strategic delivery systems by 10 percent: More than 250 Soviet missile launchers or bombers will have to be dismantled. Naturally the Soviets will choose to phase out their older systems but these systems are still formidable. The missiles, for instance, to be torn down are comparable in age and payload to our Minuteman II missiles and to our Polaris missiles, presently deployed.

Under the agreement they will not be permitted to replace these dismantled systems with modern ones. Our own operational forces have been kept somewhat below the permitted ceiling. Thus, under the agreement we could increase our force level if necessary.

SALT II will also impose the first limited but important restraints on the race to build new systems and to improve existing ones, the so-called qualitative arms race.

In short, SALT II places serious limits on what the Soviets might do in the absence of such an agreement. For example, without SALT II the Soviet Union could build up to some 3,000 strategic systems by 1985. With SALT II we will both be limited to 2,250 such weapons.

This new arms control agreement will obviously serve our national interest. It will reduce the dangerous levels of strategic arms and restrain the development of future weapons. It will help to maintain our relative strength compared to the Soviets. It will avert a costly, risky and pointless buildup of missile launchers and bombers at the end of which both sides would be even less secure.

Let me turn now to the third of the four questions: How can we know whether the Soviets are living up to their obligations under this SALT agreement?

No objective has commanded more energy and attention in our negotiations. We have insisted that the SALT II agreement be made verifiable. We are confident that no significant violation of the treaty could take place without the United States detecting it. Our confidence in the verifiability of the agreement derives from the size and the nature of activities we must monitor and many effective and sophisticated intelligence collections which we in America possess.

For example, nuclear submarines take several years to construct and assemble. Missile silos and their supporting equipment are large and quite visible. Intercontinental bombers are built at a few plants and they need major fields. Our photo reconnaissance satellites survey the entire Soviet Union on a regular basis and they give us high confidence that we will be able to count accurately the numbers of all these systems.

But our independent verification capabilities are not limited only to observing these large-scale activities. We can determine not only how many systems there are but what they can do. Our photographic satellites and other systems enable us to follow technological developments in Soviet strategic forces with great accuracy.

There is no question that any cheating which might affect our national security would be discovered in time for us to respond fully.

For many years we have monitored Soviet strategic forces and Soviet compliance with the SALT agreements with a high degree of confidence. The overall capability remains. It was certainly not lost with our observation stations in Iran, which was only one of many intelligence sources that we use to follow Soviet strategic activities.

We are concerned with that loss but we must keep it in perspective. This monitoring capability relates principally to the portion of the new agreement dealing with the modernization limits on ICBM's and to only a portion of such modernization restraints. The sensitive intelligence techniques obviously cannot be disclosed in public but the bottom line is that if there is an effort to cheat on the SALT agreement, including the limits on modernizing ICBM's, we will detect it and we will do so in time fully to protect our security.

And we must also keep in mind that quite apart from SALT limits, our security is affected by the extent of our information about Soviet strategic forces. With this SALT II treaty that vital information will be much more accessible to us. The agreement specifically forbids, for the first time, interference with the systems used for monitoring compliance and prohibits any deliberate concealment that would impede verification.

Any such concealment activity would itself be detectable and a violation of this part of the agreement would be so serious as to give us grounds to cancel the treaty itself.

As I have said many times, the stakes are too high to rely on trust. For even on the Soviets' rational inclination to act in their own best interests, the treaty must, and the treaty will be, verifiable from the first day it is signed.

And finally, how does SALT II fit into the context of our overall relations with the Soviet Union? Because SALT II will make the world safer and our own nation more secure it is in our national interest to control nuclear weapons even as we compete with the Soviets elsewhere in the world. A SALT II agreement in no way limits our ability to promote our interests or to answer Soviet threats to those interests.

We will continue to support the independence of third world nations who struggle to stay free. We will continue to promote the peaceful resolution of local and regional disputes and to oppose efforts by any others to inflame these disputes with outside force. And we will continue to work for human rights.

It's a delusion to believe that rejection of a SALT treaty would somehow induce the Soviet Union to exercise new restraints in troubled areas. The actual effect of rejecting such a treaty might be precisely the opposite. The most intransigent and hostile elements of the Soviet political power structure would certainly be encouraged to strengthen by our rejection by a SALT agreement.

The Soviets might very well feel that they then have little to lose by creating new international tensions. A rejection of SALT II would have significance far beyond the fate of a single treaty. It would mean a radical turning away from America's longtime policy of seeking world peace.

We would no longer be identified as the peace loving nation. It would turn us away from the control of nuclear weapons and from the easing of tensions between Americans and the Soviet people under the system of international law based on mutual interests.

The rejection of SALT II would result in a more perilous world. As I said at Georgia Tech on Feb. 20: "Each crisis, each confrontation, each point of friction, as serious as it may be in its own right, would take on an added measure of significance and an added dimension of danger, for it would occur in an atmosphere of unbridled strategic competition and deteriorating strategic stability. It is precisely because we have fundamental differences with the Soviet Union that we are determined to bring this most dangerous element of our military competition under control."

For these reasons we will not try to impose binding linkage between Soviet behavior and SALT. And we will not accept any Soviet attempts to link SALT with aspects of our own foreign policy of which they may disapprove.

Again, SALT II is not a favor we are doing for the Soviet Union. It's an agreement carefully negotiated in the national security interest of the United States of America.

I put these issues to you today because they need discussion and debate and because the voices of the American people must be heard.

In the months ahead we will do all in our power to explain the treaty clearly and fully to the American people. I know that members of Congress from both parties will join in this effort to insure an informed public debate.

And you, more than any other group I can imagine in the United States, share this responsibility with me and with the Congress.

During this debate it's important that we exercise care. We will be sharing with the Congress some of our most sensitive defense and intelligence secrets and the leaders in Congress must insure that these secrets will be guarded so that the debate itself will not undermine our own security.

As the national discussion takes place, let us be clear about what the issues are and are not.

Americans are committed to maintaining a strong defense. That is not the issue. We will continue to compete and compete effectively with the Soviet Union. That is not the issue. The issue is whether we will move ahead with strategic arms control or resume a relentless nuclear weapons competition.

That's a choice we face between an imperfect world with a SALT agreement or an imperfect and more dangerous world without a SALT agreement.

With SALT II we will have significant reductions in Soviet strategic forces, far greater certainty in our defense planning and in the knowledge of the threat that we might face, flexibility to meet our own defense needs, the foundation for further controls on nuclear and conventional arms, and our own self-respect and the earned respect of the world for a United States demonstrably committed to the works of peace.

Without SALT the Soviets will be unconstrained and capable and probably committed to an enormous further buildup. Without SALT there would have to be a much sharper rise in our own defense spending at the expense of other necessary programs for our people.

Without SALT we would end up with thousands more strategic nuclear warheads on both sides with far greater costs and far less security for our citizens.

Without SALT we would see improved relations with the Soviet Union replaced by heightened tensions.

Without SALT the long, slow process of arms control so central to building a safer world would be dealt a crippling and perhaps a fatal blow.

Without SALT the world would be forced to conclude that America had chosen confrontation rather than cooperation and peace.

This is the inescapable choice we face, for the fact is that the alternative to this treaty is not some perfect agreement drafted unilaterally by the United States in which we gain everything and the Soviets gain nothing. The alternative now and in the foreseeable future is no agreement at all.

I am convinced that the United States has a moral and a political will to control the relentless technology which could constantly devise new and more destructive weapons to kill human beings. We need not drift into a dark nightmare of unrestrained arms competition. We Americans have the wisdom to know that our security depends on more than just maintaining our unsurpassed defense forces.

Our security and that of our allies also depends on the strength of ideas and ideals and on arms control measures that can stabilize and finally reverse a dangerous and a wasteful arms race which neither side can win.

This is the path of wisdom. This is a path of peace.

Source: Jimmy Carter, "SALT II: The Arms Control Agreement," *Vital Speeches* 45 (15 May 1979): 450–53.

---

142. CARTER DOCTRINE
23 January 1980

The December 1979 Soviet invasion of Afghanistan prompted the Carter administration to abandon its conciliatory approach toward Moscow. During his 1980 State of the Union Message, Carter declared America's opposition to "any outside force" that might conduct "an assault on the vital interests of the United States of America," and warned that such an action could result in a military response.

MR. PRESIDENT, MR. SPEAKER, MEMBERS OF THE 96TH CONGRESS, FELLOW CITIZENS:

These last few months has not been an easy time for any of us. As we meet tonight, it has never been more clear that the state of our Union depends on the state of the world. And tonight, as throughout our own generation, freedom and peace in the world depend on the state of our Union.

The 1980s have been born in turmoil, strife, and change. This is a time of challenge to our interests and our values and it's a time that tests our wisdom and our skills.

At this time in Iran, 50 Americans are still held captive, innocent victims of terrorism and anarchy. Also at this moment, massive Soviet troops are attempting to subjugate the fiercely independent and deeply religious people of Afghanistan. These two acts—one of international terrorism and one of military aggression—present a serious challenge to the United States of America and indeed to all the nations of the world. Together, we will meet these threats to peace.

I'm determined that the United States will remain the strongest of all nations, but our power will never be used to initiate a threat to the security of any nation or to the rights of any human being. We seek to be and to remain secure—a nation at peace in a stable world. But to be secure we must face the world as it is.

Three basic developments have helped to shape our challenges: the steady growth and increased projection of Soviet military power beyond its own borders; the overwhelming dependence of the Western democracies on oil supplies from the Middle East; and the press of social and religious and economic and political change in the many nations of the developing world, exemplified by the revolution in Iran.

Each of these factors is important in its own right. Each interacts with the others. All must be faced together, squarely and courageously. We will face these challenges, and we will meet them with the best that is in us. And we will not fail. . . .

But now the Soviet Union has taken a radical and an aggressive new step. It's using its great military power against a relatively defenseless nation. The implications of the Soviet invasion of Afghanistan could pose the most serious threat to the peace since the Second World War. . . .

The region which is now threatened by Soviet troops in Afghanistan is of great strategic importance: It contains more than two-thirds of the world's exportable oil. The Soviet effort to dominate Afghanistan has brought Soviet military forces to within 300 miles of the Indian Ocean and close to the Straits of Hormuz, a waterway through which most of the world's oil must flow. The Soviet Union is now attempting to consolidate a strategic position, therefore, that poses a grave threat to the free movement of Middle East oil.

This situation demands careful thought, steady nerves, and resolute action, not only for this year but for many years to come. It demands collective efforts to meet this new threat to security in the Persian Gulf and in Southwest Asia. It demands the participation of all those who rely on oil from the Middle East and who are concerned with global peace and stability. And it demands consultation and close cooperation with countries in the area which might be threatened.

Meeting this challenge will take national will, diplomatic and political wisdom, economic sacrifice, and, of course, military capability. We must call on the best that is in us to preserve the security of this crucial region.

Let our position be absolutely clear: An attempt by any outside force to gain control of the Persian Gulf region will be regarded as an assault on the vital interests of the United States of America, and such an assault will be repelled by any means necessary, including military force.

During the past 3 years, you have joined with me to improve our own security and the prospects for peace, not only in the vital oil-producing area of the Persian Gulf region but around the world.

Source: Public Papers of the Presidents of the United States, Jimmy Carter, 1980–1981 (Washington, DC: Government Printing Office, 1981), 194–97.

143.   LEBANON AND GRENADA: THE USE OF U.S. ARMED FORCES
27 October 1983

One of the hallmarks of the Reagan administration was its willingness to deploy military forces abroad to enforce American foreign policy. As witness to this, President Reagan deployed troops to Beirut, Lebanon, as part of the international peacekeeping force, and he sent a military task force to Grenada. On 27 October 1983, after a unit of marines was attacked in Beirut on 23 October by a suicide truck bomb and after the military task force invaded Grenada on 25 October, he spoke to the nation about why it was necessary for America to be involved in other countries' conflicts.

My fellow Americans, some two months ago we were shocked by the brutal massacre of 269 men, women, and children, in the shooting down of a Korean airliner. Now, in these past several days, violence has erupted again, in Lebanon and Grenada.

In Lebanon we have some 1,600 marines, part of a multinational force that's trying to help the people of Lebanon restore order and stability to that troubled land. Our marines are assigned to the south of the city of Beirut near the only airport operating in Lebanon. Just a mile or so to the north is the Italian contingent and not far from them the French and a company of British soldiers.

This past Sunday, at 22 minutes after 6, Beirut time, with dawn just breaking, a truck looking like a lot of other vehicles in the city approached the airport on a busy main road. There was nothing in its appearance to suggest it was any different than the trucks or cars that were normally seen on and around the airport. But this one was different.

At the wheel was a young man on a suicide mission. The truck carried some 2,000 pounds of explosives, but there was no way our marine guards could know this. Their first warning that something was wrong came when the truck crashed through a series of barriers, including a chain link fence and barbed wire entanglements. The guards opened fire but it was too late.

The truck smashed through the doors of the headquarters building in which our marines were sleeping and instantly exploded. The four-story concrete building collapsed into a pile of rubble.

More than 200 of the sleeping men were killed in that one hideous insane attack. Many others suffered injury and are hospitalized here or in Europe. This was not the end of the horror.

At almost the same instant another vehicle on a suicide and murder mission crashed into the headquarters of the French peacekeeping force, an eight-story building, destroying and killing more than 50 French soldiers.

Prior to this day of horror there had been several tragedies for our men in the multinational force; attacks by snipers and mortar fire had taken their toll. I called the bereaved parents and/or widows of the victims to express on behalf of all of us our sorrow and sympathy. Sometimes there were questions. And now many of you are asking: Why should our young men be dying in Lebanon? Why is Lebanon important to us?

Well, it's true Lebanon is a small country more than five and a half thousand miles from our shores, on the edge of what we call the Middle East. But every President who has occupied this office in recent years has recognized that peace in the Middle East is of vital concern to our nation and, indeed, to our allies in Western Europe and Japan. We've been concerned because the Middle East is a powder keg. Four times in the last 30 years the Arabs and Israelis have gone to war and each time the world has teetered near the edge of catastrophe. The area is key to the economic and political life of the West. Its strategic importance, its energy resources, the Suez Canal, the well-being of the nearly 200 million people living there; all are vital to us and to world peace.

If that key should fall into the hands of a power or powers hostile to the free world, there would be a direct threat to the United States and to our allies.

We have another reason to be involved. Since 1948, our nation has recognized and accepted a moral obligation to assure the continued existence of Israel as a nation. Israel shares our democratic values and is a formidable force an invader of the Middle East would have to reckon with. For several years, Lebanon has been torn by internal strife. Once a prosperous, peaceful nation, its Government had become ineffective in controlling the militias that warred on each other.

Sixteen months ago we were watching on our TV screens the shelling and bombing of Beirut, which was being used as a fortress by P.L.O. bands. Hundreds and hundreds of civilians were being killed and wounded in the daily battles. Syria, which makes no secret of its claim that Lebanon should be part of a greater Syria, was occupying a large part of Lebanon. Today, Syria has become a home for 7,000 Soviet advisers and technicians who man a massive amount of Soviet weaponry, including SS-21 ground-to-ground missiles capable of reaching vital areas of Israel.

A little over a year ago, hoping to build on the Camp David accords, which have led to peace between Israel and Egypt, I proposed a peace plan for the Middle East to end the wars between the Arab states and Israel. It was based on U.N. Resolutions 242 and 338 and called for a fair and just solution to the Palestinian problem, as well as a fair and just settlement of issues between the Arab states and Israel.

Before the necessary negotiations could begin, it was essential to get all foreign forces out of Lebanon and to end the fighting there. So why are we there? Well, the answer is straight-forward: to help bring peace to Lebanon and stability to the vital Middle East. To that end the multinational force was created to help stabilize the situation in Lebanon until a government could be established and the Lebanese Army mobilized to restore Lebanese sovereignty over its own soil as the foreign forces withdrew.

Israel agreed to withdraw as did Syria. But Syria then reneged on its promise. Over 10,000 Palestinians who had been bringing ruin down on Beirut, however, did leave the country. Lebanon has formed a Government under the leadership of President Gemayel and that Government, with our assistance and training, has set up its own army. In only a year's time that army has been rebuilt. It's a good army composed of Lebanese of all factions.

A few weeks ago the Israeli Army pulled back to the Awali River in southern Lebanon. Despite fierce resistance by Syrian-backed forces the Lebanese Army was able to hold the lines and maintain the defensive perimeter around Beirut. In the year that our marines have been there Lebanon has made important steps toward stability and order. The physical presence of the marines lends support to both the Lebanese Government and its army. It allows the hard work of diplomacy to go forward. Indeed without the peacekeepers from the U.S., France, Italy and Britain, the efforts to find a peaceful solution in Lebanon would collapse.

As for that narrower question, what exactly is the operational mission of the marines, the answer is to secure a piece of Beirut; to keep order in their sector and to prevent the area from becoming a battlefield. Our Marines are not just sitting in an airport. Part of their task is to guard that airport. Because of their presence the airport has remained operational. In addition they patrol the surrounding area. This is their part—a limited but essential part—in a larger effort that I described.

If our marines must be there, I'm asked, why can't we make them safer? Who committed this latest atrocity against them and why? Well, we'll do everything we can to insure that our men are as safe as possible. We ordered the battleship *New Jersey* to join our naval forces offshore. Without even firing them, the threat of its 16-inch guns silenced those who once fired down on our marines from the hills. And they're a good part of the reason we suddenly had a cease-fire. We're doing our best to make our forces less vulnerable to those who want to snipe at them or send in future suicide missions.

Secretary Schultz called me today from Europe, where he was meeting with the foreign ministers of our allies and the multinational force. They remain committed to our task, and plans were made to share information as to how we can improve security for all our men.

We have strong circumstantial evidence that the attack on the marines was directed by terrorists who used the same method to destroy our embassy in Beirut. Those who directed this atrocity must be dealt justice, and they will be. The obvious purpose behind the sniping and now this attack was to weaken American will and force the withdrawal of U.S. and French forces from Lebanon.

The clear intent of the terrorists was to limit our support of the Lebanese Government and to destroy the ability of the Lebanese people to determine their own destiny. To answer those who ask if we're serving any purpose in being there, let me answer a question with a question: would the terrorists have launched their suicide attacks against the multinational force if it were not doing its job?

The multinational force was attacked precisely because it is doing the job it was sent to do in Beirut. It is accomplishing its mission.

Now then, where do we go from here? What can we do now to help Lebanon gain greater stability so that our marines can come home? I believe we can take three steps now that will make a difference.

First, we will accelerate the search for peace and stability in that region. Little attention is being paid to the fact that we have had special envoys there working literally around the clock to bring the warring factions together. This coming Monday in Geneva President Gemayel of Lebanon will sit down with other factions from his country to see if national reconciliation can be achieved. He has our firm support.

I will soon be announcing a replacement for Bud McFarlane who was preceded by Phil Habib. Both worked tirelessly and must be credited for much, if not, most, of the progress we've made.

Second, we'll work even more closely with our allies in providing support for the Government of Lebanon and for the rebuilding of a national consensus.

Third, we will insure that the multinational peacekeeping forces, our Marines, are given the greatest possible protection. Our Commandant of the Marine Corps, General Kelly, returned from Lebanon today and will be advising us on steps we can take to improve security.

Vice President Bush returned just last night from Beirut and gave me a full report of his brief visit.

Beyond our progress in Lebanon let us remember that our main goal and purpose is to achieve a broader peace in all of the Middle East. The factions and bitterness we see in Lebanon are just a microcosm of the difficulties that are spread across much of that region. A peace initiative for the entire Middle East, consistent with the Camp David accord, and U.N. Resolutions 242 and 338, still offers the best hope for bringing peace to the region.

Let me ask those who say we should get out of Lebanon: If we were to leave Lebanon now, what message would that send to those who foment instability and terrorism? If Americans were to walk away from Lebanon, what chance would there be for a negotiated settlement producing the unified, democratic Lebanon? If we turned our backs on Lebanon now, what would be the future of Israel? At stake is the fate of only the second Arab country to negotiate a major agreement with Israel. That's another accomplishment of this past year, the May 17 accord signed by Lebanon and Israel.

If terrorism and intimidation succeed, it'll be a devastating blow to the peace process and to Israel's search for genuine security. It won't just be Lebanon sentenced to a future of chaos. Can the United States, or the free world, for that matter, stand by and see the Middle East incorporated into the Soviet bloc? What of Western Europe and Japan's dependence on Middle East oil for the energy to fuel their industries? The Middle East is, as I said, vital to our national security and economic well-being.

Brave young men have been taken from us. Many others have been grievously wounded. Are we to tell them their sacrifice was wasted or that they gave their lives in defense of our national security every bit as much as any man who ever died fighting in a war?

We must not strip every ounce of meaning and purpose from their courageous sacrifice. We are a nation with global responsibilities, we're not somewhere else in the world protecting someone else's interest. We're there protecting our own.

I received a message from the father of a marine in Lebanon. He told me: "In a world where we speak of human rights, there is a sad lack of acceptance and responsibility. My son has chosen the acceptance of responsibility for the privilege of living in this country."

Certainly in this country one does not inherently have rights unless the responsibility for those rights is accepted.

Dr. Kenneth Morrison said that while he was waiting to learn if his son was one of the dead. I was thrilled for him to learn today that his son, Ross, is alive and well and carrying on his duties in Lebanon.

Let us meet our responsibilities. For longer than any of us can remember, the people of the Middle East have lived from war to war with no prospect for any other future. That dreadful cycle must be broken.

Why are we there? When a Lebanese mother told one of our ambassadors that her little girl had only attended school two of the last eight years. Now, because of our presence there, she said her daughter could live a normal life.

With patience and firmness we can bring peace to that strife-torn region and make our own lives more secure.

Our role is to help the Lebanese put their country together, not to do it for them.

Now I know another part of the world is very much on our minds. A place much closer to our shores. Grenada. The island is only twice the size of the District of Columbia with a total population of about 110,000 people. Grenada and a half-dozen other Caribbean islands here were, until recently, British colonies. They are not independent states and members of the British Commonwealth.

While they respect each other's independence they also feel kinship with each other and think of themselves as one people. In 1979 trouble came to Grenada. Maurice Bishop, a protégé of Fidel Castro, staged a military coup and overthrew the government which had been elected under the constitution left to the people by the British.

He sought the help of Cuba in building an airport, which he claimed was for tourist trade, but which looked suspiciously suitable for military aircraft, including Soviet-built long-range bombers. The six sovereign countries and one remaining colony are joined together in what they call the Organization of Eastern Caribbean States. The six became increasingly alarmed as Bishop built an army greater than all of theirs combined.

Obviously it was not purely for defense. In this last year or so, Prime Minister Bishop gave indications that he might like better relations with the United States. He even made a trip to our country and met with senior officials at the White House and the State Department. Whether he was serious or not we'll never know.

On Oct. 12, a small group in his militia seized him and put him under arrest. They were, if anything, even more radical and more devoted to Castro's Cuba than he had been. Several days later, a crowd of citizens appeared before Bishop's home, freed him and escorted him toward the headquarters of the Military Council. They were fired upon. A number, including some children, were killed and Bishop was seized. He and several members of his Cabinet were subsequently executed and a 24-hour shoot-to-kill curfew was put in effect. Grenada was without a government, its only authority exercised by a self-proclaimed band of military men.

There were then about 1,000 of our citizens on Grenada, 800 of them students in St. George's University Medical School. Concern that they'd be harmed or held as hostages, I ordered a flotilla of ships then on its way to Lebanon with Marines—part of our regular rotation program—to circle south on a course that would put them somewhere in the vicinity of Grenada in case there should be a need to evacuate our people.

Last weekend I was awakened in the early morning hours and told that six members of the Organization of Eastern Caribbean States joined by Jamaica and

Barbados had sent an urgent request that we join them in a military operation to restore order and democracy to Grenada.

They were proposing this action under the terms of a treaty, a mutual assistance pact that existed among them. These small peaceful nations needed our help. Three of them don't have armies at all and the others have very limited forces.

The legitimacy of their request plus my own concern for our citizens dictated my decision. I believe our Government has a responsibility to go to the aid of its citizens if their right to life and liberty is threatened. The nightmare of our hostages in Iran must never be repeated.

We knew we had little time and that complete secrecy was vital to insure both the safety of the young men who would undertake this mission and the Americans they were about to rescue.

The joint chiefs worked around the clock to come up with a plan. They had little intelligence information about conditions on the island. We had to assume that several hundred Cubans working on the airport could be military reserves. As it turned out the number was much larger and they were a military force. Six hundred of them have been taken prisoner and we have discovered a complete base with weapons and communications equipment which makes it clear a Cuban occupation of the island had been planned.

Two hours ago we released the first photos from Grenada. They included pictures of a warehouse of military equipment, one of three we've uncovered so far. This warehouse contained weapons and ammunition stacked almost to the ceiling, enough to supply thousands of terrorists.

Grenada, we were told, was a friendly island paradise for tourism. Well it wasn't. It was a Soviet-Cuban colony being readied as a major military bastion to export terror and undermine democracy.

We got there just in time.

I can't say enough in praise of our military. Army Rangers and paratroopers, Navy, Marine, and Air Force personnel, those who planned a brilliant campaign and those who carried it out.

Almost instantly our military seized the two airports, secured the campus where most of our students were and they're now in the mopping-up phase.

It should be noted that in all the planning, a top priority was to minimize risk, to avoid casualties to our own men and also the Grenadian forces as much as humanly possible. But there were casualties. And we all owe a debt to those who lost their lives or were wounded. They were few in number but even one is a tragic price to pay.

It's our intention to get our men out as soon as possible.

Prime Minister Eugenia Charles of Dominica—I called that wrong, she pronounces it Dom-in-EE-kuh—she is chairman of O.E.C.S. She's calling for help from Commonwealth nations in giving the people their right to establish a constitutional government on Grenada. We anticipate that the Governor General, a Grenadian, will participate in setting up a provisional government in the interim.

The events in Lebanon and Grenada, though oceans apart, are closely related. Not only has Moscow assisted and encouraged the violence in both countries, but it provides direct support through a network of surrogates and terrorists. It is no coincidence that when the thugs tried to wrest control of Grenada, there were 30 Soviet advisers and hundreds of Cuban military and paramilitary forces on the island. At the moment of our landing we communicated with the governments of Cuba and the Soviet Union and told them we would offer shelter and security to their people on Grenada. Regrettably, Castro ordered his men to fight to the death and some did. The others will be sent to their homelands.

Now there was a time when our national security was based on a standing army here within our own borders and shore batteries of artillery along our coast, and of course a navy to keep the sea lanes open for the shipping of things necessary to our well being. The world has changed. Today our national security can be threatened in far-away places. It's up to all of us to be aware of the strategic importance of such places and to be able to identify them.

Sam Rayburn once said that freedom is not something a nation can work for once and win forever. He said it's like an insurance policy; its premiums must be kept up to date. In order to keep it we have to keep working for it and sacrificing for it just as long as we live. If we do not, our children may not know the pleasure of working to keep it for it may not be theirs to keep.

In these last few days, I've been more sure than I've ever been that we Americans of today will keep freedom and maintain peace. I've been made to feel that by the magnificent spirit of our young men and women in uniform, and by something here in our nation's capital.

In this city, where political strife is so much a part of our lives, I've seen Democratic leaders in the Congress join their Republican colleagues; send a message to the world that we're all Americans before we're anything else, and when our country is threatened, we stand shoulder to shoulder in support of men and women in the armed forces.

May I share something with you I think you'd like to know? It's something that happened to the Commandant of our Marine Corps, Gen. Paul Kelley, while he was visiting our critically injured marines in an Air Force hospital. It says more than any of us could ever hope to say about the gallantry and heroism of these young men, young men who served so willingly so that others might have a chance at peace and freedom in their own lives and in the life of their country.

I'll let General Kelley's words describe the incident. He spoke of a "young marine with more tubes going in and out of his body than I have ever seen in one body. He couldn't see very well. He reached up and grabbed my four stars just to make sure I was who I said I was. He held my hand with a firm grip. He was making signals and we realized he wanted to tell me something. We put a pad of paper in his hand and he wrote: 'semper fi.' "

Well, if you've been a marine, or if, like myself, you're an admirer of the Marines, you know those words are a battle cry, a greeting and a legend in the

Marine Corps. They're Marine shorthand for the motto of the Corps: Semper Fidelis, Always Faithful.

General Kelley has a reputation for being a very sophisticated general and a very tough marine, but he cried when he saw those words, and who can blame him. That marine, and all those others like him living and dead, have been faithful to their ideals. They've given willingly of themselves so that a nearly defenseless people in a region of great strategic importance to the free world will have a chance someday to live lives free of murder and mayhem and terrorism. I think that young marine and all of his comrades have given every one of us something to live up to.

They were not afraid to stand up for their country or no matter how difficult and slow the journey might be, to give to others that last best hope of a better future.

We cannot and will not dishonor them now and the sacrifices they made by failing to remain as faithful to the cause of freedom and the pursuit of peace as they have been.

I will not ask you to pray for the dead because they are safe in God's loving arms and beyond need of our prayers.

I would like to ask you all, where ever you may be in this blessed land, to pray for these wounded young men and to pray for the bereaved families of those who gave their lives for our freedom.

God bless you and God bless America.

Source: Ronald Reagan, "Lebanon and Grenada: The Use of U.S. Armed Forces," *Vital Speeches* 50 (15 November 1983): 66–69.

---

144.   REAGAN'S "EVIL EMPIRE" SPEECH
8 March 1983

From a very early point, Ronald Reagan appeared willing to describe the Cold War in stark, moral terms. His rhetorical and substantive stance marked an abandonment of détente in favor of an American policy of confrontation more reminiscent of the Eisenhower era. Before the annual convention of the National Association of Evangelicals, Reagan called for military and moral strength in response to aggression.

There is sin and evil in the world, and we're enjoined by Scripture and the Lord Jesus to oppose it with all our might. Our nation too, has a legacy of evil with which it must deal. The glory of this land has been its capacity for transcending the moral evils of our past. For example, the long struggle of minority citizens for equal rights, once a source of disunity and civil war, is now a point of pride for all Americans. We must never go back. There is no room for racism, anti-Semitism, or other forms of ethnic and racial hatred in this country.

I know that you've been horrified, as have I, by the resurgence of some hate groups preaching bigotry and prejudice. Use the mighty voice of your pulpits and the powerful standing of your churches to denounce and isolate these hate groups in our midst. The commandment given us is clear and simple: "Thou shalt love thy neighbor as thyself."

But whatever sad episodes exist in our past, any objective observer must hold a positive view of American history, a history that has been the story of hopes fulfilled and dreams made into reality. Especially in this century, America has kept alight the torch of freedom but not just for ourselves but for millions of others around the world.

And this brings me to my final point today. During my first press conference as President, in answer to a direct question, I pointed out that, as good Marxist-Leninists, the Soviet leaders have openly and publicly declared that the only morality they recognize is that which will further their cause, which is world revolution. I think I should point out I was only quoting Lenin, their guiding spirit who said in 1920 that they repudiate all morality that proceeds from supernatural ideas—that's their name for religion—or ideas that are outside class conceptions. Morality is entirely subordinate to the interests of class war. And everything is moral that is necessary for the annihilation of the old, exploiting social order and for uniting the proletariat.

Well, I think the refusal of many influential people to accept this elementary fact of Soviet doctrine illustrates an historical reluctance to see totalitarian powers for what they are. We saw this phenomenon in the 1930s. We see it too often today.

This doesn't mean we should isolate ourselves and refuse to seek an understanding with them. I intend to do everything I can to persuade them of our peaceful intent, to remind them that it was the West that refused to use its nuclear monopoly in the forties and fifties for territorial gain and which now proposes [a] 50-percent cut in strategic ballistic missiles and the elimination of an entire class of land-based, intermediate-range nuclear missiles.

At the same time, however, they must be made to understand we will never compromise our principles and standards. We will never give away our freedom. We will never abandon our belief in God. And we will never stop searching for a genuine peace. But we can assure none of these things America stands for through the so-called nuclear freeze solutions proposed by some.

The truth is that a freeze now would be a very dangerous fraud, for that is merely the illusion of peace. The reality is that we must find peace through strength.

I would agree to a freeze if only we could freeze the Soviets' global desires. A freeze at current levels of weapons would remove any incentive for the Soviets to negotiate seriously in Geneva and virtually end our chances to achieve the major arms reductions which we have proposed. Instead, they would achieve their objectives through the freeze.

A freeze would reward the Soviet Union for its enormous and unparalleled military buildup. It would prevent the essential and long overdue modernization of United States and allied defenses and would leave our aging forces increasingly vulnerable. And an honest freeze would require extensive prior negotiations on the systems and numbers to be limited and on the measures to ensure effective verification and compliance. And the kind of a freeze that has been suggested would be virtually impossible to verify. Such a major effort would divert us completely from our current negotiations on achieving substantial reductions.

A number of years ago, I heard a young father, a very prominent young man in the entertainment world, addressing a tremendous gathering in California. It was during the time of the cold war, and communism and our own way of life were very much on people's minds. And he was speaking to that subject. And suddenly, though, I heard him saying, "I love my little girls more than anything—" And I said to myself, "Oh, no, you don't. You can't—don't say that." But I had underestimated him. He went on: "I would rather see my little girls die now, still believing in God, than have them grow up under communism and one day die no longer believing in God."

There were thousands of young people in that audience. They came to their feet with shouts of joy. They had instantly recognized the profound truth in what he had said, with regard to the physical and the soul and what was truly important.

Yes, let us pray for the salvation of all those who live in that totalitarian darkness—pray they will discover the joy of knowing God. But until they do, let us be aware that while they preach the supremacy of the state, declare its omnipotence over individual man, and predict its eventual domination of all peoples on the Earth, they are the focus of evil in the modern world.

It was C.S. Lewis who, in his unforgettable "Screwtape Letters," wrote:

The greatest evil is not done now in those sordid "dens of crime" that Dickens loved to paint. It is not even done in concentration camps and labor camps. In those we see its final result. But it is conceived and ordered (moved, seconded, carried and minuted) in clear, carpeted, warmed, and well-lighted offices, by quiet men with white collars and cut fingernails and smooth-shaven cheeks who do not need to raise their voice.

Well, because these "quiet men" do not "raise their voices," because they sometimes speak in soothing tones of brotherhood and peace, because, like other dictators before them, they're always making "their final territorial demand," some would have us accept them at their word and accommodate ourselves to their aggressive impulses. But if history teaches anything, it teaches that simpleminded appeasement or wishful thinking about our adversaries is folly. It means the betrayal of our past, the squandering of our freedom.

So, I urge you to speak out against those who would place the United States in a position of military and moral inferiority. You know, I've always believed that old Screwtape reserved his best efforts for those of you in the church. So, in your discussions of the nuclear freeze proposals, I urge you to beware the temptation of pride—the temptation of blithely declaring yourselves above it all and label both sides equally at fault, to ignore the facts of history and the aggressive impulses of an evil empire, to simply call the arms race a giant misunderstanding and thereby remove yourself from the struggle between right and wrong and good and evil.

I ask you to resist the attempts of those who would have you withhold your support for our efforts, this administration's efforts, to keep America strong and free, while we negotiate real and verifiable reductions in the world's nuclear arsenals and one day, with God's help, their total elimination.

While America's military strength is important, let me add here that I've always maintained that the struggle now going on for the world will never be decided by bombs or rockets, by armies or military might. The real crisis we face today is a spiritual one; at root, it is a test of moral will and faith.

Whittaker Chambers, the man whose own religious conversion made him a witness to one of the terrible traumas of our time, the Hiss-Chambers case, wrote that the crisis of the Western World exists to the degree in which the West is indifferent to God, the degree to which it collaborates in communism's attempt to make man stand alone without God. And then he said, for Marxism-Leninism is actually the second oldest faith, first proclaimed in the Garden of Eden with the words of temptation, "Ye shall be as gods."

The Western World can answer this challenge, he wrote, "but only provided that its faith in God and the freedom He enjoins is as great as communism's faith in Man."

I believe we shall rise to the challenge. I believe that communism is another sad, bizarre chapter in human history whose last pages even now are being written. I believe this because the source of our strength in the quest for human freedom is not material, but spiritual. And because it knows no limitation, it must terrify and ultimately triumph over those who would enslave their fellow man. For in the words of Isaiah: "He giveth power to the faint; and to them that have no might He increased strength. . . . But they that wait upon the Lord shall renew their strength; they shall mount up with wings as eagles; they shall run, and not be weary. . . ."

Yes, change your world. One of our Founding Fathers, Thomas Paine, said, "We have it within our power to begin the world over again." We can do it, doing together what no one church could do by itself.

God Bless you, and thank you very much.

Source: Public Papers of the Presidents of the United States, Ronald Reagon, 1983 (Washington DC: Government Printing Office, 1984), 362–64.

145. THE STRATEGIC DEFENSE INITIATIVE
23 March 1983

One of the key characteristics of the first Reagan administration was its willingness to confront the Soviet Union on the issue of strategic armaments. On 23 March 1983, Ronald Reagan appeared on national television to inform the public about Soviet military power and to call for an appropriate American arms buildup. Part of the response, later labeled "Star Wars," was a program designed to create a nuclear missile shield for the United States.

My fellow Americans, thank you for sharing your time with me tonight.

The subject I want to discuss with you, peace and national security, is both timely and important. Timely, because I've reached a decision which offers a new hope for our children in the 21st century, a decision I'll tell you about in a few minutes. And important because there's a very big decision that you must make for yourselves. This subject involves the most basic duty that any President and any people share, the duty to protect and strengthen the peace.

At the beginning of this year, I submitted to the Congress a defense budget which reflects my best judgment of the best understanding of the experts and specialists who advise me about what we and our allies must do to protect our people in the years ahead. That budget is much more than a long list of numbers, for behind all the numbers lies America's ability to prevent the greatest of human tragedies and preserve our free way of life in a sometimes dangerous world. It is part of a careful, long-term plan to make America strong again after too many years of neglect and mistakes.

Our efforts to rebuild America's defenses and strengthen the peace began 2 years ago when we requested a major increase in the defense program. Since then, the amount of those increases we first proposed has been reduced by half, through improvements in management and procurement and other savings.

The budget request that is now before the Congress has been trimmed to the limits of safety. Further deep cuts cannot be made without seriously endangering the security of the Nation. The choice is up to the men and women you've elected to the Congress, and that means the choice is up to you.

Tonight, I want to explain to you what this defense debate is all about and why I'm convinced that the budget now before the Congress is necessary, responsible, and deserving of your support. And I want to offer hope for the future.

But first, let me say what the defense debate is not about. It is not about spending arithmetic. I know that in the last few weeks you've been bombarded with numbers and percentages. Some say we need only a 5-percent increase in defense spending. The so-called alternate budget backed by liberals in the House of Representatives would lower the figure to 2 to 3 percent, cutting our defense spending by $163 billion over the next 5 years. The trouble with all these numbers is that they tell us little about the kind of defense program America needs or the benefits and security and freedom that our defense effort buys for us.

What seems to have been lost in all this debate is the simple truth of how a defense budget is arrived at. It isn't done by deciding to spend a certain number of dollars. Those loud voices that are occasionally heard charging that the Government is trying to solve a security problem by throwing money at it are nothing more than noise based on ignorance. We start by considering what must be done to maintain peace and review all the possible threats against our security. Then a strategy for strengthening peace and defending against those threats must be agreed upon. And, finally, our defense establishment must be evaluated to see what is necessary to protect against any or all of the potential threats. The cost of achieving these ends is totaled up, and the result is the budget for national defense.

There is no logical way that you can say, let's spend x billion dollars less. You can only say, which part of our defense measures do we believe we can do without and still have security against all contingencies? Anyone in the Congress who advocates a percentage or a specific dollar cut in defense spending should be made to say what part of our defenses he would eliminate, and he should be candid enough to acknowledge that his cuts mean cutting our commitments to allies or inviting greater risk or both.

The defense policy of the United States is based on a simple premise: The United States does not start fights. We will never be an aggressor. We maintain our strength in order to deter and defend against aggression—to preserve freedom and peace.

Since the dawn of the atomic age, we've sought to reduce the risk of war by maintaining a strong deterrent and by seeking genuine arms control. "Deterrence" means simply this: making sure any adversary who thinks about attacking the United States, or our allies, or our vital interests, concludes that the risks to him outweigh any potential gains. Once he understands that, he won't attack. We maintain the peace through our strength; weakness only invites aggression.

This strategy of deterrence has not changed. It still works. But what it takes to maintain deterrence has changed. It took one kind of military force to deter an attack when we had far more nuclear weapons than any other power; it takes another kind now that the Soviets, for example, have enough accurate and powerful nuclear weapons to destroy virtually all of our missiles on the ground. Now, this is not to say that the Soviet Union is planning to make war on us. Nor do I believe a war is inevitable—quite the contrary. But what must be recognized is that our security is based on being prepared to meet all threats.

There was a time when we depended on coastal forts and artillery batteries, because, with the weaponry of that day, any attack would have had to come by sea. Well, this is a different world, and our defenses must be based on recognition and awareness of the weaponry possessed by other nations in the nuclear age.

We can't afford to believe that we will never be threatened. There have been two world wars in my lifetime. We didn't start them and, indeed, did everything we could to avoid being drawn into them. But we were ill-prepared for both. Had we been better prepared, peace might have been preserved.

For 20 years the Soviet Union has been accumulating enormous military might. They didn't stop when their forces exceeded all requirements of a legitimate defensive capability. And they haven't stopped now. During the past decade and a half, the Soviets have built up a massive arsenal of new strategic nuclear weapons—weapons that can strike directly at the United States.

As an example, the United States introduced its last new intercontinental ballistic missile, the Minute Man III, in 1969, and we're now dismantling our even older Titan missiles. But what has the Soviet Union done in these intervening years? Well, since 1969 the Soviet Union has built five new classes of ICBM'S, and upgraded these eight times. As a result, their missiles are much more powerful and accurate than they were several years ago, and they continue to develop more, while ours are increasingly obsolete.

The same thing has happened in other areas. Over the same period, the Soviet Union built 4 new classes of submarine-launched ballistic missiles and over 60 new missile submarines. We built 2 new types of submarine missiles and actually withdrew 10 submarines from strategic missions. The Soviet Union built over 200 new Backfire bombers, and their brand new Blackjack bomber is now under development. We haven't built a new long-range bomber since our B-52's were deployed about a quarter of a century ago, and we've already retired several hundred of those because of old age. Indeed, despite what many people think, our strategic forces only cost about 15 percent of the defense budget.

Another example of what's happened: In 1978 the Soviets had 600 intermediate-range nuclear missiles based on land and were beginning to add the SS-20—a new, highly accurate, mobile missile with 3 warheads. We had none. Since then the Soviets have strengthened their lead. By the end of 1979, when Soviet leader Brezhnev declared "a balance now exists," the Soviets had over 800 warheads. We still had none. A year ago this month, Mr. Brezhnev pledged a moratorium, or freeze, on SS-20 deployment. But by last August, their 800 warheads had become more than 1,200. We still had none. Some freeze. At this time Soviet Defense Minister Ustinov announced "approximate parity of forces continues to exist." But the Soviets are still adding an average of 3 new warheads a week, and now have 1,300. These warheads can reach their targets in a matter of a few minutes. We still have none. So far, it seems that the Soviet definition of parity is a box score of 1,300 to nothing, in their favor.

So, together with our NATO allies, we decided in 1979 to deploy new weapons, beginning this year, as a deterrent to their SS-20's and as an incentive to the Soviet Union to meet us in serious arms control negotiations. We will begin that deployment late this year. At the same time, however, we're willing to cancel our program if the Soviets will dismantle theirs. This is what we've called a zero-zero plan. The Soviets are now at the negotiating table—and I think it's fair to say that without our planned deployments, they wouldn't be there.

Now, let's consider conventional forces. Since 1974 the United States has produced 3,050 tactical combat aircraft. By contrast, the Soviet Union has produced twice as many. When we look at attack submarines, the United States has produced 27 while the Soviet Union has produced 61. For armored vehicles, including tanks, we have produced 11,200. The Soviet Union has produced 54,000—nearly 5 to 1 in their favor. Finally, with artillery, we've produced 950 artillery and rocket launchers while the Soviets have produced more than 13,000—a staggering 14-to-1 ratio.

There was a time when we were able to offset superior Soviet numbers with higher quality, but today they are building weapons as sophisticated and modern as our own.

As the Soviets have increased their military power, they've been emboldened to extend that power. They're spreading their military influence in ways that can directly challenge our vital interests and those of our allies.

The following aerial photographs, most of them secret until now, illustrate this point in a crucial area very close to home: Central America and the Caribbean Basin. They're not dramatic photographs. But I think they help give you a better understanding of what I'm talking about.

This Soviet intelligence collection facility, less than a hundred miles from our coast, is the largest of its kind in the world. The acres and acres of antennae fields and intelligence monitors are targeted on key U.S. military installations and sensitive activities. The installation in Lourdes, Cuba, is manned by 1,500 Soviet technicians. And the satellite ground station allows instant communications with Moscow. This 28-square-mile facility has grown by more than 60 percent in size and capability during the past decade.

In western Cuba, we see this military airfield and its complement of modern, Soviet-built Mig-23 aircraft. The Soviet Union uses this Cuban airfield for its own long-range reconnaissance missions. And earlier this month, two modern Soviet antisubmarine warfare aircraft began operating from it. During the past 2 years, the level of Soviet arms exports to Cuba can only be compared to the levels reached during the Cuban missile crisis 20 years ago.

This third photo, which is the only one in this series that has been previously made public, shows Soviet military hardware that has made its way to Central America. This airfield with its MI-8 helicopters, anti-aircraft guns, and protected fighter sites is one of a number of military facilities in Nicaragua which has received Soviet equipment funneled through Cuba, and reflects the massive military buildup going on in that country.

On the small island of Grenada, at the southern end of the Caribbean chain, the Cubans, with Soviet financing and backing, are in the process of building an airfield with a 10,000-foot runway. Grenada doesn't even have an air force. Who is it intended for? The Caribbean is a very important passageway for our international commerce and military lines of communication. More than half of American oil imports now pass through the Caribbean. The rapid buildup of Grenada's military potential is unrelated to any conceivable threat to this island country of under 110,000 people and totally at odds with the pattern of other eastern Caribbean States, most of which are unarmed.

The Soviet-Cuban militarization of Grenada, in short, can only be seen as power projection into the region. And it is in this important economic and strategic area that we're trying to help the Governments of El Salvador, Costa Rica, Honduras, and others in their struggles for democracy against guerrillas supported through Cuba and Nicaragua.

These pictures only tell a small part of the story. I wish I could show you more without compromising our most sensitive intelligence sources and methods. But the Soviet Union is also supporting Cuban military forces in Angola and Ethiopia. They have bases in Ethiopia and South Yemen, near the Persian Gulf oil fields. They've taken over the port that we built at Cam Ranh Bay in Vietnam. And now for the first time in history, the Soviet Navy is a force to be reckoned with in the South Pacific.

Some people may still ask: Would the Soviets ever use their formidable military power? Well, again, can we afford to believe they won't? There is Afghanistan. And in Poland, the Soviets denied the will of the people and in so doing demonstrated to the world how their military power could also be used to intimidate.

The final fact is that the Soviet Union is acquiring what can only be considered an offensive military force. They have continued to build far more intercontinental ballistic missiles than they could possibly need simply to deter an attack. Their conventional forces are trained and equipped not so much to defend against an attack as they are to permit sudden, surprise offensives of their own.

Our NATO allies have assumed a great defense burden, including the military draft in most countries. We're working with them and our other friends around the world to do more. Our defensive strategy means we need military forces that can move very quickly, forces that are trained and ready to respond to any emergency.

Every item in our defense program—our ships, our tanks, our planes, our funds for training and spare parts—is intended for one all-important purpose: to keep the peace. Unfortunately, a decade of neglecting our military forces had called into question our ability to do that.

When I took office in January 1981, I was appalled by what I found: American planes that couldn't fly and American ships that couldn't sail for lack of spare parts and trained personnel and insufficient fuel and ammunition for essential training. The inevitable result of all this was poor morale in our Armed Forces, difficulty in recruiting the brightest young Americans to wear the uniform, and difficulty in convincing our most experienced military personnel to stay on.

There was a real question then about how well we could meet a crisis. And it was obvious that we had to begin a major modernization program to ensure we could deter aggression and preserve the peace in the years ahead.

We had to move immediately to improve the basic readiness and staying power of our conventional forces, so they could meet—and therefore help deter—a crisis. We had to make up for lost years of investment by moving forward with a long-term plan to prepare our forces to counter the military capabilities our adversaries were developing for the future.

I know that all of you want peace, and so do I. I know too that many of you seriously believe that a nuclear freeze would further the cause of peace. But a freeze now would make us less, not more, secure and would raise, not reduce, the risks of war. It would be largely unverifiable and would seriously undercut our negotiations on arms reduction. It would reward the Soviets for their massive military buildup while preventing us from modernizing our aging and increasingly vulnerable forces. With their present margin of superiority, why should they agree to arms reductions knowing that we were prohibited from catching up?

Believe me, it wasn't pleasant for someone who had come to Washington determined to reduce government spending, but we had to move forward with the task of repairing our defenses or we would lose our ability to deter conflict now and in the future. We had to demonstrate to any adversary that aggression could not succeed, and that the only real solution was substantial, equitable, and effectively verifiable arms reduction—the kind we're working for right now in Geneva.

Thanks to your strong support, and bipartisan support from the Congress, we began to turn things around. Already, we're seeing some very encouraging results. Quality recruitment and retention are up dramatically—more high school graduates are choosing military careers, and more experienced career personnel are choosing to stay. Our men and women in uniform at last are getting the tools and training they need to do their jobs.

Ask around today, especially among our young people, and I think you will find a whole new attitude toward serving their country. This reflects more than just better pay, equipment, and leadership. You the American people have sent a signal to these young people that it is once again an honor to wear the uniform. That's not something you measure in a budget, but it's very real part of our nation's strength.

It'll take us longer to build the kind of equipment we need to keep peace in the future, but we've made a good start.

We haven't built a new long-range bomber for 21 years. Now we're building the B-1. We hadn't launched one new strategic submarine for 17 years. Now we're building one Trident submarine a year. Our land-based missiles are increasingly threatened by the many huge, new Soviet ICBMs. We're determining how to solve that problem. At the same time, we're working in the START and INF negotiations with the goal of achieving deep reductions in the strategic and intermediate nuclear arsenals of both sides.

We have also begun the long-needed modernization of our conventional forces. The Army is getting its first new tank in 20 years. The Air Force is modernizing. We're rebuilding our Navy, which shrank from about a thousand ships in the late 1960s to 433 during the 1970s. Our nation needs a superior navy to support our military forces and vital interests overseas. We're now on the road to achieving a 600-ship navy and increasing the amphibious capabilities of our marines, who are now serving the cause of peace in Lebanon. And we're building a real capability to assist our friends in the vitally important Indian Ocean and Persian Gulf region.

This adds up to a major effort, and it isn't cheap. It comes at a time when there are many other pressures on our budget and when the American people have already had to make major sacrifices during the recession. But we must not be misled by those who would make defense once again the scapegoat of the Federal budget.

The fact is that in the past few decades we have seen a dramatic shift in how we spend the taxpayer's dollar. Back in 1955, payments to individuals took up only about 20 percent of the Federal budget. For nearly three decades, these payments steadily increased and, this year, will account for 49 percent of the budget. By contrast, in 1955 defense took up more than half of the Federal budget. By 1980 this spending had fallen to a low of 23 percent. Even with the increase that I am requesting this year, defense will still amount to only 28 percent of the budget.

The calls for cutting back the defense budget come in nice, simple arithmetic. They're the same kind of talk that led the democracies to neglect their defenses in the 1930s and invited the tragedy of World War II. We must not let that grim chapter of history repeat itself through apathy or neglect.

This is why I'm speaking to you tonight—to urge you to tell your Senators and Congressmen that you know we must continue to restore our military strength. If we stop in midstream, we will send a signal of decline, of lessened will, to friends and adversaries alike. Free people must voluntarily, through open debate and democratic means, meet the challenge that totalitarians pose by compulsion. It's up to us, in our time, to choose and choose wisely between the hard but necessary task of preserving peace and freedom and the temptation to ignore our duty and blindly hope for the best while the enemies of freedom grow stronger day by day.

The solution is well within our grasp. But to reach it, there is simply no alternative but to continue this year, in this budget, to provide the resources we need to preserve the peace and guarantee our freedom.

Now, thus far tonight I've shared with you my thoughts on the problems of national security we must face together. My predecessors in the Oval Office have appeared before you on other occasions to describe the threat posed by

Soviet power and have proposed steps to address that threat. But since the advent of nuclear weapons, those steps have been increasingly directed toward deterrence of aggression through the promise of retaliation.

This approach to stability through offensive threat has worked. We and our allies have succeeded in preventing nuclear war for more than three decades. In recent months, however, my advisers, including in particular the Joint Chiefs of Staff, have underscored the necessity to break out of a future that relies solely on offensive retaliation for our security.

Over the course of these discussions, I've become more and more deeply convinced that the human spirit must be capable of rising above dealing with other nations and human beings by threatening their existence. Feeling this way, I believe we must thoroughly examine every opportunity for reducing tensions and for introducing greater stability into the strategic calculus on both sides.

One of the most important contributions we can make is, of course, to lower the level of all arms, and particularly nuclear arms. We're engaged right now in several negotiations with the Soviet Union to bring about a mutual reduction of weapons. I will report to you a week from tomorrow my thoughts on that score. But let me just say, I'm totally committed to this course.

If the Soviet Union will join with us in our effort to achieve major arms reduction, we will have succeeded in stabilizing the nuclear balance. Nevertheless, it will still be necessary to rely on the specter of retaliation, on mutual threat. And that's a sad commentary on the human condition. Wouldn't it be better to save lives than to avenge them? Are we not capable of demonstrating our peaceful intentions by applying all our abilities and our ingenuity to achieving a truly lasting stability? I think we are. Indeed, we must.

After careful consultation with my advisers, including the Joint Chiefs of Staff, I believe there is a way. Let me share with you a vision of the future which offers hope. It is that we embark on a program to counter the awesome Soviet missile threat with measures that are defensive. Let us turn to the very strengths in technology that spawned our great industrial base and that have given us the quality of life we enjoy today.

What if free people could live secure in the knowledge that their security did not rest upon the threat of instant U.S. retaliation to deter a Soviet attack, that we could intercept and destroy strategic ballistic missiles before they reached our own soil or that of our allies?

I know this is a formidable, technical task, one that may not be accomplished before the end of this century. Yet, current technology has attained a level of sophistication where it's reasonable for us to begin this effort. It will take years, probably decades of effort on many fronts. There will be failures and setbacks, just as there will be successes and breakthroughs. And as we proceed, we must remain constant in preserving the nuclear deterrent and maintaining a solid capability for flexible response. But isn't it worth every investment necessary to free the world from the threat of nuclear war? We know it is.

In the meantime, we will continue to pursue real reductions in nuclear arms, negotiating from a position of strength that can be ensured only by modernizing our strategic forces. At the same time, we must take steps to reduce the risk of a conventional military conflict escalating to nuclear war by improving our non-nuclear capabilities.

America does possess—now—the technologies to attain very significant improvements in the effectiveness of our conventional, nonnuclear forces. Proceeding boldly with these new technologies, we can significantly reduce any incentive that the Soviet Union may have to threaten attack against the United States or its allies.

As we pursue our goal of defensive technologies, we recognize that our allies rely upon our strategic offensive power to deter attacks against them. Their vital interests and ours are inextricably linked. Their safety and ours are one. And no change in technology can or will alter that reality. We must and shall continue to honor our commitments.

I clearly recognize that defensive systems have limitations and raise certain problems and ambiguities. If paired with offensive systems, they can be viewed as fostering an aggressive policy, and no one wants that. But with these considerations firmly in mind, I call upon the scientific community in our country, those who gave us nuclear weapons, to turn their great talents now to the cause of mankind and world peace, to give us the means of rendering these nuclear weapons impotent and obsolete.

Tonight, consistent with our obligations of the ABM treaty and recognizing the need for closer consultation with our allies, I'm taking an important first step. I am directing a comprehensive and intensive effort to define a long-term research and development program to begin to achieve our ultimate goal of eliminating the threat posed by strategic nuclear missiles. This could pave the way for arms control measures to eliminate the weapons themselves. We seek neither military superiority nor political advantage. Our only purpose—one all people share—is to search for ways to reduce the danger of nuclear war.

My fellow Americans, tonight we're launching an effort which holds the promise of changing the course of human history. There will be risks, and results take time. But I believe we can do it. As we cross this threshold, I ask for your prayers and your support.

Thank you, good night, and God bless you.

Source: Public Papers of the Presidents of the United States, Ronald Reagan, 1983 (Washington, DC: Government Printing Office, 1984), 437–43.

---

146. REAGAN DOCTRINE
6 February 1985

During his 1985 State of the Union Address, President Reagan signaled his willingness to extend U.S. support to guerrilla forces engaged in a war against Communism. His administration's aid to the contra forces

fighting against Sandinista Nicaragua would pit policy makers in an on-
going battle with Congress and later mire many key Reagan aides, and
the president himself, in scandal.

. . . We cannot play innocents abroad in a world that's not innocent; nor can
we be passive when freedom is under siege. Without resources, diplomacy cannot succeed. Our security assistance programs help friendly governments defend
themselves and give them confidence to work for peace. And I hope that you
in the Congress will understand that, dollar for dollar, security assistance contributes as much to global security as our own defense budget.

We must stand by all our democratic allies. And we must not break faith with
those who are risking their lives—on every continent, from Afghanistan to Nicaragua—to defy Soviet-supported aggression and secure rights which have been
ours from birth.

The Sandinista dictatorship of Nicaragua, with full Cuban-Soviet bloc support,
not only persecutes its people, the church, and denies a free press, but arms and
provides bases for Communist terrorists attacking neighboring states. Support
for freedom fighters is self-defense and totally consistent with the OAS and
U.N. Charters. It is essential that the Congress continue all facets of our assistance to Central America. I want to work with you to support the democratic
forces whose struggle is tied to our own security.

Source: Public Papers of the Presidents of the United States, Ronald Reagan, 1985
(Washington, DC: Government Printing Office, 1988), 135.

147. INF TREATY WITH THE SOVIET UNION
6 December 1987

In late 1979, the Carter administration made the decision to deploy a new
generation of interregional nuclear weapons to Western Europe designed
to offset existing Soviet SS-20 missiles. In the meantime, American dip-
lomats continued their pursuit of an arms reduction agreement. The Rea-
gan administration embraced these policy decisions and was able to win
a treaty in 1987.

REMARKS ON SIGNING THE INTERMEDIATE-RANGE NUCLEAR
FORCES TREATY, DECEMBER 8, 1987

The President. Thank you all very much. Welcome to the White House. This
ceremony and the treaty we're signing today are both excellent examples of the
rewards of patience. It was over 6 years ago, November 18, 1981, that I first
proposed what would come to be called the zero option. It was a simple pro-

posal—one might say, disarmingly simple. Unlike treaties in the past, it didn't simply codify the status quo or a new arms buildup; it didn't simply talk of controlling an arms race.

For the first time in history, the language of "arms control" was replaced by "arms reduction"—in this case, the complete elimination of an entire class of U.S. and Soviet nuclear missiles. Of course, this required a dramatic shift in thinking, and it took conventional wisdom some time to catch up. Reaction, to say the least, was mixed. To some the zero option was impossibly visionary and unrealistic; to others merely a propaganda ploy. Well, with patience, determination, and commitment, we've made this impossible vision a reality.

General Secretary Gorbachev, I'm sure you're familiar with Ivan Krylov's famous tale about the swan, the crawfish, and the pike. It seems that once upon a time these three were trying to move a wagonload together. They hitched and harnessed themselves to the wagon. It wasn't very heavy, but no matter how hard they worked, the wagon just wouldn't move. You see, the swan was flying upward; the crawfish kept crawling backward; the pike kept making for the water. The end result was that they got nowhere, and the wagon is still there to this day. Well, strong and fundamental moral differences continue to exist between our nations. But today, on this vital issue, at least, we've seen what can be accomplished when we pull together.

The numbers alone demonstrate the value of this agreement. On the Soviet side, over 1,500 deployed warheads will be removed, and all ground-launched intermediate-range missiles, including the SS-20's, will be destroyed. On our side, our entire complement of Pershing II and ground-launched cruise missiles, with some 400 deployed warheads, will all be destroyed. Additionally, backup missiles on both sides will also be destroyed.

But the importance of this treaty transcends numbers. We have listened to the wisdom in an old Russian maxim. And I'm sure you're familiar with it, Mr. General Secretary, though my pronunciation may give you difficulty. The maxim is: *Dovorey no provorey*—trust, but verify.

The General Secretary. You repeat that at every meeting.

The President. I like it.

This agreement contains the most stringent verification regime in history, including provisions for inspection teams actually residing in each other's territory and several other forms of onsite inspection, as well. This treaty protects the interests of America's friends and allies. It also embodies another important principle: the need for *glasnost*, a greater openness in military programs and forces.

We can only hope that this historymaking agreement will not be an end in itself but the beginning of a working relationship that will enable us to tackle the other urgent issues before us: strategic offensive nuclear weapons, the balance of conventional forces in Europe, the destructive and tragic regional conflicts that beset so many parts of our globe, and respect for the human and natural rights God has granted to all men.

Source: Public Papers of the Presidents of the United States, Ronald Reagan, 1987 (Washington, DC: Government Printing Office, 1989), 1455–6.

148. THE INVASION OF PANAMA
1989

In 1989, relations between the United States and Panama had deteriorated to a crisis point. A year earlier, the ostensible leader of the country and former U.S. intelligence operative, General Manuel Noriega, had been indicted by two American grand juries on charges of drug trafficking, racketeering, and money laundering. In May 1989, Noriega voided a free election and dissolved the national assembly. Throughout the summer and fall, Noriega openly flaunted American power and publicly challenged the United States to invade. On 15 December, he took the step of declaring war on the United States. Attacks on U.S. military personnel and citizens followed the action.

Letter to the Speaker of the House of Representatives and the
President Pro Tempore of the Senate on the United States Military
Action in Panama
December 21, 1989

Dear Mr. Speaker: (Dear Mr. President.)

On December 15, 1989, at the instigation of Manuel Noriega, the illegitimate Panamanian National Assembly declared that a state of war existed between the Republic of Panama and the United States. At the same time, Noriega gave a highly inflammatory anti-American speech. A series of vicious and brutal acts directed at U.S. personnel and dependents followed these events.

On December 16, 1989, a U.S. Marine officer was killed without justification by Panama Defense Forces (PDF) personnel. Other elements of the PDF beat a U.S. Naval officer and unlawfully detained, physically abused, and threatened the officer's wife. These acts of violence are directly attributable to Noriega's dictatorship, which created a climate of aggression that places American lives and interests in peril.

These and other events over the past two years have made it clear that the lives and welfare of American citizens in Panama were increasingly at risk, and that the continued safe operation of the Panama Canal and the integrity of the Canal Treaties would be in serious jeopardy if such lawlessness were allowed to continue.

Under these circumstances, I ordered the deployment of approximately 11,000 additional U.S. Forces to Panama. In conjunction with the 13,000 U.S. Forces already present, military operations were initiated on December 20, 1989, to protect American lives, to defend democracy in Panama, to apprehend Noriega and bring him to trial on the drug-related charges for which he was indicted in 1988, and to ensure the integrity of the Panama Canal Treaties.

In the early morning of December 20, 1989, the democratically elected Panamanian leadership announced formation of a government, assumed power in a formal swearing-in ceremony, and welcomed the assistance of U.S. Armed Forces in removing the illegitimate Noriega regime.

The deployment of U.S. Forces is an exercise of the right of self-defense recognized in Article 51 of the United Nations Charter and was necessary to protect American lives in imminent danger and to fulfill our responsibilities under the Panama Canal Treaties. It was welcomed by the democratically elected government of Panama. The military operations were ordered pursuant to my constitutional authority with respect to the conduct of foreign relations and as Commander in Chief.

In accordance with my desire that Congress be fully informed on this matter, and consistent with the War Powers Resolution, I am providing this report on the deployment of U.S. Armed Forces to Panama.

Although most organized opposition has ceased, it is not possible at this time to predict the precise scope and duration of the military operations or how long the temporary increase of U.S. Forces in Panama will be required. Nevertheless, our objectives are clear and largely have been accomplished. Our additional Forces will remain in Panama only so long as their presence is required.

Sincerely,

GEORGE BUSH

Source: Public Papers of the Presidents of the United States, George Bush, 1989 (Washington, DC: Government Printing Office, 1990), 1734.

Part Ten

The Post–Cold War Era

The end of the Cold War witnessed the final demise of the bipolar boundaries of power and prompted a fundamental redefinition of international relations. For nearly five decades, the U.S.–Soviet standoff served as a benchmark for national interests, the standards that defined conflict, and the diplomacy necessary to resolve it. All were provided a collective coherence by the potential for any one to lead to a final escalation into thermonuclear war between the two superpowers.

During the 1990s this basic framework had diminished and was increasingly displaced by an array of problems apparent throughout the Cold War, but unaddressed by it. One clear dilemma present in the decade was a global economic recession. Characterized by Thomas J. McCormick as the "quiet depression," it represented a twenty-year trend, initiated by the oil crisis of 1973, that continued well after the Gulf War. For major industrial nations in both the West and the former Soviet Bloc, the period was marked by economic retrenchment of varying degrees of success. For peripheral countries dependent on raw material exports, the handicaps of debt and fluctuating commodity prices continued to undercut growth.[1] While the Pacific Rim experienced dramatic gains during this period, these did not offset the systemic limitations of the global economy, and were themselves largely negated by the Asian economic crisis of the late 1990s.[2]

The end products of this global recession extended far beyond the difficulties of debt and prosperity. Economic nationalism bordering on xenophobia gained considerable traction in countries where obsolescent industries and expensive labor were overtaken by corporations intent on moving production to lower cost areas of the world. The protests that greeted the 1993 North American Free Trade Agreement (NAFTA) and surrounded the more recent 2000 meeting of the World Trade Organization (WTO) in Seattle, Washington, reflect a resurgence of autarky. Other integration measures have faced similar difficulties. The 1993 Maastricht Treaty of European Union was ratified with a bare majority, but has suffered substantial growing pains since. Attempts to introduce a unified European currency have proceeded at an uneven pace, plagued by fluctuating values and the outright refusal of some member nations to abandon their national monetary standards.[3]

Many observers predicted at the start of the 1990s that the United States would succumb to the undertow of the global recession. Historians such as Paul Kennedy described America in 1989 as a declining empire, a power staggering under the accumulated costs of decades of Cold War defense spending.[4] Subsequent events seemed to bear Kennedy's thesis out. In the aftermath of the Gulf War, American leaders demanded foreign financial support for their military intervention against Iraq. Germany and Japan, robust economic powers in their own right who did not participate in the conflict, eventually provided $17.3 billion of the estimated $50 billion cost of the war.[5]

America's actual conduct of Operation Desert Shield/Desert Storm also revealed a nation groping for a central focus for its foreign policy. Initially, the U.S. response to the Iraqi invasion of Kuwait was a decisive act predicated by overt aggression. In the early stages of the confrontation with Baghdad, the Bush administration resorted to old historical models to explain its strategic goals. In its dire prediction that Saudi Arabia would become the next domino to fall to Iraq, the White House invoked the recently departed Cold War. In his characterization of Saddam Hussein as a Hitler-like figure, George Bush warned against the dangers of appeasing aggression. However, when pressed further to explain the geopolitical framework that guided the impending war against Iraq, Secretary of State James Baker could do little but reduce Desert Storm to the defense of American economic prosperity.

The end result of the Gulf War appeared to vindicate intervention as the guiding light of post–Cold War American foreign policy. The event embellished the conventional faith in the potency of the American military. The very brevity and lopsided nature of the war became a measure of the effectiveness of American military technology and the viability of using force to resolve conflict.[6] The Gulf War introduced an era of "brilliant" weaponry (e.g., satellite-guided munitions) that could accomplish what had not been possible in previous conflicts, particularly the Vietnam War.[7] In the afterglow of victory in 1991, projecting American power around the world via its military seemed to be a relatively effective means to pursue U.S. global interests.

Despite its unchallenged status as the last remaining superpower, American hegemony faced a considerable number of obstacles in the post–Cold War period. Some were internal. The 1992 election of Bill Clinton, a relatively obscure governor who successfully campaigned on the economic impact of a mild recession, clearly elevated domestic priorities over foreign affairs. During Clinton's first administration, lawmakers in both parties openly competed over the new budgetary opportunities provided by the so-called "peace dividend," the planned displacement of defense spending in favor of popular domestic programs. In the subsequent presidential elections of 1996 and 2000, the contemporary debate over education, public safety, and Social Security clearly overshadowed priorities overseas.

In the meantime, although America could claim a dominant place in the global hierarchy of nations, it was not alone among other major powers. Communist China emerged as perhaps the most important new American challenger of the post–Cold War era. In possession of a burgeoning economy, bolstered by both regional trade partners in "Greater China" and the United States, and a military augmented by increasing access to Western technology, the People's Republic of China presented a formidable presence. The Clinton administration's attempt at a policy of "engagement" was a measure of respect and the faith—reminiscent of U.S. treatment of the Soviet Union at the conclusion of the Second World War—that China could be successfully incorporated into the Western camp through its inclusion within the global marketplace, while the free market overtly promoted internal reforms.[8]

The nature of the global instability in the post–Cold War era also presented significant challenges to American power. Ethnic conflict—in the Balkans, Southwest Asia, Indonesia, and Africa—took on a new dimension as old rivalries arose unchecked by superpower influence. Religious fundamentalism lent a sharp edge to regional disputes in the Middle East and in the aspirations of nations such as Iran and Afghanistan. Overshadowing both was the chronic problem of economic underdevelopment, a factor which undercut stability from the former Soviet Union to sub–Saharan Africa.[9]

Subsequently, as the 1990s proceeded, intervention became an increasingly problematic option for the United States. In too many cases, American policy makers, pursuing either direct national security interests or well-intentioned policies guided by more general principles (e.g., humanitarian relief), stumbled into unforeseen consequences that prevented both success and easy extrication. In the case of Iraq, the United States combined military and economic sanctions with a U.N. inspection regime designed to root out prohibited weaponry and contain future threats to stability in the Persian Gulf. The ultimate failure of weapons inspectors to attain their goal left the Clinton administration in the tenuous position of using conventional military forces to deter an unknown nuclear and biological threat.

In the Balkans, American leaders faced the similar difficulty of imposing an external authority over an internecine internal conflict. The questionable efficacy of direct military intervention and the American public's unwillingness to endure casualties delayed U.S. intervention for years and, as was the case in Kosovo, severely circumscribed both the American military and diplomatic options.[10] In the Middle East, the Clinton administration embraced the Israeli-Palestinian peace process and the incrementalism that became a critical component of diplomacy for seven years. This discourse was dependent on the literal specificity of the surveyor's map, a far cry from the dramatic scale of the Camp David Accords a generation earlier. And, today, diplomacy still teeters on a mountain of historical and religious hatred.

The future of American foreign affairs promises additional challenges. Historian Frank Ninkovich compared America in 1999 with the country a century earlier, when "normal internationalism," defined as "liberal capitalism, democracy, and great-power cooperation, undergirded by commercial and cultural cooperation" governed the conduct of international relations.[11] However, present-day liberal capitalism finds itself at sea within a global economy still adjusting to the aftershocks of the 1997 Asian stock market collapse. Great power cooperation is currently tested by the type of regionalism best evidenced in the ongoing tensions between India and Pakistan. Cultural conflict is reflected in the growing backlash against American popular icons in Europe. In France, a political crusade has been sparked today over the proliferation of the McDonald's hamburger chain.[12]

The effectiveness of American diplomacy in the future will be measured by its capability to understand these diverse problems. It will be measured as the global nuclear family establishes a firmer foothold in Northwest Asia and policy makers weigh the problem of proliferation against the problematic security offered by a new missile defense system. It will be measured by the effectiveness of diplomacy conducted in combination with military and law enforcement agencies to counteract terrorism directed against the United States. In the future, American diplomacy will attempt what it has always pursued in the past: charting a path through a world defined by a dense mosaic of challenges and opportunities.

NOTES

1. Robert D. Kaplan, "The Coming Anarchy," in *Classic Readings of International Relations*, ed. Phil Williams, Donald Goldstein, and Jay Shafritz (New York: Harcourt Brace, 1999), 653–76.

2. Thomas J. McCormick, *America's Half-Century: United States Foreign Policy in the Cold War and After*, 2nd ed. (Baltimore: Johns Hopkins University Press, 1995), 238–41.

3. Lester C. Thurow, "New Rules: The American Economy in the Next Century," *Harvard International Review* 20 (winter 1997/1998): 54–59.

4. Paul Kennedy, *The Rise and Fall of the Great Powers: Economic Change and Military Conflict from 1500 to 2000* (New York: Vintage Books, 1989), 514–35.

5. McCormick, *America's Half-Century*, 251.

6. Rick Atkinson, *Crusade: The Untold Story of the Persian Gulf War* (New York: Houghton Mifflin, 1993), 426–48.

7. George Friedman and Meredith Friedman, *The Future of War: Power, Technology, and American World Dominance in the 21st Century* (New York: Crown Publishers, 1996), 145–46, 226–81.

8. Warren Christopher, "Advancing America's Critical Interests in the Asia-Pacific Region," *U.S. Department of State Dispatch*, vol. 7 (13 May 1996): 237–38.

9. Bruce Cumings, "The American Century and the Third World," in *The Ambiguous Legacy: U.S. Foreign Relations in the "American Century,"* ed. Michael J. Hogan (New York: Cambridge University Press, 1999), 279–301.

10. Serge Schemann, "Not Taking Losses Is One Thing: Winning Is Another," *New York Times* (3 January 1999), 4-1, 4-5.

11. Frank Ninkovich, *The Wilsonian Century: U.S. Foreign Policy since 1900* (Chicago: University of Chicago Press, 1999), 289–92.

12. Keith B. Richburg, "McDonald's Attacker Convicted in France; Farmer Vows Fight against U.S. Inroads," *Washington Post* (14 September 2000), A28.

149. THE COLLAPSE OF THE EASTERN BLOC
22 November 1989

At the conclusion of the 1980s, Soviet power had begun to crumble. A series of reforms initiated by Mikhail Gorbachev resulted in the end of Communist dominance over Soviet domestic affairs and the territory of Eastern Europe. As these events unfolded, President George W. Bush addressed the nation, acknowledging the end of the Cold War.

Like many of you, I'm spending tomorrow with family. We'll say grace, carve the turkey, and thank God for our many blessings—and for our great country. This holiday also marks the adjournment of Congress. And I've worked with Congress—extending my hand across the party aisle, advancing legislation to free our streets of fear of crime and drugs. We proposed ways to clean the air, the water and the land around us. We've joined with the Nation's Governors to enter an historic compact to better our schools. And especially touching is that so many Americans have answered the call for community service, the thousand points of light, by rolling up their sleeves and pitching in for the hopeless, the helpless—each volunteer, a beacon of light for someone who has lost his way.

This will be a very special Thanksgiving. It marks an extraordinary year. But before our families sit down tomorrow, we will give thanks for yet another reason: Around the world tonight, new pilgrims are on a voyage to freedom and for many, it is not a trip to some far-away place, but to a world of their own making.

In other Thanksgivings, the world was haunted by the images of watchtowers, guard dogs and machine guns. In fact, many of you had not even been born when the Berlin Wall was erected in 1961. But now the world has a new image—reflecting a new reality—that of Germans, East and West, pulling each other to the top of the wall—a human bridge between nations. Entire peoples all across Eastern Europe, bravely taking to the streets demanding liberty—talking democracy. This is not the end of the book of history, but a joyful end to one of history's saddest chapters.

Not long after the wall began to open, West German Chancellor Kohl telephoned, and asked me to give you, the American people, a message of thanks. He said that the remarkable change in Eastern Europe would not be taking place without the steadfast support of the United States. Fitting praise from a good friend. For 40 years, we have not wavered in our commitment to freedom. We are grateful to our American men and women in uniform. We should also be grateful to our postwar leaders. You see, we helped rebuild a continent through the Marshall Plan, and we built a shield, NATO, behind which Europeans and Americans could forge a future in freedom.

For so many of these 40 years, the test of Western resolve, the contest between the free and the unfree, has been symbolized by an island of hope behind the Iron Curtain: Berlin.

In the 1940s, West Berlin remained free because Harry Truman said: hands off. In the 1950s, Ike backed America's words with muscle. In the 1960's, West Berliners took heart, when John F. Kennedy said: I am a Berliner. In the 1970's, Presidents Nixon, Ford and Carter stood with Berlin—by standing with NATO. And in the 1980s, Ronald Reagan went to Berlin to say: Tear down this wall.

Now we are at the threshold of the 1990s. And as we begin the new decade, I am reaching out to President Gorbachev, asking him to work with me to bring down the last barriers to a new world of freedom. Let us move beyond containment, and once and for all end cold war.

We can make such a bold bid because America is strong, and 40 years of perseverance and patience are finally paying off. More recently, quiet diplomacy, working behind the scenes has achieved results. We can now dare to imagine a new world, with a new Europe, rising on the foundations of democracy.

This new world was taking shape when my presidency began with these words: "the day of the dictator is over." During the spring and summer we told the people of the world what America believes, and what America wants for the future. America believes that "liberty is an idea whose time has come in Eastern Europe." America wants President Gorbachev's reforms, known as perestroika, to succeed. And America wants the Soviets to join us, in moving "beyond containment," to a new partnership. Some wondered if all this was realistic. Now though we are still on the course we set last spring, events are moving faster than anyone imagined or predicted.

Look around the world—in the developing nations, the people are demanding freedom. Poland and Hungary are now fledgling democracies—a non-communist government in Poland, and free elections coming soon in Hungary. And in the Soviet Union itself, the forces of reform under Mikhail Gorbachev are bringing unprecedented openness and change.

But nowhere in the world today—or even in the history of Man—have the warm hearts of men and women triumphed so swiftly—so certainly—over cold stone—as in Berlin. Indeed, in all of East Germany. If I may paraphrase the words of a great poet, Robert Frost: There is certainly something in us that doesn't love a wall.

When I spoke to the German people in Mainz last May, I applauded the removal of the barriers between Hungary and Austria, saying: "Let Berlin be next." And the West German people joined us in a call for a Europe whole and free.

Just yesterday the West German Foreign Minister gave me a piece of the Berlin Wall—it is on my desk as a reminder of the power of freedom to bring down the walls between people.

It brought back memories of seven years ago, when I went to Modlareuth, a small town in Germany also knows as Little Berlin. A divided village really, its cobbled streets blocked by barbed wire and concrete—on the one side freedom, on the other despair. I talked with the townspeople, not a hundred and fifty yards from the specter of armed guards in towers. Some day I'd like to go back to Little Berlin, and see families reunited, see neighbors once apart, coming together.

Change is coming swiftly. And with this change, the dramatic vindication of free Europe's economic and political institutions; the new Europe that is coming is being built—must be built—on the foundation of democratic values. But the faster the pace, the smoother our path must be. After all, this is serious business.

The peace we are building must be different than the hard, joyless peace between two armed camps we've known so long. The scars of the conflict that began a half century ago still divide a continent. So the historic task before us now, is to begin the healing of this old wound.

During our visit to Poland and Hungary last July, I found new encouragement that we are on track—that there was, at long last, the chance for fundamental change. I saw first-hand acts of healing and reconciliation. It was in Warsaw at my lunch for General Jaruzelski and the leaders of Solidarity that I met a woman who had worked, at great personal risk, for the release of a jailed Solidarity member. She was asked: "How is it possible, after such a short time, to break bread with the men who ordered those imprisonments—why the absence of bitterness?" And she replied: "Our joy at what is happening now is more powerful than memory."

I wish you could have been there, for what we witnessed was extraordinary. The old antagonisms melted away as former adversaries stood up, often with tears in their eyes, and toasted the future. Our guests knew that history would judge them by how well they would cooperate. Well, there is a spirit of cooperation in Eastern Europe—the result—Poland and Hungary are being transformed.

They deserve our support, and they're getting it. We have matched our words with action—new loans and grants—teams of American economic experts—working to help them adjust to a free market society—clearing the way for U.S. investment and trade with Poland and Hungary. Now the people of these nations can finally expect their hard work to lead to a better life.

These same winds of change are sweeping our own hemisphere, democracy transforming the Americas with stunning speed. Regrettably, there are some exceptions—Panama, Nicaragua, and Cuba. And these last two are holding out against their people only because of the massive support of weapons and supplies from their communist allies. So when I see President Gorbachev, I'll ask him to join with us to help bring freedom and democracy to all the people of Latin America.

So as we celebrate the events of Eastern Europe, remember that some walls still remain between East and West. These are the invisible walls of suspicion. The walls of doubt, misunderstanding and miscalculation.

It was while in Eastern Europe last summer that I decided to make a personal effort to break through these lost barriers.

Back in May, I set down five steps President Gorbachev should meet if we are to take his new thinking seriously: First, reduce Soviet forces; second, support self-determination in Eastern Europe; third, work with us to end regional disputes; fourth, achieve a lasting pluralism and respect for human rights; and fifth, join with us in addressing global problems, including the international drug menace and dangers to the environment. Serious problems still remain, especially regional conflicts. The Soviet Union has made progress in these five areas. That is undeniable.

With that in mind and the momentous changes in Eastern Europe, I invited President Gorbachev to meet me ten days from now. This is a first—a time for exploration. It is not a time for detailed arms control negotiations best left for next year's summit.

I want President Gorbachev to know exactly where the United States stands. Let me be clear—America stands with freedom and democracy. We are not meeting to determine the future of Europe—after all, the peoples of Europe are determining their own future. Though there will be no surprises sprung on our Allies, we will miss no opportunities to expand freedom and enhance the peace. And to those who question our prudent pace, they must understand that a time of historic change is no time for recklessness. The peace, and the confidence, and the security of our friends in Europe—it's just too important.

We will seek President Gorbachev's assurance that this process of reform in Eastern Europe will continue. And we will give him our assurance that America welcomes reform not as an adversary seeking advantage, but as a people offering support. Our goal is to see this historic tide of freedom broadened, deepened—and sustained. We find enormous encouragement in its peaceful advance and its acceptance by the Soviet Union. We can now raise our hopes on other issues—our common environment, our common war against drugs, as well as on human rights and the regional conflicts that remain.

Immediately after my visit with President Gorbachev, I will go to Brussels to consult with our partners in NATO—the very alliance that has kept the West free for 40 years. I will assure them that no matter how dramatic the change in Eastern Europe, or in the Soviet Union itself, the United States will continue to stand with our allies and our friends.

For in a new Europe, the American role may change in form but not in fundamentals. After all, the Soviet Union maintains hundreds of thousands of troops throughout Eastern Europe. Study the map, review history and you'll see that this presence, with the Soviet Union's natural advantage of geography, cannot be ignored. So even if forces are significantly reduced on both sides, a noble goal indeed, we will remain in Europe as long as our friends want and need us.

Off the island nation of Malta, Mikhail Gorbachev and I will begin the work of years. We can help the peoples of Europe achieve a new destiny, in a peaceful Europe whole and free. I will tell President Gorbachev, the dynamic architect of Soviet reform, that America wants the people of the Soviet Union to fulfill their destiny. And I will assure him that there is no greater advocate of perestroika than the President of the United States.

When we meet, we will be on ships at anchor in a Mediterranean bay that has served as a sealane of commerce and conflict for more than two thousand years. This ancient port has been conquered by Caesar and Sultan, Crusader and King. Its forts and watchtowers survey a sea that entombs the scuttled ships of empires lost—slave galleys, galleons, dreadnoughts, destroyers. These ships once meant to guard lasting empires, now litter the ocean floor, and guard nothing more than reefs of coral.

So if the millennia offers us a lesson it is this: True security does not come from empire and domination. True security can only be found in the growing trust of free peoples.

It has been said that peace is not the work of a single day, nor will it be the consequence of a single act. Yet every constructive act contributes to its growth; every omission impedes it. Peace will come, in the end, as a child grows to maturity—slowly until we realize one day in incredulous surprise that the child is almost grown.

It is our hope that Malta will be such a constructive act—guiding brave pilgrims on their journey to a new world of freedom.

Source: George Bush, "The Events in Eastern Europe: People Are Demanding Freedom," *Vital Speeches* 56 (15 December 1989): 130–32.

---

150. BUSH, IRAQI INVASION OF KUWAIT
8 August 1990

On 2 August 1990, units of the Iraqi military crossed into the neighboring nation of Kuwait, occupying the country and posing a direct threat to the stability of the Middle East. Within hours of the invasion, American military forces were deployed to Saudi Arabia as part of a massive intervention to protect U.S. access to strategically vital petroleum resources.

In the life of a nation, we're called upon to define who we are and what we believe. Sometimes these choices are not easy. But today as President, I ask for your support in a decision I've made to stand up for what's right and condemn what's wrong—all in the cause of peace.

At my direction, elements of the 82nd Airborne Division, as well as key units of the United States Air Force are arriving today to take up defensive positions in Saudi Arabia. I took this action to assist the Saudi Arabian government in the defense of its homeland.

No one commits America's Armed Forces to a dangerous mission lightly. But after perhaps unparalleled international consultation and exhausting every alternative, it became necessary to take this action. Let me tell you why.

Less than a week ago, in the early morning hours of August 2nd, Iraqi armed forces, without provocation or warning, invaded a peaceful Kuwait. Facing negligible resistance from its much smaller neighbor, Iraq's tanks stormed in blitzkrieg fashion through Kuwait in a few short hours. With more than 100,000 troops, along with tanks, artillery and surface-to-surface missiles, Iraq now occupies Kuwait.

This aggression came just hours after Saddam Hussein specifically assured numerous countries in the area that there would be no invasion. There is no justification whatsoever for this outrageous and brutal act of aggression.

A puppet regime imposed from the outside is unacceptable. The acquisition of territory by force is unacceptable. No one, friend or foe, should doubt our desire for peace, and no one should underestimate our determination to confront aggression.

Four simple principles guide our policy. First, we seek the immediate, unconditional and complete withdrawal of all Iraqi forces from Kuwait. Second, Kuwait's legitimate government must be restored to replace the puppet regime. And third, my administration, as has been the case with every President from President Roosevelt to President Reagan, is committed to the security and stability of the Persian Gulf. And fourth, I am determined to protect the lives of American citizens abroad.

Immediately after the Iraqi invasion, I ordered an embargo of all trade with Iraq and, together with many other nations, announced sanctions that both froze all Iraqi assets in this country and protected Kuwait's assets. The stakes are high. Iraq is already a rich and powerful country that possesses the world's second largest reserves of oil and over a million men under arms. It's the fourth largest military in the world.

Our country now imports nearly half the oil it consumes and could face a major threat to its economic independence. Much of the world is even more dependent upon imported oil and is even more vulnerable to Iraqi threats.

We succeeded in the struggle for freedom in Europe because we and our allies remain stalwart. Keeping the peace in the Middle East will require no less. We're beginning a new era. This new era can be full of promise. An age of freedom. A time of peace for all peoples. But if history teaches us anything, it is that we must resist aggression or it will destroy our freedoms. Appeasement does not work. As was the case in the 1930s, we see in Saddam Hussein an aggressive dictator threatening his neighbors. Only 14 days ago, Saddam Hussein promised his friends he would not invade Kuwait. And four days ago he promised the world he would withdraw. And twice we have seen what his promises mean. His promises mean nothing.

In the last few days, I've spoken with political leaders from the Middle East, Europe, Asia and the Americas, and I've met with Prime Minister Thatcher, Prime Minister Mulroney, and NATO Secretary General Woerner. And all agree that Iraq cannot be allowed to benefit from its invasion of Kuwait.

We agree that this is not an American problem or a European problem or a Middle East problem. It is the world's problem. And that's why, soon after the Iraqi invasion, the United Nations Security Council, without dissent, condemned Iraq, calling for the immediate and unconditional withdrawal of its troops from Kuwait. The Arab world, through both the Arab League and the Gulf Cooperation Council courageously announced its opposition to Iraqi aggression. Japan, the United Kingdom, and France, and other governments around the world have imposed severe sanctions. The Soviet Union and China ended all arms sales to Iraq.

And this past Monday, the United Nations Security Council approved for the first time in 23 years mandatory sanctions under Chapter VII of the United Nations Charter. These sanctions, now enshrined in international law, have the potential to deny Iraq the fruits of aggression, while sharply limiting its ability to either import or export anything of value—especially oil.

I pledge here today that the United State will do its part to see that these sanctions are effective and to induce Iraq to withdraw without delay from Kuwait.

But we must recognize that Iraq may not stop using force to advance its ambitions. Iraq has massed an enormous war machine on the Saudi border, capable of initiating hostilities with little or no additional preparation. Given the Iraqi government's history of aggression against its own citizens as well as its neighbors, to assume Iraq will not attack again would be unwise and unrealistic.

And therefore, after consulting with King Fahd, I sent Secretary of Defense Dick Cheney to discuss cooperative measures we could take. Following those meetings the Saudi government requested our help. And I responded to that request by ordering U.S. air and ground forces to deploy to the Kingdom of Saudi Arabia.

Let me be clear. The sovereign independence of Saudi Arabia is of vital interest to the United States. This decision, which I shared with the congressional leadership, grows out of the longstanding friendship and security relationship between the United States and Saudi Arabia. U.S. forces will work together with those of Saudi Arabia and other nations to preserve the integrity of Saudi Arabia and to deter further Iraqi aggression.

Through their presence, as well as through training and exercises, these multinational forces will enhance the overall capability of Saudi armed forces to defend the Kingdom.

I want to be clear about what we are doing and why. America does not seek conflict, nor do we seek to chart the destiny of other nations. But America will stand by her friends. The mission of our troops is not wholly defensive. Hopefully, they will not be needed long. They will not initiate hostilities, but they will defend themselves, the Kingdom of Saudi Arabia, and other friends in the Persian Gulf.

We are working around the clock to deter Iraqi aggression and to enforce U.N. sanctions. I'm continuing my conversations with world leaders. Secretary of Defense Cheney has just returned from valuable consultations with President Mubarak of Egypt and King Hassan of Morocco. Secretary of State Baker has consulted with his counterparts in many nations, including the Soviet Union. And today he heads for Europe to consult with President Ozal of Turkey, a staunch friend of the United States. And he'll then consult with the NATO Foreign Ministers.

I will ask oil-producing nations to do what they can to increase production in order to minimize any impact that oil flow reductions will have on the world economy. And I will explore whether we and our allies should draw down our strategic petroleum reserves. Conservation measures can also help. Americans everywhere must do their part. And one more thing. I'm asking the oil companies to do their fair share. They should show restraint and not abuse today's uncertainties to raise prices.

Standing up for our principles will not come easy. It may take time and possibly cost a great deal. But we are asking no more of anyone than of the brave young men and women of our Armed Forces and their families. And I ask that in the churches around the country prayers be said for those who are committed to protect and defend America's interests.

Standing up for our principle is an American tradition. As it has so many times before, it may take time and tremendous effort. But most of all, it will take unity of purpose.

As I've witnessed throughout my life in both war and peace, America has never wavered when her purpose is driven by principle. And in this August day, at home and abroad, I know she will do no less.

Thank you, and God bless the United States of America.

Source: George Bush, "Iraq Invasion of Kuwait: The Defense of Saudi Arabia," *Vital Speeches* 51 (1 September 1990): 674–75.

---

151. BUSH, "THE POSSIBILITY OF A NEW WORLD ORDER"
13 April 1991

In the spring of 1991, flush with the victory over Saddam Hussein, President George Bush discussed the nature of the new world structure and

America's place in it. During a speech before a group of Air Force officers, Bush considered the new role the United States might play at this historical turning point.

Thank you all very, very much for that warm welcome. General Boyd and General McPeak, the distinguished members of the Congress with us—Senators Heflin, Shelby, and Bill Dickinson. Mayor Folmar, a nonpartisan event, but I'm glad to see some friends of long-standing over here, who were enormously helpful to me in getting to be President of the United States.

It is my great pleasure to look out across what essentially is a sea of blue, to meet this morning with the men and women of the Air University—the Air War College, the Air Command and Staff School, the Squadron Officers School, and of course, the NCO Academy. And I'm glad to see democracy in action, I see a Navy guy here or there, or maybe a Coast Guardsman, maybe the Marines, maybe the Army over here. And I think I recognize some friends from overseas, members of our coalition who helped us so much in achieving our objectives halfway around the world. They're more than welcome.

The history of aviation has been shaped here since the Wright brothers brought their strange new mechanical bird to Montgomery, and housed it in a hangar not far from where we stand. This institution from it's early days as the Air Corps Tactical School has defined the nation's air strategy and tactics that have guided our operations over the fields of Europe and the seas of the Pacific, from the first World War to the thousand hours of Desert Storm.

It falls to all of you to derive the lessons learned from this war. Desert Storm demonstrated the true strength of joint operations. Not the notion that each service must participate in equal parts in every operation in every war, but that we use the proper tools at the proper time. In Desert Storm, a critical tool was certainly air power. And every one of you can take pride in that fact. Our technology and training ensured minimal losses, and our precision, your precision, spared the lives of innocent civilians.

But our victory also showed that technology alone is insufficient. A warrior's heart must burn with the will to fight. And if he fights but does not believe, no technology in the world can save him. We and our allies had more than superior weapons; we had the will to win.

I might say parenthetically, this will is personified by the man who leads you. I know that General Boyd often speaks about what he calls the unlimited liability of the military profession. He knows because he's put it all on the line. As a veteran of Vietnam, he flew 105 combat missions before being shot down over Hanoi. And he spent almost seven years, 2,500 cruel days, in captivity. And yet he emerged brave, unbroken. He kept the faith to himself and to his nation.

And let me just say a word about this man over here on my left, General McPeak. I remember early on a meeting up at Camp David with Tony McPeak. Secretary Cheney was there; General Powell was there; Brent Scowcroft, other chiefs. The other chiefs, I believe, were with us, Tony. And in a very laid back way, typical of him with his modesty, but with total confidence, he told me exactly what he felt air power could do. And after he left, I don't mean to show my native skepticism, but I turned to my trusted National Security Advisor, who's standing over here, General Brent Scowcroft, and I said, "Brent, does this guy really know what he's talking about?"

And Lieutenant General Scowcroft—Air Force Lieutenant General, said "Yes."

And General McPeak did.

And to be doubly sure then, and he'll remember this, just before the war started, I invited General McPeak and Secretary Cheney to join me and General Scowcroft upstairs at the residence in the White House—quiet lunch there. And I asked Tony, I think he'd just come back then from the theater, the other theater. And I put the question to him, I think this is exactly what I said,

"Are you as certain now as you were up at Camp David?"

And he said,

"Even more so."

And the war started just a few days later, and history will record that General McPeak was 100 percent right, right on target.

Here at Air University it's your business to read the lessons of the past with an eye on the far horizon. And that's why I wanted to speak to you today about the new world taking shape around us, about the prospects for a new world order within our reach. For more than four decades we've lived in a world divided, East from West; a world locked in a conflict of arms and ideas called the Cold War. Two systems, two superpowers, separated by mistrust and unremitting hostility.

For more than four decades, America's energies were focused on containing the threat to the free world from the forces of communism. That war is over. East Germany has vanished from the map as a separate entity. Today in Berlin, the wall that once divided a continent, divided a world in two, has been pulverized, turned into souvenirs. And the sections that remain standing are but museum pieces. The Warsaw Pact passed into the pages of history last week. Not with a bang, but with a whimper, its demise reported in a story reported on page A16 of *The Washington Post*.

In the coming weeks I'll be talking in some detail about the possibility of a new world order emerging after the Cold War. And in recent weeks I've been focusing not only on the Gulf, but on free trade, on the North American Free Trade Agreement, the Uruguay Round trade negotiations, and the essentiality of obtaining from the United States Congress a renewal of Fast-Track authority to achieve our goals. But today I want to discuss another aspect of that order, our relations with Europe and the Soviet Union.

Twice this century, a dream born on the battlefields of Europe died after the shooting stopped. The dream of a world in which major powers worked together to ensure peace; to settle their disputes through cooperation, not confrontation. Today a transformed Europe stands closer than ever before to its free and democratic destiny. At long last, Europe is moving forward, moving toward a new world of hope.

At the same time, we and our European allies have moved beyond containment to a policy of active engagement in a world no longer driven by Cold War tensions and animosities. You see, as the Cold War drew to an end we saw the possibilities of a new order in which nations worked together to promote peace and prosperity. I'm not talking here of a blueprint that will govern the conduct of nations or some supernatural structure or institution. The new world order does not mean surrendering our national sovereignty or forfeiting our interests. It really describes a responsibility imposed by our successes. It refers to new ways of working with other nations to deter aggression and to achieve stability, to achieve prosperity and, above all, to achieve peace.

It springs from hopes for a world based on a shared commitment among nations large and small, to a set of principles that undergird our relations. Peaceful settlements of disputes, solidarity against aggression, reduced and controlled arsenals, and just treatment of all peoples.

This order, this ability to work together got its first real test in the Gulf war. For the first time, a regional conflict, the aggression against Kuwait did not serve as a proxy for superpower confrontation. For the first time, the United Nations Security Council, free from the clash of Cold War ideologies, functioned as its designers intended, a force for conflict resolution in collective security.

In the Gulf, nations from Europe and North America, Asia and Africa and the Arab world joined together to stop aggression, and sent a signal to would-be tyrants everywhere in the world. By joining forces to defend one small nation, we showed that we can work together against aggressors in defense of principle.

We also recognized that the Cold War's end didn't deliver us into an era of perpetual peace. As old threats recede, new threats emerge. The quest for the new world order is, in part, a challenge to keep the dangers of disorder at bay.

Today, thank God, Kuwait is free. But turmoil in that tormented region of the world continues. Saddam's continued savagery has placed his regime outside the international order. We will not interfere in Iraq's civil war. Iraqi people must decide their own political future.

Looking out here at you and thinking of your families, let me comment a little further. We set our objectives. These objectives, sanctioned by international law, have been achieved. I made very clear that when our objectives were obtained that our troops would be coming home. And, yes, we want the suffering of those refugees to stop, and in keeping with our nation's compassion and concern, we are massively helping. But, yes, I want our troops out of Iraq and back home as soon as possible.

Internal conflicts have been raging in Iraq for many years. And we're helping out and we're going to continue to help these refugees. But I do not want one single soldier or airman shoved into a civil war in Iraq that's been going on for ages. And I'm not going to have that.

I know the coalition's historic effort destroyed Saddam's ability to undertake aggression against any neighbor. You did that job. But now the international community will further guarantee that Saddam's ability to threaten his neighbors is completely eliminated by destroying Iraq's weapons of mass destruction.

And as I just mentioned, we will continue to help the Iraqi refugees, the hundreds and thousands of victims of this man's, Saddam Hussein's, brutality. See food and shelter and safety and the opportunity to return unharmed to their homes. We will not tolerate any interference in this massive international relief effort. Iraq can return to the community of nations only when its leaders abandon the brutality and repression that is destroying their country. With Saddam in power, Iraq will remain a pariah nation, its people denied moral contacts with most of the outside world.

We must build on the successes of Desert Storm to give new shape and momentum to this new world order, to use force wisely and extend the hand of compassion wherever we can. Today we welcome Europe's willingness to shoulder a large share of this responsibility. This new sense of responsibility on the part of our European allies is most evident and most critical in Europe's eastern half.

The nations of Eastern Europe, for so long the other Europe, must take their place now alongside their neighbors to the west. Just as we've overcome Europe's political division, we must help to ease crossover from poverty into prosperity.

The United States will do its part, we always have. As we have already in reducing Poland's official debt burden to the United States by 70 percent; increasing our assistance this year to Eastern Europe by 50 percent. But the key, the key to helping these new democracies develop is trade and investment.

The new entrepreneurs of Czechoslovakia and Poland and Hungary aren't looking to government, their own or others, to shower them with riches. They're looking for new opportunities, a new freedom for the productive genius strangled by 40 years of state control.

Yesterday, my esteemed friend, a man we all honor and salute, President Vaclav Havel of Czechoslovakia called me up. He wanted to request advice and help from the West. He faces enormous problems. You see, Czechoslovakia wants to be democratic. This man is leading them towards perfecting their fledgling democracy. Its economy is moving from a failed socialist model to a market economy.

We all must help. It's not easy to convert state-owned and operated weapons plants into market-driven plants to produce consumer goods. But these new democracies can do just exactly that with the proper advice and help from the West. It is in our interest, it is in the interest of the United States of America, that Czechoslovakia, Poland, and Hungary strengthen those fledgling democracies and strengthen their fledgling market economies.

We recognize that new roles and even new institutions are natural outgrowths of the new Europe. Whether it's the European Community or a broadened mandate for the CSCE, the U.S. supports all efforts to forge a European approach to common challenges on the continent and in the world beyond, with the understanding that Europe's long-term security is intertwined with America's, and that NATO remains the best means to assure it.

And we look to Europe to act as a force for stability outside its own borders. In a world as interdependent as ours, no industrialized nation can maintain membership in good standing in the global community without assuming its fair share of responsibility for peace and security.

But even in the face of such welcome change, Americans will remain in Europe in support of history's most successful alliance, NATO. America's commitment is the best guarantee of a secure Europe, and a secure Europe is vital to American interests and vital to world peace. This is the essential logic of the Atlantic Alliance which anchors America in Europe.

This century's history shows that America's destiny and interests cannot be separate from Europe's. Through the long years of Cold War and conflict, the United States stood fast for freedom in Europe. And now, as Eastern Europe is opening up to democratic ideals, true progress becomes possible.

The Soviet Union is engaged in its own dramatic transformation. The policies of confrontation abroad, like the discredited dogma of communism from which those policies sprang, lies dormant, if not mortally wounded. Much has changed. The path of international cooperation fostered by President Gorbachev and manifested most clearly in the Persian Gulf marks a radical change in Soviet behavior. And yet, the course of change within the Soviet Union is far less clear.

Economic and political reform there is under severe challenge. Soviet citizens, facing the collapse of the old order while the new still struggles to be born, confront desperate economic conditions; their hard-won freedoms in peril. Ancient ethnic enmities, conflict between republics and between republics and the central government add to these monumental challenges that they face.

America's policy toward the Soviet Union in these troubled times is, first and foremost, to continue our efforts to build the cooperative relationship that has allowed our nations and so many others to strengthen international peace and stability. At the same time, we will continue to support a reform process within the Soviet Union aimed at political and economic freedom. A process we believe must be built on peaceful dialogue and negotiation. This is a policy that we will advocate steadfastly, both in our discussion with the central Soviet government and with all elements active in Soviet political life.

Let there be no misunderstanding, the path ahead for the Soviet Union will be difficult and, at times, extraordinarily painful. History weighs heavily on all the peoples of the U.S.S.R., liberation from 70 years of communism, from a thousand years of autocracy. It's going to be slow. There will be setbacks. But this process of reform, this transformation from within must proceed. If external cooperation and our progress toward true international peace is to endure, it must succeed. Only when this transformation is complete will we be able to take full measure of the opportunities presented by this new and evolving world order.

The new world order really is a tool for addressing a new world of possibilities. This order gains its mission and shape not just from shared interests, but from shared ideals. And the ideals that have spawned new freedoms throughout the world have received their boldest and clearest expression in our great country the United States. Never before has the world looked more to the American example. Never before have so many millions drawn hope from the American idea. And the reason is simple: Unlike any other nation in the world, as Americans we enjoy profound and mysterious bonds of affection and idealism. We feel our deep connections to community, to families, to our faiths.

But what defines this nation? What makes us America is not our ties to a piece of territory or bonds of blood; what makes us American is our allegiance to an idea that all people everywhere must be free. This idea is as old and enduring as this nation itself, as deeply rooted, and what we are as a promise implicit to all the world in the words of our own Declaration of Independence.

The new world facing us, and I wish I were your age, it's a wonderful world of discovery. A world devoted to unlocking the promise of freedom. It's no more structured than a dream; no more regimented than an innovator's burst of inspiration. If we trust ourselves and our values; if we retain the pioneer's enthusiasm for exploring the world beyond our shores; if we strive to engage in the world that beckons us, then and only then, will America be true to all that is best in us.

May God bless our great nation, the United States of America. And thank you all for what you have done for free for our fundamental values. Thank you very much.

Source: George W. Bush, "The Possibility of a New World Order: Unlocking the Promise of Freedom," *Vital Speeches* 57 (15 May 1991): 450–52.

152. BUSH, "INITIATIVE ON NUCLEAR ARMS: CHANGING THE NUCLEAR POSTURE" 27 SEPTEMBER 1991

Efforts to limit nuclear armaments proceeded from the 1987 Intermediate-Range Nuclear Forces Treaty to include reductions in more powerful strategic weapons. In July 1990, President George Bush signed an accord with Soviet President Mikhail Gorbachev that significantly reduced the inventory of existing long-range weapons and terminated the development of a new generation of weapons systems.

Good Evening. Tonight I'd like to speak with you about our future, and the future of the generations to come. The world has changed at a fantastic pace, with each day writing a fresh page of history before yesterday's ink has even dried. And most recently, we've seen the peoples of the Soviet Union turn to democracy and freedom and discard a system of government based on oppression and fear.

Like the East Europeans before them, they face the daunting challenge of building fresh political structures, based on human rights, democratic principles, and market economies. Their task is far from easy, and far from over. They will need our help. And they will get it.

But these dramatic changes challenge our nation as well. Our country has always stood for freedom and democracy. And when the newly elected leaders of Eastern Europe grappled with forming their new governments, they looked to the United States. They looked to American democratic principles in building their own free societies. Even the leaders of the U.S.S.R. republics are reading The Federalist Papers, written by America's founders, to find new ideas and inspiration.

Today, America must lead again, as it always has, as only it can. And we will. We must also provide the inspiration for lasting peace. And we will do that, too. We can now take steps in response to these dramatic developments, steps that can help the Soviet peoples in their quest for peace and prosperity. More importantly, we can now take steps to make the world a less dangerous place than ever before in the nuclear age.

A year ago, I described a new strategy for American defenses, reflecting the world's changing security environment. That strategy shifted our focus away from the fear that preoccupied us for 40 years, the prospect of a global confrontation. Instead, it concentrated more on regional conflicts, such as the one we just faced in the Persian Gulf.

I spelled out a strategic concept, guided by the need to maintain the forces required to exercise forward presence in key areas, to respond effectively in crises, to maintain a credible nuclear deterrent, and to retain the national capacity to rebuild our forces should that be needed.

We are now moving to reshape the U.S. military to reflect that concept. The new base force will be smaller by half a million than today's military with fewer Army divisions, Air Force wings, Navy ships, and strategic nuclear forces. This new force will be versatile, able to respond around the world to challenges— old and new.

As I just mentioned, the changes that allowed us to adjust our security strategy a year ago have greatly accelerated. The prospect of a Soviet invasion into Western Europe, launched with little or no warning, is no longer a realistic threat. The Warsaw Pact has crumbled. In the Soviet Union, the advocates of democracy triumphed over a coup that would have restored the old system of repression. The reformers are now starting to fashion their own futures, moving even faster toward democracy's horizon.

New leaders in the Kremlin and the republics are now questioning the need for their huge nuclear arsenal. The Soviet nuclear stockpile now seems less an instrument of national security and more of a burden. As a result, we now have an unparalleled opportunity to change the nuclear posture of the United States and the Soviet Union.

If we and the Soviet leaders take the right steps—some on our own, some on their own, some together—we can dramatically shrink the arsenal of the world's nuclear weapons. We can more effectively discourage the spread of nuclear weapons. We can rely more on defensive measures in our strategic relationship. We can enhance stability, and actually reduce the risk of nuclear war. Now is the time to seize this opportunity.

After careful study and consultations with my senior advisors and after considering valuable counsel from Prime Minister Major, President Mitterand, Chancellor Kohl and other allied leaders, I am announcing today a series of sweeping initiatives affecting every aspect of our nuclear forces on land, on ships, and on aircraft. I met again today with our Joint Chiefs of Staff, and I can tell you they wholeheartedly endorse each of these steps.

I will begin with the category in which we will make the most fundamental change in nuclear forces in over 40 years—non-strategic or theater weapons.

Last year I canceled U.S. plans to modernize our ground-launched theater nuclear weapons. Later, our NATO allies joined us in announcing that the Alliance would propose the mutual elimination of all nuclear artillery shells from Europe, as soon as short-range nuclear force negotiations began with the Soviets. But starting these talks now would only perpetuate these systems, while we engage in lengthy negotiations. Last month's events not only permit, but indeed demand swifter, bolder, action.

I am therefore directing that the United States eliminate its entire worldwide inventory of ground-launched short-range, that is, theater nuclear weapons. We will bring home and destroy all of our nuclear artillery shells and short-range ballistic missile warheads. We will, of course, ensure that we preserve an effective air-delivered nuclear capability in Europe. That is essential to NATO's security.

In turn, I have asked the Soviets to go down this road with us—to destroy their entire inventory of ground-launched theater nuclear weapons: not only their nuclear artillery, and nuclear warheads for short-range ballistic missiles, but also the theater systems the U.S. no longer has—systems like nuclear warheads for air-defense missiles, and nuclear land mines.

Recognizing further the major changes in the international military landscape, the United States will withdraw all tactical nuclear weapons from its surface ships and attack submarines, as well as those nuclear weapons associated with our land-based naval aircraft. This means removing all nuclear Tomahawk cruise missiles from U.S. ships and submarines, as well as nuclear bombs aboard aircraft carriers. The bottom line is that under normal circumstances our ships will not carry tactical nuclear weapons.

Many of these land and sea-based warheads will be dismantled and destroyed. Those remaining will be secured in central areas where they would be available if necessary in a future crisis.

Again, there is every reason for the Soviet Union to match our actions—by removing all tactical nuclear weapons from its ships and attack submarines; by withdrawing nuclear weapons for land-based naval aircraft; and by destroying many of them and consolidating what remains at central locations. I urge them to do so.

No category of nuclear weapons has received more attention than those in our strategic arsenals. The Strategic Arms Reduction Treaty, START, which President Gorbachev and I signed last July was the culmination of almost a decade's work. It calls for substantial stabilizing reductions and effective verification. Prompt ratification by both parties is essential.

But I also believe the time is right to use START as a spring-board to achieving additional stabilizing changes.

First, to further reduce tensions. I am directing that all United States strategic bombers immediately stand down from their alert posture. As a comparable gesture, I call upon the Soviet Union to confine its mobile missiles to their garrisons, where they will be safer and more secure.

Second, the United States will immediately stand down from alert all intercontinental missiles scheduled for deactivation under START. Rather than waiting for the treaty's reduction plan to run its full seven year course, we will accelerate elimination of these systems, once START is ratified. I call upon the Soviet Union to do the same.

Third, I am terminating the deployment of the mobile Peacekeeper ICBM as well as the mobile portion of the small ICBM program. The small single-warhead ICBM will be our only remaining ICBM modernization program. And I call upon the Soviets to terminate any and all programs for future ICBMs with more than one warhead, and to limit ICBM modernization to one type of warhead missile—just as we have done.

Fourth, I am canceling the current program to build a replacement for the nuclear short-range attack missile for our strategic bombers.

Fifth, as a result of the strategic nuclear weapons adjustments that I've just outlined, the United States will streamline its command and control procedures, allowing us to more effectively manage our strategic nuclear forces.

As the system works now, the Navy commands the submarine part of our strategic deterrent, while the Air Force commands the bomber and land-based elements. But as we reduce our strategic forces, the operational command structure must be as direct as possible. And I have therefore approved the recommendation of Secretary Cheney and the Joint Chiefs to consolidate operational command of these forces into a U.S. Strategic Command, under one commander, with participation from both services.

Since the 1970s, the most vulnerable and unstable part of the U.S. and Soviet nuclear forces has been intercontinental missiles with more than one warhead. Both sides have these ICBMs in fixed silos in the ground where they are more vulnerable than missiles on submarines.

I propose that the U.S. and the Soviet Union seek early agreement to eliminate from their inventories all ICBMs with multiple warheads. After developing a timetable acceptable to both sides, we could rapidly move to modify or eliminate those systems under procedures already established in the START agreement. In short, such action would take away the single most unstable part of our nuclear arsenals.

But there is more to do. The United States and the Soviet Union are not the only nations with ballistic missiles. Some 15 have them now, and in less than a decade, that number could grow to 20.

The recent conflict in the Persian Gulf demonstrates in no uncertain terms that the time has come for strong action on this growing threat to world peace.

Accordingly, I am calling on the Soviet leadership to join us in taking immediate concrete steps to permit the limited deployment of non-nuclear defenses to protect against limited ballistic missile strike—whatever their source—without undermining the credibility of existing deterrent forces. And we will intensify our effort to curb nuclear and missile proliferation. These two efforts will be mutually reinforcing. To foster cooperation, the United States soon will propose additional initiatives in the area of ballistic missile early warning.

Finally, let me discuss yet another opportunity for cooperation that can make our world safer.

During last month's attempted coup in Moscow, many Americans asked me if I thought Soviet nuclear weapons were under adequate control. I do not believe that America was at increased risk of nuclear attack during those tense days. But I do believe more can be done to ensure the safe handling and dismantling of Soviet nuclear weapons. Therefore, I propose that we begin discussions with the Soviet Union to explore cooperation in three areas: First, we should explore joint technical cooperation on the safe and environmentally responsible storage, transportation, dismantling, and destruction of nuclear warheads. Second, we should discuss existing arrangements for the physical security and safety of nuclear weapons and how these might be enhanced. And third, we should discuss nuclear command and control arrangements, and how these might be improved to provide more protection against the unauthorized or accidental use of nuclear weapons.

My friend, French President Mitterrand, offered a similar idea a short while ago. After further consultations with the Alliance, and when the leadership in the U.S.S.R. is ready, we will begin this effort.

The initiatives that I'm announcing build on the new defense strategy that I set out a year ago—one that shifted our focus away from the prospect of global confrontation. We're consulting with our Allies on the implementation of many of these steps which fit well with the new post Cold-War strategy and force posture that we've developed in NATO.

As we implement these initiatives we will closely watch how the new Soviet leadership responds. We expect our bold initiatives to meet with equally bold steps on the Soviet side. If this happens, further cooperation is inevitable. If it does not, then an historic opportunity will have been lost. Regardless, let no one doubt we will still retain the necessary strength to protect our security and that of our allies, and to respond as necessary.

In addition, regional instabilities, the spread of weapons of mass destruction, and as we saw during the conflict in the Gulf, territorial ambitions of power-hungry tyrants, still require us to maintain a strong military to protect our national interests and to honor commitments to our allies.

Therefore, we must implement a coherent plan for a significantly smaller but fully capable military, one that enhances stability but is still sufficient to convince any potential adversary that the cost of aggression would exceed any possible gain.

We can safely afford to take the steps I've announced today, steps that are designed to reduce the dangers of miscalculation in a crisis. But to do so, we must pursue vigorously those elements of our strategic modernization program that serve the same purpose. We must fully fund the B-2 and SDI program. We can make radical changes in the nuclear postures of both sides to make them smaller, safer and more stable. But the United States must maintain modern nuclear forces including the strategic triad and thus ensure the credibility of our deterrent.

Some will say that these initiatives call for a budget windfall for domestic programs. But the peace dividend I seek is not measured in dollars but in greater security. In the near term, some of these steps may even cost money. Given the ambitious plan I have already proposed to reduce U.S. defense spending by 25 percent, we cannot afford to make any unwise or unwarranted cuts in the defense budget that I have submitted to Congress. I am counting on congressional support to ensure we have the funds necessary to restructure our forces prudently and implement the decisions I have outlined tonight.

Twenty years ago when I had the opportunity to serve this country as Ambassador to the United Nations, I once talked about the vision that was in the minds of the U.N.'s founders—how they dreamed of a new age when the great powers of the world would cooperate in peace as they had as allies in war.

Today I consulted with President Gorbachev. And while he hasn't had time to absorb the details, I believe the Soviet response will clearly be positive. I also spoke with President Yeltsin and he had a similar reaction—positive, hopeful.

Now, the Soviet people and their leaders can shed the heavy burden of a dangerous and costly nuclear arsenal which has threatened world peace for the past five decades. They can join us in these dramatic moves toward a new world of peace and security.

Tonight, as I see the drama of democracy unfolding around the globe, perhaps—perhaps we are closer to that new world than ever before. The future is ours to influence, to shape, to mold. While we must not gamble that future, neither can we forfeit the historic opportunity now before us.

It has been said,

"Destiny is not a matter of chance, it is a matter of choice; it is not a thing to be waited for, it's a thing to be achieved."

The United States has always stood where duty required us to stand. Now let them say, that we led where destiny required us to lead—to a more peaceful, hopeful future. We cannot give a more precious gift to the children of the world. Thank you, good night, and God bless the United States of America.

Source: George W. Bush, "Initiative on Nuclear Arms: Changing the Nuclear Posture," *Vital Speeches* 57 (1 November 1991): 34–36.

---

153. CLINTON, "A STRATEGY FOR FOREIGN POLICY" 1 APRIL 1992

The 1992 election campaign was largely devoid of foreign policy issues, focusing instead on the impact of an economic recession in America. Despite this, presidential candidate William J. Clinton, the governor of Arkansas with a limited record in foreign affairs, sought to establish his position on American diplomacy. He did so by criticizing the failures of the Bush administration.

Perhaps once in a generation, history presents us with a moment of monumental importance. In the aftermath of World War I, our country chose to retreat from the world, with tragic consequences. After World War II, we chose instead to lead the world and take responsibility for shaping the post-war era.

I am literally a child of the Cold War, born as it was just beginning. My parents' generation wanted nothing more than to return from a world war to the joys of work and home and family. Yet it was no ordinary moment, and history would not let them rest. Overnight, an expansionist Soviet Union summoned them into a new struggle. Fortunately, America had farsighted and courageous leaders like Harry Truman and George Marshall, who recognized the gravity of the moment and roused our battle-weary nation to the challenge. Under their leadership, we helped Europe and Japan rebuild their economies, organized a great military coalition of free nations, and defended our democratic principles against yet another totalitarian threat.

Now, we face our own moment of great change and enormous opportunity. The end of the Cold War and collapse of the Soviet empire pose an unprecedented opportunity to make our future more prosperous and secure.

It reminds us, too, of our duty to prevent the tragedies of the 20th Century—cataclysmic wars and the fear of nuclear annihilation—from recurring in the 21st Century.

Yet at the very moment America's ideas have triumphed and the whole world is rushing to embrace our way of life, our own leaders have been standing still at home and abroad. In the midst of revolutionary change, they have struggled to shore up a status quo that no longer exists.

The Bush Administration has been overly cautious on the issue of aid to Russia—not for policy considerations, but for political calculations. Now, prodded by Democrats in Congress, rebuked by Richard Nixon, and realizing that I have been raising the issue in the campaign, the President is finally . . . even now . . . as I speak . . . putting forward a plan of assistance to Russia and the other new republics. I welcome this. It's good for them and it's good for us.

I'd really like it if I could have as much influence on his domestic policy. In the coming weeks, I will be giving more speeches outlining my plan of assistance for America: to create jobs, provide health care, educate our children, and turn this country around.

In 1992, we must look forward, not backward. I seek not to be the last President of the 20th Century, but the first President for the 21st Century.

Throughout this campaign I have called for a new strategy for American engagement: to revamp our Cold War military forces to meet our nation's changing security needs; encourage the consolidation and spread of democracy abroad; and restore America's economic leadership at home and abroad. My vision for U.S. foreign policy is based on a simple premise: America must lead the world we have done so much to make.

In the months to come, I will say more about the need for American leadership to stop the spread of weapons of mass destruction, increase prosperity by opening markets to trade, and confront threats to the world environment from ozone depletion and global warming.

Today I want to discuss what America must do to secure democracy's triumph around the world, and most of all, in the former Soviet empire. No national security issue is more urgent, nowhere is our country's imperative more clear. I believe it is time for America to lead a global alliance for democracy as united and steadfast as the global alliance that defeated communism.

If we don't take the lead, no one else can, and no one else will. As we proceed, we must keep in mind three realities:

First, the end of the Cold War does not mean the end of danger in the world. Even as we restructure our defenses, we must prepare for new threats.

Where might these threats arise? From armed conflict within and among the former Soviet republics, four of which have nuclear weapons. From the spread of nuclear, chemical, and biological weapons. From regional tensions on the Korean Peninsula and in the Middle East. From terrorist attacks on Americans abroad. And from the growing intensity of ethnic rivalry and separatist violence, which could spill across borders in Yugoslavia and elsewhere.

I have laid out a defense blueprint for replacing our Cold War military structure with a more flexible mix of forces better suited to the dangers we will face in the new era. We can and must substantially reduce forces originally designed to counter the Soviet threat. But the level of defense spending must be based on protecting our enduring interests and preserving our comparative advantage in training, mobility and advanced military technology. And though we will continue to reduce our nuclear arms in tandem with Russia and the other republics, we must retain a survivable nuclear force to deter any conceivable threat.

The Commander in Chief must be prepared to act, with force if necessary, when our country's interests and values are threatened, as they were in the Gulf War. I will not shrink from using military force responsibly, and I will maintain the forces we need to win, and win decisively, should that necessity arise.

A second reality is that the irresistible power of ideas will shape the world in the Information Age. Television, cassette tapes and the fax machine helped ideas to pierce the Berlin Wall and bring it down. Look at the defining images of the past decade: Lech Walesa scaling the fence at the Lenin Shipyard; Vaclav Havel sounding the call for freedom at Wenceslas Square; Chinese students marching in Tienanmen Square; Nelson Mandela walking out of prison a free man; Boris Yeltsin standing defiantly atop a tank to face down the coup. These pictures speak of people willing to fight against all odds for their convictions, their freedom, and the right to control their own destiny.

This means that we are in a position to do more with less than at any time in our recent history. During the Cold War, we spent trillions to protect freedom where it was threatened. In this post Cold War era, the West can spend a fraction of that amount to nurture democracy where it never before existed.

America's challenge in this era is not to bear every burden, but to tip the balance. Only America has the global reach and influence to lead on the great issues confronting the world.

Third, and most important, none of this will be possible unless we restore America's economic strength. For 11 years, we've had no economic vision, no economic leadership, no national economic strategy. America's ability to lead the world and inspire others with our example has gradually been eroded by an anemic, debt-ridden economy, an inadequate education and training system, a decaying stock of public capital, and the highest crime and poverty rates of any advanced nation.

As John Kennedy put it, we can't be strong abroad if we are weak at home. It was that weakness that promoted the Japanese Prime Minister to say he felt sympathy for the United States. We must organize to compete and win in the global economy. We need a national strategy that will reward work, expand opportunity, and put people first. With more public and private investment, the world's best-educated workforce, and competitive strategies in health care, energy, and trade.

If we're not strong at home we can't lead the world we've done so much to make. In today's world, foreign and domestic policy are inseparable. But if we withdraw from the world, it will hurt us economically at home. We can't allow a false choice between domestic policy and foreign policy to hurt our country and our economy. If the President fails in either responsibility, it is not just others who will suffer but the people of the United States above all.

Anyone running for President right now—Republican or Democrat—must provide a vision for security in this new era. The President has yet to meet that test, as evidenced by his embarrassing pilgrimage to Japan illustrates the basic pattern of reactive, rudderless, and erratic U.S. diplomacy under this Administration.

I have supported the President when I have thought he was right—and will do so again. But I will differ with him when I think criticism is just. And my central criticism is this: George Bush has invoked a new world order without enunciating a new American purpose. No one doubts his long experience in diplomatic affairs or his personal ties to foreign leaders. His handling of the international coalition against Iraq was a deft display of crisis management. But for all his experience, skill and cautious professionalism, the President has failed to articulate clear goals for American foreign policy.

The lack of a positive vision has led to miscalculations and missed opportunities. In the Middle East, President Bush and Secretary of State Baker deserve credit for getting negotiations started. But they have chosen to browbeat Israel, the region's sole democracy, while nurturing ties to Syria's despotic regime. By its repeated public attacks on Israel, this Administration has damaged its ability to act as an honest broker and has encouraged the Arabs to harden their positions in the mistaken belief that Washington can or should deliver Israeli concessions without Arab concessions in return. In doing so, the Administration has damaged our strategic relationship with Israel and undermined the peace process itself.

In the Persian Gulf, first the Bush Administration made misguided efforts to purchase Saddam Hussein's goodwill through generous American assistance. Then, after America's smashing victory over Iraq, he left Saddam Hussein with enough military force to remain in power and savagely suppress uprisings by Shiites and the Kurds—who rose up after the President's promptings to do so.

In China, the President continues to coddle aging rulers with undisguised contempt for democracy, human rights, and the need to control the spread of dangerous technologies. Such forbearance on our part might have been justified during the Cold War as a strategic necessity, when China was a counterweight to Soviet power. But it makes no sense to play the China card now, when our opponents have thrown in their hand.

Most of all, the President kept America largely on the sidelines in the democratic revolution that toppled the Soviet empire and is transforming the face of world politics. Time and again, the administration sided with stability over democratic change. President Bush aligned the U.S. with Mikhail Gorbachev's efforts to prop up the stagnant and despised Soviet center, long after it was apparent that hopes for democratic reform had shifted to Boris Yeltsin and the republics. Similarly, he poured cold water on Baltic and Ukrainian aspirations for independence and still has not recognized Croatia and Slovenia despite prodding our European allies.

By failing to offer a compelling rationale for America's continued engagement in the world, the administration has invited a new birth of isolationism on the left and the right, especially at this time of economic duress, when most Americans are properly demanding that we devote more attention and money to our needs here at home. But putting our own people first cannot mean an uncritical withdrawal from the world. That's why we need a clear statement of purpose.

America deserves better than activism without vision, prudence without purpose and tactics without strategy. America needs leadership of vision, values and conviction.

I have called for greater American leadership to reinforce the powerful global movement toward democracy and market economies, as brave men and women fight for freedom in China and Haiti and South Africa. If we succeed, the world will be a safer place. The spread of free institution will make foreign rulers accountable to their people and check tyranny and external aggression. As nations free their economies from bureaucratic control they will become productive enough to satisfy more of their own material wants, and rich enough to buy more American goods and services. We have seen the spread of democracy and more open economies in Latin America; now we should seek to increase their reach around the world.

We need to respond forcefully to one of the greatest security challenges of our time, to help the people of the former Soviet bloc demilitarize their societies and build free political and economic institutions. We have a chance to engage the Russian people in the West for the first time in their history.

The stakes are high. The collapse of communism is not an isolated event; it's part of a worldwide march toward democracy whose outcome will shape the next century. For ourselves and for millions of people who seek to live in freedom and prosperity, this revolution must not fail.

I know it isn't popular today to call for foreign assistance of any kind. It's harder when Americans are hurting, as millions are today. But I believe it is deeply irresponsible to forgo this short term investment in our long term security. Being penny wise and pound foolish will cost us more in the long run in higher defense budgets and lost economic opportunities.

What does a democratic Russia mean to Americans? Lower defense spending. A reduced nuclear threat. A diminished risk of environmental disasters. Fewer arms exports and less proliferation. Access to Russia's vast resources through peaceful commerce. And, the creation of a major new market for American goods and services.

As I said at Georgetown last December,

"We owe it to the people who defeated communism, the people who defeated the coup. And we owe it to ourselves. . . . Having won the Cold War, we must not now lose the peace."

Already, chaos has threatened to engulf Russia. Its old economy lies in ruins, staples remain scarce and lawless behavior is spreading. The immediate danger is not a resurgence of communism, but the emergence of an aggressively nationalistic regime that could menace the other republics and revive the old political and nuclear threats to the West.

Boris Yeltsin has embarked on a radical course of economic reform, freeing prices, selling off state properties and cutting wasteful public subsidies. Hopes for a democratic Russia ride on these efforts, which must produce positive results before economic deprivation wears down the people's patience.

I believe America needs to organize and lead a long-term western strategy of engagement for democracy. From Russia to Central Europe, from Ukraine to the Baltics, the U.S. and our allies need to speed the transition to democracy and capitalism by keeping our markets open to these countries' products, offering food and technical assistance, and helping them privatize key industries, convert military production to civilian uses, and employ weapons experts in peaceful pursuits.

Make no mistake: Our help should be strictly conditioned on an unswerving commitment by the republics to comprehensive economic reform and on continued reductions in the former Soviet nuclear arsenal.

Russia faces two economic challenges. The short-term challenge is to stabilize the economy and stem hyperinflation, so that Russia doesn't go the way of Weimar Germany. The long-term challenge is to build a market system from the ground up—to establish private property rights, create a banking system, and modernize its antiquated capital stock, which outside the defense sector lags behind world standards.

Russia is intrinsically a rich country. What it needs is not charity but trade and investment on a massive scale. What the major financial powers can do together is help the Russians help themselves. If we do, Russia's future holds the possibility of a stronger democracy rather than a resurgent dictatorship, and a new American market rather than a new American nightmare.

We should look at this assistance not as a bail out, but a bridge loan, much as a family gets from the bank when it buys a new house before selling their old house. I propose that the U.S. must take the lead in putting together a bridge loan to help Russia make the transition from its old system to its new economy.

We must have no illusions: The West cannot guarantee Russia's prosperity. Even with our help, the future of Russia and the other republics is uncertain. But we can give President Yeltsin's reforms and Russian democracy a fighting chance.

The West should establish a $6 billion fund to help stabilize the Russian ruble. Without this fund, the ruble will continue to lose its exchange value and inflation will continue to soar. America's share would be about $1 billion, in the form of a loan, not a gift. In return, Russian leaders have to agree to tough conditions. They must rein in public spending and stop excessive printing of money. A fund of this kind is like a net for acrobats. By building confidence, it reduces the chance it will ever be used.

Russia also needs to import food, medicine and the materials required to keep the economy functioning. According to the IMF, which has just endorsed Russia's economic reform program, that country needs a minimum of $12 billion in financial assistance in 1992 to do so, primarily in the form of loans. Without this, Russia faces more than a 20 percent drop in GNP in 1992—a bigger drop than America suffered in any year of the Great Depression. This assistance should be carefully aimed at those sectors where it can do the most good, and should come from the western democracies, including Japan, and perhaps also from other countries like Saudi Arabia, Kuwait, South Korea and Taiwan. The U.S. share of these loans would be roughly 10 percent.

Finally, it is also crucial to give Russia some breathing space for servicing its external debts, at a time when it doesn't have the money to stabilize its currency or import goods.

Let me be clear: Our nation can afford this. This is not an exorbitant price to pay for a chance to create new American markets and anchor a revitalized Russia firmly in the democratic camp. The amount of money we need is available from defense and other foreign aid savings that the end of the Cold War makes possible. If Boris Yeltsin and his economic advisers stay the course, the chances are good that Russia will be in a position to pay us back in full by the latter part of the decade. Nevertheless, passing such aid will require an act of political will by the Congress and the President, and the kind of leadership from the White House we have not previously seen.

I also strongly support fulfilling the commitment America has made to our share of the IMF quota increase. Of a total increase of $60 billion, our share is 19 percent, or roughly $12 billion. But we are not talking about giving the $12 billion away. It is like a line of credit in a cooperative bank, and we earn interest on it. The quota increase was voted two years ago. It was necessary to help emerging democracies in Eastern Europe. It is all the more urgent now, with Ukraine, the Baltics, and other newly independent nations whose economic fate depends on it. Every other country in the IMF has agreed to pay their share, except the U.S. Why? Because our President has not taken the lead in persuading the Congress to authorize the necessary funds. We need a President who doesn't mind taking a little flak to seize this moment in history.

At the same time, we should encourage private American investment in the former Soviet Union. The newly independent republics, after all, are rich in human and natural resources. One day, they and Eastern Europe could be lucrative markets.

But Russia needs to do more than make the transition from state socialism to free markets. Constitutional democracy must take root firmly there as well. The popular movement for Russian democracy has been held together more by anti-communism than by a clear or common understanding of how to build a democratic society. Democracy remains an abstract and theoretical notion; there is an enormous deficit of knowledge in the former Soviet Union about the texture and dynamics of a free society.

No one on earth can fill that gap better than Americans. We need to make

our engagement for Russian democracy a matter for people, not just governments. We need person-to-person contacts: a Democracy Corps, as Rep. Dave
McCurdy has proposed, to send Americans over there; a crash program as others
have proposed to bring tens of thousands of Russians and others here to learn
how free institutions work; and a strong National Endowment for Democracy
to lead the way in spreading American values. Promoting democracy is not just
a task for the American government. For years, labor unions, universities, and
volunteer organizations in this country have nurtured the democratic revolution
around the world.

Without democratic institutions and values, economic reforms will not succeed. Our nation's greatest resource is ultimately not our dollars nor our technical expertise, but our values of pluralism and enterprise and freedom and the
rule of law—and our centuries of experience in making those values work. In
an era of fledgling democracies, those values can be our proudest export and
our most effective tool of foreign policy.

This spring, Russia is scheduled to be admitted to the IMF and the World
Bank. The lead role that such bodies will take points to a broader opportunity
at this pivotal point in history: to reinvent the institutions of collective security.

At the outset, let me be clear: I will never turn over the security of the U.S.
to the U.N. or any other international organization. We will never abandon our
prerogative to act alone when our vital interests are at stake. Our motto in this
era will be: together where we can; on our own where we must. But it is a
failure of vision not to recognize that collective action can accomplish more
than it could just a few years ago—and it is a failure of leadership not to make
use of it.

The role of the United Nations during the Gulf War was a vivid illustration
of what is possible in a new era. Too often in the past, the U.N. has looked like
New York's own Tower of Babel—a costly debating society where Soviet
client-states and others engaged in anti-American demagoguery and outra-
geously equated Zionism with racism. But the end of the East-West standoff
opens a range of new opportunities for these institutions. Through them, we can
share the burdens of making this a safer world.

For example, the U.N. has started unprecedented efforts to transform Cambodia's killing fields into a fertile place for civilian life and electoral freedom
and to bring peace in Yugoslavia. The Congress should support those efforts.
And we should build on the Desert Storm coalition and these new initiatives,
by exploring new ideas for U.N. preventive diplomacy to head off conflicts
before they break out. One such idea is a U.N. Rapid Deployment Force that
could be used for purposes beyond traditional peacekeeping, such as standing
guard at the borders of countries threatened by aggression; preventing mass
violence against civilian populations; providing humanitarian relief; and combating terrorism. It would not be a large standing army but rather a small force
that could be called up from units of national armed forces and earmarked and
trained in advance.

Together, we must also tackle problems that transcend national borders, such as threats to the earth's environment, global population growth, world trade, and weapons proliferation. We should be outraged by an indifference in the White House that could wreck the Rio Earth Summit before it has even begun. President Bush should have agreed to attend that summit long before now. The United States should lead the fight to slow global warming, instead of dragging our feet and ignoring important scientific data. We should sign a global environmental agreement to reduce carbon dioxide emissions with specific targets and timetables.

Judging by its dogged performance in tracking down Iraq's nuclear facilities since the war, the International Atomic Energy Agency is proving to be an effective weapon against proliferation. The U.S. should lead an effort to enable the IAEA to conduct surprise inspections anywhere in a member nation, to ensure that it is keeping its commitment to refrain from building nuclear weapons. We must also work harder than the administration has done to make sure that the U.S. and other countries do not export dangerous nuclear materials and technology to aspiring nuclear powers. We simply cannot afford to lose the war against nuclear proliferation.

Finally, we can make these institutions more effective and sustainable by reapportioning the burden of collective security. The answer is not to short-change our contributions to these bodies, as the President and Congress have lamentably done with the U.N. But it is also time to insist that other nations start to shoulder more of the collective burden—not just because it will reduce our expense, but because it will make these institutions more effective. We should seek to reduce our 30 percent financial share of U.N. peacekeeping operations to the 25 percent we pay for the U.N.'s regular budget. But we should also pay up—and pay up now—the past dues we owe to the U.N.

Japan and Germany should be made permanent members of the U.N. Security Council. And we should seek larger contributions from those with the greatest interest in particular efforts; for example, Japan should pay a full 30 percent of the large peacekeeping costs the U.N. will soon incur in Cambodia.

We should look to our alliances to take a more active role in the defense of their own regions. In Europe, we must maintain our ties to NATO, even as the Europeans play a stronger role both within NATO and in the evolution of future security arrangements for the continent. In this hemisphere, the Organization of American States has demonstrated more leadership than the Administration in response to the coup in Haiti.

Many of the challenges we face in this new era will call for sacrifice. All of them will test our vision. Most hold more opportunity than danger for America—if we rise to meet them.

It might be convenient to delay a debate over the contours and demands of the new era until this political season is over. But history does not grind to a halt during American presidential elections. History is calling upon our nation to decide anew whether we will lead or defer; whether we will engage or abstain; whether we will shape a new era or instead be shaped by it.

These are important choices, but they are not partisan ones. I would rather lose an issue than see America lose an opportunity. The best, boldest, and most successful moments of America's foreign policy have come when we stood together as a nation, joined not in separate parties but in common purpose.

I welcome the fact that the President—today—is announcing a program of assistance to Russia. I hope that his statement represents not only a declaration of intent, but a commitment to lead on this issue. And I tell you today, that as he does so, I will offer my support in convincing the American people and the Congress that this course is necessary for our country.

I am running for President, and I am running hard. Yet at this unique moment, just as important as our choice of national leaders is our affirmation of international leadership. That is what is at stake in 1992. After World War II, in similar circumstances, our nation proclaimed its character with an historic pledge to defend, to build, and to lead. I am confident the American people stand ready to affirm that pledge again today.

Thank you.

Source: William J. Clinton, "A Strategy for Foreign Policy: Assistance to Russia," *Vital Speeches* 58 (1 May 1992): 421–25.

154. BUSH, "CONDITIONS IN SOMALIA"
4 December 1992

At the conclusion of the Cold War, America found itself the last remaining superpower and a nation in need of new foreign policy priorities. Nearing the end of his presidency, George Bush committed America to the global mission of humanitarian relief. In December 1992, American military units were dispatched to Somalia with the objective of providing security and aiding in the distribution of food to an African country in a state of anarchy.

I want to talk to you today about the tragedy in Somalia, and about a mission that can ease suffering and save lives. Every American has seen the shocking images from Somalia. The scope of suffering there is hard to imagine. Already, over a quarter million people, as many people as live in Buffalo, New York, have died in the Somali famine. In the months ahead five times that number, one-and-a-half million people could starve to death.

For many months now, the United States has been actively engaged in the massive international relief effort to ease Somalia's suffering. All told, America has sent Somalia 200,000 tons of food, more than half the world total. This summer, the distribution system broke down. Truck convoys from Somalia's ports were blocked. Sufficient food failed to reach the starving in the interior of Somalia.

And so in August, we took additional action. In concert with the United Nations, we sent in the U.S. Air Force to help fly food to the towns. To date, American pilots have flown over 1,400 flights, delivering over 17,000 tons of food aid. And when the U.N. authorized 3,500 U.N. guards to protect the relief operation, we flew in the first of them—500 soldiers from Pakistan.

But in the months since then, the security situation has grown worse. The U.N. has been prevented from deploying its initial commitment of troops. In many cases, food from relief flights is being looted upon landing; food convoys have been hijacked; aid workers assaulted; ships with food have been subjected to artillery attacks that prevented them from docking.

There is no government in Somalia. Law and order have broken down—anarchy prevails.

One image tells the story. Imagine 7,000 tons of food aid literally bursting out of a warehouse on a dock in Mogadishu. Somalis starve less than a kilometer away because relief workers cannot run the gauntlet of armed gangs roving the city.

Confronted with these conditions, relief groups called for outside troops to provide security so they could feed people. It's now clear that military support is necessary to ensure the safe delivery of the food Somalis need to survive.

It was this situation which led us to tell the United Nations that the United States would be willing to provide more help to enable relief to be delivered. Last night the United Nations Security Council, by unanimous vote, and after the tireless efforts of Secretary General Boutros-Ghali, welcomed the United States' offer to lead a coalition to get the food through.

After consulting with my advisers, with world leaders, and the congressional leadership, I have today told Secretary General Boutros-Ghali that America will answer the call. I have given the order to Secretary Cheney to move a substantial American force into Somalia. As I speak, a Marine amphibious ready group, which we maintain at sea, is offshore Mogadishu. These troops will be joined by elements of the 1st Marine Expeditionary Force, based out of Camp Pendleton, California, and by the Army's 10th Mountain Division out of Fort Drum, New York.

These and other American forces will assist in Operation Restore Hope. They are America's finest. They will perform this mission with courage and compassion, and they will succeed.

The people of Somalia, especially the children of Somalia, need our help. We're able to ease their suffering. We must help them live. We must give them hope.

In taking this action I want to emphasize that I understand the United States alone cannot right wrongs. But we also know that some crises in the world cannot be resolved without American involvement; that American action is often necessary as a catalyst for broader involvement of the community of nations. Only the United States has the global reach to place a large security force on the ground in such a distant place quickly and efficiently and thus save thousands of innocents from death.

We will not, however, be acting alone. I expect forces from about a dozen countries to join us in this mission. When we see Somalia's children starving, all of America hurts. We've tried to help in many ways. And make no mistake about it, now we and our allies will ensure that aid gets through.

And here is what we and our coalition partners will do. First, we will create a secure environment in the hardest hit parts of Somalia, so that food can move from ships over land to the people in the countryside now devastated by starvation.

And second, once we have created that secure environment, we will withdraw our troops handing the security mission back to a regular U.N. peacekeeping force. Our mission has a limited objective—to open the supply routes, to get the food moving and to prepare the way for a U.N. peacekeeping force to keep it moving.

This operation is not open-ended. We will not stay one day longer than is absolutely necessary. Let me be very clear, our mission is humanitarian, but we will not tolerate armed gangs ripping off their own people, condemning them to death by starvation.

General Hoar and his troops have the authority to take whatever military action is necessary to safeguard the lives of our troops and the lives of Somalia's people.

The outlaw elements in Somalia must understand this is serious business. We will accomplish our mission. We have no intent to remain in Somalia with fighting forces, but we are determined to do right, to secure an environment that will allow food to get to the starving people of Somalia.

To the people of Somalia I promise this: We do not plan to dictate political outcomes. We respect your sovereignty and independence. Based on my conversations with other coalition leaders, I can state with confidence: We come to your country for one reason only, to enable the starving to be fed.

Let me say to the men and women of the Armed Forces, we are asking you to do a difficult and dangerous job. As Commander-in-Chief I assure you, you will have our full support to get the job done, and we will bring you home as soon as possible.

Finally, let me close with a message to the families of the men and women who take part in this mission. I understand it is difficult to see your loved ones go, to send them off knowing they will not be home for the holiday, but the humanitarian mission they undertake is in the finest traditions of service. So, to every sailor, soldier, airman and marine who is involved in this mission, let me say, you're doing God's work. We will not fail.

Thank you, and may God bless the United States of America.

Source: George Bush, "Conditions in Somalia: Creating a Secure Environment," *Vital Speeches* 59 (1 January 1993): 162–63

155. CLINTON, "REMARKS AT THE SIGNING CEREMONY FOR THE ISRAELI-PALESTINIAN DECLARATION OF PRINCIPLES"
13 September 1993

Early in his presidency, Bill Clinton committed the United States to fostering peace in the Middle East. After months of secret negotiations in Oslo, Norway, Israeli Prime Minister Yitzhak Rabin and PLO Chairman Yassir Arafat announced an agreement on mutual recognition and the terms of Palestinian self-government in the Gaza Strip and portions of the West Bank. Clinton presided over the final signing ceremony in Washington, D.C.

The President. Prime Minister Rabin, Chairman Arafat, Foreign Minister Peres, Mr. Abbas, President Carter, President Bush, distinguished guests.

On behalf of the United States and Russia, cosponsors of the Middle East peace process, welcome to this great occasion of history and hope.

Today we bear witness to an extraordinary act in one of history's defining dramas, a drama that began in the time of our ancestors when the word went forth from a sliver of land between the river Jordan and the Mediterranean Sea. That hallowed piece of earth, that land of light and revelation is the home to the memories and dreams of Jews, Muslims, and Christians throughout the world.

As we all know, devotion to that land has also been the source of conflict and bloodshed for too long. Throughout this century, bitterness between the Palestinian and Jewish people has robbed the entire region of its resources, its potential, and too many of its sons and daughters. The land has been so drenched in warfare and hatred, the conflicting claims of history etched so deeply in the souls of the combatants there, that many believed the past would always have the upper hand.

Then, 14 years ago, the past began to give way when, at this place and upon this desk, three men of great vision signed their names to the Camp David accords. Today we honor the memories of Menachem Begin and Anwar Sadat, and we salute the wise leadership of President Jimmy Carter. Then, as now, we heard from those who said that conflict would come again soon. But the peace between Egypt and Israel has endured. Just so, this bold new venture today, this brave gamble that the future can be better than the past, must endure.

Two years ago in Madrid, another President took a major step on the road to

peace by bringing Israel and all her neighbors together to launch direct negotiations. And today we also express our deep thanks for the skillful leadership
of President George Bush.

Ever since Harry Truman first recognized Israel, every American President,
Democrat and Republican, has worked for peace between Israel and her neighbors. Now the efforts of all who have labored before us bring us to this moment,
a moment when we dare to pledge what for so long seemed difficult even to
imagine: that the security of the Israeli people will be reconciled with the hopes
of the Palestinian people and there will be more security and more hope for all.

Today the leadership of Israel and the Palestine Liberation Organization will
sign a declaration of principles on interim Palestinian self-government. It charts
a course toward reconciliation between two peoples who have both known the
bitterness of exile. Now both pledge to put old sorrows and antagonisms behind
them and to work for a shared future, shaped by the values of the Torah, the
Koran, and the Bible.

Let us salute also today the Government of Norway for its remarkable role
in nurturing this agreement. But above all, let us today pay tribute to the leaders
who had the courage to lead their people toward peace, away from the scars of
battle, the wounds and the losses of the past, toward a brighter tomorrow. The
world today thanks Prime Minister Rabin, Foreign Minister Peres, and Chairman
Arafat. Their tenacity and vision has given us the promise of a new beginning.

What these leaders have done now must be done by others. Their achievement
must be a catalyst for progress in all aspects of the peace process. And those
of us who support them must be there to help in all aspects. For the peace must
render the people who make it more secure. A peace of the brave is within our
reach. Throughout the Middle East, there is a great yearning for the quiet miracle
of a normal life.

We know a difficult road lies ahead. Every peace has its enemies, those who
still prefer the easy habits of hatred to the hard labors of reconciliation. But
Prime Minister Rabin has reminded us that you do not have to make peace with
your friends. And the Koran teaches that if the enemy inclines toward peace,
do thou also incline toward peace.

Therefore, let us resolve that this new mutual recognition will be a continuing
process in which the parties transform the very way they see and understand
each other. Let the skeptics of this peace recall what once existed among these
people. There was a time when the traffic of ideas and commerce and pilgrims
flowed uninterrupted among the cities of the Fertile Crescent. In Spain and the
Middle East, Muslims and Jews once worked together to write brilliant chapters
in the history of literature and science. All this can come to pass again.

Mr. Prime Minister, Mr. Chairman, I pledge the active support of the United
States of America to the difficult work that lies ahead. The United States is
committed to ensuring that the people who are affected by this agreement will
be made more secure by it and to leading the world in marshaling the resources

necessary to implement the difficult details that will make real the principles to which you commit yourselves today.

Together let us imagine what can be accomplished if all the energy and ability the Israelis and the Palestinians have invested into your struggle can now be channeled into cultivating the land and freshening the waters, into ending the boycotts and creating new industry, into building a land as bountiful and peaceful as it is holy. Above all, let us dedicate ourselves today to your region's next generation. In this entire assembly, no one is more important than the group of Israeli and Arab children who are seated here with us today.

Mr. Prime Minister, Mr. Chairman, this day belongs to you. And because of what you have done, tomorrow belongs to them. We must not leave them prey to the politics of extremism and despair, to those who would derail this process because they cannot overcome the fears and hatreds of the past. We must not betray their future. For too long, the young of the Middle East have been caught in a web of hatred not of their own making. For too long, they have been taught from the chronicles of war. Now we can give them the chance to know the season of peace. For them we must realize the prophecy of Isaiah that the cry of violence shall no more be heard in your land, nor wrack nor ruin within your borders. The children of Abraham, the descendants of Isaac and Ishmael, have embarked together on a bold journey. Together today, with all our hearts and all our souls, we bid them shalom, salaam, peace.

[*At this point, Foreign Minister Shimon Peres of Israel and Mahmoud Abbas, PLO Executive Committee member, made brief remarks. Following their remarks, Foreign Minister Peres and Mr. Abbas signed the declaration, and Secretary of State Warren Christopher and Foreign Minister Andrey Kozyrev of Russia signed as witnesses. Secretary Christopher and Foreign Minister Kozyrev then made remarks, followed by Prime Minister Yitzhak Rabin of Israel and Chairman Yassir Arafat of the PLO.*]

The President. We have been granted the great privilege of witnessing this victory for peace. Just as the Jewish people this week celebrate the dawn of a new year, let us all go from this place to celebrate the dawn of a new era, not only for the Middle East but for the entire world.

The sound we heard today, once again, as in ancient Jericho, was of trumpets toppling walls, the walls of anger and suspicion between Israeli and Palestinian, between Arab and Jew. This time, praise God, the trumpets herald not the destruction of that city but its new beginning.

Now let each of us here today return to our portion of that effort, uplifted by the spirit of the moment, refreshed in our hopes, and guided by the wisdom of the Almighty, who has brought us to this joyous day.

Go in peace. Go as peacemakers.

Source: Public Papers of the Presidents of the United States, William J. Clinton, 1993 (Washington, DC: Government Printing Office, 1994), 1475–76.

156. WOOLSEY, "THREATS TO THE U.S. AND ITS INTERESTS ABROAD"
25 January 1994

The post–Cold War era required a basic reassessment of American intelligence priorities. In January 1994, CIA director R. James Woolsey testified before the Senate Select Committee on Intelligence regarding the new challenges faced by the country in the former Soviet Union, Asia, and the Middle East. Woolsey also made a point to illustrate potential emerging problems in the areas of nuclear proliferation, terrorism, and instability in the underdeveloped world.

The conclusion of the Cold War against the Soviet Union prompted American leaders to reassess the changing nature of security threats to the United States.

I welcome the opportunity to testify before this committee on the threats to the United States and its interests abroad. Much has transpired since I addressed your Senate colleagues on the Armed Services Committee on this same topic last March. Let me highlight a few of these historic events.

—In East Asia, North Korea's attempt to develop a clandestine nuclear capability, together with its military preparations and arms transfers to other countries, threatens its neighbors and our fundamental national security interests.

—In Russia and the rest of the former Soviet Union the struggle for democracy and economic reform has been intense and—as witnessed last fall in Moscow— at times, violent. Progress is occurring, but it is spotty.

—Local strife in Somalia and Haiti, and the tragedy in Bosnia, continue to threaten stability in those countries and nearby regions.

On the positive side, Mr. Chairman, in the Asia/Pacific region, Latin America, and Europe—while there are some specific difficulties, including those mentioned above—the political, security, and economic pictures are generally in the range from light gray to bright.

—In Kiev and Moscow, the President brokered an agreement with Russia and Ukraine on the disposition of the nuclear weapons stationed on Ukrainian soil. Implementation will take substantial effort, but the agreement is a step toward removing not only an obstacle to better relations between those two countries but also a source of critical concern to U.S. and Western security interests.

—On the international economic front, the GATT agreement, bringing the Uruguay Round to a successful conclusion, paves the way for a significant boost in world trade.

—Two conflicts, both of which preceded the onset of the cold war, have shown movement toward resolution, although in neither case are we yet home free. In South Africa, apartheid is being dismantled, and an historic agreement was reached last July paving the way for the first multi-racial, national, democratic election this spring. In the Middle East, Israel and the PLO concluded their famous agreement in the Rose Garden. Implementation awaits further negotiation, but here and elsewhere in the Mid-East there has been positive movement to reduce tensions between Israel and its neighbors.

The lesson that I draw from my first year as Director of Central Intelligence is that hope coexists with uncertainty, promise with danger. We had one central threat which dominated our work for nearly half a century. That threat is gone, and we gladly leave the cold war with the communist U.S.S.R. to historians and scholars.

But the end of the cold war does not mean the end of conflict, nor the end to threats to our security and to that of our friends and allies. Indeed, your invitation to me to address this committee listed no fewer than ten major issues, ranging from developments in the former Soviet Union to countering the proliferation of weapons of mass destruction. As we know, that list is by no means exhaustive.

The conflicts today may have different names and may be grouped under different banners; at times, the question which could determine war or peace may not be where you stand, politically, but who you are, ethnically. I might add that these types of conflicts are not new to U.S. intelligence: half of the stars etched into the marble wall at CIA are dedicated to those officers who lost their lives to such conflicts. And today I wear a black ribbon to honor all of those at CIA who have lost their lives in defense of their country, and particularly to commemorate the sad anniversary of the slaying of two Agency officers at our door, only five miles from where we sit today.

The task for intelligence in the post cold war era is clear:

—First, we must support policymakers working hard to nurture promise and hope, to protect the gains of the past five remarkable—indeed revolutionary—years.

—Second, we must remain vigilant against North Korea, Iran, Iraq, Libya and others throughout the globe who want to make a mockery of our goal of a more peaceful world.

—Third, we must provide the early warning and the information systems needed to keep our reduced defense forces up to the tasks they may face in an uncertain future.

—Fourth, we must be prepared for the unknown. Next year might bring a different set of headlines, and a new set of problems which can threaten our interests, task our resources, and challenge our resolve.

This afternoon I would like to highlight the critical challenges we face in the intelligence community, and the efforts underway to help counter the threats to our interests.

I want to begin my presentation on regional issues: East Asia, focusing first on North Korea and then on China; developments in Russia and in the former Soviet Union; the Middle East; Somalia; Bosnia; and Haiti. I will then turn to transnational issues: proliferation, terrorism, drug trafficking, and international economics.

I take this approach for ease of presentation only. As we know, in the real world regional and transnational problems are often intertwined, whether we speak of international economic trends constraining the ability of key nations to maintain defense capabilities, or of proliferation fueled by—and exacerbating—regional conflicts.

I. Regional Issues
The Far East: North Korea and China

Let me begin with North Korea. Mr. Chairman, in recent months North Korea has vaulted to the top of our agenda in the intelligence community. North Korea presents us and our friends and allies with three critical challenges.

First is its effort to develop its nuclear capability. As I testified publicly before the Congress on July 28 of last year, we believe that North Korea could already have produced enough plutonium for at least one nuclear weapon. Moreover, their Yongbyon reactor may be shut down soon, enabling them to extract fuel, reprocess, recover the plutonium, and use it to produce weapons. In addition, North Korea is building a larger reactor which could be completed by the mid 1990s, expanding its capability to produce even more plutonium. Even with NPT and full IAEA safeguards, North Korea will not be barred from producing, reprocessing, and stockpiling significant amounts of plutonium. We will continue to provide support to policymakers as they press for full implementation of IAEA safeguards and the 1991 North-South Non-Nuclear Agreement, which is intended to prevent the further production of fissile material on the peninsula.

We are also providing analytical support to policymakers working to resolve through diplomatic means the serious concerns raised by North Korean actions. At the same time, I have asked the intelligence community to undertake additional specific steps, in cooperation with the defense community, to ensure strong intelligence support to our military forces.

A second challenge is what North Korea calls its war preparations program, including both improvements in military capabilities and continuing efforts to bring their economy and society to a heightened state of military readiness. North Korea's deployment of rocket launchers and artillery to protected sites close to the DMZ, from which it is possible to target Seoul and South Korean defenses, is just the most recent manifestation of their steady allocation, over the last several years, of resources to the military at the expense of the needs of the North Korean people. Despite remaining readiness inadequacies affecting some North Korean forces, we are concerned with their military preparations and, as in the case of monitoring North Korea's nuclear program, here too we will continue to assign high priority to intelligence coverage.

The third challenge stems from North Korean export of missiles, including those in the 1,000 kilometer range, which can be made capable of carrying nuclear, chemical or biological weapons. Deployment and sale of such missiles provides a qualitative increase in the capabilities of both North Korea and its customers in the Mid-East. Potentially at risk is most of North East Asia as well as potential targets of North Korea's customers in the Mid-East, such as Israel, Turkey, Saudi Arabia, and other states.

Turning to China, because of its enormous population, growing economy and military strength, China will continue to play a key role in the stability not only of Asia but of much of the rest of the world as well. We are focusing our efforts on the political, economic and military evolution in China.

Politically, at some point there will of course be a change in China's leadership. Deng Xiaoping, the last of the original communist revolutionaries to serve as China's top leader, will turn 90 this August. Although formally in retirement, he is still consulted by other leaders who depend on him for cohesion, legitimacy and guidance. When Deng departs we will face a potentially unsettled period, when prospective leaders jockey for position.

Turning to economics, we see China's economy as one of the fastest growing in the world, after two years of back-to-back 13 percent real growth. Increased inflation is one concern. China's rediscovered entrepreneurial spirit has also been accompanied by unfair trading practices to which the U.S. Government has recently responded, with some success. We will continue to monitor China's trade, although decreasing central control makes some of these practices even more difficult to expose. The stakes, however, for American products—and American jobs—are enormous: we estimate that the China market will exceed $220 billion by the year 2000. At $23 billion, our bilateral trade deficit with China is already nearly half our deficit with Japan, and this deficit's size depends in part on whether the playing field is level or not.

The pace and scope of China's economic growth affect not only bilateral and world trade, but social and political life in China itself. Prosperity has not dampened the calls for reform and political freedom in China's essentially closed political system; if anything, the continued contact with outsiders, along with the freedom of the market place, has spawned a greater desire for a loosening of political controls. We have seen some evidence of small-scale social unrest in several provinces as decentralization proceeds, although certainly not on the scale we saw in Tiananmen Square in 1989. And we will continue to assist in monitoring violations of human rights. The world's ecology and fuel consumption can also be affected by China's rapid growth.

Finally, we are closely monitoring China's military modernization, as well as its attempts to export extremely potent weapons technology into some of the more unstable regions of the world such as the Middle East. The cooperation of China is essential if we are to succeed in curbing proliferation of these technologies and weapons.

Russia and the Former Soviet Union

In Russia, last December's parliamentary election reflected, to a large degree, the ambivalence of the Russian people. The Parliament which they elected—and which opened two weeks ago—contains several elements united more in their opposition to past reforms than in their interest in presenting credible alternatives to those reforms. At the same time, the Russian people gave President Yeltsin enhanced constitutional powers which he can use to help secure Russia's course. President Yeltsin and his advisors are aware that many Russians across the political spectrum believe both that the social safety net must be expanded and that the fabric of public order has frayed to an unacceptable degree.

There are four broad areas to which we have devoted our efforts.

First, we are providing critical—and sometimes unique—political and economic analysis to policymakers to warn them of potential risks facing Russia's uncertain future and to help them sort out the myriad confusing and conflicting aspects of the Russian economy.

That economy is at a critical juncture. President Yeltsin has shattered the incentives and structures of the old system: more than 95 percent of all prices are free, central planning and the State distribution system has been abolished, many controls on foreign trade and investment have been lifted, and more than a quarter of GDP is now produced by a rapidly growing private sector.

But difficult decisions remain, including whether President Yeltsin will put an end to the heavy subsidization of highly inefficient industrial and agricultural entities. Despite the December election, we believe that President Yeltsin will push ahead with reforms, but the pace will be slower as political pressures force compromise. Our major concern is that looser fiscal and monetary policies aimed at easing the pain of reform will unleash forces that could bring Russia again to the brink of destructive hyperinflation.

Second, we continue to monitor the disposition and status of Russia's 27,000 or so nuclear warheads, as well as the strategic systems still deployed to deliver these weapons.

The combination of declining morale in the military, increased organized crime, and efforts by states like Iran seeking to purchase nuclear material or expertise will make these matters a major concern for us throughout this decade and beyond. We investigate every report or claim of the illegal transfer of weapons or weapons-grade material. To date, reports of illegal transfers of weapons do not appear credible. As for weapons-grade material, we are not aware of any illegal transfers in quantities sufficient to produce a nuclear weapon. In addition to our monitoring efforts, we will continue to provide support to policymakers working with Russian officials on ways to improve the physical security of nuclear weapons and fissile material.

Third, the intelligence community continues to monitor the state of Russia's general purpose forces. As I reported last year, these forces are suffering from a host of ills: inadequate housing, erratic pay, and declining morale. Russia's military has not been immune from the vicissitudes of the country's economic, political and social transformations.

Fourth, we are closely monitoring Russia's relations with its newly independent neighbors—the other former Soviet Republics. The presence of some 25 million ethnic Russians in those states, as well as the complex legacy of economic linkages, will be key factors in the evolution of policies toward those states.

In sum, Mr. Chairman, the long existence of a system encrusted by decades of inefficiency, coupled with the stresses in an empire once held together by force and one-party rule, have had a profound impact on the Russian people. Thus, it should come as a surprise to no one that the road ahead will continue to be a long and difficult one, and that these problems will exist in some form for years to come. In the meantime, crises can occur at any point along the political, social, and regional fault lines in Russia and the rest of the former Soviet Union.

Mr. Chairman, there are other conflicts raging in the states of the former Soviet Union, including the ongoing war over Nagorno-Karabakh involving Armenia and Azerbaijan. But I want to take a few minutes to highlight a potential crisis in Ukraine. The celebration of Ukrainian independence has given way to disillusionment as a result of economic mismanagement and political drift. Reform has been nonexistent, energy shortages have become a way of life, the inflation rate for December was 90 percent, and nearly half of Ukraine's citizens are living below the poverty level. Parliamentary elections in March and a Presidential election in June could serve as barometers of how well or poorly Ukrainians are facing up to their multiple serious problems.

During his visit to Kiev, President Clinton pledged a redoubled U.S. effort to assist Ukraine through this difficult period. We will continue to provide our policymakers with the economic analysis they need to devise effective and efficient ways to help.

In addition to its economic problems, the results of a recent election in Crimea—the only region in Ukraine where ethnic Russians comprise a majority—could also lead to instability. A pro-separatist candidate who has endorsed Crimea's eventual reunification with Russia captured nearly 40 percent of the vote in the first round of a Presidential race, and is expected to win the runoff on January 30th. Any move toward secession will lead to confrontation between the Ukrainian and Crimean leadership—indeed there are already calls for President Kravchuk to declare Presidential rule in Ukraine. Ethnic tensions in Crimea would further strain Russian-Ukrainian relations, and secessionist forces would probably appeal to Moscow for support.

Along with our interest in seeing a viable, stable Ukraine, our interests are focused on the nuclear weapons still on Ukrainian soil. Mr. Chairman, Ukraine is not the only state to have inherited nuclear weapons when the U.S.S.R. dissolved in December 1991; we are also tracking the nuclear weapons in Kazakhstan, and Belarus. But, of these three states, Ukraine has the largest number of these weapons, and their disposition has been a thorny issue in Russian-Ukrainian relations and a key concern for us.

The President's efforts recently helped bring Ukraine and Russia together to resolve the dispute over the final disposition of nuclear warheads in Ukraine. We provided direct analytical support to Administration officials who worked closely with Russian and Ukrainian officials to reach the Trilateral Accord, and will continue to do so in the months ahead as the U.S. continues its engagement in the trilateral discussions on implementing the agreements that we have reached.

The accord is being heavily criticized by hardliners and nationalists in Ukraine, and is currently being examined by the Rada—the Ukrainian Parliament. The intelligence community will continue to assign high priority to tracking the debate in Ukraine over these weapons.

The Middle East

Let me turn now to the Middle East, beginning first with the peace process. American resolve over the years in standing up to extremists and opponents of the peace process, willingness to explore any avenue to advance that process, and persistence in encouraging the parties themselves to work directly together for peace, have helped to bring about this step toward an end to the Arab-Israeli conflict.

Still, much needs to be done. The road to the signing of the Israeli-PLO accord was tortuous and dramatic; the road to a comprehensive settlement will be no less arduous, and will require determination and vision. It will also require help from the United States, including help from the intelligence community. There are four ways we are assisting this process.

First, we are providing daily, intense intelligence support to our negotiators involved in the peace process.

Second, we are continuing our liaison efforts with intelligence services throughout the region to help nurture an atmosphere of confidence and trust.

Third, as we have for twenty years, we are continuing to use our unique intelligence capabilities to monitor existing peace agreements in the Sinai and Golan. If there is a breakthrough leading to a comprehensive settlement on the Golan Heights—a goal of the President's discussion earlier this month with President Assad in Geneva—we stand ready to do all we can to help monitor any agreement.

Fourth, we are continuing vigorous counter-terrorism intelligence efforts to help keep the opponents of the peace process at bay. The decades of hot war and cold peace have come at too high a price for us to allow terrorist groups and nations which support them to strangle our hopes for peace in the Middle East.

Mr. Chairman, there are other dangers in the region, especially those stemming from Iran and Iraq and their efforts to obtain weapons of mass destruction and to support terrorism.

On Iran, I wish to tell this committee that 15 years after the triumph of the extremists, the voices of hate have given way to the policies of moderation. But there is no basis for such a view. Iran remains determined to maintain its implacable hostility, to eliminate any opposition to its rule, and to undermine our security interests and those of our friends and allies in the region. Terrorism remains a central tool for Iran's leaders in seeking to accomplish these objectives, and Iranian support for Hizballah and other such groups from Algeria to Tajikistan has not abated.

We are especially concerned that Iran continues to develop its ambitious multibillion dollar military modernization program and to pursue development of weapons of mass destruction. The intelligence community estimates that left to its own devices Iran will take at least 8–10 years to build its own nuclear weapons, but that it will try to shortcut this process by buying nuclear material and ballistic missiles.

Over the past year the intelligence community has been instrumental in the ongoing, intensive, dialogue with our European allies to outline for them the continued threats posed by Iran. The Administration intends to expand these consultations with our friends and allies in the Far East as well, and we will play a key role in these discussions.

Turning to Iraq, let us be clear: without U.N. sanctions and inspections Saddam Husayn would have been well on his way by now toward rebuilding his programs for weapons of mass destruction. The importance of sanctions and monitoring cannot be overstated. Because of the unprecedented information the intelligence community has given to the U.N. Special Commission since 1991 to track down and eliminate Iraq's weapons of mass destruction, we have destroyed a far larger share of Iraq's capability in this area than was destroyed during the war itself.

Mr. Chairman, there are no easy or quick solutions to the threats posed by these two rogue regimes. For years to come, the intelligence community will continue to require the necessary resources to monitor their military programs, to uncover their attempts to establish clandestine procurement networks aimed at obtaining material and expertise for development of weapons of mass destruction, and to support terrorist activity. It was less than a year ago that Saddam attempted an audacious and outrageous crime—the assassination of a former American President. We cannot relax our guard against such governments.

Regional Conflicts: Somalia, Bosnia, Haiti

Let me now turn to three specific trouble spots which you requested that I address today: Somalia, Bosnia, and Haiti. Each one embodies human tragedy and symbolizes the intractability of conflict in our post-Cold War era.

Let me begin with Somalia. There may well be an upsurge in the fighting before American troops are withdrawn by March 31. We come to this conclusion because, to date, the key factions have failed to resolve their differences in the reconciliation talks, and appear to be arming themselves for an increase in the fighting. Moreover, we are concerned that a combination of renewed hostilities, coupled with the possibility of inadequate rainfall this spring could usher in another catastrophe for the Somali people. We continue to provide vital tactical support to U.S. forces in Somalia, as well as to U.N. authorities, but the problem in Somalia is not new and is not readily resolved.

The same can be said of Bosnia. Now suffering through another winter at war, Bosnia continues to be plagued by shortages. According to U.N. officials, less than fifty percent of the relief effort is getting through, and aid convoys are increasingly targeted by all sides. The plight of the Bosnians is exacerbated by sporadic cut-offs or reductions in supplies of gas and electricity. U.N. authorities estimate, even assuming the continuation of aid flows, a repeat of last winter, when 5,000–10,000 died of starvation and related health problems. Substantial interruption of relief would multiply these numbers many times.

As for Serbia itself, although there have been leakages in the international sanctions, the Serbian economy is in shambles. Hyperinflation has been so great that the Serbian government has had to add 18 zeros to the face of its currency over the last three years. Still, the economy functions, albeit at a primitive level, and some commercial activity continues. There is little sign of Milosevic losing his grip in the short term; his party gained seats in last December's election. However, Milosevic does want sanctions lifted and will try every means to convince the international community to accept the dismemberment of Bosnia as a fait accompli.

Turning to Haiti, the political stalemate continues. We estimate that the country probably will be out of fuel and power very shortly unless there is a significant political breakthrough.

The military, however, is hardening its position against compromise, in the apparent belief that the international community's determination to enforce the embargo will weaken once the humanitarian impact of sanctions becomes severe. International efforts are underway to bolster humanitarian relief programs inside Haiti, but those programs will become increasingly vulnerable to sabotage and diversion by the strong as food and fuel shortages become acute.

Our intelligence efforts are focused on detecting attempts to circumvent the embargo and monitoring its impact. We are also watching closely for any indication of an imminent exodus.

II. Transnational Issues
Proliferation

Mr. Chairman, I would like to move now to transnational issues, beginning with the problem of proliferation. The proliferation of weapons of mass destruction—and the means to deliver them—is not a new problem, but it is a growing one. Whether it be North Korea, Iran, Iraq, Libya, or other nations throughout the globe aspiring to acquire these weapons, all of them will be paying close attention to how we handle each individual crisis to see whether we are wavering in our commitment to nonproliferation.

I have addressed the problem of proliferation in many meetings and briefings with members of Congress. Let me reaffirm several sobering points: Ballistic missiles are becoming the weapon of choice for nations otherwise unable to strike their enemies at long ranges. Today there are 25 countries—many hostile to our interests, some of whom I have already mentioned—that are developing nuclear, biological, or chemical weapons. More than two dozen countries alone have research programs underway on chemical weapons.

Moreover, some of these countries may place little stock in the classic theory of deterrence which kept the cold war from becoming a hot one between the United States and the Soviet Union.

Biological weapons are a particular concern, especially given the ease of setting up a laboratory, and the difficulty in distinguishing between dual-use products. It is hard to get international consensus to condemn a supplier or user of such dual-use material or technology.

We have supported efforts by the Administration, in cooperation with other countries, to prevent the acquisition of materials and equipment by nations bent on developing weapons of mass destruction. To cite several examples of successful interdictions which occurred last year:

—Egyptian authorities impounded a shipment of anhydrous hydrofluoric acid enroute to Iraq for the processing of nuclear-related materials. The acid also is a known nerve agent precursor.

—The Italian Government prevented shipment of equipment to Iran which could be used in the production of chemical warfare materials. Italian officials also blocked the delivery of excavation equipment enroute to Libya for possible use in construction of an underground chemical warfare agent production facility.

—Polish Government authorities stopped the sale by Polish firms of nuclear power plant equipment and components to Iran.

Nevertheless, the task for the intelligence community will remain daunting. We need to decipher an intricate web of suppliers and end-users; we need to distinguish between legitimate and illicit purposes, particularly for dual-use technology or products; and we must help track the activities of others and work with them to see that the flow of material, technology, and know-how is interdicted. These tasks will continue to demand substantial allocation of resources and personnel for years to come.

Terrorism

Mr. Chairman, turning now to the issue of terrorism I noted earlier particularly Iranian support for terrorism. Unfortunately, as we know, terrorism does not come from one isolated regime. This year, for example, the State Department added Sudan to its list of countries which support terrorism. Nor is terrorism confined to the Middle East; it is still being used in Latin America and in Western Europe.

Terrorism has not abated: there were 427 terrorist incidents world-wide last year compared to 362 in 1992. Indeed, terrorist incidents could increase as a result of growing ethnic, religious, and regional conflicts throughout the globe.

The intelligence community will continue to support the FBI and the Justice Department here at home, as well as foreign intelligence organizations abroad, in combating terrorism. Our work must often be done out of the glare of publicity—and you will rarely find us speaking out about the successes we have had in disrupting or foiling terrorist plots. This is because we need to protect those who would provide us with vital information, and to protect methods critical to us if we are to continue to keep Americans out of harms way.

There are several cases, however, which I feel can be mentioned here today, beginning with the investigation on the attempted assassination of former President Bush in Kuwait.

—CIA used its substantial analytic capability and its technical analysis of the forensic evidence, in cooperation with the FBI and Department of Justice, to establish that the assassination attempt operation was ordered by Saddam Husayn's regime.

—One example of a terrorist brought to justice was the FBI's recent arrest of Umar Muhammed Ali Rizaq, responsible for hijacking and murder in November 1985. His crime includes shooting three Americans, killing one and leaving another suffering permanent brain damage.

—We are working closely with FBI and local law enforcement officials in the investigations surrounding last year's bombing of the World Trade Center.

—We are using our resources to provide whatever information we can to help locate and bring to justice Mir Aimal Kansi, accused of the brutal murders which occurred just one year ago outside CIA headquarters. On this day in particular, we want to let Mr. Kansi know that, as Muhammed Ali Rizaq discovered eight years after his crime, we do not forget, and we do not give up.

Drug Trafficking

Mr. Chairman, on the subject of drug trafficking, we play a constructive role around the world in countering the flow of illegal drugs into this country. We provided essential intelligence support to Colombia's Pablo Escobar Task Force.

We are focusing our efforts on obtaining the information necessary for disrupting and dismantling the entire chain of drug trafficking—transportation, finances and chain of command. We do this against traffickers both in Latin America and in the Far East. The challenge cannot be met by targeting one sector alone; nor can it be accomplished by one agency alone. Our intelligence work in support of law enforcement efforts by the DEA and FBI will continue, because we believe that only through coordinated efforts can we hope to defeat this cancer on our society.

But in this field we can never guarantee to you that we and the other U.S. agencies involved will never be betrayed by those who assist us in Latin America or Asia. Part of the unfortunate reality of the counternarcotics business is that local foreign officials sometimes succumb to the lure of drug money. Moreover, American officials—ours and those of other agencies—are not always correct in the difficult judgments that must be made in this complex area. One risk that U.S. Government employees run is sensationalist distortions in some media reports about this complex subject. We work too hard and consider this problem too important to ignore such distortions. So, let me say simply and categorically that the recent allegation made in a television report that CIA officers intentionally smuggled narcotics into the United States for distribution is flat wrong.

International Economics

In closing, Mr. Chairman, although the topic of international economics was not specifically mentioned in your invitation to me, I'd like to take the opportunity of this hearing to highlight this area of critical importance to the work of the intelligence community.

For nearly half a century, international economic issues took a back seat to our struggle against the Soviet Union and its allies. That has changed. As the President said last fall,

"More than ever, our security is tied to economics."

Interest rates, trade policies, and currency fluctuations all can have an immediate and significant impact on our economic well-being. Moreover, as industrialized nations pull themselves out of the longest recession since the depression of the 1930s, they are discovering that their economic recoveries are not accompanied by a growth in jobs, thus making the competition on the world market that much sharper.

The intelligence community is being asked to provide a strong supporting role in this new international economic arena. Let me briefly describe our tasks.

First, we are providing policymakers analytical support on world economic trends and on key international trade issues. This support includes evaluating the economic plans, intentions and strategies of foreign governments and their impact on U.S. interests and initiatives. It also includes analytical assistance to American negotiators involved in foreign trade discussions—such as GATT.

Second, we are providing analytical road maps on how well or poorly the nations in the former Soviet Union and in Eastern and Central Europe are faring with their economic reform efforts. How these nations perform economically can determine how well they do politically and whether regional and global stability will be enhanced or threatened.

Third, we are providing our expertise in trade, finance and energy to help the Administration thwart efforts by countries such as Iraq, Libya, and Serbia from circumventing United Nations sanctions.

Fourth, we are assessing how some governments violate the rules of the game in international trade. This does not mean that the CIA is in the business of economic espionage—for example, trying to learn the business plans of foreign companies in order to give such information to American firms. It does mean, however, that we are paying careful attention to those countries or businesses who are spying on our firms, to the disadvantage of American businesses and American workers, and to those governments and foreign companies that try to bribe their way into obtaining contracts that they cannot win on the merits. Frequently we are able to help the U.S. government obtain quick redress when such foreign bribery occurs or is about to occur, to the benefit, measured in billions of dollars, of American companies. Most such companies never realize that they have received our assistance and even state publicly that they do not need it. This is fine with us. It is the nature of the intelligence business.

Mr. Chairman, what I have outlined today for you and for your colleagues on the committee is far from being the sum total of our work. Nor should intelligence be viewed as an end in itself. When we try to penetrate a closed society like North Korea, when we verify dismantlement of nuclear weapons in Russia and Ukraine, or peace agreements in the Middle East, when we work to help defeat terrorists or the ambitions of Saddam Husayn, when we try to answer the "why" the "where" and the "when" of global ethnic and nationalist conflict, we do so as part of our contribution to the overall safety and security of the United States and the American people.

My year as Director of Central Intelligence has made it clear to me how critical intelligence will continue to be in helping our leaders to chart a course for our nation, to protect our interests and to keep our citizens safe.

This concludes my opening statement. I would be happy to go into greater detail on these topics and address other issues of concern to the members of this committee, here and in closed session.

Source: R. James Woolsey, "Threats to the U.S. and Its Interests Abroad: Intelligence and Security," *Vital Speeches* 60 (1 March 1994): 290–95.

---

157. CLINTON, SPEECH ON IRAQ AND HAITI
10 October 1994

Throughout the first Clinton administration, American policy makers demonstrated a willingness to utilize military force in support of American policy. On 10 October 1994, the president spoke to the nation on the use of military power to restore democracy in Haiti and deter Iraqi aggression in the Persian Gulf.

Tonight I want to speak with you about the actions we are taking to preserve stability in the Persian Gulf in the face of Saddam Hussein's provocative actions. But first, let me take just a minute to report to you on today's events in Haiti.

Three weeks ago our troops entered Haiti. They went there to keep America's, and the world community's, commitment to restore the democratically elected Government to power by Oct. 15. Today, Lieutenant General Cedras and Brigadier General Biamby, the two remaining coup leaders, have resigned. They have said they will leave Haiti shortly. I'm pleased to announce that President Aristide will return home to resume his rightful place this Saturday, Oct. 15.

I want to express again my pride in what our men and women in uniform have done in Haiti and how well they have measured up to their difficult mission. In just three weeks, the level of violence is down. The Parliament is back. Refugees are returning from Guantanamo and now the military leaders are leaving.

But I also want to caution, again, the job in Haiti remains difficult and dangerous. We still have a lot of work ahead of us but our troops are keeping America's commitment to restore democracy. They are performing their mission very, very well, with firmness and fairness and all Americans are proud of them.

The strength of America's foreign policy stands on the steadfastness of our commitments. The United States and the international community have given their word that Iraq must respect the borders of its neighbors. And tonight, as in Haiti, American troops, with our coalition partners, are the guarantors of that commitment, the power behind our diplomacy.

Three-and-a-half years ago, the men and women of our armed forces, under the strong leadership of President Bush, General Powell and General Schwarzkopf fought to expel Iraq from Kuwait and to protect our interests in that vital region. Today we remain committed to defending the integrity of that nation and to protecting the stability of the gulf region.

Saddam Hussein has shown the world before, with his acts of aggression and his weapons of mass destruction, that he cannot be trusted. Iraq's troop movements and threatening statements in recent days are more proof of this.

In 1990, Saddam Hussein assembled a force on the border of Kuwait and then invaded. Last week, he moved another force toward the same border.

Because of what happened in 1990, this provocation requires a strong response from the United States and the international community. Over the weekend, I ordered the George Washington carrier battle group, cruise missile ships, a Marine expeditionary brigade and an Army mechanized task force to the gulf.

And today I have ordered the additional deployment of more than 350 Air Force aircraft to the region. We will not allow Saddam Hussein to defy the will of the United States and the international community. Iraq announced today that it will pull back its troops from the Kuwait border. But we're interested in facts, not promises—in deeds, not words. And we have not yet seen evidence that Iraq's troops are in fact pulling back. We'll be watching very closely to see that they do so.

Our policy is clear. We will not allow Iraq to threaten its neighbors or to intimidate the United Nations as it insures that Iraq never again possesses weapons of mass destruction. Moreover, the sanctions will be maintained until Iraq complies with all relevant U.N. resolutions.

That is the answer to Iraq's sanctions problem—full compliance not reckless provocation.

I'm very proud of our troops who tonight are the backbone of our commitment to Kuwait's freedom and the security of the gulf. I'm also proud of the planners and the commanders who were getting them there so very quickly, and in such force.

They all are proof that we are maintaining and must continue to maintain the readiness and strength of the finest military in the world. That is what we owe to the men and Women of America who are putting their lives on the line today to make the world a safer place. And it is what we owe to the proud families who stand with them. They are protecting our security as we work for a post-cold war world of democracy and prosperity.

Within the last two weeks, America hosted two champions of post-cold war democracy. South African President Nelson Mandela came to thank the United States for our support of South Africa's remarkable democratic revolution and to seek a partnership for the future.

And Russian President Boris Yeltsin came to further the partnership between our two nations so well expressed by the fact that now Russian and U.S. missiles are no longer pointed at each other's people. And we are working to reduce the nuclear threat even more.

In short, we are making progress in building a world of greater security, peace and democracy.

But our work is not done. There are difficulties and dangers ahead as we see in Iraq and in Haiti. But we can meet these challenges and keep our commitments.

Our objectives are clear. Our forces are strong and our cause is right.

Thank you, and God bless America.

Source: William J. Clinton, "Iraq; Haiti," *Vital Speeches* 61 (1 November 1994): 34–35.

---

158. PERRY, "BOSNIA: WE MUST STAY THE COURSE"
9 March 1995

The collapse of Communist Yugoslavia in 1991 plunged much of the Balkans into civil war. Attempts by the United Nations, NATO, and the European Union to resolve the resulting bloodshed dragged on for years. Although initially reluctant to directly intervene, the Clinton administration eventually committed American power to an international peacekeeping effort in Bosnia. Defense Secretary William Perry explained.

Life is about choices. The playwright Arthur Miller once wrote, "Where choice begins, Paradise ends, innocence ends, for what is Paradise, but the absence of the need to choose."

You as individuals make choices every day, and you will live with the consequences of these choices—good or bad. Nations also make choices. Those choices are not as easily altered as those made by individuals. The consequences are far greater, the prices far higher.

Today, America faces distinct and very difficult choices regarding its policy in Bosnia—a place where paradise and innocence ended long ago. These choices are being actively debated in Washington. However, much of the debate on policy alternatives is taking place without an informed consideration of the consequences of these alternatives. The choice of a particular policy alternative leads us inexorably down a path, driven by an iron logic from consequence to consequence. A major part of my job is to consider and to prepare for the defense consequences of the choices we make among the alternative security policies. Today I would like to discuss these with you.

Bosnia may very well be the toughest security policy issue we face today. Under Tito, it was said that Yugoslavia consisted of seven neighbors, six republics, five nations, four languages, three religions, two alphabets, and one country. Even if Yugoslavia ever was one country, today it certainly is not. Over the past four years, Yugoslavia has completely disintegrated. The collapse of Yugoslavia left Bosnia as an independent state for the first time in its history. But Bosnia was not only a new state, it was a very unstable state. It included Muslims, Croats, Serbs, three rival ethnic groups. Bosnia's tradition of pluralism was shattered when the Serbs, who were the dominant ethnic group in the former Yugoslavia, now found themselves as the minority ethnic group in the newly independent Bosnia.

The Serbs were a minority, but they were a heavily armed minority. So in 1992 the Serbs in Bosnia decided to take advantage of their military superiority and began making war on the Bosnian government and the Bosnian Muslims who controlled the government. This has been called a civil war, but it is also a war of aggression, since the Bosnian Serbs have been supported by their ethnic cousins in Serbia.

I am not agnostic about who the victims are in this war. The Bosnian government and its supporters are the victims. The atrocities that are perpetrated by the Serbs, in particular the "ethnic cleansing," are abhorrent.

Our government and the international community support the Bosnian government. We have formally recognized the government of Bosnia-Herzegovina as a sovereign nation.

Serbia, on the other hand, is the subject of an international economic embargo and political censure for Serb actions in Bosnia. Currently, the Bosnian Serbs control about 60 percent of the territory in Bosnia. The United States, Great Britain, France, Germany, and Russia have put a proposal on the table that preserves a unified state and gives the Serbs 49 percent of the land of Bosnia, and leaves the Bosnian Muslims and Croats in control of the other 51 percent. That proposal was rejected by the Serbs.

As a consequence, I do not see the prospect of a near-term political solution.

Many people, while sympathizing with the Bosnian Muslims, find the situation too confusing, too complicated and too frustrating. Some are even tempted to throw up their hands. They say that Bosnia is a tragedy, but not our tragedy. They say that we should wash our hands of the whole situation and walk away.

This view is not only questionable from a moral standpoint, it is also flat-out wrong from a national security standpoint. It is true that we do not have what I call "vital" national security interests in Bosnia. That is to say, the survival of the United States is not threatened by actions in Bosnia. But we do have a security interest in preventing the violence from spreading and from stimulating a broader European war. We do have a security interest in limiting the violence. And we certainly have a humanitarian interest in mitigating the violence. In my view, walking away is not an option.

What are the options? Stripped to their essence, we have essentially two choices. Choice A is to stick with our current policy of limiting the threat of the war and its impact on people while we are working for peace. Choice B is to begin actively helping the Bosnian government achieve its political and its military goals.

Under Choice A, we are working to limit the spread of the conflict beyond Bosnia's borders. To that end, we have U.S. troops participating in the United Nations force in Macedonia. We are limiting the violence and the casualties by enforcing a no-fly zone over Bosnia, and by enforcing zones around urban centers where heavy weapons are excluded. We are mitigating the effects of the violence by airlifting food and medical supplies to civilian populations. Finally, we are participating in diplomatic efforts to achieve a negotiated settlement based on the plan that the multinational group has put forward.

We have had significant success with the first three of these actions. Before NATO began enforcing a no-fly zone, Bosnian cities were being bombed, with many, many casualties. Before we established a heavy weapons exclusion zone around Sarajevo, there were bombardments going on in that city, including artillery bombardments, sometimes of a thousand shells a day. In Sarajevo alone, there were 10,000 civilian casualties that resulted from this bombardment. So our efforts have saved thousands of lives; and thousands more have been saved by the delivery of food and medicine.

Fourteen nations are contributing over 12,000 United Nation troops to protect enclaves, deliver supplies, and to serve as buffers between the factions. Six nations, including the United States, are participating in a NATO air operation which enforces the no-fly zone and the weapons exclusion zone, and which delivers humanitarian supplies.

These efforts have been very well executed and have done real good, but we have not succeeded in the fourth goal—achieving a peace settlement. People find this frustrating. I find it frustrating. Many are further frustrated that our policies have not assisted the Bosnian people in their struggle to reverse Serb gains and to punish those who participate in "ethnic cleansing." These people support what I call Choice B, taking active measures to help the Bosnian government achieve its political and military goal.

My thesis today is that the active measures which have been proposed for that purpose send the United States headlong down a slippery slope. At the bottom of that slope will be American troops in ground combat; will be a humanitarian catastrophe; will be a wider war; or perhaps all three together.

Nearly everyone accepts that sending American troops for ground combat in Bosnia is a non-starter. There is no support for this idea among the public or in Congress. American casualties undoubtedly would be high—far higher than anyone could justify based on our interests. Consequently, even critics of our present policy do not propose sending American ground troops to help the Bosnian government win the war. Ironically, many of those same people have other ideas on how to help Bosnia which could very well lead to the same result.

One suggestion is that America conduct air strikes to help Bosnian military forces. But no responsible military commander believes we can change the outcome of the war with an air campaign alone. Bosnia is not Iraq. Bosnia is wooded, mountainous, and often blanketed by clouds. The Serbs spread out their weapons over a wide area and often place them in the middle of population centers. These factors combine to make it unlikely that air power by itself can be effective in stopping the Serbs. In order for an air campaign to be even partially effective, our pilots would need the assistance of trained, ground-based, forward observers to help coordinate their strikes. So we would have the prospect of captured pilots, of casualties on the ground among the observers, and of very heavy civilian casualties—including casualties among the population we are trying to help.

Another suggested way to help the Bosnian government cause, and a course which has been popular with many members of Congress, is for the United States to unilaterally lift the arms embargo which is now on the Bosnian government. The arms embargo went into effect in 1991 and it applies to all of the states of the former Yugoslavia. Its purpose, of course, is to limit the destructive power of all combatants in the region. However, because the Serbs inherited most of the weapons of Tito's Yugoslav armed forces, the embargo froze in place a military imbalance. The Bosnian government has no such inheritance and has been up against a much stronger Serb force with a significant advantage in tanks and other heavy weapons. Proponents of unilaterally lifting the embargo as it applies to the Bosnian government say they want at least to make it a fair fight. That's a strong moral argument.

This course has been called lift and leave. Its proponents like it because they believe this course is virtually risk-free for the United States—that it does not put American soldiers, sailors, and airmen in harm's way. Thus, this course appears to satisfy our urge to "do something about Bosnia" at no cost to America. These proponents also make the point that by leveling the battlefield, pressure will be brought on the Serbs to agree to a just peace.

These results are clearly desirable, but what is the likelihood that a unilateral lift without more U.S. involvement would achieve those results? More critical observers of this course call it "lift and pray" because it is a dangerously flawed proposition. If one follows this course step by step to its logical conclusion, it also leads to U.S. ground troops fighting in Bosnia—the very situation the proponents say they are trying to avoid.

Simply authorizing U.S. manufacturers to sell arms to Bosnia will not, in and of itself, level the battlefield. To truly level the battlefield, to equalize the two warring forces, will take a major commitment to ensure that the arms reach Bosnia. Since the Bosnians do not have the financial resources, either the U.S. or a third party would have to supply the funds.

Should the U.S. assume this responsibility, the financial costs are substantial, but would be the least of our problems.

We would also need to get the arms into the hands of the Bosnians. The Bosnians do not have a navy or an air force capable of coming and getting the weapons. So proponents of lifting the embargo must also assume that the United States would be responsible for delivering the weapons. Sea and land delivery would require cooperation from a third party—Croatia—which has its own interests at stake and may not cooperate. All airfields in Bosnia are within range of Bosnian-Serb artillery, so all arriving aircraft would be subject to ground fire. Realistically, then, we could expect American casualties even in the delivery of these supplies.

As we delivered these supplies, we would be in the extremely awkward position of defying the other NATO nations with forces operating in the same area who are enforcing the arms embargo against all of the states of the former Yugoslavia. Are American ships and planes supposed to evade and elude the ships and planes of our NATO allies with whom we worked these past four years trying to enforce the embargo?

Let me assume that we could find a relatively safe way to deliver arms to the Bosnian government. We'd then have to deal with the question of training the Bosnian soldiers to use these weapons. The Bosnians don't just need rifles or grenades, they need sophisticated arms to counter the Serbian advantage in heavy weapons. Using such arms takes training. We know from our own experience that it is not just arms, but training in their use that makes a force effective. So we will also have to consider using American soldiers to train the Bosnian forces.

Assuming that we can solve the arms financing, delivery, and training questions, we face a different set of issues that evolve around this question: How would the Serbs react to the prospect of arms on their way to Bosnia? What if they launched preemptive strikes to gain a military victory on the ground before the arms shipment arrived? In particular, what if the Serbs attacked the isolated U.N.-protected enclaves in Bosnia? This would result in tens of thousands of civilian casualties and hundreds of thousands of refugees.

If our decision to lift the embargo results in Serbs overrunning the enclaves and massive civilian casualties, what do we do? What is our responsibility at that point? We would face a difficult moral and political dilemma, and an even more difficult military problem. From a moral and political standpoint, there would be an enormous pressure on us to retaliate in some way to stop this carnage, but militarily, that would not be easy. Air strikes could punish the Serbs, but they could not change the outcome or stop the killing. Indeed, it would only expand the violence.

That brings us to yet another set of problems. Even if we resisted the pressure to do something and instead simply watched the enclaves being overrun, we would still have to deal with the inevitable evacuation of the U.N. peacekeeping forces. Key countries contributing peacekeepers have already firmly stated that they will not keep them in Bosnia if the United States lifts the embargo. That means humanitarian relief will stop flowing, and we would have to decide whether to take over the protection of relief operations now being done by the U.N. or simply stand by and watch people starve.

In addition, if it's decided that U.N. forces have to evacuate Bosnia, we are committed, in principle, to participating in a NATO operation to help get them out, subject to consultation with the Congress. To do this operation properly, NATO and the U.S. will have to send in substantial numbers of ground combat forces, the very situation we are trying to avoid. While it's possible that an evacuation of U.N. forces from Bosnia may become necessary down the road no matter what we do, unilaterally lifting the embargo will make that evacuation a certainty—not just a possibility.

Unilateral lift would also undermine our most important security objective in the region, which is to prevent the conflict from spreading to other parts of the former Yugoslavia, possibly leading to a much wider war in the Balkans.

In sum, unilateral lift could lead to a humanitarian disaster, it could lead to American ground troops in Bosnia, and it could lead to a wider war, or it could lead to all three of those. If the arms embargo is to be lifted, it must be done in a multilateral way because only by involving the international community generally on the side of the Bosnians can we avoid many, but not all, of the problems of unilateral lift.

In short, unilateral lift is not an alternative to intervention with ground troops, it is merely another means of reaching that same result. It is an attempt to influence the war on the cheap. It is a policy that does not help the people of Bosnia and does not advance America's interests in the Balkans.

In addition, unilateral lift is detrimental to America's interest in a wider sphere. Without question, it would drive a wedge between the United States and the rest of the NATO alliance—a wedge deeper than any in NATO's history.

Taken as a whole, these are disastrous and unacceptable consequences which bring me back to Choice A—continuing with our present policy: trying to contain the conflict, limiting the violence and its effects, and supporting negotiations to a peaceful settlement.

While we can reasonably expect this policy to continue to be successful in preventing the spread of the war, and to continue to be successful in limiting both the fighting and its effects, I confess that this policy gives me no great moral satisfaction because it does not give America much leverage on influencing a peace settlement. Our approach has been to facilitate the parties in reaching that settlement, recognizing that we do not have enough leverage to force a settlement. To force a peace on the combatants, we would have to be willing to fight a war, and that is an unacceptable level of commitment.

Bosnia is a tragedy which will end only when the parties themselves conclude that their interests are served better by a negotiated settlement than by continuing the war. We understand that this may take some time. That is why we are committed to those actions which lower the level of violence and mitigate the suffering while these peace talks continue.

I am fully aware of the short-comings of our present approach, but there are no good options. We must be very wary of the siren call coming from those who say that there are easy and painless ways for America to do something— none of them turn out to be easy. None of them turn out to be painless.

I began by talking about choices and consequences. Let me end by returning to this theme. Political life offers many opportunities for posturing, for pretending there are simple solutions to complex problems. Bosnia as a policy issue is not difficult. It is painful, but it's not difficult. When you look carefully at the consequences, it is easy to make a choice between our two options.

John Kenneth Galbraith once said,

"Politics is not the art of the possible. Rather it consists of choosing between the disastrous and the unpalatable."

Our present course in Bosnia has been called unpalatable, but the alternative—unilaterally lifting the embargo—would prove to be disastrous. It's a course of action which might make us feel good today, but result in the pointless spilling of American blood tomorrow.

I have shared with you today the consequences of alternative policy options in Bosnia. The truth, as I said, is unpalatable. It is, nonetheless, important to understand the truth. During the Second World War Winston Churchill once said,

"Men occasionally stumble over the truth, but most pick themselves up and hurry away without being affected by it."

I have tried today to make you stumble over the truth about Bosnia, and I hope that you will be affected by it.

Thank you.

Source: William Perry, "Bosnia: We Must Stay the Course," *Vital Speeches* 61 (15 April 1995): 386–89.

159. LAKE, "THE PRICE OF LEADERSHIP"
27 April 1995

*During the Clinton presidency, the White House engaged in a hotly con-
tested debate with Republican leaders who criticized the administration
for overcommitting America to the problems that populated the world.
National Security Advisor Anthony Lake offered a response to this school
of thought in April 1995.*

Let me begin with a simple but alarming fact: The United States could be on
the brink of unilateral disarmament.

Did that get your attention? I hope so, because it is true.

No, we are not about to junk our jets or scuttle our ships. Our military is
strong and ready—and there is a strong bipartisan consensus to keep it so. But
we are on the verge of throwing away—or at least damaging—many of the
other tools America has used for 50 years to maintain our leadership in the
world: aid to emerging markets, economic support for peace, international peacekeeping, programs to fight terrorism and drug trafficking, and foreign
assistance. Together with a strong military, these have been key instruments of
our foreign policy.

Presidents since Harry Truman have used these tools to promote American
interests—to preserve our security, to expand our prosperity, and to advance
democracy. Their efforts were supported by Democrats and Republicans—and
the broad majority of the American people. Congress consistently provided the
needed resources for these tasks. Because of this resolve, coupled with our
military might, we prevailed over the long haul in the Cold War, strengthened
our security, and won unparalleled prosperity for our people.

Now, I deeply believe our success is in danger. It is under attack by new
isolationists from both left and right who would deny our nation those resources.
Our policy of engagement in world affairs is under siege and American leadership is in peril.

A few of the new isolationists act out of conviction. They argue that the end
of the Soviet menace means that the serious threats are gone and that we should
withdraw behind our borders and stick to concerns at home. "Fortress America,"
they say, can shut out new dangers even though some of the new threats facing
us—such as nuclear proliferation, terrorism, rapid population growth, and environmental degradation—know no boundaries.

But most of the new isolationists do not argue such a position or even answer
to the name isolationist. They say they are part of the post-Cold War bipartisan

consensus, that their goals are its goals—democracy, security, peace, and prosperity. But they won't back up their words with deeds.

These self-proclaimed devotees of democracy would deny aid to struggling democracies. They laud American leadership, but oppose American leadership of coalitions, advocating only unilateral action instead.

Yes, they praise peace—but then they cut our help to those who take risks for peace. They demand greater prosperity—but they shy away from the hard work of opening markets for American workers and businesses. Under the cover of budget-cutting, they threaten to cut the legs out from under America's leadership.

These are the back-door isolationists—and they are much more numerous and influential than those who argue openly for American retreat: They can read the polls, and they know that the American people want the U.S. to be engaged in the world. Support for American leadership in the world is about as strong as ever—a Chicago Council on Foreign Relations survey shows two-thirds or more want us to remain deeply engaged. So these back-door isolationists and unilateralists cast themselves as the true guardians of American power, but through their actions, they could become the agents of America's retreat. They champion American leadership, but they want it the one way you can't have it—and that is, on the cheap.

They want America to turn its back on 50 years of success. They are working—whether they know it or not—to destroy part of the foundation for our peace and prosperity, the great legacy of our postwar leaders: Vandenberg, Truman, Marshall, Acheson. These men faced their own challenge from isolationists. But they saw the cost of our earlier withdrawal after Versailles was terribly, terribly damaging—saw it in the wreckage of Europe and Asia after World War II and the casualties America suffered liberating those continents. And they understood that investing in a vigorous foreign policy was the only way to prevent another catastrophe.

They knew the price of leadership. They spent what was necessary to maintain America's security. And they went further, creating the United Nations and the Bretton Woods institutions and covering those bills, pouring Marshall Plan aid into Western Europe to save it from despair and communism, and they and their successors in later administrations developed the new tool of technical assistance so that democracy and prosperity got a better chance around the world.

Look at the results: The map is almost covered with democracies, many of them strong allies. Markets that fulfill needs and dreams are expanding. A global economy supports American jobs and prosperity. These are the returns on 50 years of American political and economic investment abroad—the benefits of 50 years of bipartisan engagement. But these achievements are not cut in stone. We will not go on reaping these benefits automatically. Back-door isolationism threatens to propel us in the wrong direction at a real moment of hope—when our engagement can still make a dramatic difference by securing rather than frittering away our victory in the Cold War.

We could forfeit that victory because in many places democracy still needs nurturing. Some market economies have not sunk deep roots, and the post-Cold War era has brought into new focus real and powerful dangers that threaten what we have worked for. Aggression by rogue states, international terrorism, economic dislocation: These are new forms of an old conflict—the conflict between freedom and oppression, the conflict between the defenders of the open society and its enemies.

There is no expiration date on these lessons from five decades. Defeating these threats requires persistent engagement and hands-on policies. Defeating them demands resources. Throwing money at problems won't make them go away, but we also cannot solve problems without money. The measure of American leadership is not only the strength and attraction of our values but what we bring to the table to solve the hard issues before us. That is why President Clinton has said that he will not let the new isolationism prevail.

Make no mistake: The American people want their nation to lead. Americans know the world is growing closer, they know our security and prosperity depend on our involvement abroad. And they agree with the President, who has said before and since he took office: "For America to be strong at home, it must be strong abroad."

Plenty of Americans also say they want us to spend less abroad until they know the real numbers. Most think that we spend 15% or more of the Federal budget on foreign aid. They think 5% would be about right. They would be shocked to know that little more than 1%—$21 billion out of a $1.6-trillion budget—goes to foreign policy spending, and less than $16 billion goes to foreign assistance. That's a lot of money, but not the budget-buster that neo-isolationists pretend. It is 21% less in real terms than that spent in FY 1986. They would also be surprised to learn that others recognize the reality of necessary resources far better than we. The richest, most powerful nation on earth—the United States—ranks dead last among 25 industrialized nations in the percentage of GNP devoted to aid.

These are facts that should be better known. More of our citizens should know that our foreign policy resources are devoted to goals that the American people support.

- $6.6 billion a year promotes peace, including our efforts in the Middle East, the help we give U.S. allies to defend themselves, and our contribution to UN peacekeeping missions around the world, such as those on the Golan Heights, the Iraq-Kuwait border, and in Cambodia.

- $2.4 billion builds democracy and promotes prosperity, helping South Africa, for example, hold free elections and transform itself peacefully.

- $5 billion promotes development—that includes job programs in Haiti to increase employment, improve infrastructure, and help that nation get back on its feet.

- $1.7 billion provides humanitarian assistance, such as caring for refugee children in the former Yugoslavia—because Americans have always wanted their country to alleviate suffering in areas with the most compelling need.

- The remainder funds the State Department and other agencies that work every day to advance America's interests abroad.

This is the price of American leadership—and the backdoor isolationists don't want us to pay it. But imagine how the world would look if we did not. Take what I call the George Bailey Test. You remember George—he is the character played by Jimmy Stewart in the Christmas classic "It's a Wonderful Life." In that film, the angel Clarence shows George how Bedford Falls would have fallen apart without him.

Allow me to play Clarence briefly and take you through a world without American leadership. Imagine if:

- Ukraine, Belarus, and Kazakhstan joined the club of declared nuclear weapons states because we couldn't do the deals to denuclearize them.
- Russian missiles were still pointed at our cities because we couldn't push to detarget them.
- Thousands of migrants were still trying to sail to our shores because we had not helped restore democracy in Haiti.
- Nearly 1 million American jobs had not been created over the last three years alone because we had not promoted U.S. exports.
- We had to fight a war on the Korean Peninsula—the implied result of what some critics were urging—because we did not confront the threat of a North Korea with nuclear weapons.
- Another quarter of a million people had died in Rwanda because we had not deployed our military and they had not been able to do such a fine job in the refugee camps.
- We had paid tens of billions of dollars more and suffered more casualties because we insisted on fighting Operation Desert Storm against Iraq by ourselves.

Imagine that. Each of these efforts cost money and the hard work of building international coalitions. But you and I are safer, better off, and enjoy more freedom because America made these investments. If the backdoor isolationists have their way, much of what we have worked for for over two generations could be undone.

Speaker Gingrich recently described what the world might look like if America retreats. He described "a dark and bloody planet . . . in our absence you end in Bosnia and Rwanda and Chechnya." He added, "They are the harbingers of a much worse 21st century than anything we've seen in the half-century of American leadership."

It does not have to be that way. If we continue to invest in democracy, in arms control, in stability in the developing world, and in the new markets that bring prosperity, we can assure another half-century of American leadership.

But already, because of decisions in the last few years, we sometimes cannot make even modest contributions to efforts that deserve our support. America is a great nation, but we cannot now find the small sum needed to help support peacekeepers in Liberia, where a million people are at risk from renewed civil war, or the money to adequately fund UN human rights monitors in Rwanda. We can barely meet our obligations in maintaining sanctions on Serbia. This is no way to follow the heroic achievements of the Cold War. And I can't imagine that this fits any American's vision of world leadership. It doesn't fit mine.

Nickel-and-dime policies cost more in the end. Prevention is cheap and doesn't attract cameras. When the all-seeing eye of television finds real suffering abroad, Americans will want their government to act—and rightly so. Funding a large humanitarian effort after a tragedy or sending in our forces abroad to assist will cost many times the investment in prevention.

Some costs of short-sighted policies must be paid in our neighborhoods: In 1993, Congress cut by almost one-third our very lean request for funding to combat the flow of narcotics into our country—and that funding has been declining in real terms ever since. As a result, we are scaling back programs to wipe out production of drugs and block their importation, as well as training programs for police, Prosecutors, and judges in foreign countries. America pays a far higher cost in crime and ruined lives.

These are some of the constraints we have lived with in the past few years. Now, however, American leadership faces a still more clear and present danger. Budget legislation being prepared in Congress could reduce foreign affairs spending by nearly one-quarter, or $4.6 billion. That would mean drastic cuts in or elimination of aid to some states of the former Soviet Union and cuts in the security assistance programs that help U.S. allies and friends provide for their own defense. It would sharply reduce or eliminate our contributions to international peace operations. It would lame the agencies—such as OPIC [Overseas Private Investment Corporation] and the Eximbank—that have played a key role in expanding U.S. exports. It would threaten our non-proliferation efforts and the Arms Control and Disarmament Agency. It could eliminate assistance for some programs that save children's lives.

These cuts would cripple our legacy of leadership. The strength to lead does not fall from heaven. It demands effort; it demands resources.

A neo-isolationist budget could undercut our strategic interest in democracy in Russia and the former Warsaw Pact countries and it would directly affect America's security. We must continue to fund the farsighted programs begun by Senators Nunn and Lugar to reduce nuclear arsenals in the former Soviet Union. The $350 million in Nunn-Lugar funds made it possible for Ukraine to dismantle its arsenal and accede to the Non-Proliferation Treaty. That made it easier for us to pull back from the Cold War nuclear precipice and save some $20 billion a year on strategic nuclear forces. That is just one of the more dramatic examples of how our foreign spending literally pays off.

A neo-isolationist budget could harm our efforts to prevent rogue states and terrorists from building nuclear weapons. We are spending $35 million over three years to employ thousands of weapons scientists in the former Soviet Union on civilian research projects. That helps keep them off the nuclear labor market and from selling their skills to an Iraq or Iran.

A neo-isolationist budget could nearly end our involvement in UN peace operations around the world—operations that serve our interests. Presidents since Harry Truman supported them as a matter of common sense. President Bush, in particular, saw their value: Last year nearly 60% of our UN peace-keeping bill went to operations begun with his Administration's support. His Secretary of State, James Baker, made a strong defense for these operations when he remarked that "We spent trillions to win the Cold War and we should be willing to spend millions of dollars to secure the peace."

This is burdensharing at its best. UN peace operations:

- Save us from deploying U.S. troops in areas of great importance, for example, Cyprus or the Indian subcontinent.

- They help pick up where our troops left off, for example, along the border of Iraq and Kuwait. In Haiti, UN troops are saving us resources by replacing most of our own withdrawing troops.

- They are building democracy in Namibia, Mozambique, and Cambodia—all missions we helped design. In Cambodia, the UN negotiated the withdrawal of Vietnamese forces and then held the country's first democratic election. After the years of the Killing Fields, 90% of the electorate turned out to vote—while UN peacekeepers protected them from the Khmer Rouge.

We would pay much more if we performed even a small number of these missions unilaterally. Instead, the price we pay now in manpower and money is reasonable: Of the 61,000 UN peacekeepers deployed around the world, only some 3,300 are American. We pay the equivalent of one-half of 1% of our total defense spending for UN peace operations—less than a third of the total UN cost and less than the Europeans pay in proportion to their defense spending. We participate in these operations only after careful consideration of the command arrangements and costs—but we gain immense influence through our ability to lead multinational efforts.

A neo-isolationist budget could severely undercut our work for peace. The President has said that "America stands by those who take risks for peace." This is true in Northern Ireland, South Africa, the Middle East, and around the world.

For the Middle East peace process to continue—and for negotiations in other regions to succeed—we must have the resources to support the risk-takers. We cannot convince the holdouts from the peace process that we will stand behind a just and lasting settlement if we back away from our current commitments. That means maintaining aid to Israel, Egypt, and the Palestinians and fulfilling our pledge of debt relief to Jordan. In the Middle East, our vital security and economic interests are on the line. We must not fold our hands and leave the game to the opponents of peace just when we are on the verge of winning.

A neo-isolationist budget could throw away decades of investment in democracy. In the last 16 years, the number of democracies in the world has almost doubled and USAID provided assistance to most of the newcomers. For example, in Mozambique—a nation emerging from years of strife—USAID assistance helped register 6 million out of a possible 8 million voters and turn the polling there into a success. Now—when these societies are most fragile—is not the time to cut this lifeline for democracy.

A neo-isolationist budget would directly damage our own livelihoods. Our economy depends on new markets for U.S. goods and high-paying jobs for American workers. That is why President Clinton led efforts to expand free trade with the landmark GATT agreement, NAFTA, and the free-trade agreements in the Asia-Pacific region and in the Americas. And this Administration has worked harder, I believe, than any other to promote American exports. Imagine, for example, where we would be without the Commerce Department's efforts on this score. Secretary Brown's staff worked with other agencies last year on export deals worth $46 billion for American business—deals that support 300,000 U.S. jobs.

In many cases, we were in a position to close deals because America had been engaged in those countries for years. Consider two statistics: USAID programs in some countries have helped increase life expectancy by a decade. Every year, USAID's immunization program saves 3 million lives. These are statistics not only of humanitarian hope; they are part of efforts to help create stable societies of consumers who want to buy our goods—not masses of victims in need of relief.

In addition, our support of the multilateral development banks also helps nations grow and their economies prosper. We contribute $1.8 billion while other nations contribute $7 billion—and that capital leverages more than $40 billion in lending. If we stopped our contributions, we would lose our influence. And others might follow our lead, and that would cripple these important institutions.

The backdoor isolationists who claim they are saving America's money cannot see beyond the green of their own eyeshades: Our assistance has repaid itself hundreds and hundreds of times over. That was true when Marshall Plan aid resuscitated European markets after the war. And South Korea now imports annually U.S. goods worth three times as much as the assistance we provided over almost 30 years.

While we preserve our tradition of assistance, we are reforming its practice. USAID has become a laboratory for Vice President Gore's efforts to reinvent government—it is eliminating 27 overseas missions and cutting its workforce by 1,200.

Now, with the "New Partnership Initiative," we will improve our assistance programs even more, by focusing on the local level. This will enhance the efforts of non-governmental organizations and raise the percentage of our aid that is channeled to them to 40%. These organizations are on the ground and more responsive than distant national governments. This local focus, therefore, puts our resources to better use in helping nations so they can become self-sufficient.

Every one of us in this room knows that winning support for an activist foreign policy has never been easy in America.

Throughout the history of our Republic, Americans have never lived in literal isolation. In a world of instant communication and capital flows, we cannot do so now. That is not the issue, because literal isolationism is not an option.

What is at issue is whether we will have the policies and resources that can shape and support our involvement in ways that benefit our people in their daily lives—whether by opening markets or by preventing conflicts that could embroil us. It is at those times when our government failed to engage in such efforts that our people paid the greatest price—as in World War II, which followed a period of irresponsible American retreat.

The genius of our postwar leaders was to see that technology and American power had changed the world and that we must never again remain aloof. But they had a hard time winning support even with the memories of war still fresh.

As he put his case forward, President Truman had an uphill struggle. But a foreigner saw that it was America's moment to lead—and told us so. Winston Churchill stirred the nation with his appeal for an engaged foreign policy. Today, we remember his address as the Iron Curtain speech, but Churchill called it "The Sinews of Peace." The phrase plays on a saying of the Romans: "Money is the sinews of war." Churchill's message was that preserving peace—like waging war—demands resources.

Today, that message rings as true as ever. This is a moment of extraordinary hope for democracy and free markets. But nothing is inevitable. We must remain engaged. We must reach out, not retreat. American leadership in the world is not a luxury; it is a necessity. The price is worth paying. It is the price of keeping the tide of history running our way.

Source: Anthony Lake, "The Price of Leadership," *U.S. Department of State Dispatch*, vol. 6 (8 May 1995): 388–91.

---

160. CLINTON, "REMARKS AT THE SIGNING CEREMONY FOR THE BALKANS PEACE AGREEMENT IN PARIS"
14 December 1995

After debating the issue for months, the Clinton administration decided to commit American ground forces to Bosnia. Their mission was to enforce the conditions of a treaty that would create a federal republic comprised of Muslims, Orthodox Serbs, and Catholic Croats. Although the administration promised a U.S. troop withdrawal within a year, American combat forces remained for more than five years to ensure stability in the Balkans.

President Chirac, President Izetbegovic, President Tudjman, President Milosevic, Secretary-General Boutros-Ghali, Secretary General Solana, High Representative Bildt, Prime Minister Filali, Prime Minister Chernomyrdin, Prime
Minister Major, Prime Minister Gonzalez, Chancellor Kohl: Let me begin, on
behalf of the people of the United States, by thanking all of those whose labor
and wisdom helped to keep hope alive during the long, dark years of war, the
humanitarian relief workers, the United Nations forces from Europe and beyond.
Had it not been for their dedication and their sacrifice, the toll of the war in
Bosnia would have been even greater.

And I thank those whose work helped make this moment of peace possible,
beginning with our host, Prime Minister Chirac, for his vigor and determination;
Prime Minister Major, who was a full partner in the development of the rapid
reaction force and our NATO cooperation; and our friend Chancellor Kohl, who
has taken so many of the refugees and who now is sending German troops
beyond his border in this historic common endeavor. I thank the leaders of the
strong NATO and the determined negotiating team of Russians, Europeans, and
Americans.

All of you have brought us to this bright new day, when Bosnia turns from
the horror of war to the promise of peace. President Izetbegovic, President Tudjman, President Milosevic, by making peace you have answered the call of your
people. You have heard them say, "Stop the war. End the suffering. Give our
children the blessings of a normal life."

In this chorus for peace today we also hear the hallowed voices of the victims,
the children whose playgrounds were shelled into killing fields, the young girls
brutalized by rape, the men shot down in mass graves, those who starved in the
camps, those who died in battle, the millions taken from their homes and torn
from their families. Even from beyond the grave there are victims singing the
song of peace today. May their voices be in our minds and our hearts forever.

In Dayton, these three Balkan leaders made the fateful choice for peace. Today, Mr. Presidents, you have bound yourselves to peace. But tomorrow you
must turn the pages of this agreement into a real-life future of hope for those
who have survived this horrible war. At your request, the United States and
more than 25 other nations will send you our most precious resource, the men
and women of our Armed Forces. Their mission, to allow the Bosnian people
to emerge from a nightmare of fear into a new day of security, according to
terms you have approved, in a manner that is evenhanded and fair to all.

The international community will work with you to change the face of Bosnia:
to meet human needs; to repair and to rebuild; to reunite children with their
families and refugees with their homes; to oversee democratic elections, advance
human rights, and call to account those accused of war crimes.

We can do all these things, but we cannot guarantee the future of Bosnia. No
one outside can guarantee that Muslims, Croats, and Serbs in Bosnia will come
together and stay together as free citizens in a united country sharing a common
destiny. Only the Bosnian people can do that.

I know the losses have been staggering, the scars are deep. We feel even today that the wounds have not healed. But Bosnia must find a way, with God's grace, to lay down the hatreds, to give up the revenge, to go forward together. That is the road—indeed, that is the only road—to the future.

We see from Northern Ireland to the Middle East, from South Africa to Haiti, people turning from hatred to hope. Here in Europe, countries that for centuries fought now work together for peace. Soon the Bosnian people will see for themselves the awesome potential of people to turn from conflict to cooperation. In just a few days troops from all over Europe and North America and else-where—troops from Great Britain, France, and Germany, troops from Greece and Turkey, troops from Poland and Lithuania, and troops from the United States and Russia, former enemies, now friends—will answer the same call and share the same responsibilities to achieve the same goal, a lasting peace in Bosnia where enemies can become friends.

Why would they do this? Because their hearts are broken by the suffering and the slaughter; because their minds recoil at the prospect of needless spreading war in the heart of Europe. But they—we—do so in the face of skeptics who say the people of the Balkans cannot escape their bloody past, that Balkan hearts are too hard for peace.

But let us remember this war did violence not only to Bosnia's people but also to Bosnia's history. For Bosnia once found unity in its diversity. Generations of Muslims, Orthodox, Catholics, and Jews lived side by side and enriched the world by their example. They built schools and libraries and wondrous places of worship. Part of the population laid down their tools on Friday, part on Saturday, and part on Sunday. But their lives were woven together by marriage and culture, work, a common language, and a shared pride in a place that then they all called home. Now, if that past is any guide, this peace can take hold. And if the people of Bosnia want a decent future for their children, this peace must take hold.

Here in this City of Light, at this moment of hope, let us recall how this century—marked by so much progress and too much bloodshed, witness to humanity's best and humanity's worst—how this century began in Bosnia. At the dawn of the century, when gunfire in Sarajevo sparked the first of our two World Wars, the British Foreign Secretary, Sir Edward Cray, said these words: "The lamps are going out all over Europe. We shall not see them lit again in our lifetimes."

But they were lit again, by an extraordinary generation of Europeans and Americans. The torch of freedom they carried now shines more brightly than ever before on every continent. That torch can shine on Bosnia again, but first it must warm the hearts of the Bosnian people.

So I say to all the people of the Balkans on behalf of all of us who would come to see this peace take hold: You have seen what war has wrought. You know what peace can bring. Seize this chance and make it work. You can do nothing to erase the past, but you can do everything to build the future. Do not let your children down.

Thank you.

Source: Public Papers of the Presidents of the United States, William J. Clinton, 1995 (Washington, DC: Government Printing Office, 1996), 1889–90.

---

161. CHRISTOPHER, "ADVANCING AMERICA'S CRITICAL INTERESTS IN THE ASIA-PACIFIC REGION"
10 May 1996

Asia attracted considerable American attention after the demise of Soviet Communism. Opportunities for U.S trade and investment existed, but the region's expanding military power, particularly with respect to Communist China, was a cause for concern in Washington.

Thank you for that kind introduction. I want to thank Ed Woolard and John Bryan for their invitation to appear before the Business Council, which has done so much to deepen the dialogue between business and government. It is a great honor to be on the program with Senior Minister Lee Kwan Yew of Singapore, my distinguished predecessor Henry Kissinger, my former Carter Administration colleague Zbig Brzezinski, and Treasury Secretary Robert Rubin. Appearing in this company before this powerful audience is enough to make me look forward to another relaxing round of Middle East shuttle diplomacy.

I am particularly pleased to have the chance to speak with you about the dynamic Asia-Pacific region. As a young naval officer in the Pacific in World War II, chairman of a Los Angeles-based law firm with Asian offices, a one-time trade negotiator with Japan, and now Secretary of State, I have had the opportunity to witness—up close and personal—many of Asia's remarkable changes over the last half-century.

With all due respect to the proponents of a coming "Asian century," I am bold enough to believe that it will also be the second American century as well. As a global power with global interests, the United States has a great stake in the region's dynamism, and we have the greatest ability to sustain it in ways that benefit the American people and the world.

Let me make a few observations about the impact of this new era on the way in which we pursue our national interests.

First, accelerated change means that no company or country can take its leadership for granted. The United States won the Cold War, but, as Peter Drucker has written, no company—or country—is automatically destined to be a permanent economic superpower in the new global marketplace. We have to keep on our toes and be light on our feet.

Second, one of the most dramatic changes I have seen is the erasure of the line between domestic and foreign policy—just as in the corporate world you no longer see a bright line between a company's domestic and foreign operations. The Clinton Administration recognizes that our strengths at home and abroad are inseparable and that our ability to create jobs and growth here depends on our ability to open markets overseas. I believe that one of the signature accomplishments of our Administration will be a landmark set of market-opening agreements—from GATT and NAFTA to APEC and the Free Trade Agreement of the Americas.

Third, our economic diplomacy is not only essential to advancing our commercial interests but is also a powerful tool for achieving other core foreign policy goals. Economic development is essential to undergird peace, stability, and progress toward democracy—whether in the Middle East, Haiti, or the New Independent States of the former Soviet Union. Just as surely as our military might and our embassies overseas advance our interests, your companies' global presence extends American power and influence. Our late and much-admired colleague Ron Brown understood this concept well, and we will certainly miss him for that and for many other reasons.

Nowhere is the mutually reinforcing relationship between our economic and security interests more apparent than in the Asia-Pacific region. For the last half-century, America's military presence in Asia has provided the foundation of stability for nations to build thriving economies for the benefit of all.

There should be absolutely no doubt that we intend to remain a Pacific power. During the last three years, President Clinton has taken a number of key strategic decisions to reinforce our engagement in the region—through our five active security alliances, our forward-deployed presence, and our commitment to maintain approximately 100,000 troops in the Pacific.

The cornerstone of our engagement in the region, of course, remains our relationship with Japan. Here as elsewhere, this Administration has defied the skeptics and demonstrated that we can promote America's economic interests while strengthening our vital security relationships at the same time.

The Joint Declaration signed by the President and Prime Minister Hashimoto in Tokyo last month provides the firm foundation to ensure that our alliance can meet the challenges of the next century. Japan has agreed to increase its financial and material support for our troops stationed there. In addition, we are working well with Japan in areas such as Bosnia and the Middle East.

Our economic relationship with Japan is also becoming more balanced. Since 1993, U.S. exports to Japan have risen by 34%, with increases as high as 80% in the sectors where trade agreements have been reached. Our trade deficit fell last year by almost 10% from its level in 1994—the first time since 1990 that our bilateral trade deficit has decreased.

This progress is due to a variety of factors, including the persistent efforts of your companies to gain footholds in Japanese markets. But there can be no doubt that it is also due to our determined efforts to open markets. Over the last three years, we have reached 21 separate market access agreements with Japan in sectors as diverse as autos and auto parts, agriculture, telecommunications, and medical technology. We will be vigilant in ensuring the implementation of existing agreements and in resolving outstanding trade disputes in areas such as film, semiconductors, and insurance. We will press for further deregulation of Japan's economy, which will benefit Japanese consumers as well as American and other foreign businesses.

Of course, no nation is playing a larger role in shaping the future of Asia than China. How our relationship with China develops will have a vast impact on our future. Nobody should have any illusions about the difficulty of dealing with this emerging power during a time of transition. But nobody should have any doubt about how important a stable, open, and prosperous China is to our interests. What is vital is keeping a clear eye on our strategic interest in moving China in that direction. Your companies' capital, technology, and ideas are already playing a critical role in integrating China into the mainstream of the global economy and the international community.

The United States shares an array of important interests with China, and we have worked hard over the last three years to advance them. I have met with my counterpart Vice Premier and Foreign Minister Qian Qichen 13 times since I became Secretary of State. We have been able to work together to extend the nuclear Non-Proliferation Treaty and to resolve the threat posed by the North Korean nuclear program. We have engaged with China in our effort to ban nuclear testing, to fight drug trafficking and alien smuggling, and to protect the environment.

When we have problems with China's actions, we have pressed our interests candidly and forcefully. As you know, we have stressed to China the importance of fully implementing the agreement on protecting intellectual property rights that we concluded in March 1995. The piracy of CDs, videos, and software is growing, causing billions of dollars in losses to American companies. The President has made it clear that if the Chinese do not deal with this IPR piracy, we will have no choice but to go ahead with a carefully targeted but quite substantial list of sanctions provided for by U.S. law.

We will continue to pursue our interests vigorously, whether the issue is security, trade, non-proliferation, or human rights. Last month, for example, we sent an unmistakable signal to China that the use of force across the Taiwan Strait would be a matter of grave concern to the United States. But we reject the counsel of those who seek to contain or isolate China. Far from protecting our interests, such a course would harm them.

It is in this broad context that we will be supporting the continuation of MFN for China once again next month. The President and I will make the case that the best way to advance our interests is to maintain our engagement—an approach pursued by six presidents and now endorsed, I am pleased to note, by Senator Dole. Revoking or conditioning MFN now would not advance human rights in China. But it would damage our economy and harm Hong Kong, Taiwan, and other Asian allies and friends. That is why Hong Kong legislative leader Martin Lee and Governor Chris Patten, with whom I met yesterday morning, support MFN's unconditional renewal.

Our alliance with South Korea is also another vital relationship. During the last three years, we have developed an unprecedented degree of cooperation. Our strong partnership enabled us to forge an agreement to freeze North Korea's dangerous nuclear program and put it on course for dismantlement. We have also made great commercial progress in what is now our fifth-largest export market. We expanded our exports last year by 40% and now have a trade surplus.

As you know, to reach a durable peace on the peninsula, President Clinton and President Kim Young Sam recently offered a proposal for four-party talks among the United States, South Korea, North Korea, and China. China has said that the proposal is "reasonable" and that it will participate if North Korea does. North Korea, for its part, has indicated that it is seriously studying the proposal.

The nations of ASEAN—Singapore, Indonesia, Malaysia, Thailand, the Philippines, Brunei, and now Vietnam—are essential to our security and economic interests in Asia. Their rapidly growing markets collectively represent our fourth-largest trading partner. We are working hard in Southeast Asia to protect intellectual property rights, promote U.S. investment, and expand U.S. exports, which rose by more than 10% in 1994.

As in any other region, the Asia-Pacific region has its share of problems that make the business environment difficult. As Secretary, one of my top priorities has been to fight the corrupt practices that I know cost American companies billions of dollars in orders and contracts every year. In late 1993, I launched a global initiative through the OECD to unite supplier nations to end illicit payments. I am delighted that we have reached agreement to prevent bribes paid to foreign officials from being tax-deductible as a business expense. I hope they will soon be outlawed altogether. In a parallel effort, I have also intensified our efforts through APEC [Asia-Pacific Economic Conference] to increase the transparency of bidding practices in government procurement in this region where, as you know, there will be such massive demand over the next two decades.

During the past three years, this Administration has placed an unprecedented emphasis on our interlocking strategic and economic interests in Asia and around the world. We will continue to work with you to seize the opportunities that Asia has to offer—opportunities that are so critical to America's future.

Thank you very much.

Source: Warren Christopher, "Advancing America's Critical Interests in the Asia-Pacific Region," *U.S. Department of State Dispatch*, vol. 7 (13 May 1996): 237–38.

162. SODERBERG, "U.S. INTERVENTION IN THE POST–COLD WAR ERA" 10 July 1996

One important dilemma for U.S. policymakers in the 1990s was establishing the litmus test necessary for American global intervention. In contrast to the relatively stable threat posed by Soviet power for nearly five decades, the issues that could prompt an American response in the post–Cold War era were much less tangible. Paradoxically, policymakers also understood that America's position as the last remaining superpower placed ever greater pressure on the United States to resolve a growing list of problems created by its own Cold War victory. In July 1996, Deputy Assistant to the President for National Security Affairs, Nancy E. Soderberg, made the case for American intervention.

I would like to use my time with you to address American intervention in the post-Cold War era—how we decide to get involved in matters beyond our borders.

For more than four decades, most American foreign policy was made and measured in relation to the Soviet threat. Confronted by a fierce, ideological rival—a rival that possessed thousands of nuclear warheads—American policymakers rallied around a single mission: containment. That banner slogan became the central organizing concept for American foreign policy in the Cold War era—from where and when we intervened to the creation of security alliances to whether and to whom we gave foreign assistance.

Today, with the Cold War over, the security environment has changed. To be sure, we still face threats to our national security—threats that demand traditional uses of American power and diplomacy. During the last three years, we have met these familiar challenges with determination and success. But in this new world, we also face a new type of challenge that I would like to discuss today: The new opportunities and new responsibilities America has to make a difference. No national consensus has emerged to date on what we should do in these areas. Resources are tight, and once again, some voices are preaching the path of isolation. But I believe the Clinton Administration has laid the foundation for real progress. We have worked decisively to bolster support for American leadership in the world, not only in areas of traditional concern, but in meeting the challenges of the 21st century as well.

First, let me address those challenges that reflect the traditional focus of our power and diplomacy. The President's primary responsibility is always to protect our citizens and our shores. When matters of overriding importance to our national security and survival are at stake—such as a direct attack on our soil, our people, or our allies—we will do whatever it takes to defend our interests, including the use of decisive military force—with others where we can, and alone when we must.

When Saddam Hussein's henchmen made an attempt on President Bush's life, President Clinton took direct military action. When Iraq moved forces toward the Kuwaiti border in 1994, we sent our troops to the region and Saddam backed down. When North Korea began removing spent fuel from its nuclear reactor that same year, we broke off our negotiations and began working with our allies toward international sanctions and making plans to augment our military forces on the Peninsula. Pyongyang came back to the table, ready to talk about terminating their dangerous nuclear program.

America's armed forces are the core of our nation's power, and we have kept our military the best-trained, best-equipped, and best-prepared in the world. We have strengthened and modernized our core alliances in Europe and Asia—maintaining about 100,000 troops in each region, setting the process of NATO enlargement in motion, and forging a new security declaration with Japan. While a long-range missile threat to our shores is unlikely to arise within the next 15 years, we are committed to developing a National Missile Defense system by 2000 that can, if needed, be deployed by 2003.

Just as we have strengthened our military ability to secure our interests, we have also focused on our diplomatic power. President Clinton has seized the opportunity the end of the Cold War presents to reduce the nuclear threat by pursuing the most ambitious arms control and non-proliferation agenda in history. Today, Ukraine, Belarus, and Kazakstan have agreed to give up the nuclear weapons left on their soil. START I and START II will slash by two-thirds the nuclear arsenals that we and the Soviet Union held at the height of the Cold War. We secured indefinite extension of the NPT, are urging the earliest Senate ratification of the Chemical Weapons Convention, hope to sign a Comprehensive Test Ban Treaty this year, and have broadened international support for the Missile Technology Control Regime. These efforts and achievements are in the interest of every American security.

We have also led the fight against an increasingly interconnected array of forces of destruction—such as terrorists, drug traffickers, and organized criminals. These threats have little regard for national borders. No nation is immune, and none can defeat them alone.

Since taking office, President Clinton has marshaled our resources and galvanized world efforts against these threats. He has attacked state-sponsored terrorism with stiff sanctions on rogue nations, enacted tough counterterrorism legislation that gives law enforcement the tools they need to fight terrorists at home, and mobilized the world community—from the Summit of Peacemakers in Sharm El-Sheikh to the recent G-7 summit in Lyon. But the skeletal remains of the Khobar Towers in Dhahran are a brutal reminder that our work is far from over. As the President has said, America must not and will not be driven from this battle.

We also understand the importance of engagement with the world's other great powers—those nations that have the greatest ability to help or hinder us in our efforts. We have worked steadily and intensively with Russia to help it seize the promise of a democratic future—and last week's run-off confirmed that the Russian people want to stay the path of reform.

We have fortified our strategic dialogue with China, using the best tools available—incentives and disincentives alike—to advance American interests. That was the purpose of Tony Lake's trip over the last few days to Beijing. When we disagree with China, we defend our interests vigorously, and when China expanded its military exercises in the Taiwan Strait, we made clear that any use of force against Taiwan would have grave consequences. But by engaging China, we have helped achieve important benefits—from cooperation toward a Comprehensive Test Ban Treaty to freezing North Korea's dangerous nuclear program.

Deterring—and defending our nation if necessary—against attacks on our vital interests, reducing the nuclear threat, fighting forces of destruction such as terrorism, and staying engaged with other great powers, are clearly the most serious foreign policy challenges and also the most straightforward. In deciding how and when to meet them, the calculus is clear: We must and will marshal whatever resources we need to get the job done right. Protecting our most fundamental national security interests is always the primary focus and concern of any American president.

The second category of challenge is what I would call "new responsibilities and opportunities," which demand new responses and new thinking.

Let me divide these new responsibilities and opportunities into four general areas in which we can use our influence as the sole remaining superpower to:

promote peace;

strengthen democracy;

prevent conflicts;

and alleviate crises.

Some would argue against our engagement in areas where there is no overriding direct threat to our interests. President Clinton sees the situation differently. During the Cold War, we resisted actions that diverted our resources from the overwhelming struggle at hand. Today, we are freed from that constraint. This does not mean we should intervene everywhere or respond to every emergency. But as the world's most powerful nation—economically, militarily, and through the sheer force of our values—we cannot simply turn our backs on tragedy or opportunity.

In choosing how and when to get involved, we must ask a number of critical questions, including the following:

1. Will our efforts advance American interests and ideals?
2. Will they be successful?
3. Are they a good use of our limited resources?
4. How do our interests compare to the costs and risks?

Once we have answered these questions, we must carefully decide which tools we are willing to apply—from the power of our example—persistent diplomacy and economic aid, or sanctions to military force.

First, let me address promoting peace. The end of the Cold War has lifted the lid on religious and ethnic conflicts such as we saw in Bosnia where ethnic hatred spiraled into a war that claimed thousands of lives, threatened stability in the heart of Europe, and did violence to the values on which America stands. Early in 1993, the President decided he would only send ground troops to Bosnia to help implement a peace agreement, because the costs of intervening as combatant were too high when balanced against our interests.

However, we used every other tool in our arsenal to search for peace, prevent the war from spreading, and ease the suffering of the Bosnian people. We imposed tough economic sanctions on Serbia, stationed troops in The Former Yugoslav Republic of Macedonia to contain the spread of the fighting, provided air support for UNPROFOR, conducted the longest humanitarian airlift in history, enforced a no-fly zone, and helped to make peace between Bosnia's Muslims and Croats.

But last summer, when Bosnia's Serbs stepped up their brutality and another winter of disaster loomed, President Clinton launched his own diplomatic effort—backed by military force—to bring the warring parties to the peace table. The combination of heavy NATO air strikes and intensive American diplomacy, together with the renewed determination of our European partners and the Croat gains on the battlefield, were what made the Dayton peace conference possible.

Today, our troops are serving heroically in Bosnia—not fighting in a war, but helping to secure the peace that American leadership helped achieve. The success of our military operation in Bosnia has been strengthened by the lessons we learned in Somalia—about the importance of a clear military mission, firm deadlines, and an exit strategy.

There are other areas in which the investment of American resources has gone a long way for peace. The President has worked hard to build on the efforts of previous administrations in the Middle East, and we all admire the determined diplomacy of Secretary Christopher and his team. During the last three years, we have witnessed historic agreements between Palestinians and Israelis, and between Israel and Jordan. In Northern Ireland, the President's decision to use our leverage as a close and trusted partner of both Great Britain and Ireland has spurred unprecedented breakthroughs: a 17-month cease-fire that saved hundreds of lives and peace talks that began last month in Belfast. There remains much to be done, beginning with the restoration of the cease-fire, but we can be proud of the difference our engagement has made. In Cyprus, our special envoy Richard Beattie is working hard to resolve the problem. He is the first person to take on this important role since 1980, and will be traveling to the region with Ambassador Albright next week to try to build momentum toward a comprehensive settlement.

Second, let me address strengthening democracy. The rising tide of freedom around the world is helping shape a world in which America can thrive, but it is neither inevitable nor irreversible. It needs our support and our leadership.

In Haiti, the Administration mobilized the international community to isolate the brutal dictatorship that had overthrown the legitimate government. We had important interests in shoring up democracy in our hemisphere, ending the abuse of human rights, and stemming the tide of desperate refugees, and we tried every peaceful avenue to achieve our goals. But when it became clear that peaceful means alone would not succeed, the President decided to back his diplomacy with force. When Haiti's generals learned our planes were in the air, they stepped aside in a hurry. Our troops were able to enter Haiti peacefully and help the Haitian people reclaim their democracy. By defining our interests clearly and using the tools at our disposal effectively, we achieved all our goals with a minimum of violence. Today, Haiti has achieved the first democratic transfer of power in its history, and its people have a chance for a brighter future.

We have worked to promote democracy in other, though less dramatic ways, including tightened sanctions against Cuba, marshaling international condemnation of near coups in Paraguay and Sao Tome and Principe, and working in partnership with Europe to consolidate the gains of Central Europe's new democracies. Our assistance programs are making a difference in building judicial systems, helping monitor elections, teaching political party development, and promoting sustainable development. Democrats from Beijing to Bucharest and beyond look first to America for inspiration.

We are leading the effort to pressure those still bucking the tide of democracy—such as the military rulers in Nigeria and Burma—by isolating the leaders while trying to press them to move forward. Progress is often painfully slow, but in the end, history is on the side of democracy and we can and must push it along.

Third, as Michael Lund so thoughtfully discusses in his book, the United States can also use its influence to prevent conflicts before they erupt and become a more serious drain on our resources. I doubt many Americans are aware that we have troops on the border between Peru and Ecuador to help safeguard peace between these two friends of the United States. We helped our NATO allies Greece and Turkey avoid a conflict over the Aegean island of Imia. And we have launched an intensive diplomatic effort to prevent another Rwanda-like genocide in Burundi. In the last year alone, Ambassador Albright, Deputy Secretary Talbott, NSA Anthony Lake, Assistant Secretary Moose, Deputy Director of Central Intelligence Tenet, and now, Special Representative Howard Wolpe have all traveled to the region to help promote reconciliation.

Some may argue that we should not put so much effort in a place with so little bearing on American interests. I would argue that it is a small investment compared to the one we would have to make if Burundi exploded. In Rwanda, for example, where the international community failed to act quickly enough to prevent the genocide, the United States was spurred into action as images of the atrocities captured our attention and our conscience. I am proud that the U.S. military was able to kick-start the relief effort—delivering nearly 15,000 tons of food, medicine, and supplies to Rwanda's refugees, and then handing the operation back to the relief community. But the crisis in Rwanda was costly—first and foremost in Rwandan lives. And no matter how admirable our intervention was, we are trying to avoid the need to repeat it in Burundi.

The **fourth** area of opportunity, alleviating crises—both man-made and natural—is a simple calculation of costs and need. In Rwanda, we could not stand by as images of the disaster poured out, when we knew we had unique abilities to help. Similarly, when complex crises from the Balkans to the Caribbean to West Africa threaten the lives of hundreds of thousands, or when earthquakes result in devastation in Japan, America can and should respond. We continue to be in the forefront of international efforts to respond to humanitarian need, contributing some $1.5 billion each year for these efforts. Moreover, this level of commitment reflects a strong executive-congressional consensus. By showing the strength to be generous and humane, we reinforce our authority as the leader of the global community.

During the last three years, I believe this Administration has made a real difference for our people and others—by knowing how to use the right tool at the right time, by marshaling our resources, and leveraging our power. Our efforts may lack the simple clarity of the past. But that is not necessarily bad. In today's new world of fast-paced innovation, part of being strong means being able to adapt—to fortify old structures to withstand modern challenges, to anticipate new problems before they arise, and to make the investments that will bring greater payoffs, or prevent greater costs, down the line.

Whenever we are faced with pressures to act, we carefully balance our interests against the costs. But there are times when America, and America alone, can make the crucial difference between fear and hope. We must not shrink from our responsibility to lead, and those in Congress who would slash our modest foreign affairs budget are playing dangerous politics with America's well-being.

For 50 years, our country has been the world's greatest force for freedom and progress, and it has brought us real security and prosperity here at home. If we continue to lead, if we continue to meet the peril and seize the promise of this new era, that proud history will also be our destiny. That is President Clinton's goal—and that is what we who work with him are determined to achieve. We don't have magic solutions for every challenge we face. But at the end of the day, the bottom line is clear: Because of our efforts, our nation is more secure, our people are more prosperous, and our values are ascendant all around the world. We are laying the foundations for the 21st century to be an American century as well. Thank you.

Source: Nancy E. Soderberg, "U.S. Intervention in the Post–Cold War Era," *U.S. Department of State Dispatch*, vol. 7 (22 July 1996): 373–75.

---

163. ALBRIGHT, "ENLARGING NATO"
15 February 1997

The end of Soviet dominance in Eastern Europe created an opportunity to redraw the political, economic, and military maps of the entire continent. In early 1997, Secretary of State Madeleine Albright made the case that an expansion of the North Atlantic Treaty Organization (NATO) could also serve as a necessary precursor for free economic and political institutions in the former Soviet bloc.

It is an old diplomatic tradition that American secretaries of state begin their terms by visiting our closest allies and partners. That is why this week I will be meeting with officials in Europe, and later in Asia, to forge a common agenda. The dominant questions of the day in virtually all these countries, as in my own, involve matters close to home—educating children, building businesses, cutting deficits, fighting unemployment. At a time when much of the world enjoys relative peace, we run the risk of forgetting the decades-long work of diplomacy and institution-building that has made it possible for the great majority of people to worry about domestic improvements rather than national survival.

My message on this trip is that we have our own work to do—and quickly—if this space of tranquility is to endure and spread, rather than be written off by history as a pleasant time of tragically wasted opportunities. That message applies with special force to Europe. Today, the continent is no longer sliced in two, but dangers remain: from Bosnia to Chechnya, more Europeans died violently in the last five years than in the previous 45. From Serbia to Belarus, reminders are appearing that Europe's democratic revolution is not complete.

Even so, a goal that would have seemed like a Utopian delusion just years ago lies within our grasp: a peaceful and undivided Europe working in partnership with the United States, that welcomes every one of the continent's new democracies into our transatlantic community.

An ambitious goal, to be sure. Yet progress towards its realization has been remarkable. Western Europe is moving towards economic and monetary union. Most of Europe's fastest-growing economies lie east of the Elbe. Russia has made a choice for democracy and markets and defied the most dire predictions about its evolution. An independent and robustly democratic Ukraine is casting its lot with Europe. American and European resolve has stopped the fighting in Bosnia. The military coalition there contains so many former adversaries that no sober student of history would have predicted it: France and Germany, Poland and Lithuania, Turkey and Greece, Russia and America.

Many institutions are playing their part in this effort, and all face critical tests this year. The European Union has promised to expand again and will soon make decisions. The Organization for Economic Cooperation and Development (OECD) has taken in Poland, Hungary and the Czech Republic; it is now looking to other market democracies, including Russia. The Organization for Security and Cooperation in Europe (OSCE) is promoting the democratic standards that will enable Europe to come together; it is still treading a rough road in Bosnia.

But it is NATO, the linchpin of European security and the principal mechanism for American involvement in Europe, that is playing the leading role in bringing Europe together. It is changing its internal structure to create a stronger role for Europe. Its Partnership for Peace, under which other countries can train, plan, exercise and cooperate with NATO, has brought together old adversaries and long-time neutrals. In the wake of such changes, France and Spain are participating more fully in the alliance. NATO is now more attractive to more nations because it is addressing new challenges in Europe and beyond. The next six months will be among the most ambitious and demanding in its history.

NATO's opportunity

At the NATO summit this July in Madrid, allied leaders will reform NATO's internal structures and invite several nations to become members by 1999. President Clinton and I have no higher priority than to work with our allies, and with our people and Congress, to build this new NATO. The debate in America will be spirited, as it should be. But I am confident the American people and their representatives will affirm that a new and broader NATO serves our security as well as Europe's.

Too often, the debate about NATO's future reduces the alliance's past to a one-dimensional caricature that discounts its relevance to today's European challenges. Certainly, NATO's cold-war task was to contain the Soviet threat. But that is not all it did. It provided the confidence and security shattered economies needed to rebuild themselves. It helped France and Germany become reconciled, making European integration possible. With other institutions, it brought Italy, then Germany and eventually Spain back into the family of European democracies. It denationalized allied defense policies. It has stabilized relations between Greece and Turkey. All without firing a shot.

Now the new NATO can do for Europe's east what the old NATO did for Europe's west: vanquish old hatreds, promote integration, create a secure environment for prosperity, and deter violence in the region where two world wars and the cold war began.

Just the prospect of NATO enlargement has given Central and Eastern Europe greater stability than it has seen in this century. Hungary has settled its border and minority questions with Slovakia and Romania. Poland has reached across an old divide to create joint peacekeeping battalions with Ukraine and Lithuania. Throughout the region, support for NATO membership has rallied political parties of every ideology in favor of joining the West. Country after country has made sure that soldiers take orders from civilians, not the other way around.

To align themselves with NATO, these states are resolving problems that could have led to future Bosnias. This is the productive paradox at NATO's heart: by extending solemn security guarantees, we actually reduce the chance that our troops will again be called to fight in Europe. At the same time, we will gain new allies who are eager and increasingly able to contribute to our common agenda for security, from fighting terrorism and weapons proliferation to ensuring stability in trouble spots like the former Yugoslavia.

NATO enlargement will involve real costs to the United States, its allies and its partners. But the costs are reasonable and many would arise whether NATO expands or not. Countries aspiring to membership will have to modernize their armed forces whether they are in or out of NATO—if anything, military spending would be higher in an insecure, unattached central Europe. A decision not to enlarge would also carry costs: it would constitute a declaration that NATO will neither address the challenges nor accept the geography of a new Europe. NATO would be stuck in the past, risking irrelevance and even dissolution. Those are costs we cannot afford.

Addressing the critics

NATO and its members have laid out the reasons for enlargement. It is high time that critics came forward with a rationale that might possibly support a policy of fossilized immobility in the face of Europe's sweeping changes. Now that democracy's frontier has moved to Europe's farthest reaches, what logic would dictate that we freeze NATO's eastern edges where they presently lie, along the line where the Red Army stopped in the spring of 1945? President Clinton said it in Prague two years ago: "Freedom's boundaries now should be defined by new behavior, not old history." Or for that matter by old thinking. To define them otherwise would not only create a permanent injustice, mocking the sacrifices made in this century on both sides of the Iron Curtain. It would create a permanent source of tension and insecurity in the heart of Europe.

Some critics point out that none of NATO's prospective members faces an immediate military threat. True enough. But then, neither does Italy. Or Denmark. Or Britain. Or Iceland. Or the United States. If NATO were open only to countries menaced by aggressive neighbors, virtually no current ally would qualify.

Those who ask "where is the threat?" mistake NATO's real value. The alliance is not a wild-west posse that we trot out only when danger appears. It is a permanent presence, designed to promote common endeavors and to prevent a threat from ever arising. That is why current allies still need it and why others wish to join. NATO does not need an enemy. It has enduring purposes.

Other critics say that if we want to reunite Europe, the EU can do the job. Besides, they argue, what central Europe needs is stocks and bonds, not stock-piles and bombs. They are certainly right that EU expansion is vital. Though the United States has no vote in the process, we do have an interest in seeing it happen as rapidly and expansively as possible.

But the security NATO provides has always been essential to the prosperity the EU promises. What is more, EU enlargement requires current and new mem-bers to make vast and complex adjustments in subsidy schemes and regulatory regimes. If NATO enlargement can proceed more quickly, why wait until, say, tomato farmers in Central Europe start using the right kinds of pesticides? And because NATO, unlike the EU, is a transatlantic institution, it can ensure that a united Europe maintains its strongest link to North America. The question is not which institution strong democracies should join, but when and how they are prepared to join each.

Critics also say that NATO enlargement will somehow redivide post-cold war Europe. On the contrary, NATO has taken a range of steps to ensure that the erasure of old lines of division does not leave new ones on the map. NATO is strengthening its Partnership for Peace, reaching out to Ukraine and Russia, and giving every new democracy—whether it joins the alliance sooner, later or not at all—a say in its future through the Atlantic Partnership Council we will launch this spring.

Of course, the enlargement of NATO must begin with the strongest candi-dates; otherwise, it would not begin at all. But when we say that the first new members will not be the last, we mean it. And we expect the new members to export stability eastward, rather than viewing enlargement as a race to escape westward at the expense of their neighbors.

The core of that challenge—and one of the most important tasks for NATO—is to build a close and constructive partnership with Russia. This will take vision and political will. It requires abandoning cold-war stereotypes and no longer looking at European security as a zero-sum game.

NATO enlargement is not taking place in response to a new Russian threat. It is motivated by the imperative of creating an integrated Europe—one that includes, not excludes, Russia. The purpose of enlargement is to give Central and Eastern Europe, a region whose future stability is key to the future of Europe as a whole, the same kind of security that has become commonplace in Western Europe. Russia, no less than the rest of us, needs stability and prosperity in the center of Europe.

I recognize that many Russian leaders express opposition to NATO enlarge-ment. Yet the NATO Russia claims to oppose bears little resemblance to the alliance we are actually building. NATO's conventional and nuclear forces have been dramatically reduced. We have no plan, no need and no intention to station nuclear weapons on the territory of new members. NATO's actions over the past six years reveal an alliance focused on building co-operation, not confrontation: an alliance working shoulder-to-shoulder with Russia—as it is in Bosnia—not trying to isolate it.

We recognize that Europe cannot finally be whole and free until a democratic Russia is fully part of Europe. Now we hope that Russians will recognize that their suspicions about NATO and its enlargement are misplaced. After all, if Russia wishes to be part of an undivided Europe, then it cannot look at countries like Poland or Estonia or Ukraine as a buffer zone that separates Russia from Europe.

It is a mistake to think that the fate of Russian democracy is somehow at stake in the enlargement debate. Russia's future as a free and prosperous nation will depend upon the ability of its leaders and citizens to build an open society, to defeat crime and corruption, to spark economic growth and spread its benefits. The Russian people know that their future will be written in Moscow, in Perm, in Irkutsk—and certainly not in Brussels. Poll after poll has shown that few ordinary Russians express concern about an alliance that many of their leaders concede poses no actual military threat to the country.

It would not be in our interest to delay or derail enlargement in response to the claims of some Russians that this constitutes an offensive act. Doing so would only encourage the worst political tendencies in Moscow. It would send a message that confrontation with the West pays off. Waiting to integrate Central and Eastern Europe's new democracies would do nothing to help Russian democracy. It would make it harder, not easier, to create the kind of NATO-Russia relationship we are striving for today.

How to engage Russia

NATO has proposed defining that partnership in a charter with Russia. The charter would establish clear principles and arrangements for consultation, co-operation and joint action in peacekeeping, defense and arms control, nuclear safety, non-proliferation and emergency relief. It would establish a permanent NATO-Russia joint council. We want Russia and our other partners to participate in NATO's Combined Joint Task Forces, which will allow us to respond to crises together. We want Russian officers to help plan the missions we jointly undertake. As a nation not bound by NATO decisions, Russia would have no veto. But its voice would be sought and heard.

We are also negotiating to update the treaty governing Conventional Forces in Europe (CFE), which limits military deployments throughout the continent. We invite the Russians to join us in an agreement that will lower levels of forces and promote stability and transparency on the continent. This can assure Russia that NATO enlargement will not result in any major build-up of NATO forces along its borders. Indeed, it can ensure there is no destabilizing concentration of military equipment anywhere in Europe.

We have every chance to make progress on these issues before the July NATO summit. I will be seeing Russian leaders in Moscow on February 20th. President Clinton will meet President Yeltsin in Helsinki in March. He will be in Europe again in May for the US-EU summit. The G7 leaders will meet President Yeltsin in Denver in June. Russia has a strategic opportunity to secure its interests in an integrated Europe. It should seize it now.

I approach this challenge, and all the challenges we face in Europe over the next few years, with confidence. And why not? For half a century now, Europeans and Americans have worked together to shape events, instead of being shaped by them.

Today's Europe stands in such stark contrast to the Europe I knew as a child after the second world war. For those who were not there, it must be hard to imagine the days of Franco, Tito and Stalin, the refugees, the hunger, the constant fear that peace was just an interlude, the Europe Winston Churchill described as "a rubble heap, a charnel house, a breeding ground for pestilence and hate." Thank heaven leaders like Marshall, Monnet, Bevin and Adenauer had the fortitude to make the hard and controversial decisions needed to build the institutions that gave us 50 years of peace and prosperity. Now it's our turn.

President Clinton observed in his state-of-the-union address that a child born today will have almost no memory of the 20th century. Just the same, the children of the transatlantic community who are born today have the chance to grow up knowing a very different Europe. In that new Europe, they will know Checkpoint Charlie only as a museum, Yalta as just a provincial city in a sovereign Ukraine, Sarajevo as a peaceful mountain resort in the heart of Europe. The children of the next century will come of age knowing a very different NATO—one that masses its energies on behalf of integration, rather than massing its forces on the borders of division.

All this is possible if—and it is not a big if—we act now to strengthen the arrangements that have served half of Europe so well for so long and to extend them to new partners and allies. Then, having come together, we will be able to concentrate on what we must do together. That is a goal worth every measure of our common effort.

Source: Madeleine K. Albright, "Enlarging NATO: Why Bigger is Better," *The Economist* 342 (15 February 1997): 21–23.

---

164. THE WYE MEMORANDUM
23 October 1998

In order to facilitate the Middle East peace process, the United States sponsored a series of marathon meetings between Israeli and Palestinian representatives at the Wye River plantation in October 1998. With President Clinton presiding over many of the discussions, both sides were able to agree on the specific provisions of a memorandum that addressed ter-

ritorial reapportionment, security, and economic conditions in the West Bank and the Gaza Strip.

The following are steps to facilitate implementation of the Interim Agreement on the West Bank and Gaza Strip of September 28, 1995 and other related agreements including the Note for the Record of January 17, 1997 (hereinafter referred to as "the prior agreements") so that the Israeli and Palestinian sides can more effectively carry out their reciprocal responsibilities, including those relating to further redeployments and security, respectively. These steps are to be carried out in a parallel phased approach in accordance with the Memorandum and the attached time line. They are subject to the relevant terms and conditions of the prior agreements and do not supersede their other requirements.

I. FURTHER REDEPLOYMENTS

A. Phase One and Two Further Redeployments

1. Pursuant to the Interim Agreement and subsequent agreements, the Israeli side's implementation of the first and second F.R.D. will consist of the transfer to the Palestinian side of 13% from Area C as follows:

1% to Area (A)

12% to Area (B)

The Palestinian side has informed that it will allocate an area/areas amounting to 3% from the above Area (B) to be designated as Green Areas and/or Nature Reserves. The Palestinian side has further informed that they will act according to the established scientific standards, and that therefore there will be no changes in the status of these areas, without prejudice to the rights of the existing inhabitants in these areas including Bedouins; while these standards do not allow new construction in these areas, existing roads and buildings may be maintained.

The Israeli side will retain in these Green Areas/Nature Reserves the overriding security responsibility for the purpose of protecting Israelis and confronting the threat of terrorism. Activities and movements of the Palestinian Police forces may be carried out after coordination and confirmation; the Israeli side will respond to such requests expeditiously.

2. As part of the foregoing implementation of the first and second F.R.D., 14.2% from Area (B) will become Area (A).

B. Third Phase of Further Redeployments

With regard to the terms of the Interim Agreement and of Secretary Christopher's letters to the two sides of January 17, 1997 relating to the further redeployment process, there will be a committee to address this question. The United States will be briefed regularly.

II. SECURITY

In the provisions on security arrangements of the Interim Agreement, the Palestinian side agreed to take all measures necessary in order to prevent acts of terrorism, crime and hostilities directed against the Israeli side, against individuals falling under the Israeli side's authority and against their property, just as the Israeli side agreed to take all measures necessary in order to prevent acts of terrorism, crime and hostilities directed against the Palestinian side, against individuals falling under the Palestinian side's authority and against their property. The two sides also agreed to take legal measures against offenders within their jurisdiction and to prevent incitement against each other by any organizations, groups or individuals within their jurisdiction.

Both sides recognize that it is in their vital interests to combat terrorism and fight violence in accordance with Annex I of the Interim Agreement and the Note for the Record. They also recognize that the struggle against terror and violence must be comprehensive in that it deals with terrorists, the terror support structure, and the environment conducive to the support of terror. It must be continuous and constant over a long-term, in that there can be no pauses in the work against terrorists and their structure. It must be cooperative in that no effort can be fully effective without Israeli-Palestinian cooperation and the continuous exchange of information, concepts, and actions.

Pursuant to the prior agreements, the Palestinian side's implementation of its responsibilities for security, security cooperation, and other issues will be as detailed below during the time periods specified in the attached time line:

A. *Security Actions*

1. *Outlawing and Combating Terrorist Organizations*
a. The Palestinian side will make known its policy of zero tolerance for terror and violence against both sides.
b. A work plan developed by the Palestinian side will be shared with the U.S. and thereafter implementation will begin immediately to ensure the systematic and effective combat of terrorist organizations and their infrastructure.
c. In addition to the bilateral Israeli-Palestinian security cooperation, a U.S.-Palestinian committee will meet biweekly to review the steps being taken to eliminate terrorist cells and the support structure that plans, finances, supplies and abets terror. In these meetings, the Palestinian side will inform the U.S. fully of the actions it has taken to outlaw all organizations (or wings of organizations, as appropriate) of a military, terrorist or violent character and their support structure and to prevent them from operating in areas under its jurisdiction.
d. The Palestinian side will apprehend the specific individuals suspected of perpetrating acts of violence and terror for the purpose of further investigation, and prosecution and punishment of all persons involved in acts of violence and terror.
e. A U.S.-Palestinian committee will meet to review and evaluate information pertinent to the decisions on prosecution, punishment or other legal measures which affect the status of individuals suspected of abetting or perpetrating acts of violence and terror.

2. *Prohibiting Illegal Weapons*

a. The Palestinian side will ensure an effective legal framework is in place to criminalize, in conformity with the prior agreements, any importation, manufacturing or unlicensed sale, acquisition or possession of firearms, ammunition or weapons in areas under Palestinian jurisdiction.

b. In addition, the Palestinian side will establish and vigorously and continuously implement a systematic program for the collection and appropriate handling of all such illegal items in accordance with the prior agreements. The U.S. has agreed to assist in carrying out this program.

c. A U.S.-Palestinian-Israeli committee will be established to assist and enhance cooperation in preventing the smuggling or other unauthorized introduction of weapons or explosive materials into areas under Palestinian jurisdiction.

3. *Preventing Incitement*

a. Drawing on relevant international practice and pursuant to Article XXII (1) of the Interim Agreement and the Note for the Record, the Palestinian side will issue a decree prohibiting all forms of incitement to violence or terror, and establishing mechanisms for acting systematically against all expressions or threats of violence or terror. This decree will be comparable to the existing Israeli legislation which deals with the same subject.

b. A U.S.-Palestinian-Israeli committee will meet on a regular basis to monitor cases of possible incitement to violence or terror and to make recommendations and reports on how to prevent such incitement. The Israeli, Palestinian and U.S. sides will each appoint a media specialist, a law enforcement representative, an educational specialist and a current or former elected official to the committee.

B. Security Cooperation

The two sides agree that their security cooperation will be based on a spirit of partnership and will include, among other things, the following steps:

1. *Bilateral Cooperation*

There will be full bilateral security cooperation between the two sides which will be continuous, intensive and comprehensive.

2. *Forensic Cooperation*

There will be an exchange of forensic expertise, training, and other assistance.

3. *Trilateral Committee*

In addition to the bilateral Israeli-Palestinian security cooperation, a high-ranking U.S.-Palestinian-Israeli committee will meet as required and not less than biweekly to assess current threats, deal with any impediments to effective security cooperation and coordination and address the steps being taken to combat terror and terrorist organizations. The committee will also serve as a forum to address the issue of external support for terror. In these meetings, the Palestinian side will fully inform the members of the committee of the results of its investigations concerning terrorist suspects already in custody and the participants will exchange additional relevant information. The committee will report regularly to the leaders of the two sides on the status of cooperation, the results of the meetings and its recommendations.

C. Other Issues

1. *Palestinian Police Force*
a. The Palestinian side will provide a list of its policemen to the Israeli side in conformity with the prior agreements.
b. Should the Palestinian side request technical assistance, the U.S. has indicated its willingness to help meet their needs in cooperation with other donors.
c. The Monitoring and Steering Committee will, as part of its functions, monitor the implementation of this provision and brief the U.S.

2. *PLO Charter*
The Executive Committee of the Palestine Liberation Organization and the Palestinian Central Council will reaffirm the letter of 22 January 1998 from PLO Chairman Yasir Arafat to President Clinton concerning the nullification of the Palestinian National Charter provisions that are inconsistent with the letters exchanged between the PLO and the Government of Israel on 9/10 September 1993. PLO Chairman Arafat, the Speaker of the Palestine National Council, and the Speaker of the Palestinian Council will invite the members of the PNC, as well as the members of the Central Council, the Council, and the Palestinian Heads of Ministries to a meeting to be addressed by President Clinton to reaffirm their support for the peace process and the aforementioned decisions of the Executive Committee and the Central Council.

3. *Legal Assistance in Criminal Matters*
Among other forms of legal assistance in criminal matters, the requests for arrest and transfer of suspects and defendants pursuant to Article 11 (7) of Annex IV of the Interim Agreement will be submitted (or resubmitted) through the mechanism of the Joint Israeli-Palestinian Legal Committee and will be responded to in conformity with Article II (7) (f) of Annex IV of the Interim Agreement within the twelve week period. Requests submitted after the eighth week will be responded to in conformity with Article II (7) (f) within four weeks of their submission. The U.S. has been requested by the sides to report on a regular basis on the steps being taken to respond to the above requests.

4. *Human Rights and the Rule of Law*
Pursuant to Article XI (1) of Annex I of the Interim Agreement, and without derogating from the above, the Palestinian Police will exercise powers and responsibilities to implement this Memorandum with due regard to internationally accepted norms of human rights and the rule of law, and will be guided by the need to protect the public, respect human dignity, and avoid harassment.

III. INTERIM COMMITTEES AND ECONOMIC ISSUES

1. The Israeli and Palestinian sides reaffirm their commitment to enhancing their relationship and agree on the need to actively promote economic development

in the West Bank and Gaza. In this regard, the parties agree to continue or to reactivate all standing committees established by the Interim Agreement, including the Monitoring and Steering Committee, the Joint Economic Committee (JEC), the Civil Affairs Committee (CAC), the Legal Committee, and the Standing Cooperation Committee.

2. The Israeli and Palestinian sides have agreed on arrangements which will permit the timely opening of the Gaza Industrial Estate. They also have concluded a "Protocol Regarding the Establishment and Operation of the International Airport in the Gaza Strip During the Interim Period."

3. Both sides will renew negotiations on Safe Passage immediately. As regards the southern route, the sides will make best efforts to conclude the agreement within a week of the entry into force of this Memorandum. Operation of the southern route will start as soon as possible thereafter. As regards the northern route, negotiations will continue with the goal of reaching agreement as soon as possible. Implementation will take place expeditiously thereafter.

4. The Israeli and Palestinian sides acknowledge the great importance of the Port of Gaza for the development of the Palestinian economy, and the expansion of Palestinian trade. They commit themselves to proceeding without delay to conclude an agreement to allow the construction and operation of the port in accordance with the prior agreements. The Israeli-Palestinian Committee will reactivate its work immediately with a goal of concluding the protocol within sixty days, which will allow commencement of the construction of the port.

5. The two sides recognize that unresolved legal issues adversely affect the relationship between the two peoples. They therefore will accelerate efforts through the Legal Committee to address outstanding legal issues and to implement solutions to these issues in the shortest possible period. The Palestinian side will provide to the Israeli side copies of all of its laws in effect.

6. The Israeli and Palestinian sides also will launch a strategic economic dialogue to enhance their economic relationship. They will establish within the framework of the JEC an Ad Hoc Committee for this purpose. The committee will review the following four issues: (1) Israeli purchase taxes; (2) cooperation in combating vehicle theft; (3) dealing with unpaid Palestinian debts; and (4) the impact of Israeli standards as barriers to trade and the expansion of the A1 and A2 lists. The committee will submit an interim report within three weeks of the entry into force of this Memorandum, and within six weeks will submit its conclusions and recommendations to be implemented.

7. The two sides agree on the importance of continued international donor assistance to facilitate implementation by both sides of agreements reached. They also recognize the need for enhanced donor support for economic development in the West Bank and Gaza. They agree to jointly approach the donor community to organize a Ministerial Conference before the end of 1998 to seek pledges for enhanced levels of assistance.

IV. PERMANENT STATUS NEGOTIATIONS

The two sides will immediately resume permanent status negotiations on an accelerated basis and will make a determined effort to achieve the mutual goal of reaching an agreement by May 4, 1999. The negotiations will be continuous and without interruption. The U.S. has expressed its willingness to facilitate these negotiations.

V. UNILATERAL ACTIONS

Recognizing the necessity to create a positive environment for the negotiations, neither side shall initiate or take any step that will change the status of the West Bank and the Gaza Strip in accordance with the Interim Agreement.

This Memorandum will enter into force ten days from the date of signature.

Done at Washington, D.C. this 23d day of October 1998.

For the Government of the State of Israel: Benjamin Netanyahu	For the PLO: Yassir Arafat	Witnessed by: William J. Clinton The United States of America

Source: The White House, Office of the Press Secretary, http://www.state.gov/www/regions/nea/981023__interim__agmt.html.

---

165. ASIA-PACIFIC SECURITY AND CHINA
13 November 1998

By the second Clinton administration, the Pacific Rim had risen to occupy a critical place in U.S. strategic priorities. On 13 November 1998, Admiral Joseph W. Prueher, Commander of the United States Pacific Command, specifically addressed the importance of Asia, potential challenges to stability, and American policy in the region.

Good afternoon. Thank you for that kind introduction. I want to thank President Yang Fujia for the invitation to speak here at the famous Fudan University today. The role this university plays as a gateway between China and the rest of the world is well known.

We are especially honored to have with us representatives of the Shanghai Institute for International Studies as well as the Center for American Studies. The Center for American Studies is a long term symbol of what can be achieved through U.S.-China cooperation.

The invitation of Wang Daohan to visit Shanghai after his visit to Hawaii is a pleasure. On this, my fifth visit to China, we are continuing to gain understanding on issues and build foundations for bonds between our nations and particularly our militaries. I look forward to learning more about Shanghai.

Today, my topic is U.S. Pacific Command's perspective on Asia-Pacific security. I will give a quick assessment of the region, through U.S. eyes, an overview of the U.S. military's role as well as our U.S. Pacific Command strategy in the Asia-Pacific. Finally, I would like to finish with a few points on my own perspective of our growing relationship with China and some ideas on a way ahead.

The Region

First our region is organized in U.S. eyes as an assigned area of responsibility extending from the west coast of North America to the east coast of Africa. It includes 43 nations. Over the course of the past two years our Asia-Pacific region has seen significant change. A primary portion of this change remains the continuing economic crisis that plagues much of the region.

In addition recent developments on the Korean peninsula, tests of nuclear devices by India and Pakistan, and changes of government in the Philippines, Thailand, Korea, Indonesia, and Japan have occurred. As a Pacific nation, our U.S. economic, political and military interests in the Pacific are diverse and lasting. These interests drive our permanent and active involvement in the region . . . as partners with Asian nations.

The U.S. and Asia have become more interdependent as our trade and foreign direct investment have grown dramatically over the last generation. Trade with the region accounts for over $500 billion per year, approximately 35% of total U.S. trade, double our trade with Europe. Foreign direct investment is less but America's economic future remains merged with this region.

The region contains over 56 percent of the earth's population. Millions of American citizens living along or within the Pacific Rim add to its 65% of the world's total population. As we look to the future, solving any global problem will require that we work together with the people and governments of the Asia-Pacific.

Militarily, five of America's seven mutual defense treaties are with Asia-Pacific nations and the world's six largest militaries operate in this region. America shares with the other nations here an enduring objective that no hostile coalition arises in the AsiaPacific. It is not in our mutual interest for any state, including the United States, to become a Pacific hegemon.

The Asia-Pacific region is generally at peace, but is not free from the possibility of major conflict. Our nation has fought three major wars in this region during the last century and since 1950 the U.S. has lost more lives in Asia than in the rest of the world combined. The wars and occupations on the Asian continent in this century are well known here; the scars remain.

Other than the United Nations and regional organizations such as the ASEAN Regional Forum, there are no broader integrating regional institutions to reconcile conflicting ambitions. We must work together to develop such institutions for stability and security.

Each of these interests bind the U.S. to the Asia-Pacific region and we are committed for the long term. It is clear that both China and the U.S. enjoy a common interest in a secure, stable and prosperous Asia-Pacific region.

The Framework

Pacific Command's mission is to promote peace, to deter aggression, to respond to crises and, if necessary, to fight and win in order to guarantee security and stability throughout the Asia-Pacific region.

Our U.S. Pacific Command is tasked to plan, coordinate and direct joint operations for peace, crisis or war. We strive to be an active player, partner and beneficiary to promote a secure, prosperous and democratic Asia-Pacific community. The word "partner" is key. As we have moved from a Cold War posture to today, we are determined to work as partners with the other countries in the region.

Our military strategy derives from two fundamental premises on which I believe all can agree. The first is that there is a merge of political, economic and military aspects of security. These aspects are interdependent and are counterproductive to advance separately. Imagine three interlocking rings, if you will. Although the military tends to its ring, the Pacific Command must also operate at the center where the three rings overlap. Our task is to ensure the military focus advances in concert with the economic and political pieces.

To achieve this goal, we work very closely with our State Department and with the foreign ministries in other nations. Frequent calls with ambassadors and their country teams, to discuss regional issues—political and economic as well as military, is a good example of this cooperation.

For example, we met recently in Singapore with the U.S. Chiefs of Mission for Southeast Asia, our ambassadors and consuls general, for the region. We also helped to host the most recent ASEAN Regional Forum Inter-sessional Group meeting on confidence building measures in Honolulu where I met your country's delegates.

Our second premise is that security, especially military security, undergirds the stable conditions that are prerequisite for economic and political prosperity. In the words of Singapore's Senior Minister Lee Kuan Yew, "security is the oxygen that fuels the economic engine of Asia." Military security does not cause economic or political growth, but such cannot occur without it.

Perhaps the best illustration of this premise comes from U.S. Secretary of State Madeleine Albright who said, "Economic systems rest on political order, political order rests on military security." In the context of the current economic crisis, military security must help provide the stable conditions necessary for economic recovery to begin.

Our Strategy

The Pacific Command strategy is simple and consists of three parts: Preventive defense, crisis response, and the ability to fight and win a major conflict. The first part encompasses our normal peacetime interactions in the region— our day-to-day business. The second and third parts are designed to address the destabilizing or unpredicted events that may occur. At all levels, the concept of responsible forward presence is an essential element to our strategy—contributing directly to security and stability throughout the region.

Our concept of preventive defense is similar to the concept of preventive medicine, with which Chinese are quite familiar. The term preventive defense was coined by Dr. William Perry, our former Secretary of Defense, but the concept really dates back to Sun Tzu. In preventive medicine, we try to avoid illness before it occurs. Similarly, in preventive defense we try to reconcile conflict before it occurs.

One component of preventive defense is peacetime engagement. In peacetime we focus on those activities to build relationships which we hope, reassure the region of our commitment to security and stability. Day-to-day these activities take many forms, including meetings, high-level visits, exercises, port calls, and multinational conferences such as those hosted by our Asia-Pacific Center for Security Studies in Honolulu. It is about these activities that we have had discussions with the PLA General Staff in Beijing.

A good example is the recent Asia-Pacific Chiefs of Defense Conference we held in Hawaii. In the first meeting of its kind for our region, the top-ranking military officers from 14 nations gathered to discuss prospects for regional military cooperation as well as to keep our communications clear. Though the PLA was invited, the time was not yet right for participation. All of us hope the time will be right soon.

The second component of preventive defense is training and preparing our forces, along with those of our allies, for the next level of the strategy, crisis response. When specific events threaten to bring about crises or conflict, we try to be prepared to respond with credible and ready military forces to deter violence, reinforce diplomacy, and position critical capabilities should deterrence fail.

One example, both of preventive defense and crisis response, occurred in July 1997 when factional fighting broke out in Cambodia, endangering foreign citizens living there. After a call to the head of the Thai military, General Mongkon Ampornpisit, we were able to deploy a Joint Task Force to Thailand to prepare an evacuation. As it turned out, we didn't use the forces, but they gave our leaders and those of other nations confidence they were ready if needed.

Another example was earlier this year as rising political and economic tensions caused civil unrest and a change of government in Indonesia, many nations conducted precautionary evacuations of their citizens. Had the situation deteriorated further, an amphibious ready group was standing by to complete the evacuation, though this was not necessary. We are aware of your concern with the apparent repulsive treatment of Indonesian Chinese. This is also a great concern to us, and all responsible people, including General Wiranto, the commander of the Indonesian Armed Forces.

The last resort is our ability to fight and win. Should diplomatic efforts fail to deter conflict, we are prepared to fight and win quickly and decisively. We prefer to fight with the support of allies and coalition partners, but we will fight alone if necessary.

The best example of this component of our strategy is the situation on the Korean peninsula where we believe that our ready presence, in concert with the South Koreans and other allies has maintained the peace for 45 years. This visible capacity to fight and win enables us to focus on preventive defense day in and day out.

Our Focus—Key Issues

With that backdrop, let me now review Pacific Command's most important military security goals for the immediate future. There are five . . .

First, we are working steadily to preserve our vital security relationship with Japan. We believe our relationship with Japan, a longtime ally, is the pivotal security relationship in the Pacific and remains a significant factor for regional stability. This alliance is dedicated to the security of Japan and is not directed at any nation. We take seriously concerns about our alliance with Japan and work hard to maintain openness. Japan's significant challenges include stabilizing their leadership transition as well as the continuing impact of the economic crisis in Asia. A more galvanizing issue for Japan is the threat to security posed by the North Korean ballistic missile and potential nuclear programs. While the U.S. and Japan examine options for dealing with this emerging challenge to security in the region, our forward presence in Japan and Korea continue to remain an essential guarantor of stability.

Second, U.S. Pacific Command is laying sound foundations for our growing relationship with China. I'll focus my comments on this topic in just a moment.

Third, we are continuing to help provide a secure environment for a non-cataclysmic reconciliation on the Korean peninsula. The Korean peninsula remains the region's most potentially volatile flashpoint. The recent missile launch and infiltration efforts point to the mercurial decision-making and unpredictable nature of the North Korean regime. While the likelihood of conflict may not be high, the consequences would be severe—so we and our ROK allies must remain prepared. Our immediate objectives for the peninsula—which I think we share with China—include controlling the spread of weapons of mass destruction as well as fostering a border with reduced tensions and more stable interaction between the North and South. In the end, North Korea and South Korea must resolve this issue—one where the PRC and U.S. can have some positive influence.

Fourth, we have been looking at ways to improve our military relationship with India for the future. We work closely on this with U.S. Central Command which has responsibility for Pakistan. India is a nation of vast economic, political and military potential and is an important player in the Asia-Pacific region and in the global community. It is also a nation with which we share a democratic form of government. India's and Pakistan's regrettable decisions to resume nuclear testing was a major setback to stability in South and East Asia. It put on hold our gradually improving military-to-military ties. Our immediate goals are to help reduce those tensions, restrain further missile and nuclear activity, and encourage a substantive India-Pakistan bilateral dialogue.

And fifth, in concert with other branches of our government, we are doing our part in providing security and stability to help our friends in Asia cope with the ongoing economic crisis. The effects of this crisis are now being felt in the United States and demonstrate our growing global interdependence. The bottom line is that continuing economic decline in the region can have a decidedly negative impact on stability. This suggests that all of us must be watchful to keep communications clear and avoid military miscalculation.

With that underpinning on what U.S. Pacific Command is doing, let me now focus the remainder of my remarks on our relationship with China.

China

A secure and stable Asia is a goal that both China and the United States share. Likewise, an open, prosperous and responsible China that assumes a more active role in the region's affairs is also in the interests of the United States. That said, China's size, importance, and growing economic and military power make it the backdrop for discussions we have with all other nations in the region. To allay the concerns of neighboring nations, I recommend China continue to increase its openness in security matters as it prepares to assume this more active role. A good first step towards a more reassuring China is the recently published Defense White Paper. We have differences of opinion concerning the value to regional security of bilateral alliances—this is a good topic for future discussion between us.

Any student of China recognizes that she faces enormous challenges—especially the unique challenges of feeding, clothing, housing, employing and providing energy to 1.3 billion people—these are challenges of a magnitude few other governments can contemplate. We also recognize Taiwan is a core sovereignty issue for the Chinese people. The U.S. is committed to "One-China," as defined in the three joint communiques and the Taiwan Relations Act. It is equally important for the Chinese people to recognize the U.S. will honor its commitment to peaceful resolution of Taiwan issues. We are encouraged by the recent resumption of cross-Strait dialogue during which Wang Daohan so ably represented China. We know that the Taiwan question can only be properly settled by Chinese people on both sides of the Strait, peacefully and over time.

Now, where should our relationship go? U.S.-China relations can take several paths, from partnership to coexistence to competition. Our military and political relationship evolved, from a low point with no communication between our military leaders in March 1996, to where it is today—good and improving at a steady pace. General Zhang Wannian described this relationship as a treasure, not easily won, but of great worth. To move forward at a proper pace—which does not need to be rapid, I offer three suggestions:

As part of the "constructive strategic partnership" called for by our two Presidents, U.S. Pacific Command aims to promote military-to-military ties that bring us closer. When President Jiang Zemin visited Honolulu in 1997, he remarked, "before there can be trust there must first be understanding." So first, we want to develop and increase understanding by moving our military relationship beyond the very senior policy, foreign affairs and protocol channels and into more routine operational channels.

Today, I must pass through several layers of bureaucracy to speak directly with senior PLA officers—it is not an easy process. With other nations in the region, it is a simple process to telephone my colleagues in the military to discuss matters of mutual concern. Our U.S.-China relationship is now robust enough to sustain this type of operational contact.

Second, we want to continue expanding our contacts to bring younger, more-junior American and Chinese officers together. Our experiences with senior PLA officers are rewarding and have benefited both countries. We need younger officers to also have a dialogue for the future. Both sides agree on the benefits of this initiative. We've had mid-grade Chinese officers observe some of our exercises this year and we made more progress when General Zhang Wannian and Secretary of Defense Cohen recently signed an agreement for the exchange of mid-grade officers as students in language, field medicine and command leadership. Now it is time to move forward with these initiatives and others like them.

Finally, in a more general way, our two nations should strive to increase engagement at all levels of society—governmental, non-governmental, business, military, religious and private—again at the proper pace.

Several examples exist of relationships that are sufficiently broad enough that, regardless of the politics at the national level, these other interactions can continue. One example is our relationship with France. For over two centuries our relationship has ranged from politically adversarial to that of strong allies. Whatever the state of the national relationship, our two societies have always been close.

China will choose her own path in determining if the next century is one of conflict or cooperation. Our common goal and interests far outweigh our differences. We remain optimistic that we can forge a relationship with China that will meet our mutual interests and work to the benefit of all nations of the world. It will come only with increased understanding and clear communication.

The Future

Let me conclude by saying that as a Pacific nation, the United States remains committed to the vast and changing Asia-Pacific region for the long-term. Working in step with our political and economic counterparts, U.S. Pacific Command's focus remains on providing military security. Our strategy of Preventive Defense, along with our readiness to respond to crisis or conflict helps ensure the secure conditions that undergird regional stability.

As military professionals, we are "paid pessimists" and are expected to "keep our powder dry." However, this does not prevent us from being optimists about the future of the U.S.-China relationship. We remain convinced that by engaging in dialogue informed by mutual understanding and respect for each other's views, and by maintaining a position of strength we can best contribute to peace, stability, and prosperity in the Asia-Pacific region.

Thank you for your attention. I would like to now start the question and answer period with another Chinese proverb I have recently learned, "Under the right conditions, all things can be discussed." I believe we have the right conditions today so please ask anything you like.

Source: Admiral Joseph W. Prueher, "Asia-Pacific Security and China: A U.S. Pacific Command Perspective," *Vital Speeches* 65 (1 January 1999): 167–70.

166. CLINTON, "WHY WE'RE INVOLVED IN KOSOVO" 1 APRIL 1999

In early 1999, Serbian military clashes with the native residents of Kosovo caused hundreds of thousands of refugees to flee into neighboring Macedonia and Albania. After failing to reach a negotiated halt to the conflict, the United States and NATO began a sustained aerial bombing campaign against Serbian military units stationed in Kosovo.

The echo is pretty bad, isn't it? Well, if I speak louder, is it better or worse? No difference. I'll do the best I can.

First, I'd like to thank Secretary Cohen and General Shelton for their truly outstanding service in our administration at a difficult time. I'd like to thank Admiral Gehman, Admiral Reason, General Pace, General Keck, and the other leaders of all the forces represented here. I thank Secretary Danzig, National Security Advisor Berger, and others who came with me from the White House. Mayor Oberndorf, thank you for welcoming me to Virginia Beach.

I'd like to say a special word of appreciation to the members of Congress who are here—your representatives, Congressman Scott and Sisisky; Senator Levin, our ranking member of the Armed Services Committee; and a special thanks to my long-time friend, Senator Chuck Robb, who is one of the most courageous members of the United States Congress and Virginia is very fortunate to be represented by him.

Let me say to all of you, I came here today primarily to thank two groups of people—our men and women in uniform, and their families, for the service and sacrifice that makes America strong.

I just met a few moments ago with several members of families—spouses and children of members of four different services who are deployed away from here now. They're all over here to my right. And whatever it is you would like to say to me today, I think there's a very good chance they said it. They did a very good job for you, and I'm very proud of them.

I heard about the financial sacrifices and I heard about human sacrifices. I don't think that anyone could say it better than this lady over here with this beautiful baby in the red hat, with the "I miss you, Daddy" sign. I thank you. And this sign, "I love my TR sailor, support our troops."

I wanted to come here today because I want America to know that the sacrifices made by our men and women in uniform are fully mirrored by their families back home, by the opportunities that are missed to be with wives and husbands and children on birthdays and holidays, and just being there for the kids when they're needed at night and in the morning as they go off to school. They are fully felt in terms of the financial sacrifices of the family members left at home to pay the bills and see to the health care and other needs of the children.

And America should know that and should be very, very grateful to all of you. We are grateful and we think all Americans will be grateful as they know what you do.

Let me also say I had a chance to speak just before I came out here with the 510th Fighter Squadron at Aviano Air Base in Italy, part of our Operation Allied Force in Kosovo, to thank them and to hear of their immense pride and determination in their mission.

I know that many, many people here have friends or family members who are working hard in our mission in Kosovo. I know this port is home to 100 ships, not only the powerful battle groups now at sea led by the Enterprise and the Theodore Roosevelt, but also ships in the Adriatic—guided missile destroyers like the Gonzalez; fast-attack submarines like the Norfolk. Yes, you can clap for your ships, that's okay.

I can't name every ship or every unit, but I know that all of you are proud of all of them. Again, let me say, too, a special word of thanks to the family members of those who are deployed in the Kosovo operation now.

And let me say to all of you, we spend a lot of time—perhaps more time than you would think—in the White House, and at the Pentagon, talking about our obligations to the families of our service members. We know that we are asking more and more of you as we have downsized the military, and diversified and increased the number of our operations around the world. We know that the more we ask of you, the greater our responsibilities to you.

We know that we owe you the support, the training, the equipment you need to get the job done. We know we owe you fair pay, decent housing, and other support. Our new defense budget contains not only a substantial pay raise, but increased funding to keep our readiness razor-sharp. It is our solemn obligation to those of you who accept the dangers and hardships of our common security.

Since the Cold War ended, we have asked more and more from our Armed Forces—from the Persian Gulf to Korea, to Central America to Africa—today to stand with our allies in NATO against the unspeakable brutality in Kosovo.

Now, this is not an easy challenge with a simple answer. If it were, it would have been resolved a long time ago. The mission I have asked our Armed Forces to carry out with our NATO allies is a dangerous one, as I have repeatedly said. Danger is something the brave men and women of our country's Armed Forces understand because you live with it every day, even in routine training exercises.

Now, we all know that yesterday three Army infantrymen were seized as they were carrying out a peaceful mission in Macedonia—protecting that country from the violence in neighboring Kosovo. There was absolutely no basis for them to be taken. There is no basis for them to be held. There is certainly no basis for them to be tried. All Americans are concerned about their welfare.

President Milosevic should make no mistake: The United States takes care of its own. And President Milosevic should make no mistake: We will hold him and his government responsible for their safety and for their well-being.

But I ask you also to resolve that we will continue to carry out our mission with determination and resolve.

Over the past few weeks I have been talking with the American people about why we're involved with our NATO allies in Kosovo, and the risks of our mission and why they're justified. It's especially important that I speak to you and, through you, to all men and women in uniform about these matters.

The roots of this conflict lie in the policies of Mr. Milosevic, the dictator of Serbia. For more than 10 years now, he has been using ethnic and religious hatred as a path to personal power and a justification for the ethnic cleansing and murder of innocent civilians. That is what he did first in Bosnia and Croatia, where the United States with our allies did so much to end the war. And that is what he is doing in Kosovo today. That is what he will continue to do to his own people and his neighbors unless we and our allies stand in the way.

For months, we tried and tried and tried every conceivable peaceful alternative. We did everything we could through diplomacy to solve this problem. With diplomacy backed by the threat of NATO force, we forged a cease-fire last October that rescued from cold and hunger hundreds of thousands of people in Kosovo whom he had driven from their homes.

In February, with our allies and with Russia, we proposed a peace agreement that would have given the people of Kosovo the autonomy they were guaranteed under their constitution before Mr. Milosevic came to power, and ended the fighting for good.

Now, the Kosovar leaders, they signed that agreement—even though it didn't give them the independence they said they wanted, and that they had been fighting for. But Mr. Milosevic refused. In fact, while pretending to negotiate for peace, he massed 40,000 troops and hundreds of tanks in and around Kosovo, planning a new campaign of destruction and defiance. He started carrying out that campaign the moment the peace talks ended.

Now the troops and police of the Serbian dictator are rampaging through tiny Kosovo—separating men from their families, executing many of them in cold blood; burning homes—sometimes, we now hear, with people inside; forcing survivors to leave everything behind, confiscating their identity papers, destroying their records so their history and their property is erased forever.

Yesterday, Mr. Milosevic actually said, this problem can only be solved by negotiations. But yesterday, as he said that, his forces continued to hunt down the very Kosovar leaders with whom he was supposed to be negotiating.

Altogether now, more than half a million Kosovars have been pushed from their homes since the conflict began. They are arriving at the borders of the country, shaken by what they have seen and been through. But they also say—as a delegation of Albanian Americans, many of whom have relatives in Kosovo, told me personally in the White House yesterday—that NATO's military action has at least given them some hope that they have not been completely abandoned in their suffering.

Had we not acted, the Serbian offensive would have been carried out with impunity. We are determined that it will carry a very high price, indeed. We also act to prevent a wider war. If you saw my address to the country the other night and the maps that I showed, you know that Kosovo is a very small place. But it sits right at the dividing line of Europe, Asia and the Middle East; the dividing line between Islam and Christianity; close to our Turkish and Greek allies to the south, our new allies, Hungary, Poland and the Czech Republic to the north; surrounded by small and struggling democracies that easily could be overwhelmed by the flood of refugees Mr. Milosevic is creating.

Already, Macedonia is so threatened. Already, Serbian forces have made forays into Albania, which borders Kosovo. If we were to do nothing, eventually our allies and then the United States would be drawn into a larger conflict at far greater risks to our people and far greater costs.

Now, we can't respond to every tragedy in every corner of the world. But just because we can't do everything for everyone doesn't mean that for the sake of consistency we should do nothing for no one.

Remember now, these atrocities are happening at the door step of NATO, which has preserved the security of Europe for 50 years because of the alliance between the United States and our allies. They are happening in violation of specific commitments Mr. Milosevic gave to us, to our NATO allies, to other European countries and to Russia. They are happening to people who embrace peace and promise to lay down their own arms. They put their trust in us, and we can't let them down.

Our objective is to restore the Kosovars to their homes with security and self-government. Our bombing campaign is designed to exact an unacceptably high price for Mr. Milosevic's present policy of repression and ethnic cleansing, and to seriously diminish his military capacity to maintain that policy.

We've been doing this for seven days now—just seven days. Our pilots have performed bravely and well, in the face of dangerous conditions and often abysmal weather. But we must be determined and patient. Remember, the Serbs had 40,000 troops in and around Kosovo, and nearly 300 tanks, when they began this, before the first NATO plane got in the air. They had a sophisticated air-defense system. They also have a problem which has been festering for a decade, thanks to the efforts of Mr. Milosevic to make people hate each other in the former Yugoslavia because they are Muslims instead of Orthodox Christians or Catholics; because they're Albanians instead of Serbians or Croatians, or Bosnian Muslims, or Macedonians, or you have—whatever. It is appalling.

For decades, those people lived in peace with one another. For ten years and more, now, a dictator has sought to make himself powerful by convincing the largest group, the Serbs, that the only way they can amount to anything is to uproot, disrupt, destroy and kill other people who don't have the same means of destruction—no matter what the consequences are to everybody around them; no matter how many innocent children and their parents die; no matter how much it disrupts other countries.

Why? Because they want power, and they want to base it on the kind of ethnic and religious hatred that is bedeviling the whole world today. You can see it in the Middle East, in Northern Ireland. You can see it in the tribal wars in Africa. You can see that it is one of the dominant problems the whole world faces. And this is right in the underbelly of Europe.

We have to decide whether we are going to take a stand with our NATO allies, and whether we are prepared to pay the price of time to make him pay the price of aggression and murder. Are we, in the last year of the 20th century, going to look the other way as entire peoples in Europe are forced to abandon their homelands or die? Are we going to impose a price on that kind of conduct and seek to end it?

Mr. Milosevic often justifies his behavior by talking about the history of the Serbs going back to the 14th century. Well, I value the history of this country, and I value what happened here in the 18th century. But I don't want to take America back to the 18th century. And he acts like he wants to take Serbia back to the 14th century—to 14th century values, 14th century ways of looking at other human beings.

We are on the edge of a new century and a new millennium, where the people in poor countries all over the world, because of technology and the Internet and the spreading of information will have unprecedented opportunities to share prosperity, and to give their kids an education, and have a decent future, if only they will live in peace with the basic human regard for other people—that is absolutely antithetical to everything that Mr. Milosevic has done.

So I ask you—you say, what has this got to do with America? Remember, we fought two world wars in Europe. Remember that the unity, the freedom, the prosperity, the peace of Europe is important to the future of the children in this room today. That is, in the end, what this is about.

We're not doing this on our own. We could not have undertaken it on our own. This is something we're doing with our NATO allies. They're up there in the air, too. If there's a peace agreement, they've agreed to provide 85 percent of the troops on the ground to help to monitor the peace agreement and protect all the ethnic groups, including the Serbs.

This is something we are doing to try to avoid in the 21st century the kind of widespread war, large American casualties and heartbreak that we saw too much of in the century we are about to leave.

So this is not just about a small peace of the Balkans. But let me ask you something. When we are moved by the plight of three servicemen, when we stay up half the night hoping that our rescue teams find that fine pilot who went down when his plane was hit, when we see a sign that says, "I love my TR sailor" or "I miss my Daddy," we remember that all political and military decisions ultimately have a human component that is highly individualized.

Think how you would feel if you were part of the half million people who lived peaceably in a place, just wanted to be let alone to practice your religion and educate your children and do your work—if people came to your house and your village and said, pack up your belongings and go; we're going to burn your property records, we're going to burn your identity records. And if your husband or your son is of military service age, we might take them out behind the barn and shoot them dead—just because you have a different religion, just because you have a different ethnic background. Is that really what we want the 21st century to be about for our children?

Now, that is what is at stake here. We cannot do everything in the world, but we must do what we can. We can never forget the Holocaust, the genocide, the carnage of the 20th century. We don't want the new century to bring us the same nightmares in a different guise.

We also want to say again how proud the United States is that each of NATO's 19 members is supporting the mission in Kosovo in some way—France and Germany, Turkey and Greece, Poland and Hungary, the Czech Republic, Britain, Canada—all the others. And this is also important.

Let me finally say—I'd like to read you something. Near the end of the second world war, President Roosevelt prepared a speech to give at a holiday honoring Virginia's famous son, Thomas Jefferson. He never got to give the speech. But it still speaks to us, his last words. And to those of you who wear the uniform of our nation and to those of you who are part of the families of our uniformed service members, I ask you to heed these words.

After the long war was almost drawing to a close, these were Franklin Roosevelt's last words that he never got to deliver: "We as Americans do not choose to deny our responsibilities. Nor do we intend to abandon our determination that within the lives of our children and our children's children, there will not be a third world war. We seek peace, enduring peace. More than an end to war, we want an end to the beginnings of all wars."

That is what we are trying to achieve in Kosovo. That is what many of you in this room, perhaps, and your colleagues, did achieve in Bosnia. We want to end a war that has begun in Europe, and prevent a larger war. And we want to alleviate the burdens and the killing of defenseless people. Let us heed President Roosevelt's last words.

Let me say again, for those of you who serve and for those of you who serve as family members, and who sacrifice as wives and husbands and children: I thank you for your service and your sacrifice, and America thanks you.

God bless you.

Source: William J. Clinton, "Why We're Involved in Kosovo: It Is Time to Stop Ethnic and Religious Hatred," *Vital Speeches* 65 (15 April 1999): 386–88.

---

167. CLINTON, "A PATHWAY BACK TO NEGOTIATIONS" 17 OCTOBER 2000

In late September 2000, the Middle East peace process degenerated into an unmitigated spasm of violence and recrimination. As Israelis and Palestinians fought pitched street battles in the Gaza Strip and the West Bank, and the death toll passed one hundred, leaders met hastily in October in an attempt to restore some semblance of order in the contested territories.

Even as we meet, the situation in the territories remains tense. Yesterday again was violent. This is a reminder of the urgency of breaking the cycle of violence. I believe we have made real progress today. Repairing the damage will take time and great effort by all of us. When we leave here today, we will have to work hard to consolidate what we have agreed.

Our primary objective has been to end the current violence so we can begin again to resume our efforts toward peace. The leaders have agreed on three basic objectives and steps to realize them.

They have agreed to issue public statements unequivocally calling for an end of violence. They also agreed to take immediate, concrete measures to end the current confrontation, eliminate points of friction, ensure an end to violence and incitement, maintain calm and prevent recurrence of recent events. To accomplish this, both sides will act immediately to return the situation to that which existed prior to the current crisis in areas such as restoring law and order, redeployment of forces, eliminating points of friction, enhancing security cooperation and ending the closure and opening the Gaza airport. The United States will facilitate security cooperation between the parties as needed.

Second, the United States will develop with the Israelis and the Palestinians, as well as in consultation with the United Nations secretary general, a committee of fact finding on the events of the past several weeks and how to prevent their recurrence. The committee's report will be shared by the U.S. president with the U.N. secretary general and the parties prior to publication. The final report will be submitted under the auspices of the U.S. president for publication.

Third, if we are to address the underlying roots of the Israeli-Palestinian conflict, there must be a pathway back to negotiations and a resumption of efforts to reach a permanent status agreement based on the U.N. Security Council Resolutions 242 and 338 and subsequent understandings. Toward this end, the leaders have agreed that the United States would consult with the parties within the next two weeks about how to move forward.

We have made important commitments here today against a backdrop of tragedy and crisis. We should have no illusions about the difficulties ahead. If we are going to rebuild confidence and trust, we must all do our part, avoiding recrimination and moving forward. I am counting on each of us to do everything we possibly can in the critical period ahead.

Source: "In President's Words: 'A Pathway Back to Negotiations,' " *New York Times* (18 October 2000), A12.

Selected Bibliography

ARCHIVAL RESOURCES

The Library of Congress
Manuscript Division
Washington, DC 20540-4680
(202) 707-5387
http://www.lcweb.loc.gov/rr/mss/

Papers of George Washington, 1732–1799
Papers of Thomas Jefferson, 1743–1826
Papers of James Madison, 1751–1836
Papers of James Monroe, 1758–1831
Papers of Andrew Jackson, 1767–1845
Papers of Martin Van Buren, 1782–1862
Papers of William Henry Harrison, 1773–1841
Papers of John Tyler, 1790–1862
Papers of James K. Polk, 1795–1849
Papers of Zachary Taylor, 1784–1850
Papers of Millard Fillmore, 1800–1874
Papers of Franklin Pierce, 1804–1869
Papers of James Buchanan, 1791–1868
Papers of Abraham Lincoln, 1809–1865
Papers of Andrew Johnson, 1808–1875
Papers of Ulysses S. Grant, 1822–1885
Papers of Rutherford B. Hayes, 1822–1893
Papers of James A. Garfield, 1831–1881
Papers of Chester A. Arthur, 1829–1886
Papers of Grover Cleveland, 1837–1908
Papers of Benjamin Harrison, 1833–1901
Papers of William F. McKinley, 1843–1901
Papers of Theodore Roosevelt, 1858–1919

Papers of William Howard Taft, 1857–1930
Papers of Woodrow Wilson, 1856–1924
Papers of Warren G. Harding, 1865–1923
Papers of Calvin Coolidge, 1872–1933

The National Archives and Records Administration
8601 Adelphi Road
College Park, MD 20740-6001
(301) 713-6950
http://www.nara.gov

Records Group 59, General Records of the Department of State
Records Group 218, Records of the U.S. Joint Chiefs of Staff
Records Group 220, Records of Temporary Committees, Commissions, and Boards
Records Group 273, Records of the National Security Council
Records Group 286, Records of the Agency for International Development
Records Group 330, Records of the Office of the Secretary of Defense
Records Group 333, Records of International Military Agencies
Records Group 338, Records of U.S. Army Commands
Records Group 469, Records of U.S. Foreign Assistance Agencies

PRESIDENTIAL ARCHIVES AND COLLECTIONS

John Adams Papers
Massachusetts Historical Society
1154 Boylston Street
Boston, MA 02215-3695
(617) 536-1608
http://www.masshist.org

James Buchanan Papers
Historical Society of Pennsylvania
1300 Locust Street
Philadelphia, PA 19107-5661
(215) 732-6200
http://www.hsp.org

Rutherford B. Hayes Presidential Center
Spiegel Grove
Fremont, OH 43420-2797
(800) 998-7737
http://www.rbhayes.org

Herbert Hoover Library
210 Parkside Drive
P.O. Box 488
West Branch, IA 52358-0488
(319) 643-5301
http://www.library@hoover.nara.gov

William R. Castle Papers
Wayne Cole Papers
Hugh Gibson Papers
John F. Meck Papers
Gerald P. Nye Papers
Charles C. Tansill Papers
Francis White Papers
Hugh R. Wilson Papers
Robert E. Wood Papers

Franklin D. Roosevelt Library
511 Albany Post Road
Hyde Park, NY 12538-1999
(914) 229-8114
http://www.fdrlibrary.marist.edu

Harry S. Truman Library
500 West U.S. Highway 24
Independence, MO 64050-1798
(816) 833-1400
http://www.trumanlibrary.org

President's Secretary's Files, 1945–1953
Confidential File, 1938 (1945)–1953
Korean War File, 1947–1952
National Security Council Files, 1947–1953

Dean Acheson Papers
Edwin G. Arnold Papers
Albert H. Huntington Papers
Edgar A. Johnson Papers
Robert A. Lovett Papers
Edward R. Stettinius Papers
Henry L. Stimson Papers
Stuart Symington Papers

Dwight D. Eisenhower Presidential Library
200 Southeast Fourth Street
Abilene, KS 67410-2900
(785) 263-4751
http://www.library@eisenhower.nara.gov

Dwight D. Eisenhower, Papers as President, 1953–1961 (Ann Whitman File)
White House Office File
    National Security Council Staff, Papers, 1948–1961
    Office of the Special Assistant for National Security Affairs, 1952–1961
    Office of the Staff Secretary, 1952–1961

John M. Cabot Papers
Joseph Dodge Papers
John Foster Dulles Papers
Gordon Gray Papers

C. D. Jackson Papers
Walter Bedell Smith Papers
Samuel C. Waugh Papers

The John F. Kennedy Library
Columbia Point
Boston, MA 02125-3398
(617) 929-4500
http://www.library@kennedy.nara.gov

White House Central Files
President's Office Files
National Security Files

Robert Amory Papers
George Ball Papers
Edwin R. Bayley Papers
Jack N. Behrman Papers
David E. Bell Papers
McGeorge Bundy Papers
John M. Cabot Papers
Gordon Chase Papers
J. Harlan Cleveland Papers
Douglas C. Dillon Papers
Robert H. Estabrook Papers
John Kenneth Galbraith Papers
Lincoln Gordon Papers
Walter W. Heller Papers
Roger Hilsman Papers
Edwin M. Martin Papers
Max F. Millikan Papers
Teodoro Moscoso Papers
Dean Rusk Papers
Arthur M. Schlesinger Papers
James C. Thompson Papers

The Lyndon B. Johnson Library
2313 Red River Street
Austin, TX 78705-5702
(512) 916-5137
http://www.library@johnson.nara.gov

White House Central Files, 1963–1969
White House Central Files, Confidential File
National Security File, 1963–1969
Office Files of White House Aids

Gardener Ackley Papers
George Ball Papers
McGeorge Bundy Papers
Clark Clifford Papers
H. Barefoot Davis Papers

W. True Davis Papers
Morton H. Halperin Papers
U. Alexis Johnson Papers
William J. Jorden Papers
Robert S. McNamara Papers
Leonard H. Marks Papers
Covey T. Oliver Papers
Walt W. Rostow Papers
Anthony M. Solomon Papers
Paul C. Warnke Papers

Richard M. Nixon Presidential Materials Collection
National Archives and Records Administration
8601 Adelphi Road
Room 1320
College Park, MD 20740-6001
(301) 713-6950
http://www.nixon@arch2.nara.gov

White House Central File
    Subject Files
    Staff Member and Office Files
White House Special Files
    Staff Member and Office Files
    Subject Files
National Security Council Files

Gerald R. Ford Library
1000 Beal Avenue
Ann Arbor, MI 48109-2114
(734) 741-2218
http://www.ford.utexas.edu

White House Central Files, 1974–1977
    Subject File, 1974–1977
    Name File, 1974–1977
National Security Advisor. National Security Decision Memoranda and National Se-
    curity Study Memoranda
National Security Council Staff "Convenience" Files: Communications with the U.S.
    Embassy in Saigon
Presidential Handwriting File
Presidential Speeches: Reading Copies
U.S. Council of Economic Advisors Records

Philip W. Buchan Files
Arthur F. Burns Papers
John G. Carlson Files
James E. Connors Files
David R. Gergen Files
Robert A. Goldwin Papers
Robert T. Hartmann Files

Jimmy Carter Library
441 Freedom Parkway
Atlanta, GA 30307-1498
(404) 331-3942
http://www.library@carter.nara.gov

   White House Central File
     Countries
     Federal Government—Organizations
     Foreign Affairs
     International Organizations
     National Security—Defense
   Staff Office Files
     National Security Advisor
     Chief of Staff
   Zbigniew Brzezinski Papers
   Warren Christopher Papers

Ronald Reagan Presidential Library
40 Presidential Drive
Simi Valley, CA 93065-0699
(800) 410-8354
http://reagan.utexas.edu

   Presidential Records
     White House Office of Records Management File
       Subject File, 1981–1989
     White House Offices
       Administration, National Security Council Office of
       Arms Control Directorate, National Security Council
       Asian Affairs Directorate, National Security Council
       Chief of Staff, White House Office of the Council of Economic Advisors
       Counterterrorism and Narcotics, National Security Council
         Office of Crisis Management Center, National Security Council
       Defense Policy Directorate (including Defense Policy Planning Staff) National
         Security Council
       Defense Programs and Arms Control Directorate, National Security Council
       European and Soviet Affairs Directorate, National Security Council
       Executive Secretary, National Security Council Office of
         Intelligence Directorate, National Security Council
       International Communications and Information Directorate, National Security
         Council
       International Economic Affairs Directorate, National Security Council
       International Programs and Technology Affairs Directorate, National Security
         Council
       Latin American Affairs Directorate, National Security Council
       National Security Affairs Office of the Assistant to the President for Near East
         and South Asia Affairs Directorate, National Security Council

Planning and Evaluation Directorate, National Security Council
Political Affairs Directorate, National Security Council
Space Programs, National Security Council Office of
Non-Presidential Records
   Frank C. Carlucci Papers
   Fred C. Ikle Papers
   John H. McNeil Papers
   Donald T. Regan Papers
   Charles Z. Wick Papers

George Bush Library
1000 George Bush Drive West
College Station, TX 77845-3906
(979) 260-9554
http://www.library@bush.nara.gov

SECONDARY SOURCES

General

Barston, R. P. *Modern Diplomacy*. New York: Longman, 1988.

Boucher, David. *Political Theories of International Relations*. New York: Oxford University Press, 1998.

Challinor, Joan R., and Robert L. Beisner, eds. *Arms at Rest: Peacemaking and Peacekeeping in American History*. New York: Greenwood Press, 1987.

Cohen, Warren I. *The Cambridge History of American Foreign Relations: America in the Age of Soviet Power, 1945–1991*. Vol. 4. New York: Cambridge University Press, 1993.

Combs, Jerald A. *American Diplomatic History: Two Centuries of Changing Interpretations*. Berkeley: University of California Press, 1983.

Craig, Gordon A., and Alexander L. George. *Force and Statecraft: Diplomatic Problems of Our Time*. New York: Oxford University Press, 1990.

Dallek, Robert. *The American Style of Foreign Policy: Cultural Politics and Foreign Affairs*. New York: Oxford University Press, 1983.

Hogan, Michael J., ed. *The Ambiguous Legacy: U.S. Foreign Relations in the "American Century."* New York: Cambridge University Press, 1999.

Hunt, Michael H. *Crises in U.S. Foreign Policy: An International History Reader*. New Haven, CT: Yale University Press, 1996.

Kennan, George F. *American Diplomacy*. Chicago: University of Chicago Press, 1951.

———. *Realities of American Foreign Policy*. Princeton, NJ: Princeton University Press, 1954.

Kennedy, Paul. *The Rise and Fall of the Great Powers: Economic Change and Military Conflict from 1500 to 2000*. New York: Vintage Books, 1989.

Kolko, Gabriel. *The Roots of American Foreign Policy: An Analysis of Power and Purpose*. Boston: Beacon Hill Press, 1969.

Malloy, William. M., ed. *Treaties, Conventions, International Acts, Protocols, and Agreements between the United States of America and Other Powers, 1776–1909*. 2 vols. Washington, DC: Government Printing Office, 1910.

————. *Treaties, Conventions, International Acts, Protocols, and Agreements between the United States of America and Other Powers, 1776–1937.* 4 vols. New York: Greenwood Press, 1968.

————. *Treaties, Conventions, International Acts, Protocols, and Agreements between the United States of American and Other Powers, 1910–1923.* Vol. 3. Washington, DC: Government Printing Office, 1923.

————. *Treaties, Conventions, International Acts, Protocols, and Agreements between the United States of America and Other Powers, 1923–1937.* Vol. 4. Washington, DC: Government Printing Office, 1938.

Martel, Gordon, ed. *American Foreign Relations Reconsidered, 1890–1993.* New York: Routledge, 1994.

Miller, Hunter, ed. *Treaties and Other International Acts of the United States of America.* 5 vols. Washington, DC: Government Printing Office, 1931–1937.

Mommsen, Wolfgang. *Theories of Imperialism.* Chicago: University of Chicago Press, 1977.

Niebuhr, Reinhold. *Christian Realism and Political Problems.* New York: Charles Scribner's Sons, 1953.

Ninkovich, Frank. *The Wilsonian Century: U.S. Foreign Policy since 1900.* Chicago: University of Chicago Press, 1999.

Onuf, Peter, and Nicholas Onuf. *Federal Union, Modern World: The Law of Nations in an Age of Revolutions, 1776–1814.* Madison, WI: Madison House Publishers, 1993.

Perkins, Bradford, ed. *The Cambridge History of American Foreign Relations: The Creation of a Republican Empire.* Vol. 1. New York: Cambridge University Press, 1993.

Polanyi, Karl. *The Great Transformation: The Political and Economic Origins of Our Time.* Boston: Beacon Press, 1957.

Richardson, James D., ed. *Compilation of the Messages and Papers of the Presidents.* 17 vols. New York: Bureau of National Literature, 1897–1917.

Rosenman, Samuel I., ed. *The Public Papers and Addresses of Franklin D. Roosevelt.* 13 vols. New York: Russell & Russell, 1969.

Schick, Frank L., Renee Schick, and Mark Carroll, eds. *Records of the Presidency: Presidential Papers and Libraries from Washington to Reagan.* New York: Oryx Press, 1989.

Schurman, Franz. *The Logic of World Power: An Inquiry into the Origins, Currents, and Contradictions of World Politics.* New York: Pantheon Books, 1974.

Valone, Stephen J. *Two Centuries of U.S. Foreign Policy: The Documentary Record.* Westport, CT: Praeger, 1995.

Williams, William Appleman. *The Tragedy of American Diplomacy.* New York: Dell Publishing, 1962.

The Colonial Era

Bailyn, Bernard. "The Central Themes of the American Revolution: An Interpretation." In *Essays on the American Revolution,* ed. Stephen G. Kurtz and James H. Hutson, 3–31. New York: W. W. Norton, 1973.

Bemis, Samuel Flagg. *The Diplomacy of the American Revolution.* Bloomington: Indiana University Press, 1957.

Dull, Jonathan R. *A Diplomatic History of the American Revolution.* New Haven, CT: Yale University Press, 1985.

Gilbert, Felix. *To the Farewell Address: Ideas of Early American Foreign Policy.* Princeton, NJ: Princeton University Press, 1961.

Greene, Jack P., and J. R. Poole. *Colonial British America: Essays in the New History of the Early Modern Era.* Baltimore: Johns Hopkins University Press, 1984.

Higginbotham, Don. *The War of American Independence: Military Attitudes, Policies, and Practice.* Boston: Northeastern University Press, 1983.

Hutson, James H. *John Adams and the Diplomacy of the American Revolution.* Lexington: University Press of Kentucky, 1980.

Kaplan, Lawrence S. *Colonies into Nation: American Diplomacy, 1763–1801.* New York: Macmillan, 1972.

McDonald, Forrest. *Novus Ordo Seclorum: The Intellectual Origins of the Constitution.* Lawrence: University Press of Kansas, 1985.

Meier, Pauline. *From Resistance to Revolution: Colonial Radicals and the Development of American Opposition to Britain, 1765–1776.* New York: Vintage Books, 1974.

Mintz, Max M. *Gouverneur Morris and the American Revolution.* Norman: University of Oklahoma Press, 1970.

Morgan, Ted. *Wilderness at Dawn: The Setting of the North American Continent.* New York: Simon & Schuster, 1993.

Parsons, Lynn Hudson. *John Quincy Adams.* Madison, WI: Madison House Publishers, 1998.

Rosenfeld, Richard N. *American Aurora: A Democratic-Republic Returns.* New York: St. Martin's Press, 1997.

Schaeper, Thomas J. *France and America in the Revolutionary Era: The Life of Jacques-Donatien Leray de Chaumont, 1725–1803.* Providence, RI: Berghahn Books, 1995.

Stourzh, Gerald. *Benjamin Franklin and American Foreign Policy.* Chicago: University of Chicago Press, 1969.

The Early Republic

Ambrose, Stephen E. *Undaunted Courage: Meriwether Lewis, Thomas Jefferson, and the Opening of the American West.* New York: Simon & Schuster, 1996.

Bauer, K. Jack. *The Mexican War, 1846–1848.* Lincoln: University of Nebraska Press, 1974.

Coffman, Edward M. *The Old Army: A Portrait of the American Army in Peacetime, 1784–1898.* New York: Oxford University Press, 1986.

Field, James A. *America and the Mediterranean World.* Princeton, NJ: Princeton University Press, 1969.

Goetzman, William H. *When the Eagle Screamed: The Romantic Horizon in American Diplomacy, 1800–1860.* New York: Wiley, 1966.

Graebner, Norman A. *Traditions and Values: American Diplomacy, 1790–1865.* New York: University Press of America, 1985.

Johnson, John J. *A Hemisphere Apart: The Foundations of United States Policy toward Latin America.* Baltimore: Johns Hopkins University Press, 1990.

Lewis, James E. *The American Union and the Problem of Neighborhood: The United*

States and the Collapse of the Spanish Empire, 1783–1829. Chapel Hill: University of North Carolina Press, 1998.

Mahin, Dean B. *Olive Branch and Sword: The United States and Mexico, 1845–1848.* Jefferson, NC: McFarland Publishers, 1997.

May, Ernest R. *The Making of the Monroe Doctrine.* Cambridge, MA: Belknap Press, 1975.

Merk, Frederick. *Manifest Destiny and Mission in American History: A Reinterpretation.* New York: Knopf, 1963.

———. *The Monroe Doctrine and American Expansion, 1843–1849.* New York: Knopf, 1966.

Pappas, Paul C. *The United States and the Greek War for Independence, 1821–1828.* New York: Columbia University Press, 1985.

Shurbutt, Thomas R. *United States–Latin American Relations, 1800–1850: The Formative Generations.* Tuscaloosa: University of Alabama Press, 1991.

Varg, Paul A. *New England and Foreign Relations, 1789–1850.* Hanover, NH: University Press of New England, 1983.

Weeks, William Earl. *Building the Continental Empire: American Expansion from the Revolution to the Civil War.* Chicago: Ivan R. Dee, 1996.

The Civil War

Berwanger, Eugene H. *The British Foreign Service and the American Civil War.* Lexington: University Press of Kentucky, 1994.

Crook, D. P. *Diplomacy during the American Civil War.* New York: Wiley, 1975.

Donald, David Herbert. *Lincoln.* London: Jonathan Cape, 1995.

Ferris, Norman B. *Desperate Diplomacy: William H. Seward's Foreign Policy, 1861.* Knoxville: University of Tennessee Press, 1976.

Hanna, Alfred J., and Kathryn Abbey Hanna. *Napoleon III and Mexico: American Triumph over Monarchy.* Chapel Hill: University of North Carolina Press, 1971.

Jenkins, Brian. *Britain and the War for Union.* London: McGill-Queen's University Press, 1974.

Jones, Howard. *Union in Peril: The Crisis over British Intervention in the Civil War.* Chapel Hill: University of North Carolina Press, 1992.

———. *Abraham Lincoln and a New Birth of Freedom: The Union and Slavery in the Diplomacy of the Civil War.* Lincoln: University of Nebraska Press, 1999.

Mahin, Dean B. *One War at a Time: The International Dimensions of the American Civil War.* Washington, DC: Brassey's, 1999.

May, Robert E., ed. *The Union, the Confederacy, and the Atlantic Rim.* West Lafayette, IN: Purdue University Press, 1995.

The Gilded Age

Anderson, David L. *Imperialism and Idealism: American Diplomats in China, 1861–1898.* Bloomington, IN: Indiana University Press, 1985.

Armstrong, William M. *E. L. Godkin and American Foreign Policy, 1865–1900.* New York: Bookman, 1957.

Calhoun, Charles W. *Gilded Age Cato: The Life of Walter Q. Gresham.* Lexington, KY: University Press of Kentucky, 1988.

Crapol, Edward P. *James G. Blaine: Architect of Empire.* Wilmington, DE: Scholarly Resources, 2000.

Fry, Joseph A. *Henry S. Sanford: Diplomacy and Business in Nineteenth-Century America.* Reno, NV: University of Nevada Press, 1982.

Goldberg, Joyce S. *The "Baltimore" Affair.* Lincoln, NE: University of Nebraska Press, 1986.

Holbo, Paul Sothe. *Tarnished Expansion: The Alaska Scandal, The Press, and Congress, 1867–1871.* Knoxville, TN: University of Tennessee Press, 1983.

McFeeley, William S. *Grant: A Biography.* New York: W. W. Norton, 1982.

Nelson, William J. *Almost a Territory: America's Attempt to Annex the Dominican Republic.* Newark, DE: University of Delaware Press, 1990.

Paolino, Ernest N. *The Foundations of American Empire: William Henry Seward and U.S. Foreign Policy.* Ithaca, NY: Cornell University Press, 1973.

Plesur, Milton. *America's Outward Thrust: Approaches to Foreign Affairs, 1865–1890.* DeKalb, IL: Northern Illinois University Press, 1971.

Schoonover, Thomas D. *Dollars Over Dominion: The Triumph of Liberalism in Mexican-United States Relations, 1861–1867.* Baton Rouge, LA: Louisiana State University Press, 1978.

Taylor, John M. *William Henry Seward: Lincoln's Right Hand.* New York: HarperCollins Publishers, 1991.

Early Empire

Beal, Howard K. *Theodore Roosevelt and the Rise of America to World Power.* Baltimore: Johns Hopkins University Press, 1956.

Beisner, Robert L. *Twelve against Empire: The Anti-Imperialists, 1898–1900.* New York: McGraw-Hill, 1968.

———. *From the Old Diplomacy to the New, 1865–1900.* Arlington Heights, IL: Harlan Davidson, 1986.

Cohen, Warren I. *America's Response to China.* New York: Columbia University Press, 1990.

Collin, Richard H. *Theodore Roosevelt, Culture, Diplomacy, and Expansionism.* Baton Rouge: Louisiana State University Press, 1985.

———. *Theodore Roosevelt's Caribbean: The Panama Canal, the Monroe Doctrine, and the Latin American Context.* Baton Rouge: Louisiania State University Press, 1991.

Drake, Frederick C. *The Empire of the Seas.* Honolulu: University of Hawaii Press, 1984.

Dudden, Arthur Power. *The American Pacific: From the Old China Trade to the Present.* New York: Oxford University Press, 1992.

Foner, Philip S. *The Spanish-Cuban-American War and the Birth of American Imperialism.* New York: Monthly Press Review, 1972.

Gould, Lewis L. *The Spanish-American War and President McKinley.* Lawrence: University Press of Kansas, 1983.

Herman, Sondra. *Eleven against War: Studies in American Internationalist Thought, 1898–1921.* Stanford, CA: Hoover Institution Press, 1969.

Herrick, Walter. *The American Naval Revolution*. Baton Rouge: Louisiana State University Press, 1966.

Hunt, Michael. *The Making of a Special Relationship: The United States and China to 1914*. New York: Columbia University Press, 1983.

Iriye, Akira. *Across the Pacific*. New York: Harcourt, Brace & World, 1967.

LaFeber, Walter. *The New Empire: An Interpretation of American Expansion, 1860–1898*. Ithaca, NY: Cornell University Press, 1963.

———. *The Panama Canal: The Crisis in Historical Perspective*. New York: Oxford University Press, 1978.

May, Ernest R. *Imperial Democracy: The Emergence of America as a Great Power*. New York: Harcourt, Brace & World, 1961.

Morgan, H. W. *America's Road to Empire: The War with Spain and Overseas Expansion*. New York: Wiley, 1975.

Morris, Edmund. *The Rise of Theodore Roosevelt*. New York: Ballantine Books, 1979.

Munro, Dana. *Intervention and Dollar Diplomacy in the Caribbean, 1900–1921*. Princeton, NJ: Princeton University Press, 1964.

Schoonover, Thomas. *The United States in Central America, 1860–1911*. Durham, NC: Duke University Press, 1991.

Stanley, Peter W. *A Nation in the Making: The Philippines and the United States, 1899–1921*. Cambridge: Harvard University Press, 1974.

Trask, David F. *The War with Spain in 1898*. New York: Macmillian, 1981.

Turk, Richard W. *The Ambiguous Relationship: Theodore Roosevelt and Alfred Thayer Mahan*. New York: Greenwood Press, 1987.

Wrobel, David M., and Michael C. Steiner, eds. *Many Wests: Place, Culture, and Regional Identity*. Lawrence: University Press of Kansas, 1997.

The First World War

Ambrosius, Lloyd E. *Wilsonian Statecraft: Theory and Practice of Liberal Internationalism during World War I*. Wilmington, DE: SR Books, 1991.

———. *Woodrow Wilson and the American Diplomatic Tradition: The Treaty Fight in Perspective*. New York: Cambridge University Press, 1987.

Burk, Katherine. *Britain, America, and the Sinews of War, 1914–1918*. Boston: Allen Unwin, 1985.

Calhoun, Frederick S. *Power and Principle: Armed Intervention in Wilsonian Foreign Policy*. Kent, OH: Kent State University Press, 1986.

Cohen, Warren I. *The American Revisionists: The Lessons of Intervention in World War I*. Chicago: University of Chicago Press, 1967.

Cooper, John M. *The Warrior and the Priest: Woodrow Wilson and Theodore Roosevelt*. Cambridge: Harvard University Press, 1983.

Ferrell, Robert H. *Woodrow Wilson and World War I*. New York: Harper & Row, 1985.

Gardener, Lloyd C. *Safe for Democracy: Anglo-American Response to Revolution, 1913–1923*. New York: Oxford University Press, 1984.

Gilderhus, Mark T. *Pan American Vision: Woodrow Wilson in the Western Hemisphere, 1913–1921*. Tucson: University of Arizona Press, 1986.

Healy, David. *Gunboat Diplomacy in the Wilsonian Era: The U.S. Navy in Haiti, 1915–1916*. Madison: University of Wisconsin Press, 1976.

Heater, Derek B. *National Self-Determination: Woodrow Wilson and His Legacy.* New York: St. Martin's Press, 1994.

Jonas, Manfred. *The United States and Germany.* Ithaca, NY: Cornell University Press, 1984.

Katz, Friedrich. *The Secret War in Mexico: Europe, the United States, and the Mexican Revolution.* Chicago: University of Chicago Press, 1981.

Kennedy, David. *Over Here: The First World War and American Society.* New York: Oxford University Press, 1980.

Knock, Thomas J. *To End All Wars: Woodrow Wilson and the Quest for a New World Order.* New York: Oxford University Press, 1992.

Levin, N. Gordon. *Woodrow Wilson and World Politics: America's Response to War and Revolution.* New York: Oxford University Press, 1968.

Margulies, Herbert F. *The Mild Reservationists and the League of Nations Controversy in the Senate.* Columbia: University of Missouri Press, 1989.

May, Ernest. *The World War and American Isolation.* Cambridge: Harvard University Press, 1959.

Salzman, Neil V. *Reform and Revolution: The Life and Times of Raymond Robins.* Kent, OH: Kent State University Press, 1991.

Scholes, Walter, and Marie Scholes. *Foreign Policies of the Taft Administration.* Columbia: University of Missouri Press, 1970.

Smith, Daniel M. *The Great Departure: The United States and World War I, 1914–1920.* New York: Wiley, 1965.

Stevenson, David. *The First World War and International Politics.* New York: Oxford University Press, 1988.

Walworth, Arthur. *Wilson and the Peacemakers: American Diplomacy at the Paris Peace Conference.* New York: W. W. Norton, 1986.

The Interwar Period

Castigliola, Frank. *Awkward Dominion: American Political, Economic, and Cultural Relations with Europe, 1919–1933.* Ithaca, NY: Cornell University Press, 1984.

Cohen, Warren I. *Empire without Tears: American Foreign Relations, 1921–1933.* Philadelphia: Temple University Press, 1987.

Dallek, Robert. *Franklin D. Roosevelt and American Foreign Policy.* New York: Oxford University Press, 1979.

Diggins, John P. *Mussolini and Fascism: The Views from America.* Princeton, NJ: Princeton University Press, 1972.

Dingman, Roger. *Power in the Pacific: The Origins of Naval Arms Limitations, 1914–1922.* Chicago: University of Chicago Press, 1976.

Divine, Robert A. *The Illusion of Neutrality.* Chicago: University of Chicago Press, 1962.

Doenecke, Justus D., ed. *The Diplomacy of Frustration: The Manchurian Crisis of 1931–1933 as Revealed in the Papers of Stanley K. Hornbeck.* Stanford, CA: Hoover Institution Press, 1981.

Ferrell, Robert H. *American Diplomacy in the Great Depression: Hoover-Stimson Foreign Policy, 1929–1933.* Hamden, CT: Archon Books, 1969.

Gellman, Irwin F. *Good Neighbor Diplomacy: United States Policy in Latin America, 1933–1945.* Baltimore: Johns Hopkins University Press, 1979.

Heinrichs, Waldo. *Threshold of War: Franklin D. Roosevelt and American Entry into World War II*. New York: Oxford University Press, 1988.

Hoff Wilson, Joan. *American Business and Foreign Policy, 1920–1933*. Lexington: University Press of Kentucky, 1971.

Iriye, Akira. *After Imperialism: The Search for a New Order in the Far East, 1921–1933*. New York: Atheneum, 1969.

Jonas, Manfred. *Isolationism in America*. New York: Cornell University Press, 1966.

Langley, Lester D. *The United States and the Caribbean, 1900–1970*. Athens: University of Georgia Press, 1980.

Leffler, Melvin. *The Elusive Quest: America's Pursuit of European Stability and French Security, 1919–1933*. Chapel Hill, NC: University of North Carolina Press, 1979.

Martin, James J. *American Liberalism and World Politics, 1931–1941*. New York: Devin Adair, 1964.

Munro, Dana. *United States and the Caribbean Republics, 1921–1933*. Princeton, NJ: Princeton University Press, 1974.

Murray, Robert K. *The Harding Era*. Minneapolis: University of Minnesota Press, 1969.

Offner, Arnold A. *American Appeasement: United States Foreign Policy and Germany, 1933–1938*. Cambridge, MA: Belknap Press, 1969.

———. *The Origins of the Second World War: American Foreign Policy and World Politics, 1917–1941*. New York: Holt, Rinehart & Winston, 1975.

Pease, Neal. *Poland, the United States, and the Stabilization of Europe 1919–1933*. New York: Oxford University Press, 1986.

Rosenberg, Emily S. *Spreading the American Dream: American Economic and Cultural Expansion, 1890–1945*. New York: Hill & Wang, 1982.

Valone, Stephen J. *"A Policy Calculated to Aid China": The United States and the China Arms Embargo, 1919–1929*. New York: Greenwood Press, 1991.

The Second World War

Buhite, Russell. *Decisions at Yalta*. Wilmington, DE: Scholarly Resources, 1986.

Clemens, Diane Shaver. *Yalta*. New York: Oxford University Press, 1970.

Dallek, Robert. *Franklin D. Roosevelt and American Foreign Policy, 1933–1945*. New York: Oxford University Press, 1981.

Divine, Robert. *Second Chance: The Triumph of Internationalism in America during World War II*. New York: Atheneum, 1967.

Feis, Herbert. *Churchill, Roosevelt, and Stalin: The War They Waged and the Peace They Sought*. Princeton, NJ: Princeton University Press, 1957.

———. *Between War and Peace: The Potsdam Conference*. Princeton, NJ: Princeton University Press, 1960.

Herring, George. *Aid to Russia, 1941–1946*. New York: Columbia University Press, 1973.

Iriye, Akira. *Power and Culture: The Japanese-American War, 1941–1945*. Cambridge: Harvard University Press, 1981.

———. *The Origins of the Second World War in the Pacific*. New York: Longman, 1987.

Kimball, Warren F. *The Most Unsordid Act: Lend-Lease, 1939–1941*. Baltimore, MD: Johns Hopkins University Press, 1969.

———. *The Juggler: Franklin Roosevelt as Wartime Statesman*. Princeton, NJ: Princeton University Press, 1991.

King, F. P. *The New Internationalism: Allied Policy and the European Peace, 1939–1945*. Hamden, CT: Archon Books, 1973.

Marks, Frederick W. *Wind over Sand: The Diplomacy of Franklin Delano Roosevelt*. Athens: University of Georgia Press, 1988.

Prange, Gordon. *At Dawn We Slept: The Untold Story of Pearl Harbor*. New York: McGraw-Hill, 1981.

Sainsbury, Keith. *The Turning Point: Roosevelt, Stalin, Churchill and Chiang Kai-shek, 1943*. Oxford: Oxford University Press, 1985.

Sherwin, Martin. *A World Destroyed*. New York: Vintage Books, 1987.

Thorne, Christopher. *Allies of a Kind*. London: Hamilton, 1978.

Toland, John. *Infamy: Pearl Harbor and Its Aftermath*. Garden City, NY: Doubleday, 1982.

Woods, Randall Bennett. *A Changing of the Guard: Anglo-American Relations, 1941–1946*. Chapel Hill: University of North Carolina Press, 1990.

The Cold War

Acheson, Dean. *Present at the Creation: My Years in the State Department*. New York: W. W. Norton, 1969.

Ambrose, Stephen E. *Rise to Globalism: American Foreign Policy since 1938*. 6th ed. New York: Penguin Books, 1991.

Ameringer, Charles D. *U.S. Foreign Intelligence: The Secret Side of American History*. Lexington, MA: Lexington Books, 1990.

Anderson, David L. *Trapped by Success: The Eisenhower Administration and Vietnam, 1953–1961*. New York: Columbia University Press, 1991.

Berman, Larry. *Planning a Tragedy: The Americanization of the War in Vietnam*. New York: W. W. Norton, 1982.

Beschloss, Michael R. *The Crisis Years: Kennedy and Khrushchev, 1960–1963*. New York: Burlingame Books, 1991.

Bill, James. *The Eagle and the Lion: The Tragedy of American Iranian Relations*. New Haven, CT: Yale University Press, 1988.

Blasier, Cole. *The Hovering Giant*. Pittsburgh: University of Pittsburgh Press, 1976.

Blaufarb, Douglas S. *The Counterinsurgency Era: U.S. Doctrine and Performance, 1950 to the Present*. London: Collier MacMillan Publishers, 1977.

Boyer, Paul. *By the Bomb's Early Light: American Thought and Culture at the Dawn of the Atomic Age*. New York: Pantheon Books, 1985.

Brands, H. William. *Cold Warriors: Eisenhower's Generation and American Foreign Policy*. New York: Columbia University Press, 1988.

———. *The Wages of Globalism: Lyndon Johnson and the Limits of American Power*. New York: Oxford University Press, 1995.

Brzezinski, Zbigniew. *Power and Principle: Memoirs of the National Security Adviser, 1977–1981*. New York: Farrar, Straus & Giroux, 1983.

Bundy, William. *A Tangled Web: The Making of Foreign Policy in the Nixon Presidency*. New York: Hill & Wang, 1998.

Callahan, David. *Dangerous Capabilities: Paul Nitze and the Cold War*. New York: Harper & Row, 1990.

Caridi, Ronald. *The Korean War and American Politics.* Philadelphia: University of Philadelphia Press, 1969.

Cohen, Warren I., and Nancy Bernkopf Tucker, eds. *Lyndon Johnson Confronts the World: American Foreign Policy, 1963–1968.* New York: Cambridge University Press, 1994.

Cray, Ed. *General of the Army: George C. Marshall, Soldier and Statesman.* New York: Simon & Schuster, 1990.

Cullather, Nick. *Secret History: The CIA's Classified Account of Its Operations in Guatemala, 1952–1954.* Stanford, CA: Stanford University Press, 1999.

Cumings, Bruce. *The Origins of the Korean War.* Vol I, *Liberation and the Separate Regimes, 1945–1947.* Princeton, NJ: Princeton University Press, 1981.

———. *The Origins of the Korean War.* Vol. II, *The Roaring of the Cataract, 1947–1950.* Princeton, NJ: Princeton University Press, 1990.

Dallek, Robert. *Flawed Giant: Lyndon Johnson and His Times, 1961–1973.* New York: Oxford University Press, 1998.

Divine, Robert A. *Eisenhower and the Cold War.* New York: Oxford University Press, 1981.

Draper, Theodore. *A Very Thin Line: The Iran-Contra Affairs.* New York: Hill & Wang, 1991.

Eisenhower, Dwight D. *The White House Years.* Garden City, NJ: Doubleday, 1965.

Foot, Rosemary. *A Substitute for Victory: The Politics of Peacemaking at the Korean Armistice Talks.* Ithaca, NY: Cornell University Press, 1990.

Freeland, Richard. *The Truman Doctrine and the Origins of McCarthyism.* New York: Knopf, 1971.

Gaddis, John Lewis. *The United States and the Origins of the Cold War, 1941–1947.* New York: Columbia University Press, 1972.

———. *Russia, the Soviet Union, and the United States.* New York: Knopf, 1978.

———. *Strategies of Containment: A Critical Appraisal of Postwar American National Security Policy.* New York: Oxford University Press, 1982.

———. *The Long Peace: Inquiries into the History of the Cold War.* New York: Oxford University Press, 1987.

Garthoff, Raymond L. *Détente and Confrontation: American-Soviet Relations from Nixon to Reagan.* Washington, DC: Brookings Institution, 1994.

Giglio, James N. *The Presidency of John F. Kennedy.* Lawrence: University Press of Kansas, 1991.

Gimbel, John. *The Origins of the Marshall Plan.* Stanford, CA: Stanford University Press, 1976.

Gleijeses, Piero. *Shattered Hope: The Guatemalan Revolution and the United States, 1944–1954.* Princeton, NJ: Princeton University Press, 1991.

Gormley, James L. *From Potsdam to the Cold War: Big Three Diplomacy, 1945–1947.* Wilmington, DE: SR Books, 1990.

Green, David. *The Containment of Latin America.* Chicago: Quadrangle Books, 1971.

Greene, John Robert. *The Limits of Power: The Nixon and Ford Administrations.* Indianapolis: University Press, 1992.

Harbutt, Frasier J. *The Iron Curtain: Churchill, America, and the Origins of the Cold War.* New York: Oxford University Press, 1986.

Heiss, Mary Ann. *Empire and Nationhood: The United States, Great Britain, and Iranian Oil, 1950–1954.* New York: Columbia University Press, 1997.

Herring, George. *America's Longest War: The United States and Vietnam, 1950–1975.* New York: Wiley, 1979.

Higgins, Trumbull. *The Perfect Failure: Kennedy, Eisenhower, and the Bay of Pigs.* New York: W. W. Norton, 1987.

Hixson, Walter. *George F. Kennan: Cold War Iconoclast.* New York: Columbia University Press, 1989.

Hoff, Joan. *Nixon Reconsidered.* New York: Basic Books, 1994.

Hogan, Michael J. *The Marshall Plan: America, Britain, and the Reconstruction of Western Europe, 1947–1952.* New York: Columbia University Press, 1987.

Immerman, Richard H. *The CIA in Guatemala: The Foreign Policy of Intervention.* Austin: University of Texas Press, 1982.

Iriye, Akira. *The Cold War in Asia.* Englewood Cliffs, NJ: Prentice-Hall, 1974.

Issacson, Walter. *Kissinger.* New York: Simon & Schuster, 1992.

Johnson, Haynes. *Sleepwalking through History: America in the Reagan Years.* New York: W. W. Norton, 1991.

Jones, Howard. *"A New Kind of War": America's Global Strategy and the Truman Doctrine in Greece.* New York: Oxford University Press, 1989.

Kahin, George. *Intervention: How America Became Involved in Vietnam.* New York: Knopf, 1986.

Kaplan, Lawrence S. *The United States and NATO.* Lexington: University of Kentucky Press, 1984.

Kaufman, Burton I. *Trade and Aid: Eisenhower's Foreign Economic Policy, 1953–1961.* Baltimore: Johns Hopkins University Press, 1982.

———. *The Korean War.* Philadelphia: Temple University Press, 1986.

Kearns, Doris. *Lyndon Johnson and the American Dream.* New York: Harper & Row, 1976.

Kissinger, Henry. *Nuclear Weapons and Foreign Policy.* New York: Harper, 1957.

Kolko, Gabriel. *Confronting the Third World: United States Foreign Policy, 1945–1980.* New York: Pantheon Books, 1988.

Kunz, Diane B., ed. *The Diplomacy of the Crucial Decade: American Foreign Relations during the 1960's.* New York: Columbia University Press, 1994.

———. *Guns and Butter: America's Cold War Economic Diplomacy.* New York: Free Press, 1997.

LaFeber, Walter. *America, Russia, and the Cold War, 1945–1984.* New York: Knopf, 1985.

Larson, Deborah. *Origins of Containment.* Princeton, NJ: Princeton University Press, 1985.

Leffler, Melvyn P. *A Preponderance of Power: National Security, the Truman Administration, and the Cold War.* Stanford, CA: Stanford University Press, 1992.

Litwak, Robert. *Détente and the Nixon Doctrine.* New York: Cambridge University Press, 1984.

Mastny, Vojtech. *Russia's Road to the Cold War.* New York: Columbia University Press, 1979.

McCormick, Thomas J. *America's Half-Century: United States Foreign Policy in the Cold War and After.* 2nd ed. Baltimore: Johns Hopkins University Press, 1995.

McCoy, Donald. *The Presidency of Harry S. Truman.* Lawrence: University Press of Kansas, 1984.

McCullough, David. *Truman.* New York: Simon & Schuster, 1992.

Millikan, Max F. *A Proposal: Key to an Effective Foreign Policy.* New York: Harper & Brothers, 1957.

Moffett, George. *The Limits of Victory: The Ratification of the Panama Canal Treaties.* Ithaca, NY: Cornell University Press, 1985.

Morley, Morris. *Imperial State and Revolution: The United States and Cuba, 1952–1987.* New York: Cambridge University Press, 1987.

Mower, A. Glen. *Human Rights and American Foreign Policy: The Carter and Reagan Experience.* New York: Greenwood Press, 1987.

Ninkovich, Frank. *Germany and the United States: The Transformation of the German Question since 1945.* Boston: Twayne Publishers, 1988.

Osgood, Robert. *Limited War: The Challenge to American Strategy.* Chicago: University of Chicago Press, 1957.

———. *NATO: The Entangling Alliance.* Chicago: University of Chicago Press, 1962.

Pach, Chester J. *Arming the Free World: The Origins of the United States Military Assistance Program, 1945–1950.* Chapel Hill: University of North Carolina Press, 1991.

Packenham, Robert. *Liberal America and the Third World: Political Ideas in Foreign Aid and Social Science.* Princeton, NJ: Princeton University Press, 1973.

Patterson, Thomas. *On Every Front: The Making and Unmaking of the Cold War.* New York: W. W. Norton, 1979.

Pollard, Robert A. *Economic Security and the Origins of the Cold War.* New York: Columbia University Press, 1983.

Powaski, Ronald E. *The Cold War: The United States and the Soviet Union, 1917–1991.* New York: Oxford University Press, 1998.

Rabe, Stephen G. *Eisenhower and Latin America.* Chapel Hill: University of North Carolina Press, 1988.

Rostow, Walt W. *The Stages of Economic Growth: A Non-Communist Manifesto.* Cambridge, MA: Cambridge University Press, 1959.

Rotter, Andrew J. *The Path to Vietnam: Origins of the American Commitment to Southeast Asia.* Ithaca, NY: Cornell University Press, 1987.

Rubin, Barry. *Paved with Good Intentions: The American Experience and Iran.* New York: Penguin Books, 1981.

Schaller, Michael. *The United States and China in the Twentieth Century.* New York: Oxford University Press, 1979.

———. *Douglas MacArthur: The Far Eastern General.* New York: Oxford University Press, 1989.

———. *Reckoning with Reagan.* New York: Oxford University Press, 1992.

Schlesinger, Stephen C., and Stephen Kinzer. *Bitter Fruit: The Untold Story of the American Coup in Guatemala.* Garden City, NY: Doubleday, 1982.

Schulzinger, Robert D. *Henry Kissinger.* New York: Columbia University Press, 1989.

Sheehan, Neil. *A Bright Shining Lie: John Paul Vann and America in Vietnam.* New York: Vintage Books, 1988.

Sheehan, Neil, Hedrick Smith, E. W. Kenworthy, and Fox Butterfield, eds. *The Pentagon Papers.* New York: Bantam Books, 1971.

Smith, Gaddis. *Morality, Reason, and Power: American Diplomacy in the Carter Years.* New York: Hill & Wang, 1986.

Stephenson, Anders. *Kennan and the Art of Foreign Policy.* Cambridge: Harvard University Press, 1989.

Talbott, Strobe. *Reagan and Gorbachev*. New York: Vintage Books, 1987.

Thornton, Richard. *The Nixon-Kissinger Years: The Reshaping of American Foreign Policy*. New York: Paragon House, 1989.

Walker, Martin. *The Cold War: A History*. New York: Henry Holt & Co., 1993.

Welch, Richard W. *Response to Revolution: The United States and the Cuban Revolution, 1959–1961*. Chapel Hill: University of North Carolina Press, 1985.

Williams, William Appleman, Thomas J. McCormick, Lloyd Gardner, and Walter La-Feber, eds. *America in Vietnam: A Documentary History*. New York: Anchor Books, 1985.

Young, Marilyn B. *The Vietnam Wars, 1945–1990*. New York: HarperCollins, 1991.

The Post–Cold War Era

Allan, Pierre, and Kjell Goldman, eds. *The End of the Cold War: Evaluating Theories of International Relations*. Boston: Martinus Nijhoff Publishers, 1992.

Apter, David E. *Rethinking Development: Modernization, Dependency, and Postmodern Politics*. London: Sage Publications, 1987.

Atkinson, Rick. *Crusade: The Untold Story of the Persian Gulf War*. New York: Houghton Mifflin, 1993.

Bert, Wayne. *The Reluctant Superpower: United States' Policy in Bosnia, 1991–95*. New York: St. Martin's Press, 1997.

Callahan, David. *Between Two Worlds: Realism, Idealism, and American Foreign Policy after the Cold War*. New York: HarperCollins, 1994.

Chace, James. *The Consequences of the Peace: The New Internationalism and American Foreign Policy*. New York: Oxford University Press, 1992.

Cyr, Arthur I. *After the Cold War: American Foreign Policy, Europe, and Asia*. New York: New York University Press, 1997.

Dumbrell, John. *American Foreign Policy: Carter to Clinton*. Basingstoke, UK: Macmillan, 1997.

Friedman, George, and Meredith Friedman. *The Future of War: Power, Technology, and American World Dominance in the 21st Century*. New York: Crown Publishers, 1996.

Gaddis, John Lewis. *The United States and the End of the Cold War: Implications, Reconsiderations, Provocations*. New York: Oxford University Press, 1992.

———. *We Now Know: Rethinking Cold War History*. New York: Clarendon Press, 1997.

Galbraith, John Kenneth. *The Culture of Contentment*. Boston: Houghton Mifflin, 1992.

Gilbert, Alan. *Must Global Politics Constrain Democracy? Great-Power Realism, Democratic Peace, and Democratic Internationalism*. Princeton, NJ: Princeton University Press, 1999.

Haass, Richard. *The Reluctant Sheriff: The United States after the Cold War*. New York: Council on Foreign Relations Press, 1997.

Hutchings, Robert L., ed. *At the End of the American Century: America's Role in the Post–Cold War World*. Baltimore: Johns Hopkins University Press, 1998.

Iriye, Akira. *Japan and the Wider World: From the Mid-Nineteenth Century to the Present*. New York: Longman, 1997.

Johnson, Robert H. *Improbable Dangers: U.S. Conceptions of Threat in the Cold War and After*. New York: St. Martin's Press, 1994.

Kaufman, Daniel J., David S. Clark, and Kevin P. Sheehan, eds. *U.S. National Security Strategy for the 1990's*. Baltimore: Johns Hopkins University Press, 1991.

Lieber, Robert J., ed. *Eagle Adrift: American Foreign Policy at the End of the Century*. New York: Longman, 1997.

Melanson, Richard A. *American Foreign Policy since the Vietnam War: The Search for Consensus from Nixon to Clinton*. Armonk, NY: Sharpe, 2000.

Natsios, Andrew S. *U.S. Foreign Policy and the Four Horsemen of the Apocalypse: Humanitarian Relief in Complex Emergencies*. Westport, CT: Praeger, 1997.

Nolan, Janne E. *An Elusive Consensus: Nuclear Weapons and American Security after the Cold War*. Washington, DC: Brookings Institutions Press, 1999.

Payne, Richard J. *The Clash with Distant Cultures: Values, Interests, and Force in American Foreign Policy*. Albany: State University of New York Press, 1995.

Robinson, William I. *Promoting Polyarchy: Globalization, U.S. Intervention, and Hegemony*. New York: Cambridge University Press, 1996.

Rothkopf, David J. *The Price of Peace: Emergency Economic Intervention and U.S. Foreign Policy*. Washington, DC: Carnegie Endowment for International Peace, 1998.

Ruggie, John G. *Winning the Peace: America and World Order in the New Era*. New York: Columbia University Press, 1996.

Steel, Ronald. *Temptations of a Superpower*. Cambridge: Harvard University Press, 1996.

Weber, Cynthia. *Faking It: U.S. Hegemony in a "Post Phallic" Era*. Minneapolis: University of Minnesota Press, 1999.

UNPUBLISHED SOURCES

Aguilar, Manuela. "Cultural Diplomacy and Foreign Policy: German-American Relations, 1955–1968." Ph.D. diss., University of Kansas, 1993.

Asselin, Pierre. "The Quest for a Negotiated Settlement of the Indochinese Crisis: North Vietnamese–American Secret Diplomacy, 1968–1973." Ph.D. diss., University of Hawaii, 1997.

Banerjee, Paula. "Neither Antagonist Nor Ally: Indo-American Relations between 1954 and 1968." Ph.D. diss., University of Cincinnati, 1993.

Beck, Michael W. "Big Stick Diplomacy: American Politics and the Panama Canal." Ph.D. diss., University of Houston–Clear Lake, 1997.

Bowditch, Thomas A. "Force and Diplomacy: The American Failure in Lebanon, 1982–1984." Ph.D. diss., University of Virginia, 1999.

Bradley, Mark P. "Imagining Vietnam and America: Vietnamese Radicalism, the United States, and the Cultural Construction of the Cold War, 1919–1950." Ph.D. diss., Harvard University, 1996.

Chang, Junkab. "United States Mediation in South Korean–Japanese Negotiations, 1951–1965: A Case Study in the Limitations of Embassy Diplomacy." Ph.D. diss., Mississippi State University, 1998.

Citino, Nathan J. "Eisenhower, King Sa'ud, and the Politics of Arab Nationalism: United States–Saudi Relations, 1952–1960." Ph.D. diss., Ohio State University, 1999.

Coutinho, Charles G. "A Complex Interregnum: Anglo-America Relations, 1950–1956." Ph.D. diss., New York University, 1997.

Dawson, Peter M. "Liberal Hegemony and Democratic Peace." Ph.D. diss., Rice University, 1996.

Engerman, David C. "America, Russia, and the Romance of Economic Development." Ph.D. diss., University of California–Berkeley, 1998.

Esselstrom, Erik W. " 'Of Such Local Significance:' Culture, Diplomacy and the Tientsin Incident of 1919." Ph.D. diss., University of Oregon, 1996.

Forslund, Catherine M. "Woman of Two Worlds: Anna Chennault and Informal Diplomacy in United States–Asian Relations, 1950–1990." Ph.D. diss., Washington University, 1997.

Franklin, Douglas A. "Aspirations for Greatness: John Foster Dulles, Anthony Eden, and the Conduct of Anglo-American Diplomacy, 1951–1956." Ph.D. diss., University of Kentucky, 1990.

Jwaied, Mahmoud M. "History and Diplomacy: The United States and the Hashimite Kingdom of Jordan, 1947–1960." Ph.D. diss., City University of New York, 1996.

Kilroy, David P. "Extending the American Sphere to West Africa: Dollar Diplomacy in Liberia, 1908–1926." Ph.D. diss., University of Iowa, 1995.

Kim, Ilsu. "The President and International Security: Korea, Containment, and Change." Ph.D. diss., Miami University, 1998.

Kim, Stephen J. "The Carrot and the Leash: Eisenhower, Syngman Rhee, and the Dual Containment of Korea." Ph.D. diss., Yale University, 1999.

Kim, Yungho. "Power and Prestige: Explaining American Intervention in the Korean War." Ph.D. diss., University of Virginia, 1996.

Lowry, Paul T. "The Truman Administration Policy in Palestine, November 1947–December 1952." Ph.D. diss., University of Minnesota, 1997.

MacDonald, Kenneth S. "The Toughest Decision: Rolling the Iron Dice, Historical Analogies, and Decisions to Use Force." Ph.D. diss., University of Southern California, 1997.

Martin, Ian C. "But Not in Shame: American Diplomacy with Japan, 1852–1941." Ph.D. diss., Southern Connecticut State University, 1999.

Mills, Penny B. "Diplomatic Recognition as Coercive Diplomacy: The Inter-American Experience." Ph.D. diss., University of Arizona, 1999.

Mulanax, Richard B. "South Africa and the United States at the End of the 19th Century: The Boer War in American Politics and Diplomacy." Ph.D. diss., Florida State University, 1992.

Paek, Tae Youl. "United States–Japan Influence Relations, 1945–1990: An Analysis of the Politics of Demand, Concession, and Compromise." Ph.D. diss., Southern Illinois University at Carbondale, 1996.

Parides, Panajiotis K. "The Politics of the Atom: Nuclear Diplomacy, National Security, and the Anglo-American Alliance, 1939–1945." Ph.D. diss., State University of New York at Stony Brook, 1997.

Pennacchio, Charles F. "The United States and Berlin, 1945–1949." Ph.D. diss., University of Colorado at Boulder, 1996.

Rice, Michael D. "Nicaragua and the United States: Policy Confrontations and Cultural Interactions, 1893–1933." Ph.D. diss., University of Houston, 1995.

Rigby, David J. "The Combined Chiefs of Staff and Anglo-American Strategic Coordination in World War II." Ph.D. diss., Brandeis University, 1997.

Rorvig, Paul E. "The Controversial Contribution: American Diplomacy, Western European Security, and the Problem of German Rearmament, 1949–1955." Ph.D. diss., University of Missouri–Columbia, 1993.

Russell, Richard L. "George F. Kennan's Realism: A Theory of American Foreign Policy." Ph.D. diss., University of Virginia, 1997.

Sarieddine, Farida Abu Izzeddin. "Reagan's Foreign Policy: A Case Study of Lebanon, 1982–1984." Ph.D. diss., Boston University, 1999.

Schulten, Susan. "The Transformation of World Geography in American Life, 1880–1950." Ph.D. diss., University of Pennsylvania, 1995.

Schwartz, Thomas A. "Missionary Capitalist: Nelson Rockefeller in Venezuela." Ph.D. diss., Vanderbilt University, 1996.

Sharoni, Simona. "United States Foreign Policy and Persuasive Diplomacy: The Lessons of Selected Cases of Diplomatic Persuasion, Compellence, and Deterrence." Master's thesis, The American University, 1995.

Siegel, Katherine A. S. "Loans and Legitimacy: Soviet-American Trade and Diplomacy, 1919–1929." Ph.D. diss., University of California–Santa Barbara, 1991.

Skinner, Kiron K. "The Politics of Weakness and the Politics of Strength: American Use of Security Linkage during the Carter Era." Ph.D. diss., Harvard University, 1994.

Smith, Robert W. "Keeping the Republic: Ideology and the Diplomacy of John Adams, James Madison, and John Quincy Adams." Ph.D. diss., The College of William and Mary, 1997.

Soman, Appu Kuttan. "An Unequal Fight? Nuclear Diplomacy toward the Non-Nuclear: The United States and China, 1950–1958." Ph.D. diss., Vanderbilt University, 1995.

Veeser, Cyrus R. "Remapping the Caribbean: Private Investment and United States Intervention in the Dominican Republic, 1890–1908." Ph.D. diss., Columbia University, 1997.

Walko, John W. "American Rejection of German Reunification in 1952: An Investigation of the United States' Response to the Stalin Note of March 10." Ph.D. diss., Southern Connecticut State University, 1996.

Wood, Molly M. "An American Diplomat's Wife in Mexico: Gender, Politics, and Foreign Affairs Activism, 1907–1927." Ph.D. diss., University of South Carolina, 1998.

Zhu, Pingchao. "The Road to an Armistice: An Examination of the Chinese and American Diplomacy during the Korean War Cease-Fire Negotiations, 1950–1953." Ph.D. diss., Miami University, 1998.

Index

About the Author

MICHAEL D. GAMBONE is Assistant Professor of History at Kutztown University of the Pennsylvania State System of Higher Education. He is the author of *Eisenhower, Somoza, and the Cold War in Nicaragua, 1953–1961* (Praeger, 1997) and *Capturing the Revolution: The United States, Central America, and Nicaragua* (Praeger, 2001).